HARDEN'S

London
Party Guide

Publisher's announcements

Other Harden's titles

London Restaurants
UK Restaurants
Hotel Guide
London Bars & Pubs
Good Cheap Eats in London
London Baby Book
London for Free

The ideal corporate gift

Harden's London Restaurants, *Harden's UK Restaurants*,
Harden's Hotel Guide and *Harden's London Bars & Pubs* are
available in a range of specially customised corporate gift
formats.

For further information on any of the above, please call
(020) 7839 4763 or visit www.hardens.com.

party@hardens.com
Attention new venues/services!
The next edition of this guide will go to press in late-2004.
New venues and services are invited to supply proposed
details for publication to party@hardens.com as soon
as possible.

Thanks to Finishing Touch for providing the cover photographs

Production Manager: Elizabeth Warman
Research Manager: Frances Gill

© Harden's Limited, 2004

ISBN 1-873721-56-0

British Library Cataloguing-in-Publication data:
a catalogue record for this book is available from the British Library.

Printed and bound in Italy by
Printer Trento

Harden's Limited
14 Buckingham Street
London WC2N 6DF

CONTENTS

HOW TO USE

Price bands

The price bands indicate, in the most general terms, the overall minimum level of expenditure per head you are likely to incur in giving a party at a particular venue.

£B – Budget: it should be possible to organise a drinks party for about the same cost per head as an evening in a wine bar, or a party with food and drink for about the same cost as eating in a modestly priced restaurant.

£M – Medium: the costs of a party with wine and food will generally run at, or a little above, those of providing similar catering in a middle to high class restaurant. Drinks parties will probably cost as much per head as a meal in a modestly priced restaurant.

£E – Expensive: outside the budget of most private individuals and mainly, therefore, used for corporate events.

Where two levels are shown (eg £B-M), the likely range of expenditure straddles two bands.

Capacities – eg (150, 100,–,125)

The maximum normal capacity of the venue for a private function is given in bold type at the beginning of each entry.

Individual room capacities are given in the small print. This list of rooms may not be exhaustive – details are given only for the more important or interesting rooms, or, in some cases, rooms which are representative of other similar rooms.

We list capacities of which we are aware in the following format:

(standing, seated, dinner-dance, theatre)

Where we do not hold information to intimate suitability in the relevant configuration a dash (–) appears – this does not necessarily mean that the room is unsuitable for that purpose.

Smoking, amplified music and dancing

Permitted, unless otherwise indicated. The fact that no restrictions are noted does not imply that 'anything goes'.

Restrictions on use

Any explicit restrictions upon hirers or types of function are noted. The absence of such a note does not, of course, mean that the venue may not be selective about the functions and hirers which it will accept.

Catering

Restaurants, hotels, wine bars and pubs will generally expect to provide all the food and drink for any event on their premises.

For other venues, we give a guide to stipulations re catering arrangements, as follows:

"in-house catering" – there is a resident caterer, the use of which (unless an alternative is stated) is generally obligatory.

"xco catering" – using the specified caterer is obligatory.

"list of caterers" – one of a list of approved outside caterers must be used.

"hirer's choice of caterer" – you can, in principle, bring in the caterer of your choice (though some venues may wish to vet your proposed arrangements).

Even where there is no obligation to use a particular caterer, you may find that there is a resident caterer which is able to offer keener prices than an outsider.

Finishing times

There are venues where the finishing time for functions is not at all open to negotiation, and others which are almost completely flexible. For many, the question is a grey area – you may find that there is a 'preferred' finishing time, but that, for an extra payment, a later conclusion is perfectly feasible. For venues which have a meaningful general rule about the finishing time for events, we give the time in the small print – we must emphasise, however, that this can be no more than a broad indication. In some cases, the time given is subject to a licensing extension being obtained, but this will generally be dealt with by the venue.

Days and times available and annual closures

Except as indicated (immediately after the finishing time, where applicable), venues are generally available daily throughout the year for day and evening functions. Many venues, however, close around Christmas and the New Year, and many City venues have an August holiday.

CHECKLIST

This is a list for a ball — many of the same issues will arise for smaller parties.

Getting the ball rolling

Venue
Theme
Timetable for evening
Set-up schedule
Marquee
Loos
Furniture
Guest list
Invitations (and other information for guests)
Seating plan
Programme
Place cards
Menus
Inform police/neighbours

Food

Cooking facilities
Special food, eg cake
Snack food
Utensils
Crockery
Table linen/napkins
Catering for bands, performers and staff
Ashtrays

Drink

Cold storage
Glasses
Ice
Mixers and soft drinks
Fruit for cocktails, etc.
Serving trays

Decoration

Balloons, streamers
Flower, fruit or ice displays

Entertainments

Dance floor
Disco & DJ
Bands
Performers
Fireworks/laser
Diversions, eg casino, funfair attractions
Retiring room for bands and performers

Transport

Parking space
Signs to parking, and from parking to event
Cars, buses, train, helicopter

Staff

Security
Car parking
Reception
Cloakroom
Loos
Waiters/waitresses
Toastmaster
Seamstress
Clearing up

Cleaning up

Brushes
Water/buckets
Detergents
Cloths

Don't forget

Plan entry procedure
Insurance
Access for furniture/ equipment
Photography
Power ("3 phase"?)

Icing on the cake

Gifts for guests
Accommodation for guests

INTRODUCTION

First published in 1993, this is the fifth edition of London's only regularly published guide dedicated to parties and events. Over the intervening decade, the party world has got bigger and better, more vibrant and more professional.

We hope that this guide – now for the first time in full colour – reflects the ever-greater professionalism of the business. The number of venues and services who choose to advertise gets bigger too. These advertisements help us to give a better flavour of the different venues and services, so we hope that readers will agree that they are an ornament, not a distraction.

Harden's is best known for restaurant guides, but readers will find only a few advertisements in this guide of restaurants as venues. The reason for this is simply that, though it might seem rather prissy to refuse such advertisements at all, we do not actively search out such advertising lest anyone wrongly fear we might compromise the independence of our 'flagship' guides.

We should also note an important difference between our restaurant guides and this one. In the restaurant guides, the subjective judgements are fundamental. In this guide, the occasional subjective judgements are by the bye – this is an objective guide to help you locate the venues and services which may be suitable for your particular party or event. We make no editorial recommendation that one venue or service is better than another, not least because venues, in particular, are often what you make of them.

To state another obvious point, we have accepted advertisements from, and listed, only services and venues we believe to be respectable and professional. If any reader should have any concerns regarding anyone or anywhere found with the aid of this guide, we would be most grateful if they would bring this to our attention.

Richard Harden   **Peter Harden**

COSTS

Introduction

Giving a party at the venues listed in this book can cost anything from £10 to £1000 a head – more if you really try. If you are organising a major party for the first time, the following guidelines on expenditure may help to set you in the right direction.

Do ensure that you keep an eye on the "big picture" – it is very important not to compare specific costs in isolation. Look at the total costs involved in plan A and compare them with the total costs involved in plan B. For example, you may find that one venue is apparently, on the basis of its hire charge, cheaper than another but that, after taking the respective catering costs into account, the true picture is entirely different.

Where choice is possible, you should, of course, always get competing estimates for each of the different items.

Catering and drink will almost inevitably consume the greater part of a party budget. The other main costs are usually venue hire and decoration. Sometimes, a marquee and/or entertainments can make up a significant part of the total cost.

Catering and drink

As a rule of thumb, expenditure on food and drink provided by an outside caterer will be roughly the same as eating in a restaurant providing comparable fare. (The difference, of course, is that generally you also have to bear the cost of the venue.) Caterers' charges vary widely in just the same way as restaurants do.

The quite significant wine mark-ups and/or high corkage charges sometimes demanded can make quite a difference to total costs and you should make sure you include them in your sums.

Entertainments

Examples: a disco can cost anything from £250 to £1000, although you should be able to get something very respectable for £750 or so. A top after-dinner speaker might command £5,000 and up for a night's work.

A 'dance band' might charge anything from £1000 to ten times that amount.

Venue hire

The costs of hiring the venues themselves usually fall within the following ranges:

£0-£100 – most pubs and wine bars. You may have to guarantee a certain level of total 'spend'.

£100-£2,500 – most of the private venues listed in this book.

£2,500-£15,000 – grander galleries, museums, houses and livery halls, and large nightclubs.

£15,000 and up – the top 25 or so largest and most prestigious venues listed.

Hire charges can be affected by the day of the week, length of hire, purpose of hire and time of year (prices in the quiet first quarter of the year often being 'softer'). In some cases, hire charges will be greater if you do not use the services of the resident caterer. Some, but certainly not all, venues will make an allowance if you wish to use a venue to less than its full capacity. Don't be afraid to negotiate.

Decoration and theming

It is worth bearing in mind that seemingly inexpensive venues may be less of a bargain when you factor in the expenditure on decoration which will be required to make them festive. Apparently expensive venues which are decorated to a high standard can be better value than they initially appear because they require much less work and expense to get them ready for a party.

To dress a medium size ballroom, you can spend several hundred pounds on balloons and other decoration. For floral decoration on any scale it is not difficult to spend several thousand pounds – you *can* spend tens, or even hundreds of thousands of pounds, if you really want to.

The cost of fully theming a party can be very considerable, especially if a set is to be built. A more economical option is to find a venue that comes ready-themed, at least to an extent, and to build on the base which it offers.

Marquee hire

As an example, the hire of a frame marquee large enough to hold a dinner dance for 100 people will generally cost something in the range of £2,000 to £3,000.

PARTY PEOPLE

Sonja Waites is a director of Pulbrook & Gould, and has many years' experience advising and organising functions both large and small.

At every event there is always a *focal point* and it is wise to take advice and be guided by your florist. It is more important to have one large arrangement to give impact than to have two or three small ones. Do not place flowers in corners or low on the ground as they will not be seen.

Flowers in the home

The first thing that you notice is the area where you will be greeted – ie the Hall – and so to have a large arrangement there is important. The drinks area is also important, but if people are standing, something that is at eye level will be seen or use tall vases if the space will allow. At dinner, table centres are very important as this is where most of the evening will be spent, so make them lavish. Choose flowers to complement the colours of the room or the table cloths, use candles if possible as candlelight is very flattering and gives atmosphere to the party.

Venues

Once you have chosen your venue, whether it is a boat or a grand hall, and the type of function – reception, buffet or dinner – talk to your florist and caterer so that you can *co-ordinate* the cloths and colours with the flowers. Determine the reception and drinks areas so as to plan your focal points (as in the home, above). If the venue is very large with high ceilings, don't be afraid to add extra height to the flowers, but do *not* block the view across the tables.

Marquees

Today most marquees are metal-framed with lowish ceilings and it therefore follows that your focal points will be the entrance area and then the tables. Lighting is also important and will give added atmosphere. Concentrate on the tables which can be lavish or simple, but do use candles if possible. Try to create a theme by using a combination of flowers and plants with lighting, music and colour which will give impact and your guests a talking point.

Colours

It is important to use colours wisely. Try to use flowers in season. Whether your floral colour scheme is pale or vibrant, soft lighting will usually show it to the best advantage. Take care with blues and lilacs as they can change colour in night light.

Pulbrook and Gould, Liscartan House, 127 Sloane Street, SW1X 9AS
☎ 020 7730 0030 ⌁ sales@pulbrookandgould.co.uk

PARTY PEOPLE

Jon Kellet is managing director of Starlight Design – party planners and one of the country's leading lighting, fireworks and theme creation companies.

Most parties are evening affairs, which means that once the sun sets lighting can play an extraordinarily important part in the event, adding to the sense of occasion, and transforming the mundane into the spectacular.

The point of arrival should be the start of 'The Drama', and marking the entrance with a pair of giant flares, an avenue of flickering torches or even beams of light pointing skywards immediately alerts your guests that this is no normal night.

Within the party, lighting levels should be carefully controlled. With a little effort any existing lights can be adjusted, refocused and even gelled subtle colours to give a suitable ambience. Dim lighting is cool, glamorous and 'edgy'; warm glows and candlelight are flattering and the soft light of a 100 lamps and lanterns can add a sense of mystery and the exotic.

The added benefit of low lighting is that it allows 'focal points' to be created by simple highlighting. A single spot focused onto a floral feature, downlighters over a bar or multiple up-lighters picking out architectural details will make these chosen items the centre of attention, leaving more mundane elements out of focus.

Parties are like theatrical occasions and benefit from lighting suited to the various scenes. A reception in Act I is where people meet and mingle and should be bright enough for guests to see and be seen. In Act II dinner should be dimmer, cosier and intimate, with the focus being a soft pool of light emanating from the table, akin to candlelight. After dinner comes Act III: entertainment moves to the fore with music and dancing requiring a more dramatic ambience. Now lighting really can show off with a wealth of hi-tech gizmos to bring West End Magic to any location and create a focus for the remainder of the night's revelries.

The atmosphere should bleed off the dance floor and into the surrounding areas, but leave sufficient dark and intimate areas around the edges for those wishing to retreat from the action.

The magic of lighting is that it allows rooms to be instantly repainted, and transformed at the flick of a switch. Thus the formal reception room can become a funky, chilled out club lounge.

The importance of lighting is easy to overlook, but used properly it can be a secret weapon for a successful evening, dramatically improving ambience. If you do nothing else for a party, turn off the fluorescent lights, remove the energy saving bulbs and light a candle... you'll be amazed at the effect!

Starlight Design, 120 Gateway Trading Est, Hythe Road, NW10
☎ 020 8960 6078 ∘ info@starlightdesign.co.uk

AM & PM CATERING. *Established in 1981, the firm is experienced in all forms of corporate and private entertaining. Here they provide a few top tips for working successfully with your caterer.*

1) Choose your caterer carefully
In the absence of a personal recommendation, ask for references. Much can also be gained from meeting your prospective caterer face to face. Do you feel comfortable and confident in their ability to deliver your requirements?

Quotations too, can be a good indicator. If it looks professional, so, probably, will be the standard of service.

A visit to their kitchens/offices might also be useful – do they have proper, commercial premises and public liability insurance? Do they have temperature controlled vehicles for food deliveries? Silly questions perhaps, but some so-called caterers have no insurance and operate out of unregistered Aga-style farmhouse kitchens transporting food in the back of dog-hairy 4 x 4s.

2) Set a realistic budget and try to stick to it
Beware of quotations which are just too low – the reason will probably become apparent too late.

3) Listen to your caterer
You're paying them for their years of experience, and their advice – especially on the menu – is invaluable, so make good use of it.

4) How much drink to order
There is no exact science when it comes to calculating drink quantities, as more often than not common sense prevails, perhaps with an element of educated guesswork. Your caterer should be willing to offer you their advice based on experience and anyway, if they are providing the drink, this becomes their problem. Ensure that drink is charged as consumed, on a sale or return basis.
NB If the event is being held in your own home, do not accept a 'corkage' charge for the service of your own drink – if necessary, choose another caterer. A charge for the hire of glasses and bar equipment, and the provision of ice, would however, be reasonable in these circumstances.

5) Are pre-dinner canapés important?
It all depends upon the duration of the pre-dinner reception. Anything longer than half an hour would, in an ideal world, require the service of canapés and for anything over an hour, it would be a little irresponsible not to do so!

6) Should we ask for a tasting?
If someone cooked a fantastic meal for two people, would you assume that they could do the same for two hundred? Probably not, which is the reason why 'tastings' have to be of limited or no value. Save your money (the cost has to be built in somewhere along the line) and ask for references instead.

AM & PM CATERING, 10 Lower Richmond Rd, London SW15
☎ **020 8789 4447** 🖱 **info@ampmcatering.co.uk**

PRIVATE VENUES

Abbaye EC1
£B-M, (350,160,160,–)
55 Charterhouse St
☎ (020) 7253 1612
🖥 (020) 7251 5259
This large Belgian restaurant in Smithfield is well suited to a big party – especially one that's to go on till late. The cellars are particularly characterful. / 2 am; Basement Restaurant (200,125,–,–); Wine Bar (150,60,–,–).

The Academy WC1
£M-E, (30,18,–,14)
21 Gower St
☎ (020) 7631 4115
🖥 (020) 7636 3442
🖳 www.theetongroup.com
🖃 academy@etongroup.com
Intimate spaces for a variety of functions, in a Bloomsbury hotel recently converted from five Georgian townhouses. Its amenities include a small garden. / in-house caterers; smoking restricted; Conservatory (30,–,–,–); Boardroom (20,18,–,14); Library (10,5,–,–); Garden (40,–,–,–).

Academy of Live & Recorded Arts SW18
£B-M, (300,250,200,250)
The Royal Victoria Patriotic Bldg, Trinity Rd
☎ (020) 8870 6567
🖃 marklegothique@aol.com
Particularly popular for weddings, this extraordinarily overblown Victorian building, in a Wandsworth park, houses a large, mirrored rehearsal room with one of the largest sprung wooden floors in London. It's a characterful space, and opens off the very pretty cloister garden. / midnight; in-house caterers; Great Hall (300,250,200,250); Le Gothique (150,90,150,–).

Adam Street WC2
£M, (350,200,90,65)
9 Adam St
☎ (020) 7379 8000
🖳 www.adamstreet.co.uk
🖃 reception@adamstreet.co.uk

Intriguingly located in c18 vaults beneath the Strand, this members club comprises a restaurant, a club bar, a dance floor and private dining rooms. You can hire the whole place only on Sat (day) and Sun. / members club; 1 am; in-house caterers; Gallery (100,55,–,65); Rehearsal Rm (80,–,–,50); Dining Rm (–,10,–,–).

Addington Palace, Surrey
£M-E, (1200,1000,800,1000)
Gravel Hill, Addington Village
☎ (020) 8662 5000
🖳 www.addington-palace.co.uk
🖃 info@addington-palace.co.uk
This imposing listed Palladian building, once the country retreat of the Archbishops of Canterbury, is set in 163 acres of grounds landscaped by Capability Brown. The bright and airy Winter Garden is licensed for weddings, and, for larger events, it can be combined with the Great Hall. The maximum capacities shown can only be achieved by erecting a marquee. / in-house caterers; Great Hall (200,120,80,200); Winter Garden (100,70,50,90); Library (50,40,–,80); Wellington Rm (50,50,–,60); Empire Rm (40,30,–,50); Lecture Rm (80,60,–,70); Music Rm (50,40,–,40).

CAPACITIES: (Standing, Seated, Dinner dance, Theatre-style)

Adelphi Theatre WC2
£M, (–,–,–,1500)
Strand
☎ (020) 7836 1166
🖰 www.rutheatres.com
📧 mike.townsend@
rutheatres.com
A thirties theatre, available for private hire subject to the constraints of the current show ('Chicago' for the foreseeable future). / available subject to constraints of current production.

Aeonian WC1
£M, (–,130,–,130)
Shropshire House, 2nd Floor,
2-10 Capper St
☎ (020) 7631 1272
🖰 www.aeonian.co.uk
📧 aeonian@
shropshire-house.co.uk
Modern training and conference rooms, handily located just off Tottenham Court Road. We've listed only a selection of the accommodation available. / 6pm; in-house caterers; no amplified music; no dancing; no smoking; Dining Rm (–,130,–,130); Rm 1 (–,–,–,100); Rm 2 (–,–,–,80); Rm 3 (–,–,–,30).

Africa Centre WC2
£B, (–,120,–,–)
38 King St
☎ (020) 7836 1973
🖰 www.africacentre.org.uk
📧 roomhire@
africacentre.org.uk
This quirky, atmospheric place, just off Covent Garden, has as its main space a c18 galleried hall which, with a little decoration, could be used for fairly traditional events. With catering from the on-site restaurant (Calabash), however, it makes a good venue for a sit-down event. / companies only; in-house caterers; no music; no dancing; Main Hall (–,120,–,–).

The Agency WC2
£M, (100,40,–,16)
112 St Martins Ln
☎ (020) 7379 1717
🖷 (020) 7379 6336
🖰 www.theagencyclub.co.uk
📧 peter@theagencyclub.co.uk
If you're looking for an intimate venue in the heart of the West End, it's worth checking out this small members' club, opposite the Coliseum. At the weekends, you can take the whole place. / 2 am; in-house caterers; Main Bar (70,40,–,–); Conference Rm (–,16,–,16); Board Rm (–,–,–,10); Library (–,–,–,6).

Albery Theatre WC2
£M, (150,–,–,800)
St Martin's Ln
☎ (020) 7369 1730
🖷 (020) 7438 9711
🖰 www.theambassadors.com
📧 alberymanager@
theambassadors.com
An Edwardian theatre, available for hire subject to the constraints of the current production. / 11pm; available subject to constraints of current production; in-house caterers; smoking restricted.

Aldwych Station WC2
£M-E, (280,–,–,–)
Cnr Strand & Surrey St
☎ (020) 7222 5600
The ticket hall of this disused underground station makes an unusual, and central, venue for a party. The platforms and so on below may also be hired, but are mainly used for filming. / very restricted availability; hirer's choice of caterer.

Aldwych Theatre WC2
£M, (200,–,–,1200)
Aldwych
☎ (020) 7379 6736
🖷 (020) 7240 0633
🖰 www.aldwychtheatre.co.uk
📧 email@aldwychtheatre.co.uk
A large theatre (opened in 1905), available for hire subject to the constraints of the current production. / hirer's choice of caterer; no dancing; smok-

*ing restricted; Auditorium (–,–,–,1200);
Bar (200,–,–,–).*

Alexandra Palace & Park N22
£M, (7250,5500,5000,–)
Alexandra Palace Way, Wood Gn
☎ (020) 8365 2121
🖰 www.alexandrapalace.com
🖂 info@alexandrapalace.com
*They boast that parties of between
10 and 7,250 can be catered for at
this enormous Victorian hall complex,
set in 196 acres of park (with great
views over London and parking for
2000 cars). What's impressive –
apart from the sheer scale of the
place, of course – is that they really
do have rooms of suitable scale for
almost any function.* / 2 am; in-house
caterers; Great Hall (6500,5500,5000,–);
West Hall (2500,2200,2000,–); Palm
Court (1500,–,–,–); Palace
Restaurant (400,250,200,–); Loneborough
Rm (200,130,100,–); Palm Court
5 (100,50,–,–); Palm Court 1 (25,10,–,–).

Alexandra Palace Ice Rink N22
£M, (1750,–,–,–)
Alexandra Palace Way, Wood Gn
☎ (020) 8365 2121
🖰 (020) 8444 3439
🖰 www.alexandrapalace.com
🖂 ice.rink@alexandrapalace.com
*You can take over the whole Ally
Pally rink by the hour. You could use
it for ice-go-karting (40 people per
session) or a skating birthday party.
It has even hosted a wedding reception.* / 1 am; hirer's choice of caterer
(in-house available); smoking restricted.

Alma SW18
£B, (80,60,–,–)
499 Old York Rd
☎ (020) 8870 2537
🖰 (020) 8488 6603
🖰 www.thealma.col.uk
🖂 drinks@thealma.co.uk
*A popular Wandsworth pub with
something of a name for its solid
grub. There's an upstairs parlour
available for presentations, dinners*

*and drinks and – perhaps rather sur-
prisingly – also for weddings.* / 11pm.

The Almeida N1
£M-E, (140,98,–,–)
30 Almeida St
☎ (020) 7354 4777
🖰 (020) 7354 2777
🖰 www.almeida-restaurant.co.uk
*One of the better-reputed restau-
rants in the Conran empire, this
'70s-retro Gallic establishment is
especially well placed for functions
related to Islington's Almeida Theatre
(opposite).* / Private Rm (–,16,–,–).

Amadeus Centre W9
£M, (250,160,100,–)
50 Shirland Rd
☎ (020) 7286 1686
🖰 www.amadeuscentre.co.uk
🖂 amadeus@
amadeuscentre.co.uk

*This converted c19 century chapel in
Little Venice offers a characterful
space, with good natural light for
receptions, parties and private
events. An ideal combination is a dinner in the Upper Hall and
disco/dancing in the Lower Hall.* / 2
am; list of caterers; Upper
Hall (250,160,100,–); Lower
Hall (120,60,60,–).

CAPACITIES: (Standing, Seated, Dinner dance, Theatre-style)

Amber W1
£B-M, (135,–,–,–)
6 Poland St
☎ (020) 7734 3094
🖰 www.amberbar.com
A modern, two-floor Soho bar, whose stylish neutral décor, layout and sound system suit it to a range of occasions. Upstairs there are tables and booths, and in the basement a dance-floor, making the place very suitable for exclusive hires.

Amberley Castle, W Sussex
£M-E, (40,55,–,40)
Nr Arundel
☎ 01798 831992
🖨 01798 831998
🖰 www.amberleycastle.co.uk
🖂 info@amberleycastle.co.uk
If you're looking for a defensive location for your gathering, this storybook castle – complete with portcullis – may well be just the place for you. / children 12+ only; midnight; in-house caterers; smoking restricted; Queens Rm (–,55,–,–); King Charles Rm (12,12,–,12); Great Rm (40,40,–,40).

The Anchor SE1
£B-M, (400,150,150,–)
34 Park St, Bank End
☎ (020) 7407 1577
🖨 0870 9906403
A well-known South Bank tavern, four centuries old, but ever-evolving. The Shakespeare Room has a great view of the river and 200-year-old panelling. Mrs Thrale's Room is an intimate, characterful private bar. In summer, barbecues can be arranged. / 11pm; Terrace (400,–,–,–); Mrs Thrale's Rm (50,–,–,–); Upper Chart Rm (–,50,–,–); Lower Chart Rm (–,30,–,–); Shakespeare Rm (–,22,–,–).

Annabel's W1
£E, (250,125,125,–)
44 Berkeley Sq
☎ (020) 7629 1096
🖨 (020) 7491 1860
A grand and comfortable Mayfair nightclub that's been a legend for decades, and which has recently had some success in cultivating a rather 'younger' image. It makes an ideal venue for a small to medium-sized party, but the active involvement of a member will be required. / 3 am; in-house caterers.

The Antelope SW1
£B-M, (60,25,–,–)
22 Eaton Ter
☎ (020) 7824 8512
🖂 antelopeSW1@aol.com
A famous pub, whose character is strongly defined by its pukka location just off Eaton Square. A comfortable upstairs room is available for civilised stand-ups and dinners. / 11.30pm; no amplified music; no dancing.

The AOP Gallery EC2
£M, (300,100,–,–)
The Association of Photographers, 81 Leonard St
☎ (020) 7739 6669
🖨 (020) 7739 8707
🖰 www.the-aop.org
🖂 gallery@aophoto.co.uk
In a warehouse in the heart of trendy Shoreditch, a contemporary photographic gallery available for private events and parties. / 11pm; closed Sun; hirer's choice of caterer; no smoking.

Apartment 195 SW3
£B-M, (100,60,60,15)
195 Kings Rd
☎ (020) 7351 5195
🖨 (020) 7376 5076
🖰 www.apartment195.co.uk
🖂 info@apartment195.co.uk
A new Chelsea bar that's been a great success (including being the Evening Standard's Bar of the Year). It offers a choice of cosy, clubby spaces for private events, or you can take the whole place. / 11pm; hirer's choice of caterer (in-house available); no amplified music; Lounge (100,60,60,–); Cellar (25,15,–,15); TV Rm (10,–,–,10).

PRIVATE VENUES

Apollo Victoria Theatre SW1

£M, (300,–,–,2572)
17 Wilton Rd
☎ (020) 7529 4323
🖨 0870 7493198
⌖ www.victoria-apollo.co.uk
✉ venue.bookings@
clearchannel.co.uk
*If you're looking for a place for a
large, central gathering – and can
accommodate the timings of the current show (likely to be 'Bombay
Dreams' throughout the currency of
this guide) – this Art Deco palace
(originally, the New Victoria Cinema,
1930) may be for you.* / available subject to constraints of current production;
no smoking; Whole Theatre (300,–,–,2572).

Apothecaries' Hall EC4

£M-E, (200,130,–,–)
Blackfriars Ln
☎ (020) 7236 1180
🖨 (020) 7329 3177
⌖ www.apothecaries.org
✉ beadle@apothecaries.org
*With its lovely approach (through a
small, cream-coloured courtyard, off
a cobbled lane), its charming hall, its
sober Court Room and its Parlour
decorated with apothecaries' jars
through the centuries, this ancient
building offers one of London's most
delightful settings.* / 11pm; not available
Sat eves & Sun; Party Ingredients; no amplified music; no dancing; no smoking;
Hall (200,130,–,–); Court Rm (50,22,–,–);
Parlour (50,–,–,–).

Aquarium EC1

£M, (500,–,–,–)
256-260 Old St
☎ (020) 7251 6136
🖨 (020) 7253 9131
⌖ www.clubaquarium.co.uk
*London's only nightclub with integral
swimming pool and Jacuzzi (towels
provided) can be booked in its entirety in the early days of the week. On
Fri night, hire the Star Bar and your
guests have access to the (almost)
all-night action in the main club.* / 3
am Mon-Wed, 4 am Thu-Sat, midnight Sun;
not available weekends; in-house caterer or

hirer's choice by negotiation; Club (500,–,–,–);
Café Bar (250,–,–,–).

Aquarium E1

£M, (400,100,–,–)
Aquarium: Ivory House, St
Katharine-by-the-Tower
☎ (020) 7480 6116
🖨 (020) 7480 5973
⌖ www.theaquarium.co.uk
✉ info@theaquarium.co.uk
*This smart, rather modernistic fish
and seafood restaurant (which
changed hands in late-2003) benefits
from a particularly pleasant location
in the centre of the Tower Bridge-
side marina. Additional facilities not
themselves part of the restaurant
make this a surprisingly flexible and
capacious party space.* / 11pm;
Restaurant (150,100,–,–); Bang
Bar (150,50,–,–); Waterside
Terrace (100,–,–,–).

Aragon House SW6

£B-M, (180,55,55,–)
247-249 New King's Rd
☎ (020) 7736 1856
⌖ www.aragonhouse.net
✉ info@aragonhouse.net
*Part of the British Legion building
overlooking Parson's Green has been
converted into this trendy-looking
lounge bar. From summer 2004, an
additional facility will be available for
larger functions such as wedding
receptions.* / midnight; in-house caterers;
Function Rm (80,–,–,–).

Archduke Wine Bar SE1

£B-M, (300,200,–,–)
153 Concert Hall Approach
☎ (020) 7928 9370
🖨 (020) 7928 0839
⌖ www.thearchduke.co.uk
✉ manager@thearchduke.co.uk
*Handy for the Eye and for the cultur-
al attractions of the South Bank, this
wine bar/restaurant – beneath railway arches – has long been a useful
rendezvous. There are two large
niches available for private hire. On
Saturday morning and Sunday, the
whole place can be taken.* / midnight;

CAPACITIES: (Standing, Seated, Dinner dance, Theatre-style)

Bridge Rm (50,30,–,–);
Conservatory (30,20,–,–).

The Argyll Arms W1
£B, (70,30,–,–)
18 Argyll St
☎ (020) 7734 6117
Ornately decorated Victorian pub,
just by Oxford Circus, with a pleasant private room – the Palladium
Bar. / 11pm; no music; no dancing.

Armourers' &
Braisers' Hall EC2
£M-E, (125,80,–,–)
81 Coleman St
☎ (020) 7374 4000
🖨 (020) 7606 7481
On London Wall, this fine, but not
overbearingly grand livery hall
(1840s) is notable for its distinctive
decoration. Guests are generally
received in the rich comfort of the
gilt-walled Drawing Room and proceed to the armour-lined, vaulted
hall, lit by the candles of the impressive c18 chandeliers. / no weddings,
birthdays or stag nights; 11pm; not available
weekends; list of caterers; no amplified music;
no dancing; Livery Hall (125,80,–,–); Drawing
Rm (100,–,–,–); Court Rm (–,20,–,–).

Arts Club W1
£M-E, (200,160,120,80)
40 Dover St
☎ (020) 7290 3554
🖥 www.theartsclub.co.uk
📧 functions@theartsclub.co.uk
A popular Mayfair address, whose
manageable size and layout make
for conviviality, and where the mixed
traditional and modern styles of the
rooms produce an atmosphere of
easy-going charm. A paved garden
leads off the dining room. / 2 am; dining & drawing rms not available Wed eve;
hirer's choice of caterer (in-house available);
Dining Rm (200,150,120,–); Bar &
Conservatory (100,–,–,–); Drawing
Rm (80,26,–,–); Garden Rm (100,60,60,80);
Board Rm (30,12,–,30).

Arts Theatre WC2
£B-M, (150,60,–,360)
Great Newport St
☎ (020) 7836 2132
🖨 (020) 7240 7018
🖥 www.artstheatre.com
📧 info@artstheatre.com
A small and very central playhouse
(with extensive bar and restaurant
facilities), available for hire subject to
the constraints of current productions. / available subject to constraints of
current production; list of caterers;
Auditorium (–,–,–,360);
Restaurant (150,60,–,–); Bar (150,–,–,–).

The Artworkers
Guild WC1
£B-M, (120,150,–,–)
6 Queen Sq
☎ (020) 7713 0966
An unaltered early-c18 Bloomsbury
house (listed Grade II*), mainly used
for lectures with an artistic leaning,
but also available for hire for social
and business events. / 10.30pm; closed
Sun; hirer's choice of caterer; no amplified
music; no dancing; smoking restricted.

Arundel House WC2
£M-E, (200,140,100,200)
13-16 Arundel St
☎ 0870 780 9639
🖨 (020) 7653 6653
🖥 www.cbvs.co.uk
📧 helpme@cbvs.co.uk
The home of the International
Institute for Strategic Studies is a
remodelled Victorian building by
Temple tube. It boasts state-of-the-
art conference and presentation facilities. / 11pm; in-house caterers; no dancing;
Rm With A View (200,140,100,200);
Conference Rm (50,40,–,80); 4th Floor
Conference Rm (40,40,–,45).

Ascot Racecourse,
Berks
£M, (1500,1200,1000,–)
Ascot
☎ 01344 878555
🖥 www.ascot.co.uk
📧 banquets@ascot.co.uk
Ascot is an all-year fixture, function-
wise, offering a large range of spaces

for social events (and even a new Exhibition Hall). Events of most sizes can be accommodated here – the list of rooms given is far from exhaustive. NB closed for rebuilding from October 2004 until 2006. / *midnight; not available on race days; Sodexho; Ascot Pavilion (subdivisible) (1500,1200,1000,–); Royal Enclosure Suite (600,500,450,–); Paddock Balcony (350,250,200,–); King Edward VII (50,40,–,–).*

Athenaeum Hotel W1
£M, (100,60,40,55)
116 Piccadilly
☎ (020) 7499 3464
🖷 (020) 7493 1860
🕾 www.athenaeumhotel.com
🖃 info@athenaeumhotel.com

Very comfortable modern Mayfair hotel, in fairly traditional style. Two of the function rooms (Ardmore and the Bowmore) have views of Green Park. For a small and discreet gathering, consider one of the hotel's apartments, which are located in converted Edwardian townhouses. / *midnight; Macallan (100,60,40,55); Richmond Suite (20,8,–,–); Ardmore (20,12,–,–); Bowmore (–,12,–,–); Apartments (–,6,–,–).*

Atlantic Bar & Grill W1
£M-E, (500,300,–,–)
20 Glasshouse St
☎ (020) 7734 4888
🖷 (020) 7734 5400
🕾 www.atlanticbarandgrill.com
This atmospheric Art Deco basement bar/restaurant, near Piccadilly Circus, is on an enormous scale. There is a stylish private room ('Chez Cup') and a cocktail lounge ('Dick's Bar') or, for a big-budget event, you could take over the whole place. / *3 am; Chez Cup (70,70,–,–); Dicks Bar (70,50,–,–).*

The Atlas SW6
£B, (120,40,40,–)
16 Seagrave Rd
☎ (020) 7385 9129
🖃 theatlas@btopenworld.com
A popular 'gastropub', near Earl's Court 2, with a good reputation for its cooking. It has two private party rooms (not available independently), one with its own bar.

Atrium SW1
£M, (–,24,–,–)
4 Millbank
☎ (020) 7233 0032
🖷 (020) 7233 0010
Proximity to Parliament's media centre makes this Westminster restaurant an ideal venue for those wishing to combine a little lobbying with their entertaining. / *Private Rm (–,24,–,–); Private Rm (–,12,–,–).*

Audi Forum W1
£M-E, (250,80,–,40)
74-75 Piccadilly
☎ 0870 780 9478
🖷 (020) 8870 1818
🕾 www.createfood.co.uk
🖃 charlotteb@createfood.co.uk
"Vorsprung durch Technic", as they say in, er, Mayfair – if you're looking for a haven of Teutonic taste, this prominently located car showroom may be just the place. / *11pm; evenings only; in-house caterers; Whole Space (250,80,–,–); Meeting Rm (–,–,–,40).*

The Avenue SW1
£M-E, (400,180,–,–)
7-9 St James's St
☎ (020) 7321 2111
🖷 (020) 7321 2500
🕾 www.egami.co.uk
🖃 avenue@egami.co.uk
The Manhattanite décor of this large and airy St James's restaurant – which may be taken over in its entirety for suitable events – makes an impressive backdrop for a stylish party.

CAPACITIES: (Standing, Seated, Dinner dance, Theatre-style)

Avenue House N3
£M, (90,70,70,74)
17 East End Rd
☎ (020) 8346 7812
🖑 www.avenuehouse.org.uk
📠 info@avenuehouse.org.uk
This Victorian villa in Finchley was partly rebuilt in 1989 after a major fire. There is a variety of function rooms for 30–70 people. Some are definitely suitable only for business meetings, but the Drawing Room is licensed for weddings. / 11pm weekdays, midnight weekends; hirer's choice of caterer (in-house available); no smoking; Drawing Rm (90,70,70,74); Stephens Rm (–,69,–,50); Salon (45,30,45,30); Dining Rm (45,30,–,30).

Babylon W8
£M-E, (–,120,–,–)
99 Kensington High St
☎ (020) 7368 3993
🖳 (020) 7938 2774
🖑 www.roofgardens.com
If you want altitude (and are prepared to pay for it), the restaurant above Kensington's amazing Roof Gardens offers an intriguing venue (for sit-down functions only). / Private Rm (–,12,–,–).

BAC SW11
£B-M, (600,400,400,650)
Lavender Hl
☎ (020) 7326 8211
🖳 (020) 7585 0704
🖑 www.venuesatbac.org.uk
📠 venues@bac.org.uk
This impressive Victorian building in Battersea is best known as an arts centre, but it also does big business in weddings and other events. Having what is apparently the largest sprung dance floor in the country, it is also eminently suitable for dances. / midnight; hirer's choice of caterer; Grand Hall (600,400,400,650); Lower Hall (200,120,120,180).

BAFTA W1
£M, (200,200,200,213)
195 Piccadilly
☎ (020) 7734 0022
🖑 www.bafta.org
📠 pollyc@bafta.org
While their décor is now modern, the club bars of the erstwhile 'Royal Institute of Painters in Watercolours' retain traces of c19 grandeur, adding to their attractiveness for receptions. This period character is absent from the function room, however, though it does enjoy good views of St James's churchyard. / I am; Roux Fine Dining; dancing in bar areas only; David Lean Rm (200,200,–,200); Foyer Bar (200,–,–,–); Club Bars (200,–,–,–); Princess Anne Theatre (–,–,–,213).

Bakers' Hall EC3
£B-M, (150,75,–,100)
9 Harp Ln
☎ (020) 7623 2223
🖑 www.bakers.co.uk
📠 clark@bakers.co.uk
Located a short step from the Tower, this modern livery hall stands at the foot of the company's own office block. The livery hall is a dark room, with deep-blue stained glass windows, while the basement Court Room is more conventional, with light wood panelling and furniture. / 11pm; list of caterers; no dancing; Livery Hall (120,77,–,100); Court Rm (60,22,–,60); Ante Rm (70,14,–,–).

Balham Bar & Kitchen SW12
£M, (40,16,–,–)
15-19 Bedford Hill
☎ (020) 8675 6900
The Soho House team have made a great initial success of the first destination for which Balhamites might claim some sort of 'destination' status. While not totally private, there's an elevated area at rear well suited to informal parties, as well as a basement bar. / Playroom Bar (40,–,–,–).

Balls Brothers SW1
£B

20 St James's St, SW1A
- ☎ (020) 7321 0882 (300,–,–,–)
- ✉ stjames@ballsbrothers.co.uk

34 Brook St, W1
- ☎ (020) 7499 4567 (200,12,–,–)
- ✉ brookst@ballsbrothers.co.uk

13-14 Cork St, W1X
- ☎ (020) 7409 1370 (–,50,50,–)
- ✉ jallison@ballsbrothers.co.uk

24 Southwark St, SE1
- ☎ (020)7403 6851 (350,140,120,–)
- ✉ hopcel@ballsbrothers.co.uk

158 Bishopsgate, EC2
- ☎ (020) 7426 0567 (250,–,–,–)
- ✉ bishgate@ballsbrothers.co.uk

Bow Ln, EC4
- ☎ (020) 7489 9895 (200,60,–,–)
- ✉ utc@ballsbrothers.co.uk

Hays Galleria, Tooley St, SE1
- ☎ (020) 7407 4301(150,100,100,–)
- ✉ haysgal@ballsbrothers.co.uk

11 Blomfield St, EC2
- ☎ (020) 7588 4643 (60,12,–,–)
- ✉ blomst@ballsbrothers.co.uk

King Arms Yd, EC2R
- ☎ (020) 7796 3049 (60,–,–,–)
- ✉ kingsarm@ballsbrothers.co.uk

6-8 Cheapside, EC2V
- ☎ (020) 7248 2708 (80,–,–,–)
- ✉ cheapside@ballsbrothers.co.uk

5-6 Carey Ln, EC2
- ☎ (020) 7600 2720 (200,60,60,–)
- ✉ careylane@ballsbrothers.co.uk

52 Lime St, EC3M
- ☎ (020) 7283 0841 (200,90,–,10)
- ✉ limest@ballsbrothers.co.uk

Mark Ln, EC3R
- ☎ (020) 7623 2923 (120,16,–,–)
- ✉ marklane@ballsbrothers.co.uk

2 St Mary-at-Hill, EC3R
- ☎ (020) 7626 0321 (250,60,60,–)
- ✉ stmary@ballsbrothers.co.uk

Bucklersbury Ho, 3-6 Budge Row, Cannon St, EC4
- ☎ (020) 7248 7557 (300,40,–,–)
- ✉ cannonst@ballsbrothers.co.uk

Minster Court, Mark Ln, EC3R
- ☎ (020) 7283 2838 (120,90,90,–)

81 Old Broad St, EC2M
- ☎ (020) 7920 9645 (120,90,90,–)
- ✉ gows@ballsbrothers.co.uk

This well-known chain of wine bars makes its branches available, given sufficient numbers, on an exclusive basis, particularly at the weekends. You can go direct to the individual wine bars, or call the party service on ((020)) 7739 6466.

Baltic SE1
£M, (400,100,–,–)

74 Blackfriars Rd
- ☎ (020) 7928 1111
- 🖨 (020) 7928 8487
- 🖱 www.balticrestaurant.co.uk

A dramatic conversion of these premises near Tate Modern has helped make a great success of this Polish restaurant and cocktail bar. There's a private room overlooking the main eating area, or you can hire the venue in its entirety. / Private Dining Rm (–,30,–,–).

Baltic Exchange EC3
£M-E, (100,50,60,70)

38 St Mary Axe
- ☎ (020) 7369 1665
- 🖱 www.balticexchange.com
- ✉ enquiries@
  balticexchange.co.uk

The "new" Baltic Exchange has, since 1995, occupied an the impressive Art Deco building, which offers a number of options for businesslike gatherings. For obvious reasons, the dining room is not available on weekday lunchtimes. / 10.30pm; in-house caterers; Churchill (–,12,–,–); Dining Rm (100,50,60,70); Boardroom (–,24,–,–); Chairman's Rm (–,20,–,–).

Bam-Bou W1
£M-E, (150,80,–,–)

1 Percy St
- ☎ (020) 7323 9130
- 🖨 (020) 7323 9140
- 🖱 www.bam-bou.co.uk
- ✉ reservations@bam-bou.co.uk

The clubby Fitzrovia Vietnamese restaurant has been lavishly furnished, and has something of a reputation as a beautiful people hangout. It has three private areas, or you could take the whole place. / Black Lounge Bar (50,20,–,–); Private Rms (2) (–,14,–,–).

CAPACITIES: (Standing, Seated, Dinner dance, Theatre-style)

Bank of England Sports Club SW15
£M, (260,180,180,60)
Priory Ln
☎ (020) 8876 8417
🖨 (020) 8878 7007
🖱 www.greatvenue.co.uk
📧 marianna.karakousheva@ bankofengland.co.uk
Set in 42 acres of woodlands and with every type of sports field, this very well-maintained Roehampton 'country-club' is tailor-made for grown-up sports days (including go-karting and the like). The Redgates Lodge is suitable for a wide variety of functions, including weddings. / 11pm; Searcy's; Redgates Lodge (150,80,–,–); Green Rm (80,50,–,60); Balcony Bar (80,40,–,–); Restaurant (250,180,180,–).

Bank Westminster SW1
£M, (250,140,140,–)
45 Buckingham Gt
☎ (020) 7379 9797
🖨 (020) 7240 7001
🖱 www.bankrestaurants.com
📧 westres@ bankrestaurants.com
This Victoria offshoot of the Aldwych restaurant has an impressive modern layout, including two private rooms. For a larger party, you could take the whole place – especially attractive in summer, when the conservatory comes into its own. / Private Rms (combined) (–,40,–,–); Private Rms (x2) (–,20,–,–).

Bankside Gallery SE1
£B-M, (150,70,–,–)
48 Hopton St
☎ (020) 7928 7521
📧 bankside@freeuk.com
A pleasant, simple, red-walled gallery, this Southwark institution – home to the Royal Watercolour Society and Royal Society of Painter-Printmakers – is at the foot of a modern block, set back from the river. / 11pm; available Wed-Sun after 5pm, Tue after 8pm; hirer's choice of caterer; no amplified music; no dancing; no smoking.

Bankside Restaurant SE1
£B-M, (250,150,–,–)
32 Southwark Br Rd
☎ (020) 7633 0011
📧 kelvin@ banksiderestaurants.co.uk
If you're looking for a venue on the South Bank – and certainly one that's convenient for Tate Modern – this large and reasonably-priced basement restaurant is one of the relatively few choices available.

Banqueting House SW1
£M-E, (500,400,380,–)
Whitehall
☎ (020) 7839 8918
🖨 (020) 7930 8268
🖱 www.hrp.org.uk
📧 mike.nicholas@hrp.org.uk
The sole remaining fragment of the Palace of Whitehall, Inigo Jones's stately c17 hall (with Rubens ceiling) offers just the venue if you're setting out to impress. The undercroft is an elegant space, available separately. / no weddings, 18ths or 21sts; list of caterers; some restrictions on music; smoking restricted; Main Hall (500,400,380,–); Undercroft (375,150,–,–).

Bar Bourse EC4
£M, (220,100,–,–)
67 Queen St
☎ (020) 7248 2200
🖨 (020) 7248 2211
🖱 www.barbourse.com
📧 barbourse@aol.com

A bright and stylish establishment, in a basement near Mansion House, described in one guidebook as "the Rolls-Royce of City bars". It is in fact both a bar and restaurant, and private function use includes wedding receptions.

Bar M SW15
£B-M, (250,130,–,–)
4 Lower Richmond Rd
☎ (020) 8788 0345
🖰 www.bar-m.uk.com
✉ bmputney@glendola.co.uk

A landmark pub, near Putney Bridge, which been stripped down and converted into a modern, minimalist space, with good river views. / River Rm (250,130,–,–); Bar M (250,100,–,–); The Cellar Bar (70,–,–,–).

Bar Red
£B-M, (250,–,–,–)
4 Greek Street
☎ (020) 7434 3417
🖷 (020) 7434 3418
🖰 www.bar-red.com
A popular two-floor West Soho lounge bar, which makes a very central venue for a stand-up event. / Downstairs (100,–,–,–).

Barbarella SW6
£M, (–,–,150,–)
428 Fulham Rd
☎ (020) 7385 9434
🖷 (020) 7381 0895
🖰 www.barbarella-restaurant.co.uk
A long-established Fulham dine-and-disco venue, highly suitable for taking over in its entirety. / 3 am; not available Sat.

Barber-Surgeons' Hall EC2
£M, (250,130,–,180)
Monkwell Sq
☎ 0870 780 9639
🖷 (020) 7653 6653
🖰 www.cbvs.co.uk
✉ helpme@cbvs.co.uk

This light, panelled livery hall, near the Barbican, was remodelled in the '60s in traditional style. It is available primarily for business and livery functions. / 10.30pm; not available weekends; Chester Boyd; no amplified music; no dancing; smoking restricted; Great Hall (250,130,–,180); Reception Rm (100,–,–,55); Court Rm (–,12,–,25).

Barbican Art Gallery EC2
£M, (500,–,–,–)
Barbican Centre, Silk St
☎ (020) 7382 7246
🖷 (020) 7382 7237
🖰 www.barbican.org.uk
✉ conferences@barbican.org.uk
This twin-level gallery is quite reasonably priced by City standards and is a popular venue, especially in the summer. Depending on the layout of the current exhibition, access to the external Sculpture Court may be possible. NB now booking from April 2004, after renovation. / evenings and weekends; Searcy's; no amplified music; no smoking.

Barbican Centre EC2
£M-E, (550,288,260,–)
Barbican Centre
☎ (020) 7382 7246
🖷 (020) 7382 7247
🖰 www.barbican.org.uk
✉ searcys@barbican.org.uk
The huge, jungle-like Conservatory would not be out of place in Kew Gardens and makes a dramatic setting for a grand event. It can be used in combination with the Barbican Art Gallery (see above). / sound limits in garden rm; midnight; evenings and weekends; Searcy's; some restrictions on music; smoking restricted; Garden Rm (400,288,260,–); Conservatory (200,150,–,–); Conservatory Terrace (120,66,–,–).

CAPACITIES: (Standing, Seated, Dinner dance, Theatre-style)

Barnard's Inn Hall EC1
£M-E, (80,50,–,–)
Holborn
☎ (020) 7831 0575
🖷 (020) 7831 5208
🖱 www.gresham.ac.uk
✉ enquiries@gresham.ac.uk
As a walk-on rôle in 'Great
Expectations' confirms, this Inn of
Chancery – a hall with c14 origins –
has quite a history. Substantially
refurbished by owners the Mercers'
Company, it has only recently
become available for hiring. / 11pm;
hirer's choice of caterer; no amplified music.

Basil Street Hotel SW3
£M, (250,140,120,–)
8 Basil St
☎ (020) 7581 3311
🖷 (020) 7495 1163
🖱 www.thebasil.com
✉ enquiries@
westburymayfair.com
This well-known Knightsbridge
Edwardian establishment has a
peaceful charm and lots of creaky
'country house' character. The large
Parrot Club (downstairs) can be used
for dancing. / midnight; parrot club available eves & weekends only; smoking restricted; Parrot Club (250,140,120,–); Basil
Rm (50,30,–,–).

The Battersea Barge Bistro SW8
£B-M, (200,100,100,–)
Nine Elms Ln
☎ (020) 7498 0004
🖷 (020) 7622 9729
🖱 www.batterseabarge.com
✉ info@batterseabarge.com
It's not exactly easy to find – behind
the FedEx building, near New Covent
Garden Market – but this restaurant
in a Dutch barge makes a cosy and
atmospheric place for a party, and is
very reasonably priced. / no stag nights;
2 am; Upper Deck (50,–,–,–).

Battersea Park SW11
£M, (5000,2000,2000,–)
Battersea Park
☎ (020) 7223 6241
🖱
www.wandsworth.gov.uk/events
✉ asmith@wandsworth.gov.uk
The only one of the more central
parks to enjoy a river frontage offers
some useful spaces for the erection
of marquees, especially large ones.
For the park's only permanent party
venue, see Pump House Gallery.
/ 2am; boules area 10pm; hirer's choice of
caterer; British Genius
Site (5000,2000,2000,–); Boules
Area (600,500,–,–).

Beach Blanket Babylon W11
£B-M, (300,100,–,–)
45 Ledbury Rd
☎ (020) 7229 2907
🖷 (020) 7313 9525
🖱 www.beachblanketbabylon.uk.com
Even after over a decade, the amazing Gothic interior of this Notting Hill
bar is still one of the more striking in
town. You can only take the whole
place, or the bar at less-busy times,
but there's a curtained off bar area
available on all but the busiest days.
/ 2 am; Bar (200,–,–,–); Bar Area (60,–,–,–);
Restaurant (–,45,–,–); Chapel (–,35,–,–).

Bedroom Bar EC2
£B-M, (100,–,–,–)
62 Rivington St
☎ (020) 7613 5637
🖷 (020) 7256 1242
For a NYC-style loft apartment look
in fashionable Hoxton, this upstairs
warehouse-conversion is perfect. It's
a hip bar most of the time, but you
can also hire it for private parties
and events. / 3 am; in-house caterers.

Belair House SE21
£M-E, (150,85,85,–)
Gallery Rd, Dulwich Village
☎ (020) 8299 9788
🖷 (020) 8299 6793
🖱 www.belairhouse.co.uk
✉ info@belairhouse.co.uk
A picture postcard pretty Georgian

house by Dulwich Park which, as a wedding venue, is something of a 'natural'. The capacities given are for the building, though some people boost numbers by adding a marquee in the grounds. / midnight; Restaurant (100,85,85,–); Bar (70,40,–,–); Conservatory (–,14,–,–).

HMS Belfast SE1
£M, (400,144,96,–)
Hay's Galleria
☎ (020) 7403 6246
🖷 (020) 7404 0708
⌂ www.conference-online.co.uk
✉ hms.belfast@sodexho.co.uk
This WWII cruiser, permanently moored by Tower Bridge, offers a range of possibilities for medium-sized events, including weddings. The decks afford a very central location for a summer drinks party. / 11.30pm; Sodexho Prestige; Quarter Deck (Summer Evenings) (350,–,–,–); Ship Co's Dining Hall (240,144,96,–); Gun Rm (120,60,60,–); Admiral's Quarters (35,20,–,–).

Belvedere W8
£M, (250,150,–,–)
off Abbotsbury Rd
☎ (020) 7734 7333
🖷 (020) 7734 0033
⌂ www.whitestarline.org.uk
✉ sales@whitestarline.org.uk
This beautifully-situated Holland Park restaurant is one of Marco Pierre White's most glamorous establishments. It's ideal for a reception after a wedding at the nearby Orangery (or you can have the ceremony here too). / 2 am; Lower level (150,60,–,–); Top level (100,80,–,–); Mezzanine (–,24,–,–).

Benares W1
£M-E, (300,150,–,–)
12 Berkeley Hse, Berkeley Sq
☎ (020) 7629 8886
🖷 (020) 7491 8883
⌂ www.benaresrestaurant.com
A smart, businesslike and discreet new Indian restaurant, with a handy location in the heart of Mayfair. It has a number of private rooms. / Private Rm (–,20,–,–); Private Rm (–,12,–,–); Private Rm (–,8,–,–).

Bengal Clipper SE1
£M, (–,170,–,–)
31 Shad Thames
☎ (020) 7357 9001
🖷 (020) 7357 9002
⌂ www.bengalrestaurant.com
✉ clipper@bengalrestaurant.com
A modern, airy Indian restaurant near Tower Bridge, which can be taken over in its entirety for functions. / 11.30pm.

Bentleys W1
£M, (–,50,–,–)
11-15 Swallow St
☎ (020) 7734 4756
🖷 (020) 7287 2972
This very pretty, old-established English fish restaurant boasts a civilised, light first-floor private room. For larger events, half of the restaurant's main dining room, which is effectively a private space, can be used. / Private Rm (–,14,–,–).

The Berkeley SW1
£M-E, (400,200,160,–)
Wilton Pl
☎ (020) 7235 6000
⌂ www.savoygroup.com
✉ info@the-berkeley.co.uk
A modern Savoy Group hotel in Knightsbridge. Styling is generally fairly conventional, but the Mulberry Room has recently been revamped in subdued contemporary style. / midnight; list of caterers; Ballroom (400,200,160,–); Belgravia (150,54,–,–); Mulberry (40,20,–,–); Knightsbridge (10,10,–,–).

The Berkshire W1
£M, (50,26,–,–)
350 Oxford St
☎ (020) 7845 8680
⌂ www.radissonedwardian.com
✉ londonmeetings@radisson.com
The pretty, panelled top-floor Sonning Suite – suitable for dinners and smaller receptions – is the more richly-furnished and better-proportioned room available in this modern, wedge-shaped hotel. / 2 am; Sonning

CAPACITIES: (Standing, Seated, Dinner dance, Theatre-style)

Suite (50,26,–,–); Sandhurst
Suite (30,12,–,–).

The Berners Hotel W1

£M-E, (250,160,120,–)
10 Berners St
☎ (020) 7666 2000
🖱 www.thebernershotel.co.uk
✉ berners@berners.co.uk
This hotel, not far from Oxford Street, was built in 1835 and converted to its present form at the turn of the century. It's a comfortable, traditional sort of place, with a reasonable choice of medium-sized accommodation, and would make quite a good wedding venue. / 11pm; Thomas Ashton Suite (250,160,120,–); Fitzrovia Suite (120,80,–,–); Tyburn Rm (60,40,–,–).

Berry Bros & Rudd SW1

£M-E, (100,60,–,–)
3 St James St
☎ (020) 7396 9600
🖷 (020) 7396 9619
🖱 www.bbr.com
✉ thecellars@bbr.com
A section of the extensive cellars of this long-established wine merchant, by St James's Palace, have been tastefully converted into a dining (or tasting) room. See advertisement on page 32 / 11pm; in-house caterers; no dancing.

BFI London IMAX Cinema SE1

£M-E, (350,–,–,450)
1 Charlie Chaplin Walk,
South Bank
☎ (020) 7960 3130
🖷 (020) 7960 3112
🖱 www.bfi.org.uk/imax
✉ lucy.jennings@bfi-org.uk
This state-of-the-art South Bank cinema boasts a screen the size of five double decker buses, and is available for special events and corporate hire. / 11pm; in-house caterers; no dancing; no smoking; no alcohol in auditorium.

Big Brother House, Herts

£M-E, (120,80,–,–)
Elstree Film Studios, Shenley Rd,
Borehamwood
☎ (020) 8254 1500
🖱 www.skybridgegroup.com/
bigbrother
From Aug 2004 – when filming for a new series is planned to come to an end – you too can party at the nation's most famous reality TV studio. Perhaps paradoxically, the venue seems to be popular for teambuilding exercises. / companies only; 8pm Mon-Thu, midnight Fri-Sat; not available Sun; in-house caterers.

Bishopsgate Institute EC2

£B-M, (350,120,100,–)
230 Bishopsgate
☎ (020) 7247 6844
🖷 (020) 7392 9250
🖱 www.bishopsgate.org.uk
✉ reception@
bishopsgate.org.uk
A Victorian institute, by Liverpool Street station, whose large, wooden-floored main hall has very high ceilings and wood floors. It makes a very handy location for a corporate bash. / 2 am; in-house caterers; no smoking.

Le Bistrot de L'Institut Français SW7

£B-M, (100,40,–,–)
17 Queensbury Pl
☎ (020) 7589 5433
✉ bistrot@ambafrance.org.uk
You can hire these modern South Kensington premises separately from or together with the Institut Français (in whose building it is housed). It's quite a stylish room, with light wood fittings, and particularly suitable for cocktail parties. / 11pm; in-house caterers.

'If you imagined a wine merchant in a story book, it would look something like these wonderful premises near St. James's Palace. The candle-lit cellar is a fabulously romantic venue for 50, or drinks for 100, and the facilities and catering are excellent.'
The Independent

Blackheath Concert Halls SE3
£B-M, (1000,600,300,–)
23 Lee Rd
☎ (020) 8318 9758
🖰 www.blackheathhall.co.uk
📠 marketing@
   blackheathhall.co.uk
These characterful Victorian halls (claiming to be the first purpose-built concert halls in the country) are well appointed, and a local favourite for a whole range of events from wedding receptions to college balls. The Café Bar is also available for hire. / midnight; list of caterers; Great Hall (600,600,300,–); Recital Rm (150,100,100,–); Café Bar (75,50,–,–).

Bleeding Heart EC1
£M, (100,140,140,–)
Bleeding Heart Yd, off Greville St
☎ (020) 7242 8238
It may be difficult to find, but this Gallic restaurant/wine bar, in the thin area north of Holborn, is extremely popular. At weekends, you can hire the whole place. / 1 am; in-house caterers; Bistro (ground floor) (70,40,–,–); Private Rm (60,50,–,–); The Tavern (100,70,–,–).

Blenheim Palace, Oxon
£E, (750,320,320,120)
Woodstock
☎ 01993 813874
🖶 01993 810580
🖰 www.blenheimpalace.com
📠 alexandra.howden@
   blenheimpalace.com
The home of the 11th Duke of Marlborough (and birthplace of Sir Winston Churchill) is one of the finest houses in England. A few miles north of Oxford, and set in 2,100 acres of Capability Brown gardens, its state rooms offer unparalleled opportunities to impress. / Sodexho; no red wine for standing receptions ; State Rms (750,320,320,–); Orangery (300,230,–,–); Marlborough (180,90,–,120); Spencer Churchill (–,–,–,70); Audenarde Rm (–,32,–,30); Ramillies (–,32,–,30); Malplaquet (–,32,–,30).

Bloomsbury Square Training Centre WC1
£M, (90,30,60,120)
2-3 Bloomsbury Sq
☎ (020) 7212 7510
🖶 (020) 7212 7550
🖰 www.bloomsburysquare.co.uk
📠 natasha.james@uk.pwc.com
The name may sound uninviting, but accountants Pricewaterhouse Coopers' listed Bloomsbury building has some surprisingly characterful accommodation, including the Ascham Room (with its six chandeliers). The Cellars Restaurant is an atmospheric place for evening functions (including discos). / 11pm; in-house caterers; smoking restricted; Ascham Rm (80,–,–,–); Cellars Restaurant (90,30,60,–); Milton Auditorium (–,–,–,120).

Bloomsbury Theatre WC1
£B-M, (100,–,–,550)
15 Gordon St
☎ (020) 7679 2777
🖶 (020) 7383 4080
🖰 www.thebloomsbury.com
📠 blooms.theatre@ucl.ac.uk
This modern theatre is a flexible space equipped to a high standard, and it's handy for the emerging 'Midtown' area between the City and the West End. Hire is of course subject to the constraints of current productions. Dinners cannot be provided on the premises, but can be arranged in university premises nearby. / 11pm; available subject to constraints of current production; in-house caterers; no smoking; Venue (–,–,–,550); Foyer (100,–,–,–).

BMA House WC1
£M-E, (200,100,100,100)
Tavistock Square
☎ (020) 7383 6750
🖶 (020) 7383 6645
🖰 www.bmahouse.org.uk
📠 specialevents@bma.org.uk
Designed by Sir Edwin Lutyens, this impressive Bloomsbury building has a wide variety of rooms celebrating famous physicians (of which we list only a representative selection

VISIT US AT: www.hardens.com

below). Attractive outdoor areas contribute to its suitability for weddings. / 10.30pm; in-house caterers; no smoking; Prince's Rm (100,36,–,70); Members Dining Rm (200,100,100,100); Douglas Black (150,–,–,100); Edward Jenner (–,–,–,20); Joseph Lister (–,–,–,14); Alexander Fleming (–,–,–,20); James Young Simpson (–,–,–,16).

Boisdale SW1
£M, (–,80,–,–)
15 Eccleston St
☎ (020) 7730 6922
🖷 (020) 7730 0548
⌂ www.boisdale.co.uk
✉ info@boisdale.co.uk
Managing to be both cosy and quite fashionable, this Scottish restaurant, near Victoria Station, has a number of areas available for private hire. Live jazz nightly is a feature. / 1 am; Back Bar (–,28,–,–); Jacobite Rm (–,22,–,–).

Bombay Bicycle Club SW12
£M, (–,70,–,–)
95 Nightingale Ln
☎ (020) 8673 6217
🖷 (020) 8673 9100
This high quality Indian restaurant near Wandsworth Common has a ground floor private room, or, in the earlier part of the week, you can take over the whole restaurant. / 12.30 am; available eves only; Private Rm (–,22,–,–).

Bombay Brasserie SW7
£M, (–,250,–,–)
Courtfield Rd
☎ (020) 7370 4040
🖷 (020) 7835 1669
⌂ www.bombaybrasserielondon.com
✉ bombay1brasserie@aol.com
An Indian restaurant built on an imperial scale – if you guarantee 150 people, you can use the whole of the impressive conservatory. / Conservatory (–,150,–,–); Main (–,100,–,–).

Threadneedles EC2
£M-E, (450,76,–,–)
5 Threadneedle St
☎ (020) 7657 8088
🖷 (020) 7657 8100
⌂ www.theetongroup.com
✉ resthreadneedles@theetongroup.com
This popular design-hotel – converted from a bank in the heart of the City – offers a fair choice of private dining and event possibilities. / midnight; Stirling or Capital (25,16,–,–); Traders (–,8,–,–).

The Bonnington in Bloomsbury WC1
£M, (250,150,150,250)
92 Southampton Row
☎ (020) 7400 3808
⌂ www.bonnington.com
✉ sales@bonnington.com
One of the nicer Bloomsbury hotels, which, with its 14 function rooms, can accommodate a wide variety of functions. / 11pm; in-house caterers; Derby Suite (250,150,150,250); York Rm (120,70,70,120); Derby (100,50,–,100); Balmoral (100,40,–,–); Jubilee (100,40,–,100); Jack Frame (50,30,–,40); Committee Rm (20,–,–,20).

Borscht & Tears SW3
£B, (120,100,–,–)
46 Beauchamp Pl
☎ (020) 7589 5003
This rowdy Russian restaurant in Knightsbridge seems oblivious to the whims of fashion, and remains a popular destination for the more boisterous sorts of parties. / Restaurant (–,55,–,–); Downstairs (–,30,–,–).

Il Bottaccio SW1
£M-E, (400,200,150,250)
8/9 Grosvenor Place
☎ (020) 7235 9522
🖷 (020) 7235 9577
⌂ www.bottaccio.co.uk
✉ ieda@bottaccio.co.uk
Occupying an impressive c19 building, this Italianate club-cum-art gallery offers a very central location,

CAPACITIES: (Standing, Seated, Dinner dance, Theatre-style)

and views over the gardens of Buckingham Palace . / 2 am; hirer's choice of caterer (in-house available); Gallery (400,200,150,250); Club Gallery (150,60,60,50).

Boudin Blanc W1
£B-M, (–,20,–,–)
5 Trebeck St
☎ (020) 7499 3292
🖥 (020) 7584 8625
It's no longer the inexpensive bistro as which some may still remember it, but this rustic Shepherd Market restaurant remains very popular nonetheless. It has two cosy private rooms. / 11pm; Private Rm (–,20,–,–); Private Rm (–,14,–,–).

Bow Wine Vaults EC4
£B-M, (80,50,–,–)
10 Bow Church Ln
☎ (020) 7248 1121
🖥 (020) 7248 0318
🖰 www.motcombs.co.uk
A City restaurant/wine bar, charmingly situated behind St Mary-le-Bow – its basement restaurant has recently been refurbished. / 11pm; no dancing; Restaurant (–,50,–,–); Bistrot (60,30,–,–).

Bramah Tea & Coffee Museum SE1
£B-M, (100,–,–,–)
40 Southwark Street
☎ (020) 7403 5650
🖥 (020) 7403 5650
🖰 www.bramahmuseum.co.uk
🖂 e.brahmah@virgin.net
A South Bank social history museum (recently relocated), dedicated to two of the world's oldest beverages. Displays include over 1000 teapots and coffee-making machines.
/ 10.30pm; available from 6.30pm; hirer's choice of caterer; no amplified music; no dancing; no smoking.

Bonchurch Brasserie W10
£B-M, (60,40,–,–)
349 Portobello Rd
☎ (020) 8968 5828
🖥 (020) 8960 8978
The downstairs private room at this amiable North Kensington bistro (formerly known as the Brasserie du March aux Puces) makes a congenial place for an informal party. / midnight; Private Rm (60,40,–,–).

Brasserie St Quentin SW3
£M, (–,80,–,–)
243 Brompton Rd
☎ (020) 7589 8005
🖥 (020) 7584 6064
A grand Gallic brasserie in Knightsbridge, with a pleasant downstairs private room, in Deco-esque style. Very occasionally, the whole place is hired. / no music; no dancing; Private Rm (–,18,–,–).

Break For The Border W1
£B-M, (450,300,250,–)
8-9 Argyll St
☎ (020) 7734 5776
🖥 (020) 7437 5140
🖰 www.bftb.com
🖂 oxfordcircusbfb@ sfigroup.co.uk
A brash and brightly coloured restaurant-cum-nightclub, occupying extensive cellars, just off Oxford Street – the place has a very unusual 'feel' to it. / 3 am.

Brewers' Hall EC2
£M, (200,80,80,–)
Aldermanbury Sq
☎ (020) 7606 1301
🖥 (020) 7796 3557
🖂 courtsecretary@ brewershall.co.uk
The Brewers' Company is reasonably flexible about the use of its elegant, panelled hall which – together with its adjoining rooms – suits a range of smaller functions. / 11pm; list of caterers; no smoking; Livery Hall (150,80,80,–); Court Rm (80,20,–,–); Committee Rm (10,6,–,–).

The Brewery EC1
£M, (850,660,550,–)
Chiswell St
☎ 0800 068 1288
🖷 (020) 7638 5713
🖰 www.thebrewery.chiswell
   street.com
📧 info@thebrewery.co.uk
*Whitbread's former City brewery is
now a leading conference and function venue. The star attraction is the
Porter Tun – built in the c18 as a
storehouse, and boasting an unob-
structed floor space of 8,400 square
metres. The rooms do tend to be
rather businessy in feel, though the
airy Sugar Rooms are attractive
enough for purely social functions.* / /
am; not available Sun; in-house caterers;
Porter Tun (850,660,550,–); King George
III (700,400,300,–); Queen
Charlotte (250,180,120,–); Sugar
Rms (150,100,100,–); City
Cellars (80,45,40,–).

Bridewell
Theatre EC4
£B-M, (200,–,–,–)
Bride Ln
☎ (020) 7583 0259
🖷 (020) 7589 5289
🖰 www.bridewelltheatre.co.uk
📧 admin@
   bridewelltheatre.co.uk
*Just off Fleet Street, this graceful the-
atre (adapted from an Edwardian
swimming pool) offers an interesting
space, with technical back-up including full lighting and sound systems.
Seating arrangements are adaptable,
but you may be constrained by tim-
ing and other requirements of the
current production.* / available subject to
constraints of current production; hirer's
choice or caterer, list available;
smoking restricted; Theatre (200,–,–,–);
Bar (100,–,–,–).

The Bridge SE1
£B-M, (1500,350,–,350)
Weston St
☎ (020) 7940 6060
🖷 (020) 7940 6081
🖰 www.the-ultimate.co.uk
📧 sales@the-ultimate.co.uk
A lot of space – in the arches below

*London Bridge – which can be
turned to almost any sort of event or
function requirement.* / in-house caterers;
Rm4 (200,50,–,50); Rm 3 (300,80,–,100);
Rm 2 (500,200,–,200); Rm
1 (1500,350,–,350).

Bridges Wharf SW11
£M, (550,250,250,–)
Unit 10 (off York Rd)
☎ (020) 7223 9666
🖷 (020) 7924 5358
🖰 www.bridgeswharf.co.uk
📧 jodie@bridgeswharf.co.uk
*Opposite Chelsea Harbour, an
impressive riverside warehouse-conversion, which offers a full 'one-stop-
shop' event service.* / list of caterers.

Brighton Royal
Pavilion, E Sussex
£M-E, (200,90,–,180)
Brighton
☎ 01273 290900
🖷 01273 292871
🖰 www.royalpavilion.brighton.org.uk
📧 louise.crittell@brighton-
   hove.gov.uk
*George IV's splendid seaside palace
offers the ideal setting for a Regency
banquet, or for a range of other
functions, including weddings.* / companies only in the evening, no food or drink in
music rm; 11pm; list of caterers; no amplified
music; no dancing; smoking restricted;
Banqueting Rm (and Great
Kitchen) (200,90,–,–); Queen Adelaide
Suite (100,80,–,–); Great
Kitchen (90,40,–,–); King William IV
Rm (70,60,–,–); Music Rm (–,–,–,180); Small
Adelaide (40,30,–,–); Large
Adelaide (70,50,–,–).

Brinkley's SW10
£M, (–,45,–,–)
47 Hollywood Rd
☎ (020) 7351 1683
🖷 (020) 7376 5083
🖰 www.brinkleys.com
📧 winegallery@
   brinkleys.fsnet.co.uk
*The appeal of this airy, modern
British restaurant, off the Fulham
Road, is wide-ranging, and this must
be the nicest restaurant in London to*

CAPACITIES: (Standing, Seated, Dinner dance, Theatre-style)

be notorious for stag and hen parties
(the less sober of which are held in
the "Brinkley bomb room"). / 12.30
am; no live bands; Private Rm 1 (–,45,–,–);
Private Rm 2 (–,20,–,–); Private Rm
3 (–,20,–,–).

Britannia International Hotel E14
£M, (600,500,450,550)
163 Marsh Wall
☎ (020) 7712 0100
🖷 (020) 7712 0099
🖱 www.britanniahotels.com
🖃 rubi.purnomo@
britanniahotels.com
Modern Docklands hotel – bizarrely
furnished in 'traditional' style –
boasting a wide range of banqueting
accommodation. / 1 am; list of caterers;
Grand Suite (600,500,450,550); Royal
Lounge (250,170,120,200);
Buckingham (100,70,72,80);
Beaufort (40,20,–,30);
Queens (50,22,24,40);
Blenheim (50,22,36,40);
Balmoral (60,22,–,30).

The British Library NW1
£M, (250,255,120,255)
Conference Office, 96 Euston Rd
☎ (020) 7380 1934
🖱 www.bl.uk
🖃 conferences@bl.uk
Given its scale, and its importance
for the English Speaking World, it's
perhaps surprising that this enormous building by St Pancras doesn't
have more function capability/busi-
ness. / 10.30pm; Leith's; no dancing; no
smoking; Auditorium & Foyer (–,255,–,255);
Terrrace Restaurant (250,150,120,–).

British Museum WC1
£E, (2000,450,–,320)
Great Russell St
☎ (020) 7323 8747
🖱 www.thebritishmuseum.ac.uk
Possibly the world's greatest museum
of antiquities offers some high-pres-
tige options for corporate entertaining. The Egyptian Sculpture Gallery is
one of the most suitable for receptions, though other possibilities
include the the Nereid Gallery and
the Hotung Gallery of Oriental
Antiquities. The Great Court is one
of London's greatest spaces – indeed,
so vast it's difficult to see quite what
to do with it! / corporate partners & exhibition sponsors only; most facilities available
Mon-Wed; list of caterers; no amplified music;
no dancing; no smoking; Great
Court (2000,300,–,–); Hotung
Gallery (1000,80,–,–); Egypt & Nereid
Rms (350,170,–,–);
Restaurant (200,150,–,–).

The Broadgate Club EC2
£M, (200,100,–,–)
1 Exchange Place
☎ (020) 7422 6400
🖷 (020) 7422 6401
🖱 www.broadgate-club.co.uk
🖃 info.broadgate@
broadgateclub.com
Situated next to Liverpool Street station, this City sports club has two
rooms overlooking the pool. Both are
quite corporate. / 9.30pm; in-house caterers; no amplified music; no dancing; no smoking; Rest (200,100,–,–); Private
Dining (35,20,–,–).

Broadgate Estates EC2
£M-E, (200,–,–,–)
Broadgate Centre
☎ (020) 7505 4000
🖷 (020) 7382 9854
🖱 www.broadgateestates.co.uk
Sites available for corporate receptions, launches, and the like at this
Manhattanite city complex include
the Arena and – hidden away north
of Liverpool Street – Exchange
Square. / companies only; 11pm; hirer's
choice of caterer; Arena (200,–,–,–);
Exchange Square (100,–,–,–).

PRIVATE VENUES

Brockwell Lido SE24
£B, (350,300,–,–)
Brockwell Park, Dulwich Rd
☎ (020) 7274 3088
Go retro and hold your summer party at this 30s-style south London site with huge (50m) pool. It's ideal for parties with an indoor and an outdoor element, as there is a 70m x 20m marquee site. / 1 am; available from 7pm, Summer only; in-house caterers; Café-restaurant (150,100,–,–); Marquee Site (350,300,–,–).

Brompton Oratory – St Wilfrid's Hall SW7
£B-M, (140,100,–,–)
Brompton Rd
☎ (020) 7808 0900
🖷 (020) 7584 1095
St Wilfrid's Hall is a gracious and central Victorian setting (next to the V&A) for receptions and recitals. Facilities include a grand piano and a large billiards room. / 11pm; not available Sun; hirer's choice of caterer; no amplified music; no dancing; St Wilfrid's Hall (and Billiards Rm) (140,100,–,–).

Brown's Hotel W1
£M, (100,72,–,60)
Albemarle St
☎ (020) 7493 6020
⌐🖰 www.brownshotel.com
🖂 sgosselin.brownshotel@
rfhotels.com
A Mayfair stalwart – in a row of townhouses long ago converted to an hotel – epitomising a certain creaky, pleasantly worn, traditional English style. It has been taken over in recent times by Rocco Forte, so changes may be afoot. / 11.30pm; in-house caterers; no amplified music; Clarendon (100,72,–,60); Niagara & Roosevelt combined (100,70,–,–); Kipling (60,40,–,15); Niagara (40,40,–,–); Lord Byron (20,20,–,–); Roosevelt (80,40,–,30).

Browns W1
£M, (200,150,–,–)
47 Maddox St, W1R
☎ (020) 7491 4565
🖷 (020) 7491 4564
⌐🖰 www.browns-restaurant.com
🖂 browns.maddox@mbplc.com
These premises just off Savile Row started life as tailors and the original fittings have been retained at what is now a branch of the English brasserie chain. The three original fitting rooms have been preserved and are available for private hire. / Private Rm (–,14,–,–); Private Rm (–,10,–,–); Private Rm (–,8,–,–); Private Rm (–,4,–,–).

Browns WC2
£M, (120,100,–,–)
82-84 St Martin's Ln, WC2N
☎ (020) 7497 5050
🖷 (020) 7497 5005
⌐🖰 www.browns-restaurant.com
This Grade II listed building in Covent Garden was a real courtroom between 1890 and 1995 – the judge's and witness boxes and jurors' bench are still in situ. Now it's become a branch of the English brasserie chain. / 1 am; Courtroom 1 (120,100,–,–); Courtroom 2 (80,60,–,–); Courtroom 3 (50,40,–,–); Courtroom 4 (–,10,–,–).

Browns Club WC2
£B-M, (200,–,–,–)
4 Great Queen St
☎ (020) 7831 0802
🖷 (020) 7831 2228
🖂 info@badabing.uk.com
A large nightclub, stylishly decorated, in a handy Covent Garden location. It is a popular venue for receptions. / 3 am; hirer's choice of caterer (in-house available); Ground Floor Bar & Dance Floor (200,–,–,–); Brown's Studio (120,–,–,–); VIP Rm I (100,–,–,–); VIP Rm II (70,–,–,–).

CAPACITIES: (Standing, Seated, Dinner dance, Theatre-style)

Burgh House NW3
£B-M, (90,50,–,60)
New End Sq
☎ (020) 7431 0144
🖨 (020) 7435 8817
🖰 www.burghhouse.org.uk
✉ burghhouse@talk21.com
A charmingly-located Queen Anne house in Hampstead, with a very pretty ground floor music room which is especially suited to weddings and more sedate receptions. / 10pm; not available Mon & Tue; in-house caterers; no amplified music; no smoking; Music Rm (90,50,–,60); Library (–,20,–,–).

Busabong Too SW10
£M, (–,25,–,–)
1a Langton St
☎ (020) 7352 7414
🖨 (020) 7352 7414
A cheerfully decorated Thai restaurant in Chelsea. If you supply enough people to more-or-less fill the mezzanine floor – where you sit barefoot on floor cushions – you can have it to yourself. / available eves only; Mezzanine (–,25,–,–).

Bush Bar & Grill W12
£M, (80,50,–,–)
45a Goldhawk Rd
☎ (020) 8746 2111
Shepherd's Bush's trendiest restaurant maintains quite a following among west London media types. It has a large private room at the rear. / Private Dining Rm (80,50,–,–).

The Business Design Centre N1
£M-E, (1500,1500,–,500)
52 Upper St
☎ (020) 7359 3535
🖨 (020) 7288 6444
🖰 www.businessdesigncentre.co.uk
✉ max@
businessdesigncentre.co.uk
Modern exhibition premises in Islington, sometimes used for large-scale corporate events. / companies only; midnight; in-house caterers; smoking restricted; Main Hall (1500,1500,–,–); Gallery Hall (400,400,–,500);
Auditorium (–,–,–,500); Executive Centre (60,–,–,–).

Butchers' Hall EC1
£M, (280,170,110,180)
87 Bartholomew Close
☎ 0870 780 9639
🖨 (020) 7653 6653
🖰 www.cbvs.co.uk
✉ helpme@cbvs.co.uk
This Smithfield livery hall in traditional style offers flexible accommodation which is much used both for business affairs and socially. / 11pm; in-house caterers; no discos; Great Hall (250,165,110,180); Reception Rm (165,–,–,–); Court Suite (190,60,–,100); Taurus Suite (100,70,–,80); Library (8,8,–,8); George Adams (6,6,–,6); Committee Rm (14,14,–,14).

Buzz Bar WC2
£B-M, (800,–,–,–)
49 Whitcomb St
☎ (020) 7839 8939
American retro-decoration gives this centrally-located bar a slightly touristy feel (though it has been refurbished by new owners). It seems best suited to a large, unthemed party where all you need is a space to bring people together. / Bourbon Street (150,–,–,–).

Cabinet War Rooms SW1
£M-E, (320,320,320,140)
King Charles St
☎ (020) 7747 8334
🖨 (020) 7930 5847
🖰 www.iwm.org.uk
✉ cwr@sodexho.co.uk
This is really two venues in one. Churchill's actual subterranean bunker, off Whitehall, is a fascinating venue composed of 21 tiny rooms (and the corridors which snake between them) and is best enjoyed, on an exclusive basis (after 6.30pm). A new high-tech conference centre, however, has added all-day facilities, suited to larger events. Note that capacities will be somewhat reduced from May 2004, when the Churchill Room becomes a museum. / in-house

caterers; no smoking;
Auditorium (200,140,120,140); Plant
Rm (150,80,60,50); Churchill
Museum (320,320,320,–).

Cabot Hall E14
£M, (800,400,350,400)
Canary Wharf
☎ (020) 7418 2780
🖷 (020) 7512 9117
🖲 www.cabothall.com
📧 cabothall@canarywharf.com
*This impressive Canary Wharf hall
(overlooking Cabot Square through a
lofty bay window) is a very modern
space, equipped to a high standard.
/ midnight; list of caterers;
Hall (800,400,350,400); Sebastian
Rm (100,60,–,80); St Lawrence
Rm (70,40,–,50); Cape Breton
Rm (30,12,–,25); Newfoundland
Rm (20,12,–,15).*

Cactus Blue SW3
£M, (75,60,–,–)
86 Fulham Rd
☎ (020) 7823 7858
*This impressively-designed Chelsea
bar and restaurant (southwest
American) has a suite for private
parties, the Blue Room. For less private affairs, you can also hire the
mezzanine of the main restaurant.
/ midnight; Mezzanine (–,60,–,–); Blue
Rm (75,40,–,–).*

The Cadogan SW1
£M, (80,50,–,–)
75 Sloane St
☎ (020) 7235 7141
🖲 www.cadogan.com
📧 info@cadogan.com
*A welcoming and fashionably-located,
if somewhat old-fashioned,
Knightsbridge hotel. The main dining
room (for a maximum of 50 sitting)
may sometimes be used for parties
too large for the Langtry private
rooms. Get married here, and you
may be able to use the square gardens for your photos! / midnight; no
amplified music; Langtry Dining (50,36,–,–);
Langtry Sitting (30,18,–,–).*

Café de Paris W1
£M-E, (715,240,–,–)
3 Coventry St
☎ (020) 7935 5534
🖲 www.cafedeparis.com
📧 parties@cafedeparis.com
*Although this '30s Society ren-
dezvous has been relaunched as a
contemporary nightclub/bar/restau-
rant, much of the period elegance
lingers, and the establishment is now
licensed for civil weddings. The VIP
suite offers a brace of rooms and its
own bar. / 3 am; not available Fri & Sat; in-
house caterers; Restaurant &
Mezzanine (160,240,–,–);
Restaurant (120,–,–,–); VIP Rm (90,–,–,–);
Blue Bar (65,–,–,–); Red Bar (35,–,–,–).*

Café du Jardin WC2
£M, (120,70,–,–)
28 Wellington St
☎ (020) 7836 8769
🖷 (020) 7836 4123
🖲 www.lecafedujardin.com
*The downstairs part of this Covent
Garden restaurant, long a popular
pre-theatre destination, makes a convenient and central rendezvous for a
not-too-pricey party. / no amplified
music; no dancing; Downstairs (120,70,–,–).*

Café du Marché EC1
£M, (120,60,–,–)
22 Charterhouse Sq
☎ (020) 7608 1609
🖷 (020) 7336 7459
*A popular French restaurant, occupy-
ing a 'designer-rustic' warehouse conversion near Smithfield market. Its
has two rooms well suited to social
(and less formal business) occasions.
/ midnight; not available Sun;
Upstairs (120,60,–,–);
Rendezvous (80,40,–,–).*

Café Lazeez SW7
£M, (100,100,–,–)
93-95 Old Brompton Rd
☎ (020) 7581 9993
🖷 (020) 7581 8200
🖲 www.cafelazeez.com
📧 sl@cafelazeez.com
*A modernistic Indian restaurant in
South Kensington, whose upstairs*

CAPACITIES: (Standing, Seated, Dinner dance, Theatre-style)

room makes quite an elegant party venue. / 1 am; Downstairs (–,60,–,–); Upstairs (–,50,–,–).

Caper Green SE10
£B-M, (250,200,–,–)
The Teahouse, Greenwich Park
☎ (020) 8858 9695
🖷 (020) 8853 4774
Formerly called the Park Café, this is a cafeteria with a wonderful location. Although its private room is probably best suited to kids' parties, it has its own garden which would make a good spot for an outdoors evening party/barbecue for grown-ups. You can have the disco inside. A major refurbishment was under way at press time, so all details are provisional. / midnight; available from 7.30pm (winter from 4.30pm); including Garden (250,200,–,–); inside only (150,100,–,–).

Café Royal W1
£M, (3000,2500,450,540)
68 Regent St
☎ (020) 7437 9090
🖰 www.lemeridien.com
🖂 amanda.christie@ lemeridien.com
Eight remarkable floors of ballrooms, banqueting chambers, wine bar and restaurant, offering size, flexibility and grandeur. The first three (Victorian) floors have more character than the 1920s extension upward. Some rooms are licensed for weddings. Bookings for the ornate ground-floor Grill Room are dealt with by Elysium nightclub (see also). / 11.30pm; list of caterers, in-house available; Empire Napoleon (540,540,450,540); Dubarry & Dauphin (600,400,450,360); Louis (350,240,180,220); Dauphin (250,120,–,100); Derby & Queensbury (150,100,80,120); Grill Rm (120,80,60,–).

The Caledonian Club SW1
£M-E, (200,120,120,–)
9 Halkin St
☎ (020) 7235 5162
🖷 (020) 7235 4635
🖰 www.caledonian-club.org.uk
🖂 banqueting@ caledonianclub.com
This welcoming Belgravia club lacks some of the stuffiness of its St James's cousins and its ideal for many kinds of receptions and dinners (and reeling is possible, in the Members Dining Room). The sponsorship of a member is required, but for an event with a genuine Scottish link, it may be worth approaching the Secretary. / no children's parties; 2 am; members dining rm available eves only; no discos; Members Dining Rm (200,120,60,–); Stuart (65,52,–,–); Selkirk (40,22,–,–); Oval (–,12,–,–).

Calthorpe Arms WC1
£B, (60,36,–,–)
252 Grays Inn Rd
☎ (020) 7278 4732
Friendly Bloomsbury pub with quite a smart, well-maintained private room. / 11pm; not available weekday lunch; Private Rm (60,36,–,–).

The Camden Palace NW1
£M, (1500,250,250,–)
1a Camden High St
☎ 09062 100200
🖷 (020) 7388 8850
Characterful converted theatre premises, now well equipped to host many types of gathering, business or social. / 2.30pm Tue, Fri-Sat 6am; hirer's choice of caterer; Main Auditorium (800,250,250,–); Balcony (200,–,–,–); Royal Box (50,–,–,–).

PRIVATE VENUES

Canal Café Theatre W2
£B-M, (–,–,–,60)
Bridge House, Delamare Terrace
☎ (020) 7289 6056
🖳 (020) 7266 1717
🖱 www.newsrevue.com
📧 mail@canalcafetheatre.com
"The longest-running live comedy show in Britain". For your party, perhaps you'd like to block-book one of their twice-nightly shows. / 11.15pm; hirer's choice of caterer (in-house available); no dancing; Theatre (–,–,–,60).

The Candid Arts Trust EC1
£B-M, (200,100,–,–)
3 Torrens St
☎ (020) 7837 4237
🖱 www.candidarts.com
📧 info@candidarts.com
The banquet room at this idiosyncratic art gallery, near Angel tube, is one of the top bargains in town for an atmospheric party on a budget, offering flexible and reasonably priced accommodation for a whole range of functions. / 2 am; hirer's choice of caterer (in-house available); Ground Floor Gallery (200,100,–,–); Basement Gallery (200,100,–,–); Banquet Rm (50,29,–,–).

Canning House SW1
£B-M, (150,80,–,120)
2 Belgrave Sq
☎ (020) 7235 2303
🖱 www.canninghouse.com
📧 cknott@canninghouse.com
The first floor rooms of the Hispanic and Luso Brazilian Council, which overlook the square, are extremely popular for drinks parties. They offer affordable grandeur at a very smart address, a stone's throw from Hyde Park Corner. / 10pm; hirer's choice of caterer; no amplified music; no dancing; Drawing Rm (150,80,–,120); Library (70,–,–,70).

Cannizaro House SW19
£M-E, (120,100,60,–)
West Side, Wimbledon Common
☎ (020) 8879 1464
🖳 0870 333 9224
🖱 www.thistlehotels.com
📧 cannizarohouse@thistle.co.uk
A Georgian mansion-hotel, prettily situated in Cannizaro Park on the edge of Wimbledon Common. It offers a good range of function rooms of various sizes. / 11pm; smoking restricted; Viscount Melville Suite (120,96,60,–); Queen Elizabeth Rm (60,36,–,–); Oak Rm (30,18,–,–); Blue Rm (40,30,–,–); Boardroom (–,10,–,–).

Canonbury Academy N1
£M-E, (120,55,–,90)
6 Canonbury Place, Islington
☎ (020) 7359 6888
🖱 www.canonburyacademy.co.uk
📧 canonburyacademy@
btinternet.com
A beautifully refurbished c16 Benedictine priory standing in its own gardens. Each individually decorated room – of which there are 25 – has antique furniture and overlooks the gardens. This is a venue best suited to quieter corporate events. / companies only; 9.30pm; weekdays only; hirer's choice of caterer (in-house available); no amplified music; no dancing; no smoking; Long Gallery (120,55,–,90); Queen Elizabeth (60,30,–,32); Wentworth (35,24,–,–); Denby Suite (70,40,–,50).

The Capital SW3
£M-E, (30,22,–,–)
Basil St
☎ (020) 7589 5171
🖳 (020) 7225 0011
🖱 www.capitalhotel.co.uk
📧 carol@capitalhotel.co.uk
The private dining rooms of this chic, small hotel – right by Harrods – are in a fairly traditional style. Its restaurant has long had a reputation well above average. / Eaton (30,10,–,–); Cadogan (–,22,–,–).

CAPACITIES: (Standing, Seated, Dinner dance, Theatre-style)

Captain Kidd E1
£B, (60,50,50,–)
108 Wapping High St
☎ (020) 7480 5759
One of the most popular places for food and drink in the Docklands, this olde worlde riverside pub has one function room – the second floor Observation Deck (which has large windows overlooking the river). Parties of up to 30 can take a corner of the Gallows restaurant. / 11pm; not available Sun; The Observation Deck (60,50,–,–).

Cargo EC2
£B-M, (500,–,–,–)
83 Rivington St
☎ (020) 7739 3440
🖷 (020) 7739 3441
🖱 www.cargo-london.com
Huge converted railway arches – now a large venue complete with major sound system that has become a lynchpin of the ever-more trendy Shoreditch scene.

Carlton Club SW1
£M-E, (600,180,180,150)
69 St James's St
☎ (020) 7399 0904
🖷 (020) 74954090
🖱 www.carltonclub.co.uk
📧 catering@carltonclub.co.uk
The spiritual home of the Tory party, this elegant St James's club – which has a wonderful staircase – makes a very congenial venue for those of a rightwards persuasion. It has a good range of accommodation, but all events require the sponsorship of a member. / midnight; in-house caterers; Churchill Rm (200,92,92,150); Disraeli Rm (50,24,–,35); Macmillan Rm (50,24,–,35); Cabinet Rm (70,36,–,36); Library (40,18,–,30).

The Carlton Mitre Hotel, Surrey
£M-E, (140,90,90,120)
Hampton Court
☎ (020) 8979 9988
🖱 www.carltonhotels.co.uk
📧 gmmitre@carltonhotels.co.uk
Over three centuries old, this Thames-side hotel, with views over Hampton Court Palace, has pleasant function facilities. Should you choose to arrive or depart by boat, the Landings Bar benefits from its own private mooring. / no 18ths, 21sts or stag nights; midnight; Pavilion (140,90,70,120); Cardinal Wolsey (30,–,–,30); (–,–,–,–).

Carlton Tower SW1
£M-E, (670,400,360,–)
Cadogan Pl
☎ (020) 7235 1234
🖷 (020) 7823 1708
🖱 www.carltontower.com
📧 events@carltontower.com
The ballroom of this modern but fairly traditionally luxurious Belgravia hotel was remodelled in 1996. If you're looking for something a little different, you might consider the Water Garden, a semi-tropical room, next to the swimming pool. / 1 am; Ballroom (670,400,360,–); Garden Rm (100,60,–,–); Water Garden (80,30,–,–); Boardroom (–,16,–,–).

Carpenters' Hall EC2
£M, (350,220,–,220)
Throgmorton Av
☎ (020) 7382 1670
🖷 (020) 7382 1683
🖱 www.thecarpenterscompany.co.uk
Forming the arch over the London Wall end of Throgmorton Avenue, this livery hall, in distinctive '60s style, makes quite an impressive venue. / no weddings; 11pm; not available weekends; list of caterers; no amplified music; no dancing; smoking restricted; Livery Hall (350,220,–,220); Reception Rm (230,–,–,–); Luncheon Rm (–,32,–,–).

Cavalry & Guards Club W1
£M, (350,130,–,–)
127 Piccadilly
☎ (020) 7499 1261
🖷 (020) 7495 5956
🖱 www.cavgds.co.uk
📧 functions@cavgds.co.uk
This carefully maintained Edwardian club, overlooking Green Park, has a number of charming traditional rooms. / midnight; not available Sun; in-

*house caterers; Coffee Rm (300,130,–,–);
Peninsula Rm (140,84,–,–); Waterloo
Rm (60,18,–,–); Double Bridle Rm (20,8,–,–).*

The CBI Conference Centre WC1

£M, (–,–,–,200)
Centre Point, 103 New Oxford St
☎ (020) 7395 8014
🖰 www.etcvenues.co.uk
🖂 nghani@etcvenues.co.uk
*At the bottom of the landmark
Centre Point tower, a flexible suite of
rooms suitable for conferences and
for business entertaining generally.
/ in-house caterers; no smoking;
Methven (–,–,–,200); Rms 1, 2 &
3 (–,–,–,75); Rm 1 (–,–,–,25); Rm
2 (–,–,–,25).*

CC Club W1

£M, (1000,150,100,200)
13 Coventry St
☎ (020) 7297 3234
🖨 (020) 7297 3201
🖰 www.cc-club.co.uk
🖂 events@cc-club.co.uk
*Popular in the media 'n' fashion
worlds, this handily-located West End
club-venue offers flexible accommodation for functions. / list of caterers; Bar
M (250,50,30,50).*

Cecil Sharp House NW1

£B-M, (500,300,300,–)
2 Regent's Park Rd
☎ (020) 7485 2206
🖨 (020) 7284 0534
🖰 www.efdss.org
🖂 hire@efdss.org
*The Primrose Hill home of the
English Folk Dance and Song Society
has two panelled halls which are
available for private receptions and
dances (semi-sprung floors). There is
a small, attractive walled garden.
/ 11pm; in-house caterers; smoking restricted;
Kennedy Hall (500,300,300,–); Trefusis
Hall (140,100,100,–); Bar (65,–,–,–); Storrow
Hall (50,25,–,–).*

Central Hall Westminster SW1

£M, (700,2350,300,2350)
Storey's Gate
☎ (020) 7222 8010
🖰 www.c-h-w.com
🖂 events@c-h-w.com
*If you're looking for a central meeting
place, this vast Viennese Baroque
confection opposite Westminster
Abbey certainly lives up to its name,
and it offers a number of options for
events on quite a scale. No booze,
though. / hirer's choice of caterer (in-house
available); no smoking; no alcohol; Great
Hall (–,550,–,2350); Lecture
Hall (700,500,300,500);
Library (700,500,300,500);
Westminster (350,250,180,250);
Assembly (200,150,80,150).*

The Chainstore E14

£B-M, (2000,1000,1000,–)
Trinity Buoy Wharf
☎ (020) 7377 8001
🖰 www.mask.co.uk
🖂 enquiries@mask.co.uk
*Across the Thames from the
Millennium Dome, a venue compris-
ing London's only lighthouse plus a
restored warehouse offers accommodation on a considerable scale. If
that's not enough for you, there's
also a two-acre marquee site. / hirer's
choice of caterer.*

Charlotte Street Hotel W1

£M-E, (67,20,–,67)
15 Charlotte St
☎ (020) 7806 2000
🖨 (020) 7806 2002
🖰 www.firmdalehotels.com
🖂 charlotte@firmdale.com
*A boutique hotel in a street long
famous for restaurants, just north of
Soho. It offers a range of options for
intimate gatherings, with a private
screening room a particular feature.
/ midnight; in-house caterers; no dancing;
Private Screening Rm (–,–,–,67);
Rm1 (67,20,–,25); Rm 2 (25,12,–,12);
Library (10,–,–,–); Private Dining
Rm (–,12,–,–).*

CAPACITIES: (Standing, Seated, Dinner dance, Theatre-style)

Chartered Accountants' Hall EC2
£M, (400,250,200,325)
Moorgate Pl
☎ (020) 7920 8613
⌂ www.cahall.co.uk
✉ ebolling@icaew.co.uk
An elegant, attractive and extremely well-maintained City complex, which includes two interesting, traditional-style rooms (Members' and Main Reception) and a tasteful modern hall. / midnight; in-house caterers; Great Hall (400,250,200,325); Main Reception Rm (100,50,–,70); Members' Rm (70,28,–,40); Small Reception Rm (35,18,–,–); Restaurant (250,80,80,80).

Chartered Institute of Public Finance & Accountancy WC2
£M, (40,40,–,40)
3 Robert St
☎ (020) 7543 5612
⌂ www.cipfa.org.uk
✉ conference.centre@cipfa.org
Though perhaps a little institutional, this Adam house offers a fine view over the Embankment from its fourth-floor committee room, which is suitable for receptions or dinners. There are lower-floor rooms, which are really only suited to business entertaining. / 10.30pm; not available weekends; Owen Bros; no smoking; Committee Rm 4 (40,24,–,40); Council Chamber (40,34,–,–); Committee Rm 5 (10,12,–,–).

Chatham Hall SW11
£B, (100,80,–,–)
152 Northcote Rd
☎ (020) 8871 6394
🖷 (020) 8871 6391
⌂ www.wandsworth.gov.uk/publichalls
Former Battersea stables, available for events including children's parties (around 50 youngsters) or cocktail parties. / 11pm; hirer's choice of caterer; no amplified music.

The Chelsea Gardener SW3
£B-M, (400,150,–,–)
125 Sydney St
☎ (020) 7352 9881
🖷 (020) 7352 9809
✉ daphne@chelseagardener.demon.co.uk
There are few half-acre sized gardens in Chelsea, so this one – the garden centre at The Chelsea Gardeners' Market – is popular for summer soirées. If it rains, you can always shelter in the conservatory. / 10.30pm; available from 6.30pm, not available Fri; list of caterers; no dancing; smoking restricted.

Chelsea Old Town Hall SW3
£B-M, (400,180,140,400)
King's Rd
☎ (020) 7361 2207
🖷 (020) 7361 3164
⌂ www.rbkc.gov.uk
✉ hall-let@rbkc.gov.uk

For a large event, this civic hall is grand, well-maintained, centrally-located and affordable. The adjoining register office has always been a fashionable wedding venue – now the Main and Small Halls of the Town Hall itself are also available for this purpose. / midnight; list of caterers; Main Hall (400,180,140,400); Small Hall (150,100,80,150); Cadogan Suite (120,–,–,–).

PRIVATE VENUES

Chelsea Physic Garden SW3

£M, (400,80,–,100)
66 Royal Hospital Rd
☎ (020) 7352 5646
⌂ www.cpgarden.demon.co.uk
✉ maureen@
cpgarden.demon.co.uk
This 3.5 acre botanical garden, hidden away in Old Chelsea, has been here since 1673. It makes a fascinating spot for a summer drinks party, but not – thanks to the dual hazards of deadly nightshade and ponds – with kids present. / 10.30pm; available May-Sep, Mon-Thu eves & Sat; list of caterers; no amplified music; no dancing; smoking restricted; with Marquee (Sat in Jun-Sep only) (300,250,–,–); Reception Rm (150,60,–,–); Lecture Rm (–,–,–,100).

Chelsea Village SW6

£M-E, (1500,500,400,300)
Stamford Bridge, Fulham Rd
☎ (020) 7565 1400
🖶 (020) 7915 1914
⌂ www.chelseavillage.com
✉ conference@
chelseavillage.com
A modern Fulham venue, overlooking the Chelsea FC ground, with flexible function facilities and exhibition space. / 1 am; in-house caterers; Exhibition Space (1500,500,400,–); Drakes Suite (650,300,220,–); Jimmys (130,60,–,–); Galleria (800,450,400,300); Trophy Rm (175,80,70,60).

Chessington World of Adventures, Surrey

£M-E, (300,300,250,250)
Chessington, Surrey
☎ 01372 731595
🖶 01372 725050
⌂ www.chessington.co.uk
✉ events@chessington.co.uk
With easy access to the M25, a theme park providing an adventurous setting for a (probably corporate) day out. / midnight; Alexander Catering; Hospitality Marquee (300,300,250,200); Glade (300,300,250,250); Keg (150,120,100,–).

The Chesterfield Mayfair W1

£M, (150,120,90,–)
35 Charles St
☎ (020) 7491 2622
⌂ www.redcarnationhotels.com
✉ meeting@chesterfield.
redcarnationhotels.com

A clubby and comfortable hotel near Shepherd Market offering a good range of quite characterful rooms – from a panelled library to a conservatory. / 1 am; hirer's choice of caterer (in-house available); Royal Suite (150,120,90,–); Conservatory (60,30,–,–); Library (30,16,–,–); Stanhope Suite (25,8,–,–).

Cheyne Walk Brasserie SW3

£M, (200,80,–,–)
50 Cheyne Wk
☎ (020) 7376 8787
🖶 (020) 7876 5878
⌂ www.cheynewalkbrasserie.com
Perhaps one of the Chelsea restaurants most obviously suited to hiring as a whole, this lovely building (once a pub) doesn't just benefit from one of the smartest street-addresses in town. Its loungey upstairs bar has lovely river views.
/ Salon/lounge/bar (60,–,–,–).

Chez Bruce SW17

£M, (–,16,–,–)
2 Bellevue Rd
☎ (020) 8672 0114
🖶 (020) 8767 6648
This Wandsworth restaurant – unchallenged as the best in south London – has a pleasant room upstairs, overlooking the common. It is available for private functions only at lunchtime. / available lunchtime only; no smoking; Private Rm (–,16,–,–).

CAPACITIES: (Standing, Seated, Dinner dance, Theatre-style)

Chez Gérard, Dover Street W1
£B-M, (35,25,–,–)
31 Dover St
☎ (020) 7499 8171
🖨 (020) 7491 3818
🖱 www.sante.co.uk
✉ doverstreet@
   groupechezgerard.co.uk
The Mayfair branch of the steak/frites chain has a particularly nice downstairs room. More extensive (semi-) private dining facilities are afforded by the mezzanine.
/ 11.30pm; Private Rm (30,15,–,–); Mezzanine (–,30,–,–).

Chez Gérard, Opera Terrace WC2
£B-M, (150,–,–,–)
The Market, The Piazza, Covent Garden
☎ (020) 7379 0666
🖨 (020) 7497 9060
🖱 www.sante.co.uk
The terrace of this branch of the Chez Gérard steak-frites chain overlooks the Royal Opera House, and offers one of the most central alfresco venues. As a private hire venue, it's suitable only for drinks and canâpés. / 11.30pm.

China White W1
£M-E, (400,250,–,–)
6 Air St
☎ (020) 7343 0040
🖨 (020) 7343 0041
🖱 www.chinawhite.com
This louche, oriental basement near Piccadilly Circus still cultivates its (once formidable) reputation as a celeb-magnet. It doesn't market itself as a venue, and declined to answer all our fact-checking questions – if your event's face fits, though, you might find an enquiry worthwhile.
/in-house caterers.

Chintamani SW1
£M-E, (350,130,100,–)
122 Jermyn St
☎ (020) 7839 2020
🖨 (020) 7839 7700
With its lavish and groovy, Turkish-inspired décor, this large, new St James's restaurant lends itself to use for private functions. It comes equipped with a sound system (and space can be made for dancing).
/ 1 am.

Chiswick House W4
£E, (150,80,80,–)
Burlington Ln
☎ (020) 7973 3292
🖨 (020) 7973 3443
🖱 www.heritagehospitality.org.uk
✉ jane.coughlan@english-
   heritage.org.uk
A grand Palladian villa (1729) with a suite of interconnecting first-floor rooms. You might dine in the octagonal Domed Saloon, with its coffered domed ceiling – other rooms feature period paintings and furniture.
/ 11pm; available summer from 6.30pm, winter from 4.30pm; list of caterers; no smoking; no red wine for standing receptions ; 1st floor (6 Rms) (150,80,–,–); Domed Saloon (80,48,–,–); Courtyard Marquee (185,150,130,–).

Christie's SW1
£M-E, (700,200,–,–)
8 King St
☎ (020) 7389 2205
🖨 (020) 7839 1611
🖱 www.christies.com
✉ sburridge@christies.com
The grand galleries of this St James's auctioneer are, subject to other requirements, sometimes made available for functions. / midnight; available Mon-Fri from 6pm; hirer's choice of caterer; no amplified music; no dancing; no smoking; Great Rm (500,200,–,–); Rm 1 (200,70,–,–); Rm 2 (150,70,–,–).

PRIVATE VENUES

Christopher's WC2
£M-E, (250,100,–,–)
18 Wellington St
☎ (020) 7834 1888
🖷 (020) 7834 1188
🖰 www.christophersgrill.com
📧 jofirth@christophersgrill.com
This upmarket American restaurant – which occupies a very impressive Victorian building in Covent Garden, which was once apparently a brothel – has a fully private basement dining room and also a bar available for hire. The Small Dining Room benefits from a location on the light and impressive 'piano nobile', but is rather less private. / Private Dining Rm (80,40,–,–); Small Dining Rm (–,26,–,–); Bar (80,–,–,–).

Chuen Cheng Ku W1
£B, (–,400,–,–)
17 Wardour St
☎ (020) 7437 1398
🖷 (020) 7434 0533
Vast, gaudy, Chinatown restaurant set in a building some of whose rooms retain quite a degree of period grandeur. Any of the rooms (for groups of 30 people and up) may be taken privately. / Rm 1 (–,180,–,–); Rm 2 (–,100,–,–); Rm 3 (–,60,–,–); Rm 4 (–,40,–,–).

Church House SW1
£M, (250,200,120,200)
Dean's Yd
☎ (020) 7460 7500
🖷 (020) 7390 1591
🖰 www.churchhouseconf.co.uk
📧 sales@churchhouseconf.co.uk
The Conference Centre at Church House has an impressive location near Westminster Abbey, and is well appointed, if in a rather understated way. Perhaps oddly, you can have a civil wedding here too! / midnight; not available Sun; Crown Catering; no amplified music; Harvey Goodwin Suite (250,150,120,200); Hoare Memorial Hall (250,130,–,–); Bishop Partridge Hall (160,80,–,–); Westminster (30,20,–,–); Jubilee (15,10,–,–).

Churchill W1
£M, (300,240,180,–)
30 Portman Sq
☎ (020) 7486 5800
🖰 www.interconti.com
📧 churchill@interconti.com
The banqueting facilities of this '70s hotel north of Oxford Street were completely refurbished in 2001. The Library and the Chartwell Suites are licensed for weddings. / 1 am; Chartwell Suite (300,240,180,–); Chartwell 1 (200,144,80,–); Library (120,50,–,–); Marlborough Suite (80,50,–,–); Randolph (40,30,–,–).

Cibo W14
£M, (–,60,–,–)
3 Russell Gdns
☎ (020) 7371 6271
🖷 (020) 7602 1371
🖰 www.ciborestaurant.co.uk
An Olympia Italian restaurant with rather unusual décor and good food. It can be hired in its entirety for parties, or alternatively there are two (fairly) private rooms. / 1 am; Private Rm (–,16,–,–); Private Rm (–,12,–,–).

Cicada EC1
£M, (70,–,–,–)
132-136 St John St
☎ (020) 7608 1550
🖷 (020) 7608 1551
🖰 www.cicada.nu
📧 mark@cicada.nu
This trendy Smithfield bar restaurant has a pleasant downstairs party room, decorated in opium den style. / 1 am; available Mon-Sat.

CAPACITIES: (Standing, Seated, Dinner dance, Theatre-style)

48

The Cinnamon Club SW1

£M, (400,150,–,–)
Great Smith St
☎ (020) 7222 2555
🖷 (020) 7222 1333
🖱 www.cinnamonclub.com
🖂 info@cinnamonclub.com

This Indian restaurant in Westminster has created quite a reputation for its Indian food presented European-style, and its setting – in a converted library, with some books still in situ – would make an ideal setting for an event. Hire the mezzanine, or take over the whole place.
/ Private Dining Rm (80,50,–,–); Mezzanine (50,30,–,–).

The Circus W1
£M-E, (200,140,–,–)
1 Upper James St
☎ (020) 7534 4000
🖷 (020) 7534 4010
The bar of this impressively designed modern restaurant in Soho is well suited to private parties, and for smaller dinners there is a private room. Alternatively, for a large do, you can take the whole place. / Private Dining Rm (–,22,–,–).

Circus Space N1
£M-E, (500,320,320,310)
Coronet St
☎ (020) 7613 4141
🖱 www.thecircusspace.co.uk
🖂 louisemarchant@
thecircusspace.co.uk
This huge, high-ceilinged City-fringe venue is a training area for circus acts. It can be hired for corporate events (when a certain amount of theming will almost certainly be required). / restricted availability; 12.30

am; hirer's choice of caterer; Combustion Chamber (500,320,320,310); Generating Chamber (350,110,110,200).

Cittie of Yorke WC1
£B, (300,100,100,–)
22 High Holborn
☎ (020) 7242 7670
🖷 (020) 7405 6371
The main bar of this large pub by the entrance to Gray's Inn is one of the largest and most characterful of any pub in London – with brass pipes, wooden alcoves and a high wooden ceiling. You can also hire the Cellar Bar (a long, thin, white-walled vault) or the rather ordinary Front Bar. / 1 am; Main Bar (300,100,100,–); Cellar Bar (120,65,40,–); Front Bar (80,40,–,–).

City Club EC2
£M, (500,115,90,–)
19 Old Broad St
☎ (020) 7588 8558
🖷 (020) 7374 2020
🖱 www.cityclub.uk.com
🖂 banq@cityclub.uk.com
A charming, early-Victorian institution (the oldest club in the City) whose first-floor smoking room is one of a number of fine period rooms for entertaining. There are also some nice modern rooms around a terrace garden. You can now get married here too. / 1 am; in-house caterers; Main Dining Rm (300,115,90,–); Upper Smoking Rms (200,–,–,–); Garden Rm (100,50,–,–); Salisbury Rm (50,40,–,–); Masterman/Wellington Rms (20,14,–,–); Hardwick Rm (–,10,–,–).

City Conference Centre EC2
£M, (150,125,–,140)
80 Coleman St
☎ (020) 7382 2626
🖱 www.cityconferencecentre.co.uk
🖂 andy@
cityconferencecentre.co.uk
As you would expect, most of the rooms at this City conference centre are fairly businesslike in style. The Council and Committee Rooms, however, occupy elegant period rooms,

and have been decorated in an understated traditional style. / 10pm; weekdays only; in-house caterers; no amplified music; no dancing; no smoking; Parsons Rm (–,–,–,140); Ocean Suite (150,125,–,–); Council Rm (60,32,–,32); Indian (30,20,–,25); Arctic (30,20,–,25); Committee Rm (20,10,–,–).

City Hall - London's Living Room SE1
£M-E, (250,100,–,120)
The Queens Walk
☎ (020) 7983 4088
🖷 (020) 7983 4137
📧 hannah.mcmorran@
   london.gov.uk
London's Living Room is situated on the top floor of City Hall (the 'headlamp') and offers stunning panoramic views of the London skyline. Organisations will need permission from Mr Mayor. / restricted availability; in-house caterers; no dancing; no smoking; London's Living Rm (250,100,–,120).

City Inn Westminster SW1
£M, (120,64,64,100)
30 John Islip St
☎ (020) 7630 1000
🖰 www.cityinn.com/westminster
The Sky Lounge, with its impressive views, is the highlight attraction at this large new hotel, near Tate Britain. / midnight; in-house caterers; smoking restricted; Private Dining (120,64,64,100); Sky Lounge (–,12,–,–).

City Miyama EC4
£M-E, (–,10,–,–)
17 Godliman St
☎ (020) 7489 1937
🖷 (020) 7236 0325
For a private Japanese dinner in the City this is one of the smartest places (and priced accordingly). / 10pm; not available Sat eves & Sun; Private Rm (–,10,–,–); Private Rm (–,6,–,–); Private Rm (x2) (–,4,–,–).

The City Presentation Centre EC1
£M, (80,–,–,120)
4 Chiswell St, Finsbury Sq
☎ (020) 7628 5646
🖷 (020) 7628 6776
🖰 www.thecity
   presentationcentre.co.uk
The name says it all – a venue mainly used for financial world presentations. / 7pm; weekdays only; in-house caterers; no music; no dancing; no smoking; no spirits; Theatre (80,–,–,120).

City University EC1
£B-M, (300,250,–,360)
Event Management Service, Northampton Sq
☎ (020) 7040 5060
🖷 (020) 7040 8592
🖰 www.city.ac.uk/ems
📧 events@city.ac.uk
The university has a number of theatres and meeting rooms for hire. Most of the facilities – but not the Level Six Suite – are only available out of term. / restricted availability; 11pm; in-house caterers; no music; no dancing; no smoking; Oliver Thompson Lecture Theatre (–,–,–,360); Level Six Suite (300,184,–,184); Tait Meeting Rms (–,22,–,22).

The Clachan W1
£B, (70,40,–,–)
34 Kingly St
☎ (020) 7494 0834
With its own street-entrance, this Soho pub (behind Liberty) has an upstairs function room which is comfortably furnished, by pub standards. A further attraction includes a variety of real ales. / 11.20pm; Highland Bar (70,40,–,–).

Claridge's W1 ✳
£M-E, (400,240,192,–)
Brook St
☎ (020) 7629 8860
🖰 www.claridges.co.uk
📧 banqueting@claridges.co.uk
This Mayfair dowager has in recent years become one of London's most consistently successful grand hotels,

CAPACITIES: (Standing, Seated, Dinner dance, Theatre-style)

and it has some very elegant function facilities (especially the Ballroom). Catering is in the hands of chef-of-the-moment Gordon Ramsay. / midnight; in-house caterers; Ballroom (400,240,192,–); Drawing Rm, French Salon or Mirror Rm (200,96,–,–); Kensington (80,50,–,–); St James's (25,18,–,–); Amarillis (–,30,–,–); Salon (–,10,–,–); Davies (–,12,–,–); Chef's Table (–,6,–,–).

The Clink SE1
£B-M, (200,160,160,–)
1 Clink St
☎ (020) 7403 6515
🖰 www.clink.co.uk
A stone's throw from London Bridge, this former prison (yes, the original) and erstwhile brothel is now a tourist attraction – exhibitions follow prostitution through the ages. The entrance is marked with a gibbet (complete with corpse). Take the whole place or, in the evening, the museum or the medieval-style Winchester Hall. / 2 am; list of caterers.

Cliveden, Berks
£E, (250,170,–,20)
Berry Hill, Taplow
☎ 01628 668561
🖷 01628 661837
🖰 www.clivedenhouse.co.uk
The Astors' Thames-side palazzo, set in National Trust grounds, is now one of the UK's most luxurious hotels. One possibility is to take the whole place over for a house party, though for more 'modest' events the French Dining Room (whose c18 panelling was removed from a château near Paris) is a particular attraction. / in-house caterers; Great Hall (170,–,–,–); Terraced Dining Rm (–,110,–,–); French Dining Rm (75,60,–,–); Macmillan Boardroom (–,20,–,20).

Clothworkers' Hall EC3
£M-E, (350,224,–,–)
Dunster Court, Mincing Ln
☎ (020) 7623 7041
🖷 (020) 7387 0107
🖰 www.clothworkers.co.uk
One of the grandest halls in the City – it is made available on a limited basis, primarily for business, livery and charity functions. Guests proceed from a contemporary hall up to the elegant first-floor Reception Room. Off this opens the Livery Hall – a '50s chamber, decorated on traditional lines. / no weddings; 11pm; not available Fri-Sun; list of caterers; no amplified music; no dancing; smoking restricted; Livery Hall (350,224,–,–); Reception Rm (200,–,–,–).

The Cobden Club W10
£M, (350,110,90,–)
170-172 Kensal Rd
☎ (020) 8960 4222
🖰 www.cobdenclub.co.uk
🖃 info@cobdenclub.co.uk
A fashionable North Kensington hang-out, housed above a still-functioning working men's club. The main party space is the 'retro-baroque' Grand Hall – like all the facilities, it may be made available to non-members at 'off-peak' times. / 1.30 am; not available Sun; in-house caterers; The Grand Hall (180,100,–,–); Restaurant (150,120,–,–); Private Rm (–,18,–,–).

Cochrane Theatre WC1
£B-M, (–,–,–,314)
Southampton Row
☎ (020) 7269 1600
🖷 (020) 7831 5476
🖃 info@cochranetheatre.co.uk
A modern theatre, well suited to presentations, but subject to the constraints of the current shows. / available subject to constraints of current production; hirer's choice of caterer; smoking restricted; Auditorium (–,–,–,314).

The Coliseum WC2
£B-M, (200,80,95,100)
St Martin's Ln
☎ (020) 7836 0111
🖷 (020) 7845 9272
🖳 www.eno.org
✉ marketing@eno.org
Europe's largest lyric theatre was undergoing an ongoing renovation programme at press time. In the circumstances the capacities given should be regarded as strictly provisional. / in-house caterers; no dancing; no smoking; Terrace Bar (200,80,80,100); Dutch Bar (200,90,95,–); Stoll Rm (30,14,–,14); Arlen Rm (12,8,–,–); Chairman's (45,20,–,20).

The Collection SW3
£M-E, (350,200,–,–)
264 Brompton Rd
☎ (020) 7225 1212
🖷 (020) 7225 1050
🖳 www.the-collection.co.uk
With its wonderfully posey catwalk entrance, this glossy South Kensington address is ideally suited a private venue for 'look-at-me' events. You can hire the whole place, or just the mezzanine dining space overlooking the large bar. / ; 1 am; in-house caterers; Mezzanine (250,200,–,–).

College of Arms EC4
£M, (200,–,–,–)
Queen Victoria St
☎ (020) 7236 7708
🖳 www.college-of-arms.gov.uk
If you're looking for a fascinating venue with real history, this c17 City college – the ultimate arbiter on all matters heraldic – is available for book-launches or for other fairly sedate events held by charities or those with an interest in heraldry or genealogy. / 9pm; available weekdays from 5pm; list of caterers; music by agreement only; no dancing; smoking restricted; Earl Marshal's Court (60,–,–,–); Waiting Rm (40,–,–,–).

Le Colombier SW3
£M, (–,30,–,–)
145 Dovehouse St
☎ (020) 7351 1155
🖷 (020) 7351 0077
A well-reputed mid-range traditional French restaurant in Chelsea, which benefits from a light and unusually well-proportioned first-floor private room. / Private Rm (–,30,–,–).

The Comedy Store SW1
£M, (400,400,–,400)
1a Oxendon St
☎ (020) 7839 6642
🖳 www.thecomedystore.co.uk
✉ charlotte@thecomedystore.co.uk
A comics' venue, near Piccadilly Circus, available for private hire. In-house video facilities, too. / available Mon all day & Tue, Thu & Fri afternoon; hirer's choice of caterer, alcohol in-house.

Comedy Theatre SW1
£M, (–,–,–,790)
Panton St
☎ (020) 7321 5312
🖳 www.theambassadors.com
✉ comedymanager@theambassadors.com
A Victorian theatre, last reconstructed in the 1950s, available for hire subject to the constraints of the current production. / available subject to constraints of current production; in-house caterers; smoking restricted.

The Commonwealth Club WC2
£M-E, (650,224,170,150)
18 Northumberland Ave
☎ (020) 7766 9224
🖷 (020) 7766 9888
🖳 www.rcsint.org
✉ events@rcsint.org
A suspended glass dining room – unique in London, apparently – is one of the features of the extensive function facilities at this modern club building, just off Trafalgar Square. / 11.30pm; in-house caterers; Lower Ground Hall (250,120,100,–); Thorne

CAPACITIES: (Standing, Seated, Dinner dance, Theatre-style)

Rm (–,–,–,120); Cinema Rm (100,64,–,80); Blue Rm (70,60,–,60); Glass Dining Rm (–,16,–,–).

Commonwealth Conference & Events Centre W8
£M, (1500,1500,1500,460)
Kensington High St
☎ (020) 7603 3412
🖨 (020) 7603 9634
🖱 www.commonwealth.org.uk
📧 info@commonwealth.org.uk
There are few sorts of corporate events for which this unusual Holland Park building, set in three acres of gardens, is not well suited. Don't delay, though – it's sadly scheduled to shut down in July 2004. / 1 am; in-house caterers; smoking restricted; Commonwealth Galleries (1500,1500,1500,–); Exhibition Hall (450,240,250,–); Bradley (100,70,–,–); Tweedsmuir (50,30,–,–); Main Auditorium (–,–,–,460); Gillette (130,120,100,170); JBR (175,100,80,100).

Congress Centre WC1
£M, (800,220,200,500)
23-28 Gt Russell St
☎ (020) 7467 1318
🖨 (020) 7467 1313
🖱 www.congresscentre.co.uk
📧 congresscentre@tuc.org.uk
It's not just champagne socialists who can party at the TUC's fine '50s memorial building. The glass-walled Marble Hall, overlooked by a huge Epstein statue, is an elegant modern reception space, while the Congress Hall suits dinners and dances. You can even get married here. / hirer's choice of caterer (in-house available); smoking restricted; Congress Hall (800,220,200,500); Marble Hall (200,–,–,–); Council Chamber (200,80,–,160); Invision Suite (120,–,–,135).

The Connaught W1
£M-E, (–,22,–,–)
Carlos Pl
☎ (020) 7499 7070
🖱 www.gordonramsay.com
📧 privatedining@ angelahartnett.com
This small and discreet grand hotel has nothing so brash as a ballroom. There are two sharply contrasting private dining rooms – the extraordinarily pretty Regency Carlos Suite, including a small glazed ante-room, and the smaller, rather sober Georgian room. / in-house caterers; Regency Carlos Suite (–,22,–,–); Georgian Rm (–,12,–,–).

Conrad Hotel SW10
£M, (350,200,180,–)
Chelsea Harbour
☎ (020) 7823 3000
🖱 www.conradhotels.com
📧 lonch-salesadm@hilton.com
This modern waterside hotel has the benefit – or disadvantage – of feeling much further from the centre of town than it actually is. There is a wide range of facilities for functions which, though rather corporate in feel, are fitted to a high standard. / 2 am; Drake Suite (350,200,180,–); Henley Suite (250,200,160,–); Henley 1 (150,70,–,–); Harbour (75,50,–,–); Aquasia (–,60,–,–).

The Conservatory SW11
£B-M, (100,50,–,–)
Ransome's Dock, 35-37 Parkgate
☎ (020) 8874 8505
🖨 (020) 8874 0715
🖱 www.theconservatoryvenue.co.uk
📧 maggie@ theconservatoryvenue.co.uk
A modern rooftop conservatory (fully heated in winter), perched on top of a building by Albert Bridge (and accessed via a spiral staircase). It boasts plants, sculptures and terraces. / midnight; hirer's choice of caterer; no amplified music; no dancing.

Conway Hall WC1
£B-M, (350,192,275,500)
25 Red Lion Sq
☎ (020) 7242 8032
🖷 (020) 7242 8036
🕆 www.conwayhall.org.uk
On the corner of a Bloomsbury square, the South Place Ethical Society (the UK's largest humanist group) occupies a 1930s Art Deco hall. This offers a range of characterful, if not especially smart, accommodation, suitable for a wide range of functions. / midnight; hirer's choice of caterer; smoking restricted; Large Hall (350,192,275,500); Small Hall (100,40,40,100).

Ochre EC4
£B, (200,120,–,–)
2-3 Creed Ln
☎ (020) 7248 7799
🖷 (020) 7329 0215
🕆 www.coolin.co.uk
🖃 coolinbar@hotmail.com
A modern City bar/restaurant, with a basement private room. On Saturday night, you can hire the whole place. / in-house caterers; Function Rm (60,40,–,–).

Coopers Arms SW3
£B-M, (–,25,–,–)
87 Flood St
☎ (020) 7376 3120
🖷 (020) 7352 9187
🕆 www.thecoopers.co.uk
🖃 drinks@thecoopers.co.uk
An attractive Chelsea pub with a pleasant party room upstairs, where two dozen people can sit around a ship's dining table. / 11.45pm; available eves only; no music; no dancing; Private Rm (–,25,–,–).

Coopers' Hall EC2
£M, (60,32,–,30)
13 Devonshire Sq
☎ (020) 7247 9577
🖷 (020) 7377 8061
🖃 clerk@coopers-hall.co.uk
Livery hall – Georgian in origin – used for some business functions as well as livery dinners. It is available primarily to an established circle of former users but applications from

newcomers will be considered. / 10.30pm; not available weekends; Party Ingredients; no amplified music; no dancing.

Coq d'Argent EC2
£M-E, (300,150,–,–)
1 Poultry
☎ (020) 7395 5000
🖷 (020) 7395 5050
🕆 www.conran.com
Conran's grand top-floor restaurant boasts views and an impressive garden, overlooking the Bank of England, and impressive outdoor terraces. It has no private dining as such, but the whole place would make quite a spectacular venue for a (City boy and girl's) wedding. / 1 am; Outdoor Terraces (300,150,–,–).

Coram's Fields WC1
£M-E, (2800,1400,1200,1400)
Russell Square, Guilford St
☎ 0870 011 1991
🖷 0870 011 1446
🕆 www.europeangroup.co.uk
🖃 enquiries@ europeangroup.co.uk
Generally a Bloomsbury sanctuary for kids and their minders, this large site becomes a corporate Christmas playground every December. / 1 am; available December only; list of caterers; Split Facility (1400,700,700,700); Party Chalet 2 (250,125,125,125); Party Chalet (150,75,75,75).

Corney & Barrow
£B,
🕆 www.corney-barrow.co.uk
9 Cabot Sq, Canary Wharf, E14
☎ (020) 7512 0397 (300,90,–,–)
🖃 canary.wharf@ winebar-corbar.co.uk
5 Exchange Sq, Broadgate, EC2
☎ (020) 7628 4367 (70,70,–,–)
🖃 exchange.square@ winebar-corbar.co.uk
111 Old Broad St, EC2
☎(020) 7448 3700 (150,100,150,–)
🖃 old.broad.street @winebar-corbar.co.uk
19 Broadgate Circle, EC2

CAPACITIES: (Standing, Seated, Dinner dance, Theatre-style)

☎ (020) 7628 1251 (400,60,–,–)
📧 broadgate.circle@
winebar-corbar.co.uk
16 Royal Exchange, EC3
☎ (020) 7929 3131 (60,90,–,–)
📧 royal.exchange@
winebar-corbar.co.uk
1 Leadenhall Pl, EC3
☎ (020) 7621 9201 (150,50,–,–)
📧 lloyds@winebar-corbar.co.uk
2b Eastcheap, EC3M
☎ (020) 7929 3220 (200,80,–,–)
📧 monument@
winebar-corbar.co.uk
3 Fleet Pl, EC4
☎ (020) 7329 3141 (100,44,–,–)
📧 fleet.place@
winebar-corbar.co.uk
Mason's Av, EC2
☎ (020) 7726 6030 (120,80,–,–)
📧 masons.avenue@
winebar-corbar.co.uk
37 Jewry St, EC3
☎ (020) 7448 3700 (120,90,–,–)
📧 jewry.street@
winebar-corbar.co.uk
Well-known chain of superior City wine bars; Cannon St is best suited to discos, though their flagship is impressively situated above the Broadgate skating rink (where use of the terrace is also possible, see Broadgate Estates). The Lloyds building wine bar (with the benefit of an outside terrace) is particularly stylish.

Costa's Grill W8
£B, (–,25,–,–)
12-14 Hillgate St
☎ (020) 7229 3794
This popular Notting Hill stalwart restaurant offers solid Greek food at knock-down prices, and has a basement room for cheap and cheerful celebrations. / 11.30pm; not available Sun; Private Rm (–,25,–,–).

Cottons Atrium SE1
£M, (250,200,200,–)
Tooley St
☎ (020) 7940 7700
🖱 www.haysgalleria.co.uk
📧 marketing@samaprop.co.uk
This large, lofty riverside conservatory-like office-block foyer is a smart place with impressive views across to the City. Waterfalls and palm trees help create a tranquil ambience. / 12.30 am; available eves only; hirer's choice of caterer.

Courtauld Gallery WC2
£E, (400,80,–,–)
Somerset House, Strand
☎ (020) 7848 2526
🖷 (020) 7848 2589
🖱 www.courtauld.ac.uk
📧 galleryinfo@courtauld.ac.uk
England's finest collection of Impressionist paintings provides an impressive backdrop for entertaining in this world-famous gallery. / 11pm; available from 6.30pm, not available weekends; list of caterers; no amplified music; no dancing; no smoking; Fine Rms (250,80,–,–); Great Rm (250,–,–,–).

The Coronet SE1
£M, (2100,350,300,570)
28 New Kent Rd
☎ (020) 7703 2698
🖷 (020) 7377 8009
🖱 www.spacehire.com
📧 info@spacehire.com
Near Elephant & Castle, a stylishly restored '20s cinema, with Art Deco features, now a dedicated function space. A very good website shows you what's available. / 3 am; list of caterers.

Covent Garden Hotel WC2
£M-E, (75,30,–,53)
10 Monmouth St
☎ (020) 7806 1000
🖷 (020) 7287 5551
🖱 www.firmdalehotels.com
📧 events@firmdale.com
The private dining facilities at this elegant boutique hotel on the fringe of Covent Garden are ideal for smaller gatherings. Or give your own film show in the screening room.

/ 11.30pm; in-house caterers; no amplified music; Meeting Rm 1 (75,30,–,–); Meeting Rm 2 (45,14,–,–); Private (20,10,–,–); Screening Rm (–,–,–,53).

Covent Garden Market WC2
£M, (500,–,–,–)
c/o Nelson Bakewell,
41 The Market
☎ (020) 7836 9136
🖳 www.coventgardenmarket.co.uk
📠 info@coventgardenmarket.co.uk
For a gathering on a summer evening, you might like to consider this famous central marketplace. Entertainment by the market's own street-performers can be arranged.
/ hirer's choice of caterer; Central Avenue (300,–,–,–); North Hall (500,–,–,–); East Terrace (100,–,–,–).

Crazy Larry's SW10
£B-M, (400,100,–,–)
533 King's Rd
☎ (020) 7376 5555
🖳 (020) 7352 1659
🖳 www.crazylarrys.co.uk
📠 crazyradio@atlas.co.uk
A funky Chelsea nightclub, available early in the week for exclusive hire.
/ 2.30 am; hirer's choice of caterer, alcohol in-house; Vip Rm (50,–,–,–).

The Criterion W1
£M-E, (250,160,160,–)
Piccadilly Circus
☎ (020) 7734 7333
🖳 (020) 7734 0033
🖳 www.whitestarline.org.uk
📠 sales@whitestarline.org.uk
Hugely impressive, gilded and mosaicked neo-Byzantine restaurant, off Piccadilly Circus – now part of Marco Pierre White's restaurant empire. Available only on an all-or-nothing basis, it is really only suitable for events where budget is no particular constraint. / 1 am.

The Cross N1
£B-M, (800,–,–,–)
Arches 27-31 Kings Cross Goods Yard, York Way
☎ 0845 4561556
🖳 0845 4561557
🖳 www.the-cross.co.uk
📠 jennifer@jiantmarketing.co.uk
A series of railway arches provide a characterful setting for this King's Cross nightclub – the website has a particularly good tour, if you want to get a feel of the place. There are a number of niches suited to smaller events, and also a wooden decked garden, suitable for barbecues and so on. Car parking for up to 200 cars. / 6 am; available Mon-Thu; hirer's choice of caterer; Garden (200,–,–,–).

The Cross Keys SW3
£B-M, (120,70,–,–)
1 Lawrence St
☎ (020) 7349 9111
🖳 (020) 7349 9333
🖳 www.thexkeys.co.uk
📠 xkeys@fsmail.net
This very much smartened-up Chelsea pub/restaurant has an impressive conservatory dining room at the rear, and a First Floor Gallery which is a popular drinks party venue. / midnight; Conservatory (–,70,–,–); First Floor Gallery (120,40,–,–).

Crown & Greyhound SE21
£B, (150,80,80,–)
73 Dulwich Village
☎ (020) 8299 4976
The only pub in Dulwich Village has a second floor private room with its own entrance. Of its kind, it is one of London's best, boasting a dance floor, a PA system and a large TV, as well as overhead projectors, and this is one of the few pubs that's grand enough to have been granted a licence for civil weddings. / 11pm; smoking restricted; Private Rm (large) (120,80,80,–); Garden (300,–,–,–).

CAPACITIES: (Standing, Seated, Dinner dance, Theatre-style)

The Crown & Two Chairmen W1
£B, (120,40,–,–)
31 Dean St
☎ (020) 7437 8192
Well-known Soho media watering-hole whose upstairs room – set up as a sports bar for normal use – is available for hire. / *11pm; not available weekends except Jul & Aug; no dancing; Upstairs Bar (120,40,–,–).*

The Crown Tavern EC1
£B, (150,–,–,–)
43 Clerkenwell Gn
☎ (020) 7253 4973
At weekends, this pleasant recently updated pub, peacefully situated north of Smithfield, can be taken over in its entirety if you have sufficient numbers. For the rest of the week, a function room is available. / *no 18ths, 21sts or stag nights; 11pm; available Sat only, Sun by arrangement; Function Rm (50,–,–,–); Outside (100,–,–,–).*

Crystal Palace Park SE20
£B-M, (2000,1500,1000,–)
Thicket Rd
☎ (020) 8778 7148
🖱 www.bromleyknowledge.co.uk
✉ andy.heydon@bromley.gov.uk
A greenfield site and open-air amphitheatre with a permanent concert platform (with stage, roof, kitchen and changing room facilities). The concert bowl is a secure and private place for a marquee, but local concerns about noise enforce an early cut-off time. / *10.30pm; hirer's choice of caterer.*

Cuba Libre N1
£M, (100,60,60,–)
72 Upper St
☎ (020) 7354 9998
🖨 (020) 7354 9890
Earlier on in the week, you can take over the whole of this Islington bar/restaurant. It's a vibrant, get-up-and-dance sort of place, particularly suited to a buffet. / *2 am; not available weekends.*

Cumberland Hotel W1
£M-E, (1000,750,600,–)
Marble Arch
☎ (020) 7724 0087
🖱 www.thecumberland.co.uk
✉ conference.cumberland@ forte-hotels.com
The Production Box at this large hotel at the end of Oxford Street offers 3000 cubic metres of space, with a very high level of technical facilities and support, so you can create a set for anything from a fully-themed ball to a car launch. NB closed until June 2004, with all details subject to change. / *2 am; Production Box (1000,750,600,–); Carlisle Suite (500,400,360,–); Gloucester (200,100,–,–); Clarence (150,96,–,–).*

Curwen Gallery W1
£M, (80,30,–,–)
4 Windmill Street
☎ (020) 7636 1459
🖨 (020) 7436 3059
🖱 www.curwengallery.com
✉ emma@curwengallery.com
An understated contemporary art gallery, with a handy location not far from Regent Street. It's available for a variety of private events. / *10pm; hirer's choice of caterer; no smoking.*

Cutty Sark SE10
£M-E, (180,80,100,–)
King William Walk
☎ (020) 8858 2698
🖱 www.cuttysark.org.uk
✉ info@cuttysark.org.uk
In its riverside Greenwich dry-dock, the world's most famous tea clipper plays host to many types of function. The pillars and permanent displays reduce the space available, but in summer, access to the open top deck offers much compensation. / *available from 6pm (winter 5pm); list of caterers; no smoking; Tween Decks (180,80,–,–); Lower Hold (180,–,100,–); Master's Saloon (–,12,–,–).*

Da Mario SW7
£B-M, (130,130,130,–)
15 Gloucester Rd
☎ (020) 7584 9078
🖷 (020) 7823 9026
🖱 www.damario.co.uk
This long-established pizzeria near the Albert Hall has a late-night disco basement, with the option of individual tables to sit differing sizes of party (from 8 to 30 or 40). Or you can take over the whole cellar.
/ in-house caterers.

Dali Universe SE1
£M-E, (1000,300,300,150)
County Hall, Riverside Bldg
☎ 0870 780 6648
🖱 www.dalievents.com
📧 info@dalievents.com
By the London Eye, Dali Universe presents a collection of masterpieces by Spanish Surrealist Salvador Dali (and also works by Picasso and Chagall). White Space, with its contemporary collection, is also a popular space for entertaining. See advertisement on the front flap. / 1 am; hirer's choice of caterer (in-house available); Dali A (350,200,200,–); Dali B (150,100,–,–); Modern Masters (200,100,–,70); White Space (250,100,100,150).

Dan's SW3
£M, (–,70,–,–)
119 Sydney St
☎ (020) 7352 2718
🖷 (020) 7352 3265
Near Chelsea Town Hall, a long-established Anglo/French townhouse restaurant whose particular attractions are the conservatory and garden. / no amplified music; Conservatory (–,30,–,–); Restaurant (–,46,–,–); Private Rm (–,12,–,–); Garden (–,40,–,–).

Dartmouth House W1
£M, (350,140,140,–)
37 Charles St
☎ (020) 7529 1554
🖷 (020) 7495 1886
🖱 www.esu.org
📧 julia.dalgleish@compass-group.co.uk

The imposing Georgian/Victorian Mayfair HQ of the English Speaking Union offers some characterful rooms, particularly suitable for weddings and for receptions. The (rare) marbled courtyard makes an impressive setting for summer events. / midnight; Leith's; some restrictions on music; Long Drawing Rm (150,100,–,–); Ballroom (100,80,–,–); Small Drawing Rm (50,50,–,–); Restaurant (–,60,–,–); Courtyard (150,–,–,–).

Davy's Wine Bar
£B
🖱 www.davy.co.uk
57 High Holborn, WC1
☎ (020) 7242 4318 (250,–,–,–)
2-12 Wilson St, EC2
☎ (020) 7377 6326 (250,200,–,–)
1 St Mary at Hl, EC3
☎ (020) 7283 4443
53-60 Holborn Viaduct, EC1
☎ (020) 7248 2157 (–,12,–,–)
17 The Arches, WC2
☎ (020) 7930 7737 (200,–,–,–)
7 Moorfields High Walk, EC2
☎ (020) 7588 4766 (200,85,–,–)
120 Fenchurch St, EC3
☎ (020) 7623 3251 (250,120,–,–)
Lower Thames St, EC3
☎ (020) 7621 0619 (150,–,–,–)

CAPACITIES: (Standing, Seated, Dinner dance, Theatre-style)

Foster Ln, EC1
☎(020) 7606 2110 (300,150,150,–)
190-196 City Rd, EC1
☎ (020) 7608 0925 (250,120,–,–)
48-50 Tooley St, SE1
☎ (020) 7403 5775 (150,50,50,–)
20 King St, SW1
☎ (020) 7930 6157 (250,120,–,–)
10 Creed Ln, EC4
☎ (020) 7236 5317 (200,100,–,–)
50-54 Blandford St, W1
☎ (020) 7486 3590 (120,65,–,–)
2-3 Artillery Passage, E1
☎ (020) 7247 8215 (40,–,–,–)
27 Spring St, W2
☎ (020) 7723 3351 (–,30,–,–)
65 Crutched Friars, EC3
☎ (020) 7481 1131 (200,100,–,–)
White Hart Yd, Borough
High St, SE1
☎ (020) 7407 2829 (200,70,70,–)
4 Gt Portland St, W1
☎ (020) 7636 5287 (200,100,–,–)
63 Worship St, EC2
☎ (020) 7377 1574 (150,100,–,–)
42 Tooley St, SE1
☎(020) 7407 9189 (250,100,100,–)
3 Brewers Gn,
Buckingham Gt, SW1
☎ (020) 7222 0561 (150,75,–,–)
Off Bury Pl, WC1
☎ (020) 7404 5338 (200,80,–,–)
1 St Katharine's Wy, E1
☎ (020) 7480 6680 (250,100,–,–)
90-92 Wigmore St, W1
☎ (020) 7224 0170 (250,80,–,–)
10c Hanover St, W1
☎ (020) 7499 7569 (200,100,–,–)
10-20 Redcross Way, SE1
☎ (020) 7407 1184 (100,10,–,–)
161 Greenwich High Rd, SE10
☎ (020) 8853 0585 (200,100,–,–)
27 The Market,
Covent Gdn, WC2
☎ (020) 7836 1415 (–,23,–,–)
31-35 Fishermans' Wlk,
Cabot Sq, Canary Wharf, E14
☎ (020) 7363 6633 (–,60,–,–)
165 Greenwich High Rd, SE10
☎ (020) 8858 7204 (–,8,–,–)
5 William IV St, Strand, WC2
☎ (020) 7836 9839 (200,–,–,–)
91-93 Moorgate, EC2
☎ (020) 7920 0857 (200,80,–,–)
It may be true that if you've seen
one branch of Davy's you've seen
'em all, but if you're looking to hire a
weekend venue at a reasonable cost,
London's leading wine bar chain

offers a wide (if City-slanted) variety
of locations and capacities. For function hire there is a central enquiry
number ((020)) 8858 6011.

The De Vere Cavendish St James's SW1
£M, (120,80,60,80)
81 Jermyn St
☎ (020) 7930 2111
🖷 (020) 7839 4369
🖰 www.devereonline.co.uk
📧 ronny-yvonne.strasser@
devere-hotels.com
*The banqueting facilities at this long-
established St James's hotel were
expanded and updated in 2003. All
of the rooms are on the first floor,
and have natural light.*
/ smoking restricted; Meeting Rm
1 (120,80,60,80); Meeting Rm
2 (10,10,–,–); Meeting Rm 3 (80,50,–,–);
Meeting Rm 4 (40,20,–,25); Meeting Rm
5 (40,20,–,25).

Deca W1
£M-E, (–,18,–,–)
23 Conduit St
☎ (020) 7493 7070
🖷 (020) 7493 7090
*A Mayfair Gallic restaurant, run by
the Ladenis family (of 'Nico' fame),
where the style – smart and elegant,
but arguably a little cold – is perhaps
more suited to business than plea-
sure. There is a first-floor private
room. / Private Rm (–,18,–,–).*

The Decorium N22
£M, (1000,540,500,826)
22 Western Rd
☎ (020) 8365 8181
🖰 www.decorium.co.uk
📧 sales@decorium.co.uk
*A stone's throw from Alexandra Park,
a vaulted purpose-built function
venue, in neo-classical/Regency style.
It's licensed for civil weddings. / midnight; hirer's choice of caterer; Emperor
Suite (1000,520,466,826); Ante
Suite (35,20,–,35); Caesar
Suite (300,186,150,230).*

PRIVATE VENUES

Delfina Galleries SE1
£M, (500,260,250,–)
50 Bermondsey St
☎ (020) 7564 2400
🖨 (020) 7357 0250
🖱 www.delfina.org.uk
📧 events@delfina.org.uk

A bright and spacious South Bank gallery, which makes a flexible venue for corporate and social events. / *in-house caterers; Exhibition Gallery (350,250,200,–); Café Gallery (200,150,100,–); Studio Gallery (60,40,–,–).*

Denbies Wine Estate, Surrey
£M, (200,200,200,175)
London Rd, Dorking
☎ 01306 876616
🖱 www.denbiesvineyard.co.uk
📧 info@denbiesvineyard.co.uk
England's largest wine-producing estate is in the Mole Valley of the North Downs. The Denbies Suite is a purpose-built, naturally-lit function room with an arched roof. Tours and tastings as part of an event are encouraged. / *midnight; closed Sun; in-house caterers; no smoking; Garden Atrium Conservatory (200,200,200,–); Denbies Suite (–,–,–,175); Lecture Rm (–,–,–,40).*

Denim WC2
£M, (300,50,50,50)
4a Upper St Martins Lane
☎ (020) 7831 7899
🖨 (020) 7831 2228
📧 reservations@mintbar.co.uk
The striking design of this glazed-fronted Theatreland bar has made it an ongoing success, and it remains much in demand as a venue for media-world parties. / *1 am; in-house caterers; Mezz (60,30,30,20); Basement (150,50,50,50); VIP Rm (60,–,–,–).*

Depot SW14
£B-M, (–,135,–,–)
Mortlake High St
☎ (020) 8878 9462
By the water, on a bend of the river, this Barnes restaurant has an especially charming location. You can take it over in its entirety for suitable events.

Design Museum SE1
£M, (250,200,200,200)
28 Shad Thames
☎ (020) 7940 8756
🖨 0870 909 1909
🖱 www.designmuseum.org
📧 specialevents@designmuseum.org
Next to Butler's Wharf, Sir Terence Conran's International-style museum has a large, white-walled foyer available for parties – if desired, the collections above can be left open to view. Summer receptions can spill through the large floor-to-ceiling windows on to the riverside area, which has a magnificent view of Tower Bridge. / *11pm; available from 6.30pm; list of caterers; smoking restricted; no drinking in galleries; Entrance Hall (250,–,–,–); Collection Gallery (–,200,–,200); Meeting Rm (–,–,–,60).*

Detroit WC2
£B-M, (175,–,–,–)
35 Earlham St
☎ (020) 7240 2662
🖨 (020) 7240 8084
This interestingly decorated, sci-fi-cave-style bar/restaurant in Covent Garden makes an unusual setting for a drinks party. It's available in the early part of the week or (less frequently) at weekends. For smaller parties, the bar subdivides into smaller areas. / *midnight.*

Devonport House SE10
£M, (100,90,70,100)
King William Walk
☎ (020) 8269 5454
🖨 (020) 82695422
🖱 www.devonport-isc.co.uk
📧 devonport@

CAPACITIES: (Standing, Seated, Dinner dance, Theatre-style)

theinitialstyle.co.uk
An imposing neo-Georgian building in Greenwich, near the Thames. It's mainly used as a conference venue but also attractive enough for weddings. / in-house caterers; smoking restricted; Nelson & Hamilton (100,90,70,100); Drake (60,50,40,60); Churchill (–,12,–,–); Collingwood (40,20,–,24).

Dickens Inn E1
£B-M, (200,160,160,–)
St Katherine's Wy
☎ (020) 7488 2208
🖷 (020) 7702 3610
🖰 www.dickensinn.co.uk
Prettily located, at the edge of St Katherine's Dock, this sizable inn has a large warehouse-conversion function room used for discos and wedding receptions. For fine days, there's also a beer garden, and open air balconies. / midnight; Nickleby Suite (200,160,160,–).

The Dickens' House Museum WC1
£B-M, (50,15,–,–)
48 Doughty St
☎ (020) 7405 2127
🖷 (020) 7831 5175
🖰 www.dickensmusuem.com
🖂 info@dickensmusuem.com
Oliver Twist's Bloomsbury birthplace is a four-floor c19 house, for the most part filled with display cabinets detailing his life and that of his creator. Entertaining takes place in the atmospheric basement Library, whose period bookcases are filled with rare editions of the Great Novelist's work. / 11pm; available eves, all day Sun; hirer's choice of caterer; no amplified music; no dancing; no smoking.

Digress W1
£B-M, (340,–,–,–)
10 Beak St
☎ (020) 7437 0239
🖰 www.digress.co.uk
🖂 info@digress.co.uk
A clubby three-floor Soho venue, with spaces to suit most sorts of stand-up party. / 3 am; in-house caterers;

Basement (208,–,–,–); Lounge (50,–,–,–); Booths x 5 (20,–,–,–).

Diorama NW1
£B, (200,50,–,50)
34 Osnaburgh St
☎ (020) 7916 5467
🖰 www.diorama-arts.org.uk
No longer occupying the splendid building near Regent's Park from which it takes its name, this charity arts centre offers a good range of rooms if you're looking for rehearsal, workshop or audition space. Facilities include an art gallery for hire and a theatre studio. / 11pm; hirer's choice of caterer; no amplified music; no dancing; no smoking.

Docklands Sailing & Watersports Centre E14
£B-M, (200,150,–,30)
235a Westferry Rd
☎ (020) 7537 2626
🖷 (020) 7537 7774
🖰 www.dswc.org
🖂 judi@dswc.org
Purpose-built Docklands premises with one large and one smaller room on the first floor for hire. The main hall, which is very bright and has huge windows and a balcony overlooking Millwall Dock, is suitable for wedding receptions. There are also sailing and dragon boat racing possibilities. / midnight; list of caterers; Function Rm (200,150,–,–); Teaching Rm (40,24,–,30); Bar (100,70,–,–).

The Dog & Duck W1
£B, (30,–,–,–)
18 Bateman St
☎ (020) 7494 0697
A media-heartland pub with original tiles and mirrors. Its attractive upstairs bar is available for exclusive hire. / 11.20pm; no amplified music; no dancing.

Doggetts Coat & Badge SE1

£M, (300,70,–,24)

1 Blackfriars Bridge Rd
☎ (020) 7633 9081
🖶 (020) 7620 0143

This huge, Thames-side, modern pub complex has some excellent views of the City and St Paul's. The Terrace Bar offers a barbecue facility. / 11pm;
Wine Bar (300,70,–,–); Terrace Bar (150,40,–,–); Doggetts Bar (120,60,–,–); Boardroom (–,24,–,24).

Dolphin Square Hotel SW1

£B-M, (200,105,50,85)

Dolphin Sq, Chichester St
☎ (020) 7834 3800
🖰 www.dolphinsquarehotel.co.uk
🖂 events@
    dolphinsquarehotel.co.uk

The low-ceilinged Chichester Suite at this landmark apartment building in Pimlico is available for hire. It is licensed for civil weddings. / midnight;
in-house caterers; no amplified music;
Chichester (100,70,–,85);
Anson (50,24,–,43); Blake (15,–,–,20);
Restaurant (200,105,50,80).

Dominion Theatre W1

£M, (100,–,–,2190)

269 Tottenham Court Rd
☎ (020) 7529 4323
🖰 www.london-dominion.co.uk

If you're looking for a venue with more than a hint of Deco, the facilities of this enormous West End theatre may be worth checking out.
/ 11pm; available subject to constraints of current production; in-house caterers; no dancing; smoking restricted;
Auditorium (–,–,–,2190); Smirnoff Bar (100,–,–,–); Garland Suite (50,–,–,–); Milburn Suite (20,–,–,–).

The Don EC4

£M, (120,100,–,–)

20 St Swithin's Ln
☎ (020) 7626 2606
🖶 (020) 7626 2616
🖂 bookings@
    thedonrestaurant.co.uk

The site of the former Sandeman Port bottling cellar (from 1798 to 1969) provides the intriguing setting for this new restaurant near the Bank of England. The brick-vaulted Bistro is a congenial function space, and there is an attractive private room. At weekends, you can take the whole place. / midnight; evenings only; no amplified music; no dancing;
Restaurant (60,50,–,–); Bistro (60,40,–,–); Private Rm (30,24,–,–).

The Dorchester W1

£M-E, (1000,510,450,–)

53 Park Ln
☎ (020) 7629 8888
🖰 www.dorchesterhotel.com
🖂 mpeters@
    dorchesterhotel.com

Glamorous opulence distinguishes the rooms at this Mayfair hotel – all of them have real style, from the subtly-mirrored Ballroom down (or rather up) to the extraordinary fairy-tale setting of the eighth floor penthouse with terrace, fountain and spectacular view. All of the larger rooms are licensed for weddings. / 1 am;
Ballroom (1000,510,450,–);
Orchid (250,150,120,–); The Terrace (200,100,80,–); Park Suite (100,60,50,–); Holford (100,50,–,–); Pavilion (60,40,–,–); Penthouse (40,18,–,–); Library (10,–,–,–).

CAPACITIES: (Standing, Seated, Dinner dance, Theatre-style)

Dover Street Restaurant & Bar W1
£M-E, (400,340,–,–)
8-10 Dover St
☎ (020) 7491 7509
🖷 (020) 7491 2958
🖰 www.doverst.co.uk
Surprisingly, one of London's few good places to dine and dance (to live jazz, blue and soul). They can offer alcoves and spaces (non-exclusively) for various size of party, or you can exclusively hire one of the bars or the whole venue (in which case they will advise on bands and music accordingly). / ; 3 am; in-house caterers; Upper Bar (65,50,–,–); Lower Bar (150,120,–,–); Alcove (–,24,–,–).

Dr Johnsons' House EC4
£B-M, (100,25,–,–)
17 Gough Sq
☎ (020) 7353 3745
🖰 www.drjohnsonshouse.org
🖃 curator@drjohnsonshouse.org
Apart from its literary associations (and associated bric-à-brac), the charm of this four-storey house is that it is a plain Georgian house – with authentically neutral décor – hidden away just off Fleet Street. The house is generally available only for early evening receptions, but occasionally for wedding receptions and the like. / 9pm ; available from 6.30pm, Sun by arrangement; hirer's choice of caterer; no dancing; no smoking.

Drapers' Hall EC2
£M-E, (400,250,–,375)
Throgmorton Av
☎ (020) 7588 5001
🖰 www.thedrapers.co.uk
🖃 banqueting@thedrapers.co.uk
Behind the Bank of England, this livery hall, remodelled in Victoria's day, is one of the City's finest. / midnight; closed late July-early Sept; in-house caterers; no amplified music; no dancing; smoking restricted; Livery Hall (400,224,–,375); Court Rm (120,72,–,100); Court Dining (130,96,–,100).

Drones SW1
£M, (175,80,–,–)
1 Pont St
☎ (020) 7734 7333
🖷 (020) 7734 0033
🖰 www.whitestarline.org.uk
🖃 sales@whitestarline.org.uk
A long-established Belgravia restaurant, taken over in recent times by Marco Pierre White and given an understated make-over by top restaurant designer David Collins. There's a private room, or you could take the whole place. / midnight; Private Rm (–,40,–,–).

Duchess Theatre WC2
£M, (–,–,–,470)
Catherine St
☎ (020) 7494 5200
🖷 (020) 7434 1217
🖰 www.rutheatres.com
🖃 mike.townsend@rutheatres.com
Designed in 1929 in a vaguely Tudor style, a theatre available for presentations and so on, subject to the dictates of the current production. / available subject to constraints of current production; in-house caterers; smoking restricted.

Duke of Albemarle W1
£B, (40,30,–,–)
6 Stafford St
☎ (020) 7355 0321
Comfortable, slightly old-fashioned, room over a Mayfair pub, available, without charge, for functions. / 11pm; available Mon-Sat.

Duke of York's HQ SW3
£B-M, (350,300,250,200)
King's Rd
☎ (020) 7825 5577
🖃 secretary@reserve-forces-london.org.uk
This fashionably-located TA HQ, a stone's throw from Sloane Square, now has a shiny new shopping mall as a neighbour. The once popular Cadogan Hall venue is no more, but the London Irish Mess and Hall sur-

vive. / 1 am; hirer's choice of caterer; London Irish Mess (240,72,–,–); London Irish Hall (–,–,–,200).

Dukes Hotel SW1
£M-E, (120,60,45,60)
35 St James's Pl
☎ (020) 7491 4840
⌂ www.dukeshotel.com
✉ kdennis@dukeshotel.co.uk
A late-Victorian St James's hotel with two conventional private rooms, which suit intimate dinners or perhaps a wedding. / midnight; Marlborough Suite (120,64,45,60); Sheridan Rm (25,12,–,15).

Dulwich College SE21
£B-M, (400,350,300,400)
Dulwich Common
☎ (020) 8299 9284
⌂ www.dulwich.org.uk/ enterprises
✉ enterprises@dulwich.org.uk
An impressively equipped Victorian school – in extensive and leafy grounds – which offers a variety of possibilities for functions and entertainments (especially sports-related). Moderate prices are helped by a no-corkage policy – as long as catering is in-house. The Old Library has a wedding licence. / midnight; hirer's choice of caterer (in-house available); smoking restricted; Christison Hall and Upper Dining Rms (400,350,300,450); Great Hall (200,200,200,486); Pavilion Salle (120,75,60,80); Lower Hall (150,90,60,120); Old Library (80,–,–,110).

Dulwich Picture Gallery SE21
£M-E, (500,150,–,120)
Gallery Rd
☎ (020) 8299 8711
🖷 (020) 8299 8700
⌂ www.dulwichpicturegallery.org.uk
✉ i.evens@ dulwichpicturegallery.org.uk
England's oldest, purpose-built picture gallery houses a magnificent collection of old masters (and a mausoleum for its founders). It is set in five acres of gardens and has recent-ly undergone extensive refurbishment, including the installation of an elegant glazed cloister. / midnight; available Mon all day, otherwise from 5pm; list of caterers; no amplified music; no dancing; no smoking; no red wine for standing receptions ; Soane Building (350,150,–,–); Linbury Rm (150,60,–,120).

Durrants Hotel W1
£M, (80,60,60,–)
George St
☎ (020) 7935 8131
⌂ www.durrantshotel.co.uk
✉ enquiries@ durrantshotel.co.uk
One of London's few surviving privately-owned, hotels of character, these comfortable Marylebone premises were built in 1790 as townhouses. There are two old-fashioned, panelled, ground-floor rooms which are particularly attractive. / midnight; Edward VII Rm (80,50,–,–); Oak Rm (40,24,–,–); Armfield Rm (20,12,–,–).

Dyers' Hall EC4
£M-E, (–,57,–,–)
10 Dowgate Hl
☎ (020) 7236 7197
🖷 (020) 72480774
A small, early-Victorian hall, available to suitable hirers for luncheons and dinners only. / 11pm; in-house caterers; no amplified music; no dancing.

E&O W11
£M, (–,18,–,–)
14 Blenheim Cr
☎ (020) 7229 5454
🖷 (020) 7229 5522
⌂ www.eando.nu
Few places are more hip and happening than this Notting Hill bar/restaurant, with its interesting oriental tapas menu. At least in these days, they won't make the whole place available for hire, so the only option is the basement private room.

CAPACITIES: (Standing, Seated, Dinner dance, Theatre-style)

Ealing Town Hall W5
£M, (500,375,375,175)
14-16 Uxbridge Rd,
New Broadway
☎ (020) 8825 5000
🖷 (020) 8825 6066
🖰 www.ealing.gov.uk
🖃 halls@ealing.gov.uk
*This impressive Victorian Town Hall
is unusually well geared-up for function business, and offers a variety of
settings – from the council chambers
themselves to small meeting rooms.*
*/ 2 am; hirer's choice of caterer; Princes
Hall (220,220,220,–); Queens
Hall (175,132,100,175); Victoria
Hall (500,375,375,–); Nelson
Rm (80,75,–,80).*

Earlsfield
Library SW18
£B, (120,80,–,–)
Magdalen Rd
☎ (020) 8871 6389
🖰 www.wandsworth.gov.uk
*The library has a pleasant barrel-
vaulted art gallery, made available
for social functions. NB Closed at
press time, but scheduled to re-open
in April 2004. / 11.30pm; hirer's choice of
caterer; no amplified music; no smoking.*

East India Club SW1
£M, (250,150,–,–)
16 St James's Sq
☎ (020) 7930 1000
🖃 eastindia@globalnet.co.uk
*This imposing St James's Club makes
no efforts to market its facilities to
non-members. However, if you can
find one of their number (6,000 or
so) to act as host (and be present),
its rooms make convivial places for
dinners and receptions. / midnight; in-
house caterers; no amplified music.*

East
Wintergarden E14
£M-E, (700,500,450,–)
43 Bank St
☎ (020) 7418 2725
🖰 www.eastwintergarden.com
🖃 eastwintergarden
    @canarywharf.com
Part of Canary Wharf's continuing

*sprawl – a large, vaulted, glazed
space, precisely in keeping with its
name. / no access until 4pm for setup;
11pm; evenings only; in-house caterers.*

Easthampstead Park
Conference
Centre, Berks
£M, (200,180,110,180)
Wokingham
☎ 01189 780686 ext 503
🖷 01189 793870
🖰 www.eastpark.co.uk
🖃 info@eastpark.co.uk
*A Victorian house set in 60 acres of
parkland, offering accommodations
for everything from conferences to
weddings. / in-house caterers; no smoking;
Downshire (200,110,–,180);
Tawney (40,25,–,40); Harwich (–,36,–,50);
Windsor (–,30,–,30); Wylie (–,25,–,30).*

The East Hill SW18
£B, (25,25,–,–)
21 Alma Rd
☎ (020) 8874 1833
🖰 www.geronimo-inns.co.uk
*A Wandsworth pub with an upstairs
function room, whose style suits
more sedate gatherings (or more
informal business meetings). / 11pm.*

Eddalino W1
£M, (–,60,–,–)
10 Wigmore St
☎ (020) 7637 0789
🖷 (020) 7637 2163
🖰 www.eddalino.com
*The only truly private option at this
ambitious Italian restaurant, near the
Wigmore Hall, is to take the whole
place. The room is divided into two,
though, and If you don't need complete privacy, you could take half of
it.*

Egg N7
£B-M, (1000,300,200,278)
200 York Way, Kings Cross
☎ (020) 7609 8364
🖷 (020) 7619 0402
🖰 www.egglondon.net
🖃 events@egglondon.net
An impressive three-floor nightclub,

near King's Cross, whose features include a courtyard garden. / list of caterers; Loft Bar (200,–,–,–); Middle Floor (278,100,100,278); Ground Floor (240,100,100,240); Courtyard (140,140,140,140).

Eight Over Eight SW3
£M, (–,14,–,–)
392 King's Rd
☎ (020) 7349 9934
🖷 (020) 7351 5157
🖰 www.eightovereight.nu

Will "E&O" Ricker's latest Chelsea project is decked out in his hallmark, hip clean-lined style and provides similar oriental-inspired fare. Its private dining room comes complete with its own sound sytem.

Electric Ballroom NW1
£B, (1200,–,–,–)
184 Camden High St
☎ (020) 7485 9006
🖰 www.electricballroom.co.uk
🖃 mags@electricballroom.co.uk

A rather nice, old-established, Camden Town dance hall. It's located right by the tube station, and ideal for a large dance or major themed event. / 2.30 am; not available Fri-Sun; hirer's choice of caterer, alcohol in-house.

Electric Brasserie (& Electric House Club) W11
£M, (35,14,–,98)
191 Portobello Road
☎ (020) 7908 9696

This hip and happening redevelopment of the Electric Cinema (the UK's oldest cinema screen) into a bar/brasserie and member's club – run by Soho House – has become a linchpin of Notting Hill life. Events can be combined with screenings in the cinema – either your own film or one from their programme. / ; 2 am; cinema available 8am-6pm, occasionally evenings; in-house caterers; Study (25,10,–,–); Playroom (35,14,–,–); Cinema (–,–,–,98).

Elena's L'Etoile W1
£M, (–,24,–,–)
30 Charlotte St
☎ (020) 7636 7189
🖷 (020) 7637 0122

This long-established Fitzrovia French restaurant still maintains quite a degree of period charm, and offers a choice of private rooms. / Private Rm (–,24,–,–); Private Rm (x2) (–,16,–,–).

Elstree Film Studio, Herts
£M, (400,270,270,–)
Shenley Rd, Borehamwood
☎ (020) 8953 1600
🖃 info@elstreefilmtv.com

A film studio usually offers a blank space in which you have the opportunity (and cost) of building your own set. The attraction here is precisely the opposite – it's a smart, conventional banqueting suite, offering the (unusual) option of bringing in your own caterer. / 1.30 am; hirer's choice of caterer (in-house available); Oscars Bar (200,100,–,–); Restaurant (350,270,–,–); Marquee (120,80,–,–); The White House (100,45,–,–); Board/Green Rm (25,25,–,–).

Eltham Palace SE9
£E, (250,200,150,300)
Courtyard
☎ (020) 8294 2577
🖷 (020) 8294 2621
🖰 www.heritagehospitality.org.uk
🖃 johanna.ashley-down@ english-heritage.org.uk

This intriguing building was the boyhood home of Henry VIII. The hall ultimately became the home of the Courtauld family, who made some celebrated Art Deco additions. / no stilettos; midnight; list of caterers; no smoking; no red wine for standing receptions ; Great Hall (250,200,150,300); Drawing Rm (120,60,–,80); Dining Rm (80,50,–,–).

CAPACITIES: (Standing, Seated, Dinner dance, Theatre-style)

Elysium W1
£M-E, (720,110,110,–)
Café Royal, 68 Regent St
☎ (020) 7439 7770
🖨 (020) 7287 4292
🖰 www.elysiumlounge.co.uk
📧 samantha@
    elysiumlounge.co.uk
They've aimed for a feel "like an Indonesian palace", at this large basement nightclub on the fringe of Soho. It certainly makes a good venue for a loungey cocktail party. Also manage bookings for the Café Royal Grill Room (see also). / over 21s only; 3 am; available Mon & Tue only; hirer's choice of caterer (in-house available); Club Rm (250,–,–,–); Amber Bar (100,–,–,–); Restaurant & VIP Rm (150,110,–,–).

Embargo SW10
£B-M, (200,70,–,–)
533b Kings Rd
☎ (020) 7351 5038
🖰 www.ponana.co.uk
📧 embargo@ponana.co.uk
In the early evening (till 11pm), you can hire this intimate Chelsea nightclub for a drinks or dinner party. Such of your guests as wish to can then stay on for the rest of the evening. / over 21 only; 2 am; hirer's choice of caterer.

The End WC1
£B-M, (800,–,–,–)
18 West Central St
☎ (020) 7419 9199
🖨 (020) 7419 4099
🖰 www.the-end.co.uk
📧 hire@the-end.co.uk
A centrally located nightclub, with a minimalist modern interior, set inside the converted vaults of a c19 post office. / in-house caterers.

The Energy Clinic E1
£M-E, (350,200,–,140)
132 Commercial St
☎ (020) 7650 0718
🖨 (020) 7650 0719
🖰 www.energyclinicuk.com
📧 contract@energyclinicuk.com
Feng shui looms large at this new venue, which is divided into five areas, each decorated according to a different elemental theme (and with appropriate music). It seems to have a surprisingly wide appeal, with many clients seeming to have nothing obviously New Agey about them at all! / hirer's choice of caterer (in-house available); no music after 11pm; no smoking; Lobby (350,80,–,–); Largest Area (–,50,–,140); Smallest Area (20,–,–,–).

Engineer NW1
£B-M, (–,30,–,–)
65 Gloucester Av
☎ (020) 7722 0950
🖨 (020) 7483 0592
🖰 www.the-engineer.com
A fashionable Primrose Hill gastropub, with quite ambitious grub. It has two private dining rooms upstairs. / 12.30 am; Large Rm (–,30,–,–); Mirror Rm (–,18,–,–).

Epsom Downs Surrey
£M, (600,400,360,–)
Epsom
☎ 01372 726311
🖨 01372 748253
🖰 www.epsomderby.co.uk
📧 epsom@rht.net
Two separate multi-level buildings – the Queen's Stand and the Grandstand – together offer a panoply of choice for anything from a small event or a large-scale exhibition. / not available most race days; in-house caterers; Blue Riband Rm (600,400,360,–); Derby Suite (400,200,180,–); Jockey Club Rm (200,140,120,–); Boardroom (–,70,70,–); Coronation Cup (60,48,–,–); Double Boxes (40,36,–,–); Single Boxes (20,10,–,–).

Equinox at the Empire WC2
£B-M, (2180,800,600,–)
Leicester Sq
☎ (020) 7437 1446
🖰 www.nightclub.co.uk/equinox
📧 davejoyce21@hotmail.com
This nightclub, with the largest dance floor in the West End, boasts all the hi-tech gizmos you would expect. It is used for a large range of day and evening functions. / available weekdays during day and Sun-Thurs eves; hirer's choice

of caterer (in-house available); Empire
Lounge (150,50,60,–).

L'Escargot W1
£M, (–,60,–,–)
48 Greek St
☎ (020) 7437 2679
🖷 (020) 7734 0033
🕆 www.whitestarline.org.uk
✉ sales@whitestarline.org.uk
Long-established Soho restaurant,
with two good quality private rooms.
One, the barrel-vaulted room, is particularly distinctive. / not available Sun L;
Barrel Vault Rm (–,60,–,–); Private
Rm (–,30,–,–).

Estorick Collection N1
£M-E, (200,80,–,70)
39a Canonbury Sq
☎ (020) 7704 9522
🖷 (020) 7704 9531
🕆 www.estorickcollection.com
✉ curator@
estorickcollection.com
The Estorick Collection of Modern
Italian Art (Modigliani, Morandi and
the Futurists among others) is on display in a recently converted Georgian
villa – an intimate but stylish setting
for an event. / 9.30pm; available day Mon
& Tue otherwise eves; hirer's choice of caterer
(in-house available); no dancing; no smoking;
no red wine.

Eton College (Dorney Lake), Berks
£M, (200,120,–,–)
Eton
☎ 01753 832756
🖷 01753 851767
🕆 www.etoncollege.org.uk
✉ dorneylake@
etoncollege.org.uk
The school boathouse is available for
external events and functions. The
main room has a balcony overlooking
the new rowing lake. / hirer's choice of
caterer (in-house available); no smoking;
Main Rm (200,120,–,–);
Clubroom (40,25,–,–).

ExCel E16
£B-M, (1064,–,–,–)
London Docklands
☎ (020) 7069 4782
🕆 www.excel-
london.co.uk/excel/
✉ info@excel-london.co.uk
Part of the great revival of the East,
this new centre claims to provide
London with the "world-class, state-
of-the-art venue" it has long needed.
Apart from 65,000 square metres of
exhibition space, there are 3,700
square metres of conference and
banqueting space and roughly the
same again of outside event space.
/ Platinum Suite (1064,–,–,–); Waterfront
Rms (228,–,–,–).

Fabric EC1
£B-M, (1800,200,200,200)
77a Charterhouse St, Farringdon
☎ 0845 456 1556
🖷 0845 4561557
🕆 www.fabricevents.com
✉ jennifer@jiantmarketing.co.uk
The enormous nightclub by
Smithfield market is intriguingly laid
out in a former cold store (for New
Zealand lamb, if you're interested).
Facilities include three dance floors,
five sound systems, six bars and a
VIP lounge. / available Mon-Thu; hirer's
choice of caterer (in-house available).

Fan Museum SE10
£M-E, (80,30,–,–)
12 Crooms Hl
☎ (020) 8305 1441
🕆 www.fan-museum.com
✉ admin@fan-museum.org
Very pretty all round – both the fine
collection of fans (housed in two converted c18 Greenwich townhouses)
and the mirrors-and-murals décor of
the Orangery annexe where food is
served. The venue is ideal for smaller
wedding receptions. / 11pm; list of caterers; no amplified music; no dancing; no smoking; no alcohol on 1st floor;
Museum (80,–,–,–); Orangery (40,30,–,–).

CAPACITIES: (Standing, Seated, Dinner dance, Theatre-style)

Farmers' & Fletchers' Hall EC1
£M, (220,125,120,150)
3 Cloth St
☎ 0870 7809639
🖷 (020) 7653 6653
🖰 www.cbvs.co.uk
📧 helpme@cbvs.co.uk
Modern livery hall, decorated in a traditional style – quite an adaptable venue for smaller and medium-sized events. / 1 am; in-house caterers; Livery Hall (200,125,120,150); Reception Rm (50,–,–,–); Court Rm (30,18,–,30).

Fashion & Textile Museum SE1
£M, (250,150,100,–)
83 Bermondsey St
☎ (020) 7407 8664
🖷 (020) 7403 5333
🖰 www.ftmlondon.org
📧 admin@ftmlondon.org
Favourite dresses from 70 of the world's top designers adorn Zandra Rhodes's new South Bank museum, strikingly designed by a Mexican architect. / 1 am; list of caterers; no smoking.

Fifteen05 EC4
£B-M, (450,220,200,–)
Allhallows Ln, Upper Thames St
☎ (020) 7283 1505
🖷 (020) 7283 9312
🖰 www.fifteen05.com
📧 contact@fifteen05.com
Lofty arches beneath Cannon Street railway bridge, well suited to a party, reception or dinner. / 2 am; in-house caterers; Great Hall (220,150,120,–); Gallery of City Bar (70,40,–,–).

FireHouse SW7
£M-E, (200,55,–,–)
3 Cromwell Rd
☎ (020) 7584 7258
🖷 (020) 7584 9768
Though it's a club, this townhouse opposite the Natural History Museum has a restaurant which is available to non-members, which would make an atmospheric venue for a medium-sized dinner (for 40-55 people). You can use the club's other facilities afterwards, till late. For non-dining events, you'll need the sponsorship of a member. / 3 am.

Firepower - The Royal Artillery Museum SE18
£M-E, (300,100,–,100)
Royal Arsenal West, Woolwich
☎ (020) 8855 7755
🖷 (020) 8855 7100
🖰 www.firepower.org.uk
📧 info@firepower.org.uk
A recently-opened museum of the history of gunnery, which provides a number of spaces suitable for corporate entertaining. / hirer's choice of caterer (in-house available); Gunnery Hall (300,100,–,–); History Gallery (150,–,–,–); Theatre (–,100,–,100).

First Bowl Queensway W2
£B, (500,–,–,–)
17 Queensway
☎ (020) 7229 0172
🖷 (020) 7229 5207
🖰 www.queensiceskating.com
The action at Central London's only ice rink is no longer limited to falling over on a slippery, cold surface – you can hire the entire Bayswater centre and try Sega World, ten-pin bowling and pool too / 11.30pm; in-house or hirer's choice by negotiation; smoking restricted; Sega World (500,–,–,–); Ice Rink (400,–,–,–); 10 Pin Bowling (per game) (144,–,–,–).

Fishmongers' Hall EC4
£E, (450,180,–,–)
London Bridge
☎ (020) 7626 3531
One of London's finest halls, included for completeness only – it is generally unavailable to third parties, except sometimes to national charities. / charities only; 11pm; weekdays only; no dancing; smoking restricted.

PRIVATE VENUES

Fitzroy Square W1
£M-E, (100,60,–,–)
Fitzroy Sq
☎ (020) 7434 2067
🖨 (020) 7281 0944
🖱 www.spteventsltd.co.uk
📧 schattalov@spteventsltd.co.uk

A Grade 1 listed Georgian house, in a tranquil Marylebone square, ideal for smaller-scale events. / 11.30pm; hirer's choice of caterer (in-house available); no amplified music; no dancing;
1st Space (60,–,–,–); 2nd Space (–,60,–,–).

5 Cavendish Square W1
£M-E, (300,80,–,–)
5 Cavendish Sq
☎ (020) 7079 5000
🖨 (020) 7079 5001
'Townhouse' is really too small a word for this palace, just north of Oxford Street, which has recently been renovated as a bar/club/restaurant in no-expense-spared style. As a (slightly glitzy) venue to impress, it has few peers in the West End. / 1 am; Nightclub (180,–,–,–); Ground Floor Bar (150,–,–,–); Restaurant (150,80,–,–); Black Bar (30,–,–,–); Private Dining Rm (–,24,–,–).

Footstool SW1
£B-M, (250,120,–,–)
St John's, Smith Sq
☎ (020) 7222 2779
🖨 (020) 7222 5221
🖱 www.digbytrout.co.uk
📧 stjohns@digbytrout.co.uk
St John's light, flower-filled crypt is a lunch-spot popular with MPs (it has a division bell) and, in the evenings, with concert-goers. At other times, it's available for most types of function. / 1 am.

Fortnum & Mason W1
£M-E, (800,120,120,–)
181 Piccadilly
☎ (020) 7734 8040
🖨 (020) 7437 9278
🖱 www.fortnumandmason.com
📧 restaurants@
    fortnumandmason.co.uk
After nearly 300 years in business, the Queen's grocers decided to open a dedicated function room, on the fourth floor of the shop. After hours, you can hire the St James's Room (restaurant), or you might take over the famous food hall. / 1 am; in-house caterers; smoking restricted; Food Hall (500,–,–,–); St James's Rm (200,120,120,–); Burlington Rm (75,56,–,–).

Fortune Theatre WC2
£M, (80,–,–,432)
Russell St
☎ (020) 7369 1737
🖨 (020) 7010 7879
🖱 www.theambassadors.com
📧 fortunetheatre@hotmail.com
An Art Deco theatre in Covent Garden, available for presentations during the day (and on Sun) – event use is subject to the constraints of the resident show, but as 'The Woman in Black' has now been running for 13 years the pattern of likely availability is fairly well established! / 5pm; available Mon-Sat 10am-5pm, Sun all day; smoking restricted; Auditorium (–,–,–,432); Bar (80,–,–,–).

CAPACITIES: (Standing, Seated, Dinner dance, Theatre-style)

Forty Hall, Middx
£M, (250,160,120,150)
Enfield
☎ (020) 8363 4774
🖷 (020) 8363 8252
📧 info@fortyhall.demon.co.uk

A Grade I listed house set in a beautiful landscape garden. Banqueting takes place in the Tudor Barn, but hirers also get use of the courtyard and garden patio. / midnight; list of caterers; no smoking; Banqueting Suite (250,160,120,150).

The Founders' Hall EC1
£M, (100,80,–,80)
I Cloth Fair
☎ 0870 780 9639
🖷 (020) 7653 6653
🖱 www.cbvs.co.uk
📧 helpme@cbvs.co.uk
This small, modern (1987) Smithfield hall combines a large number of decorative styles into a surprisingly small space. The Livery Hall itself boasts striking contemporary décor, / 11pm; Chester Boyd; some restrictions on music; some restrictions on dancing; Livery Hall (100,80,–,80); Parlour (50,25,–,25); Masters & Clerks (–,14,–,–).

Four Seasons Canary Wharf E14
£M-E, (200,200,160,200)
Westferry Circus
☎ (020) 7510 1860
🖷 (020) 7510 1998
🖱 www.fourseasonscanary wharf.com
The grandest hotel in the environs of Canary Wharf offers a range of function rooms. Though it's in a fairly businesslike style, it apparently does big business in weddings and bar

mitzvahs. / 1 am; Ballroom (200,200,160,200); River Rm (80,60,–,75); City Rm (55,30,–,30).

Four Seasons Hotel W1
£M-E, (650,400,300,–)
Hamilton Pl
☎ (020) 7499 0888
🖱 www.fourseasons.com
📧 nicholas.smith@ fourseasons.com
A large, '70s hotel overlooking Hyde Park. The c18-panelled Pine Room is a grand setting for smaller dinners, and the larger Oak Room is also atmospheric. The Ballroom, Park and Garden Rooms are less distinctive (though the last benefits from access to a garden). Most rooms are licensed for weddings. / 2 am; Ballroom (650,400,300,–); Garden Rm (300,150,120,–); Oak Rm (150,95,60,–); Pine Rm (60,48,–,–).

Fox & Anchor EC1
£B-M, (–,25,–,–)
115 Charterhouse St
☎ (020) 7253 5075
🖷 (020) 7255 0696
Famous, atmospheric Smithfield pub – the best known of those serving early breakfast with ale. For parties of 10-25 people you can order breakfasts, grill lunches and dinners to be taken in the agreeable upstairs parlour. / not available weekends; Private Rm (–,25,–,–).

The Fox Club W1
£M-E, (65,20,–,–)
46 Clarges St
☎ (020) 7495 3656
🖷 (020) 7495 3626
📧 mia@thefoxclub.co.uk
A rather old-fashioned club, in a Georgian Mayfair townhouse, offering a number of rooms suited to smaller functions. / 11pm; in-house caterers.

Foxtrot Oscar SW3
£B-M, (–,34,–,–)
79 Royal Hospital Rd
☎ (020) 7351 7179
🖨 (020) 7357 1667
This comfortably dated restaurant – a Chelsea in-crowd hang-out – remains popular for its relaxed atmosphere. The basement is available for hire.

Frederick's N1
£M, (200,140,120,–)
106 Camden Passage
☎ (020) 7359 3902
🖨 (020) 7359 5173
🖱 www.fredericks.co.uk
📧 eat@fredericks.co.uk
A grand and spacious Islington restaurant with two private rooms. The Clarence Room is an elegant first floor room, which is a pleasant place for a dinner or small reception. It is also licensed for civil weddings for up to 40 people. For larger events, it may be possible to use the whole restaurant, with its impressive conservatory. / Garden Rm (Main Restaurant) (100,70,–,–); Clarence Rm (–,32,–,–); Sussex Rm (–,18,–,–).

The Freemason's Arms WC2
£B, (100,50,–,–)
81-82 Long Acre
☎ (020) 7836 3115
🖨 (020) 7497 0583
📧 j.annetts@virgin.net
Covent Garden pub with a large, pleasant upstairs bar used for much more than typical pub functions. / 11pm.

Freud Museum NW3
£M, (120,30,–,–)
20 Maresfield Gdns
☎ (020) 7435 2002
🖱 www.freud.org.uk
📧 freud@gn.apc.org
Spacious '20s Hampstead villa in which the great man lived his last days and where his daughter, Anna, lived until the '80s. Its domestic ambience makes it ideal for intimate gatherings, especially in summer when the charming garden can be used. / 11pm; available Wed-Sun from 5pm, Mon & Tue all day; hirer's choice of caterer; no amplified music; no dancing; no smoking; House (80,30,–,–).

The Fridge SW2
£B, (1100,–,–,–)
Town Hall Parade, Brixton Hl
☎ (020) 7326 5100
🖨 (020) 7274 2879
🖱 www.fridge.co.uk
📧 info@fridge.co.uk
Large, well-known Brixton nightclub, available for exclusive hire. / 6 am; not available Fri & Sat; in-house or hirer's choice by negotiation.

Frocks E9
£B-M, (–,30,–,–)
95 Lauriston Rd
☎ (020) 8986 3161
🖨 (020) 8986 5601
This intimate English restaurant near the East End's Victoria Park has a cosy downstairs section, which would make a good place for a birthday party. / Basement (–,30,–,–).

Froebel College SW15
£B-M, (160,100,–,–)
Roehampton Ln
☎ (020) 8392 3305
🖨 (020) 8392 3331
🖱 www.roehampton.ac.uk
📧 jrochford@roehampton.ac.uk
Grove House, in leafy Roehampton, is home of Froebel College. Set in 25 acres it has grounds and gardens including a large lake. The attractive Terrace and Portrait Rooms are popular for wedding receptions. / midnight; in-house caterers; smoking restricted; Portrait Rm (160,100,–,–); Terrace Rm (120,60,–,–).

Fulham House SW6
£B-M, (200,140,110,100)
87 Fulham High St
☎ (020) 7384 4670
🖨 (020) 7384 4679
📧 marketing@reserve-forces-london.mod.uk
This listed Georgian house – the oldest in Fulham apparently, and com-

CAPACITIES: (Standing, Seated, Dinner dance, Theatre-style)

plete with defensive cannon – accommodates a branch of the TA and is also a popular party venue. The main hall (a more recent extension) is a flexible gym-type space with a glass-canopied ceiling. The Dining Room is formal. / 2 am; hirer's choice of caterer; smoking restricted; Main Hall (200,140,110,100); Dining Rm (80,30,–,50).

Fulham Palace SW6
£M, (130,80,80,–)
Bishops Av
☎ (020) 8748 3020 extn 4930
🖷 (020) 8753 3913
🖑 www.lbhf.gov.uk
This listed medieval palace, with courtyard, was the home of the Bishops of London until the '70s. It is prettily situated in a park and potentially a very charming setting. / midnight; hirer's choice of caterer; no smoking; Great Hall (100,80,80,–); Drawing Rm (100,80,–,–); Ante Rm (30,–,–,–).

Fulham Town Hall SW6
£B-M, (500,250,230,300)
Fulham Broadway
☎ (020) 8748 3020
🖷 (020) 8753 2353
🖑 www.lbhf.gov.uk
🖃 helen.pinnington@lbhf.gov.uk
Fulham Town Hall (right by the tube) has been restored in recent years to its Edwardian splendour, and the Grand Hall with its vaulted ceiling and period chandeliers is certainly very impressive. The Concert Hall shares many of the attractions of the Great Hall, but on a smaller scale. Both halls are licensed for weddings. / 2 am; hirer's choice of caterer; no amplified music in concert hall; Grand Hall (500,250,230,300); Concert Hall (250,150,100,200).

Funland W1
£M-E, (250,–,–,–)
The London Trocadero, Piccadilly Circus
☎ (020) 7292 0700
🖷 (020) 7287 2570
🖑 www.funland.co.uk
🖃 info@funland.co.uk
For a (usually corporate) day out that involves going no further than Piccadilly Circus, you might like to consider hiring this high-tech amusement centre. / midnight; in-house & list of approved caterers; no live music; no dancing; smoking restricted.

Gainsborough Studios N1
£M-E, (450,250,250,300)
1 Poole St
☎ (020) 7749 4451
🖷 (020) 7739 5133
🖑 www.gainsboroughstudios.co.uk
Alfred Hitchcock made "The Lady Vanishes" at these Islington studios, whose uses nowadays include cocktail parties, corporate events and fashion shows. / 3 am; hirer's choice of caterer (in-house available); smoking restricted; South Studio (200,150,150,170); North Studio (70,40,40,50).

Le Gavroche W1
£M-E, (100,70,–,–)
43 Upper Brook St
☎ (020) 7408 0881
🖷 (020) 7491 4387
London's longest-established, grand non-hotel restaurant has now sadly lost its elegant private dining room. For suitable occasions, though, you can hire the whole restaurant.

Gay Hussar W1
£M, (–,24,–,–)
2 Greek St
☎ (020) 7437 0973
🖷 (020) 7437 4631
The atmosphere of this venerable, creaky Hungarian restaurant – long a haunt of Soho's socialist intelligentsia – permeates as far as the cosy upper-floor private rooms. / not available Sun; no music; no dancing; First Floor (–,24,–,–); Second Floor (–,12,–,–).

PRIVATE VENUES

Geffrye Museum E2
£M-E, (250,70,–,–)
136 Kingsland Rd
☎ (020) 7739 9893
🖨 (020) 7729 5647
🖲 www.geffrye-museum.org.uk
📧 info@geffrye-museum.org.uk
Charming former c18 almshouses, now an interesting museum of the history of the English domestic interior, not far from Liverpool Street station. Availability for functions has increased in recent years. / 10pm; evenings only Tue-Thu; in-house caterers & list of approved caterers; no amplified music; no dancing; no smoking; Museum Galleries (250,70,–,–).

The Geological Society of London W1
£M, (180,20,–,185)
Burlington House, Piccadilly
☎ (020) 7434 9944
🖨 (020) 7494 0579
🖲 www.geolsoc.org.uk
📧 enquiries@geolsoc.org.uk
A central and impressively-housed venue (adjacent to the Royal Academy), where a range of smaller-scale facilities come at relatively reasonable cost. / 10pm; in-house caterers; no music; no dancing; no smoking; Lecture Theatre (–,–,–,185); Lower Library (180,–,–,–); Council Rm (20,20,–,20); Arthur Homes Rm (12,12,–,–).

George Inn SE1
£B-M, (350,150,–,–)
77 Borough High St
☎ (020) 7407 2056
🖨 (020) 7403 6956
🖲 www.laurelpubco.com
📧 george.southwark@laurelpubco.com
National Trust pub, just south of London Bridge – the only remaining galleried coaching inn in town. It has two pleasant private rooms, but the restaurant, part of which may be taken privately, is more characterful. Best of all, however, is the Old Bar which, for upwards of 25 people, is available on an exclusive basis. / 11pm; George (–,55,–,–); Talbot (–,34,–,–); Old Bar (50,–,–,–); Courtyard (300,–,–,–).

Gibson Hall EC2
£M-E, (600,300,260,–)
13 Bishopsgate
☎ (020) 7334 3983
🖨 (020) 7334 3981
🖲 www.gibsonhall.com
📧 sales@gibsonhall.com
A sumptuous (going on garish) City hall, dominated by crystal chandeliers. The Garden Room is plain in comparison, but it does have lots of natural light and overlooks the secluded garden – ideal for summer receptions for up to 400. / 1 am; hirer's choice of caterer (in-house available); Hall (600,300,260,–); Garden Rm (200,100,–,–); Garden (300,–,–,–).

The Gilbert Collection WC2
£E, (350,100,–,–)
Somerset House, Strand
☎ (020) 7845 4618
🖲 www.somerset-house.org.uk
📧 corporate.events@somerset-house.org.uk
In the bowels of Somerset House, this museum specialising in ornate and precious objects makes an intriguing location for an event. / 11.30pm; list of caterers; no dancing; no smoking; Silver Gallery (350,180,–,–); Russian Gate Rm (–,15,–,–).

Glassblower W1
£B, (150,50,–,–)
42 Glasshouse St
☎ (020) 7734 8547
This pub on the fringe of Soho has a large, relaxed upstairs lounge bar. Except at weekends, you can also hire the whole place. / 11pm; no dancing; Top Bar (100,50,–,–).

The Glasshouse Stores W1
£B, (150,–,–,–)
55 Brewer St
☎ (020) 7287 5278
Cosy wine bar beneath a Soho pub – either or both arms of its U-configuration may be used privately. / 11.20pm; not available last Fri & Sat of the month; no live music; no dancing; Large Side (80,–,–,–); Small Side (50,–,–,–).

CAPACITIES: (Standing, Seated, Dinner dance, Theatre-style)

Glaziers' Hall SE1
£M, (500,250,200,300)
9 Montague Close
☎ (020) 7403 3300
🖰 www.glaziershall.co.uk
✉ sales@glaziershall.co.uk
A '70s renovation left this early c19 South Bank building with a rather 'flat' feel. The River Room's view more than compensates, however, and the hall and other rooms offer flexible, not-too-expensive accommodation on a good scale. / 2 am; list of caterers; Hall (500,250,200,300); River Rm (200,120,–,100); Library & Court Rm (120,100,80,125).

Goldsmiths College SE14
£B-M, (700,–,–,–)
Lewisham Way
☎ (020) 8692 1406
🖶 (020) 8694 9789
🖰 www.goldsmiths.ac.uk
✉ j.hicks@gold.ac.uk
One of London's finest art schools, unglamorously located in New Cross. The students' union has two bars, both recently refurbished, with full nightclub facilities. / restricted availability; 2 am; in-house or hirer's choice by negotiation; smoking restricted; Bar Revolution (300,–,–,–); Stretch Bar (700,–,–,–).

The Golden Hinde SE1
£M, (120,60,–,–)
St Mary Overie Dock, Cathedral St
☎ 0870 011 8700
🖶 (020) 7403 0123
🖰 www.goldenhinde.co.uk
✉ info@goldenhinde.co.uk
Full-scale reconstruction of Sir Francis Drake's galleon, moored between Southwark and London Bridge. The rigging is floodlit at night enhancing the setting, and you can go out on deck in the summer. You can get married in the hold or the great cabin. / hirer's choice of caterer; no amplified music; no smoking.

Goldsmiths' Hall EC2
£M-E, (700,220,100,–)
Foster Ln
☎ (020) 7606 7010
🖶 (020) 7606 1511
🖰 www.thegoldsmiths.co.uk
✉ theclerk@thegoldsmiths.com
The epitome of majestic, classically-styled grandeur, this gilded early c19 livery hall, a stone's throw from St Paul's, manages to be stately rather than stiff in atmosphere. It is available for hire primarily by an established circle of former users for special events, but applications from newcomers will always be considered. / 11pm; not available Fri-Sun; in-house caterers; Livery Hall (500,220,100,–); Drawing Rm & Exhibition Rm (200,70,–,–).

The Golden Lion SW1
£B, (120,40,–,–)
25 King St
☎ (020) 7925 0007
This St James's pub is usually closed for weekend evenings, but for parties of more than 80 it will open for you exclusively. Discos can be arranged in the nicer-than-usual upper room, the Theatre Bar, which is also available independently during the week for parties of 25-45 people. / 11pm; available Mon-Fri eves, weekends all day; Theatre Bar (45,25,–,–).

Goodenough College WC1
£M, (550,300,125,450)
23 Mecklenburgh Square
☎ (020) 7769 4727
🖶 (020) 7837 9321
🖰 www.goodenough.ac.uk
✉ club@goodenough.ac.uk
In a leafy part of Bloomsbury, an academic institution with pleasant function facilities, including a panelled great hall, on quite a scale and not too expensive. / ; midnight; in-house caterers; no amplified music; no dancing; Great Hall (350,200,125,300); Common Rm (200,100,–,150).

Goolies W8
£M, (60,50,40,–)
21 Abingdon Rd
☎ (020) 7938 1122
🖷 (020) 7937 6121
🖰 www.goolies-bar.com
📧 david@goolies-bar.com
Bright modern British restaurant, just off Kensington High Street, available for exclusive hire. See their advertisement above. / *midnight.*

Le Gothique SW18
£B-M, (400,250,200,–)
The Royal Victoria Patriotic Bldg, Fitzhugh Gr, off Trinity Rd
☎ (020) 8870 6567
The particular appeal of this French restaurant is its access to the very pretty cloister garden of its extraordinarily Victorian building, in a Wandsworth common. For larger events, the restaurant can also make use of the Academy of Live and Recorded Arts (see also). / *midnight; Patio (250,150,–,–).*

The Goring SW1
£M, (100,100,–,–)
Beeston Pl
☎ (020) 7396 9000
🖷 (020) 7834 4393
🖰 www.goringhotel.co.uk
📧 reception@goringhotel.co.uk
Surprisingly tranquil for Victoria, this is one of the few family-owned quality hotels in town. It has some pretty rooms for entertaining, including two panelled dining rooms. At weekends only, wedding receptions for up to 100 can be accommodated in the Restaurant. / *Archive Rm (100,50,–,–); Drawing Rm (25,12,–,–); Breakfast Rm (–,8,–,–).*

The Grafton W1
£M, (200,140,120,100)
130 Tottenham Court Rd
☎ (020) 7388 4131
🖰 www.radissonedwardian.com
📧 graftcb@radisson.com
Edwardian hotel on the fringe of Bloomsbury, with a good variety of smaller to medium-size function rooms (including quite a number not listed), decorated in traditional style. / *11pm; smoking areas; Warren Suite (200,140,120,–); Grafton (125,80,80,100); Arlington Suite (60,40,–,–); Torrington (–,12,–,–).*

CAPACITIES: (Standing, Seated, Dinner dance, Theatre-style)

Gray's Inn WC1
£M-E, (300,170,170,–)
High Holborn
☎ (020) 7458 7830
🖷 (020) 7458 7935
🖑 www.graysinn.org.uk
🖂 banqueting.functions@
graysinn.org.uk
*The attractively cloistered surround-
ings of this Inn of Court make a
good setting for social and business
events. You might have dinner in the
simply decorated but attractive c17
hall and adjourn for coffee to the
Large Pension Room, before returning to the Hall for dancing. / midnight;
not available Sun; in-house caterers;
Hall (300,170,170,–); Large Pension
Rm (150,90,–,–).*

Great Eastern Dining Rooms EC2
£M, (200,–,–,–)
54 Great Eastern Street
☎ (020) 7613 4545
🖷 (020) 7613 4137
*Will Ricker's sleek corner bar/restau-
rant (now serving Pan-Asian food)
was one of the first to help put
Shoreditch on the map. In the basement there's a large, night-clubby
space (Below 54), with lots of sofas.
/ 1 am; Below 54 (200,–,–,–).*

Great Eastern Hotel EC2
£M-E, (700,230,176,200)
Liverpool St
☎ (020) 7618 5000
🖷 (020) 7618 5001
🖑 www.great-eastern-hotel.co.uk
🖂 sales@great-eastern-
hotel.co.uk
*This was the first grand hotel to
open in the City in recent decades. It
is Conran-designed and managed,
and offers quite a range of accommodation. / 1 am; Great
Eastern (400,230,176,200);
Chancery (50,40,–,50);
Bishopsgate (140,88,80,80);
Moorgate (25,30,–,40);
Broadgate (25,14,–,–); Monument (–,10,–,–).*

Great Fosters, Surrey
£M-E, (200,180,160,40)
Stroude Rd, Egham
☎ 01784 433822
🖑 www.greatfosters.co.uk
🖂 conferences@
greatfosters.co.uk
*Once reputedly a Royal hunting lodge
in the heart of Windsor Forest, this
Grade I listed building is now an
hotel. It offers an impressive setting
for a corporate gathering or a wedding. / midnight; in-house caterers; no amplified music; Tithe Barn & Painted
Hall (200,180,160,–);
Orangery (150,80,70,–); Conference
Centre (–,–,–,40).*

Greenwich Playhouse SE10
£B-M, (150,80,80,84)
189 Greenwich High Rd
☎ (020) 8858 9256
🖑 www.galleontheatre.co.uk
🖂 boxoffice@
galleontheatre.co.uk
*The auditorum of what claims to be
London's newest purpose-built studio
theatre offers flexible space, useful
for presentations and rehearsals.
Downstairs, the bar is well suited to
social gatherings. / 1 am; available subject to constraints of current production; in-
house caterers; smoking restricted;
Bar (150,80,80,–); Theatre (–,–,–,84).*

Greenwich Theatre SE10
£B-M, (100,45,–,420)
Crooms Hl
☎ (020) 8858 4447
🖑 www.greenwichtheatre.org.uk
🖂 d.cleveland@
greenwichtheatre.org.uk
*Recently refurbished, the auditorium
here suits presentations and conferences. Alternatively, the bar would
make quite a convivial rendezvous
for a social gathering. / midnight; available subject to constraints of current production; in-house caterers; smoking restricted;
Bar (100,45,–,–).*

Greenwich Yacht Club SE10
£M, (250,120,110,140)
Peartree Wharf, 1Peartree Way
☎ (020) 8244 9393
🖰 www.greenwichyachtclub.co.uk
Intriguingly located on stilts, halfway between the Millennium Dome and the Thames Barrier, this striking modern clubhouse offers a rather intriguing venue for an event. To make best use of it, make sure you arrive/leave by boat. / midnight; hirer's choice of caterer; Club House (150,120,–,100); Function Rms (250,140,110,140).

Grocers' Hall EC2
£M-E, (250,160,–,–)
Princes St
☎ (020) 7606 3113
🖳 (020) 7600 6121
🖰 www.grocershall.co.uk
🖃 sarah@grocershall.co.uk
Rebuilt in 1970, the Grocers Company's accommodation, by the Bank of England, emerged relatively unscathed by the period's style-horrors. The Piper Room, named after the designer of its striking modern wall-hangings, may be used for a reception or dinner. The Livery Hall (with medieval gates) is an unusual modern re-creation of traditional style. / no weddings; 11pm; not available Sat/Sun; in-house caterers; some restrictions on music; some restrictions on dancing; Livery Hall (250,160,–,–); Piper Rm (150,100,–,–).

The Grosvenor House Hotel W1
£M-E, (1700,1700,1700,–)
86-90 Park Ln
☎ (020) 7499 6363
🖳 (020) 7493 3341
🖰 www.lemeridian-grosvenor house.com
🖃 grosvenor.reservations@ lemeridian.com
The Great Room – an enormous two-storey, unpillared space with chandeliers, originally built as an ice-rink – is the largest hotel room in Europe (it is said) and hosts many major events. Its fame tends to over-shadow the other facilities here, which include a pretty ballroom, and 86 Park Lane – a complex of 18 dining and reception rooms, all with natural light (catering for parties from six to 120) in a variety of styles, but principally clubby English. */ 2 am; list of caterers; in-house available; Great Rm (1700,1700,1700,–); Ballroom (800,500,500,–); Albemarle (150,120,100,–); Stratton Suite (125,70,40,–); Spencer Rm (80,40,–,–).*

Groucho Club W1
£M, (500,120,–,–)
45 Dean St
☎ (020) 7439 4685
🖳 (020) 7434 9540
🖰 www.thegrouchoclub.com
🖃 privatereceptions@ grouchoclub.com
This Soho media-world club has a variety of rooms, suitable for many types of function. Facilities can be hired by non-members. / 1 am; whole club available Sat and Sun, 1st or 2nd floors Sat eves; in-house caterers; First Floor (entire) (350,120,–,–); Soho Rm (200,90,–,–); New Rm (50,35,–,–); Gennaro Rm (60,50,–,–); Mackintosh (–,18,–,–).

The Grove, Herts
£M-E, (–,500,450,300)
Chandler's Cross, Rickmansworth
☎ 01923 807807
🖳 01923 221008
🖰 www.thegrove.co.uk
A new 'groovy grand' country house hotel, handy for the metropolis. It is well endowed with facilities of all types, including for events. / 1 am; Amber (–,500,450,300); Ivory (–,120,110,140); Silk (–,40,–,90); Garden Rm (–,20,–,–); Zebrano (–,14,–,–).

Guards Museum SW1
£M, (180,80,–,–)
Wellington Barracks,
Birdcage Walk
☎ (020) 7414 3271
🖳 (020) 7414 3429
Below the concrete of the Guards' parade ground, right by Buck House, these modern galleries of regimental dress, weapons and regalia make a

CAPACITIES: (Standing, Seated, Dinner dance, Theatre-style)

colourful backdrop for a function. There is space for a free-standing marquee in the square, which increases capacity and permits danc-ing. / 10.30pm; list of caterers; no amplified music; no dancing; no smoking; Royal Gallery (180,80,–,–).

Guildhall EC2
£M-E, (1500,704,704,–)
PO Box 270, Aldermanbury
☎ (020) 7332 1462
🖰 www.cityoflondon.gov.uk
📧 michaela.whilbread@
    corpoflondon.gov.uk
The City's imposing c14 HQ is the venue for many state and civic occa-sions. City (and notable London) organisations can also apply, but use of the cathedral-like Great Hall is limited to special events such as milestone anniversaries. Other rooms include the lofty, churchy Library and the Crypts which – with their painted ceilings and stained glass windows – are not at all gloomy. Dancing is allowed, but discouraged by the early closing time. / 11pm; not available Sun; list of caterers; smoking restricted; Great Hall (900,704,704,–); Old Library (600,380,225,–); The Crypts (250,160,160,–); Art Gallery (300,–,–,–).

The Guinea Grill W1
£M, (50,30,–,–)
30 Bruton Pl
☎ (020) 7499 1210
🖶 (020) 7491 1442
🖰 www.youngs.co.uk
Pleasantly old-fashioned Mayfair pub which is one of the relatively few steakhouses in London, and one of the fewer tolerable ones. For a com-fortable, traditional meal it has a first-floor, panelled boardroom. / boardroom not available Sat lunch, closed Sun; Boardroom (50,30,–,–).

Gunnersbury Park W3
£B-M, (120,80,–,–)
Gunnersbury Park
☎ (020) 8992 1612
🖶 (020) 8752 0686
🖰 www.cip.org.uk
📧 gp-museum@cip.org.uk
A huge park, just north of Kew Bridge, with three simple buildings available for wedding receptions and similar events – the Small Mansion possibly enjoys the nicest position. / 1 am; hirer's choice of caterer; smoking restrict-ed; Terrace Rm (100,60,–,–); Orangery (120,80,–,–); Temple (60,35,–,–).

Guy's Hospital SE1
£B-M, (180,120,80,–)
St Thomas's St
☎ (020) 7955 5000 extn 4490
🖶 (020) 7955 4181
On the 29th floor of one of London's tallest blocks, the Robens Suite is the highest venue available for hire in London. The view is, predictably, magnificent (while the walk through the building to reach the suite is, predictably, not). The earth-bound Court Room, part of a much older building, is suitable for formal din-ners. / 1 am; in-house caterers; Robens Suite (180,120,80,–); Court Rm (50,40,–,–); Emily MacManus Hse (–,12,–,–); Lounge (–,12,–,–); Atrium (200,–,–,–).

Haberdashers' Hall EC1
£M-E, (350,210,–,240)
18 West Smithfield
☎ 0870 780 9629
🖶 (020) 7653 6653
🖰 www.cbvs.co.uk
📧 helpme@cbvs.co.uk
A new livery hall, designed by Sir Michael Hopkins, which uses tradi-tional materials and building skills to create a building in thoroughly mod-ern style. / 11pm; in-house caterers; Livery Hall (300,210,–,240); Reception Gallery (180,–,–,–); Court Rm (75,74,–,90); Luncheon Rm (18,18,–,18); Courtyard Orangery (350,–,–,–).

PRIVATE VENUES

Hakkasan W1
£M-E, (215,200,–,–)
8 Hanway Pl
☎ (020) 7907 1888
A continuing success both critically speaking and as a haunt for the beautiful people, this subterranean oriental restaurant has a very striking setting. The Lounge Bar is available for drinks parties, but otherwise the only real option is to hire the whole place – cheaper during the day. / Lounge Bar (70,–,–,–).

The Halkin
£M-E, (150,80,–,–)
5 Halkin St
☎ (020) 7333 1234
🖨 (020) 7233 1100
🖰 www.halkin.co.uk
The hotel's options for functions all revolve around its Thai-fusion restaurant Nahm, run by celebrated aussie chef David Thompson. There's a private room, or – for a stand-up – you can take over the whole restaurant, plus the hotel's cocktail bar. / midnight; no amplified music; no dancing; Private Dining Rm (55,36,–,–).

Ham House, Surrey
£M-E, (250,250,250,–)
Ham Richmond
☎ (020) 8940 1950
🖨 (020) 8332 6903
🖰 www.nationaltrust.org.uk/
hamhouse
✉ hamhouse@
nationaltrust.org.uk
A c17 National Trust house, whose Great Hall makes an impressive setting for a civil wedding. You might use the Orangery's Tea Room for drinks, moving to the Restaurant (in the same building) for dining. The Tea Garden beside the Restaurant is available for alfresco events, and there is a marquee site in the Orangery Garden. / 10.30pm; available Fri & Sat only; Fair Catering; no amplified music; smoking restricted; no drinking in house; Orangery (Restaurant) (70,60,–,–); Orangery Garden (Marquee) (250,250,–,–).

Ham Polo Club, Surrey
£M, (250,260,–,–)
Petersham Rd, Petersham
☎ (020) 8334 0001
🖨 (020) 8948 8443
🖰 www.hunt-kendall.com
✉ emma@hunt-kendall.com
London's only polo club, ten miles from the West End, has space for a marquee of virtually any size. Or you can take over the colonial-style clubhouse, with its floor-to-ceiling glass doors, which open onto vine-clad verandas on either side of the building. / midnight; not available Sun during polo season; Hunt Kendall; Club House (250,260,–,–); Marquee (–,1200,–,–).

Hamilton House EC4
£M, (65,18,–,30)
1 Temple Av
☎ (020) 7353 4212
🖨 (020) 7489 2001
This bright, lofty room, nicely decorated in traditional style, has windows on three sides and an excellent view of the Inner Temple Garden. Its location in an office building and the absence of cooking facilities restrict its function use to drinks parties. / not available weekends; hirer's choice of caterer; no amplified music; no dancing; smoking restricted.

Hamleys Playground W1
£M, (350,–,–,–)
188-196 Regent St
☎ (020) 7479 7332
🖰 www.hamleys.com
✉ esaltman@hamleys.co.uk
It's playtime for adults... The Sega Park in this world-famous toy shop claims to offer the "latest and greatest" in interactive games. Alternatively, rent the whole store to give your friends free run at the shopping! / 11pm; available from 7pm; Leith's; smoking restricted.

CAPACITIES: (Standing, Seated, Dinner dance, Theatre-style)

Hammersmith Apollo W6
£M, (300,–,–,3719)
Queen Caroline St
☎ (020) 7529 4323
🖨 0870 7493198
🖱 www.cclive.co.uk
📧 venue.bookings@ clearchannel.co.uk
If you need to make a presentation to a lot of people, you might like to consider this enormous Hammersmith theatre, available subject to the constraints of the current show. / available subject to constraints of current production.

Hammersmith Palais W6
£B-M, (2230,–,–,–)
230 Shepherds Bush Rd
☎ (020) 8600 2300
🖨 (020) 8600 2332
🖱 www.ponanahammersmith.co.uk
If you're looking for a west London venue on quite a scale, this famous club may well be the answer. As you would expect, it's technically equipped to a high standard. / 3 am; not available Fri-Sat eve; hirer's choice of caterer (in-house available).

Hammersmith Town Hall W6
£B-M, (1000,400,350,950)
King St
☎ (020) 8753 2135
🖱 www.lbhf.gov.uk
📧 helen.pinnington@lbhf.gov.uk
The panelled Assembly Hall itself is a huge, atmospheric '30s room, suitable for a large ball. The other rooms, including the Marble Gallery, are also impressive. The panelled Council Chamber (which seats 130) is licensed for weddings. / 2 am; hirer's choice of caterer; Assembly Hall (1000,400,350,950); Small Hall (150,80,–,–); Marble Gallery (100,–,–,–).

Hampshire Hotel WC2
£M-E, (120,100,60,10)
Leicester Sq
☎ (020) 7451 0228
🖨 (020) 7451 0159
🖱 www.radissonedwardian.com
📧 hampastcb@radisson.com
With its view towards Trafalgar Square, the Penthouse is the special feature of this Theatreland hotel. / 11pm; Penthouse (120,100,60,–); Romsey (30,16,–,–); Drawing Rm (40,10,–,10); Burley (30,16,–,–); Milton (–,8,–,–).

Hampton Court Palace, Surrey
£E, (500,750,–,–)
East Molesey
☎ 0870 751 5182
🖱 www.hrp.org.uk
📧 jill.macdonald@hrp.org.uk
Wolsey's magnificent palace, adopted by Henry VIII, is occasionally used for major corporate and charity dinners. On a more intimate scale, the delightful Banqueting House in the grounds is used relatively frequently for medium-sized dinners. / charities & companies only; available eves only; list of caterers; no amplified music; no dancing; no smoking; Great Hall (400,280,–,–); Cartoon Gallery (350,220,–,–); Public Dining Rm (150,50,–,–); Banqueting House (80,50,–,–).

Hampton Court Palace (The Tiltyard), Surrey
£M, (300,200,160,–)
East Molesey
☎ (020) 8943 3666
🖨 (020) 8943 5457
🖱 www.conference-online.co.uk
A purpose-built function-room, the 'Garden Room' – adjacent to the '20s-style tearooms and the c14 Tiltyard Tower – is the only part of the palace within most budgets. / midnight; Sodexho Prestige; no amplified music.

Harrington Hall SW7
£M-E, (400,240,200,–)
5-25 Harrington Gdns
☎ (020) 7396 1717
🖰 www.harringtonhall.co.uk
✉ sales@harringtonhall.co.uk
*This modern South Kensington hotel
– decorated in a smart, fairly traditional style – is well provided with
panelled banqueting rooms of vary-
ing sizes.* / 1 am; in-house caterers; no
amplified music; Harrington (400,240,200,–);
Turner & Constable (180,100,85,–); Reynolds
& Landseer (150,110,70,–);
Stubbs (70,45,–,–); Sutherland (50,45,–,–).

Harrods SW1
£M-E, (1000,500,–,–)
87-135 Brompton Rd
☎ (020) 7225 6736
🖰 www.harrods.com
✉ emeline.bernard@
    harrods.com
*The eminent Knightsbridge depart-
ment store has long had its enormous Georgian restaurant available
as a venue for functions. What's less
well known is that it also offers a
more general party service, so if you
want to hold a a reception in the
world-famous food halls, for example, it's certainly worth enquiring.* / 2
am; smoking restricted; Georgian
Restaurant (1000,500,–,–); Food
Halls (1000,–,–,–).

Harrow
School, Middx
£B-M, (1000,850,500,750)
5 High St, Harrow On The Hill
☎ (020) 8426 4638
🖰 www.harrowschool.org.uk/
    enterprises
✉ enterprises@
    harrowschool.org.uk
*When school's out you can hire vari-
ous rooms around this well-known
seat of learning.* / 11pm; available outside
term time only; in-house caterers; no amplified music; smoking restricted; Shepherd
Churchill Hall (1000,850,500,–); Speech
Rm (–,–,–,750); Shepherd Churchill
Rm (200,86,–,–).

The Hatton EC1
£M, (200,150,–,–)
51-53 Hatton Gdns
☎ (020) 7242 4123
🖨 (020) 7242 1818
🖰 www.etcvenues.co.uk
✉ hatton@etcvenues.co.uk
*In an Art Deco building near
Holborn, 22 rooms suitable for training and conferences. Entertaining
takes place in the restaurant.* / in-
house caterers; no dancing; no smoking;
Restaurant (200,150,–,–).

Haymarket
Theatre SW1
£M, (–,–,–,895)
Haymarket
☎ (020) 7930 8890
🖰 www.trh.co.uk
✉ nigel@trh.co.uk
*With its Nash façade, the Theatre
Royal (as it is also known) is one of
the most elegant playhouses in
London. The auditorium offers a
grand setting for a daytime presentation.* / available daily until 6pm (setting up
from 11pm night before), except Wed & Sat;
hirer's choice of caterer (in-house available);
no music; no dancing; no smoking.

Hayward Gallery SE1
£M-E, (1000,–,–,–)
Belvedere Rd
☎ (020) 7921 0979
🖨 (020) 7928 2189
🖰 www.hayward.org.uk
✉ sasmiths@hayward.org.uk
*This Brutalist South Bank gallery has
five different indoor spaces, and provides a good range of accommodation for events. Usage, however, is of
course subject to the constraints of
the current show.* / evenings only; list of
caterers; no smoking.

Heights Bar &
Restaurant W1
£M, (130,70,–,–)
Langham Pl
☎ (020) 7580 0111
*The St George's Hotel is not the cap-
ital's most glamorous address (even
if, being next door to Broadcasting
House, it does draw in the BBC*

CAPACITIES: (Standing, Seated, Dinner dance, Theatre-style)

crowd). It does, though – unusually – have a 15th floor bar and restaurant with good views over central London. / 12.30 am; in-house caterers.

Hellenic Centre W1
£M, (200,200,180,–)
16-18 Paddington St
☎ (020) 7487 5060
🖰 www.helleniccentre.org
This impressive Marylebone building may not feel even vaguely Greek, but it does offer smart and characterful accommodation at relatively reasonable cost. / 12.30 am; in-house caterers; no music after 11.30pm; smoking restricted; Great Hall (200,200,180,–); Conference Rm (50,50,–,–).

The Hempel W2
£M-E, (700,300,80,100)
31-35 Craven Hill Gdns
☎ (020) 7298 9000
🖷 (020) 7402 4666
🖰 www.the-hempel.co.uk
🖃 sonal.cara@the-hempel.co.uk
Ultra-minimalist Hyde Park hotel, with a private garden square whose soundproof marquee can cater for up to 300 diners. The I-Thai restaurant can be hired in its entirety. / 1 am; Garden Square (400,300,–,–); Room No 17 (150,42,–,50); I-Thai Restaurant (and Shadow Bar) (175,80,60,100); Jade Rm (25,16,–,20).

Hendon Hall Hotel NW4
£M, (350,240,200,350)
Ashley Ln
☎ (020) 8203 3341
🖷 (020) 8457 2502
🖰 www.thistlehotels.co.uk
🖃 hendonhall@thistle.com
This imposing, Victorian style, mid-c18 building was once the home of actor David Garrick. To the rear is the purpose-built Pembroke Suite, licensed for weddings. There is also a terrace suitable for summer functions. / 11pm; hirer's choice of caterer (in-house available); no smoking; Pembroke Suite (350,240,200,350); Garrick (60,40,30,50); Sheridan (40,30,–,35); Johnson (35,30,–,35).

Henry J Beans SW3
£B-M, (50,–,–,–)
195 King's Rd
☎ (020) 7352 9255
🖰 www.henryjbeansgroup.co.uk
🖃 admin@
  henryjbeansgroup.co.uk
This dark Chelsea burger parlour houses a great surprise – an attractively laid out beer garden, available for exclusive hire.

Hever Castle, Kent
£M-E, (250,150,130,150)
Nr Edenbridge
☎ 01732 861744
🖰 www.hevercastle.co.uk
🖃 tudor@hevercastle.co.uk
Rich with Tudor historical associations, this intimate moated castle was substantially rebuilt by the Astors at the beginning of the c20 – it now benefits from an adjacent Tudor Village which makes it especially suitable for residential events. No dancing in the castle itself, but facilities are available in the grounds. / 11.30pm; in-house caterers; no amplified music; no dancing; smoking restricted; Pavilion (250,150,130,150); Tudor Suite (100,64,–,64); Inner Hall (70,–,–,–); Castle Dining Rm (–,40,–,–); Music Rm (20,–,–,–).

Highgate School N6
£B-M, (400,300,300,160)
Cholmeley House,
3 Bishopswood Rd
☎ (020) 8347 3586
🖷 (020) 8340 7674
🖰 www.highgateschool.org.uk
🖃 bob.jones@
  highgateschool.org.uk
The Victorian buildings of this north London school can provide a pleasant setting for a social event, now including weddings. / hirer's choice of caterer; smoking restricted; Big School (200,160,200,160); School Dining Hall (400,300,300,–); Undercroft (60,40,–,–).

PRIVATE VENUES

Hilton London Docklands SE16
£M, (400,300,250,–)
265 Rotherhithe St
☎ (020) 7231 1001
🖷 (020) 7064 4469
🕾 www.hilton.com
✉ joanne.smith@hilton.com
On the south bank of the Thames in Rotherhithe, this modern hotel and conference centre overlooks the eponymous dock and – across the water – Canary Wharf. Part of the hotel (including the Copenhagen Room, with river terrace) occupies converted c18 warehouses. / midnight; London (400,300,250,–); Thames Suite (250,200,180,–); Battersea (80,–,–,–); Westminster (55,–,–,–); Albert (35,–,–,–); Copenhagen (–,24,–,–).

Hilton London Paddington W2
£M-E, (450,200,200,380)
Praed St
☎ (020) 7850 0500
🕾 www.hilton.com
✉ leanne_halliday@hilton.com
The former Great Western Hotel, by Paddington Station, has now been restored to its former ('20s) grandeur, with function rooms in both contemporary and traditional styles. / 2 am; hirer's choice of caterer (in-house available); Great Western Suite (450,200,200,380); Thunderbolt (50,48,32,72); Red Star (30,40,24,48); McGyver (35,48,28,60).

Hilton on Park Lane W1
£M-E, (1250,1250,1000,–)
22 Park Ln
☎ (020) 7493 8000
🖷 (020) 7208 4145
🕾 www.hilton.com
This landmark hotel has one of the capital's largest ballrooms and also a full range of other accommodation for functions (especially dinner-dances). The fourth-floor Serpentine Room has one of the best views of any function room in London. / 2 am; Grand Ballroom (1250,1250,1000,–); Wellington Ballroom (700,300,200,–); Coronation Suite (200,140,100,–); Serpentine Rm (80,45,–,–); Argyll Rm (40,16,–,–).

RS Hispaniola WC2
£M, (300,220,150,100)
Victoria Embankment
☎ (020) 7839 3011
🕾 www.hispaniola.co.uk
✉ info@hispaniola.co.uk
Moored by Hungerford Bridge for the last 30 years, this erstwhile Clyde steamer is quite a smart place to entertain. The Top Deck has outside areas, front and rear, while the Main Deck has an external area at the side. / 11.30pm; Main Deck (300,220,–,100); Top Deck (150,90,70,60); Board Rm (100,–,–,50).

Hogarth's House W4
£M, (60,–,–,–)
Hogarth's Ln, Great West Rd
☎ (020) 8994 6757
🕾 www.cip.org.uk/heritage/hogarth
The home of engraver and painter William Hogarth contains memorabilia of the great man's life, work and circle, and examples of his work – most famously, the 'Rake's Progress' and 'Marriage à la Mode'. There is an attractive garden. / 10pm; available Tue-Fri from 6pm, weekends from 6pm; hirer's choice of caterer; no amplified music; no dancing; no smoking; no red wine.

Holiday Inn London Regent's Park W1
£M, (400,270,250,–)
Carburton St
☎ (020) 7874 9007
🖷 (020) 7388 3198
🕾 www.london-regentspark.holiday-inn.com
Quietly situated, and rather Continental in feel, a modernish Marylebone hotel (inevitably not adjacent to the Park). / 1 am; smoking restricted; Cambridge & Oxford Suites (400,–,250,–); Oxford (250,150,130,–); Cambridge (150,80,80,–); Trinity Suite (60,50,–,–); Somerville (50,40,–,–);

CAPACITIES: **(Standing, Seated, Dinner dance, Theatre-style)**

Pembroke Suite (10,10,–,–);
Churchill (10,10,–,–).

Holiday Inn – Mayfair W1
£M, (90,50,–,–)
3 Berkeley St
☎ (020) 7493 8282
🖷 (020) 7412 3001
🖑 www.mayfair.holiday-inn.com
🖂 jackie@gc.com
An hotel that benefits from a very central position, just off Piccadilly. The banqueting accommodation is decorated in traditional style.
/ 10.30pm; no amplified music; no dancing; Stratton Suite (90,50,–,–); Presidential Suite (40,20,–,–); Burlington (20,12,–,–); Buckingham (20,12,–,–).

Hollands W11
£B, (75,60,–,–)
6 Portland Rd, Holland Park
☎ (020) 7229 3130
🖑 www.hollandswinebar.
    villaconiglio.com

The airy conservatory at the rear of this Holland Park Thai and Filipino restaurant and wine bar makes an ideal spot for an informal drinks party. / midnight; in-house caterers; Conservatory (75,40,–,–); Balcony Bar (–,20,–,–).

Home EC2
£B-M, (400,110,–,–)
100-106 Leonard Street
☎ (020) 7684 8618
🖷 (020) 7684 1491
A funky Shoreditch lounge bar (basement) and restaurant (ground floor). The bar in particular suits parties,

although for large events, or for sit-down meals the restaurant can also be made available. / 2 am; Basement Bar (250,–,–,–); Ground Floor Restaurant (200,110,–,–).

Home House W1
£E, (1000,150,120,70)
20 Portman Square
☎ (020) 7670 2000
🖷 (020) 7670 2020
🖑 www.homehouse.co.uk
🖂 isturrock@homehouse.co.uk
Overlooking Portman Square, this stately Georgian townhouse (these days a members' club) has some extremely impressive rooms – not least a glittering, first-floor ballroom. Availability to non-members is very restricted, but if you can find a member they can sponsor your event (of – if they like the cut of your jib – you could always join). / midnight, garden 10pm; in-house caterers; Front Parlour (80,40,–,–); Eating Rm (80,72,–,70); Front & Eating Rm (160,120,120,–); Asylum (200,–,–,–); Drawing Rm (200,–,–,–); Garden (200,150,–,–).

Honourable Artillery Co EC1
£B-M, (3000,2500,2500,2000)
Armoury Hs, City Rd
☎ 0870 780 9639
🖷 (020) 7653 6653
🖑 www.cbvs.co.uk
🖂 helpme@cbvs.co.uk
Armoury House, the HAC's intriguing north-City home, looks on to 6 acres of fields surrounded by office buildings. Options include the atmospheric, if basic, Queen's Room, the Albert Room (a large drill hall used for parties, often with a marquee liner as decoration) and, for smarter events, the Long Room (using the fine Medal or Court Room for pre-dinner drinks). Organisers of mega-functions (for up to 2,500) should consider using the huge amount of kit the HAC assembles for its annual June ball while it is still up – a rig much cheaper than you could possibly DIY. / 11pm; in-house caterers; Albert Rm (350,270,300,300); Long Rm (250,172,120,130); Queen's

Rm (60,46,–,50);
Marquee (3000,2500,2500,2000).

Hop Cellars SE1
£B, (330,100,100,–)
24 Southwark St
☎ (020) 7403 6851
🖱 www.ballsbrothers.co.uk
✉ hopcell@ballsbrothers.co.uk
Close to London Bridge, this large,
pleasant wine bar beneath the
imposing façade of the Hop
Exchange (see below) has two inter-
connecting private function rooms
and a restaurant and bar for hire.
Parties of 100 or more can hire the
facilities at weekends. / midnight; Porter
Rm (150,90,–,–); Bar (150,–,–,–);
Restaurant (–,55,–,–); Malt Rm (75,50,–,–).

Hop Exchange SE1
£M, (400,250,200,–)
24 Southwark St
☎ (020) 7940 8900
🖨 (020) 7403 6848
✉ mail@peergroup.co.uk
In the hinterland to London Bridge,
this lofty, cream and green Victorian
hall – with wrought iron galleries and
a modern, translucent roof – offers a
large and atmospheric venue for
those prepared to think a little about
lighting and decoration. / midnight; avail-
able from 7pm, weekends all day; hirer's
choice of caterer (in-house available); smok-
ing restricted.

The Hop Farm Country Park, Kent
£M, (250,250,200,–)
Nr Paddock Wood
☎ 01622 872068
🖨 01622 872630
🖱 www.thehopfarm.co.uk
✉ joanna@thehopfarm.co.uk
The largest collection of Victorian
oast houses in existence forms the
centrepiece of this 250 acre park. It
offers a variety of accommodation
for both in-and outdoor events. / Dray
Museum (500,300,250,–); White Banqueting
Suite (300,220,150,–); Roundels (30,25,–,–).

Horniman Museum SE23
£M, (1000,300,300,400)
100 London Rd, Forest Hill
☎ (020) 8291 8689
🖨 (020) 8291 5506
🖱 www.horniman.ac.uk
✉ hire@horniman.ac.uk

Set in 16 acres of impressive gar-
dens, this intriguing museum offers
flexible space in curious surround-
ings. A major recent revamp has left
it much more suitable for functions,
and it now has some striking con-
temporary spaces. For something a
little different, why not dine "with the
mummies" in the Egyptian room.
/ midnight; list of caterers; smoking restricted;
no red wine; Victoria
Conservatory (100,80,80,100); Gallery Sq &
Centenary Gallery (250,80,80,80); Music
Gallery (100,60,–,60); Exhibition
Gallery (400,300,300,400); African
Worlds/Natural History (120,–,–,–);
Performance Space (30,20,–,30).

The House of St Barnabas-in-Soho W1
£B-M, (120,60,–,–)
1 Greek St, Soho Sq
☎ (020) 7434 2067
🖱 www.spteventsltd.co.uk
✉ schattalou@spteventsltd.co.uk

Grade I listed, this c18 house in the
heart of Soho offers three historic
rooms, impressively decorated in
rococo style. / 11.30pm; list of caterers; no

CAPACITIES: (Standing, Seated, Dinner dance, Theatre-style)

amplified music; no dancing; Council
Rm (80,60,–,–); Withdrawing
Rm (40,20,–,–); Records Rm (20,10,–,–).

Hoxton Hall N1
£B-M, (300,80,80,140)
130 Hoxton St
☎ (020) 7684 0060
🖰 www.hoxtonhall.co.uk
🖂 office@
    hoxtonhall.dabsol.co.uk
*The only saloon-type music hall left
in London in its original form (1863),
this theatrical space is available for
hire subject to the constraints of the
current performance.* / available subject
to constraints of current production; hirer's
choice of caterer (in-house available); smoking restricted; Theatre (140,80,–,140);
Whole Ground Floor (300,80,80,140).

Hoxton Square Bar & Kitchen N1
£B-M, (300,40,–,–)
2 Hoxton Square
☎ (020) 7613 0709
*This large, designer-concrete bar in
Hoxton is, of course, trendy, but it
also seems very professionally run.
Its loungey style (it's lined with sofas)
make it a good place to take over,
but they've also recently added a private room for small functions.* / 12.30
am; Private Rm (80,40,–,–).

Hurlingham Club SW6
£M-E, (500,380,380,400)
Ranelagh Gdns
☎ (020) 7471 8220
🖳 (020) 7736 7167
🖰 www.hurlinghamclub.org.uk
🖂 events@
    hurlinghamclub.org.uk
*An elegant Georgian 'country club' in
its own extensive Fulham grounds
(which, implausibly, was where polo
was first played in England). It is one
of the prettiest places near to central
London and has an impressive suite
of rooms well suited to weddings,
dances or summer barbecues, in all
of which they do big business.
Sponsorship by a member must be
obtained.* / ; 2 am; Searcy's; Quadrangle

Suite (500,380,380,400); Broom House
Suite (500,360,280,400).

ICA SW1
£M, (350,120,80,168)
The Mall
☎ (020) 7766 1414
🖳 (020) 7306 0122
🖰 www.ica.org.uk
🖂 info@ica.org.uk
*Certainly an imposing venue, occupy-
ing an impressive terrace overlooking
the Mall. It has a wide variety of
facilities for hire, including two
impressive reception rooms with balconies overlooking the mall, a theatre, two cinemas and a new media
centre.* / I am; in-house caterers; Nash &
Brandon Rms (250,120,80,80); Cinema
I (–,–,–,185); Cinema 2 (–,–,–,45);
Theatre (350,–,–,168).

Ikkyu W1
£B-M, (–,16,–,–)
67a Tottenham Court Rd
☎ (020) 7636 9280
🖳 (020) 7436 6169
*This impossible-to-locate Japanese
basement, near Goodge Street tube,
has a reputation for serving unusually affordable Japanese food of good
quality. It has a traditional (shoes off)
private tatami room.* / 10.30pm; not
available Sat or Sun L; Tatami Rm (–,16,–,–).

The Imagination Gallery WC1
£M-E, (350,140,140,–)
South Crescent, 25 Store St
☎ (020) 7323 3300
🖳 (020) 7323 5810
🖰 www.imagination.com
🖂 gallery@imagination.com

*One of London's most impressive
spaces. You cross a sci-fi-style, appar-*

PRIVATE VENUES

ently fragile, metal bridge which spans the building's atrium to reach the light and airy fifth-floor gallery (which has a very good view of Bedford Square from its full-length balcony). The Atrium is also available for hire. / no children; 11pm; in-house caterers; no discos; Atrium and Restaurant (350,100,–,–); Gallery (250,100,–,–).

Imperial China WC2
£B-M, (–,500,–,–)
25a Lisle St
☎ (020) 7734 3388
🖻 (020) 7734 3833
Intriguingly located in Chinatown (behind a small courtyard), this light multi-floor restaurant (which is undergoing an ongoing improvement programme) offers very flexible accommodation for parties large and small (including some surprisingly smart private rooms). / Private Rm (–,50,–,–); Private Rms (x2) (–,20,–,–).

Imperial City EC3
£M, (–,16,–,–)
Cornhill, Royal Exchange
☎ (020) 7626 3437
🖻 (020) 7338 0125
🖰 www.imperialcity.co.uk
This stylish City Chinese restaurant has an excellent location (beneath the Royal Exchange) – a side vault is available for private lunches and dinners. / not available weekends; Private Vault (–,16,–,–).

Imperial College SW7
£B-M, (500,420,–,67)
Watts Way, Prince's Garden
☎ (020) 7594 9494
🖻 (020) 7594 9504
🖰 www.imperial.ac.uk/ conferences
🖃 conference@imperial.ac.uk
Imperial College has a range of facilities for social occasions. Most imposing (but also most restrictive) is the Rector's residence at 170 Queensgate – the Council Chamber is the most used room, but the Music Room (or Solar), with French windows to the garden, is the most

pleasant. Elsewhere, the Main Dining Hall, with its wooden floor and function bar, is used for formal dining and dinner dances. Patio doors lead on to Queen's Lawn, popular for garden parties and barbecues. / 11pm; available weekends by rector's permission, Mon-Fri eves except council rm all day; in-house caterers; smoking restricted; Main Dining Hall (500,420,–,–); Council Rm (–,66,–,67); Solar (40,–,–,–); Dining Rm (–,40,–,–).

Imperial War Museum SE1
£M-E, (1000,400,350,50)
Lambeth Rd
☎ (020) 7416 5394
🖻 (020) 7416 5457
🖰 www.iwm.org.uk/ lambeth/venue
🖃 hospitality@iwm.org.uk
This historic site (which includes part of the original Bedlam hospital) is a most impressive venue, and comes ready-themed with guns, planes and tanks. Various galleries can be added to the lofty central atrium for extra reception space, while the Trench and Blitz Experiences can also be open during events. / midnight; available from 7.30pm; list of caterers; no smoking; Main Atrium (400,300,250,–); Boardroom 1 (70,40,–,50); Boardroom 2 (30,14,–,25).

L'Incontro SW1
£M-E, (–,32,–,–)
87 Pimlico Rd
☎ (020) 7730 6327
🖻 (020) 7730 5062

An opulent Italian restaurant in Pimlico, with a basement dining room and bar kitted out by David Linley (whose shop is nearby). / 11am; Private Rm (–,32,–,–).

CAPACITIES: (Standing, Seated, Dinner dance, Theatre-style)

Inmarsat EC1
£M, (300,–,–,300)
99 City Rd
☎ (020) 7728 1259
🖨 (020) 7728 1765
🖰 www.inmarsat.com/
conferences
📧 conference_services@
inmarsat.com

A dozen rooms, convenient for the City, accommodating between 10 and 300 people for conferences and presentations. / 10pm; weekdays only; in-house caterers; no music; no dancing; no smoking.

Inner Temple Hall EC4
£M-E, (750,250,–,250)
Temple
☎ (020) 7797 8230
🖨 (020) 7797 8227
🖰 www.innertemple.org.uk
📧 catering@innertemple org.uk

The three main rooms at this Inn of Court are interconnected – you might have drinks in the Hall, followed by dinner in the Luncheon Room and Parliament Chamber. The Garden makes a charming venue for a summer party. / 1 am; available eves and weekends; in-house caterers; no amplified music in garden; Hall (400,250,–,250); Parliament Chamber (200,90,–,120); Luncheon Rm (120,50,–,70); Garden (750,–,–,–).

Innholders' Hall EC4
£M-E, (250,87,–,120)
30 College St
☎ (020) 7236 6703
🖨 (020) 7236 0059
🖰 www.innholders.co.uk
📧 mail@innholders.co.uk

Sombre but striking, this c17 hall, near Cannon Street, was substantially restored after the Blitz. It is accessed via a pretty hall and reception room, both of recent construction. / 11pm; not available weekends; in-house caterers; no amplified music; no dancing; Hall (150,87,–,120); Court Rm (30,25,–,–).

Institut Français SW7
£B-M, (100,50,–,–)
17 Queensberry Pl
☎ (020) 7073 1366
🖨 (020) 7073 1355
🖰 www.institut-francais.org.uk
📧 francoise.faulkner@
ambafrance.org.uk

The Salon de Réception of this South Kensington centre is quite a large, light, first floor room that suits smartish receptions and dinners, and the Art Deco Library is sufficiently notable to have listed building status. The café is run separately, as Brasserie de l'Institut Francais (see also). / midnight; hirer's choice of caterer; no amplified music; no dancing; Library (100,50,–,–); Salon de Réception (80,30,–,–).

Institute of Directors SW1
£M-E, (400,250,180,300)
116 Pall Mall
☎ (020) 7451 3107
🖨 (020) 7930 9060
🖰 www.iod.co.uk/116
📧 caroline.gregory@iod.com

The full stateliness of this large, white Nash edifice in St James's – built as a gentlemen's club – is most apparent in the Waterloo and Nash rooms, both of which lead off the magnificent staircase. For business-related functions particularly, the Institute offers affordable grandeur. Events must be sponsored by one of the 55,000+ members. / 11pm;

in-house caterers; Nash (400,250,180,300);
Burton (160,80,60,120);
Waterloo (160,60,40,100); Trafalgar II/St
James II (60,50,–,50); Trafalgar
I (50,40,–,40); St James's II (40,30,–,30).

Institute of Electrical Engineers WC2
£M, (450,260,200,460)
Savoy Place
☎ (020) 7344 5479
⌂ www.iee.org/savoyplace
✉ facilities@iee.org.uk
*The home of the Institute of
Electrical Engineers, by the Savoy
Hotel, has now relaunched itself as a
fully-fledged venue for corporate pre-
sentations and entertaining.* / 11pm;
in-house caterers; smoking restricted; Lecture
Theatre (–,–,–,460); Riverside
Restaurant (450,220,200,–); Lancaster
Rm (100,–,–,–); Maxwell Suite (100,60,–,–);
Common Rm (100,30,–,–).

The Insurance Hall EC2
£M, (300,180,120,100)
20 Aldermanbury
☎ (020) 7417 4417
🖶 0870 6067805
⌂ www.cii.co.uk
✉ insurance.co@cii.co.uk
*A cosy institution, behind the
Guildhall, which is, by City standards,
quite a flexible venue. Although the
hall has quite a capacity, it is much
less imposing than some of its local
competition – which may be no bad
thing – and the feel inside is of a
small Edwardian town hall. The
Council Chamber (with a small
museum attached) is an atmospheric
corner room.* / 11pm; Crown Catering;
smoking restricted; Great
Hall (300,160,120,–); New
Rm (120,60,40,–); Council
Chamber (100,23,–,–); Oftler
Suite (150,90,–,100); President's
Rm (–,8,–,–).

InterContinental London W1
£M-E, (1400,750,650,–)
1 Hamilton Pl, Hyde Park Corner
☎ (020) 7409 3131
⌂ www.london.intercontinental.com
✉ london@interconti.com
*Banqueting facilities at this impres-
sively-located modern hotel have
been transformed in the last few
years – it now offers rooms, mainly
decorated in traditional style, of a
size appropriate to almost any function. Most impressive, perhaps, is the
seventh floor Windsor suite, with its
commanding views.* / 2 am; Grand
Ballroom (1400,750,650,–);
Westminster (800,430,300,–); Byron & Parks
Suites (750,200,–,–); Piccadilly (400,220,–,–);
Windsor Suite (80,40,–,–).

International Coffee Organisation W1
£M, (–,–,–,284)
22 Berners St
☎ (020) 7580 8591
⌂ www.ico.org
✉ maqueda@ico.org
*Purpose-built to meet the needs of
one particular business, this central
venue offers very central facilities for
meetings, lectures and conferences.*
/ hirer's choice of caterer; Council
Chamber (–,–,–,284); Boardroom (–,–,–,101);
Meeting Rms (–,–,–,25); Committee
Rm (–,–,–,26).

The Irish Centre W6
£B-M, (300,160,110,140)
Black's Rd, Hammersmith
☎ (020) 8563 8232
🖶 (020) 8563 8233
⌂ www.ibh.gov.uk/irishcentre
*A simple Hammersmith space, with
sprung dance-floor and cream walls
– a relatively inexpensive venue for a
dance, a dinner or a wedding reception.* / midnight; hirer's choice of caterer;
Hall (300,160,110,140).

CAPACITIES: (Standing, Seated, Dinner dance, Theatre-style)

Ironmongers' Hall EC2
£M, (250,168,–,150)
Shaftesbury Pl, Barbican
☎ (020) 7776 2300
🖳 (020) 7600 3519
🖰 www.ironhall.co.uk
📧 hallmanager@ironhall.co.uk
It may be surrounded by the Barbican, but – from the inside at least – this 1920s faux-medieval hall (complete with panelling, stone flags and stained glass) manages to feel surprisingly antique. The Drawing Room and Livery Hall are particularly impressive. / 11pm; list of caterers; no amplified music; no dancing; smoking restricted; Hall (250,168,–,150); Drawing Rm (100,60,–,–); Luncheon Rm (80,50,–,30); Court Rm (80,50,–,70).

The Ivy WC2
£M, (120,60,–,–)
1 West St
☎ (020) 7379 6077
🖳 (020) 7497 3644
🖰 www.caprice-holdings.co.uk
Truly a legend in its own lunchtime, this discreet Theatreland restaurant has now enjoyed almost a decade at the top of the popularity pops. It is never available for hire as a whole, though there is a large private room. / 1 am; Private Rm (120,60,–,–).

Jackson's Lane Community Centre N6
£B, (150,75,75,167)
269a Archway Rd
☎ (020) 8341 4421
🖰 www.jacksonslane.org.uk
📧 mail@jacksonslane.org.uk
A converted Highgate church, with a number of rooms suitable for parties. / 1 am; hirer's choice of caterer (in-house available); smoking restricted; Dance Studio (120,75,75,–); Multi-purpose Rm (80,40,40,–); Youth Space (25,–,–,–); Theatre (–,–,–,167).

Jason's W9
£M, (95,60,–,–)
Blomfield Rd, Little Venice
☎ (020) 7286 6752
🖳 (020) 7266 2656
🖰 www.jasons.co.uk
📧 enquiries@jasons.co.uk
A fish and seafood restaurant that has an unusual canal-side location in Maida Vale. You might go for drinks on one of the restaurant boats (see Moving Venues), and then have dinner at the restaurant. / midnight; Restaurant (60,40,–,–).

Jerwood Space SE1
£M-E, (450,150,–,–)
171 Union Street
☎ (020) 7654 0171
🖳 (020) 7654 0172
🖰 www.jerwoodspace.co.uk
📧 space@jerwoodspace.co.uk
A light modern building recently created from an old Victorian school. It makes a good venue for a drinks party, and is a popular spot for media events. / 1 am; in-house caterers; smoking restricted; Gallery & Glasshouse (300,100,–,–); Space 1 (150,80,–,–); Space 2 (150,80,–,–).

Jolly Hotel St Ermins SW1
£M, (350,200,150,–)
Caxton St
☎ (020) 7222 7888
🖳 (020) 7227 7758
🖰 www.jollyhotels.co.uk
📧 stermins@jollyhotels.co.uk
The very characterful, old-fashioned ballroom is the most striking feature of this hotel by St James's Park tube. The proximity to Westminster makes its smaller rooms favourites for political entertaining. / 1 am; Ballroom (200,180,150,–); Balcony (With Ballroom Only) (150,100,–,–); York or Clarence (40,30,–,–); Cameo (50,40,–,–).

PRIVATE VENUES

Jongleurs (Battersea) SW11
£M, (300,–,–,–)
49 Lavender Gdns
☎ 0870 0111960
🖷 0870 0111970
🖱 www.jongleurs.com
✉ dan.foley@jongleurs.com
Originally a '20s ballroom, this venue in its current use has helped to launch the careers of some of the biggest names in comedy. You can hire the whole place as a shell for a private party, or use the in-house service to hold a private comedy night or workshop. / 1 am; available Mon-Thu; hirer's choice of caterer (in-house available); Bar Risa (200,–,–,–).

Jongleurs at Bow Wharf E3
£M, (300,–,–,270)
Bow Wharf, 221 Grove Rd
☎ 0870 0111960
🖷 0870 0111970
🖱 www.jongleurs.com
✉ dan.foley@jongleurs.com
The large main room in this East End comedy club – set in a Victorian warehouse conversion – would require theming for function use. At the junction of Regent and Grand Union Canals, it's an interesting space, popular for product launches. / 2 am; available Mon-Thu; hirer's choice of caterer (in-house available); Bar Risa (250,–,–,–).

Jongleurs at Camden Lock NW1
£M, (450,60,–,300)
Middle Yard, Camden Lock
☎ 0870 011 1960
🖷 0870 011 1970
🖱 www.jongleurs.com
✉ dan.foley@jongleurs.com
The flagship Jongleurs comedy venue. With its interesting waterfront location, it's often used for music events and parties. / 2 am; available Mon-Thu; hirer's choice of caterer (in-house available); Jongleurs (250,200,–,–); Riverside Bar (150,–,–,–); Roof Terrace (60,60,–,–).

Julie's Restaurant & Wine Bar W11
£M, (–,70,–,–)
133-137 Portland Rd
☎ (020) 7229 8331
🖷 (020) 7229 4050
🖱 www.juliesrestaurant.com
This seductive, eclectically-decorated Holland Park labyrinth is one of London's best known party-restaurants, and – now that the neighbouring wine bar has been "rolled in" – can accommodate rather larger gatherings than before. The best rooms are the panelled Banqueting Room (with its single oval table) and the Garden Room. / 1 am; Gothic Rm (–,45,–,–); Garden Rm (–,34,–,–); Banqueting Rm (–,24,–,–); Conservatory (–,16,–,–); Moroccan Rm (–,12,–,–); The Gallery (–,10,–,–).

Just Gladwins EC3
£M-E, (200,120,–,–)
Minster Court, Mark Ln
☎ (020) 7444 0004
🖷 (020) 7444 0001
🖱 www.justgladwins.co.uk
A smart and bright – that is to say, quite businessy – City basement restaurant, available for exclusive hire (usually in the evenings).

Just St James SW1
£M-E, (800,470,–,–)
16 St James's St
☎ (020) 7976 2222
🖷 (020) 7976 2020
🖱 www.juststjames.com

A St James's bar and restaurant, housed in a grandly-marbled Edwardian banking hall. The Gallery makes an unusual venue for a cocktail party, or you can hire the whole place. / Just St James (500,200,–,–); Just Oriental (280,150,–,–); Just The Gallery (200,140,–,–).

CAPACITIES: (Standing, Seated, Dinner dance, Theatre-style)

Just The Bridge EC4
£M, (200,120,120,–)
1 Paul's Walk
☎ (020) 7236 0000
🖷 (020) 7329 9299
🖰 www.thebridgerestaurant.co.uk
A view of Tate Modern (and of the 'wobbly bridge') distinguishes this modern City brasserie. In the evenings, you could hire the whole place, or, in summer, the Bar and Terrace.

Ken Lo's Memories of China SW1
£M, (–,100,–,–)
67-69 Ebury St
☎ (020) 7730 7734
🖷 (020) 7730 2992
One of the few quality restaurants in the immediate vicinity of Victoria, serving pricey oriental cuisine. Recently refurbished, it has two private rooms (which can be used together), or you can hire the whole place. / Private Rms (combined) (–,25,–,–); Private Rm (x2) (–,12,–,–).

The Kenilworth WC1
£M, (150,120,100,–)
97 Great Russell St
☎ (020) 7666 2322
🖷 (020) 7631 1330
🖰 www.radissonedwardian.com
✉ markencb@radisson.com
A medium-sized hotel near the British Museum, recently refurbished in contemporary style. It offers good, standard accommodation for events of a middling sort of scale. / 11pm; smoking restricted; Bloomsbury Suite (150,120,100,–); Kenilworth Suite (120,80,80,–).

Kensington Palace W8
£M-E, (300,150,–,340)
☎ (020) 7376 2452
🖷 (020) 7376 0198
🖰 www.hrp.org.uk
✉ helena.impett@hrp.org.uk
A royal residence longer than Buckingham Palace, the palace is available for events where a suitable degree of formality is required. See also the Orangery (Kensington Palace). / no weddings; 10.30pm; evenings only; list of caterers; no amplified music; no dancing; no smoking; State Apartments (170,–,–,340); Victorian Garden Rms (80,–,–,150); Queens Gallery (170,–,–,–); Orangery (300,150,–,–).

Kensington Place W8
£M, (90,48,–,–)
201-205 Kensington Church Rd
☎ (020) 7727 3184
🖷 (020) 7229 2025
🖰 www.egami.co.uk
✉ kpparty@egami.co.uk
This ever-popular 'goldfish bowl' of a restaurant has an impressive private dining room, with its own street entrance. / no dancing; Private Rm (90,48,–,–).

Kensington Rooms SW7
£M-E, (200,100,–,90)
Courtfield Gardens,
131-137 Cromwell Rd
☎ (020) 7598 7979
🖷 (020) 7598 7981
🖰 www.kensingtonrooms.co.uk
✉ info@kensingtonrooms.co.uk
A new contemporary-style hotel in South Kensington, offering a range of function accommodation. / midnight; in-house caterers; smoking restricted; Rm 9 (200,100,–,90); Media Rm (150,84,–,70); Studio Rm (60,25,–,20).

Kensington Town Hall W8
£M, (600,500,400,860)
Hornton St
☎ (020) 7361 2220
🖷 (020) 7361 3164
🖰 www.rbkc.gov.uk
✉ hall-let@rbkc.gov.uk
Kensington's low-rise red-brick Town Hall offers accommodation on quite a scale. It's perhaps most obviously suited to conferences, but events of all types, including civil weddings, can be accommodated. / list of caterers; Great Hall (600,500,400,860); Small Hall (250,100,70,190).

Kent House SW7
£M-E, (300,100,–,100)
Rutland Gardens
☎ (020) 8993 9978
🖷 (020) 8993 9884
🖰 www.evolve-events.com
🖃 io@evolve-events.com

An impressive Knightsbridge house, recently restored. It has an imposing staircase, and providing an elegant space for entertaining. / midnight; list of caterers; smoking restricted; The Sanctuary (300,200,–,180); Marbled Foyer (80,–,–,–); Library (60,40,–,40); Rutland Rm (80,90,–,70).

Kenwood House NW3
£E, (250,80,–,–)
Hampstead Ln
☎ (020) 7973 3507
🖃 enquiries@
   kenwoodhospitality.co.uk
This beautiful neo-classical house at the top of Hampstead Heath. Replete with artistic treasures, it is available for functions of a more sedate nature. / midnight; list of caterers; no smoking; no red wine; Orangery (250,80,–,–).

Kenwood House, Old Kitchen NW3
£M, (180,80,–,–)
Hampstead Ln
☎ (020) 8341 5384
🖷 (020) 8569 9978
🖰 www.corporate@ksbm.org
🖃 enquiries@
   kenwoodhopitality.co.uk
If you're not looking for the 'full-on' grandeur of Kenwood House itself,

you might like to consider the Old Kitchen and Brew House Restaurant – an airy and attractive, stone-flagged room, often used for civil weddings, or receptions. / 11pm; in-house caterers; no smoking; Brew House (120,80,–,–); Old Kitchen (100,80,–,–).

Kettners W1
£B, (250,90,–,–)
29 Romilly St
☎ (020) 7734 6112
🖷 (020) 7434 1214
It may now be an upmarket PizzaExpress, but this impressive Soho building – which once housed a very grand English restaurant – offers a characterful central location at relatively reasonable cost. / 1 am; Edward Rm (100,50,–,–); Blue Rm (–,30,–,–); Soho Rm (–,12,–,–).

Kew (Royal Botanic) Gardens, Surrey
£M-E, (300,200,200,220)
Kew, Richmond
☎ (020) 8332 5641
🖷 (020) 8332 5667
🖰 www.rbgkew.org.uk
🖃 k.innes@rbgkew.org.uk
If you want to entertain in the grand style, the Temperate House is the most suitable of the famous glasshouses – other possibilities include use of the art gallery, or erecting a marquee. You can get married in the pretty, listed Cambridge Cottage (with up to 80 people in attendance). / midnight; list of caterers; no amplified music; no smoking; Temperate House (300,200,200,–); Gallery (entire ground floor) (150,80,120,–); Cambridge Cottage Lounge (60,50,–,80); New Palace Marquee Site (800,600,600,–); Lecture Theatre (–,–,–,220).

Kew Bridge Steam Museum, Middx
£M, (150,120,100,–)
Green Dragon Ln, Brentford
☎ (020) 8568 4757
🖷 (020) 8569 9978
🖰 www.kbsm.org
🖃 corporate@kbsm.org

CAPACITIES: (Standing, Seated, Dinner dance, Theatre-style)

A dramatic setting – with working steam engines – much in demand for occasions ranging from wedding receptions to themed company events. / no college events or under-30 birthdays; I am; available eves, day sometimes; hirer's choice of caterer; smoking restricted.

King's College WC2
£B-M, (350,140,140,250)
138-142 Strand
☎ (020) 7848 1700
🖰 www.kcl.ac.uk
🖂 vacbureau@kcl.ac.uk
A very central site. The college's main hall is well maintained, quite grand and suitable for a wide range of functions. / 11pm; in-house caterers; no smoking; Great Hall (350,140,140,250); Council Rm (75,–,–,50); Committee Rm (30,–,–,30).

King's College School SW19
£B-M, (300,180,180,–)
Southside, Wimbledon Common
☎ (020) 8255 5401
🖷 (020) 8255 5409
🖰 www.kcs.org.uk
🖂 ents@kcs.org.uk
Facilities at this Wimbledon school include the panelled Great Hall to accommodate barbecues, the Dalziel Room (with access to a terrace and private lawn) and the Boathouse club room (overlooking the river at Putney). / midnight; Great Hall available outside term time only; hirer's choice of caterer; no smoking; Great Hall (300,180,180,–); Dalziel Rm (100,40,–,–); Boathouse (100,40,–,–).

King's College, King's Cuisine Restaurant SE1
£B-M, (400,250,150,–)
150 Stamford St
☎ (020) 7848 3800
A student dining facility that's worth considering if you're looking to entertain a fair number of people at modest cost. / in-house caterers; no smoking.

King's Head Theatre N1
£B, (–,–,–,120)
115 Upper St
☎ (020) 7226 1916
🖰 www.kingsheadtheatre.org
🖂 kingsheadtheatre@btclick.com
If you're looking for somewhere with a lot of olde worlde atmosphere for a daytime presentation, you might consider this famous Islington theatre-pub. / 6pm; available daily until 6pm; in-house caterers.

Kingsway Hall WC2
£M, (200,150,120,150)
Great Queen St
☎ (020) 7309 0909
🖰 www.kingswayhall.co.uk
🖂 kingswayhall@compuserve.com
This modern Covent Garden hotel has a panelled banqueting suite (subdivisible), or for suitable occasions it may be possible to take over the light and airy restaurant at the front of the hotel. / midnight; Keats & Milton Rms (180,100,70,150); Restaurant (120,150,120,–); Chaucer (30,12,–,26).

Kingswood House SE21
£B-M, (250,180,40,–)
Kingswood Estate, Seeley Dr, Dulwich
☎ (020) 8761 7239
🖷 (020) 8766 7339
A c18 castle now run by Southwark Council as a library and community centre, but retaining much of the opulence of its original decorative style. It is available for weddings. / midnight; hirer's choice of caterer; no smoking; Golden Rm, Jacobean Rm (250,180,–,–); Charles Suite (100,80,40,–); Vestey (50,–,–,–); Hannen Rm (20,–,–,–).

PRIVATE VENUES

LABAN SE8
£M-E, (450,240,200,294)
Creekside
☎ (020) 8691 8600
🖨 (020) 8691 8400
🖰 www.laban.org
📧 events@laban.org

Housing one of Europe's leading institutions for contemporary dance artist training, this new Lewisham venue won the 2003 RIBA Stirling prize for its architects Herzog & de Meuron, thereby making it an ideal backdrop for events of a fashionable or artistic nature. / 11pm; restricted availability in term time; list of caterers, in-house available; no smoking; Bonnie Bird Theatre (300,240,200,294); Amphitheatre (450,240,200,200); Concourse (450,–,–,–); Studio Theatre (300,240,200,100); Medium Studio (100,90,60,80); Meeting Rm (30,20,–,30).

The Lamb Tavern EC3
£B, (100,70,–,–)
10-12 Leadenhall Mkt
☎ (020) 7626 2454
One of the City's best pubs – in the centre of an atmospheric, covered market – with two bars available for private early-evening hire, without charge. / 10pm; not available weekends; no amplified music; no dancing; Dining Rm (100,70,–,–); The Dive (100,–,–,–).

Lancaster House SW1
£E, (350,150,–,200)
Stable Yard, St James's
☎ (020) 7210 6853
🖰 www.fco.gov.uk
The St James's palace has "entertained more heads of state than any other", and parts of it are ornamented to a degree that seems more French than English. It is primarily used for government events, but is also made available for suitably august third-party events. / very restricted availability; list of caterers; no amplified music; no dancing; no smoking; Long Gallery (350,150,–,200); Grand Hall (200,–,–,–); State Dining Rm (120,67,–,–); Gold Rm (40,16,–,–); Eagle Rm (50,24,–,–); Music Rm (150,78,–,–).

The Landmark NW1
£M-E, (500,360,310,–)
222 Marylebone Rd
☎ (020) 7631 8000
🖰 www.landmarklondon.co.uk
📧 sales@thelandmark.co.uk
An impressive hotel where skillful updating of a Victorian building (once the Great Central Hotel) has provided London with some of its grandest public rooms – the marbled Ballroom and the oak-panelled Drawing Room are especially impressive, as is the eight-storey atrium. / 1 am; Ballroom (500,408,348,–); Music Rm (350,340,180,–); Drawing Rm (300,180,120,–); Empire Rm (250,180,120,–); Gazebo (in the Atrium) (250,90,–,–); Champagne Rm (70,36,–,–); Tower Suite (60,36,–,–).

The Lanesborough SW1
£M-E, (180,100,60,100)
Hyde Park Corner
☎ (020) 7259 5599
🖨 (020) 7259 5606
🖰 www.lanesborough.com
📧 info@lanesborough.com
A neo-classical landmark, converted into a glossy hotel and furnished in a rather overblown Regency style. For functions, a variety of lofty, medium-sized rooms and a prettified wine cellar are available. Many rooms are licensed for weddings. / 1 am; in-house caterers; Belgravia (180,100,60,100); Wellington Rm (100,60,40,80); Westminster Rm (60,40,–,55); Wilkins Rm (30,20,–,35); Wine Cellar (–,12,–,–).

CAPACITIES: (Standing, Seated, Dinner dance, Theatre-style)

Langham Hilton W1
£M, (450,300,220,–)
1c Portland Pl
☎ (020) 7636 1000
🖷 (020) 7436 7418
🖱 www.langham.hilton.com
London's first purpose-built Victorian hotel has an extremely grand Grand Ballroom, with access to the courtyard in fine weather. You can marry in the Palm Court (with its fountain, fronds and pillars) or the Ambassador Room. / am;
Ballroom (450,300,220,–); Palm Court (250,–,–,–); Portland Suite (150,100,–,–); Regent/Welbeck Rms (50,40,–,–); Cumberland Rm (15,–,–,–); Ambassador Rm (50,40,–,–).

The Langley WC2
£B-M, (500,100,–,–)
5 Langley St
☎ (020) 7836 5005
🖷 (020) 7836 5775
🖱 www.latenightlondon.co.uk
🖂 info@thelangley.com
Rambling cellars beneath Covent Garden make this large bar/restaurant eminently suitable as a "groovy" (their word) party venue. Of the various areas which can be hired, the most private is The Vault. Or you could take the whole place. / The Vault (50,–,–,–).

Lansdowne Club W1
£M, (250,150,120,150)
9 Fitzmaurice Pl
☎ (020) 7629 7200
🖱 www.lansdowneclub.com
🖂 enquiries@
  lansdowneclub.com

A Mayfair club, recently refurbished, with a very handy location, some impressive Art Deco interiors and a good range of facilities for functions. / 12.30 am; in-house caterers;

Ballroom (250,150,–,150); Sun Rm (22,12,–,–); Shelburne Rm (80,40,–,60); Findlay Rm (30,20,–,30).

Latchmere Theatre SW11
£B-M, (120,60,60,80)
503 Battersea Park Rd
☎ (020) 7978 7040
🖷 (020) 7978 7041
🖱 www.latchmeretheatre.com
🖂 info@latchmeretheatre.com
If you're looking for a presentation space around Battersea, this recently modernized Victorian pub-theatre is well worth considering. / available subject to constraints of current production; smoking restricted.

Lauderdale House N6
£B-M, (180,100,100,–)
Waterlow Park, Highgate Hl
☎ (020) 8348 8716
🖱 www.lauderdale.org.uk
🖂 admin@lauderdale.org.uk
A pretty c16 Highgate house, overlooking the park, much used for weddings, receptions and other social events. / midnight; in-house caterers; no smoking.

Launceston Place W8
£M, (–,80,–,–)
1a Launceston Pl
☎ (020) 7937 6912
🖷 (020) 7938 2412
🖂 lpr@egami.co.uk
One of the most discreet, comfortable and English of restaurants, hidden away in Kensington, with a comfortable private room and also a larger semi-private area. / Private Area (–,30,–,–); Private Rm (–,14,–,–).

The Law Society WC2
£M-E, (300,220,150,–)
113 Chancery Ln
☎ (020) 7316 5760
🖷 (020) 7320 5616
🖱 www.
  uniquevenue.lawsociety.org.uk
🖂 mande@lawsociety.org.uk
This fine early c19 building, sensitively developed over the years and very

well maintained, has a comfortable grandeur and surprising degrees of charm and flexibility. The Old Council Chamber stands out, but there is a good range of rooms – they claim 24 in total – for most occasions. / 11pm; only available for parties of 100+ at weekends; Leith's; Common Rm (300,160,150,–); Old Council Chamber (120,55,–,–); Chancery (60,50,–,–); Fleet (45,30,–,–).

Leadenhall Wine Bar EC3
£B, (150,100,–,–)
27 Leadenhall Mkt
☎ (020) 7623 1818
In the evening you can hire either of the two rooms of this comfortable City wine bar, which looks down into Leadenhall Market. / available Mon-Fri eves, closed weekends; Main Rm (100,60,–,–); Top Floor (50,40,–,–).

Lee Valley Cycle Circuit E10
£B-M, (–,–,–,–)
Quarter Mile Ln, Stratford
☎ (020) 8534 6085
✉ cycle@leevalleypark.org.uk
On a circuit of 48 acres, there is space for marquees of virtually unlimited capacity at this east London venue. / 10pm; hirer's choice of caterer; no smoking.

Legoland Windsor, Berks
£M-E, (500,300,280,400)
Winkfield Rd, Windsor
☎ 01753 626102
🖨 01753 626200
🌐 www.legoland.co.uk
✉ lisa.hogg@legoland.co.uk
With 150 acres of mature parkland and over 50 rides, shows and attractions, this theme park can accommodate a wide range of meetings, events and corporate fun days. / midnight; in-house caterers; smoking restricted; no spirits; The Pavilions (500,300,280,400); JFK Drawing Rm (120,60,60,80); Creation Centre (120,40,–,–); Boardroom (–,20,–,–).

Leighton House W14
£M-E, (150,80,–,–)
12 Holland Park Rd
☎ (020) 7603 1123
🖨 (020) 7371 2467
🌐 www.rbkc.gov.uk/ leightonhousemuseum
An idiosyncratic 1870s Holland Park house – built for Frederic Lord Leighton as a showcase for Aesthetic taste – which is ideally suited to more intimate grand events. The highpoint is the Arab Hall, featuring a fountain and intricately patterned c16 and c17 tiles. / 11pm; available eves, not Sun, garden available Apr-Sep; list of caterers; no amplified music; no dancing; no smoking; Studio (150,80,–,–); Arab Hall (70,–,–,–); Dining Rm (–,30,–,–).

Lemonia NW1
£B-M, (–,40,–,–)
89 Regent's Park Rd
☎ (020) 7586 7454
🖨 (020) 7483 2630
For an informal party, the private room of this popular Primrose Hill Greek institution is a very handy size for many events. The whole restaurant is no longer available for hire. / Private Rm (–,40,–,–).

Levant W1
£B-M, (200,120,120,–)
Jason's Court, 76 Wigmore St
☎ (020) 7224 1111
An exotic feel makes this stylish North African basement restaurant just north of Oxford Street a 'natural' party venue. There are lots of useful corners for informal parties, but if you want your 'own' space the only option is to take the whole place.

Leven is Strijd E14
£M, (50,20,–,–)
West India Quay, Hertsmere Rd
☎ (020) 7987 4002
🌐 www.theleven.co.uk
✉ info@theleven.co.uk
This permanently-moored barge in the Docklands (which has been moved from its previous site) caters for dinners for ten or more people in

CAPACITIES: (Standing, Seated, Dinner dance, Theatre-style)

comfortable and unusually private surroundings. / 2 am.

Lightship E1
£M-E, (100,100,–,–)
5a Katharine's Way,
St Katharine's Dock
☎ (020) 7481 3123
🖳 (020) 7702 0338
⌁ www.lightshipx.com
For something a little 'different' – but still very handy for the City – this intriguing 19th century lightship, now moored and in use as a restaurant, makes an obvious choice. / midnight; Main Deck (–,30,–,–); Lower Deck (–,70,–,–).

The Lincoln Centre WC2
£M, (150,50,–,160)
18 Lincoln's Inn Fields
☎ (020) 7936 1300
🖳 (020) 7396 3535
⌁ www.thelincolncentre.co.uk
✉ info@thelincolncentre.co.uk
In an elegant building overlooking Lincoln's Inn Fields, a centre for conference and presentations of a businesslike nature. / 7pm; list of caterers; no smoking; Central Boardroom (–,–,–,12); Break-out Area (150,50,–,–); Presentation 1 (–,–,–,160); Presentation 2 (–,–,–,40); .

Lincoln's Inn WC1
£M-E, (600,320,280,–)
☎ (020) 7405 5969
⌁ www.lincolnsinn.org.uk
✉ catering@lincolnsinn.org.uk
For 'medieval' magnificence, the great hall (1845), set in the quiet of the Inn's gardens, is difficult to better. The real c15 Old Hall across the lawn is smaller and, in its way, more atmospheric. Summer functions on the terrace will be considered. / 11pm; hirer's choice of caterer (in-house available); Great Hall (600,320,280,–); Old Hall (250,130,90,–).

Lindsay House W1
£M, (–,37,–,–)
21 Romilly St
☎ (020) 7439 0450
🖳 (020) 7437 7349
⌁ www.lindsayhouse.co.uk
A discreet Soho townhouse restaurant, redecorated in modernistic style. It's now part of the Searcy's empire, and a showcase for the talents of Irish chef Richard Corrigan. For parties of 30-37 people, you can take the whole of the first floor. / no dancing; Private Rm (–,20,–,–); Private Rm (–,14,–,–).

Liquid Lab EC1
£B-M, (150,–,–,–)
20 City Rd
☎ (020) 7920 0372
⌁ www.liquidlab.co.uk
Arranging "an appointment with the Doctor" means something a little out of the ordinary at this medical-themed cocktail bar north of Finsbury Square. It's a cool-looking, white-walled space decorated with X-rays and test tubes – there's a mezzanine and basement for private hire, but you can hire the whole place at weekends. / 1 am; Mezzanine or Basement (50,–,–,–).

The Litten Tree SW15
£B, (120,–,–,–)
14 Putney High St
☎ (020) 8785 3081
The private room at this younger scene boozer has the advantage of being self-contained (with its own entrance, bar and loo). The basement, however, has the advantage of being licensed till 1am at weekends. / 11pm, basement 1am; in-house caterers; Function Rm 1 (120,–,–,–); Basement Bar (80,–,–,–).

Little Angel Theatre N1
£B-M, (–,–,–,100)
14 Dagmar Passage Cross St
☎ (020) 7226 1787
⌂ www.littleangeltheatre.com
✉ angel@littleangeltheatre.co.uk
Once a temperance hall, this is now the only specialist puppet theatre in London (in business for 40 years). It offers an intimate space, which can be used for smaller meetings and presentations. Fixed seating is something of a drawback, although it may be possible to take drinks outside on a nice evening. / available evenings only; hirer's choice of caterer; no dancing; smoking restricted; Auditorium (–,–,–,100).

The Little Ship Club EC4
£B-M, (200,100,100,–)
Upper Thames St
☎ (020) 7236 7729
⌂ www.little-ship-club.co.uk
✉ cluboffice@little-ship-club.co.uk
Redeveloped in 1991, this comfortable and smart river-side yachtclubs' only real disadvantage is to share its entrance with a car park (though guests may be welcomed at the river entrance). It enjoys wonderful views. / 11pm; Aramark; Club Rm Bar (100,–,–,–); Dining Rm (120,100,–,–); Library (70,40,–,–); Claude Worth Rm (–,14,–,–); Chart Rm (–,8,–,–).

The Little Square W1
£B-M, (–,14,–,–)
3 Shepherd Mkt
☎ (020) 7355 2101
🖷 (020) 7355 2170
Not a bad choice if you're looking for a budget dining possibility in Mayfair – the upstairs room of a welcoming small restaurant, in Shepherd Market.

Lloyd's Club EC3
£M-E, (170,40,–,–)
3 Carlisle Ave
☎ (020) 7480 7135
A club with contemporary décor – its restaurant, available for hire in the evenings, makes a handy venue for a City cocktail party. / 11pm; evenings only; in-house caterers; no amplified music; Restaurant (170,40,–,–).

Lloyd's of London EC3
£M, (800,330,300,–)
1 Lime St
☎ (020) 7327 6321
🖷 (020) 732 5014
⌂ www.avenanceatlloyds.co.uk
✉ eventcatering@lloyds.co.uk
The large ground-floor Captain's Room of Lord Rogers's remarkable building is available at night for functions. For receptions, another possibility is the Old Library – a panelled hall from the market's old building transplanted into the frame of the new. / 11pm; evenings only Mon-Fri, conference rm available all day ; Avenance Caterers; Captain's Rm (800,330,300,–); Conference Rm (80,50,–,–); Old Library (120,–,–,–).

London Aquarium SE1
£M-E, (1500,250,250,250)
County Hall, Riverside Bldg, Westminster Bridge Rd
☎ (020) 7401 8747
🖷 (020) 7620 2982
⌂ www.londoncountyhall.com
✉ info@londoncountyhall.com
London's fishiest venue is its aquarium – one of the largest in Europe. Guests can enjoy their drinks and canapés while wandering among the examples of aquatic life. / 11pm; available from 6.30pm; list of caterers; smoking restricted; Atlantic (300,250,250,250); Shark Tank (150,60,–,60); Rainforest (75,30,–,–); Terrace (with marquee) (400,200,200,200).

CAPACITIES: (Standing, Seated, Dinner dance, Theatre-style)

The London Art House N1
£M-E, (300,200,200,250)
2-18 Britannia Row
☎ (020) 7359 5195
🖨 (020) 7704 0171
🖱 www.londonarthouse.com
✉ kathryn@
londonarthouse.com
A versatile Islington venue for events. Each of the dozen rooms is decorated in accordance with a different artistic style. / midnight; list of caterers; smoking restricted; Manor Garden Hall (300,200,200,250); Tadema Terrace (100,–,–,–); Rococo Rm (100,60,–,70); Baroque Hall (100,60,–,80); Art Studio (–,–,–,40); Orangery (50,40,–,48); Redon Rm (–,14,–,–); Albert Moore Lounge (–,10,–,20).

London Astoria WC2
£B-M, (2000,–,–,2000)
157 Charing Cross Rd
☎ (020) 7434 9592
🖨 (020) 7437 1781
🖱 www. meanfiddler.com
A central rock venue, used almost exclusively for concerts, but which has potential, especially with theming, for use by large, loud parties. / 4 am; available Tue-Wed only; hirer's choice of caterer.

The London Canal Museum N1
£M, (200,100,–,–)
12-13 New Wharf Rd
☎ (020) 7713 0836
🖨 (020) 7689 6679
🖱 www.canalmuseum.org.uk
✉ info@canalmuseum.org.uk
With the help of one of the companies which organises canal trips, guests can arrive at this waterside museum (a former warehouse, recently refurbished) by boat. / 1 am; available from 4.30pm Tue-Sun, all day Mon; hirer's choice of caterer; no smoking; 1st Floor (200,100,–,–); Private Rm (–,15,–,–).

London Capital Club EC4
£M-E, (150,60,–,–)
15 Abchurch Ln
☎ (020) 7203 6951
🖨 (020) 7717 0099
🖱 www.londoncapitalclub.co.uk
✉ privaterooms@
londoncapitalclub.co.uk
A listed building (1917), formerly known as the Gresham Club, with a number of rooms available for private events. / no 18ths or 21sts; 10pm; available Mon-Fri from 7am; in-house caterers; Oriental Rm (150,60,–,–); Boardroom (65,20,–,–); Gresham Rm (30,14,–,–); Marco Polo (10,10,–,–); Wren (10,8,–,–).

The London Dungeon SE1
£M-E, (400,120,100,–)
28-34 Tooley St
☎ (020) 7334 3965
🖱 www.london-dungeon.com
✉ thelondondungeon@
crownsociety.co.uk
Boasting "a perfectly horrible experience", this highly-successful London Bridge attraction is great fun (though the high-ceilinged vaults are at their best when full). Add fun to your evening with a Judgement Day boat-ride or, best of all, a Jack the Ripper experience. / 1 am; available summer from 7.30pm, winter from 6.30pm; London Catering Services.

London Eye SE1
£M, (500,–,–,–)
Riverside Building, County Hall, Westminster Bridge Rd
☎ 0870 220 2223
🖨 0870 990 8882
🖱 www.ba-londoneye.com
✉ corporate.event@
ba-londoneye.com
Would you like to fly in British Airways' beautiful, er, capsules? Take one for your own party, complete with champagne and canapés. Or you can even get married. / no smoking; per capsule (25,–,–,–).

The London Hippodrome WC2
£B-M, (1855,450,450,–)
Leicester Sq
☎ (020) 7437 4311
🖷 (020) 7434 4225
🖰 www.londonhippodrome.com
✉ hippodromeevents@
    hotmail.com
London's best-known central night-club is sufficiently well maintained that it would suit any crowd. It boasts an extremely impressive light system and is technically well equipped for major corporate events, in which it does big business. / 3 am; in-house & list of approved caterers; Auditorium (1855,450,450,–); Balcony Restaurant (300,175,175,–); Private Function Rm (100,50,–,–).

London Marriott W1
£M, (1000,600,570,–)
Grosvenor Sq
☎ (020) 7493 1232
🖰 www.marriott.com
✉ events.countyhall@
    marriotthotels.co.uk
Thanks to its unusual barrel-vaulted ceiling, this Mayfair hotel's ballroom offers one of the largest pillar-free function spaces in central London. / no smoking; Westminster Ballroom (1000,600,570,–); Hamilton Rm (65,40,–,–); John Adams Suite (40,25,–,–); Grosvenor Suite (30,15,–,–).

London Marriott County Hall Hotel SE1
£M-E, (100,60,–,–)
County Hall
☎ (020) 7928 5200
🖷 (020) 7902 8026
🖰 www.marriotthotels.com
✉ events.countyhall@
    marriotthotels.co.uk
This Thames-side hotel is situated in the grandest parts of the former GLC Building. Private functions are accommodated in a series of eight imposing Edwardian rooms, with much panelling and many marble fireplaces. / smoking restricted; George V (100,60,–,–); Library Lounge (100,40,–,–);

Queen Mary (50,20,–,–); Boardroom (–,12,–,–).

London Marriott Hotel Park Lane W1
£M-E, (90,40,30,24)
140 Park Lane
☎ (020) 7493 7000
🖷 (020) 7493 8333
🖰 www.marriotthotels.com/
    lonpl
✉ london.salesoffice@
    marriott.com
One of the few truly new hotels on Park Lane, recently opened, and with a range of facilities for smaller events. / 11pm; in-house caterers; smoking restricted; Hyde Park Suite (40,34,–,24); Oxford Suite (divisable by 3) (90,40,30,72); Meeting Foyer (40,–,–,–).

London Metropole W2
£M, (1900,1100,900,1700)
Edgware Rd
☎ (020) 7402 4141
🖰 www.hiltonlondonmet.com
✉ monica.castedo@
    londonmet.stakis.co.uk
Boasting over 1000 rooms after a recent expansion, this businesslike Bayswater hotel offers more event facilities than any other in town, including 37 meeting rooms of 44,000 square feet in total (including two suites each capable of hosting dinners for over 1000). / 1 am; list of caterers, in-house available; Monarch or King's Suite (1900,1100,900,1700); Palace Suite (1100,600,600,1100); Windsor (300,250,140,250); Park Suite (160,144,–,130).

London Palladium W1
£M, (150,50,–,–)
8 Argyll St
☎ (020) 7494 5200
🖷 (020) 7434 1217
🖰 www.rutheatres.com
✉ mike.townsend@
    rutheatres.com
Atop the main staircase of this famous theatre, the large, light Cinderella bar attracts a fair number of daytime receptions. You can even

CAPACITIES: (Standing, Seated, Dinner dance, Theatre-style)

get married here. / 1 am; Sodexho;
smoking restricted; Variety Bar (150,50,–,–);
Cinderella Bar (100,50,–,–); VIP
Rm (40,30,–,–); Argyll Suite (30,–,–,–).

The London Planetarium NW1
£M-E, (300,130,130,–)
Marylebone Rd
☎ (020) 7487 0224
⌂ www.madame-tussauds.com
✉ events@madame-tussauds.com
An auditorium which can genuinely claim to be unique, at least in the capital, and which comes complete with the latest multimedia facilities. There are quite extensive banqueting facilities attached. / 1 am; available from 7pm; list of caterers.

London Rowing Club SW15
£B, (250,100,100,–)
Embankment, Putney
☎ (020) 8788 1400
🖨 (020) 8788 8643
⌂ www.lrcvenue.org.uk
✉ manager@lrcvenue.org.uk
The first of the line of boathouses on the Putney 'hard', 'London' is a good and economical spot for receptions and business meetings. / midnight; hirer's choice of caterer.

London School of Economics WC2
£B-M, (450,100,–,–)
Houghton St
☎ (020) 7955 7087
🖨 (020) 7955 6272
⌂ www.lse.ac.uk
✉ event.services@lse.ac.uk
Central and reasonably priced accommodation for meetings, conferences, and events. / no weddings; 10pm; available from 6pm; in-house caterers; no amplified music; no dancing; smoking restricted; Senior Dining Rm (200,70,–,–); Senior Common Rm (60,20,–,–).

London Scottish SW1
£B-M, (300,180,150,224)
95 Horseferry Rd
☎ (020) 7630 0411
🖨 (020) 7414 3487
⌂ www.reserve-forces-london.org.uk
✉ secretary@reserve-forces-london.org.uk
A very unusual Pimlico TA hall, reconstructed from pieces transported from the regiment's old building. With the messes also available, it can suit many different types of event. / 1 am; not available Tue or some weekends; hirer's choice of caterer; Hall (300,180,150,224); Queen Elizabeth Rm (60,30,–,44); Officers' Mess (60,20,–,40).

London Stock Exchange EC2
£M-E, (250,90,90,80)
Old Broad St
☎ (020) 7797 2040
🖨 (020) 7920 4783
⌂ www.london stockexchange.com/media
✉ events@londonstockexchange.com
The Exchange offers a range of spaces for events of a corporate nature, especially where broadcast/media facilities are required. Capacity will be somewhat expanded at the new building, near St Paul's, scheduled for occupation in mid-2004. / companies only; midnight; weekdays only; in-house caterers; no smoking; Blue Rm (80,28,–,40); Theatre (–,–,–,80); Syndicate Rm (–,10,–,10); Video Conference Rm (–,–,–,12); Top Floor (250,90,90,75).

London Transport Museum WC2
£M, (400,120,100,70)
Covent Gdn
☎ (020) 7379 6344
⌂ www.ltmuseum.co.uk
✉ corphire@ltmuseum.co.uk
Originally a Victorian flower market, this airy, iron and glass museum facing Covent Garden is home to a collection of old buses, tubes, trams and trains. It attracts a lot of (mainly corporate) function business. / mid-

PRIVATE VENUES

night; available from 6.30pm; list of caterers; no smoking; Main Gallery (400,120,100,–); Lecture Theatre (–,120,100,70).

The London Underwriting Centre EC3
£M-E, (500,220,–,–)
3 Minster Court, Mincing Ln
☎ (020) 7617 5000
🖰 www.luc.co.uk
✉ events@luc.co.uk
An eight storey atrium, housing Europe's tallest free-standing escalator – it makes an interesting venue for larger City events. / 11pm; in-house caterers; smoking restricted; Atrium (500,220,–,–); Hospitality Suite (120,60,–,–).

The London Welsh Centre WC1
£B, (250,150,150,200)
157-163 Grays Inn Rd
☎ (020) 7837 3722
🖷 (020) 7837 6268
The light, gym-type Bloomsbury hall is largely used for rehearsals, but also for parties. The bar upstairs is suitable for informal get-togethers. / midnight; not available Sun; in-house caterers; no music after 11pm; dancing in hall only; Main Hall (250,150,150,200); Bar (100,–,–,–).

London Wetland Centre SW13
£M, (150,100,100,130)
Queen Elizabeth's Walk
☎ (020) 8409 4407
🖷 (020) 8409 4401
🖰 www.wwt.org.uk/london/functions
✉ holly.moore@wwt.org.uk
Over a hundred acres of lakes, pools and lagoons – and all within the range of a Zone 2 Travelcard! Quite extensive function facilities, too. / midnight; in-house caterers; no smoking; Meeting Rm (–,–,–,22); Waters Edge (130,100,100,130); Observatory (150,30,–,–); Audio Visual Centre (–,–,–,80); Bird Hide (–,30,–,–).

London Zoo NW1
£M-E, (380,240,240,–)
Regent's Park
☎ (020) 7449 6374
🖷 (020) 7722 0388
🖰 www.londonzoo.co.uk
✉ londonzoo@compass-group.co.uk
Few are immune to the delight of partying among the animals, so this really is a venue for children of all ages. There are two banqueting suites (licensed for weddings) but the real attraction is to be out barbecuing among the tigers or drinking among the reptiles – 'animal encounters' can be arranged. / midnight; animal houses available eves only; Leith's; no amplified music; Prince Albert Suite (380,240,240,–); Aquarium (380,–,–,–); Bugs (300,–,–,–); Lion Terrace (250,–,–,–); Reptile Hse (250,–,–,–); Raffles Suite (150,100,–,–); Bear Mountain (150,–,–,–).

Lonsdale W11
£M, (170,50,–,–)
48 Lonsdale Road
☎ (020) 7727 4080
🖷 (020) 7727 6030
An atmospheric Notting Hill bar whose slick retro décor – complete with oddly studded walls – is slightly reminiscent of a setting for Dr Who. There's an upstairs club (where you can dance), and – at non-peak times – you can also hire the downstairs. / midnight, 1 am upstairs; dancing only upstairs; Genevieve (upstairs) (70,20,–,–); Downstairs (120,–,–,–).

Lord's NW8
£M, (1000,700,350,500)
St John's Wood Rd
☎ (020) 7286 2909
🖰 www.conference-online.co.uk
✉ susanne.schroeder@sodexho-uk.com
The home of cricket boasts a modern, purpose-built banqueting centre. / 1 am; Sodexho Prestige; dancing in banqueting suite only; smoking restricted; Banqueting Suite (500,400,350,300); Nursery Pavilion (1000,700,–,500); Media Centre (100,50,–,–); Long Rm (–,200,–,–).

CAPACITIES: (Standing, Seated, Dinner dance, Theatre-style)

104

Loungelover E1
£M, (200,60,60,–)
1 Whitby St
☎ (020) 7012 1234
🖷 (020) 7012 1236
🖑 www.loungelover.co.uk
📧 craig@loungelover.co.uk
*Eccentric and eclectic, and filled with
antiques and original pieces, this new
bar has made quite a name for its
funky 'maximalist' style, and would
make a cool setting for a party.* / 2
am; in-house caterers; Rustic
Area (38,38,–,–); Baroque Rm (20,–,–,–);
Red Area (50,20,20,–).

LSO St Luke's EC1
£M-E, (350,64,–,360)
Old St
☎ (020) 7490 3939
🖷 (020) 7566 2881
🖑 www.lso.co.uk/lsostlukes
📧 swales@lso.co.uk
*In an impressive Grade 1 c18
church, recently refurbished, the
London Symphony Orchestra's
rehearsal space offers flexible facilities for events.* / 1 am; list of caterers;
no smoking; Jerwood Hall (350,–,–,360);
Clore Rms (–,–,–,20); Crypt
Café (150,64,–,–).

PRIVATE VENUES

Lyceum Theatre WC2
£M, (150,–,–,2100)
21 Wellington St
☎ (020) 7420 8100
🖰 www.cclive.co.uk
Behind its grand façade, this Covent Garden theatre (home for the foreseeable future to 'The Lion King') was recently rebuilt. During the day, it offers a large, central auditorium, available for hire. / available subject to constraints of current production; no dancing; no smoking; Theatre (–,–,–,2100); Function Rm (150,–,–,–).

Madame Tussaud's NW1
£M-E, (600,400,350,–)
Marylebone Rd
☎ (020) 7487 0224
🖰 www.madame-tussauds.com
📧 events@madame-tussauds.com
London's longest-running tourist attraction is also one of the top party venues. Recent refurbishments have created two new areas – Blush and World Stage – with a more contemporary style than the (rather charming) period feel of the rest of the place. See advertisement on page 105. / 1 am; available from 7pm; list of caterers; World Stage (600,400,350,–); Blush (250,100,–,–).

The Magic Circle NW1
£M, (130,80,–,162)
12 Stephenson Way
☎ (020) 7387 2222
🖶 (020) 7387 5114
🖰 www.themagiccircle.co.uk
📧 sheila@magic-circle.fsnet.co.uk
The home of magic has recently become available for corporate entertaining, for which it offers quite an atmospheric setting, adorned with magical artefacts. The auditorium is equipped to a high level. / 10.30pm; in-house caterers; no amplified music; no dancing; no smoking; Auditorium (–,–,–,162); Devant Rm (130,80,–,100); Club Bar (60,50,–,50).

Mall Galleries SW1
£B-M, (500,250,–,–)
The Mall
☎ (020) 7930 6844
🖶 (020) 7839 7830
🖰 www.mallgalleries.org.uk
📧 info@mallgalleries.com
A short step from Admiralty Arch, the Main Gallery at the Federation of British Artists offers an impressive and central function space. The East Gallery is smaller and rather more cosily proportioned. / 11pm; available from 5pm; hirer's choice of caterer; no amplified music; no dancing; Main Gallery (500,250,–,–); East Gallery (100,75,–,–); North Gallery (80,50,–,–).

Mandarin Oriental Hyde Park SW1
£M-E, (400,230,200,–)
66 Knightsbridge
☎ (020) 7235 2000
🖶 (020) 7235 2001
🖰 www.mandarinoriental.com
The interior of this externally overbearing redbrick Knightsbridge edifice boasts much charming Edwardian detail, and offers one of the most impressive suites of interconnecting entertaining rooms in London. Decorated in cream, blue and gold, they have splendid views of the park and are popular for grander weddings and receptions. / 2 am; Ballroom (400,230,200,–); Carlyle Suite (250,150,70,–); Roseberry Rms (100,40,–,–); Balfour Rm (70,30,–,–); Asquith Rm (70,30,–,–).

Mao Tai SW6
£M, (–,130,–,–)
58 New King's Rd
☎ (020) 7731 2520
🖶 (020) 7471 8992
🖰 www.maotai.co.uk
This long-established Parson's Green spot has a reputation as a good all-rounder (with a much more comfortable and stylish atmosphere than many Chinese restaurants). Its private room is an ideal size for birthday parties and the like. For quite a fee, you can also take the whole of

CAPACITIES: (Standing, Seated, Dinner dance, Theatre-style)

the ground floor. / 1.30 am; no music; no dancing; Private Rm (–,28,–,–).

Marble Hill House, Surrey
£M-E, (40,25,–,–)
Richmond Rd, Twickenham
☎ (020) 8892 5115
🖷 (020) 8607 9976
🖰 www.english-heritage.org.uk
Fine early c18 house, whose grounds are bordered by the Thames, and which afford a very elegant site for a marquee. The Great Room (based on the Cube Room at Wilton House) is decorated in white and gilt and adorned with period paintings and furniture. / midnight; hirer's choice of caterer; no dancing; no smoking; no red wine; Tetra Hall (40,25,–,–).

Marriott Maida Vale NW6
£M-E, (250,180,110,200)
Plaza Parade
☎ (020) 7543 6000
🖰 www.marriott.com/lonwh
✉ events.maidavale@marriotthotels.co.uk
A new Maida Vale/Kilburn border hotel (150 bedrooms), which brings modern facilities to a part of town without too many quality meeting places. / midnight; Regent Suite (250,180,110,200); Hamilton Suite (–,18,–,–); Carlton Suite (40,26,–,40).

The Mary Sumner House SW1
£B-M, (150,40,–,160)
24 Tufton St
☎ (020) 7222 5533
🖷 (020) 7799 2735
🖰 www.themothersunion.org
✉ conference@themothersunion.org
The facilities of this '20s building in Westminster, home of the Mothers' Union, are mainly used for conferences. For social events, however, they do offer bring-your-own-caterer space, very centrally. / 11pm; hirer's choice of caterer; no smoking; Conference

Hall (150,100,–,160); Mary Sumner Rm (40,25,–,40); Syndicate Rm (14,12,–,–).

The Mayfair Club W1
£M, (600,250,250,–)
15 Berkeley St
☎ (020) 7629 0010
🖷 (020) 7499 2566
🖰 www.mayfairclub.net
✉ kellymunnelly@mayfairclub.net
In the heart of Mayfair, a nightclub which offers flexible facilities for private events. / 2 am; hirer's choice of caterer (in-house available); Satellite Bar & Cabaret (400,250,–,–); Living Rm Bar (250,100,100,–); VIP Rm (150,35,–,–).

Mayfair Conference Centre W2
£M, (125,75,–,130)
17 Connaught Place
☎ (020) 7706 7700
🖷 (020) 7706 7711
🖰 www.mayfairconference.com
✉ enquiries@mayfairconference.com
A smart and businesslike conference centre, near Marble Arch. / 5.30pm; in-house caterers; no music; no dancing; no smoking; Conservatory (125,75,–,130).

The Mayfair Inter-Continental W1
£M-E, (400,320,250,–)
Stratton St
☎ (020) 7629 7777
🖷 (020) 7629 1459
🖰 www.interconti.com
✉ mayfair@interconti.com
A large and quite grand '20s Mayfair hotel whose distinctive function room is the large rose-hued Crystal Room – named in honour of its three huge, modern chandeliers. / 1 am; Crystal Rm (400,320,250,–); Danziger Suite (200,120,80,–); Berkeley Suite (50,30,–,–); Mayfair Theatre (–,292,–,–).

The Mean Fiddler WC2
£B, (1000,–,–,–)
165 Charing Cross Rd
☎ (020) 7434 9592
🖶 (020) 7437 1781
🖰 www.meanfiddler.com
Large, subterranean central dive where a large dance-floor is surrounded by a gallery. Smaller parties, of up to 500, could take over a balcony. / 6 am; in-house or hirer's choice by negotiation.

The Medieval Banquet E1
£M, (500,500,500,–)
Ivory House, St Katharine's Dock
☎ (020) 7480 5353
🖶 (020) 7709 0499
🖰 www.medievalbanquet.com
✉ info@medievalbanquet.com
Vaulted archways give character to this City-fringe tourist attraction. Themed entertainment, dancing and (on regular nights) unlimited wine and beer are part of the attraction. You can take over an alcove, or hire the whole place. / Alcove (–,50,–,–).

Mega Bowl SW2
£M, (650,–,–,–)
142 Streatham Hl
☎ (020) 8678 6007
🖶 (020) 8674 1706
🖰 www.megabowl.co.uk
✉ salestreatham@ megabowl.co.uk
If a mega bowling party (up to 216 people at any one time) is your idea of a fun, this is the place. You can hire a single lane, or one or both floors. Though there is no drinking on the 36 lanes, there are fair-sized bar areas on each floor around which to stage festivities. As an alternative you might consider the Zapp Zone – a hi-tech laser game in semi-darkness with futuristic lighting, for up to 25 people. / 1 am; in-house caterers; 1st floor (500,–,–,–); Balcony (30,–,–,–).

Mela WC2
£B-M, (120,74,–,–)
152-156 Shaftesbury Av
☎ (020) 7836 8635
🖰 www.melarestaurant.co.uk
A bright modern Indian restaurant that's already made something of a name for its cooking. Other attractions include reasonable prices and a location right in the heart of town, just north of Cambridge Circus. / Ground Floor (120,74,–,–); Private Rm (downstairs) (70,34,–,–).

Mercers' Hall EC2
Ironmonger Ln
☎ (020) 7726 4991
🖶 (020) 7600 1158
🖰 www.mercers.co.uk
✉ mail@mercers.co.uk
What is probably the richest of the livery companies tells us that its hall is never available to outsiders (unless you are a member of another livery company, however, in which case your application may be graciously considered). / very restricted availability.

Merchant Taylors' Hall EC2
£M-E, (600,280,300,400)
30 Threadneedle St
☎ (020) 7450 4445
🖶 (020) 7450 4455
🖰 www.merchant-taylors-catering.co.uk
✉ rdent@merchant-taylors-catering.co.uk
In the heart of the City, this very grand, reconstructed (post-War) medieval hall is one of the most imposing of the livery halls to be made available to outsiders with reasonable frequency. It comes complete with cloisters and paved garden. / midnight; not available Sun; hirer's choice of caterer (in-house available); smoking restricted; Great Hall (500,290,250,400); Parlour (200,80,–,120); Cloisters (200,–,–,–); Library (50,30,–,20); Drawing Rm (200,80,–,100); Kings Gallery (50,30,–,50).

CAPACITIES: (Standing, Seated, Dinner dance, Theatre-style)

Le Mercury N1

£B, (–,50,–,–)
140 Upper St
☎ (020) 7354 4088
🖩 (020) 7359 7186
Atmospheric, bargain-basement Islington bistro, with a private room upstairs. / 1 am; Private Rm (–,50,–,–).

Le Meridien W1

£M-E, (400,250,210,–)
21 Piccadilly
☎ (020) 7734 8000
🖰 www.lemeridien-piccadilly.com
📧 nicolas.billerot@lemeridien.com
The elegant and understated Georgian and Adam rooms are the function accommodation highlights of this smart, central hotel, which has quite a range of facilities for business and social events. / 1 am;
Georgian (245,240,210,–);
Edwardian (200,180,150,–);
Regency (120,100,70,–); Adam (90,70,–,–);
Chelsea (30,25,–,–); Mayfair (30,20,–,–).

Le Meridien Russell Hotel WC1

£M, (650,350,300,–)
Russell Sq
☎ (020) 7837 6470
🖩 (020) 7897 2857
🖰 www.lemeridien.com
A splendid (going on overbearing) Victorian hotel in Bloomsbury, where most of the rooms – many of which are marbled – retain an impressive period charm. The adjoining Warncliffe and Woburn suites are used for dinner-dances. The Library is suitably clubby. / midnight;
smoking restricted; Warncliffe
Suite (650,350,300,–); Bedford
Suite (80,36,–,–); Ormond Suite (60,48,–,–);
Library (60,50,–,–).

Le Meridien Selsdon Park, Surrey

£M-E, (200,180,150,–)
Addington Rd, Sanderstead,
South Croydon
☎ (020) 8657 8811
🖩 (020) 8657 3401
🖰 www.lemeridien.com
📧 sales.selsdonpark@lemeridien.com
Set in 200 acres, this ivy-clad, neo-Jacobean mansion near Croydon has a number of function rooms, with dance floors. / midnight; Terrace
Suite (200,180,150,–); Kent Rm (90,50,–,–);
Solarium (50,–,–,–); Surrey Rm (100,60,–,–);
Sir Edward Heath Rm (150,80,80,–).

Mermaid Theatre EC4

£B-M, (400,150,150,–)
Puddle Dock, Blackfriars
☎ (020) 7236 1919
🖰 www.the-mermaid.co.uk
📧 info@the-mermaid.co.uk
The function room of this modern City-fringe theatre offer unusually good river views, especially from the second-floor Blackfriars Room. You might hold a reception in the River Room, move to dine in the Blackfriars Room, and return to the River Room for a disco. / 2 am; hirer's choice of caterer (in-house available); no music after 11pm; no dancing after 11pm; Blackfriars Rm (400,150,150,–); River Rm (120,60,–,–); Studio (–,–,150,–).

The Metropolitan W1

£M-E, (150,45,–,–)
Old Park Ln
☎ (020) 7447 1040
🖩 (020) 7447 1042
🖰 www.metropolitan.co.uk
📧 richardm@metropolitan.co.uk
A Minimalist Mayfair hotel, which has a single, top-lit function room. The well-known Met Bar doesn't market itself as a venue, but it does do events during Fashion Week, and will consider others that measure up to its fashionista aspirations. / no dancing; Dining-Meeting Rm (80,40,–,–); Met Bar (150,–,–,–).

Middle Temple Hall EC4
£M-E, (725,392,225,400)
Temple
☎ (020) 7427 4820
🖷 (020) 7427 4821
🖱 www.middletemple.org.uk
✉ banqueting@
   middletemple.org.uk
The fine Tudor hall of this Inn of Court is an impressive, historic setting for dinners and receptions of all types. More intimate are the Bench Apartments, available separately. The garden is a charming venue much used for summer parties. / mid-night; closed Aug; hirer's choice of caterer (in-house available); Hall (500,300,225,400); Parliament Chamber (125,70,–,70); Queen's Rm (75,22,–,50); Smoking Rm (100,–,–,–).

The Milestone Hotel & Apartments W8
£M-E, (60,34,–,–)
1 Kensington Court
☎ (020) 7917 1000
🖷 (020) 7917 1133
🖱 www.redcarnationhotels.com
✉ jlecordeur@rchmail.com
This small hotel occupies a lavishly converted Victorian house near Kensington Gardens. Most rooms are in a panelled, traditional style, and there is quite a range of accommodation for smaller parties. For something a little different, you might consider a themed evening in the self-explanatory Safari Suite. / Windsor Suite (60,24,–,–); Cheniston Restaurant (50,28,–,–); Safari Suite (20,12,–,–); Conservatory (15,10,–,–); Oratory (–,8,–,–); Map Rm (–,8,–,–).

Millennium Gloucester Hotel SW7
£M-E, (640,432,348,–)
Harrington Gdns
☎ (020) 7373 6030
🖱 www.millenniumhotels.com
✉ mcc.events@mill-cop.com
A South Kensington hotel offering flexible banqueting facilities. These have been much extended with the Conservatory, an impressive open space with great scope for theming, and the Millennium Conference Centre. The latter offers two floors of column-free space, capable of a number of different configurations. / in-house caterers; no amplified music in conservatory; Century Suite (640,432,348,–); Decade Suite (500,300,250,–); Cotswold Suite (500,310,250,–); Conservatory (300,200,150,–); Ashburn Suite (200,100,70,–); Boardroom (–,12,–,–).

Millennium London Mayfair W1
£M-E, (700,460,360,450)
Grosvenor Sq
☎ (020) 7629 9400
🖷 (020) 7408 0699
🖱 www.millenniumhotels.com
✉ eventsales.mayfair@
   mill-cop.com

A discreetly-located hotel, which boasts quite a range of accommodation for functions. The ballroom benefits from a private entrance. / 2 am; Ballroom (700,460,360,450); Manhattan (100,60,40,75); Turner Fine Dining Rm (120,80,50,90); Waterloo Rm (80,60,40,72); Grosvenor Suite (40,20,–,–).

Mimmo d'Ischia SW1
£M-E, (–,30,–,–)
61 Elizabeth St
☎ (020) 7730 5406
🖷 (020) 7730 9439
A sociable, upmarket Belgravia Italian restaurant of long standing, run by the jovial Mimmo as a quasi-club. The private rooms are upstairs. / Private Rm (–,30,–,–); Private Rm (–,12,–,–).

CAPACITIES: (Standing, Seated, Dinner dance, Theatre-style)

The Townhouse SW3
£M, (60,–,–,–)
31 Beauchamp Pl
☎ (020) 7589 5080
🖰 www.lab-townhouse.com
A trendy Knightsbridge cocktail bar. For private parties you can take over the (more characterful and larger) first floor, or the basement. / First Floor (60,–,–,–); Basement (30,–,–,–).

The Ministry of Sound SE1
£B, (1500,900,160,220)
103 Gaunt St
☎ (020) 7740 8728
🖨 (020) 7403 5348
🖰 www.ministryofsound.com/ privatehire
✉ met@ministryofsound.com
An all-black room, the Box, at this converted warehouse near Elephant and Castle houses Europe's loudest sound system and it can be hired for functions. It is used in conjunction with the Main Bar. For smaller events you can take one of the smaller bars. For a major extravaganza you might take over the whole club, which is licensed for alcohol until 2am. / 6 am; not available Fri, Sat; list of caterers; Main Bar (500,160,160,–); Balcony Bar (200,150,–,–); VIP Bar (170,–,–,60); Box (700,200,–,220); Baby Box (80,30,–,–).

Mint Leaf SW1
£M-E, (500,200,–,–)
1 Suffolk Pl
☎ (020) 7930 9020
🖨 (020) 7930 6205
🖰 www.mintleafrestaurant.com
If Hakkasan is not available, this large new basement Indian bar/restaurant, just off the Haymarket – with its dark finishes, subdued lighting and screens – gives a similarly sleek impression. Sadly, it doesn't seem to be very much cheaper! / Private Rm (–,60,–,–).

Mirabelle W1
£M-E, (250,130,–,–)
56 Curzon St
☎ (020) 7734 7333
🖨 (020) 7734 0033
🖰 www.whitestarline.org.uk
✉ sales@whitestarline.org.uk
Classic Mayfair restaurant, now part of the Marco Pierre White empire, and boasting two private rooms. The Pine Room is the more elegantly proportioned of the two, the Chinese room the more interestingly furnished. Alternatively, you could take the whole place. / Chinese (–,48,–,–); Pine Rm (–,33,–,–).

Mitsukoshi SW1
£M-E, (–,20,–,–)
14-20 Regent St
☎ (020) 7930 0317
🖨 (020) 7839 1167
A little bright and efficient it may appear, but by Japanese standards this smart basement (below the department store) is welcoming and stylish. There are two private rooms, one Japanese-style (tatami) and one western. / Western Rm (–,20,–,–); Tatami Rm (–,12,–,–).

Momo W1
£M-E, (200,100,100,–)
25 Heddon Street
☎ (020) 7434 4040
🖨 (020) 7287 0404
🖰 www.momoresto.com
This lavish Moroccan is a key West End party place, especially for the fashion world. Exclusive hire possibilities are to hire the bar only, or to take the whole place (using the bar for dancing). / Kemia Bar (80,–,–,–).

Mon Plaisir WC2
£M, (–,28,–,–)
21 Monmouth St
☎ (020) 7836 7243
🖨 (020) 7240 4774
🖰 www.mon-plaisir.co.uk
A classic Theatreland restaurant, half a century old, with great character and a very convenient location. / not available Sat L or Sun; Private Rm (–,28,–,–).

PRIVATE VENUES

Monkey Island Hotel, Berks
£M-E, (150,120,120,150)
Old Mill Lane, Bray
☎ 01628 623400
🖷 01628 784732
🖰 www.monkeyisland.co.uk
✉ monkeyisland@
  btconnect.com
An idyllic four-acre islet, accessible only by footbridge or boat. The hotel – in a building early c18 in origin – has some charming rooms and a lovely garden, making this quite a nice place for a civil wedding. / 1 am; River Rm (150,120,120,150); Boardroom (16,16,–,–); Spencer Rm (36,18,–,40); Garden Rm (45,30,–,44); Wedgewood (10,10,–,–); Temple (6,8,–,–).

The Montcalm Hotel W1
£M, (120,60,60,80)
Gt Cumberland Place
☎ (020) 7402 4288
🖷 (020) 7724 9180
🖰 www.montcalm.co.uk
✉ sales@montcalm.co.uk
A comfortable hotel in converted Georgian townhouses, not far from Marble Arch, offering a range of luxury accommodation in a traditional style. / Maquis De Montcalm (120,60,60,80); Montagu Suite (–,16,–,30); Portman Suite (–,16,–,30).

Monte's SW1
£M-E, (100,80,80,–)
164 Sloane St
☎ (020) 7235 0555
🖰 www.montes.co.uk
✉ pam@montes.co.uk
A modern Belgravia club-cum-restaurant, nicely located and styled for a small but swanky private event. / members club; 2 am; not available Sun; in-house caterers; Restaurant (100,80,–,–); Nightclub (50,–,–,–); Private Dining Rm (–,16,–,–).

Mosimann's Academy SW11
£M-E, (80,40,–,50)
5 William Blake Hs, Bridge Ln, The Lanterns
☎ (020) 7326 8344
🖷 (020) 7326 8340
🖰 www.mosimann.com
✉ paul.scannell@mosimann.com
Star chef Anton Mosimann's Battersea HQ, which occupies a converted Victorian school building. It offers (well-catered) event possibilities, as well as cookery courses. / 10pm; in-house caterers; no music; no dancing; smoking restricted; Demonstration Kitchen (–,–,–,50); Library (40,20,–,–); Thinking Rm (80,40,–,–).

Mosimann's Belfry SW1
£M-E, (180,115,105,–)
11b West Halkin St
☎ (020) 7326 8344
🖰 www.mosimann.com
✉ sales.enquiries@
  mosimann.com
Celebrity chef Anton Mosimann's converted Belgravia chapel, now a private dining club, has a number of private rooms decorated in the colours of the respective corporate sponsor. Non-members may hire the main restaurant (in its entirety) as well as the private rooms. / 1 am; no dancing in private dining rms; Dining Rm (–,115,85,–); Coutts Rm (180,50,–,–); Parmigiani Fleurier Rm (70,30,–,–); Veuve Cliquot Rm (25,10,–,–); Gucci Rm (–,14,–,–); Davidoff Rm (–,4,–,–); Mont Blanc Rm (–,2,–,–).

Motcomb's Townhouse SW1
£M-E, (130,30,–,–)
23 Motcomb St
☎ (020) 7235 3092
🖷 (020) 7245 6351
🖰 www.motcombs.co.uk
✉ motcombs@dial.pipex.com
The Belgravia restaurant of the same name has its own townhouse for private dining. There is an attractive pine-panelled dining room especially suited to parties of a dozen or more around a single table, and a sepa-

CAPACITIES: (Standing, Seated, Dinner dance, Theatre-style)

rate reception room. / midnight; no
music; no dancing; Belgravia Rm (50,30,–,–);
Mclue Suite (40,20,–,–); Lounge (40,–,–,–).

The Mountbatten WC2
£M, (80,80,50,–)
Seven Dials, 20 Monmouth St
☎ (020) 7836 4300
🖰 www.raddissonedwardian.com
✉ londonmeetings@
   radisson.com
Off the foyer, the elegant Broadlands
Suite (limited availability) is this
Theatreland hotel's best point. / Earl
Suite (80,60,50,–); Viceroy (40,20,–,–).

Mr Kong WC2
£B-M, (–,40,–,–)
21 Lisle St
☎ (020) 7437 7341
🖨 (020) 7437 7923
This Chinatown basement looks
nothing special, but it's pleasant
enough, and the good, affordable
food and easy-going service make it
one of London's best places for a
Chinese feast. / Private
Basement (–,40,–,–).

Mudchute Park & Farm E14
£B, (200,40,–,–)
Pier St, Isle of Dogs
☎ (020) 7515 5901
🖨 (020) 7538 9530
✉ info@mudchute.org
Set in 32 acres of open space (with
28 resident foxes), this Docklands
city farm has a café seating up to
60, which is especially suitable for
children's parties. Other events may
be accommodated (though alcohol
may only be served with food).A popular venue for summer barbeques
and softball tournaments, apparently.
/ 11pm; in-house or hirer's choice by negotiation; no smoking; Café (60,30,–,–).

Museum of Garden History SE1
£M, (400,250,150,50)
Lambeth Palace Rd
☎ (020) 7401 8865
🖨 (020) 7401 8869
🖰 www.museumofgardenhistory.org
✉ info@museumofgardenhistory.org
This deconsecrated church building
has quite a handy location, by
Lambeth Palace. It is now available
for function hire, welcoming wedding
receptions, corporate events and
press launches. / midnight; list of caterers;
no smoking; Lecture Rm (–,–,–,50);
Garden (100,–,–,–).

Museum of London EC2
£M-E, (800,100,100,270)
London Wall
☎ (020) 7814 5613
🖨 (020) 7600 1058
🖰 www.museumoflondon.org.uk
✉ specialevents@
   museumoflondon.org.uk
This colourful museum of the capital's history is quite well suited to
function use. You might have your
reception in the Lord Mayor's Coach
Gallery and a disco in the museum's
reception area that overlooks it. The
large, well laid-out central garden is
available in summer. / 11pm; available
from 6.30pm; list of caterers; no smoking;
Lord Mayor's Gallery (250,–,100,–); Medieval
Gallery (150,40,–,–); World City Gallery
(350,–,–,–); Eighteenth Century
Gallery (100,60,–,–); Lecture
Theatre (–,–,–,270); London Befort
Gallery (350,–,–,–).

The Music Room W1
£B-M, (350,160,–,180)
26 South Molton Ln
☎ (020) 7629 8199
🖰 www.themusicroom.co.uk
✉ info@themusicroom.co.uk
This unusual venue – under new
ownership, renovated and technically
upgraded – is located in a Victorian
building, above a Mayfair antiques
market. It now offers flexible and
central space suited to most types of
events. / hirer's choice of caterer; Exhibition
Hall (350,160,–,160); Gallery (60,50,–,20).

PRIVATE VENUES

Museum in Docklands E14
£M, (800,160,160,165)
No. 1 Warehouse, West India
Quay, Hertsmere Rd
☎ (020) 7001 9816
🖳 (020) 7001 9801
🖰 www.museumindocklands.org.uk
📧 specialevents@
museumindocklands.org.uk
*A listed warehouse building within
sight (and a short stroll) of Canary
Wharf. It offers characterful space
on quite a scale, especially for drinks
parties. / 11pm; list of caterers; no smoking; Wilberforce Theatre (–,–,–,165); Thames
Highway Gallery (150,50,–,–); 3rd Floor
Galleries (350,–,–,–); 2nd Floor
Galleries (500,–,–,–); Chris Ellmers
Gallery (200,160,160,–).*

MVH SW13
£M-E, (100,40,40,–)
5 White Hart Ln
☎ (020) 8392 1111
🖳 (020) 8878 1919
*An amazingly-themed Heaven &
Hell-style bar/restaurant, somewhat
incongruously located in Barnes. Its
baroque style of cooking is something
else again and for a small, lavish,
OTT party the place – though not
cheap – has a lot to recommend it.
You can take over just the bar (Hell),
or the restaurant (Heaven) too. / 1
am; Hell (30,15,–,–).*

Namco SE1
£M, (1200,–,–,–)
County Hall,
Westminster Bridge Rd
☎ (020) 7967 1067
🖳 (020) 79671060
🖰 www.namcostation.co.uk
📧 countyhall@namco.co.uk
*"Fun and games on a massive scale"
is the promise at this "pleasure-
drome of interactive entertainment".
Ten pin bowling, an American pool
hall and over 200 video games are
among the attractions, not to mention "Europe's fastest bumper cars".
/ midnight; list of caterers; smoking restricted;
no alcohol upstairs; Substation (lower
level) (500,–,–,–); Private Party
Area (150,–,–,–).*

National Army Museum SW3
£M, (300,140,–,250)
Royal Hospital Rd, Chelsea
☎ (020) 7730 0717 extn 2210
🖳 (020) 7823 6573
🖰 www.national-army-
museum.ac.uk
📧 events@national-army-
museum.ac.uk
*If you are looking for a venue with
martial associations in a smart area
(next to Chelsea's Royal Hospital),
this building with some fine military
treasures and works of art. They can
help you warm to the theme – war
games are a popular diversion, and
you can book a Napoleonic-times
soldier as your Master of
Ceremonies. / midnight; list of caterers; no
smoking; Art Gallery (300,140,–,250);
Templer Galleries (70,40,–,50); Council
Chamber (100,38,–,78); Modern Army
Gallery (300,–,–,–); Lecture
Theatre (150,50,–,120);
Atrium (300,140,–,–).*

National Liberal Club SW1
£M-E, (300,150,140,–)
Whitehall Pl
☎ (020) 7930 9871
🖳 (020) 7839 4768
🖰 www.nlc.org.uk
📧 banqueting@nlc.org.uk
*Especially at weekends (when access
to the larger rooms is more easily
obtained) this august Victorian building, just off Whitehall, makes an
interesting venue for events as dis-
parate as a wedding or a ball. It has
the special advantage of a large outside terrace, overlooking the river.
/ in-house caterers; David Lloyd
George (250,130,90,–); Lady
Violet (60,30,30,–); Smoking Rm (300,–,–,–);
Dining Rm (300,120,–,–);
Terrace (250,–,–,–).*

CAPACITIES: (Standing, Seated, Dinner dance, Theatre-style)

National Maritime Museum SE10

£M-E, (1000,500,500,120)

Romney Rd, Greenwich

☎ (020) 8312 6693

🖷 (020) 8312 6572

🖱 www.nmm.ac.uk

✉ events@nmm.ac.uk

A refurbishment gave this impressive Greenwich museum a large event space, the Neptune Court, and it also has a number of other striking function spaces. See also Queen's House. / 11pm; list of caterers; no smoking; no red wine for standing receptions in Queen's House; Neptune Court (1000,500,–,–); Orangery (150,50,–,–); Southern Parlours (150,50,–,–); Royal Observatory (150,60,–,–); Lecture Theatre (–,–,–,120).

National Portrait Gallery WC2

£E, (350,100,200,200)

2 St Martin's Pl

☎ (020) 7312 2453

🖷 (020) 7306 0058

🖱 www.npg.org.uk

✉ eaggmanning@npg.org.uk

Compared to many of London's major galleries, the NPG has a relatively intimate scale suited to entertaining, and a choice of interesting medium-sized spaces. The top-floor Portrait Restaurant has a particularly interesting panoramic view of the

West End. / *no weddings; midnight; available from 6.30pm; list of caterers; no dancing; smoking restricted; red wine in restaurant only; Contemporary Galleries (350,80,200,–); Victorian Galleries (150,100,–,–); Tudor Gallery (100,–,–,–); Portrait Restaurant (150,100,–,–); (–,–,–,–).*

ambassadors.com
Completed in 1913, the original home of 'The Mousetrap' can be hired for presentations and conferences. / *4pm; daytime only; in-house caterers; no smoking.*

Natural History Museum SW7
£M-E, (1200,600,600,120)
Cromwell Rd
☎ (020) 7942 5434
🖷 (020) 7942 5070
🖱 www.nhm.ac.uk/functions
🖃 functions@nhm.ac.uk
The monumental Victorian Main Hall – complete with prehistoric creatures – particularly lends itself to dramatic, big-budget parties. Some of the individual galleries, particularly the striking Earth Galleries (with their own entrance) also offer interesting possibilities. See advertisement on page 115. / *1 am; list of caterers; Central Hall (1200,600,600,–); Earth Galleries (500,180,180,–); North Hall (250,180,150,–); Spencer Gallery (–,120,–,120); Darwin Centre (150,100,–,120).*

Neal's Lodge SW18
£M, (80,50,–,–)
On The Common, Wandsworth
☎ (020) 8874 9386
🖃 info@
  commongroundcafe.org.uk
Natural light, lots of plants, and French windows opening on to a terrace impart a countrified feeling to this former farmhouse, right on Wandsworth Common. Seating is in the Conservatory, with the Maple Room available for dancing. / *11pm; evenings only; in-house caterers.*

New Ambassadors Theatre WC2
£M, (30,–,–,403)
West St
☎ (020) 7395 5401
🖷 (020) 7395 5411
🖱 www.ambassador
  theatregroup.com
🖃 newambassadorstheatre@

The New Cavendish Club W1
£M, (100,80,–,80)
44 Great Cumberland Pl
☎ (020) 7723 0391
🖷 (020) 7262 8411
🖃 jeanpaulncc@aol.com
Near Marble Arch, a club building whose rooms may be used for company meetings and a range of social events. For summer drinks parties, you can use the roof garden. / *midnight; in-house caterers; no dancing; smoking restricted; Jubilee Rm (100,80,–,80); Ante-rm (60,40,–,40); Library (20,12,–,20); Boardroom (–,11,–,–).*

New Connaught Rms WC2
£B-M, (1000,530,380,700)
Gt Queen St
☎ (020) 7405 7811
🖱 www.newconnaughtrooms.co.uk
🖃 sales@
  newconnaughtrooms.co.uk
One of London's oldest sets of banqueting suites, two centuries old, is now mainly used by business and the Masons – this was once an annexe of the neighbouring Temple. The Grand Hall, with three huge chandeliers, is particularly impressive but, with 29 rooms to choose from, there is accommodation for most sizes of event. / *in-house caterers, but hirer's choice on Sun; Balmoral (450,230,160,300); Edinburgh (350,250,170,300); York (250,150,100,210); Grand Hall & Balmoral (1000,530,380,700); Durham (60,50,–,55); Penthouse (50,40,–,40).*

CAPACITIES: (Standing, Seated, Dinner dance, Theatre-style)

New End Theatre NW3

£B-M, (–,–,–,77)

27 New End

☎ (020) 7472 5800

🖷 (020) 7472 5808

🖰 www.newendtheatre.co.uk

✉ mail@newendtheatre.co.uk

Karl Marx was laid out in this building, which at the time was a mortuary for the New End Hospital. Converted to a theatre in 1974, it now offers an intimately scaled venue, available subject to the constraints of performances. / available subject to constraints of current production; hirer's choice of caterer (in-house available); no music after 11pm; no dancing; smoking restricted.

New World W1

£B-M, (–,700,–,–)

Gerrard Pl

☎ (020) 7734 0677

🖷 (020) 7287 3994

For a big party relatively inexpensively, how about a feast for all your friends on one of the floors of this vast Chinatown spot? Or if you've really got a lot of friends, take the whole place! / midnight; no dancing; no smoking; Private Rm (–,200,–,–).

Newham City Farm E16

£B, (50,50,–,–)

King George Av, Custom Hse

☎ (020) 7474 4960

The Visitors Centre of this city farm has a room particularly suited to children's parties. The whole venue, could, however, be made available for a suitable function. / 4pm winter, 5pm summer; available from 10am; hirer's choice of caterer; no smoking; no alcohol; Rm (50,50,–,–).

The Newsroom EC1

£M-E, (220,70,50,90)

60 Farringdon Rd

☎ (020) 7713 4971

🖷 (020) 7239 9766

🖰 www.guardian.co.uk/ newsroom

✉ newsroomevents@ guardian.co.uk

Originally built as a bonded warehouse in 1875, this Farringdon structure was completely renovated and re-opened (as the Guardian's archive building) in 2002. It makes an interesting setting for an event, especially with an historical or literary theme. / 11pm; hirer's choice of caterer; no smoking; Lecture Theatre (220,70,50,90); Exhibition (90,–,–,–); Scott Rm (90,–,–,90).

Niksons SW11

£M, (–,32,–,–)

172-174 The Highway

☎ (020) 7228 2285

This impressive Battersea restaurant, with a charming lofty rear dining room. Its scale is pretty much perfect for many private events.

No 4 Hamilton Place W1

£M, (300,280,150,–)

4 Hamilton Pl

☎ (020) 7670 4314

🖷 (020) 7670 4319

🖰 www.4hp.org.uk

Although now slightly institutional in feel, much of the original grandeur of this impressive c19 townhouse, just off Hyde Park Corner, remains. A terrace opens off the Argyll room. / midnight; in-house caterers; Argyll Rm & Hawker Rm (200,120,80,–); Council Rm & Bar (150,60,–,–); Lecture Theatre (250,250,150,–); Sopwith Rm (60,40,–,–).

Noble Rot W1

£M-E, (300,115,65,–)

3-5 Mill St

☎ (020) 7629 8877

🖷 (020) 7629 8878

🖰 www.noblerot.com

A stylish Mayfair restaurant whose darkly-decorated basement functions as a private member's bar. At lunch and during the week (and very occasionally at weekends) you can hire the bar privately, or you may be able to take over the whole place. / 3 am; generally not available at weekends; in-house caterers; Member's Bar (120,50,–,–).

Notting Hill Brasserie W11

£M-E, (–,55,–,–)
92 Kensington Park Rd
☎ (020) 7229 4481
🖨 (020) 7221 1246
This imposing townhouse-restaurant – it was long known as Leith's, but has now had a very contemporary make-over – offers a flexible range of private dining opportunities. / no live entertainment; no dancing; Main Restaurant (–,55,–,–); Semi-Private Areas By Bar (–,32,–,–); Large Private Rm (–,22,–,–); Small Private Rm (–,8,–,–).

Number Sixteen SW7

£M-E, (30,10,–,–)
16 Sumner Place
☎ (020) 7589 5232
🖨 (020) 7584 8615
🖰 www.numbersixteenhotel.co.uk
📧 reservations@
   numbersixteenhotel.co.uk
A small South Kensington hotel, whose conservatory is a popular venue for summer drinks parties. / 10pm; in-house caterers; no dancing; Conservatory (30,10,–,–).

Nylon EC2

£M, (475,200,–,–)
1 Addle St
☎ (020) 7600 7771
🖨 (020) 7600 7772
🖰 www.styleinthecity.com
It may have a Citified location, at the food of Royex House just south of London Wall, but this large, '70s-looking venue is quite cool by Square Mile standards, and offers a good option for a large bash, with the possibility of dancing. / 2 am.

The October Gallery WC1

£B, (150,80,60,–)
24 Old Gloucester St
☎ (020) 7831 1618
🖰 www.theoctobergallery.com
This former C of E girls' school, which has a small courtyard, is a good size to be taken over in its entirety, or the individual galleries could suit a wide range of smaller

functions. *Events with some kind of artistic tie-in are particularly encouraged.* / 10pm, Fri & Sat 11pm ; hirer's choice of caterer (in-house available); no amplified music; no smoking; Main Gallery (150,80,60,–); Top Floor Theatre (80,50,–,–); Club (40,10,–,–).

Odette's NW1

£M, (–,30,–,–)
130 Regent's Park Rd
☎ (020) 7586 5486
🖨 (020) 7586 2575
This multi-mirrored, Primrose Hill favourite – still probably north London's smartest restaurant – has one of the sweetest private rooms, with an atmosphere akin to that of a cosy cupboard. The downstairs conservatory can also be hired. / not available Sat L & Sun; no music; no dancing; Conservatory (–,30,–,–); Private Rm (–,10,–,–).

Old Billingsgate EC3

£M-E, (2430,1400,1000,–)
1 Old Billingsgate Walk
☎ (020) 7283 2800
🖨 (020) 7626 1095
🖰 www.billingsgateassociates.com
📧 jon@billingsgate.biz
On the site of the ancient fishmarket, a very large and flexible space, not too distant from Tower Bridge, and with some impressive river views. / 3 am; hirer's choice of caterer; Grand Hall (2430,1400,1000,–); Terrace (750,500,–,–); Mezzanine (500,300,–,–); Gallery (500,300,–,–); Arches (750,–,–,–); Well (200,–,–,–).

The Old Operating Theatre, Museum & Herb Garret SE1

£B-M, (60,–,–,–)
9a St Thomas's St
☎ (020) 7955 4791
🖰 www.thegarret.org.uk
📧 curator@thegarret.org.uk
Bizarre and fascinating, a c19 operating theatre, up tortuous spiral stairs in the belfry of a church near London Bridge. It now houses a collection of surgical instruments and

CAPACITIES: (Standing, Seated, Dinner dance, Theatre-style)

pickled internal organs – tough to beat for a drinks party with a touch of the macabre. / hirer's choice of caterer (in-house available); no amplified music; no dancing; no smoking.

The Old Palace, Herts
£M-E, (300,220,180,300)
Hatfield Park, Hatfield
☎ 01707 262055
🖰 www.theoldpalace.co.uk/banquets
📧 banquets@theoldpalace.co.uk
Originally built in the late c15, the Palace, also known as Hatfield House, has been added to throughout the centuries. It provides a suitably grand setting for events of all sizes (including Elizabethan banquets). / in-house caterers; The Old Riding School (300,220,160,300); Great Hall (300,220,180,300).

The Old Royal Naval College SE10
£M-E, (600,500,500,60)
Old Royal Naval College, Greenwich
☎ (020) 8269 2131
🖻 (020) 8269 2723
🖰 www.greenwichfoundation.org.uk
📧 leiths.greenwich@compassgroup.co.uk
Recognised by UNESCO as a site of worldwide significance, this baroque set piece offers a setting as magnificent as any in London. The Painted Hall is described by its owners, with only a modest degree of hyperbole, as "probably the finest dining hall in the Western world". For events for which this might be a little over-the-top, the King William Restaurant (in an undercroft to the hall) offers plainer, but still elegant, accommodation. / 1 am; in-house caterers; smoking restricted; Painted Hall (600,500,–,–); Queen Mary Ante Rm (500,–,–,–); King William Restaurant (150,120,100,–); Admirals Residence (100,50,40,60).

The Old Sessions House EC1
£M, (200,120,70,180)
Clerkenwell Grn
☎ (020) 7250 1212
🖻 (020) 7253 2302
🖰 www.sessionshouse.com
📧 conference@sessionshouse.com
An imposing building overlooking Clerkenwell Green, this former courthouse offers a range of function accommodation, in quite a traditional style. / in-house caterers; smoking restricted; Westminster (200,120,–,180); London Rm (100,40,40,70); Judges (100,70,70,75); Justices (40,30,–,40); Recorder Rm (40,30,–,40); Jailers Rm (80,60,–,60); Clerks (25,–,–,25).

Old Spitalfields Market E1
£M-E, (1000,1000,1000,–)
Commercial St
☎ (020) 7251 6661
🖰 www.amazingspace.co.uk
All year round, this covered City space, managed by Amazing Space, is available for suitable semi-outdoor functions. In winter, though, you need a marquee as protection against the cold – offering a central site with a large capacity. / midnight; available Mon-Sat from midday; hirer's choice of caterer; With marquee (1000,1000,1000,–).

The Old Thameside Inn SE1
£B, (300,–,–,–)
Clink St
☎ (020) 7403 4243
🖻 (020) 7407 2063
A South Bank riverside pub, with a large, stone-floored cellar bar available for private parties (and where you can also have a disco). A section of the terrace overlooking the river can be roped off for 40 or so people. / 11pm; Ground Floor (300,–,–,–); Cellar Bar (150,–,–,–).

On Anon W1
£B-M, (1495,–,–,–)
London Pavilion
☎ (020) 7287 8008
🖰 www.latenightlondon.co.uk
✉ info@onanon.co.uk
If you really want to be at the heart of things, this collection of eight bars over 4 floors actually overlooks Piccadilly Circus. If you take the whole place, it offers quite a capacity, too. / in-house caterers.

One Aldwych WC2
£M-E, (100,48,–,60)
1 Aldwych
☎ (020) 7300 1000
🖶 (020) 7300 0501
🖰 www.onealdwych.com
✉ mickbishop@onealdwych.com
A very central location is just one of the distinguishing features of this comfortably understated – and very highly-regarded – Covent Garden design-hotel, which offers a selection of smaller accommodation. / in-house caterers; Rms 1 & 2 (100,48,–,60); Rm 3 (50,30,–,25); Screening Rm (–,–,–,30); Dome Suite (–,10,–,–); Suite 500 (15,–,–,–).

One Birdcage Walk SW1
£M, (200,150,–,214)
1 Birdcage Walk
☎ (020) 7973 1248
🖰 www.onebirdcagewalk.com
✉ v_dobson@imeche.org.uk
Although the common parts and entrance of this prettily-located St James's institute (of Mechanical Engineers) are rather, well, institutional, the panelled Council room, the Hinton room (park views) and the odd but striking Marble Hall are all well suited to quite grand entertaining – the last being the best place for receptions. / 1 am; Crown Catering; smoking restricted; Marble Hall (200,150,–,–); Hinton Rm (80,60,–,60); Council (90,60,–,70); Lower Dining Rm (–,70,–,–); Courses Rm (–,70,–,40); Lecture Theatre (–,–,–,214).

1 Blossom Street E1
£M, (180,100,–,–)
1 Blossom St
☎ (020) 7247 6530
This Italian restaurant, not far from Liverpool Street, boasts an intriguing, rather hidden-away basement location, off a courtyard garden. There are three private rooms, or you could take the whole place. / available Mon-Fri only; Grand Salon (–,26,–,–); Garden Salon (–,12,–,–); Red Rm (no smoking) (–,6,–,–).

One Great George Street SW1
£M, (700,260,220,400)
1 Gt George St
☎ (020) 7665 2323
🖰 www.onegreatgeorge
street.co.uk
✉ oggs@ice.org.uk
The high-ceilinged lobby, staircase, and, in particular, the huge marbled Great Hall of this impressive building, just off Parliament Square, all possess much neo-classical ('30s) grandeur. They can suit a whole range of events, from grand dinners to weddings, and the whole would make a good setting for a ball. Extensive meeting facilities are also available. / in-house caterers; Great Hall (400,260,220,400); Smeaton Rm (150,100,60,150); Brunel Rm or Council Rm (100,80,–,100); Stephenson Rm & President's Dining Rm (30,30,–,30); Telford Theatre (–,–,–,241).

1 Lombard Street EC3
£M-E, (400,170,–,–)
1 Lombard St
☎ (020) 7497 4321
🖶 (020) 7929 6622
🖰 www.1lombardstreet.com
Herbert Berger's ambitious City restaurant, in a converted, listed banking hall with neo-classical interior. For fully private events, the choice is to take the private room or the whole place. / Private Rm (60,40,–,–).

CAPACITIES: (Standing, Seated, Dinner dance, Theatre-style)

One New Inn Square EC2
£M-E, (100,35,35,40)
8-13 New Inn Sq
☎ 0845 4561556
🖷 0845 4561557
⌖ www.jiantmarketing.co.uk
📧 jennifer@jiantmarketing.co.uk
An impressive 'NY-style' Shoreditch loft apartment – the home of eminent personal chef David Vanderhook – available for private hire. / 1 am; in-house caterers.

115 at Hodgson's WC2
£M, (150,70,70,–)
115 Chancery Ln
☎ (020) 7242 2836
🖷 (020) 7831 6113
⌖ www.115.uk.com
This rather intriguing 'Midtown' space was built as a Victorian auctioneer's showroom. With its glazed double-height roof, it would perhaps be particularly of interest for a summer drinks party. For more informal affairs, the cellar wine bar (with its own private room) is also available. / Mezzanine (40,30,–,–); Cellar Wine Bar (100,–,–,–); CWB Private Rm (–,20,–,–).

One Whitehall Place SW1
£M-E, (400,228,228,220)
One Whitehall Pl
☎ (020) 7839 3344
⌖ www.thistlehotels.com
📧 meetingplan.whitehall@ thistle.co.uk
A sumptuous Grade I listed Victorian building, now exclusively used for functions (including weddings). The balconies of the River Room and the Reading and Writing Rooms have views of Whitehall Gardens and the Thames, and there is a fine library, with minstrels' gallery. It may also be possible to hire the terrace of the adjacent National Liberal Club (see also). / 1 am; hirer's choice of caterer (in-house available); Gladstone Library (400,228,228,220); Whitehall Suite (300,220,160,200); Reading And Writing Rms (250,150,70,120); Meston Suite (80,72,–,65); River Rm (80,68,–,65); Cellar (50,12,–,–); Thames Suite (–,20,–,–).

Opium W1
£M-E, (250,60,–,–)
1a Dean St
☎ (020) 7287 9608
🖷 (020) 7437 3500
This opulent Vietnamese restaurant in north Soho would make an ideal venue for a loungey party. There's no private room, so you would have to take the whole place.

L'Oranger SW1
£M-E, (–,55,–,–)
5 St James's St
☎ (020) 7839 3774
🖷 (020) 7839 4330
This comfortable St James's restaurant would particularly suit a grand business dinner. There is a private room downstairs, or you can take the whole place. / Private Rm (–,20,–,–).

Orangery (Holland Park) W8
£M, (150,80,–,–)
Holland Park
☎ (020) 7603 1123
This must be one of the prettiest spots in London – an enchanting c18 building, on an intimate scale and glazed on three sides. / 11.30pm; list of caterers; no amplified music; no dancing.

Orangery (Kensington Palace) W8
£M-E, (300,150,–,–)
Kensington Palace
☎ (020) 7376 2452
🖷 (020) 7376 0198
⌖ www.hrp.org.uk
📧 helena.impett@hrp.og.uk
Beautifully situated, at the back of the Palace, this lovely, long, white-painted, Queen Anne summer house is made available 20 or so times a year for prestigious celebrations. See also Kensington Palace. / no weddings; 10.30pm; available eves only; list of caterers; no amplified music; no dancing; no smoking.

PRIVATE VENUES

Osterley Park & House, Middx
£M-E, (60,60,–,100)
Jersey Rd, Isleworth
☎ (020) 8232 5050
🖥 www.nationaltrust.org.uk
📧 osterley@nationaltrust.org.uk
Set in 300 acres of landscaped park and farmland with ornamental lakes and woodland, this house, which was built in 1575 and transformed two hundred years later, is one of London's best-kept secrets. Put up a marquee, and you can have a dinner dance for up to 300. / no stilettos; in-house caterers & list of approved caterers; no smoking; Brewhouse (60,60,–,100); Hall (–,–,–,80).

The Oval SE11
£M, (350,240,180,–)
Kennington
☎ (020) 7735 6884
🖥 www.surreycricket.co.uk
📧 meetingpoint@surreyccc.co.uk
A banqueting suite adjacent to the Dennington cricket ground, overlooking the pitch. / 1 am; Letheby & Christopher; no music in long rm; no dancing in long rm; Banqueting Suite (350,240,180,–); Long Rm (120,80,–,–); KBCC (350,350,300,–).

Oxford & Cambridge Club SW1
£M, (80,70,60,–)
71 Pall Mall
☎ (020) 7930 5151
🖥 www.oxfordand cambridgeclub.co.uk
📧 club@ oxfordandcambridgeclub.co.uk
Those who spent their salad days at the Varsity (or who have friends who did) should bear this imposing St James's institution in mind. A member must be present at any function. / members club; midnight; in-house caterers; no amplified music; Marlborough (80,70,–,–); Edward VII (25,18,–,–).

Pacha SW1
£M, (800,180,160,160)
205 Victoria St
☎ 0845 4561556
🖨 0845 4561557
🖥 www.jiantmarketing.co.uk
📧 jennifer@jiantmarketing.co.uk
"The most glamorous nightclub in the world" – well, that's what they say – now occupies the old dance-hall site which older groovers may remember as the SW1 Club. Now substantially upgraded, it can cater for a large variety of events at this very central site, adjacent to Victoria Station. / 6 am; available Mon-Thu.

Painshill, Surrey
£M-E, (60,–,–,–)
Cobham
☎ 01932 868113
🖥 www.painshill.co.uk
📧 info@painshill.co.uk
If you're looking for a marquee site of more than usual charm and historical interest, this recently restored c18 garden – whose points of interest include a Gothic temple, a Chinese bridge, a ruined abbey and a remarkable grotto – has much to commend it. / midnight; hirer's choice of caterer (in-house available); no music after 11.30pm; Visitor Building (60,–,–,–).

Painters' Hall EC4
£M, (250,180,180,200)
9 Little Trinity Ln
☎ (020) 7236 6258
🖥 www.painters-hall.co.uk
📧 beadle@painters-hall.co.uk
This hall, near Mansion House tube, is quite modest compared to some of its grand City brethren (and a lot more flexible in its outlook too). The décor of the hall itself (re-opened in the '60s) is quite sparse, but the small Painted Chamber is particularly charming. / 11pm; Chelsea Catering; Livery Hall (250,180,–,200); Court Rm (100,35,–,60); Painted Chamber (–,14,–,–).

CAPACITIES: (Standing, Seated, Dinner dance, Theatre-style)

Palace Theatre W1
£M, (100,–,–,1396)
Cambridge Circus
☎ (020) 7494 5200
🖷 (020) 7434 1217
🖰 www.rutheatres.com
🖃 info@rutheatres.com
Sunday evening concerts and post-film launch parties are among the private events accommodated at this impressive theatre (opened in 1891 as the Royal English Opera House), on the fringe of Soho. / available until 4.30pm & after shows; in-house caterers; smoking restricted; Auditorium (–,–,–,1396); Dress Circle Bar (100,–,–,–).

Paxton's Head SW1
£B-M, (80,40,–,–)
153 Knightsbridge
☎ (020) 7589 6627
🖰 www.thespiritgroup.com
🖃 paxtonshead@
   thespiritgroup.com
This palatial Knightsbridge boozer offers a couple of party possibilities in very different styles (and both different from what you'd expect from the ground-floor bar). Upstairs, there's a elegant modern oriental restaurant, downstairs a loungey bar. / no dancing; Basement Bar (80,–,–,–); Pan-Asian Canteen (–,40,–,–).

La Paquerette EC2
£B, (100,60,–,–)
Finsbury Sq
☎ (020) 7638 5134
🖷 (020) 7638 1706
By the green at the centre of Finsbury Square, this small bar/café has a garden and is available for barbecues, parties and bowling evenings. At the weekends, you can take over the whole place. / 1 am; Terrace (100,50,–,–).

Park Crescent Conference Centre W1
£B, (600,220,–,320)
International Students House, 229 Great Portland St
☎ (020) 7631 8306
🖰 www.ish.org.uk

🖃 conference@ish.org.uk
Impressively-housed student hostel, geared to student and club discos (as well as conference business). The cafeteria is surprisingly stylish, with the gym-like theatre (removable seating) standing out among the other rooms. Worthy organisations may be able to organise summer parties in the Park Crescent garden. / 3 am; in-house caterers; no music after 11pm; smoking restricted; Theatre (600,220,–,320); Portland Rm (250,80,–,110); Gulbenkian (150,–,–,–); Bistro (150,70,–,–).

Park Lane Hotel W1
£M-E, (1200,650,500,22)
Piccadilly
☎ (020) 7290 7294
🖷 (020) 7290 7566
🖰 www.sheraton.com
🖃 events.centrallondon@
   sheraton.com
Charming Mayfair hotel, where the star is the large Art Deco Ballroom, with its superb entrance. Some of the other rooms, for example the imposing Oak Room, also offer some unusually characterful possibilities. / 2 am; Ballroom (1200,650,500,–); Tudor Rose Rm (250,200,150,–); Oak Rm (120,80,50,–); Smart Rms (–,22,–,22); Orchard Suite (60,50,–,–); Mirror Rm (50,50,–,–); Drawing Rm (30,20,–,–).

Pasha N1
£M-E, (150,60,–,–)
301 Upper St
☎ (020) 7226 1454
🖷 (020) 7226 1617
With its seductive décor, this well-known South Kensington Moroccan restaurant provides an opulent backdrop to an event. With a guaranteed minimum spend, it can be taken privately. / in-house caterers.

Patio W12
£B, (–,80,–,–)
5 Goldhawk Rd
☎ (020) 8743 5194
🖷 (020) 8743 5194
Fun Shepherd's Bush institution – a Polish party restaurant – whose cheap prices for hearty nosh and

vodka, plus charming service have earned it a deserved festive reputation. For exclusive hires, you can take over the basement or whole place. / 12.30 am; in-house caterers; no dancing; Basement (–,40,–,–).

Pattersons W1
£M, (200,90,90,–)
4 Mill St
☎ (020) 7499 1308
🖨 (020) 7491 2122
🗑 www.pattersonsrestaurant.com
📧 enquiries@
   pattersonsrestaurant.com

A new restaurant in Mayfair, in contemporary style. Being family-run, it's a touch more personal in its approach than many of the venues which have such central locations. The private function room downstairs is suitable for quiet dinners and discos alike. / midnight; in-house caterers; smoking restricted; Function Rm (60,30,30,–).

Jamies Pavilion EC2
£M, (150,35,–,–)
Finsbury Circus Gardens,
Finsbury Circus
☎ (020) 7628 8224
🗑 www.jamiesbars.co.uk
📧 info@jamiesbars.co.uk
Set in one of the largest garden squares in the City, a wine bar with a very handy location. At weekends, you can hire the whole place. / midnight; available restaurant eves; wine bar weekends; no music; no dancing; Restaurant (40,25,–,–); Wine Bar (100,35,–,–).

Pennyhill Park Hotel, Surrey
£M-E, (200,170,170,–)
London Rd, Bagshot
☎ 01276 471774
🗑 www.exclusivehotels.co.uk
📧 nicky@pennyhillpark.co.uk
A Victorian manor house, now converted to a 123 bedroom hotel, standing in 120 acres of parkland. The décor has a traditional feel with wood panelled rooms. / midnight; Balmoral (200,170,170,–); Windsor & Eton (120,100,80,–); Parkview (60,48,–,–).

Penshurst Place & Gardens, Kent
£M-E, (600,150,150,200)
Penshurst, Tonbridge
☎ 01892 870307
🗑 www.penshurstplace.com
📧 banqueting@
   penshurstplace.com
The Sidney family home since 1552 and substantially still a medieval building. You can get married in the Sunderland Room then go downstairs to the Baron's Hall for dinner and dancing. / midnight; Letheby & Christopher; smoking restricted; Baron's Hall (400,150,–,200); Sunderland Rm (120,84,–,120); Buttery (70,30,–,–).

The People's Palace SE1
£M-E, (400,240,–,–)
South Bank Centre
☎ (020) 7928 9999
🖨 (020) 7928 2355
🗑 www.capitalgrp.co.uk
📧 info@peoplespalace.co.uk
The enormous main dining room of the Royal Festival Hall, overlooking the Thames, can be taken in its entirety for functions. The prohibition, for obvious reasons, of music during performances precludes many uses for which the place would otherwise be suitable. / no music; no dancing.

CAPACITIES: (Standing, Seated, Dinner dance, Theatre-style)

The Petersham, Surrey
£M-E, (80,40,–,–)
Nightingale Ln, Richmond
☎ (020) 8940 7471
🖳 (020) 8939 1098
🖰 www.petershamhotel.co.uk
📠 enq@petershamhotel.co.uk

An intriguing Victorian building, prettily located, and with a number of pleasantly furnished rooms for functions, some with charming views. The Claret Room is appropriately housed, in the cellars. / in-house caterers; River Rm (70,40,–,–); Terrace Rm (50,40,–,–); Rose Rm (15,10,–,–); Cellars (–,16,–,–); Meeting Rm (80,–,–,–).

Pétrus SW1
£M-E, (–,14,–,–)
Wilton Pl
☎ (020) 7235 1200
🖳 (020) 7235 1011
Now in Knightsbridge, Marcus Wareing's ambitious Gallic restaurant offers swanky private dining facilities, in a ground-floor room.

Pewterers' Hall EC2
£M, (125,70,–,–)
Oat Ln
☎ (020) 7606 9363
🖳 (020) 7600 3896
🖰 www.pewterers.org.uk
📠 beadle@pewterers.org.uk
This mid-sized '60s livery hall – but with panelling from an earlier hall – is sometimes made available for dinners and receptions. / no weddings; 10.30pm; list of caterers; no amplified music; no dancing; Livery Rm (125,70,–,–); Court Rm (125,70,–,–).

Phene Arms SW3
£B, (60,35,–,–)
9 Phene St
☎ (020) 7352 3294
The ever-popular Chelsea back street corner pub was reaching the end of major works to extend and upgrade its facilities as this guide went to press. Its lovely garden survives, and there are two inside spaces which may be taken privately. / 11pm; Upstairs Rm (60,30,–,–); Bistro (20,–,–,–); Upstairs Terrace (20,16,–,–); Garden (150,–,–,–).

Philbeach Hall SW5
£B, (300,220,–,–)
51 Philbeach Gdns
☎ (020) 7373 4631
Especially in the 'fashionable SWs', it's no easy task to find do-your-own-catering venues with fully-equipped kitchens. All the more worth knowing about this well decorated church hall, in a listed building just two minutes from Earl's Court tube. / midnight; hirer's choice of caterer.

Phoenix Artist Club WC2
£M, (150,50,–,–)
1 Phoenix St, Charing Cross Rd
☎ (020) 7836 1077
🖳 (020) 7497 1080
🖰 www.thephoenixartistsclub.co.uk
📠 mail@
thephoenixartistsclub.co.uk
A restaurant and bar located in the original dressing and rehearsal rooms of the Phoenix Theatre (where Laurence Olivier made his stage début in 1930). / 3 am; in-house caterers; Dining Rm (150,50,–,–).

Phoenix Theatre WC2
£M, (–,1046,–,–)
Charing Cross Rd
☎ (020) 7438 9600
🖳 (020) 7438 9611
🖰 www.theambassadors.com
This elegantly furnished '30s theatre is available for private hire, subject to the constraints of the current production. It is used mainly for media

events and photo-shoots. / in-house caterers; smoking restricted.

Photographers' Gallery WC2
£B-M, (150,80,–,–)
5 Great Newport St
☎ (020) 7831 1772
🖷 (020) 7836 9704
⌐ www.photonet.org.uk
✉ info@photonet.org.uk
A modern gallery, on the fringe of Covent Garden, most obviously suited to receptions. / midnight; available Mon-Fri 7pm onwards; list of caterers; no amplified music; no dancing; no smoking; no red wine.

Pinewood Studios, Bucks
£M, (500,500,500,–)
Pinewood Rd, Iver
☎ 01753 651110
🖷 01753 651113
⌐ www.pinewood-studios.co.uk
✉ pinewoodsales@aol.com
The country house at the centre of this famous studio complex accommodates large parties in its Ballroom (using the adjoining theatre for dancing). Smaller get-togethers happen in its Great Gatsby or Green Rooms. For big gatherings – perhaps after a marriage in the house itself – a marquee can be erected. / 1 am; in-house caterers; Ballroom (200,150,150,–); Green Rm (125,100,–,–); Great Gatsby Rm (100,70,–,–).

Pissarro's on the River W4
£M, (150,120,–,–)
Corney Reach Way
☎ (020) 8994 3111
🖷 (020) 8994 3222
⌐ www.pissarro.co.uk
A beautiful riverside location and a conservatory with a retractable roof set an away-from-it-all tone at this usual restaurant (available for private hire), set on the towpath amidst a development in deepest Chiswick. For a touch of style, arrive by boat on the nearby pier. / 12.30 am; in-house caterers; no amplified music; no dancing.

Pizza On The Park SW1
£B-M, (–,100,–,–)
11 Knightsbridge
☎ (020) 7235 5273
🖷 (020) 7235 6853
The subterranean room of this large, fashionably-located pizzeria – used nightly for cabaret – may be hired privately at lunchtimes.

PizzaExpress NW8
£B-M
⌐ www.pizzaexpress.co.uk
   39 Abbey Rd, NW8
☎ (020) 7624 5577 (85,55,–,–)
   7 Beauchamp Pl, SW3
☎ (020) 7589 2355 (25,16,–,–)
   30 Coptic St, WC1A
☎ (020) 7636 3232 (–,40,–,–)
   10 Dean St, W1D
☎ (020) 7439 8722
   35 Earls Court Rd, W8
☎ (020) 7937 0761 (200,120,–,–)
   94 Golders Green Rd, NW11
☎ (020) 8455 9556 (45,30,–,–)
   70 Heath St, NW3
☎ (020) 7433 1600 (40,30,–,–)
   99 High Holborn, WC1V
☎ (020) 7831 5305 (100,55,–,–)
   335 Upper St, N1
☎ (020) 7226 9542 (–,70,–,–)
   187 Kentish Town Rd, NW1
☎ (020) 7267 0101 (50,25,–,–)
   152 Kings Rd, SW3
☎ (020) 7351 5031 (120,60,–,–)
   230 Lavender Hl, SW11
☎ (020) 7223 5677 (60,35,–,–)
   125 Alban Gate, EC2
☎ (020) 7600 8880 (–,200,–,–)
   23 Bruton Place, W1X
☎ (020) 7495 1411 (80,45,–,–)
   137 Notting Hill Gt, W11
☎ (020) 7229 6000
   46 Moreton St, SW1V
☎ (020) 7592 9488 (50,35,–,–)
   144 Upper Richmond Rd, SW15
☎ (020) 8789 1948 (30,30,–,–)
   227 Finchley Rd, NW3
☎ (020) 7794 5100 (60,40,–,–)
   78-80 Wapping Ln, E1W
☎ (020) 7481 8436 (120,76,–,–)
This well-known chain makes some of its restaurants available for exclusive hire, while many offer private rooms for larger bookings.

CAPACITIES: (Standing, Seated, Dinner dance, Theatre-style)

PJ's Bar & Grill SW3
£M, (70,40,–,–)
52 Fulham Rd
☎ (020) 7581 0025
Unlike most of the venues we list, this mezzanine of this buzzy Chelsea American restaurant is only semi-private, but it makes a fun venue for an informal party.

The Place Below EC2
£B-M, (–,80,–,–)
St Mary-le-Bow, Cheapside
☎ (020) 7329 0789
🖨 (020) 7248 2626
🕙 www.theplacebelow.co.uk
📧 info@theplacebelow.co.uk
In the evenings, parties of 20 or more can take over this high-quality City crypt vegetarian restaurant. / 11.30pm; no smoking.

The Place WC1
£M, (150,80,–,100)
17 Dukes Rd
☎ (020) 7387 0161
🕙 www.theplace.org.uk
Home of London's Contemporary Dance School, this recently refurbished venue near Euston offers a variety of spaces for studio hire, as well as a bar and theatre for more traditional corporate events. / restricted availability; 11pm; in-house caterers; no smoking; Theatre Bar (70,–,–,30); Founders Studio (150,30,–,100); Café (150,80,–,–).

Plateau E14
£M-E, (130,90,–,–)
Canada Pl
☎ (020) 7715 7100
🖨 (020) 7715 7110
🕙 www.conran.com
Conran's new futuro-retro restaurant, in Canary Wharf. There's a private room, or you can take the whole place. / Private Rm (40,24,–,–).

The Player W1
£M, (120,–,–,–)
8-12 Broadwick St
☎ (020) 7494 9125
🖨 (020) 7494 9126
🕙 www.thplyr.com
A nothing-looking doorway adds to the thrill of discovering this superior (and well-known, for those in-the-know) Soho cocktail bar. Now part of members' bar Milk & Honey, it can – at certain times – be hired privately. / 1 am; in-house caterers.

The Plough WC1
£B, (45,30,–,–)
27 Museum St
☎ (020) 7636 7964
Friendly, creaky well-worn pub across from the British Museum. If you are happy to do without a private bar, the room comes free. / 11pm; no amplified music; no dancing.

Poetry Society WC2
£B-M, (70,40,–,–)
22 Betterton St
☎ (020) 7420 9887
🕙 www.poetrysociety.org.uk
📧 poetrycafe@
   poetrysociety.org.uk
A Covent Garden society whose HQ is, as one might expect, is most used for book launches and readings, but where the café is also used for more social occasions. / members club; 11pm; not available Sun; in-house caterers; no amplified music; smoking restricted; Restaurant & Basement (70,40,–,–).

Poissonnerie de l'Avenue SW3
£M, (–,20,–,–)
82 Sloane Av
☎ (020) 7589 2457
🖨 (020) 7581 3360
📧 info@poissonnerie.co.uk
A long-established Chelsea fish and seafood parlour, with a comfortable upstairs private dining room. The bar area can also be privately booked. / not available Sun; Private Rm (–,20,–,–); Bar (–,20,–,–).

Polish Club SW7
£B-M, (350,130,–,–)
55 Exhibition Rd
☎ (020) 7589 4635
🖨 (020) 7581 7926
📧 markgeliak@aol.com
*For old-fashioned charm, this South
Kensington emigrés' club scores highly. Parts have been recently refurbished but it remains a characterful,
quite grand, mid-priced venue for
most kinds of event. The Restaurant
has an outside terrace, and is popular for summer cocktails. / 1 am; ballroom available Fri-Sun; in-house caterers;
Ballroom (200,130,–,–);
Restaurant (200,120,–,–);
Terrace (80,30,–,–).*

Polish Social &
Cultural
Association W6
£B, (750,200,200,–)
238-246 King St
☎ (020) 8741 3225
*As with many emigrés' clubs, it's the
time-warp atmosphere which some
may find a particular attraction of
this basic '60s building in
Hammersmith. On the social side,
the club hosts a fair number of wedding receptions. / 1 am; restaurant not
available Sat D & Sun L; in-house, but Club
Disco may be at hirer's choice; Lowiczanka
Restaurant (200,150,110,–); Malinova
Rm (200,200,200,–); Ball Rm (–,–,160,–);
Club Disco (150,–,–,–).*

Polka Theatre for
Children SW19
£B-M, (200,–,–,300)
240 The Broadway
☎ (020) 8545 8328
🖰 www.polkatheatre.com
📧 boxoffice@polkatheatre.com
*London's only theatre for children
with its own permanent base comes
complete with a small but attractive
playground. It's used for a wide
range of (adult) readings and receptions. The studio theatre is popular
for children's events. / 10pm; evenings
only Sun & Mon; hirer's choice of caterer
(in-house available); no smoking; Studio
Theatre (200,–,–,80); Foyer (200,–,–,–);
Main Theatre (–,–,–,300).*

Polygon Bar &
Grill SW4
£M, (65,65,–,–)
4 The Polygon,
Clapham Old Town
☎ (020) 7622 1199
🖨 (020) 7622 1166
🖰 www.thepolygon.co.uk
📧 polygon@dial.pipex.com
*This unusually stylish Clapham
restaurant – a little way from the
busy main drag - is available during
the day for private parties.*

Pomegranates SW1
£M, (–,12,–,–)
94 Grosvenor Rd
☎ (020) 7828 6560
🖨 (020) 7828 2037

*Patrick Gwynn-Jones's Pimlico base-
ment restaurant of long standing (est
1974) has quite a name for its old-
style-eclectic cooking. The management speculates that its off-the-beat-
en-track location – "perfect for political plotting or high-powered deal
making" – is part of its appeal! / not
available Sat L or Sun; Private Rm (–,12,–,–).*

Le Pont de la
Tour SE1
£M-E, (–,20,–,–)
36d Shad Thames, Butlers Wharf
☎ (020) 7403 8403
🖨 (020) 7403 0267
🖰 www.conran.com
*The private room of the leading
restaurant of Conran's Tower Bridge-
side restaurant complex may lack
the spectacular view of the main dining room, but proximity to the City*

CAPACITIES: (Standing, Seated, Dinner dance, Theatre-style)

makes it a popular business rendezvous. / Private Rm (–,20,–,–).

Porchester Centre W2
£B-M, (630,450,450,–)
Queensway
☎ (020) 7792 2823
🖷 (020) 7641 4493
⌂ www.porchester.hall@
    cannons.co.uk
An ornate, panelled Art Deco ballroom – a gem hidden away in a
municipal-looking Bayswater building
– which is not very expensive, has
lots of character, and has recently
benefited from refurbishment. The
famous marbled Turkish baths in the
same building are available only for
product launches (and photo shoots).
/ midnight; hirer's choice or caterer, list available; Ballroom (630,450,450,–);
Baths (150,–,–,–).

La Porte des Indes W1
£M-E, (500,300,200,–)
32 Bryanston St
☎ (020) 7224 0055
🖷 (020) 7224 1144
⌂ www.pilondon.net
This vast Indian restaurant near
Marble Arch is extremely flexible as
a function venue, and offers obvious
theming potential. One or other of
the restaurant's two floors can be
used to accommodate parties of anywhere between 100 and 200, and
there are some smaller private
rooms. / Private Rm 1 (–,14,–,–); Private
Rm 2 (–,10,–,–).

Portland Place Conference Centre W1
£M-E, (–,40,–,40)
17 Portland Place
☎ (020) 7323 9084
🖷 (020) 7580 6945
⌂ www.initialstyle.co.uk
🖃 portland@initialstyle.co.uk
An Adam-style building near Oxford
Circus, which offers a range of meeting rooms which have natural light,
as well as a full range of audio-visual
equipment and technical support.
/ in-house caterers; no music; no dancing;
no smoking; Tavistock (–,–,–,40);
Grosvenor (–,–,–,40); Chiswick (–,–,–,24);
Cavendish (–,–,–,35).

Portman Hotel W1
£M-E, (700,550,500,80)
22 Portman Sq
☎ (020) 7208 6000
🖷 (020) 7224 4928
⌂ www.radissonsas.com
🖃 neil.barton@radissonsas.com
The banqueting facilities of this modern hotel reflect a certain confer-
ence-orientation (though it does have
a wedding licence). There's a good
variety of rooms, though, most with
floor-to-ceiling windows. / 1 am;
in-house caterers; Ballroom (700,550,500,–);
Gloucester Suite (100,80,–,80); Berkeley
Suite (50,50,–,–); Library (30,24,–,–);
Bryanston Suite (50,50,–,–).

Prenelle Gallery E14
£M, (150,60,60,70)
West India Quay, Hertsmere Rd
☎ (020) 7093 0628
⌂ www.prenelle.co.uk
🖃 amy@prenelle.com
A 130ft Dutch barge, moored in the
East End, which claims to be
London's only floating contemporary
art gallery. It is used for a wide variety of shows, launches & parties.
/ 11.30pm; hirer's choice of caterer; smoking restricted; Main Gallery (150,60,60,70);
Library (30,–,–,–); Outer Deck (150,60,–,–).

HMS President EC4
£B-M, (350,200,160,–)
Victoria Embankment
☎ (020) 7583 1918
⌂ www.hmspresident.com
🖃 enquiries@hmspresident.com
For a special occasion, this WWI, Q-
class boat, moored just above
Blackfriars Bridge, offers good value
and the sense of occasion that being
afloat brings. / 2 am; hirer's choice of
caterer (in-house available);
Ballroom (350,200,160,–); Ward
rm (120,70,–,–); Embankment
Bar (80,40,–,–); Quarter Deck (150,–,–,–).

Prince of Wales NW1
£B, (100,–,–,–)
Chalcot Rd
☎ (020) 7722 0354
🖨 (020) 7483 2770
A prettily-located Primrose Hill pub, with a cellar bar, sometimes available for hire in its entirety. / I am; no amplified music.

Prism EC3
£M-E, (300,120,120,–)
147 Leadenhall St
☎ (020) 7256 3875
🖨 0870 238 6345
🖰 www.harveynichols.com
📧 emma.morrison@
harveynichols.com
A converted banking hall now provides the impressive setting for this Harvey Nichols group restaurant in the heart of the City. It has a number of rooms for private hire, or the whole venue is quite well suited to a small dance. / Mezzanine (70,40,–,–); Library (40,20,–,–); Cocktail Bar (80,–,–,–).

Proud Galleries WC2
£B-M, (180,–,–,–)
5 Buckingham St
☎ (020) 7839 4942
🖨 (020) 7839 4947
🖰 www.proud.co.uk
📧 nina@proud.co.uk
A small photographic gallery, just off the Strand, which does quite a lot of business as a venue for corporate and media-world drinks parties.
/ hirer's choice of caterer (in-house available).

The Pump House Gallery SW11
£B, (70,70,–,–)
Battersea Park
☎ (020) 7350 0523
📧 pump_house@lineone.net
Prettily located on the lakeside in Battersea Park, this square tower (converted into four levels) makes an attractive and rather unusual place for a wedding or cocktail party. For a sit-down, you can boost the ground floor area with a marquee. / 11pm; hirer's choice of caterer; dancing in marquee only; no smoking.

Putney Bridge SW15
£M, (30,–,–,–)
Lower Richmond Road
☎ (020) 8780 1811
🖨 (020) 8780 1211
🖰 www.putneybridge
restaurant.com
📧 information@
putneybridgerestaurant.com
This architecturally striking modern landmark, near the start of the Boat Race, has a glass-walled area at the end of its ground floor bar that can be hired privately.

The Queen Elizabeth II Conference Centre SW1
£M-E, (800,880,600,–)
Broad Sanctuary, Westminster
☎ (020) 7222 5000
🖰 www.qeiicc.co.uk
📧 info@qeiicc.co.uk
The appeal of this purpose-built centre by Westminster Abbey is perhaps more obvious for conferences than for social events. In fact, however, the place is quite geared up for the latter, even to the extent of having a wedding licence. / midnight; Leith's; Fleming & Whittle Rms (–,880,–,–); Benjamin Britten Lounge (800,500,–,–); Fleming Rm (–,500,600,–).

TS Queen Mary WC2
£M, (700,150,120,–)
Victoria Embankment
☎ (020) 7240 9404
🖰 www.queenmary.co.uk
📧 info@queenmary.co.uk
This converted steamer, moored by Waterloo Bridge, has a variety of bars, two function rooms, a nightclub and a sundeck. / 2 am; in-house caterers; Admirals Suite (170,150,120,–); Captains Quarters (90,80,70,–).

Queen Mary College E1
£B, (800,200,–,–)
Mile End Rd
☎ (020) 7882 7881
🖨 (020) 8983 0146
🖰 www.qmul.ac.uk
📧 conference@qmul.ac.uk

CAPACITIES: (Standing, Seated, Dinner dance, Theatre-style)

This London University college has several venues – all at different East End sites, and in different styles ancient and modern – which are available for hire. The Octagon is the plushest. / *restricted availability; in-house caterers; smoking restricted; The Octagon (300,200,–,–); The Gallery (–,150,–,–); The Old Library (200,200,–,–); Bar Med (200,140,–,–); Charterhouse Square (500,–,–,–).*

Queen Mary Garden NW1
£B-M, (500,150,–,–)
Inner Circle, Regent's Park
☎ (020) 7935 5729
🖨 (020) 7224 5014
The Prince Regent room of this park café is available for civil weddings, and opens onto a large rose garden area. (The owners also run the tea rooms and cafés in Hyde and Greenwich Parks with space for a marquee, though the Rose Garden Restaurant is the only area suitable for formal seated occasions. Contact the telephone number given for details of the other venues.) / *Prince Regent Rm (75,50,–,–); Rose Garden Restaurant (–,150,–,–).*

Queen Mary Students' Union E1
£B, (750,180,–,–)
University Of London,
432 Bancroft Rd
☎ (020) 7882 5390
🖨 (020) 8981 0802
🖱 www.qmsu.org
✉ su-genoss@qmul.ac.uk
During vacations, the Union has two venues for hire at its East End campus – The Drapers Arms (a modern bar) and the e1 Nightclub. / *11.30pm; available outside term time only; hirer's choice of caterer (in-house available); e1 Nightclub (750,–,–,–); Drapers Arms (275,180,–,–).*

Queen's Eyot, Berks
£M, (250,150,150,60)
Monkey Island Ln, Windsor
☎ 01753 671219
🖨 01753 671219
🖱 www.etoncollege.com
✉ queenseyot@
   etoncollege.org.uk
Eton College's island retreat has an impressive modern clubhouse reached by ferry. Uses of the eyot range from corporate sports days to wedding receptions. / *11.30pm; closed Oct-Mar; in-house caterers; no smoking; Marquee (250,150,150,–); Clubhouse (80,60,–,60).*

Queen's House SE10
£M-E, (300,120,150,35)
National Maritime Mus
☎ (020) 8312 6644
🖱 www.nmm.ac.uk
✉ egoody@nmm.ac.uk
Sandwiched picturesquely between the Royal Naval College and Greenwich Park, a highly unusual house (by Inigo Jones et al), comprehensively restored. The lofty, cubic Great Hall and pretty Orangery are the areas most used, and are ideal for an evening wedding reception. / *11pm; available from 6pm; list of caterers; no amplified music outside; no smoking; no red wine for standing receptions ; Great Hall (150,120,–,–); Orangery Suite (80,40,–,–); Undercroft (120,–,–,–); SW Parlour (100,50,–,35); Loggia (30,–,–,–).*

Queen's Theatre WC2
£M, (80,–,–,990)
Shaftesbury Av
☎ (020) 7494 5200
🖨 (020) 7434 1217
🖱 www.rutheatres.com
✉ mike.townsend@
   rutheatres.com
This Edwardian theatre was reconstructed after the war, and therefore strikes a rare '50s note. It can be made available for presentations. / *smoking restricted; Auditorium (–,–,–,990); Stalls Bar (80,–,–,–); Dress Circle Bar (40,–,–,–).*

VISIT US AT: www.hardens.com

PRIVATE VENUES

Quilon SW1
£M, (125,100,–,–)
41 Buckingham Gt
☎ (020) 7821 1899
🖷 (020) 7828 5802
🖰 www.thequilonrestaurant.com
In the thin area around Victoria Street, this smart, rather businesslike modern Indian restaurant makes quite a popular venue for entertaining. There's no private room, but you can hire the whole place.

Quo Vadis W1
£M-E, (150,90,–,–)
26-29 Dean St
☎ (020) 7734 7333
🖷 (020) 7734 0033
🖰 www.whitestarline.org.uk
🖃 sales@whitestarline.org.uk
A Soho outpost of the Marco Pierre White restaurant empire, in a house in which Karl Marx once lived. Its four private rooms have the unusual advantage of natural light. / 1 am; no amplified music; no dancing; Warhol Rm (150,90,–,–); Modigliani (50,30,–,–); Giacommeti (–,15,–,–); Rossini Rm (–,12,–,–).

Raffles SW3
£M-E, (200,70,70,–)
287 King's Rd
☎ (020) 7352 1091
🖷 (020) 7352 9293
🖰 www.rafflesnightclub.co.uk
🖃 info@rafflesnightclub.co.uk
This intimate Chelsea nightclub, with separate Dining Room, is decorated in contemporary style. It is available for hire by non-members before 11pm and all day on Sunday. / 3 am; list of caterers.

The Ramada Jarvis London West W5
£M, (200,180,180,10)
Ealing Common
☎ (020) 8992 5399
🖷 (020) 8896 8424
🖰 www.ramadajarvis.co.uk
🖃 c.sales.londonwest@ ramadajavis.co.uk
Modern hotel in west London whose conference facilities double up for weddings, receptions and the like.

The ballroom features a stage. / midnight; Ballroom (200,180,180,–); Park View Rm (40,40,–,–); Park Mews (–,14,–,–); Boardroom (–,–,–,10).

La Rascasse W1
£M-E, (500,170,–,–)
50a Berkeley St
☎ (020) 7629 0808
🖷 (020) 7409 4708
🖰 www.cafegrandprix.com
Monaco – Beaux Arts styling and all – comes to Mayfair at this impressively-scaled new restaurant. Its sweeping style might well suit a corporate bash, or indeed a grand (probably winter) wedding reception. / Restaurant (500,170,–,–); Private Rm (–,40,–,–); Semi-private Area (–,45,–,–).

Raven's Ait Island, Surrey
£M-E, (400,300,300,200)
Portsmouth Rd, Surbiton
☎ (020) 8390 3554
🖰 www.ravensait.co.uk
🖃 info@ravensait.co.uk
Located between Kingston and Surbiton, this Thames islet makes an ideal venue for a larger events, not too far from the capital, and in slightly unusual surroundings. / midnight; in-house caterers; Britannia Suite (250,220,220,200); Thames Suite (150,100,100,100); Lambourne Rm (60,50,50,–).

Red Cube WC2
£M, (670,200,200,–)
1 Leicester Place
☎ (020) 7287 8050
🖰 www.redcubebarandgrill.com
🖃 info@redcubebarandgrill.com
A clubby bar/restaurant, just off Leicester Square. It would make a very central location for a large party. / in-house caterers; Dance Floor (400,–,–,–); Restaurant (–,147,–,–); Lounge Bar (420,150,–,–).

CAPACITIES: (Standing, Seated, Dinner dance, Theatre-style)

Red Rose Comedy Club N7

£M, (200,–,–,150)

129 Seven Sisters Rd,
Finsbury Park

☎ (020) 7281 3051

🖱 www.redrosecomedy.co.uk

✉ info@redrosecomedy.co.uk

Established in 1987, the Red Rose Comedy Club has presented virtually every current UK comedy star you can think of. You can hire the whole place for a private comedy night, or use the function room for a party with a band or DJ. / 11pm; hirer's choice of caterer.

The Regalia EC4

£M, (400,250,250,–)

Swan Pier, Swan Ln

☎ (020) 7623 1805

🖳 (020) 7283 4002

🖱 www.thamesleisure.co.uk

✉ info@thamesleisure.co.uk

A lunchtime watering-hole for younger City types, this permanently moored barge is an ideal place for a large and casual get-together. / 2 am; in-house caterers.

Regency Banqueting Suite N17

£B-M, (600,400,300,–)

113 Bruce Grove

☎ (020) 8885 2490

🖳 (020) 8885 1739

🖱 www.regencybanqueting.com

✉ info@regencybanqueting.com

It started off as a ballroom in the mid-20s, then became a cinema, and for the last 20 years these ivory, gold and white Tottenham premises – complete with crystal chandeliers – have been a banqueting suite. / hirer's choice of caterer (in-house available); Main Banquet Rm (600,400,–,–); Amber Rm (200,120,–,–).

Regent's College NW1

£M, (400,200,200,–)

Inner Circle, Regent's Park

☎ (020) 7487 7540

🖳 (020) 7487 7657

🖱 www.regents.ac.uk/
conferences

✉ conferences@regents.ac.uk

A great position, in the heart of the Park, makes this a very attractive venue. The rooms available are light and airy, in good decorative order, and only somewhat institutional. The Tuke Common Room has a particularly leafy prospect. / 11pm; in-house caterers; no amplified music outside; Refectory (400,200,200,–); Herringham Hall (200,100,100,–); Tuke Common Rm (100,50,50,–); Knapp Gallery (150,50,50,–); Gardens (500,400,400,–).

The Rembrandt Hotel SW7

£M, (–,180,180,200)

11 Thurloe Pl

☎ (020) 7589 8100

🖳 (020) 7225 3476

🖱 www.sarova.com

✉ rembrandt@sarova.co.uk

This Edwardian Hotel with modern facilities, near the V&A, offers good, flexible banqueting accommodation, all licensed for civil weddings. / Elizabeth & Victoria (Queen Suite) (–,60,40,90); Elizabeth (–,50,–,60); Princes (–,30,–,–); Victoria (–,10,–,–).

Renaissance London Chancery Court Hotel WC1

£M-E, (450,330,270,–)

252 High Holborn,

☎ (020) 7829 9888

🖳 (020) 7829 9889

🖱 www.marriott.com/loncc

✉ saleschancerycourt@
renaissancehotels.com

Built in 1914 as the impressive headquarters of the Pearl Assurance Company, this grand hotel is a recent arrival in the 'Midtown' area between the City and the West End. It offers a large variety of function and conference rooms, many of

which interconnect. / 2 am;
Ballroom (450,330,270,–); Lower Ground
Floor Suite (100,70,50,–); Staple Inn Rm &
Gray's Inn Rm (55,40,–,–); Ground Floor
Suite (90,64,40,–).

Rex Cinema & Bar W1
£M, (190,–,–,75)
Rupert St
☎ (020) 7287 0102
🖷 (020) 7478 1501
🖱 www.rexcinemaandbar.com
📧 info@rexcinemaandbar.com
*"A state-of-the-art 75-seat cinema,
together with a 1930s style lounge
bar" — an ideal Soho destination for
a screening.* / in-house caterers;
smoking restricted; Cinema (–,–,–,75);
Bar (190,–,–,–).

RICS SW1
£M, (150,100,–,–)
12 Gt George St
☎ (020) 7334 3781
🖷 (020) 7334 3871
🖱 www.rics.org/
    resources/venues
📧 venues@rics.org
*Just off Parliament Square, the home
of the Royal Institution of Chartered
Surveyors offers traditional Victorian
rooms with an easy-going atmosphere. The dark-panelled Lecture
Theatre is the best room and is popular for receptions. The much smaller York Room, also panelled, has
marble columns and is filled with
antiques.* / midnight; in-house caterers; no
amplified music; no dancing; smoking restricted; Lecture Hall (150,100,–,–); Members
Club Rm (100,–,–,–); Gloucester (40,24,–,–).

The Ritz W1
£M-E, (100,50,–,–)
150 Piccadilly
☎ (020) 7493 8181
🖱 www.theritzlondon.com
📧 enquire@theritzlondon.com
*The Ritz's strength is in stylish small-
to medium-sized rooms — in décor,
the Marie Antoinette suite lives up to
its name, and the Trafalgar Suite is
also impressive. There is no ballroom.* / no amplified music; Marie

Antoinette Suite (100,50,–,–); Trafalgar
Suite (–,20,–,–); Garden (100,–,–,–).

River & Rowing Museum, Oxon
£M-E, (300,100,100,–)
Mill Meadows, Henley-on-Thames
☎ 01491 415610
🖱 www.rrm.co.uk
📧 museum@rrm.co.uk
*This architectural-award-winning
museum offers a very pleasant space
for functions, benefiting from river
views.* / in-house caterers; no smoking;
Thames Rm (200,100,100,–); Henley
Rm (–,10,–,–).

Riverside Studios W6
£B-M, (1200,400,250,–)
Crisp Rd, Hammersmith
☎ (020) 8237 1000
🖱 www.riversidestudios.co.uk
📧 info@riversidestudios.co.uk
*A TV studio and arts centre, offering
flexible space. The studios are without windows, but the café-bar and
gallery are quite light and bright, and
the terrace has views towards
Hammersmith Bridge.* / 11.30pm; in-
house caterers; no amplified music on terrace; Studios 1 & 2 (600,400,250,–); Studio
3 (250,150,–,–); Café-Bar (200,120,–,–);
Terrace (150,100,–,–).

Robert Wilson Black Centre SW1
£M, (–,–,–,60)
Alliance House, 12 Caxton St
☎ (020) 7222 4001
🖷 (020) 7799 2510
🖱 www.ias.org.uk/rwb.htm
*A businesslike small hall, suitable for
presentations, near St James's Park
tube.* / 6pm; closed weekends & evenings;
no smoking; no alcohol; Main Hall (–,–,–,60).

Rock Garden WC2
£B, (300,80,–,–)
6-7 The Piazza
☎ (020) 7836 4052
🖱 www.rockgarden.co.uk
📧 kerry@rockgarden.co.uk
*Though it's better-known for its
touristy upstairs burger joint over-*

CAPACITIES: (Standing, Seated, Dinner dance, Theatre-style)

looking Covent Garden, the vaults here are among London's older rock venues. It's all very clean-cut, and offers combinations for parties of many sizes. Bigger events are organised in conjunction with the neighbouring nightclub, the *Gardening Club*. / *over 18s only; 3 am; in-house caterers; Rock Garden (250,–,–,–); Gardening Club Nightclub (300,–,–,–); Ground Floor Restaurant (–,40,–,–); Piazza Seating Restaurant (–,80,–,–); 1st Floor Restaurant (–,36,–,–).*

Rocket W1
£B-M, (250,30,–,–)
4-6 Lancashire Court, Brook Pl
☎ (020) 7629 2889
Bargains in Mayfair are hardly ten a penny, so it's well worth knowing about this smart, quite funky pizza (and more) restaurant, just off Bond Street. Unsurprisingly, its two private rooms are much in demand. / *Private Rm (–,30,–,–); Private Rm (–,10,–,–).*

Roehampton Club SW15
£M-E, (200,180,180,140)
Roehampton Ln
☎ (020) 8480 4225
🖷 (020) 8480 4222
🖰 www.roehamptonclub.com
It's not necessary to be a member to book function facilities at this impressive club. Sports facilities include an 18-hole golf course, 28 tennis and five squash courts, three croquet lawns, pools indoor and outdoor, and a gymnasium. The Roehampton and Garden Rooms benefit from huge windows overlooking the garden. / *11pm; in-house caterers; Roehampton Rm (140,120,120,140); Garden Rm (60,50,50,60); Centenary Board Rm (40,14,–,40).*

Ronnie Scotts W1
£M, (50,250,–,–)
47 Frith St
☎ (020) 7439 0747
🖷 (020) 7437 5081
🖰 www.ronniescotts.co.uk
🖃 ronniescotts@ronniescotts.co.uk

This famous Soho jazz night club is available for private hire in the day only. It is most commonly used for product launches and record company showcases. / *7pm; daytime only, Tue-Fri; hirer's choice of caterer (in-house available).*

The Roof Gardens W8
£M-E, (500,220,180,–)
99 High St Kensington
(entrance off Derry St)
☎ (020) 7937 7994
🖷 (020) 7938 2774
🖰 www.virgin.com/roofgardens
🖃 events@roofgardens.virgin.co.uk
A nightclub set in two acres of beautiful gardens would be a popular venue anywhere. Six floors above Kensington it seems all the more remarkable, and the place is constantly in demand for all types of events. / *1 am; not available Thu eves or Sat eves; in-house caterers; no amplified music outside.*

Royal Academy of Arts W1
£E, (800,250,–,–)
Burlington Hs, Piccadilly
☎ (020) 7300 5701
🖰 www.royalacademy.org.uk
🖃 entertaining@royalacademy.org.uk
The c18 private rooms of the Royal Academy are among the most charmingly impressive of any in London. It may also be possible to organise functions around gallery exhibitions (particularly the Summer Exhibition). Sit-down events are for corporate members only. / *charities & companies only; 11pm; available from 6.30pm, not available weekends; list of caterers; no dancing; no smoking; Summer Exhibition (800,250,–,–); Private Rms (400,100,–,–); General Assembly Rm (–,40,–,–).*

Royal Academy of Engineering SW1
£M-E, (90,80,–,–)
29 Great Peter St
☎ (020) 7222 2688
🖷 (020) 7233 0054
🖱 www.raeng.org.uk
📧 luceyj@raeng.co.uk
The Academy's Westminster HQ benefits from a very central location. It's best suited to corporate functions – all the rooms are in a businessy modern style. / 10pm; not available weekends; in-house caterers; no amplified music; no dancing; no smoking; Dining Rm (80,40,–,–); Conference Rm (80,80,–,–); Council Chamber (–,30,–,–); Meeting Rm 1 (–,10,–,–); Meeting Rm 2 (–,10,–,–).

The Royal Air Force Club W1
£M, (250,140,120,140)
128 Piccadilly
☎ (020) 7499 3456
🖷 (020) 7629 1316
🖱 www.rafclub.org.uk
📧 admin@rafclub.com
Functions need to be sponsored (and attended) by a member but, once you're in, this club is more flexible than many others as it has a ballroom and also a bar/disco area. The Mezzanine Suite offers adaptable accommodation, and in the basement, the Running Horse (the 'pub within the club') and Millennium Suite are suitable for discos, dances and wedding receptions. / members club; 1 am; in-house caterers; Ballroom (250,140,–,140); Presidents Rm (80,60,–,55); Drawing Rm (40,20,–,30); Mezzanine Suite (40,20,–,30); Boardroom (–,8,–,–); Running Horse/Millennium Suite (120,–,120,–).

Royal Air Force Museum NW9
£M-E, (1400,400,400,–)
Grahame Park Way, Hendon
☎ (020) 8205 2266
🖷 (020) 8358 4981
🖱 www.rafmuseum.com
📧 events@rafmuseum.com
Although other galleries are available, the Battle of Britain Hall of this Hendon venue is the most popular for functions. As well as dining underneath the wings of a flying boat, it has interesting displays on the Blitz, making it a natural for themed events. / list of caterers; smoking restricted; Loching Rm (300,130,130,–); Main Aircraft Hall (1000,400,–,–); Battle of Britain Hall (400,280,280,–); The Halton Gallery (300,170,170,–); Art Gallery (200,100,–,–); Cosford Rm (312,170,170,–).

Royal Albert Hall SW7
£M-E, (1500,1600,1000,5200)
Kensington Gore
☎ (020) 7589 3203
🖱 www.royalalberthall.co.uk
📧 admin@royalalberthall.com
You can entertain huge numbers in great style here, although, once more than just the arena is used, it is necessary to use the stalls and the boxes – a rather odd arrangement. Smaller events may be arranged in private rooms – the Prince of Wales and Henry Cole are particularly attractive. The maximum capacity figures require the setting up of the exhibition floor and terrace and should not be regarded as 'everyday' figures. / 1 am; Letheby & Christopher; smoking restricted; Cabaret or Ball (1500,1600,1000,5200); Arena (–,360,–,750); The Gallery (500,–,–,–); Victoria Rm (100,70,–,–); Henry Cole Rm (30,20,–,–); Prince Of Wales (35,25,–,–).

Royal Astronomical Society W1
£M-E, (–,–,–,15)
Burlington House Piccadilly
☎ (020) 7734 4582
🖷 (020) 7494 0766
🖱 www.ras.org.uk
Not a reception venue, but worth knowing about if you want a small, central conference followed by lunch. Next to the Royal Academy. / 5.30pm; open weekdays only; in-house caterers; no amplified music; no dancing; no smoking; wine only; Meeting Rm (–,–,–,15).

CAPACITIES: (Standing, Seated, Dinner dance, Theatre-style)

Royal College of Art SW7
£B-M, (600,450,350,–)
Kensington Gore
☎ (020) 7590 4118
🖰 www.rca.ac.uk
📧 galleries@rca.ac.uk
Large, white-walled galleries looking on to Kensington Gardens, which offer large, open spaces for modest-budget events – from a private view to a party – or are an ideal blank canvas within which to stage more lavish themed events. The third-floor Fellows' rooms suit smaller, formal occasions. / 2 am; available subject to constraints of current production; hirer's choice of caterer; smoking restricted; no red wine; Henry Moore Gallery (500,400,350,–); Gulbenkian Upper Gallery (350,200,100,–); Gulbenkian Lower Gallery (150,80,70,–); Senior Common Rm Dining Rm (150,80,–,–); Entrance Gallery (150,–,–,–).

Royal College of Music SW7
£M, (350,300,–,468)
Prince Consort Rd
☎ (020) 7591 4353
🖰 www.rcm.ac.uk
📧 jemptage@rcm.ac.uk
The Concert Hall and Britten Theatre of this grand institution by the Albert Hall are available for hire, particularly out of term time. / restricted availability, no weddings; list of caterers; no dancing; no smoking; Concert Hall (350,300,–,468); Britten Theatre (250,–,–,400).

Royal College of Pathologists SW1
£M-E, (150,80,–,100)
2 Carlton House Terr
☎ (020) 7451 6715
🖰 www.rcpath.org
📧 conference@rcpath.org
This Nash Terrace house was elegantly refurbished in understated modern style (maple panelling and pale grey walls) in 1993. It offers a prestigious central venue, whose terrace has an exceptional view.
/ 10.30pm; not available weekends; in-house caterers; no music; no dancing; no smoking;

Lecture Rm (150,80,–,100); Council Rm (100,50,–,50); Seminar Rm (40,20,–,30).

Royal College of Physicians NW1
£M-E, (500,240,–,320)
11 St Andrew's Place,
Regent's Park
☎ (020) 7935 1174
🖷 (020) 7224 0900
🖰 www.rcplondon.ac.uk
📧 meetingsandevents@
rcplondon.ac.uk
A Grade I listing makes this striking modern edifice, beside Regent's Park, quite a rarity. It also boasts a large garden. / 11pm; closed Aug; in-house caterers; no amplified music; no smoking; Osler Rm (400,240,–,320); Dorchester Library (300,–,–,–); Platt Rm (150,100,–,–); Garden (500,–,–,–).

Royal College of Radiologists W1
£M-E, (50,24,–,–)
38 Portland Pl
☎ (020) 7636 4432
🖷 (020) 7323 3110
🖰 www.rcr.ac.uk/enquiries
📧 enquiries@rcr.ac.uk
The basement of this Adam townhouse (circa 1776) has been modernised, but most of the remainder retains its original features and is decorated in country house style. Only the Council Chamber is really suitable for entertaining. / midnight; not available weekends; in-house caterers; no music; no dancing; no smoking; Council Chamber (–,24,–,–); Robens Rm (30,14,–,–).

Royal Court Theatre SW1
£M, (230,130,130,70)
Sloane Sq
☎ (020) 7565 5050
🖷 (020) 7565 5001
🖰 www.royalcourttheatre.com
📧 info@royalcourttheatre.com
An expensively revamped Victorian theatre, offering good facilities for a presentation in a smart location. It is available subject to constraints of the current production. / hirer's choice of caterer; smoking restricted; Balcony

Bar (70,–,–,70); Main Restaurant (230,130,130,–).

Royal Garden Hotel W8
£M-E, (650,426,360,550)
2-24 Kensington High St
☎ (020) 7937 8000
🖰 www.royalgardenhotel.co.uk
📠 banqueting@
royalgardenhotel.co.uk
Sweeping views over Kensington Gardens distinguish many of the rooms at this large, modern hotel. It has accommodation suitable for all but the largest functions, and is licensed for weddings. / I am; Palace Suite (550,426,360,550); Kensington Suite (130,108,80,120); 'The Tenth' Restaurant (–,110,110,–); Lancaster Suite (80,72,40,60); Bertie's Bar (50,–,–,–).

Royal Geographical Society SW7
£B-M, (400,230,130,750)
I Kensington Gore
☎ (020) 7591 3090
🖰 www.rgs.org/roomhire
📠 n.leevers@rgs.org
*A characterful building with a great South Kensington address, and quite reasonably priced too. The large garden will not again be available for summer functions until June 2004.
/ midnight; Lodge Catering; smoking restrict-*

ed; Main Hall (150,100,–,–); New Map Rm (150,60,–,–); Tea Rm (60,40,–,–); Council Rm (60,24,–,–); Theatre (–,–,–,750); Education Centre (–,130,–,–).

Royal Green Jackets W1
£B-M, (350,200,150,–)
56 Davies St
☎ (020) 7629 3674
🖷 (020) 7414 3488
This Mayfair TA outpost, just off Oxford Street, offers a large recently refurbished hall – is suited to Dinner Dances and Wedding Receptions and the like. The Club Bar is worth considering for stag nights, discos and so on. / restricted availability; I am; in-house caterers; Hall (350,200,150,–); Club Bar (100,–,–,–).

Royal Holloway College, Surrey
£B-M, (250,200,170,–)
Egham Hl, Egham
☎ 01784 443046
🖰 www.rhul.ac.uk/fm
📠 sales-office@rhul.ac.uk
The impressive Picture Gallery of this extraordinary Victorian confection (which claims to house the country's top collection of art of the period) makes a great venue for a dinner. Out of term you can use the adjoining Dining Hall, which is larger and,

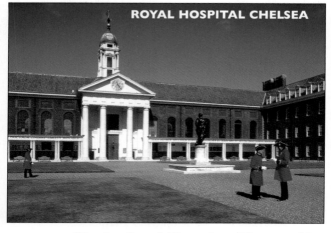

ROYAL HOSPITAL CHELSEA

CAPACITIES: (Standing, Seated, Dinner dance, Theatre-style)

when dressed, almost as impressive.
/ I am; in-house caterers; some restrictions
on music; some restrictions on dancing; no
smoking; Founder's Dining
Hall (250,200,170,–); Picture
Gallery (250,120,–,–).

Royal Horticultural Halls SW1
£B-M, (1800,800,750,200)
80 Vincent Sq
☎ (020) 7828 4125
⌂ www.horticultural-halls.co.uk
✉ maugiel@rhs.org.uk
The RHS has two very different halls.
The grander of the two is the Lindley,
which has recently been extensively
refurbished and upgraded. Over the
road, the '30s Lawrence Hall is a
glass and concrete hangar which
would not be wholly out of place in a
sci-fi 'B' movie. Both are much in
demand for fairs and events. / 11pm;
list of caterers; Lawrence
Hall (1800,800,750,–); Lindley
Hall (700,450,350,–); Lecture
Theatre (–,–,–,200).

Royal Hospital Chelsea SW3
£M-E, (500,300,–,400)
Royal Hospital Rd
☎ (020) 7881 5298
🖷 (020) 7881 5319
⌂ www.chelsea-pensioners.org.uk
✉ eventsao@chelsea-
    pensioners.org.uk
Charles II founded this impressive
hospital, designed by Wren, as a
home for old soldiers. That primary
role today – as the home of the
Chelsea Pensioner – continues to this
day. Its impressive buildings sit in 66
acres of charming grounds. A number of event facilities are available.
See the advertisement opposite. / list
of caterers; no smoking; Great
Hall (500,300,–,–); Chapel (–,–,–,400); State
Apartments (250,100,–,–);
Grounds (10000,–,–,–).

Royal Institute of British Architects W1
£M-E, (500,284,–,100)
66 Portland Pl
☎ (020) 7307 3888
⌂ www.riba-venues.com
✉ venues@inst.riba.org
This is an elegant '30s building, and
its central (Florence) hall is now once
again available as an impressive
venue for receptions and dinners. A
large terrace and an impressive café
space are among other accommodation also available for hire. / 11pm; not
available Sun; Milburns; no smoking; Florence
Hall (500,250,–,–); Jarvis Hall (–,284,–,–);
South Rm (70,30,–,70); Conference
Rm (100,70,–,100); Committee
Rm (–,20,–,40); Aston (–,22,–,40); Student
Gallery (–,10,–,10); Professional
Gallery (–,15,–,25); Canal
Chamber (–,20,–,60).

Royal Institution of Great Britain W1
£B-M, (150,90,–,430)
21 Albemarle St
☎ (020) 7409 2992
⌂ www.rigb.org
✉ nicola@rigb.org
The Mayfair institution, where
Faraday discovered electricity, offers
impressive accommodation with lots
of creaky charm. / 10pm; not available
weekends; Owen Bros; no dancing; no smok-
ing; Ante Rm (70,–,–,–); Main
Library (120,90,–,50); Council
Rm (35,20,–,–); Conversation
Rm (80,35,–,–); Long Library & Red
Corridor (150,–,–,–); Faraday Lecture
Theatre (–,–,–,430); Bernard Sunley
Theatre (–,–,–,100).

Royal Lancaster W2
£M-E, (2500,1050,1000,–)
Lancaster Terr
☎ (020) 7262 6737
🖷 (020) 7724 3191
⌂ www.royallancaster.com
✉ sales@royallancaster.com
This blot on the Hyde Park landscape has one of the largest ballrooms in town (and the whole building is very much nicer than the exte-
rior might lead one to expect). Some
smaller function rooms are being cre-

ated during 2004. / 2 am; Nine Kings
Suite (1500,780,650,–); Westbourne
Suite (1300,1000,520,–); Gloucester
Suite (200,70,70,–).

Royal Majestic Suite NW6

£M, (300,220,180,–)
196 Willesden Ln
☎ (020) 8459 3276
🖷 (020) 8451 0902
📧 hgroyalmajestic@ad.com
*Pleasant, well-maintained kosher
banqueting hall in Willesden.* / 12.30
am; not available Fri, not Sat in Summer; in-
house caterers; Ground
Floor (300,220,180,–); First
Floor (200,70,70,–).

Royal National Theatre SE1

£M, (1200,240,–,1150)
South Bank
☎ (020) 7452 3560
🖷 (020) 7452 3565
🖰 www.nationaltheatre.org.uk
📧 functions@
    nationaltheatre.org.uk
*Most entertaining here happens
around shows, but at other times the
theatre's spaces are available for
events. The Mezzanine restaurant
and the Terrace Bar café suit functions best (being used particularly for
daytime parties), while the Olivier
Stalls offer a pleasant, lofty foyer-
space for a reception (with access to
an outside terrace).* / 1 am; available
subject to constraints of current production;
in-house caterers; smoking restricted; Olivier
Stalls Foyer (500,160,–,80); Terrace
Café (220,120,–,–);
Mezzanine (180,110,–,–); Olivier Circle
Foyer (50,–,–,–); Richardson
Rm (25,14,–,20); Ashcroft (30,30,–,35);
Lyttelton Exhibition Level (350,240,–,300).

Royal Observatory SE10

£E, (150,60,–,–)
The Avenue, Greenwich Park
☎ (020) 8312 6693
🖷 (020) 8812 6572
🖰 www.nmm.ac.uk/hospitality
📧 events@nmm.ac.uk

*Survey London from this lofty 0° van-
tage-point in Greenwich Park. The
charming, top-floor Octagon room is
one of the few surviving Wren interiors, and its long, narrow windows
have one of the best views of the
metropolis. Guests can enjoy tele-
scope viewings, with the
Observatory's team of astronomers.*
/ midnight; available eves only; list of caterers;
no amplified music; no dancing; no smoking;
no red wine.

Royal Opera House WC2

£M-E, (600,350,–,400)
Bow St
☎ (020) 7219 9150
🖷 (020) 7212 9172
🖰 www.royaloperahouse.org
📧 sarahphilips@roh.org.uk
*Even if you leave the artistic attrac-
tions out of account, the new ROH is
a major entertainment centre, and
includes civil weddings (and kosher
weddings) and barbecues among its
private activities. The main constraint, of course, is that most of the
facilities are not available during performances. The house is dark some
evenings, though, and the Clore
Studio can often be made available
regardless.* / Searcy's; no smoking; Vilar
Floral Hall (600,350,–,350); Clore
Studio (–,200,–,170); Royal Opera House
Café & Restaurant (–,150,–,–); Linbury
Studio Theatre (–,–,–,400); Crush
Rm (160,120,–,–); Trust Dining Rms (x8, of
which 4 interlink) (–,10,–,–);
Terrace (400,–,–,–).

Royal Over-Seas League SW1

£B-M, (200,200,100,–)
Park Pl, St James's St
☎ (020) 7495 2282 extn 322
🖰 www.rosl.org.uk
📧 thanmer@rosl.org.uk
*A reasonable degree of grandeur, rel-
atively affordably, is the attraction of
this clubby establishment near the
Ritz. The smaller rooms of the older
buildings, overlooking Green Park,
are better suited to entertaining than
the larger ones in the '30s annexe.*
/ 11pm; in-house caterers; Hall of India &

CAPACITIES: (Standing, Seated, Dinner dance, Theatre-style)

Pakistan (200,200,100,–); St Andrew's
Hall (150,80,80,–); Wrench (45,40,–,–);
Mountbatten Rutland (45,32,–,–); Bennet-
Clark (30,16,–,–); Park (15,11,–,–).

Royal Parks Agency W2
Rangers Lodge, Hyde Park
☎ (020) 7298 2113
🖨 (020) 7402 3298
🖑 www.royalparks.gov.uk
✉ events@royalparks.gsi.gov.uk
The Royal Parks (which include
Hyde, Green, St James's and
Greenwich) were traditionally averse
to corporate functions, but nowadays
applications for suitable corporate
uses will be entertained. Private functions, however, will still not be considered. / charities & companies only; list of
caterers.

Royal Society of Arts WC2
£M, (250,120,100,200)
8 John Adam St
☎ (020) 7839 5049
🖑 www.theplacetomeet.org.uk
✉ conference@rsa.org.uk
Five converted c18 houses, just off
the Strand, whose vaults offer most
flexibility for functions (even if the
space is rather broken up). The other
accommodation comprises white-
walled galleries and period rooms. / 1
am; in-house caterers; smoking restricted;
Great Rm (–,–,–,200); Benjamin Franklin
Rm (150,100,60,75); Vault 1 (100,60,–,–);
Tavern Rm (50,30,–,40); Folkestone
Rm (50,30,–,–); Gallery (70,–,–,–).

Royal Statistical Society EC1
£M, (150,100,–,200)
12 Errol St
☎ (020) 7614 3947
🖑 www.rss.org.uk
✉ j.lewis@rss.org.uk
Following conversion of a former
Victorian school, the Barbican headquarters of the Royal Statistical
Society now provides a light, airy
working environment for meetings
and small conferences. / 10pm; hirer's
choice of caterer (in-house available);

no smoking; Lecture
Theatre (250,100,–,200); Council
Chamber (80,40,–,60); New Meeting
Rm (25,16,–,20); Old Meeting Rm (–,14,–,–);
Basement (150,50,–,–).

RSJ SE1
£M, (–,45,–,–)
13A Coin St
☎ (020) 7928 4554
🖨 (020) 7401 2455
🖑 www.rsj.uk.com
✉ sallywebber@rsj.uk.com
This modern British South Bank
restaurant offers good value for
money (and, for wine enthusiasts, a
collection of 250 wines from the
Loire). The ground floor private room
benefits from natural light. / no cigars
or pipes; Private Rm (Basement) (–,45,–,–);
Private Rm (Ground Floor) (–,24,–,–).

The Rubens SW1
£M, (250,160,160,–)
39 Buckingham Palace Rd
☎ (020) 7834 6600
🖨 (020) 7233 6037
🖑 www.redcarnationhotels.com
✉ meetrb@rchmail.com
Facing the Royal Mews, this Victoria
hotel has agreeable banqueting facilities that are fairly traditional in style.
/ midnight; Old Masters
Restaurant (200,160,160,–); Rembrandt
Rm (80,60,–,–); Rubens (40,30,–,–);
Library (35,17,–,–); Van Dyke (90,80,–,–).

Rules WC2
£M, (24,24,–,–)
35 Maiden Ln
☎ (020) 7379 0258
🖨 (020) 7497 1081
🖑 www.rules.co.uk
✉ pr@rules.co.uk
Claiming to be London's oldest
restaurant, this ultra-traditional, panelled English establishment in Covent
Garden has very attractive private
dining rooms. / Green Rm (24,24,–,–);
King Edward VII Rm (–,18,–,–); Charles
Dickens Rm (–,16,–,–).

PRIVATE VENUES

RUSI Building SW1
£M, (200,150,50,150)
Whitehall
☎ (020) 7747 2622
🖰 www.rusi.org
📧 venue@rusi.org
The airy D-shaped Lecture Theatre at these Whitehall premises is particularly suited to receptions (and has held discos). The clubby Library (with books, for once) is a cosy and interesting place for a formal dinner, and the Council Room would elegantly accommodate a dinner party. / Lodge Catering; smoking restricted; Lecture Theatre (200,150,–,–); Reading Rm (80,40,–,–); Library (100,60,–,–); Duke of Wellington Rm (180,80,50,150).

The Saatchi Gallery SE1
£M-E, (1500,250,–,400)
County Hall, Belvedere Rd
☎ (020) 7608 0080
🖰 www.timebased.co.uk
📧 events@timebased.co.uk
Views of the Thames, the London Eye and Houses of Parliament are among the attractions of this gallery now housed in the former GLC building, whatever you happen to think of the art on display at the time. / midnight; list of caterers; no dancing; no smoking; Main Gallery (750,250,–,400); Council Chamber (–,–,–,725); Members Terrace (1000,–,–,–).

Saddlers' Hall EC2
£M-E, (250,139,–,–)
40 Gutter Ln
☎ (020) 7726 8661
🖷 (020) 7600 0386
🖰 www.saddlersco.co.uk
📧 hallmanager@
saddlersco.co.uk
This traditional livery company hall, erected in the '50s, is now made available to a less restrictive range of hirers than was once the case. / charities & companies only; 11pm; weekdays only; list of caterers; no amplified music; no dancing.

Sadler's Wells Theatre EC1
£M-E, (300,200,–,180)
Rosebery Av
☎ (020) 7863 8065
🖷 (020) 7863 8061
🖰 www.sadlerswells.com
📧 events@sadlerswells.com
A striking modern theatre on the fringe of Islington, with a good range of rooms for presentations, dinners and receptions. / 11pm; in-house caterers; no smoking; Lillian Bayliss Theatre (–,–,–,180); Cable & Wireless Rm (200,90,–,100); Fonteyn Rm (–,30,–,30); Sackler Rm (–,15,–,–); Cripplegate Rm (–,15,–,–); Mezzanine Area (300,–,–,–); Cahn Lecture Th (75,–,–,–); Rehearsal Studios (100,–,–,–).

St Mary's Church W1
£M, (600,300,300,600)
Wyndham Place, Off York St
☎ (020) 7431 7375
🖷 (020) 7794 9655
🖰 www.platinumevents.co.uk
📧 jr@platinumevents.co.uk
Near Bryanston Square, a recently refurbished deconsecrated church, suited to event hire. / 6pm Mon-Fri,10.30pm Sat; not available Sun; Scott Harris; no smoking.

Salters' Hall EC2
£M-E, (300,120,–,120)
4 Fore St
☎ (020) 7588 5216
🖰 www.salters.co.uk
📧 beadle@salters.co.uk
The Salters' Company now makes its intriguingly designed 1970s hall rather more available for functions than was once the case. This may in due course include being licensed for civil weddings. / hirer's choice of caterer; no dancing; Mail Hall (200,120,–,120); Court Rm (100,30,–,60).

CAPACITIES: (Standing, Seated, Dinner dance, Theatre-style)

The Sanctuary WC2
£M-E, (200,100,–,–)
12 Floral St
☎ (0870) 063 0300
🖳 (01442) 430301
🖱 www.thesanctuary.co.uk
✉ info@thesanctuary.co.uk
This luxury Covent Garden health spa is among the most exotic settings central London affords. You can twist by the pool (complete with palms and tropical fish). Private drinks parties are, in fact, the only times men are allowed on the premises. / 11pm; available after 6pm, Mon & Tue; in-house caterers; no amplified music; no dancing; smoking restricted.

The Savoy WC2
£M-E, (800,500,375,–)
Strand
☎ (020) 7836 4343
🖱 www.savoy.com
✉ imichman@the-savoygroup.co.uk
This famous riverside hotel remains the default choice for many grander corporate and social events – it has a range of characterful accommodation in differing period styles, some with a river view. / 1am; Lancaster Rm (800,500,375,–); Abraham Lincoln & Manhattan Rms (400,200,150,–); River Rm (350,120,120,–); Beaufort (120,80,–,–); Pinafore (80,50,–,–); Gondoliers (50,30,–,–); Mikado (35,18,–,–); Patience (30,24,–,–); Iolanthe (25,12,–,–); Sorcerer (18,6,–,–).

Sartoria W1
£M-E, (150,150,120,–)
20 Savile Row
☎ (020) 7534 7000
🖳 (020) 7534 7070
This smart Conran restaurant draws its tailoring theme from the world-famous street in which it is situated. There are two interconnecting private rooms, or you may be able to hire the whole place. / Private Rms (both) (70,40,–,–); Private Rm (x2) (35,20,–,–).

School of Pharmacy WC1
£B-M, (300,150,100,–)
29-39 Brunswick Sq
☎ (020) 7753 5800
🖱 www.ulsop.ac.uk
✉ glenda.bray@ulsop.ac.uk
A large hall – with large windows facing onto Brunswick Square – with potential for many kinds of function. / midnight; available eves, weekends; in-house caterers; Refectory (300,150,100,–).

Science Museum SW7
£M-E, (2000,500,450,430)
Exhibition Rd
☎ (020) 7942 4340
🖱 www.sciencemuseum.org.uk
✉ science.eventsoffice@nmsi.ac.uk
A vast museum offering flexible party and facilities. The galleries have the added bonus of being pre-themed. / 11.30pm; list of caterers; smoking restricted; Flight Gallery (500,350,300,–); East Hall (600,200,200,–); Space Gallery (250,90,–,–); Directors Suite (–,90,–,100); Imax Cinema (–,–,–,430); Challenge of Materials (400,250,–,–); Making The World Modern (2000,500,350,–); Wellcome Wing (2000,500,450,–).

Savile Club W1
£M-E, (300,160,160,110)
69 Brook St
☎ (020) 7629 5462
🖳 (020) 7499 7087
🖱 www.savileclub.co.uk
✉ info@savileclub.co.uk
A Georgian Mayfair house, remodelled in opulent Gallic style at the end of the 19th century, offering a characterful setting for private events. / midnight; in-house caterers; Members Dining Rm & Ballroom (300,160,160,110); Ballroom (100,60,60,110); Members Dining Rm (150,60,60,110); Elgar Rm (30,12,–,25).

PRIVATE VENUES

Scotch Malt Whisky Society EC1
£M, (50,35,–,35)
Members' Room, 19 Greville St
☎ (020) 7831 4447
🖰 www.smws.com
✉ events@smws.com
You don't have to finish with a whisky tasting if you entertain in these elegant Clerkenwell rooms. Rude not to, though! / *11pm; in-house caterers; no amplified music; no dancing; Members' Rm (50,35,–,–); Tasting Rm (27,16,–,24); Still Rm (40,24,–,35).*

Scotts W1
£M-E, (220,140,–,–)
20 Mount St
☎ (020) 7629 5248
🖨 (020) 7499 8246
This famous and long-established Mayfair restaurant, which has been through a couple of changes of ownership in recent times, is a smart venue well suited to a party. There's only one private room (downstairs), but you can also hire the restaurant itself, or the smartly refurbished cocktail bar. / *Restaurant (220,140,–,–); Cocktail Bar (60,–,–,–); Club Rm (–,22,–,–).*

Seashell NW1
£B, (–,30,–,–)
49-51 Lisson Grove
☎ (020) 7724 1063
🖨 (020) 7724 9071
If you want to make a party feast on our national dish, London's most famous chippy has a downstairs private room. / *not available Sun eves; Downstairs Rm (–,30,–,–).*

The Selfridge Hotel W1
£M, (300,216,200,200)
Orchard St
☎ (020) 7408 2080
🖨 (020) 7499 8358
🖰 www.thistlehotels.com
✉ mande.marblearch@ thistle.co.uk
The Drawing Room (a large, light, traditional dining room) of this woody modern hotel behind the department store is the best function facility. The long, divisible Selfridge Suite offers very flexible space. / *11pm; Selfridge Suite (300,216,200,–); Drawing Rm (35,20,–,–); Conservatory (25,10,–,–); Chitten (40,25,–,42); Cleaveland (120,96,60,–); Cheviot (100,72,–,–); Cotswold (–,36,–,–).*

Serpentine Gallery W2
£M-E, (350,150,–,–)
Kensington Gdns
☎ (020) 7402 6075
🖨 (020) 7402 4103
🖰 www.serpentinegallery.org
✉ elizabeth@ serpentinegallery.org
The Gallery, with its idyllic location for a summer function, is well suited to sedate corporate entertaining. From Jun-Sep, capacity is extended by the addition of a temporary 'structure', designed by a world renowned architect. / *companies, patrons & benefactors only; 11pm; available from 6.30pm; list of caterers; no amplified music; no dancing; no smoking.*

76 Portland Place W1
£M, (170,130,100,170)
76 Portland Place
☎ (020) 7470 4884
🖰 www.76portlandplace.com
✉ enquiries@ 76portlandplace.com
The conference and banqueting facility of the Institute of Physics is marketed as an independent venture. The Rutherford Room is a flexible conference or presentation space, complemented by a separate catering suite, which can also be used independently. / *10pm; evenings only; smoking restricted; Rutherford Suite (–,–,–,170); Catering Suite (170,140,100,–); Franklin (70,–,–,100); Herschel (–,30,–,40); Faraday Rm (–,12,–,–).*

CAPACITIES: (Standing, Seated, Dinner dance, Theatre-style)

Shaftesbury Theatre WC2
£M, (150,100,–,1402)
210 Shaftesbury Av
☎ (020) 7379 3345
🖷 (020) 7836 8181
📠 mhone@
    toc.dltentertainment.co.uk
Large Edwardian theatre, near Piccadilly Circus, available for hire subject to the constraints of performances. / available subject to constraints of current production; hirer's choice of caterer (in-house available); smoking restricted; Bars (150,100,–,–).

Shakespeare's Globe SE1
£M, (550,270,270,270)
21 New Globe Walk
☎ (020) 7902 1503
🖷 (020) 7902 1460
🖰 www.shakespeares-globe.org
📠 events@
    shakespearesglobe.com
The original theatre may have survived for only a decade and a half (1599-1613), but Sam Wanamaker's Southwark re-creation has certainly captured people's imaginations. It offers a number of interesting venues for events. The airy Balcony Room has a view of St Paul's. For a more obviously theatrical setting, the Foyers are available (but the main one is only during the winter season). / 11.30pm; in-house caterers; no amplified music during theatre season; no smoking; Balcony Rm (120,70,–,70); Upper Foyer (120,–,–,–); Main Foyer (300,–,–,–); Café (–,100,–,–); Lecture Theatre (–,–,–,110).

Shakespeare's UnderGlobe SE1
£M-E, (650,270,270,270)
New Globe Walk
☎ (020) 7902 1503
🖷 (020) 7902 1460
🖰 www.shakespeares-globe.org
📠 events@
    shakespearesglobe.com
Beneath the South Bank's 'new' Globe Theatre, an exhibition devoted to the life of the Bard. This large and flexible space is most suitable for awards ceremonies and large dinners. / no costumes; 11.30pm; in-house caterers; no smoking; Underglobe (650,270,270,270).

Shampers W1
£B, (100,45,–,–)
4 Kingly St
☎ (020) 7437 1692
🖷 (020) 7287 1097
You can organise private dinners and receptions in the basement restaurant of this comfortably worn-in Soho wine bar. At weekends, the whole place is available. / midnight; Restaurant (60,45,–,–).

Shelleys W1
£B, (70,40,–,–)
10 Stafford St
☎ (020) 7493 0337
The pleasant basement bar of this Mayfair inn is suitable for informal functions. / 11.30pm, Fri & Sat 1am.

Shepherd's SW1
£M, (–,32,–,–)
Marsham Court, Marsham St
☎ (020) 7834 9552
🖷 (020) 7233 6047
🖰 www.langansrestaurants.co.uk
Bright, art-filled and clubby, this English restaurant in Westminster has a comfortable private salon, which is a shade grander than the main dining room. / Private Rm (–,32,–,–).

Sheraton Belgravia SW1
£M, (75,22,–,–)
20 Chesham Pl
☎ (020) 7235 6040
🖷 (020) 7290 7566
🖰 www.sheraton.com
📠 events.centrallondon@
    sheraton.com
For a small dinner or reception this discreetly-located Belgravia hotel has some serviceable private rooms. / 1.30 am; no amplified music; no dancing; Study and Library (75,18,–,–); Meeting Rm (–,8,–,–); Restaurant (–,30,–,–); Study (–,8,–,–).

Sheraton Park Tower SW1
£M-E, (150,120,80,80)
101 Knightsbridge
☎ (020) 7235 8050
🕭 www.sheraton.com
✉ fiona.rae@sheraton.com
Prominent, cylindrical Knightsbridge luxury hotel with a range of first floor function rooms in '70s/traditional style. The Trianon Room has the benefit of a terrace overlooking Lowndes Square, which may be used for barbecues. / I am; Trianon Rm (150,120,80,80); Buckingham Rm (60,36,–,40); Explorers (40,16,–,25); Balmoral (40,12,–,20).

Ship SW18
£B-M, (30,20,–,–)
41 Jews Row
☎ (020) 8870 9667
🕭 (020) 8874 9055
🕭 www.theship.co.uk
✉ drinks@theship.co.uk
This very popular younger-scene Wandsworth pub has a permanent marquee attached, which can be used for private functions. In summer, you can also have drinks parties outside. / 11pm; Garden (60,–,–,–).

Shillibeer's N7
£B-M, (400,320,–,–)
Carpenter's Mews, North Road
☎ (020) 7700 1858
🕭 (020) 7700 2710
Locations don't come more recherché than this converted industrial building in the no-man's-land between Islington and Holloway (created as the garage for the world's first-ever horse-drawn buses). It's a funky space, though, with the option of a private room, or for a large 'do' taking the whole place. Lots of parking is an added plus. / no amplified music; no dancing; Private Room (75,55,–,–).

Shumi SW1
£M-E, (–,8,–,–)
23 St James's St
☎ (020) 7747 9380
🕭 (020) 7747 9839
🕭 www.shumi-london.com
If Hush (same backers) is anything to go by, this new Italo/Oriental restaurant – in the St James's landmark building recently occupied by Che – is set to be quite a fashionable success. The only private dining option, however, is the chef's table.

CAPACITIES: (Standing, Seated, Dinner dance, Theatre-style)

Simon Drake's House of Magic SE17
£M, (180,95,–,–)
PO Box 20457
☎ (020) 7735 4777
🖱 www.houseofmagic.co.uk
📧 info@houseofmagic.co.uk
Guests are ferried to a 'secret location' in blacked-out buses before being entertained by magic, fortune telling, and tours of the haunted cellar. / list of caterers; no live bands; no dancing.

Simpsons Tavern EC3
£B, (50,74,–,–)
Ball Court, 38 1/2 Cornhill
☎ (020) 7626 9985
🖨 (020) 7626 3736
This popular Dickensian City institution offers two compact bars for function use. The restaurant is characterful, but the boothed seating reduces suitability for functions. / no music; Amy's Bar or Wine Bar (40,–,–,–); Restaurant (–,74,–,–); Grill (–,48,–,–); Courtyard (60,–,–,–).

Simpsons-in-the-Strand WC2
£M, (500,270,200,–)
100 Strand
☎ (020) 7836 9112
🖨 (020) 7836 1381
🖱 www.savoy-group.co.uk
A famously solidly Edwardian English restaurant. The Bishops' Room downstairs is one of the oldest in London, and perfect for a mid-sized dinner. / 1 am; Regency Rm (200,150,80,–); Bishops' Rm (150,50,–,–).

Singapura
£M
🖱 www.singapuras.co.uk
📧 john@singapuras.co.uk
31 Broadgate Circle, EC2
☎ (020) 7256 5045 (80,50,50,–)
1-2 Limeburner Ln, EC4
☎ (020) 7329 1133(250,150,–,150)
78-79 Leadenhall St, EC3
☎ (020) 7929 0089
A chain of City Singaporean restaurants, where friendly service has long been a particular plus. See the advertisement opposite. / 11pm; Main Rm (150,120,80,120); Private Rm (12,12,–,12).

Sir John Soane's Museum WC2
£E, (80,30,–,–)
13 Lincoln's Inn Fields
☎ (020) 7405 2107
🖨 (020) 7831 3957
🖱 www.soane.org
📧 jbrock@soane.org.uk
On a very restricted basis, one of the most remarkable houses in the world is made available, at quite an expense, for parties of between 24 and 30 people. A pre-dinner tour of Soane's Egyptian treasures and paintings (including the original Rake's Progress) can be arranged, and dinner is served in the dark, candlelit and very antique dining room and library. / very restricted availability; midnight; evenings only Tue-Sat; list of caterers; no amplified music; no dancing; no smoking.

Six Hamilton Place W1
£M, (220,120,120,100)
6 Hamilton Pl, Park Ln
☎ (020) 7499 6555
🖱 www.sixhamiltonplace.com
📧 lmead@london-clubs.co.uk
A discreet Mayfair venue. NB Being refurbished during 2004. / 3 am; in-house caterers; Red Rm (220,120,–,100).

PRIVATE VENUES

606 Club SW10
£B-M, (165,135,–,–)
90 Lots Rd
☎ (020) 7352 5953
🖱 www.606club.co.uk
✉ jazz@606club.co.uk

*Cellar jazz club/restaurant,
intriguingly located down an
anonymous staircase, opposite
Chelsea's Lots Road power station.
For private hires there is no fee –
just a minimum catering-spend. / 2
am; not available Fri & Sat; in-house caterers.*

Six-13 W1
£M, (300,70,–,–)
19 Wigmore St
☎ (020) 7629 6133
🖱 www.six13.com
*Central London's only upmarket
kosher restaurant offers flexible
accommodation for dinners of various sizes. / Lower Ground Floor (–,60,–,–);
Private Rm (–,20,–,–).*

Sketch W1
£M-E, (700,150,150,200)
9 Conduit Street
☎ 0870 777 4488
🖨 0870 777 4400
✉ emilyg@sketch.uk.com
*Did they spend £10m or £20m
doing up this Grade I listed Mayfair
building as a trendy bar/restaurant?
Whichever rumour is correct, it's certainly been a hit with the meejah
crowd, with the SciFi ground bar particularly lending itself to events. If
you have really deep pockets you can
have a meal in the stratospherically
expensive Lecture room (either privately or in the semi-private Library
section)... or just take over the
whole building. / ; in-house caterers;
Gallery (250,150,150,200); Lecture Rm
(Library) (–,24,–,–); Lecture Rm (–,45,–,–);
Parlour (120,37,–,–).*

Skinners' Hall EC4
£M-E, (300,170,170,–)
8 Dowgate HI
☎ (020) 7213 0553
🖨 (020) 7213 0568
🖱 www.skinnershall.co.uk
✉ sales@skinnershall.co.uk

*Imposing but charming, the Skinners'
Company's accommodation near
Cannon Street, entered via a courtyard, offers a number of possibilities.
The restored c17 Hall (with Victorian
murals) is rich and red. Other rooms
are grand, in a relaxed country
house style, and there is a modern
roof garden, with fountain, for fair-
weather receptions. A wedding
license has been applied for. / midnight; not available Sun; Party Ingredients;
no smoking; Banquet Hall (300,170,120,–);
Old Court Rm (120,50,–,–); Roof
Garden (120,–,–,–); Outer Hall (120,–,–,–);
Parlour (50,12,–,–).*

Slug & Lettuce N1
£B, (130,50,–,–)
1 Islington Gn
☎ (020) 7226 3864
🖱 www.slugandlettuce.co.uk
✉ islingtonsl@sfigroup.co.uk
*Above a branch of the bar chain, a
warm and homely room, with sofas,
overlooking Islington Green. / 11pm.*

Smith's of
Smithfield EC1
£M-E, (900,130,130,–)
67-77 Charterhouse St
☎ (020) 7236 7666
🖨 (020) 7236 0488
🖱 www.smithsofsmithfield.com
✉ natasha@
smithsofsmithfield.com
This four-floor Smithfield warehouse-

CAPACITIES: (Standing, Seated, Dinner dance, Theatre-style)

conversion bar/restaurant offers a variety of settings for events. Most spectacular is the top floor, with its open-air terrace. / *Cocktail Bar (150,–,–,–); Private Rm (50,26,–,–); Top Floor (300,80,80,–).*

So.uk Soho W1
£M, (400,–,–,–)
93-107 Shaftesbury Avenue
☎ (020) 7494 3040
🖥 (020) 7494 3050
🖲 www.so-uk.co.uk
This Moroccan-themed venue is the successor to Teatro restaurant (whose adjacent members' bar continues under that name). The clubby décor is fairly similar throughout, and events generally take place in the loungey bar/restaurant. For large events, they will sometimes – given sufficient notice for their members – make the whole venue available. / ; 3 am; in-house caterers; So.uk Restaurant (250,–,–,–).

Soho House W1
£M, (120,30,–,–)
40 Greek St
☎ (020) 7734 5188
🖲 www.sohohouse.com
🖂 reception@sohohouse.com
Although this is mainly a (trendy) members' club, it does offer three rooms available for general hire. / members club; 3 am; not available Sun; in-house caterers; Bar (120,–,–,–); Dining Rm (–,30,–,–); Roof Deck (80,–,–,–).

Somerset House WC2
£M-E, (200,100,–,–)
Strand
☎ (020) 7836 8686
🖥 (020) 7836 7613
🖲 www.somerset-house.org.uk
🖂 corporate.events@ somerset-house.org.uk
This great c18 palace of bureaucracy now comprises one of the nicest spaces in the heart of London, and offers a couple of interesting possibilities for entertaining. / 11pm; evenings only; list of caterers; no dancing; no smoking; Seamen's Waiting Hall (200,100,–,–);

Hermitage Rms (60,22,–,–); Courtyard (2000,850,–,–).

Sotheby's W1
£M-E, (400,250,–,–)
34 New Bond St
☎ (020) 7293 5000
🖲 www.sothebys.com
🖂 jennifer.conner@ sothebys.com
The Mayfair auctioneers restricts function use of their galleries to a few occasions a year, generally by companies or charities. / very restricted availability; midnight; list of caterers; no amplified music; no dancing; no smoking.

Souk WC2
£B-M, (–,110,–,–)
27 Litchfield St
☎ (020) 7240 1796
🖥 (020) 7240 3382
🖲 www.souk.net
For a budget party meal in the heart of the west end, it's hard to best this younger-scene Moroccan a few doors down from the Ivy. It has lots of nooks and crannies for different sized tables, or – so long as you are close to their capacity – you could book the whole place out in advance.

Sound W1
£M, (625,300,300,200)
Swiss Centre, Leicester Sq
☎ (020) 7287 1010
🖲 www.soundlondon.com
🖂 info@soundlondon.com
Formerly called Sound Republic, this centrally-located, high-tech venue includes a bar/restaurant, a disco and a broadcast studio. / 3 am; in-house caterers; Restaurant & Bar (600,300,300,200); Blue Rm (125,80,–,60); Club Sound (625,200,–,150); Sound Bar (125,60,–,–).

PRIVATE VENUES

South London Gallery SE5
£M, (300,200,150,–)
65 Peckham Rd
☎ (020) 7703 6120
🖷 (020) 7252 4730
🖑 www.southlondongallery.org
🖂 mail@southlondongallery.org
A purpose-built Victorian gallery, naturally top-lit, associated with some of the BritArt 'greats'. NB Available from spring 2004. / no stag nights; hirer's choice of caterer; no amplified music; no smoking; Inside (300,200,150,–); Inside And Marquee (400,250,–,–).

Southwark Cathedral SE1
£B-M, (400,80,–,80)
Montague Close
☎ (020) 7367 6722
🖑 www.dswark.org/cathedral
🖂 cathedral@dswark.org.uk
A recent renovation has smartened up this ancient cathedral, and added a pleasant new library, which is a harmonious space for smaller gatherings. / 10.30pm; not available Sun; in-house caterers; no amplified music; no dancing; no smoking; Restaurant (120,80,–,–); Library (120,60,–,80); Seminar Rm (50,20,–,40); Courtyard (400,–,–,–).

Southwark Tavern SE1
£B, (70,30,–,–)
22 Southwark St
☎ (020) 7403 0257
By Borough Market, a traditional boozer with an atmospheric, if quite cramped, cellar bar, available for hire. / 11pm; Cellar Bar (70,30,–,–).

Spaghetti House W1
£B, (–,150,–,–)
15 Goodge St
☎ (020) 7636 6582
🖷 (020) 7436 4908
A three-floor Fitzrovia monument to '50s Italian restaurant-kitsch, offering two floors for private hire. / no music; no dancing; Private Floor (x 2) (–,40,–,–).

Spencer House SW1
£E, (450,150,132,–)
27 St James's Pl
☎ (020) 7514 1964
🖷 (020) 7409 2952
🖑 www.spencerhouse.co.uk
🖂 events@ritcap.co.uk
A great c18 palace, bordering Green Park, restored in the mid-'80s to its former glory (with paintings from the Royal collection and furniture on loan from the V&A). Dancing can occasionally be arranged in a marquee in the garden or on the terrace. / no stilettos; midnight; evenings only Sun; in-house caterers; dancing on terrace only; smoking restricted; Great Rm (–,90,–,–); Lady Spencer's Rm (–,36,–,–); Dining Rm (–,24,–,–); Music Rm (–,24,–,–).

Spring Grove House, Middx
£M, (120,80,–,–)
West Thames College, London Rd, Isleworth
☎ (020) 8569 7173
🖷 (020) 8847 2421
🖑 www.west-thames.ac.uk
🖂 ianb@west-thames.ac.uk
The Georgian house of Sir Joseph Banks (creator of Kew Gardens), remodelled in Victorian times, and now part of West Thames College. It is used for social and business events. The Winter Garden Room, licensed for weddings, features potted palms, a domed glass ceiling and a mosaic floor. / no 21sts; midnight; closed Sun; hirer's choice of caterer (in-house available); smoking restricted; Winter Garden Rm (100,80,–,–); Music Rm (50,50,–,–); Banks Suite (60,60,–,–); Board Rm (–,20,–,–); Directors Rm (–,12,–,–); Captain Cook's Rm (–,15,–,–).

The Square W1
£M-E, (–,18,–,–)
6-10 Bruton St
☎ (020) 7495 7100
🖷 (020) 7495 7150
🖑 www.squarerestaurant.com
🖂 info@squarerestaurant.com
One of London's leading French restaurants, especially popular for business. Its Mayfair premises have

CAPACITIES: (Standing, Seated, Dinner dance, Theatre-style)

an internal private room. / Private
Rm (–,18,–,–).

SS Great Britain, Bristol
£M, (200,150,150,–)
Great Western Dock
☎ 01179 225737
🖷 01179 255788
⌖ www.ss-great-britain.com
✉ enquiries@
ss-great-britain.com
No longer ruling the waves, the
world's first iron-hulled, screw pro-
peller-driven, steam-powered passen-
ger liner offers an unusual venue for
your party (or quite an unusual place
to get married). / midnight; in-house
caterers; no smoking; Dining
Saloon (200,150,150,–); Hayward
Saloon (70,50,–,–).

St Andrew's Court House EC4
£M, (130,80,–,60)
5 St Andrew St
☎ (020) 7353 5200
⌖ www.standrewholborn.org.uk
✉ della@
standrewholborn.org.uk
This 1870 courthouse (refurbished in
1996), located just off Holborn
Circus, incorporates remains of earlier buildings – the ornate and colourful fireplace in the Court Room, for
example, is Jacobean. / no weddings or
stag nights; list of caterers; no amplified
music; no dancing; Court Rm (130,80,–,60);
Archive Rm (50,20,–,15).

St Bartholomew's Hospital EC1
£M, (300,190,–,–)
West Smithfield
☎ (020) 7601 7871
🖷 (020) 7601 7080
Ascend the Hogarth staircase to find
one of the most atmospheric halls in
London (c18), all cream, gold and
dark wood. / 11.30pm; in-house caterers;
no amplified music; no smoking; Great
Hall (300,190,–,–); Henry VIII Committee
Rm (50,18,–,–); Peggy Turner
Rm (40,14,–,–); Treasurer's Rm (40,18,–,–).

St Botolph's Hall EC2
£B-M, (150,80,50,100)
Bishopsgate
☎ (020) 7588 1053
🖷 (020) 7638 1256
✉ gibson.verger@care4free.net
An oak-panelled Victorian church
hall, next to Liverpool Street Station,
used for receptions, dinners and
Christmas parties by City firms. The
lower hall could be used for a disco
or for children's entertainment.
/ 10pm; closed Sun; hirer's choice of caterer;
Upper Hall (150,80,50,100); Lower
Hall (45,–,–,–).

St Bride Foundation Institute EC4
£B, (200,100,100,150)
Bride Ln, Fleet St
☎ (020) 7353 3331
🖷 (020) 7353 1547
⌖ www.stbrideinstitute.org
✉ emma@stbrideinstitute.org
A bright and characterful, Victorian
institution, attractively situated near
the 'wedding cake' church of the
same name, just off Fleet Street.
/ 10pm; hirer's choice of caterer (in-house
available); no smoking; Bridewell
Hall (200,100,100,150); Farringdon
Rm (80,50,50,60); Salisbury
Rm (40,14,14,25); Blackfriars
Rm (80,50,50,60); Caxton (15,6,–,12).

St Etheldreda's Crypt EC1
£B, (170,120,100,–)
14 Ely Pl, Holborn Circus
☎ (020) 7242 8238
✉ thecrypt@bleedingheart.co.uk

As the scene of the wedding feast of
Henry VIII and Catherine of Aragon
in 1531, this atmospheric space
boasts a long and colourful entertaining history. You can have a reception
in the crypt after getting married in
the Church above. Arrangements and
catering are via the Bleeding Heart

*restaurant. / midnight; Bleeding Heart
restaurant.*

St John EC1
£M, (150,100,–,–)
26 St John's St
☎ (020) 7251 0848
🖨 (020) 7251 4090
🖱 www.stjohnrestaurant.co.uk
*This Smithfield smokehouse has been
converted to a bare, bright white
English restaurant (whose motto is,
famously, "nose-to-tail-eating") – it
makes an interesting function space.
/ Private Rm (–,18,–,–); Bar (100,–,–,–).*

St John's Gate EC1
£M, (260,100,–,–)
St John's Ln
☎ (020) 7324 4083
🖨 (020) 7490 8835
🖱 www.sja.org.uk
📧 alan.beggs@nhq.sja.org.uk
*North of Smithfield market, this
romantic medieval gatehouse –
home to the Order of St John – is a
local landmark. The stately Chapter
Hall is a lofty, panelled room used
for dinners and receptions. The
Council Chamber, actually in the
gatehouse, is similar but much smaller. / 11pm; closed Sun; hirer's choice of
caterer; no dancing; no smoking; Chapter
Hall (200,100,–,–); Council
Chamber (–,15,–,–); Prior's Dining
Rm (20,12,–,–).*

St Martin In The Fields WC2
£B-M, (350,150,110,–)
6 St Martin's Pl
☎ (020) 7839 4342
🖨 (020) 7839 5163
🖱 www.stmartin-in-the-fields.org
📧 cafeinthecrypt@smithf.co.uk
*This atmospheric cafe in the crypt of
the impressive church on Trafalgar
Square offers an interesting venue
for a central party. / 2 am; evenings only,
closed Sun; in-house caterers; no spirits;
Gallery (150,70,50,–).*

St Martin's Lane Hotel WC2
£M-E, (350,200,60,90)
45 St Martin's Lane
☎ (020) 7300 5500
🖨 (020) 7300 5537
🖱 www.ianschragerhotels.com
📧 sml@ianschragerhotels.com
*Ian Schrager's Covent Garden-fringe
design hotel. It offers quite a range
of accommodation suited to event
use. / 1 am; in-house caterers; no live bands;
Light Bar (150,–,–,–); The
Studio (150,90,60,90); The
Backroom (70,48,–,60); Board Rm (–,–,–,16);
Front Rm (–,–,–,18);
Restaurant (350,200,–,–).*

St Moritz W1
£B, (120,–,–,–)
159 Wardour St
☎ (020) 7734 3324
*Despite its fame as a rock music
venue, this Soho basement of Swiss
grottoes – dance-floor, bar, and seating areas – lends itself well to other
types of parties. / 3 am; not available
Thu-Sun; hirer's choice of caterer, alcohol
in-house.*

St Paul's Cathedral EC4
£M, (350,200,–,80)
The Chapter House,
St Paul's Churchyard
☎ (020) 7246 8346
🖨 (020) 7248 3104
🖱 www.stpauls.co.uk
📧 duncan@
   stpaulscathedral.org.uk
*The conference room in the crypt of
St Paul's is certainly an original location for any event you're planning,
and hire can be combined with guided tours of the cathedral. The beehive is a domed antechamber. / 10pm;
in-house caterers; no dancing; no smoking;
Conference Rm (120,70,–,80);
Beehive (40,15,–,–); Crypt (350,200,–,–).*

CAPACITIES: (Standing, Seated, Dinner dance, Theatre-style)

St Paul's Church W1
£B-M, (–,130,–,270)
Robert Adam St
☎ (020) 7935 5941
🖨 (020) 7935 7486
*If you're organising a daytime gather-
ing (of a suitably uplifting nature), it
may be worth considering the Blue
Lounge room of this modern church,
behind Selfridges.* / 10pm; closed Sun,
restricted weekday evenings; no amplified
music; no dancing; no smoking; Blue
Lounge (–,60,–,90); Church
Rm (–,130,–,270); Portman Rm (–,20,–,30).

St Peter's Hall W11
£B-M, (100,80,–,–)
59a Portobello Rd
☎ (020) 7792 8227
🖨 (020) 7792 8227
📧 stjohnandstpeter@
btinternet.com
*This Victorian school building in
Notting Hill, built around a small
central courtyard, makes an atmospheric place for a party. The Upper
Hall is a lofty room, ideal for receptions, as is the Café (which opens
onto the courtyard). The North Hall
is reserved for kids' parties.* / 11pm;
North Hall not available Fri & Sat; hirer's
choice of caterer (in-house available); no
amplified music after 7pm; Upper
Hall (100,80,–,–); Café (100,50,–,–); North
Hall (60,30,–,–).

St Stephen's Club SW1
£M, (300,120,120,90)
34 Queen Anne's Gate
☎ (020) 7222 1382
🖨 (020) 7222 8740
🖳 www.ststephensclub.co.uk
📧 info@ststephens.co.uk
*This pleasant building overlooking St
James's Park was spruced up by its
new owners at the beginning of
2003. It is a nice size to be taken
over in its entirety, say for a wedding
reception, and imparts a sense of
occasion without stuffiness. Numbers
can be much increased by erecting a
marquee.* / 1 am; in-house caterers; Dining
Rm (200,120,120,90); Bar (70,–,–,–);
Garden Rm (90,32,–,–); Garden (150,–,–,–).

St Thomas' Hospital SE1
£M, (300,200,150,200)
2 Lambeth Palace Rd
☎ (020) 7928 9292 extn 2400
📧 soraya.rahim@
gstt.sthames.nhs.uk
*Though situated among the rather
drab buildings of this hospital (opposite the Houses of Parliament), the
hall and committee room offer quite
grand settings for many types of
function.* / midnight; in-house caterers;
smoking restricted; Governors'
Hall (250,125,90,200); Grand Committee
Rm (50,24,–,–); Shepherd
Hall (300,200,150,–); Consultant's Dining
Rm (80,26,–,–).

The Stafford SW1
£M-E, (75,44,–,–)
16 St James's Pl
☎ (020) 7493 0111
🖨 (020) 7493 7121
🖳 www.thestaffordhotel.co.uk
📧 info@thestaffordhotel.co.uk
*Dinner in the wonderful, musty wine-
cellars (heading for four centuries
old, but still very much in use) is this
cosy St James's hotel's special attraction, though it also has a good range
of other traditionally-furnished function rooms.* / 12.30 am; no amplified
music; Panel Rm & Sutherland
Rm (50,40,–,–); The Cellar (75,44,–,–);
Sutherland Rm (40,24,–,–); Pink Rm & Argyll
Rm (30,14,–,–); Argyll Rm (20,14,–,–); Panel
Rm or Pink Rm (–,8,–,–).

Staple Inn WC1
£M, (250,120,80,160)
High Holborn
☎ (020) 7632 2165
🖳 www.actuaries.org.uk
📧 joanneg@actuaries.org.uk
*Prettily situated off a cobbled court-
yard, this panelled Victorian
medieval-style hall (the home of the
Institute of Actuaries) is lofty, plain
and handsome. A marquee can be
erected over the award-winning rose-
garden. See advertisement on page
154.* / midnight; hirer's choice of caterer; no
smoking; Hall (250,120,–,160); Council
Chamber (80,40,–,60).

$\mathcal{S}$taple Inn Hall

A magnificent dining hall, graced with a great hammer-beam roof, rich oak panelling and priceless Elizabethan and Jacobean stained-glass windows.

Catering for up to 120 guests silver service, 200 stand-up buffet. Bring your own caterer or we can suggest a few.

*For further information or an appointment to view contact **Joanne Gordon** Telephone: 0207 632 2165/2127 e-mail: joanneg@actuaries.org.uk*

Staple Inn Hall

High Holborn, London WCIV 7QJ

Star Tavern SW1
£B, (50,37,–,–)
6 Belgrave Mews West
☎ (020) 7235 3019
The private bar is available for hire, at this famous, if hidden away, public house near Belgrave Square. / no music; no dancing; Bar (50,37,–,–).

The Station W10
£B-M, (400,80,–,–)
41 Bramley Rd
☎ (020) 7229 1111
🖷 (020) 7229 3331
🖰 www.priorybars.com
A gritty urban view, of the Latimer Road tube viaduct, sets the tone at this above-average gastropub. All the more surprise then to find a huge and attractive garden out back which they hire for a BBQ (or even erect a marquee). There's also a basement private room and – probably open by the time you read this – a conservatory. / ; 1 am; in-house caterers; no amplified music outside; Garden (400,–,–,–); Conservatory (120,70,–,–); Private Rm (80,80,–,–).

CAPACITIES: (Standing, Seated, Dinner dance, Theatre-style)

Stationers' Hall EC4
£M-E, (400,205,175,196)
Ave Maria Ln
☎ (020) 7248 2934
⌖ www.stationers.org
✉ marketing@stationers.org
One of the more accommodating of the livery halls – even dancing is permitted, if at an extra charge. The c17 hall itself is dark-panelled and bannered, and the gilded Court Room and the plainer Stock Room are also agreeable. / midnight; list of caterers; smoking restricted; Livery Hall (400,205,175,196); Court Rm (150,80,–,120); Stock Rm (80,46,–,60); Ante Rm (–,20,–,–).

Stoke Newington Town Hall E8
£B-M, (500,400,400,–)
Town Hall, Mare St
☎ (020) 8356 3299
🖨 (020) 8356 3236
⌖ www.hackney.gov.uk
✉ ricky.chan@hackney.gov.uk
The wooden-floored Assembly Room is regularly used for wedding receptions and other fairly large-scale celebrations. Theming is advised. / 11pm; evenings only Mon-Thu; hirer's choice of caterer; smoking restricted; Assembly Rm (500,400,400,–).

Stonor, Oxon
£M-E, (500,350,300,–)
Henley-on-Thames
☎ 01491 614321
🖨 01491 614455
⌖ www.stonor.com
✉ alina@britwellpartnership.co.uk
A magnificent historic house nestling in Chiltern Hills an hour from Central London. Georgian facade, formal gardens and deer park provide a perfect backdrop for marquee wedding receptions. A variety of wedding packages coordinated by Britwell Partnership (with a private chapel available for Roman Catholic weddings). Ideal for Corporate events/ private parties, 25 years experience. / midnight; list of caterers; Croquet Lawn (300,220,200,–); Front Lawn (500,350,300,–).

Strand Palace Hotel WC2
£B-M, (200,140,140,180)
Strand
☎ (020) 7257 9029
⌖ www.strandpalacehotel.co.uk
✉ meetings@strandpalacehotel.co.uk
The banqueting facilities of this central hotel have been revamped in a crisp modern style which is much more suited to business than social events. / 1 am; no smoking; Exeter Suite (200,140,140,180); Essex Suite (70,56,56,60); Grenville Suite (70,56,56,60); Drake Suite (50,48,48,40).

Stratford Old Town Hall E15
£B-M, (490,250,200,70)
29 The Broadway
☎ (020) 8534 7835
🖨 (020) 8534 8411
If you want old-fashioned chandeliers-and-ornate-ceilings elegance, these east London premises might well fit the bill. The Courtyard (not generally open as part of a function let) can be used for a marquee. / midnight, Sat 2am; in-house caterers weekdays, hirers choice of caterer on weekends; Main Hall (490,250,200,70); Council Chamber (80,80,60,–); Conference Rm (70,40,–,70); Mayor's Parlour (20,–,–,20).

Streatham Ice Arena SW16
£B-M, (1500,50,–,–)
386 Streatham High Rd
☎ (020) 8769 7771
🖨 (020) 8769 9979
⌖ www.streathamicearena.co.uk
✉ starburstltd@lineone.net
For a skating party, numbers here are limited to 900, but if you board over the ice, you can accommodate 1,500. There is a function room, complete with kitchen, suitable for smaller parties. / 11pm; hirer's choice of caterer; no alcohol; Function Rm (80,50,–,–).

PRIVATE VENUES

Strictly Hush W1
£M-E, (–,80,–,–)
2nd Floor, 8 Lancashire Court,
Brook St
☎ (020) 7659 1500
🖨 (020) 7659 1501
🖰 www.hush.co.uk
🖃 info@hush.co.uk
The private dining floor of the fash-
ionable Hush restaurant, in a mews
just off Bond Street, has a brand
identity separate from the main
establishment. There are three
rooms, decorated in African themes
(though the cooking is a little more
international in inspiration).
/ Zanzibar (–,80,–,–); Kenya (–,20,–,–);
Tangiers (–,15,–,–).

Studio 33 SE11
£B-M, (800,–,–,–)
100-102 The Arches, Tinworth St,
Albert Embankment
☎ (020) 7820 1702
🖨 (020) 7820 1775
🖃 kcut33@aol.com
The three arches of this nightclub
have been given a slightly Greek
mythological slant. It offers lofty
space to accommodate a variety of
functions (but mainly stand-ups). / 5
am; hirer's choice of caterer; Cristal
Rm (140,–,–,–); Champagne Bar (70,–,–,–);
Lounge Bar (140,–,–,–); Upper
Lounge (77,–,–,–); Purple Rm (186,–,–,–).

Sugar Hut SW6
£M, (–,80,–,–)
374 North End Rd
☎ (020) 7386 8950
🖨 (020) 7386 8428
🖰 www.sugarhutfulham.com
A lavishly decorated Thai restaurant
near Fulham Broadway, whose dis-
creet style (it's hidden from the
street), seductive bar and opulent
décor make it a good private hire
venue. / 12.30 am; in-house caterers; no
dancing.

Sugar Reef W1
£M, (1000,300,–,–)
42-44 Great Windmill St
☎ (020) 7851 0800
🖰 www.sugarreef.net
🖃 info@sugarreef.net
A large Soho night club makes its
facilities available for private hire on
non-club nights. Several areas are
available for smaller parties, as well
as a new club-lounge and private
dining room. / available Mon-Sat; in-house
caterers; Restaurant (450,300,–,–);
Bar (650,–,–,–); Private Dining Rm (–,20,–,–).

The Sun WC2
£B-M, (90,40,–,–)
66 Long Acre
☎ (020) 7836 4520
Bright function room, decorated in
modern style, over a Covent Garden
pub.

Le Suquet SW3
£M, (–,30,–,–)
104 Draycott Av
☎ (020) 7581 1785
🖨 (020) 7225 0838
West London's most authentic French
fish restaurant transports you from
Chelsea to Cannes – not least in the
two upstairs private rooms. The ser-
vice is no less Gallic than the atmos-
phere. / Private Rm 1 (–,30,–,–); Private Rm
2 (–,16,–,–).

Surrey Docks Watersports Centre SE16
£B-M, (120,80,–,–)
Rope St, Off Plough Way
☎ (020) 7237 4009/5555
🖨 (020) 7525 1007
The light and bright first floor Quay
Room and Lounge at this Rotherhithe
venue overlook the Thames. Suitable
for buffets, birthday parties and
wedding receptions. / midnight; hirer's
choice of caterer; smoking restricted; Quay
Rm/Quay Lounge (120,80,–,–).

CAPACITIES: (Standing, Seated, Dinner dance, Theatre-style)

Sutton House E9
£M, (–,–,–,100)
2-4 Homerton High St
☎ (020) 8986 2264
🖰 www.nationaltrust.org.uk
✉ suttonhouse@
nationaltrust.org.uk
*The oldest house in Hackney
(1535), this National Trust property
has interiors ranging from dark oak
panelling to lighter Georgian additions, and an enclosed courtyard. It
offers an interesting setting for a civil
wedding – the reception however
must be held elsewhere - or a corporate meeting place.* / wedding ceremonies and meetings only; 5pm; not available
Mon & Tue; no food; no amplified music; no
dancing; no smoking; Wenlock Barn (including
Café-Bar/Linenfold Parlour) (–,–,–,100);
Marriage Suite (Great and Little
Chambers) (–,–,–,50); Linenfold
Parlour (–,–,–,18).

Sway WC2
£M, (670,120,–,–)
61-65 Great Queen St
☎ (020) 7404 6114
🖷 (020) 7404 6003
🖰 www.latenightlondon.co.uk
✉ info@swaybar.co.uk
*In Covent Garden, a large basement
nightclub, with four different themed
areas.* / 3 am; evenings only;
in-house caterers.

Sweetings EC4
£M, (90,30,–,–)
39 Queen Victoria St
☎ (020) 7248 3062
*This quirky City fish parlour is a
famous lunching place. It is less well-
known that it will do private evening
parties, at which optional extras
include live jazz, and cod 'n' chips
wrapped in the newspaper of your
choice.* / midnight; available Mon-Fri
evenings only.

Swissôtel London the Howard WC2
£M-E, (180,120,80,150)
Temple Pl
☎ (020) 7836 3555
🖰 www.swissotel.com
✉ claire.tagger@swissotel.com
*This small, luxurious, modern hotel
by the Temple offers fairly compact
accommodation for functions. The
ground floor Fitzalan Suite has a
view of the pleasant (and rather
unexpected) courtyard garden.*
/ in-house caterers; Fitzalan
Suite (180,120,80,150); Arundel
Suite (100,90,50,120).

Syon Park (Conservatory), Middx
£M, (200,150,150,150)
Brentford
☎ (020) 8758 1888
🖰 www.syonpark.co.uk
✉ pam@syonpark.co.uk
*Vast and imposing 1820s glasshouse,
suitable for a range of events and
very popular (especially for wedding
receptions). Hire includes access to
the Capability Brown garden.* / Apr-Oct
only, corporate only; midnight; not available
from mid-October until April; list of caterers;
Great Conservatory (200,150,150,150);
Private Dining Rm (–,22,–,–); Public
Rms (90,90,90,90).

Syon Park (House), Middx
£E, (120,120,80,–)
Syon Park, Brentford
☎ (020) 8758 1777
🖷 (020) 8568 0936
🖱 www.syonpark.co.uk
✉ louise@syonpark.co.uk

The Duke of Northumberland's London home is a fine example of Robert Adam's interior design. It is the only great house in the capital still privately occupied, and can be made available for suitably lavish entertaining. / no wedding receptions; I am; list of caterers; no amplified music; no smoking; Great Hall (–,120,80,–); Long Gallery (120,–,–,–); State Dining Rm (–,80,–,–).

Tallow Chandlers' Hall EC4
£M, (120,97,–,–)
4 Dowgate HI
☎ (020) 7248 4726
🖷 (020) 7236 0844
Charming c17 livery hall, set back in its own courtyard. It's quite grand, but has a very relaxed atmosphere. / no weddings; 11.15pm; not available week-ends; Payne & Gunter; no amplified music; no dancing; Livery Hall (100,100,–,–); Parlour (60,30,–,–).

Tantra W1
£M, (550,120,130,–)
62 Kingly St
☎ (020) 7434 0888
🖱 www.tantraclub.co.uk
✉ mail@tantraclub.co.uk
"Europe's biggest underlit dance floor (for that music video feel)", a mirrored ceiling, a 'boudoir' with seven semi-private beds not to mention a catwalk & stage – this Soho club's suitability for certain types of private hire events is self-evident. / 4.30 am; in-house caterers; VIP Area (80,–,–,–); Red Rm (100,–,–,–); Private Dining Rm (–,20,–,–).

Tate Britain SW1
£E, (600,200,–,190)
Millbank
☎ (020) 7887 8689
🖱 www.tate.org.uk
✉ corporate.hospitality@ tate.org.uk

BRITAIN
TATE

Tate Britain, the most prestigious arts venue for entertaining, invites all companies to take advantage of its new events packages. Tate Britain boasts eight unique entertaining spaces, which are perfect for a range of events, from dinner for 50 to receptions for 600. Ranging from classical and formal galleries to the clean and contemporary lines of the new Manton Entrance. Tate Britain is one of the most stunning venues in London. / companies only; 11pm; evenings only; list of caterers; no dancing; no smoking; Auditorium (–,–,–,190); Sackler Octagon (350,–,–,–); Clore Gallery Foyer (200,–,–,–); Lodge (25,10,–,–); Rm 9 (400,200,–,–); Rm 15 (400,200,–,–); Rex Whistler Restaurant (120,80,–,–); Manton Entrance (600,–,–,–).

Tate Modern SE1
£M-E, (500,400,–,100)
Bankside
☎ (020) 7887 8689
🖷 (020) 7887 8702
🖱 www.tate.org.uk
✉ corporate.hospitality@ tate.org.uk
The Turbine Hall, the level 3 Gallery and the East Room – many and varied are the entertaining possibilities at this monumentally popular gallery ... but only if you are (or become) a Corporate Sponsor. / corporate sponsors

CAPACITIES: (Standing, Seated, Dinner dance, Theatre-style)

only; list of caterers; no dancing; no smoking; Turbine Hall (500,400,–,–); Level 3 (150,100,–,–); Level 3 Concourse (400,–,–,–); Members Rm (150,–,–,–); Cafe 7 (300,200,–,–); East Rm (150,100,–,100).

Tatsuso EC2
£M, (–,8,–,–)
32 Broadgate Circle
☎ (020) 7638 5863
🖨 (020) 7638 5864
The basement of this modern City Japanese (one of the very best in town) is much less slick than its ground floor and has two private rooms – one is a traditional tatami room and the other is in ordinary western style. / not available weekends; Western (–,8,–,–); Tatami Rm (–,6,–,–).

The Tattershall Castle SW1
£B, (250,–,–,–)
Victoria Embankment
☎ (020) 7839 6548
This former tourist paradise – a paddle steamer/pub near Hungerford Bridge – was away for a major wash and brush-up at press time, and details of its proposed, smarter future life were not clear. It's scheduled to be back at its moorings from April 2004.

Teca W1
£M, (120,75,–,–)
54 Brooks Mews
☎ (020) 7495 4774
Just off Bond Street, a modern Italian restaurant that's acquired something of a 'hidden gem' status amongst those in the know. There's no private room, but if you're looking for quality cooking for your party, it might be well worth considering hiring the whole place.

Temple Island, Oxon
£M-E, (50,40,120,–)
c/o Henley Royal Regatta HQ
☎ 01491 572153
🖰 www.hrr.co.uk
A fantasy location, this restored Georgian island folly, picturesquely sited at the start of the Henley Regatta course, can be reached only by boat. It's difficult to beat for summer entertaining. / list of caterers; Indoors (50,40,–,–); Outdoors (with marquee) (–,–,120,–).

Texas Embassy Cantina SW1
£B-M, (500,240,–,–)
1 Cockspur St
☎ (020) 7925 0077
🖨 (020) 7925 0444
🖰 www.texasembassy.com

The lofty premises of this centrally located Tex/Mex restaurant are well suited to use for functions. Fully themed evenings can be arranged. / midnight; Upstairs (250,120,–,–).

Theatre Museum WC2
£M-E, (300,100,100,80)
1e Tavistock St
☎ (020) 7943 4744
🖨 (020) 7943 4777
🖰 www.theatremuseum.org
✉ c.malbor@vam.ac.uk
Guests on their way to this converted Covent Garden flower market can match their handprints with those of celebrities in the Wall of Fame. For a drinks reception or dinner you might hire the deep-red Gallery. Smaller groups might take the Foyer. The Studio Theatre can be used for dis-

PRIVATE VENUES

cos. / evenings only; hirer's choice of caterer; no smoking; Paintings Gallery (250,100,100,–); Foyer (120,80,–,–); Beard Rm (30,–,–,–); Studio Theatre (–,–,–,80).

Theatre Royal, Drury Lane WC2
£M, (300,120,–,–)
Catherine St
☎ (020) 7494 5200
🖷 (020) 74341217
🖰 www.rutheatres.com
🖃 productions@rutheatres.com
A crimson-and-gilt Covent Garden theatre – the current building, dating from 1812, is on a monumental scale. The impressive Grand Saloon is regularly used for events during the daytime and on Sundays. / 6.30pm; Grand Saloon & Rotunda (300,120,–,–); Royal Retiring Rm & Ante Rm (20,–,–,–); Boardroom (40,30,–,–).

30 Pavilion Road SW1
£M-E, (240,120,120,–)
30 Pavilion Rd
☎ (020) 7823 9212
🖰 www.searcys.co.uk
🖃 30pr@searcys.co.uk
Caterers Searcy's Knightsbridge address which – for those without their own townhouse – makes an excellent place in which to entertain (or to get married). The homely-scale but quite grandly furnished accommodation suits a variety of (especially social) entertaining (and there are even bedrooms for those who can't drag themselves away). / 1 am; Searcy's; Stone Hall (120,90,–,–); Ballroom (120,120,–,–); Library (60,28,–,–).

32 Craven St WC2
£M-E, (120,48,48,70)
32 Craven St
☎ (020) 7653 6666
🖷 (020) 7653 6653
🖰 www.venuesolutionsdirect.com
Craven Street is a quiet Georgian street, just a few paces from the hubbub of Charing Cross, and one of its houses has been elegantly revamped as a venue for entertaining, corporate and otherwise.

Perhaps surprisingly, the house apparently has something of a niche in the small-scale dinner-dance market. / midnight; list of caterers; Level 1 (80,50,–,70); Level 2 (20,12,–,15); Level 3 (–,10,–,–).

Thistle Kensington Palace Hotel W8
£M, (250,160,120,–)
De Vere Gdns
☎ (020) 7937 8121
🖷 (020) 7368 8129
🖰 www.thistlehotels.com
🖃 m&e.kensingtonparkpalace@thistle.co.uk
Facing Kensington Gardens, the rosily-bland function rooms of this mid-range hotel are pleasant of their type. / midnight; Duchess (250,160,120,–); Marchioness (100,70,50,–); Countess (38,20,–,–); Princess (30,20,–,–); Baroness (25,15,–,–).

Thistle Victoria Hotel SW1
£M, (150,100,80,200)
101 Buckingham Palace Rd
☎ (020) 7834 9494
🖰 www.thistlehotels.com
🖃 mande.victoria@thistle.co.uk
Victoria's grand Victorian railway hotel has some very attractive, atmospheric period rooms, including one 'find' – the imposing, very bright Bessborough Room, a double-height treasure, complete with ornamental minstrel's gallery. / 1 am; Gallery Rm (150,100,80,200); Bessborough Rm (80,60,–,100); Warwick Rm (35,20,–,40); Belgrave (30,16,–,30); Wilton Rm (20,12,–,25); Hanover (12,8,–,20).

Thomas Goode W1
£M-E, (200,80,–,–)
19 South Audley St
☎ (020) 7499 2823
🖷 (020) 7629 4230
🖰 www.thomasgoode.com
🖃 info@thomasgoode.co.uk
If you're looking for an imposing Mayfair venue for a cocktail party (in particular), London's grandest china shop is sometimes made available.

CAPACITIES: (Standing, Seated, Dinner dance, Theatre-style)

/ very restricted availability; midnight; available Mon-Fri; hirer's choice of caterer; Shop (200,80,–,–); Chairman's Rm (–,36,–,–).

Thorpe Park, Surrey
£M-E, (900,650,600,600)
Staines Rd, Chertsey
☎ 01932 577109
🖷 01932 566367
⁶ www.thorpepark.co.uk
✉ events@thorpepark.co.uk
A hundred rides await you at this adventure park, located just off the M25. For a mega-event you could take over the whole place, or alternatively hire one of the individual facilities and give your guests the run of the place. Some attractions only function in the summer. / midnight; Alexander Catering; Lake Side Hospitality Area (400,300,280,300); Thorpe Belle (250,200,180,60); Neptunes Chamber (80,50,–,60); Dome (900,650,600,600).

Throgmorton's EC2
£B-M, (200,100,100,–)
27 Throgmorton St
☎ (020) 7588 5165
🖷 (020) 7256 8956
Amazing Victorian City labyrinth of underground restaurants and bars, behind the Bank of England. Only the Oak Room is currently in use. / Oak Rm (200,100,100,–).

Tiger Tiger SW1
£M, (1770,–,–,–)
29 Haymarket
☎ (020) 7930 1885
🖷 (020) 7930 3060
⁶ www.tigertiger.co.uk
This large West End nitespot is available in its entirety during the day for corporate functions and drinks parties. In the evening it's open to the public, but you can hire several of the bars or booth areas for smaller social gatherings. / 3 am; in-house caterers.

Tower Bridge SE1
£M-E, (250,120,120,–)
Tower Bridge
☎ (020) 7407 9222
🖷 (020) 7403 4477
⁶ www.towerbridge.org.uk
✉ enquiries@ towerbridge.org.uk
This symbol of the capital is now available for social as well as corporate events. You can stage your dinner or reception either on the walkways linking the towers or in the engine room. / 1 am; walkways & engine rooms available from 6.30pm; list of caterers; Walkways (250,120,120,–); Engine Rms (100,60,70,–); Bridge Master's Dining Rm (20,12,–,–).

HM Tower of London EC3
£E, (300,240,–,–)
London
☎ (020) 7488 5762
🖷 (020) 7480 5543
⁶ www.hrp.org.uk
✉ sam.melton@hrp.org.uk
For a very grand cocktail party, hirers can use one of London's most historic buildings. Areas available include the Norman White Tower, with its display of arms, and armour. There is also the possibility of a private visit to the Crown Jewels (or, rather less appealingly, to the instruments of torture). / charities, companies & gov only; 10.30pm; available from 6pm winter, 6.30pm summer; list of caterers; no amplified music; no dancing; no smoking; White Tower (250,–,–,–); Medieval Palace (150,–,–,–); Royal Fusiliers Association Rm (100,70,–,–); Jewel House (80,–,–,–); New Armouries (300,240,–,–).

Tower Thistle E1
£M, (550,500,450,550)
St Katharine's Wy
☎ (020) 7481 2575
⁶ www.thistlehotels.com
✉ meetingplan.tower@ thistle.co.uk
Some of the views (of the Tower and Tower Bridge) from the banqueting rooms of this monolithic '70s hotel are most impressive, and it offers a good range of accommodation for

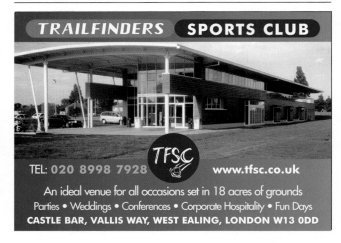

smaller to medium-size events
(including weddings). / 1 am; Tower
Suite (550,500,450,550); Raleigh or
Spencer (50,40,–,50); Mortimer
Suite (40,30,–,35); Beaufort (35,20,–,25);
Lewin (14,6,–,–).

tion rooms feel much more like those
of a county town hotel than of a
boozer, making it an attractive wedding (or reception) venue. / 2 am;
Nelson Suite (300,200,180,–); Hawke &
Howe Bar (80,–,–,–); Trafalgar
Club (100,40,–,–).

The Trafalgar SW1
£M-E, (65,40,–,22)
2 Spring Gdns
☎ (020) 7870 2914
🖥 (020) 7870 2911
🖱 www.hilton.co.uk/trafalgar
📧 anja.ramisch@hilton.com
Locations don't come much more
central than this Hilton group design-
hotel (whose rooftop bar makes a
rather intriguing venue). The style of
the boardroom is more traditional
than the rest of the building.
/ Boardroom (60,30,–,18);
Strategy (50,20,–,18);
Resolution (60,40,–,22); Roof & Bar
Garden (65,–,–,–).

Trafalgar Sports Club W13
£B-M, (250,160,160,–)
Castle Bar Sports Ground,
Vallis Way
☎ (020) 8998 7928
🖥 (020) 8998 8006
🖱 www.tfsc.co.uk
Trailfinders Sports Club offers superb
venue facilities for both private and
corporate functions. Whether you
are organising a party, wedding or
conference, their experienced and
friendly team are here to help
ensure your event is a complete suc-
cess-from planning through to when
your guests depart. TFSC has two
unique venues set in 18 acres of
grounds. See advertisement above.
/ Pavilion Hall (250,160,160,–);
Marquees (2000,–,–,–).

Trafalgar Tavern SE10
£B-M, (300,200,180,–)
Park Row
☎ (020) 8858 2437
🖥 (020) 8858 2507
🖱 www.trafalgartavern.co.uk
📧 info@trafalgartavern.co.uk
This historic Thames-side Greenwich
pub has spectacular views. Its func-

CAPACITIES: (Standing, Seated, Dinner dance, Theatre-style)

The Tram Studios NW1
£M, (800,400,400,400)
104 Arlington Road
☎ (020) 7482 7044
🖳 (020) 7482 7055
🖰 www.thetramstudios.com
📧 events@thetramstudios.com
In a Victorian tram building, a contemporary Camden Town interior mainly used as an art gallery and a business centre, and suited to a variety of event uses. / 11pm; list of caterers; no amplified music; Studio 104 (800,400,400,400).

Tricycle Theatre NW6
£B-M, (–,–,–,300)
269 Kilburn High Rd
☎ (020) 7328 1000
🖳 (020) 7328 0795
🖰 www.tricycle.co.uk
📧 admin@tricycle.co.uk
Although there is a theatre, built in the 1980s, it is the plush adjacent cinema (with stage) which is this establishment's main attraction for those organising presentations and private views. / available subject to constraints of current production; hirer's choice of caterer (in-house available); smoking restricted; Cinema (–,–,–,300); Theatre (–,–,–,240).

Trinity House EC3
£M, (120,120,120,–)
Trinity Sq, Tower Hl
☎ (020) 7481 6931
🖳 (020) 7702 4983
🖰 www.trinityhouse.co.uk
📧 kinge@thcorp.co.uk
Fine, late-Georgian HQ of the UK's lighthouse authority. The Court Room is an elegant and ornate chamber, and the view of the Tower of London from the Library is magnificent. / 1 am; list of caterers; smoking restricted; Court Rm (120,60,–,–); Library (120,120,–,–); Reading Rm (–,10,–,–); Luncheon Rm (–,20,–,–).

Les Trois Garçons EC2
£M, (–,50,–,–)
1 Club Row
☎ (020) 7613 1924
Stuffed animals wearing tiaras may seem an odd decorative theme, but it's helped turn this impressively converted former East End boozer into quite a 'destination' restaurant, and (over-)priced accordingly. There's a small private room downstairs, but hiring the whole place probably makes more sense. / Private Rm (–,10,–,–).

Turnmills EC1
£B, (1500,200,–,–)
63b Clerkenwell Rd
☎ (020) 7250 3409
🖰 www.turnmills.co.uk
📧 toanyone@turnmills.co.uk
This Farringdon nightclub, with 24-hour dance-licence, is self-evidently suited to a certain type of large bash. There are also smaller spaces which are suitable for less grandiose events. / not available Fri or weekends eves; in-house caterer or hirer's choice by negotiation; Juno Lucina (300,200,–,–); Café Gaudi (–,80,–,–); Las Brassas (–,80,–,–).

Tuttons WC2
£B-M, (75,50,–,–)
11-12 Russell St
☎ (020) 7240 3228
🖳 (020) 7379 9979
🖰 www.tuttons.com
📧 bookings@tuttons.com
Below this large English brasserie overlooking Covent Garden, the white-painted brick vaults are very atmospheric (even if the cooking is unlikely to excite). / 11.30pm; Larger Vault (75,30,–,–); Smaller Vault (–,20,–,–).

20th Century Theatre W11
£B-M, (240,120,–,–)
291 Westbourne Grove
☎ (020) 7229 4179
🖳 (020) 7243 1526
🖰 www.20thcenturytheatre.com
📧 missy@ 20thcenturytheatre.com

PRIVATE VENUES

In the heart of Notting Hill, a Victorian building which has had such famous names as Charles Dickens and Lawrence Olivier grace its stage. The word 'theatre' is in fact a bit misleading, as this is an elegant, untiered space, well-suited to event use (and popular in the fashion world). / 11pm; hirer's choice of caterer; Reception Rm (100,50,–,–).

28 Portland Place W1
£M-E, (120,84,84,90)
28 Portland Place
☎ 0870 7809639
🖨 (020) 7653 6653
🖱 www.cbvs.co.uk
📧 helpme@cbvs.co.uk
The headquarters of the Royal Institute of Public Health. The buildings, dating from 1775 and designed by the Adam Brothers, are claimed as among the finest examples of townhouses of the period. / 11pm; in-house caterers; smoking restricted; Adam's Rm (70,60,–,70); Sainsbury's Rm (120,84,84,90); Harben Rm (100,72,–,80); Heggie Rm (120,84,84,90); Founder's Rm (–,14,–,14).

Twickenham Experience, Middx
£M, (700,400,320,400)
Rugby Rd, Twickenham
☎ (020) 8831 7976
🖱 www.rfu.com
📧 twickenhamexperience@rfu.com
Substantial rebuilding of the home of rugby has expanded facilities, including those of the purpose-built banqueting suite. Hire can include tours of the grounds and visits to the Museum, and – no doubt every bride's dream – one can now get married here. / 2 am; not available match days; Payne & Gunter; Rose Rm (450,400,300,400); Members Lounge (330,–,–,–); England Rugby International's Club Rm (120,80,60,50); Committee Rm (80,–,–,–); Spirit Of Rugby (400,320,280,250); Invincibles (400,400,320,200); Norm Try Line (700,350,300,200).

Two Chairmen SW1
£B, (50,–,–,–)
39 Dartmouth St
☎ (020) 7222 8694
The upstairs bar of a quaint Westminster pub, available for evening hire or (for suitable size parties) at lunch. / available Mon-Fri; no amplified music; no dancing.

291 Gallery E2
£M, (750,250,200,400)
291 Hackney Rd
☎ (020) 7613 5676
🖱 www.291gallery.com
📧 admin@291gallery.com
An attractive neo-Gothic former church in Bethnal Green, whose current uses include as a bar and art gallery. It includes some attractive spaces, suitable for a whole variety of functions. / midnight Sun-Thu, 2 am Fri-Sat; hirer's choice of caterer (in-house available); Main Gallery (500,250,200,400); South Wing (150,85,–,80); Restaurant (–,50,–,–); Bar (140,–,–,–).

Two Temple Place WC2
£E, (400,100,100,150)
2 Temple Pl
☎ (020) 7836 3715
🖱 www.twotempleplace.co.uk
📧 enquiries@twotempleplace.co.uk
Built to elaborate specification by the first Viscount Astor in 1895, this extraordinary house by Temple Tube offers comfortably neo-Gothic grandeur in an amazingly convenient location. Now owned by a trust, it is available for events both private and corporate. / list of caterers; smoking restricted; Long Gallery (–,–,–,150); The Great Hall (200,100,100,150).

UCS Theatre NW3
£M, (–,–,–,230)
Frognal Hampstead
☎ (020) 7435 2215
🖨 (020) 7433 2143
🖱 www.ucs.org.uk
A Hampstead theatre which you can hire for meetings, musical productions, and theatrical events. / in-house

CAPACITIES: (Standing, Seated, Dinner dance, Theatre-style)

caterers; no dancing; no smoking;
Theatre (–,–,–,230).

Union Chapel N1
£B-M, (220,220,220,1000)
Compton Av
☎ (020) 7226 3750
⌂ www.unionchapel.org.uk
✉ spacehire@
unionchapel.org.uk
This rather remarkable neo-Gothic
building offers a number of areas
available for hire, including an
octagonal auditorium, and number of
other lofty and atmospheric spaces.
/ midnight; hirer's choice of caterer (in-house
available); no dancing in main auditorium;
smoking restricted; auditorium (–,–,–,1000);
auditorium (downstairs) (–,–,–,600); Studio
Theatre (220,220,220,220).

The Union Club W1
£M, (80,60,–,60)
50 Greek St
☎ (020) 7734 4113
🖷 (020) 7439 0329
⌂ www.unionclub.co.uk
✉ michaela@unionclub.co.uk
In a Georgian house in Soho, a small
members' club whose facilities can
sometimes be made available to
non-members. / members club; / am;
in-house caterers; no dancing; Dining
Rm (80,60,–,60).

United Grand Lodge of England WC2
£M-E, (200,–,–,80)
Freemasons Hall, Great Queen St
☎ (020) 7395 9265
🖷 (020) 78931 6021
⌂ www.ugle.org.uk
✉ info@ugle.org.uk
The Freemasons' imposing Covent
Garden HQ is used for a greater
variety of events than you might
expect. At the time of writing, for
example, their website proudly notes
that a Westlife – that's a popular
band, apparently – video has just
been recorded there. The place is
also available for conferences and
drinks parties. No sit-downs, though.
/ hirer's choice of caterer; smoking restricted;

Vestibule (200,–,–,80); Board
Rm (150,–,–,80); Drawing Rm (60,–,–,60).

University of London Union WC1
£B, (600,100,–,220)
Malet St
☎ (020) 7664 2020
🖷 (020) 7436 4604
⌂ www.ulu.lon.ac.uk
✉ conference@ulu.lon.ac.uk
The main hall (now called Room 101
in homage to Orwell, who used to
write in the neighbouring Senate
House) is sound-proofed (how appro-
priate) and air-conditioned, and has
a disco lighting system. The smaller
wine bar is popular for receptions,
discos and lunches. / 11pm, Fri & Sat
1am ; not available weekends in term time;
in-house caterers; Rm 101 (600,100,–,220);
Palms Rm (120,–,–,130); Bar
101 (150,–,–,–); Gallery Bar (200,–,–,–).

University of Westminster NW1
£B-M, (250,120,–,350)
35 Marylebone Rd
☎ (020) 7911 5799
🖷 (020) 7911 5141
⌂ www.wmin.ac.uk
✉ dipalmmo@wmin.ac.uk
The University has a number of
meeting and party spaces, mainly
around its Regent Street site. The Art
Deco Portland Hall has recently been
refurbished. Numerous small rooms
are available for conferences and
seminars. / 5pm weekends, 9pm weekdays;
restricted availability in term time; in-house
caterers; no smoking; Old
Cinema (–,–,–,350); Deep
End (200,120,–,–); Fyvie
Hall (150,80,–,125); Portland Hall
AD (–,–,–,190).

University Women's Club W1
£M, (100,50,–,70)
2 Audley Sq
☎ (020) 7499 2268
⌂ www.universitywomensclub.com
✉ uwc@uwc-london.com
With a member's sponsorship, many
kinds of events are possible at this

Mayfair club, which is ideal for smaller wedding receptions. Attractions include a pretty garden. / midnight; in-house caterers; smoking restricted; Library (100,50,–,70); Drawing Rm (80,50,–,70).

Upstairs at the Gatehouse N6

£B-M, (–,–,–,130)
Cnr North Rd & Hampstead Ln
☎ (020) 7387 2342
🖳 (020) 8340 3466
🖰 www.upstairsatthegatehouse.com
✉ gatehouse@
      ovationproductions.com
Formerly a ballroom of a Victorian pub – the pub's still there – and now a busy small theatre. Might be worth considering if you're looking for an unusual venue for a presentation in north London. / available subject to constraints of current production; hirer's choice of caterer; no smoking.

The Vale W9

£B-M, (60,34,–,–)
99 Chippenham Rd
☎ (020) 7266 0990
🖳 (020) 7286 7224
✉ thevalew9@hotmail.com
Useful to know about in Maida Hill – an area not over-endowed with restaurants – a modern British establishment well equipped to handle smaller and medium-size gatherings. / 11pm; Private Rm (–,34,–,–); Private Rm (–,14,–,–); Bar (60,–,–,–).

Vanderbilt Hotel SW7

£M, (140,100,80,100)
68-86 Cromwell Rd
☎ (020) 7589 2424
🖰 www.radissonedwardian.com
✉ vandcb@radisson.com
The listed Vanderbilt Suite of this South Kensington hotel is decorated in extraordinary French château style. The other accommodation is all much more businessy. / Edwardian (60,50,30,50); Vanderbilt (40,12,–,–); Victoria & Albert Suite (140,100,80,100); Cleo's (100,90,50,50).

Vats WC1

£B, (130,75,–,–)
51 Lamb's Conduit St
☎ (020) 7242 8963
🖳 (020) 7831 7299
Convivial, street-level Bloomsbury wine bar, whose back room, recently revamped, has long been a popular spot for get togethers. On Saturdays the whole place can be hired. / no music; no dancing; no beer; Restaurant (80,50,–,–).

Victoria & Albert Museum SW7

£E, (700,400,250,–)
Cromwell Rd
☎ (020) 7942 2646
🖳 (020) 7942 2645
🖰 www.vam.ac.uk
✉ p.dacunha@vam.ac.uk
The English Silver Gallery and austere Raphael Gallery are among the impressive rooms available for functions. The ornate Gamble Room and, in summer, the Pirelli Garden are popular for more social events, such as wedding receptions. Dancing is only possible in the Dome, which is a major event space in its own right. / 2 am; limited availability in opening hours, not available Wed; list of caterers; no smoking; Dome (700,250,250,–); Raphael Gallery (400,400,–,–); Gamble Rm (300,150,–,–); Silver Gallery (300,–,–,–); Morris Rm (60,40,–,–).

Victory Services Club W2

£B-M, (450,250,220,80)
63-79 Seymour St
☎ (020) 7616 8305
🖳 (020) 7724 1134
🖰 www.vsc.co.uk
✉ events@usc.co.uk
The Club (for current and former members of the armed services) has a number of rooms for hire – all available to non-members – at its Marble Arch premises. Facilities are available in styles both traditional and modern. The El Alamein Room has full AV facilities. / in-house caterers; Carisbrooke Hall (300,220,220,–); El Alamein Rm (100,90,–,–); Trafalgar

CAPACITIES: (Standing, Seated, Dinner dance, Theatre-style)

Rm (80,70,–,80); Allenby Rm (50,–,–,30); Chetwode Rm (25,–,–,25).

The Villiers Theatre WC2
£B-M, (250,150,–,250)
The Arches, Villiers St
☎ (020) 7930 6601
🖷 (020) 7930 6602
🖰 www.playerstheatre.co.uk
📧 chris@
  villierstheatre.fsnet.co.uk
Intimate and charming theatre (whose auditorium seats 258 people), under the Arches at Charing Cross. Formerly called the Players Theatre, it has recently been refurbished in plush Victorian style. / 11pm; in-house caterers; smoking restricted; Lower Supper Rm/Bar (200,104,–,–); Mezzanine Supper Rm (100,48,–,–); Auditorium (–,–,–,250).

Vinopolis – City of Wine SE1
£M, (700,550,450,400)
1 Bank End
☎ (020) 7940 8322
🖰 www.vinopolis.co.uk
📧 events@vinopolis.co.uk
The world's first adult 'theme attraction' dedicated to wine, set beneath railway arches on the South Bank. Licensed for civil weddings. / 11am; list of caterers; Great Halls (700,550,450,250); Mezzanine (450,350,270,400); Wine Odyssey Rms (350,80,–,–).

Waldorf Hotel WC2
£M, (700,420,420,270)
Aldwych
☎ 0870 400 8484
🖷 (020) 7240 9277
🖰 www.hilton.com
For large receptions and dinner-dances – or perhaps for a fashion show or product launch – this fringe-of-Covent Garden hotel will close its rightly famous Palm Court, and can accommodate events up to the maximum overall capacity shown. Smaller rooms are also available at this characterful property, recently taken over by Hilton. / Adelphi Suite & Palm Court (700,420,420,270);

Aldwych (60,–,–,30); Westminster (20,–,–,–); Executive Boardroom (40,30,–,–).

Walkers of St James's SW1
£B, (150,100,80,–)
32a Duke St
☎ (020) 7321 0854
A St James's cellar wine bar (owned by Mitchells & Butler), available in its entirety at the weekend. If you are having food, they can usually get an extension until 1am.

Wallace Collection W1
£E, (300,120,–,–)
Hertford Hse, Manchester Sq
☎ (020) 7563 9546
🖷 (020) 7563 9581
🖰 www.wallacecollection.org
The sumptuous rooms of this enormous Victorian townhouse – home to 6,000 works of fine and decorative art – are available for receptions and dinners. The glazed-roofed courtyard is available for events all year. / no weddings; 11pm; available from 6.30pm; list of caterers; no amplified music; no dancing; no smoking; no red wine in galleries; Main Galleries (300,120,–,–); Sculpture Garden (250,100,–,–); Great Gallery (–,120,–,–); Dining Rm (–,40,–,–); State Rm (–,40,–,–).

Wandsworth Civic Suite SW18
£B, (800,520,460,748)
Wandsworth High St
☎ (020) 8871 6394
🖷 (020) 8871 6391
🖰 www.wandsworth.gov.uk
📧 publichalls@
  wandsworth.gov.uk
Remodelled '30s suite of rooms, comfortably decorated in municipal style, and ideal for a dinner-dance. / midnight; hirer's choice of caterer; smoking restricted; Civic Suite (800,520,460,748); Civic Hall (–,280,220,428); Banqueting Hall (–,240,240,350); Reception Rm (30,–,–,30).

Wapping Food E1
£M, (500,175,–,–)
Hydroelectric Power Station,
Wapping Wall
☎ (020) 7680 2080
✉ ben@wapping-wpt.com
This East End arts site occupies impressive post-industrial premises, and its restaurant has made quite a name in its own right. Use for functions is subject to the constraints of the current installation. / Private Rm (50,25,–,–).

Warren House, Surrey
£M, (40,22,80,70)
Warren Rd,
Kingston Upon Thames
☎ (020) 8547 1777
✆ www.warrenhouse.com
✉ carolyn@warrenhouse.com
Just five miles from London, this Victorian country house (formerly the ICI conference centre) is set in four acres of landscaped gardens, and has been tastefully restored and updated for meetings and banqueting. / midnight; in-house caterers; no spirits; Conference Rm 1 (–,–,50,70); Conference Rm 2 (40,–,–,40); Meeting Rm 1 (–,–,–,12); Meeting Rm 2 (–,14,–,–); Meeting Rm 3 (–,22,–,–); Meeting Rm 4 (–,8,–,–); Library (–,6,–,–).

The Washington W1
£M, (550,130,120,110)
5 Curzon St
☎ (020) 7499 7000
🖨 (020) 7495 6172
✆ www.washington-mayfair.co.uk
✉ conference@washington-mayfair.co.uk
This modern Mayfair hotel is perhaps more obviously suited to corporate than social use. It is possible to use the restaurant for a small dinner-dance. / in-house caterers; Richmond Suite (120,70,62,110); Richmond 1 (Winchester) (60,30,–,–); Richmond 2 (Fairfax) (40,25,–,–); Restaurant (Madisons) (–,130,120,–).

Watermen's Hall EC3
£M, (170,72,–,–)
16-18 St Mary-at-Hill
☎ (020) 7283 2373
🖨 (020) 7283 0477
✆ www.watermenshall.org
✉ info@watermenshall.org
An appealing mix of charm, a flexible attitude and a fair degree of stateliness makes this – the only Georgian livery hall in the square mile – ideal for a wide variety of business and social events. / 11pm; list of caterers; no amplified music; no smoking; Freemen's Rm (110,72,–,–); Court Rm (70,37,–,–).

Waterstone's Piccadilly W1
£M, (200,150,–,140)
30 Jermyn St
☎ (020) 7851 2419
🖨 (020) 7851 2401
✆ www.waterstones.co.uk
✉ events@piccadilly.waterstones.co.uk
If you're looking for a very central venue (especially with a literary flavour), Europe's biggest bookshop – occupying the former splendid Art Deco premises of Simpson's of Piccadilly – has a number of rooms for events. All the rooms apart from the Red Room (the in-house restaurant) are on the upper floors. The Boardroom has a balcony overlooking Piccadilly. / 10pm; Searcy's; smoking restricted; Simpson's Rm (200,150,–,140); Red Rm (200,100,–,60); Emberton Rm (75,50,–,16); Boardroom (–,16,–,14).

Wax Chandlers' Hall EC2
£M-E, (120,60,–,80)
Gresham St
☎ (020) 7606 3591
🖨 (020) 7600 5462
✆ www.waxchandlershall.co.uk
✉ info@waxchandlershall.co.uk
The Wax Chandlers' sixth hall (on a site they have occupied for over 500 years) is a postwar building. It's not as grand as some of the halls, but its style is comfortably traditional. / 11pm; list of caterers; no amplified music;

CAPACITIES: (Standing, Seated, Dinner dance, Theatre-style)

no dancing; Hall (120,60,–,80);
Courtroom (60,20,–,30).

Waxy O'Connors W1
£M, (720,90,–,–)
14-16 Rupert St
☎ (020) 7287 0255
🖷 (020) 7287 3962
🖰 www.waxyoconnors.co.uk
🖂 saleslondon@
   waxyoconnors.co.uk
*Huge central bar, where the Irish
theming is done surprisingly well. For
a lavish party during normal opening
hours they might be persuaded to let
you take over the whole place.* / in-
house caterers; Cottage Bar (150,90,–,–);
Mezzanine (45,30,–,–);
Restaurant (–,50,–,–).

HQS Wellington WC2
£M-E, (250,180,150,180)
Victoria Embankment,
Temple Stairs
☎ 0870 780 9639
🖷 (020) 7653 6653
🖰 www.cbvs.co.uk
🖂 helpme@cbvs.co.uk
*The Master Mariners' hall, a Second
World War naval sloop, boasts a fine
location (opposite the National
Theatre). Its hall, in the bowels of
the ship, gives little clue that you are
afloat, but the other rooms are more
nautical in flavour (with superb mod-
els of ships) and have an airy charm.
The decks make a good choice for a
summer party.* / 11pm; in-house caterers;
Court Rm (180,150,150,180);
Quarterdeck (250,50,–,–); Model
Rm (120,30,–,40).

Wellington Arch W1
£M-E, (80,36,36,–)
Hyde Park Corner
☎ (020) 7973 3292
🖷 (020) 7973 3443
🖰 www.english-heritage.org.uk
🖂 jane.coughlan@
   english-heritage.org.uk
*This prominent monument (erected
in 1826, and now bearing the largest
bronze sculpture in the UK) makes
an intriguing place for a party.* / no

political events; midnight; list of caterers;
no smoking.

The Wellington Club SW1
£M-E, (200,38,–,–)
116a Knightsbridge
☎ 0845 4561556
🖷 0845 4561557
🖰 www.jiantmarketing.co.uk
🖂 jennifer@jiantmarketing.co.uk
*A Knightsbridge private members
club (with a high-profile member-
ship), spread over two floors, which
you can hire exclusively for private
functions.* / in-house caterers.

The Wells NW3
£M, (–,10,–,–)
30 Well Walk
☎ (020) 7794 3785
🖷 (020) 7794 6817
🖰 www.thewellshampstead.co.uk
*This charmingly-located and much-
above-average new Hampstead gastropub has made quite a splash. Its
upstairs private room, The Study,
would make a very pleasant location
for a small dinner.*

Wessex House SW11
£B, (200,150,–,–)
1A St John's Hl
☎ (020) 7622 6818
🖂 pamela.price@lineone.net
*A characterfully seedy dance hall, at
Clapham Junction.* / 3 am; in-house caterers.

West Wycombe Caves, Bucks
£M, (200,50,50,–)
Park Ln, Land End, High
Wycombe
☎ 01494 883808
🖷 01494 883733
🖰 www.westwycombe.co.uk
🖂 info@westwycombe.co.uk
*The caves – legacy of a c18 job-cre-
ation scheme – were the meeting
place for the Hell-Fire Club and are
used for a variety of functions.* / 2 am;
available from 6.30pm; in-house caterers; no
smoking; Banqueting Hall (200,50,50,–).

The Westbury W1
£M, (150,80,60,–)
Conduit St
☎ (020) 7629 7755
🖷 (020) 7495 1163
🖱 www.westbury-london.co.uk
📧 westburyhotel@
compuserve.com
This smartly-located '50s hotel pro-
vides four pleasant function rooms
which possess a fair degree of
charm. / smoking restricted; Mount Vernon
Rm (150,80,60,–); Pine Rm (120,60,40,–);
Brighton Rm (60,30,–,–); Regency
Rm (40,20,–,–).

Westminster Cathedral Hall SW1
£B, (300,200,–,–)
Ambrosden Ave
☎ (020) 7798 9064
🖱 www.westminster
cathedral.org.uk
📧 barrypalmer@rcdow.org.uk
This attractive and colourful
Edwardian hall behind the cathedral
was refurbished in 1995. It has an
arched roof, natural wood floor and
period chandeliers. / no weddings; 11pm;
evenings only Sun; hirer's choice of caterer;
no amplified music.

Westminster Abbey Garden SW1
£M-E, (500,230,–,–)
The Chapter Office, 20 Dean's
Yd, Westminster Abbey
☎ (020) 7654 4846
🖷 (020) 7233 2072
🖱 www.westminster-abbey.org
📧 matthew.arnoldi@
westminster-abbey.org
A gem of a site of just over an acre.
Medicinal herbs were once grown
there – it was the property of the
Infirmarer of the Abbey – and it now
contains statues and many fine trees.
You should ideally book at least a
year ahead. Also available, St
Catherine's Chapel garden. / 10pm;
available evenings only Jun-Jul, Mon-Thu; list
of caterers; no amplified music; no dancing;
smoking restricted; College
Garden (500,230,–,–); St Catherine's Chapel
Garden (100,–,–,–).

Westway Studios W11
£M-E, (750,500,500,–)
8 Olaf St
☎ (020) 7221 9041
🖷 (020) 7221 9399
🖱 www.sanctuarystudios.co.uk
📧 morseassociates@aol.com
Notting Hill film studios with large,
empty spaces that are ideal for
theme evenings – these are usually
organised by Morse Associates.
/ hirer's choice of caterer; Studio
2 (590,300,–,–); Studio 4 (300,200,–,–);
Studio 3 (150,100,–,–).

Westminster Boating Base SW1
£B-M, (350,160,160,–)
136 Grosvenor Rd
☎ (020) 7821 7389
Located on the river at Pimlico, the
base offers an unusually central loca-
tion which can be turned to most
types of function. Prices are reason-
able and there are good facilities,
including a modern pavilion, sited on
the piers. For major events, mar-
quees may be erected in the adjoin-
ing park. / 1 am; hirer's choice of caterer
(in-house available).

Whipsnade Wild Animal Park, Beds
£M, (600,400,400,600)
Dunstable
☎ 01582 873831
🖱 www.zsl.org
📧 marketingwwap@gn.apc.org
The park, home to 2,500 creatures,
makes an interesting location for a
variety of events. Packages can
include tours in an open top double-
decker bus or on a narrow-gauge
railway. The two light, bright, rather
functional, modern suites each have
a private lawn. / midnight; in-house caterers; Griffin Suite (300,200,200,300); Phoenix
Suite (300,200,200,300);
Pegasus (–,10,10,30); Unicorn (–,30,20,40).

CAPACITIES: (Standing, Seated, Dinner dance, Theatre-style)

White Hart Lane Conference Centre N17

£B-M, (600,400,300,500)
Bill Nicholson Way,
748 High Rd, Tottenham
☎ (020) 8365 5006
🖶 (020) 8365 5156
🖰 www.spurs.co.uk
📧 events@spurs.co.uk
*Range of 13 conference and ban-
queting suites, most overlooking the
famous Tottenham Hotspur pitch.*
/ *in-house caterers; Whites
Suite (600,400,300,500); Box
Norm (300,160,120,250); Oak
Rm (150,100,90,80).*

White House Hotel NW1

£M, (200,160,150,–)
Albany St, Regent's Park
☎ (020) 7391 3000
🖶 (020) 7388 8040
🖰 www.solmelia.com
📧 adolfo.almagro@solmelia.com
*A pleasant, vaguely Art Deco
Marylebone hotel, which has been
substantially refurbished in recent
years.* / *I am; hirer's choice of caterer
(in-house available); Albany (200,160,150,–);
Chester (150,90,80,–);
Osnaburgh (120,70,50,–).*

The White Horse SW6

£B, (80,50,–,50)
1-3 Parsons Gn
☎ (020) 7736 2115
🖶 (020) 7610 6091
🖰 www.whitehorseSW6.com
*A well-known, atmospheric pub over-
looking Parsons Green. It has a large
upstairs private room. There is a
pleasant terrace, but it is only made
available very occasionally for private
parties.* / *food must be served; 12.30 am;
Private Rm (80,50,–,50);
Restaurant (–,35,–,–); Winter
Marquee (–,65,–,–).*

White's EC4

£M-E, (150,80,–,–)
New St Sq
☎ (020) 7583 1313
🖶 (020) 7353 1662
*Marco Pierre White's relaunch of the
first-floor City-fringe restaurant site
long known as City Rhodes. There is
no private room, but you can hire
the whole place.*

The White House SW4

£B-M, (250,50,–,–)
65 Clapham Park Rd
☎ (020) 7498 3388
🖶 (020) 7498 5588
🖰 www.thewhitehouse
london.co.uk
📧 info@
thewhitehouselondon.co.uk
*Rooms for private parties are a fun-
damental part of the set-up of this
trendy bar/club/restaurant, which
aims to keep the flame of "West
End sophistication" alive in deepest
Clapham.* / *2 am; Private Rm (–,28,–,–);
Private Rm (–,8,–,–).*

Whitechapel Art Gallery E1

£B-M, (1500,400,–,104)
80-82 Whitechapel High St
☎ (020) 7522 7888
🖰 www.whitechapel.org
📧 info@whitechapel.org
*A spacious Art Nouveau gallery on
the fringes of the City, which is particularly suitable for early evening
receptions.* / *available subject to constraints
of current exhibits; 11pm; available eves &
Mon all day, closed Thu; hirer's choice of
caterer (in-house available); no smoking;
Upper Gallery (650,200,–,–); Lower
Gallery (800,400,–,–); Lecture
Theatre (–,–,–,104); Café (80,60,–,–).*

Winchester House

AM & PM Catering
Winchester House
10 Lwr Richmond Rd
Putney
London SW15 1JN
Tel: (020) 8789 4447
www.ampmcatering.co.uk
info@ampmcatering.co.uk

A Recipe for Successful Wedding Receptions

Whitelands College SW15
£B-M, (300,200,150,200)
West Hill
☎ (020) 8392 3505
⌂ www.roehampton.ac.uk
✉ v.ruocca@roehampton.ac.uk
A Roehampton college, standing in its own grounds, with a characterful '30s interior, and popular for wedding receptions and parties. / midnight; in-house caterers; smoking restricted; Ruskin Dining Hall (300,200,150,200); Boardroom (100,–,–,–); Lecture Theatre (–,–,–,154).

Whitewebbs Museum of Transport, Middx
£B-M, (100,80,80,50)
Whitewebbs Rd, Enfield
☎ (020) 8367 1898
🖷 (020) 8363 1904
⌂ www.whitewebbsmuseum.co.uk
✉ museum@whitewebbs.fsnet.co.uk
You can hold receptions – and sometimes other functions – among the veteran vehicles on display in this former Victorian pumping station. / midnight; in-house caterers or hirer's choice by negotiation; no smoking.

Will's Art Warehouse SW6
£B-M, (250,150,120,–)
Unit 3, Heathmans Rd
☎ (020) 7371 8787
🖷 (020) 7371 0044
⌂ www.wills-art.com
✉ info@wills-art.com

This contemporary art gallery, housed in a Victorian building in Parson's Green, is well suited to entertaining. If the current show is not decoration enough, theming can be arranged. / available from 6pm; hirer's choice of caterer.

William IV NW10
£B-M, (400,150,–,–)
786 Harrow Rd
☎ (020) 8969 5944
🖷 (020) 8964 9218
⌂ www.william-iv.co.uk
A Kensal Green gastropub, which – thanks to a couple of function rooms and a heated garden – lends itself particularly to party use. / midnight, Sat

CAPACITIES: (Standing, Seated, Dinner dance, Theatre-style)

I am; Function Rm (120,40,–,–); Bar I (150,–,–,–); Restaurant (–,70,–,–); Garden (100,100,–,–).

Wiltons SW1
£M-E, (–,18,–,–)
55 Jermyn St
☎ (020) 7629 9955
🖷 (020) 7495 6233
🖰 www.wiltons.co.uk
✉ wiltons@wiltons.co.uk
This famously clubby, old-established St James's English restaurant is the sort of place which has just had a major make-over, but which stresses that everything is still exactly the same! There is a private room on the ground floor. / 10.30pm; not available Sun; Private Rm (–,18,–,–).

Winchester House SW15
£M, (180,180,180,–)
10 Lower Richmond Rd
☎ (020) 8789 4447
🖰 www.winchesterhouse.co.uk
✉ info@ampmcatering.co.uk
Occupying an unrivalled position on the banks of the river Thames and set within its own walled grounds, Winchester House is the most fabulous place for events of all kinds – conferences, Christmas parties, dinners and dances, the choice is yours. Under the professional management of AM & PM CATERING since 1983, this venue really is a bit of gem and viewing is strongly recommended. See advertisement opposite. / I am; AM & PM Catering; River Rm (180,120,–,–); Turner Rm (–,16,–,–); Library (40,–,–,–); River Lawn (–,180,180,–); Front Lawn (–,130,–,–).

Windsor Guildhall, Berks
£M-E, (150,120,120,–)
High St, Windsor
☎ 01628 796033
🖷 01628 689543
🖰 www.rbwm.gov.uk
✉ richard.heyward@rbwm.gov.uk
A fine c17 building, (completed by Wren), popular for wedding recep-

tions and dinners. The Ascot Room features stained glass windows, paintings and a chandelier. The imposing Guildhall retains the aspect of a court-room and boasts a sequence of royal portraits spanning four centuries. / in-house caterers; no amplified music; no dancing; Guildhall Chamber (150,120,120,–); Maidenhead Rm (100,40,–,–); Ascot Rm (30,26,–,–).

Wine Gallery SW10
£B-M, (–,45,–,–)
49 Hollywood Rd
☎ (020) 7352 7572
🖷 (020) 7376 5083
🖰 www.brinkleys.com
This cosily unchanging, informal restaurant on the fringe of Chelsea has nooks and crannies to accommodate smaller parties, as well as a couple of private rooms. You may also be able to party in the pleasant paved garden, at the rear. / Private Rm (–,45,–,–); Private Rm (x2) (–,20,–,–).

Winston Churchill's Britain at War SE1
£M, (120,–,–,–)
64-66 Tooley St
☎ (020) 7403 3171
🖷 (020) 7403 5104
🖰 www.britainatwar.co.uk
✉ britainatwar@dial.pipex.com
Life in Britain during WWII is the theme of this museum near London Bridge. Events take place among the exhibits, which include a re-creation of the Blitz, where sounds and smells produce a "realistic" atmosphere. / 11.30pm; available from 6:30pm; hirer's choice of caterer; no dancing; smoking restricted.

WKD NW1
£B, (255,60,60,–)
18 Kentish Town Rd
☎ (020) 7267 1869
🖷 (020) 7284 3660
🖰 www.wkdclub.co.uk
✉ info@wkdclub.co.uk
What was part of the Camden Town Sainsbury's car-park has been reclaimed with a building that serves as a Thai restaurant by day and a

nightclub by night. You might take the mezzanine, with a view of the stage, for a private bash. / 2 am, 3 am weekends; in-house caterers; Mezzanine (120,60,60,–).

Wódka W8
£M, (–,70,–,–)
12 St Albans Grove
☎ (020) 7937 6513
🖨 (020) 7937 8621
🖑 www.wodka.co.uk
📧 info@wodka.co.uk
This bare but chic Polish restaurant in Kensington is a good place to take over in its entirety. Alternatively, smaller groups can use the downstairs private room. / 1.30 am; no amplified music; no dancing; Private Rm (–,32,–,–).

Woody's W9
£M, (330,–,–,–)
41-43 Woodfield Rd
☎ (020) 7266 3030
🖑 www.woodysclub.com
An atmospheric club, physically just outside Notting Hill, but spiritually very much within it – a good, and quite flexible, location for a stand-up party. / Individual Floors (x3) (100,–,–,–).

The Worx SW6
£B-M, (2000,200,200,250)
10 Heathmans Rd
☎ (020) 7371 9777
🖑 www.theworx.co.uk
📧 enquiries@theworx.co.uk
Though primarily designed as photographic studios, these Parson's Green facilities (which range from 400-25,000 sq ft) are, with theming, suitable for receptions and corporate events. There is a soundproofed area suitable for dancing. / 2 am; hirer's choice of caterer; Studio 1 (300,100,100,200); Studio 2 (350,150,–,200); Studio 3 (30,10,–,20); Studio 4 (100,30,–,50).

Wrotham Park, Herts
£E, (150,120,–,150)
Barnet
☎ (020) 8441 0755
🖑 www.wrothampark.com
📧 info@wrothampark.com
An elegant, privately-owned Palladian mansion, just within the M25. It's set in 300 acres of parkland and therefore highly suitable as a marquee site or for events involving activities. / no children; midnight; list of caterers; no smoking; Drawing Rm (150,120,–,150); Dining Rm (100,70,–,100); Saloon (50,–,–,–).

Wyndham's Theatre WC2
£M, (–,–,–,782)
Charing Cross Rd
☎ (020) 7438 9700
🖨 (020) 7438 9761
A medium-sized theatre, decorated in shades of blue and cream. It's available for presentations and the like, subject to the constraints of the current show. / available subject to constraints of current production; in-house caterers; smoking restricted.

Ye Olde Cheshire Cheese EC4
£B, (150,60,–,–)
145 Fleet St
☎ (020) 7353 6170
🖑 www. yeoldecheshirecheese.com
📧 info@ yeoldecheshirecheese.com
A rambling, historic, atmospheric pub – rebuilt after the Great Fire – many of whose nooks and crannies can be used for lunches, dinners or drinks. Larger parties (in the Cellar Bar) can only be accommodated on Saturdays. / 11.20pm; no music; no dancing; Cellar Bar (150,60,–,–); Williams Rm (–,60,–,–); Johnson's Bar (70,–,–,–); Director's Rm (25,10,–,–).

CAPACITIES: (Standing, Seated, Dinner dance, Theatre-style)

Yming W1
£M, (–,40,–,–)
35-36 Greek St
☎ (020) 7734 2721
🖨 (020) 7437 0292
🖱 www.yming.com
Soho's best Chinese restaurant bar none – its private room could make a good birthday party venue, for example.

Zen Central W1
£M-E, (–,20,–,–)
20-22 Queen St
☎ (020) 7629 8089
🖨 (020) 7493 6181
Grand, minimalist Chinese restaurant, in the heart of Mayfair, offering food of high quality. Its style is perhaps more suited to corporate than social entertaining. / Private Rm (–,20,–,–).

ZeNW3 NW3
£M, (–,150,–,–)
83-84 Hampstead High St
☎ (020) 7794 7863
🖨 (020) 7794 6956
🖱 www.zenw3.com
This very stylish, minimalist Hampstead Chinese restaurant has a top floor private room, or you might be able to take the whole place. / Private Rm (–,25,–,–).

MOVING VENUES

MOVING VENUES

Floating Boater W2
£B-M, (80,45,–,–)
The Waterside, Warwick
Crescent
☎ (020) 7266 1066
🖷 (020) 7266 4665
🖱 www.floatingboater.co.uk
*For entertaining on the Regent's
Canal, from Little Venice to Camden
Lock, you can choose between 'The
Prince Regent' (an Edwardian-style
boat for parties of 12-80) or
'Lapwing' a 90 year old narrow boat
now used for private dining for 12-30
guests. All the craft are weather-
proof, centrally heated and available
all year round. / in-house caterers; Prince
Regent (80,45,–,–); Lapwing (30,22,–,–).*

The Lady
Daphne EC1
£B-M, (75,35,–,–)
5-7 St. Helen's Place
☎ (020) 7562 7656
🖱 www.lady-daphne.co.uk
*A wooden vessel built in 1923 and
still sailing. Spend a day on the
Thames, perhaps boarding at Hays
Galleria, and sailing under Tower
Bridge (which will be raised for you
on the way) en route to Greenwich or
the Thames Barrier. Alternatively,
hold a reception in dock. / no stilettos;
1am; hirer's choice of caterer;
Stationary (75,35,–,–); Afloat (54,35,–,–).*

Jason's Trip W9
£B-M, (50,36,36,–)
Opposite No. 60, Bloomfield Rd
☎ (020) 7286 3428
🖱 www.jason.co.uk

*An operator of traditional style,
brightly painted narrow boats on
Regent's Canal. The smaller Lace
Plate and Lady Rose restaurant boats
accommodate more formal sit down
functions. / midnight; Apr-Oct, Lace Plate &
Lady Rose all year; in-house or hirer's choice;
Lady Rose (50,36,36,–); Lace
Plate (36,28,24,–); Jason (35,–,–,–);
Holland (48,–,–,–).*

Maidenhead Steam
Navigation
£B-M, (140,80,110,–)
Taplow Boatyard, Mill Lane,
Taplow, Berkshire
☎ (01628) 621770
🖱 www.maidenheadsteam.co.uk
*Four boats for cruising the upper
reaches of the Thames between
Henley and Windsor. The SL "Belle"
(a century old cruiser) offers the
classic experiences while the
"Mississippi", "Southern Comfort"
and "Pink Champagne" are packed
with character. The executive
"Georgian" offers style and comfort.
Full Bar facilities throughout at pub
prices, fully heated for winter
months. / 11.30pm; hirer's choice of caterer
(in-house available); smoking restricted;
Georgian (140,80,80,–); Southern
Comfort (110,60,60,–); Belle (80,28,–,–);
Fringilla (12,12,–,–); Pink
Champagne (50,28,50,–).*

CAPACITIES: (Standing, Seated, Dinner dance, Theatre style)

Thames Luxury Charters SW15
£B-M, (520,400,50,–)
5 The Mews, 6 Putney Common
☎ (020) 8780 1562
🖰 www.thamesluxury
  charters.co.uk

London's largest boat, the "Dixie Queen" and the "Elizabethan" offer upmarket facilities, plus a unique night club atmosphere for dining and dancing. The "Salamander" and "Edwardian" are useful for events and transfers. Competitive price structure, cruises and pick up from Kew to the Thames Barrier. Full bar facilities throughout and fully heated for the winter months. / hirer's choice of caterer (in-house available); smoking restricted; Golden Salamander (150,70,150,–); Elizabethan (235,180,230,–); Dixie Queen (520,400,520,–); Edwardian (100,60,100,–).

SERVICES

Services directory

Note: Unlike the Venues directory, this is an advertorial section. Though we have tried to impose a reasonably uniform style, the concepts and claims expressed are those of the advertisers concerned.

1. **Party planners**
2. **Food & beverage**
3. **Theme & equipment**
4. **Entertainment**
5. **Insurance**
6. **Invitations**
7. **Photographers**
8. **Transport**
9. **Attire**

I. PARTY PLANNERS

If you are organising a big party there is a lot to be said for bringing in the professionals. With an event of any scale, it is a full-time job to ensure that everything comes together on the night – a party planner will do the worrying for you, and let you get on with enjoying yourself. In addition, assuming you choose the right planner you may get a better party for your money, with greater flair and professionalism.

The term 'party planner' covers a multitude of sins. Many party planners have grown out of caterers or entertainers and their party planning business often emphasises their original speciality. Others are independent experts who have no formal links with any particular caterers or other suppliers and are completely free to help you choose the right contractors for your event.

Some planners will get right down to the detail, for example ensuring that invitations are correctly addressed and organising the 'placement' (table seating). Others will regard their job as done if they organise a good dinner and the band plays.

Some planners work on commission, others will charge a fee. Consider the level of service you want. As with all aspects of planning a party, try to be reasonably clear in advance about what you are looking for and how much you are prepared to pay for it, and don't be afraid to ask the planner about their experience of similar events – there should be no objection if you ask to speak to previous clients.

The descriptions adopted by those who organise parties and other events are becoming more and more confusing. In the corporate sphere, the term 'event managers' (or sometimes 'event designers') is usually preferred to the more social-sounding 'party planner'.

Absolute Taste
14 Edgel Street, London SW18
☎ (020) 8870 5151
🖷 (020) 8870 9191
🖰 www.absolutetaste.com
✉ info@absolutetaste.com
A stylish and innovative event design and catering company, creating delicious food, imaginatively presented. Their passion is "in the detail", covering everything from unique menus to full production facilities, fabulous styling and professional service, for parties, launches, weddings or film premieres. Catering at Grand Prix events, worldwide, a speciality.

The Admirable Crichton
5 Camberwell Trading Est, Denmark Rd, London SE5 9LB
☎ (020) 7326 3800
🖷 (020) 7326 3801
🖰 www.admirable-crichton.co.uk
"The name behind the world's best parties". The Admirable Crichton has

been at the cutting edge of the London food scene for over twenty years and has built an unrivalled reputation for delicious, original and inspired food and innovative and stylish party design. See advertisement on page 194.

Alternative Occasions
172 Brox Road, Ottershaw, Surrey KT16 0LQ
☎ (020) 7610 1060,
(01932) 872115
🖱 www.stressfreeday.com
✉ info@stressfreeday.com

One of the UK's most established wedding and private party organisers, run by people with professional project management backgrounds, and operating across Britain and overseas. Services include party design and management, catering, venue finding, venue decoration, theming and lighting.

Annie Fryer
134 Lots Rd, London SW10 0RJ
☎ (020) 7352 7693
🖨 (020) 7352 4890
🖱 www.anniefryer.com
✉ annie@anniefryer.com
A catering companies and party planner with one of the most established names in the business. "Good food and party design for exclusive events."

Banana Split
11 Carlisle Rd, London NW9 0HD
☎ (020) 8200 1234
🖱 www.banana-split.com
Providing a professional party planning facility for any evening in both London and internationally, the company has built a reputation for excellent quality and personal service. By carefully selecting suppliers, they ensure that customers come back time and time again.

William Bartholomew Party Organising
23 The Talina Centre, Bagleys Ln, London SW6 2BW
☎ (020) 7731 8328
🖨 (020) 7384 1807
🖱 www.wbpo.com
✉ mail@wbpo.com

One of the top party planners – see advertisement on back flap.

Beadon Daniel Events
5 Spice Court, Plantation Wharf, London SW11 3UE
☎ (020) 7978 7400
🖱 www.beadondaniel.co.uk
An inspiring party planning company, where a sense of professionalism, efficiency and attention to detail is paramount. They provide both private and corporate clients with a creative and cutting edge event production and management service, using their fully integrated, client-focused, competitive team.

Bluebird Events

350 Kings Rd, London SW3 5UU
☎ (020) 7559 1110
🖱 www.conran.com
📧 bluebirdevents@bluebird-store.co.uk

Bluebird
EVENTS

Bluebird events, Conran's outside catering and party service, is particularly proud of the 'Where do you find them?' question so regularly asked about their young, articulate and well-groomed staff. Whilst best known for a contemporary style, they have also demonstrated an ability to be classic or fun, formal or frivolous.

Brand & Deliver

The Factory,14c Shepherdess Walk, London N1 7LB
☎ (020) 7851 8521
🖱 www.brandanddeliver.co.uk
📧 info@brandanddeliver.co.uk

brand&deliver

Created to offer a fresh, clever & economical approach to live events,

this highly experienced and energetic company produces everything from large corporate brand experiences to high-profile parties.

Gill Branston & Associates

137 Hale Lane, Edgware, Middlesex HA8 9QP
☎ (020) 8906 4664
🖨 (020) 8959 2137
🖱 www.eventsbygillbranston.com
📧 info@gillbranston.com
Imaginative, cost-effective and seamlessly organised events. Corporate events (30 to 1000+) a speciality - awards dinners and conferences, product launches, promotional events, corporate parties, training seminars and incentive days out – in the UK and abroad.

Caprice Events

28-30 Litchfield St, London WC2H 9NL
☎ (020) 7557 6339
🖨 (020) 7497 3644
🖱 www.caprice-events.co.uk
📧 carmen@caprice-events.co.uk
See advertisement below.

With the continuing success of The Ivy, Le Caprice, J.Sheekey and Daphne's, Caprice Holdings have now launched Caprice Events.

We offer a bespoke catering and hospitality service, bringing the style and sophistication from the restaurants to your home or event.

Contact Jo Harris Events Co-ordinator on 020 7557 6091 or Carmen Hannemann, Events Manager on 020 7557 6339

Chance

321 Fulham Rd, London
SW10 9QL
☎ (020) 7376 5995
🖰 www.chanceorganisation.co.uk
✉ info@chanceorganisation.co.uk

Chance

With over 20 years' experience, this is a highly respected party planning and event management company. They have developed an unequalled reputation for planning and implementing exciting tailor-made events – including private & corporate parties, charity events and award ceremonies – throughout the United Kingdom & Europe.

Chaplin's Party and Conference Planners

Trafalgar House, Grenville Place, London NW7 3SA
☎ 020 8959 2070
🖷 020 8959 2867
🖰 www.chaplinproductions.co.uk
✉ info@chaplinproductions.co.uk
"One of London's leading party planners", with every party individually planned to suit each client's personal requirements.

Chevalier Event Design

Studio 4-5, Garnet Close, Watford
WD24 7GN
☎ (01923) 211703
🖷 (01923) 211704
🖰 www.chevalier.co.uk
✉ enquiries@chevalier.co.uk
"All the things you never thought you would find in one place" – practical imaginers, orderly flexibility, experienced innovators, approachable professionals...and they also create and cater for quite simply "the most wonderful events in the world"!

Complete Events

5 Beechmore Rd, London
SW11 4ET
☎ (020) 7610 1770
🖰 www.completeevents.co.uk
✉ info@completeevents.co.uk
A party organiser specialising in large parties, private and corporate, particularly those involving marquees.

costinpank

36 Fortnam Rd, London N19 3NR
☎ (020) 7272 8545
✉ event@dircon.co.uk
Established by Simon Costin and Anna Pank, this company brings a dynamic flair to every aspect of events from conception to completion, providing art direction and set production, graphic design, locations, catering, flowers, light, sound entertainment, photography, transport and security.

ESC Events

The Clockhouse, St Johns Lye, St Johns, Woking, Surrey GU21 7SE
☎ (01483) 722225
🖰 www.esc-events.co.uk
✉ info@esc-events.co.uk
A well established firm which provides a wide ranging social and corporate event services.

Event Fusion

81 Honeywell Road, London
SW11 6ED
☎ (020) 7228 1374
🖰 www.eventfusion.co.uk
✉ charlottewb@
   eventfusion.co.uk
Charlotte Wolseley Brinton is a discreet and independent organiser of weddings, private parties and corporate events of all requirements, sizes and budgets. She offers a personal service and attention to detail combined with energy and enthusiasm.

VISIT US AT: www.hardens.com

Event Network

5 Albert Drive, London SW19 6LP
☎ (020) 8780 5270
🖷 (020) 8780 5273
🖃 events@
  eventnetwork.demon.co.uk
Specialists in project management for a wide variety of bespoke events – corporate, charity, sporting, society and private – offering a complete range of services, from planning through to total event organisation.

Evolve Events

First Floor, 24 Summerlands Avenue, London W3 6ER
☎ (020) 8993 9978
🖷 (020) 8993 9884
🖱 www.evolve-events.com
🖃 info@evolve-events.com

EVOLVE EVENTS

Specialists in transforming unique venues, this firm provides a comprehensive party planning and event management service to clients looking for imaginative, high-quality occasions for between 50 and 2000 guests. Venues include warehouses, car parks, lofts, derelict theatres, Georgian houses, photographic studios and galleries.

Fait Accompli

212 The Plaza, 535 King's Rd, London SW10 0SZ
☎ (020) 7352 2777
🖱 www.faitaccompli.co.uk

"One of the leading party organisers – worldwide". Their reputation is based on discretion, excellence and meticulous attention to detail. "Flair and innovation coupled with their reputation for sticking to the budget has proved a winning formula for countless private and corporate clients."

The Finishing Touch

4 Coval Passage, London SW14 7RE
☎ (020) 8878 7555
🖷 (020) 8878 8444
🖱 www.finishingtouchevents.co.uk
🖃 events@
  finishingtouchevents.co.uk
Established in 1989, this is one of the countries most established event management companies. Specialising in corporate events, they offer an extensive selection of themed and character venues for Summer and

---

- Company Anniversaries
- Christmas Parties
- Summer Balls
- Company BBQ's

- Conferences
- Management Offsites
- Team Events
- Family Days

THE FINISHING TOUCH

CORPORATE EVENTS & CONFERENCE MANAGEMENT

Tel : 020-8878-7555
events@finishingtouchevents.co.uk
www.finishingtouchevents.co.uk

Christmas parties, catering for numbers from 40 to 3000 guests. See advertisement opposite.

Fisher Productions

118 Garratt Lane, London
SW18 4DJ
☎ (020) 8871 1978
🖷 (020) 8871 1988
🖰 www.fisherproductions.co.uk
✉ info@fisherproductions.co.uk
Established in 1985 this is a firm which really can claim a wealth of experience in producing a wide variety of events – large and small. Their enthusiastic team provide a professional service, with creative flair, putting their clients' wishes first and producing events to an exceptional standard.

Gekko Events

103 Thomas More House,
Barbican, London EC2Y 8BU
☎ 07816 921186
🖷 (020) 7053 2143
🖰 www.gekkoevents.com
✉ info@gekkoevents.com

A company specialising in bespoke creative event management and production, valued by clients for its creativity, attention to detail, personalised service, professionalism, experience, approachability and enthusiasm. Events of which they have experience include awards ceremonies, charity balls, gala dinners, backstage parties, roadshows and conferences.

Hares & Graces

2 Lilac Pl, London SE11 5QQ
☎ (020) 7820 1277,
Mobile 07710 352789
A party-planning business whose assignments are often either purely social or sometimes with a PR flavour. Intimate tapas evenings are a speciality.

I.D.E.A.S.

Trident Business Centre, 89
Bickersteth Rd, London
SW17 9SH
☎ (020) 8767 7264
🖰 www.ideasevents.co.uk
✉ mail@ideasevents.co.uk
Want IDEAS for your event? How about a champagne reception in a London palace? Wine tasting in a country mansion? A murder mystery in Monte Carlo? A treasure hunt in Cyprus? Husky racing in Lapland? The list is endless… whatever your event – they have the answer!

Inneventive

Victory House, 10-14 Leicester
Place, London WC2H 7BZ
☎ (020) 7432 4460
🖷 (020) 7287 7831
🖰 www.inneventive.co.uk
✉ events@inneventive.co.uk

The complete event design, management and production services catering for corporate and private parties. Theatrical entertainment and a full event planning service are specialities. Actors, singers and dancers from the stage will perform at your event – provide the script, or they can do the words and music for you.

Inventive Events

The Studio, 61 Elm Bank Gdns,
London SW13 0NX
☎ (020) 8392 9222
🖰 www.inventiveevents.com
✉ enquiries@
    inventiveevents.com

*Inventive and highly creative events
are the speciality of "one of London's
top event companies" (whose regular
clients include British Airways, AOL,
Carlton Television and M&C Saatchi).
Large-scale events and unusual briefs
are a speciality.*

Edmond James

37 Marlborough, 5 Inner Park Rd,
London SW19 6DX
☎ (020) 8789 8240
🖰 www.
    edmondjameshospitality.com
*" It is possible to be a guest at your
own party!" Edmond James Walshe
– or "Eddie", as he's know in the
trade – has over 35 years'
experience in hotels, restaurants and
private parties, and his firm offers a
staff of quality butlers for any
occasion. Whether you are having an
intimate dinner or a corporate
function you can rely on Eddie to
arrange it all for you down to the
finest detail.*

Lillingston Associates

The Studio, 2a Kempson Rd,
London SW6 4PU
☎ (07000) 710131
🖰 www.lillingston.co.uk
✉ sophiel@lillingston.co.uk

*Over 10 years experience in
organising spectacular events for high
profile corporate and private clients
including dinners in palaces,
weekends in private stately homes,
weddings on romantic Italian clifftops
and parties in the Moroccan desert!
"Renowned for discretion, personal
service, attention to detail, and above
all, creative flair!"*

MacGregor & Co

72 Wilton Road, London
SW1V 1DE
☎ (020) 7834 2080
🖰 www.macevents.co.uk
✉ cm@macevents.co.uk
*An event management company
specialising in the logistical
organisation and delivery of a large
range of inspired and professionally
managed entertainment events.
Creative design, impeccable taste and
a personal attention is brought to the
party-planning process, in either
London or Edinburgh.*

Maiden Management

1 Elysium Gate, 126-128 New
Kings Rd, London SW6 4LZ
☎ (020) 7610 6234
🖨 (020) 7610 9234
🖰 www.maidenmanagement.com
✉ info@maidenmanagement.com

MAIDEN MANAGEMENT

*Established in 1997, an independent
event management company and
production house specialising in sport*

and entertainment. Experts in producing shows, parties and live events and a market leader in managing fundraising events.

Mask Entertainments

Studio 302, Lana House, 118 Commercial St, London E1 6NF
☎ (020) 7377 8001
🖰 www.mask.co.uk
📠 enquiries@mask.co.uk

MASK

EVENT DESIGN & PRODUCTION

Formed in 1988, the company has a wealth of experience, and a reputation for professionalism, innovative ideas and skillful production. It has a very large following in the private and corporate sector in the UK and further afield, and has worked at many of the venues in this marvellous guide (their comment, Ed). Call Arthur Somerset for more information.

Mosimann's

4 William Blake Hse, Bridge Ln, London SW11 3AD
☎ (020) 7326 8344
🖰 www.mosimann.com
📠 sales.enquiries@ mosimann.com
A creator of exclusive, unique and memorable occasions around the world, from banquets in palaces to Oriental picnics, elegant cocktail parties and glorious Summer luncheons during the Season. From 10 guests to 1000 they ensure meticulous attention to detail, innovative cuisine and highly professional service.

Mushroom Events Services

3 Encon Court, Owl Close, Moulton Park Industrial Estate, Northampton NN3 6HZ
☎ (01604) 790900
🖰 www.mushroomevents.co.uk
Lighting, design, sales and hire, with the benefit of 30 years of experience worldwide. Also floodlighting, staging, trussing sound and drapes. Technical production and stage management of all types of events.

Party Packages

62 Beechwood Road, South Croydon, Surrey CR2 0AA
☎ (020) 8657 2813
🖰 www.partypackagesltd.co.uk
📠 info@partypackagesltd.co.uk
With 30 different themes – including Wild West, Hollywood, James Bond, Arabian and Space – this company has the props, backdrops, games, bands, table decorations and so on to offer you a complete package. Or if you don't want to go for a 'package', you can have a 'pick and mix' deal.

Party Planners

56 Ladbroke Gr, London W11 2PB
☎ (020) 7229 9666
🖷 (020) 7727 6001
🖰 www.party-planners.co.uk
📠 lea@party-planners.co.uk
Lady Elizabeth Anson - often claimed to be the inventor of the whole party-planning concept - maintains her position as doyenne of the London party scene. She is not tied to any particular suppliers and emphasises her willingness to accommodate smaller budgets.

The Persuaders

1st Floor, 30 Orange St, London WC2H 7LZ
☎ (020) 7331 2306, Mobile 07984 437517
🖰 www.thepersuadersltd.co.uk
📠 andy@thepersuadersltd.co.uk
Private parties, product launches, corporate events… "From hands-on organisation to design consultation, discover The Persuaders difference."

Planit Events
15 Nottingham Rd, London
SW17 7EA
☎ (020) 8682 4900
⌂ www.planitevents.co.uk
✉ sales@planitevents.co.uk
*Available November and December
only. Themed marquee structure
ideal for corporate Christmas parties,
Charity Balls and Award ceremonies.
This large versatile venue is available
through party planners Planit Events.
Planit will also be running a number
of shared night parties at the venue
for bookings of 10 guests upwards.*

Powwow Conference & Event Management
2nd Floor Mortimer House,
230-236 Lavender Hill, London
SW11 1LE
☎ (020) 7228 9463
🖨 (020) 7228 9469
⌂ www.powwow.org.uk
✉ info@powwow.org.uk
*Are you looking for something
different? This professional
conference and events agency
specialises in the creation and
management of "truly memorable,
bespoke events".*

VISIT US AT: **www.hardens.com**

Roebuck Webb

4 Drake House, Dolphin Square,
London SW1V 3NN
☎ (020) 7798 8579,
Mobile 07771 727586
✉ roebuckwebb@aol.com
A company specialising in organising events, parties and weddings with style, discretion and the personal touch. Their unique knowledge and experience comes from many years working in the worlds of rock music, PR and Formula One motor sport. Recent work includes high-profile UK weddings and Pink Floyd's "Interstellar" exhibition in Paris.

Starlight Design

12 Gateway Trading Est, Hythe Rd,
London NW10 6RJ
☎ (020) 8960 6078
🖰 www.starlightdesign.co.uk
✉ info@starlightdesign.co.uk
A long established company that has been behind the scenes at major parties and shows worldwide for the past 15 years. Solid practical experience in scenery, lighting, pyrotechnics and entertainment has given rise to an enviable reputation for organising stylish and sophisticated events that illustrate their special creativity and originality. See their advertisement opposite.

Table Talk

Friars Court, 17 Rushworth St,
London SE1 0RB
☎ (020) 7401 3200
🖷 (020) 7401 9500
🖰 www.tabletalk.co.uk
✉ info@tabletalk.co.uk
A top event and food design company, with an outstanding reputation for creative and delicious food, imaginative design and an attention to detail that is second to none. From finding a venue and turning it into a full-blown casino, or transforming your dining room into an Aladdin's Cave, no event is too large or too small for their dedicated event team.

Theme Traders

The Stadium, Oaklands Rd,
London NW2 6DL
☎ (020) 8452 8518
🖰 www.themetraders.com
✉ projects@themetraders.com
See advertisement below.

Carolyn Townshend & Associates

☎ (020) 7235 1946
🖰 www.
    ladycarolyntownshend.co.uk
Specialising in stunningly imaginative events, film premiere parties and charity galas in exciting venues from

royal palaces to circus big tops! All events are tailor-made to meet clients' needs and budgets.

urban productions

63-65 Goldney Rd,
London W9 2AR
☎ (020) 7286 1700
🖨 (020) 7286 1709
🖱 www.urban-productions.co.uk
📧 events@urban-productions.co.uk

"An invitation to an event designed by urban productions is a ticket to the exceptional." They are equally willing to provide a specialist service or an all-encompassing event design and production service.

Lorraine Walters

32 Marryat Rd, Wimbledon,
London SW19 5BD
☎ (020) 8947 0494
📧 lorraine.walters1@virgin.net

A general party planning business offering a personal touch, and specialising in social events.

Zest Events

2 Swan Mews, Parsons Green Lane, London SW6 4QT
☎ (020) 7384 9336
🖨 (020) 7384 9337
🖱 www.zestevents.com
📧 parties@zestevents.com

z e s t   e v e n t s   l i m i t e d

"One of the more creative party planners, known for its chic, originality and fun!" Headed by Wonkie Hills, the company gives a personalised service, with attention to detail that's second to none – for events both private and corporate, in the UK and Europe.

2. FOOD & BEVERAGE

2.1 Caterers
2.2 Cakes
2.3 Catering equipment
2.4 Staff
2.5 Wine
2.6 Bars

2.1 CATERERS

The choice of caterer is one of the most important decisions to make. Not only do you have to choose a firm at the appropriate price point, but also one whose approach suits you and your event. Many firms have websites which are useful for obtaining a variety of different initial impressions. Alternatively, ring up a few firms with some initial questions – you should soon get a "feel" for the firms which you would be happiest to work with.

Most caterers listed here hold themselves out as catering for most types of occasion. Caterers are generally only too pleased to have the opportunity to quote – it should soon emerge, in their attitude or their prices, if they are appropriate for the sort of work you are enquiring about.

The following list is necessarily selective and omits many excellent local firms who do not generally take on anything but small dinner or drinks parties. For such events, the best recommendation is to ask around. For larger events too, don't hesitate to speak to friends or others who have organised functions recently.

Different caterers charge for food, wine, service and crockery hire in different ways. When comparing companies, it is essential to ensure that you are comparing like with like – make sure, for example, that all estimates include VAT.

Almost all caterers offer some degree of party-planning service and can – to differing extents – coordinate a marquee, flowers and even entertainment in addition to the catering. Firms differ, however, in the extent to which they will involve themselves in the non-catering aspects of events, so it's important to gauge their approach at an early stage.

Above The Salt
Unit 10 Business Centre, 103 Lavender Hill, London SW11 5QL
☎ (020) 7801 0694
🖷 (020) 7801 0399
🖰 www.abovethesalt.net
✉ abovethesalt@
   compuserve.com

Above the Salt - established in 1986, a favourite caterer with City firms and private clients alike. Lorna Dunhill and her team create delicious dinners and truly excellent canapés, for which they are well known.

Market ingredients inspire modern British and European menus and many varieties of oriental canapés.

Absolute Taste
14 Edgel Street, London SW18
☎ (020) 8870 5151
🖷 (020) 8870 9191
🖰 www.absolutetaste.com
✉ info@absolutetaste.com
A stylish and innovative event design and catering company, creating delicious food, imaginatively presented. Their passion is "in the detail", covering everything from unique menus to full production facilities, fabulous styling and professional service, for parties, launches, weddings or film premieres. Catering at Grand Prix events, worldwide, a speciality.

Alexander Catering
Branksome House, Filmer Grove, Godalming, Surrey GU7 3AB
☎ 01483 523 900
🖰 www.alexandercatering.com
✉ info@alexandercatering.co.uk
A well-established company providing catering for large corporate or other events in London and the South East.

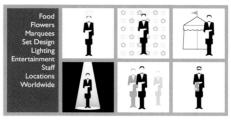

VISIT US AT: **www.hardens.com**

AM PM Catering

10 Lower Richmond Rd, London
SW15 1JN
☎ (020) 8789 4447
🖨 (020) 8785 2737
🖰 www.ampmcatering.co.uk
📧 info@ampmcatering.co.uk

*Although it has been the appointed
caterer at Winchester House – a
fabulous riverside venue in Putney –
since 1983, AM & PM is primarily an
outside catering company, with
offices in both London and
Hampshire. Their reputation for first-
class catering and service is
evidenced by numerous testimonials
from the many past happy clients. A
brochure is available on request.*

Blistering Group

Unit 2, Imex Business Centre,
Ingate Place, London SW8 3NS
☎ (020) 7720 7678
🖰 www.blisteringbarbecues.co.uk
📧 info@theblisteringgroup.co.uk

theblisteringgroup

*Blistering Barbecues have won
respect for their heroic all-weather
barbecuing themed events, relaxed
professionalism and, most
importantly, outstanding food cooked
fresh from charcoal barbecues and
wood-fired ovens. Electric Food, set
up in 2002, brings the unique
flavours, panache and
professionalism of Blistering
Barbecues inside - minus the
barbecues!*

Annie Fryer Catering

134 Lots Road, London SW10 0RJ
☎ (020) 7352 7693
🖨 (020) 7352 4890
🖰 www.anniefryer.com
📧 annie@anniefryer.com

Annie Fryer

C A T E R I N G

*"Understated excellence" is the aim
of this company which – with more
than 30 years' experience – has
more evidence to back up its claims
than most. Inspired by food and with
a love of people and parties, each
event is unique, and styled to reflect
the party-giver.*

Blue Strawberry

Unit 53-54, South Bank
Commercial Centre,
140 Battersea Park Rd, London
SW11 4NB
☎ (020) 7498 0017
🖰 www.bluestrawberry.co.uk
📧 alex@bluestrawberry.co.uk

BLUE STRAWBERRY

*Private and corporate event caterers
noted for their client service, very
high standards of food and their
beautiful presentation. They also
bring a high level of logistical know-
how, and have a venue list including
English Heritage, the V&A and the
National Portrait Gallery.*

VISIT US AT: **www.hardens.com**

Bovingdons

16 Edgel St, London SW18 1SR
☎ (020) 8874 8032
🖱 www.bovingdons.co.uk

An intense passion for food, a
genuine desire to please and a
distinctively personal approach to
contemporary event planning and
creative menu design has created a
loyal client base for this company,
both corporate and private. They're
delighted to work up from "the
smallest seed of an idea".

Butter & Co

108 Lansdowne Rd, London W11 2LS
☎ 07900 691632
🖱 www.butterandco.com
✉ info@butterandco.com
A recently established catering firm
specializes in providing interesting
menus for clients both corporate and
private.

By Word of Mouth

22 Glenville Mews, Kimber Rd,
London SW18 4NJ
☎ (020) 8871 9566
🖱 www.bywordofmouth.co.uk
✉ office@bywordofmouth.co.uk
A leading name at the top end of
catering and party design, capable of
handling every aspect of food and
production, whatever the size of the
event. A great reputation for
fashionable, contemporary parties
and a truly bespoke service.

Carluccio's

12 Great Portland St, London
W1W 8QN
☎ (020) 7580 3050
🖱 www.carluccios.com
✉ headoffice@carluccios.com
Authentic Italian foods freshly
prepared from the Carluccio's kitchen
and food shop to your place of work
for any event (from a busy business
lunch to a product launch). Menus
start from £5 per person for simple
finger food, to filled platters for a
buffet lunch from £10. A full range of
drinks can be supplied to accompany
the food. If you're in the area of one
of their caffès, lunchtime delivery is
free (further afield charges at cost).

The Cellar Society

Unit 1, Bard Rd, London W10 6TP
☎ (020) 8960 2622
🖱 www.cellarsociety.com
✉ adam@cellarsociety.com
Canapés elevated "to an art form"
are the speciality of this "rising star".
Ultra slick events, exquisite
presentation and free-thinking chefs
who are obsessed with taste, texture
and the natural theatre of food and
drink have created an enviable client
list, including the likes of YSL, Paul
Smith, Donna Karan, Jade Jagger,
Asprey, Montblanc and Estée Lauder.

Clare's Kitchen

41 Chalcot Rd, London NW1 8LS
☎ (020) 7722 9833
🖱 www.clareskitchen.co.uk
✉ clottedcream@
    blueyonder.co.uk
Clare Latimer has provided catering
for all types of events for 30 years,
for between eight and 400 people.
Most work comes by word of mouth.
When you ring, ask to speak to Clare
or Zoe.

Compleat Cooking

Unit 31/32, Alexandra House,
140 Batersea Park Road,
London SW11 4NB
☎ (020) 7627 8407
🖱 www.compleatcooking.co.uk
"Sometimes you need a little help to
achieve perfection." That's the creed
of this young and creative event
management and catering company,

where innovative ideas are combined with imagination and professionalism to create unique events on any scale.

Create Food & Party Design
Unit 4, The Kimber Centre,
54 Kimber Rd, London SW18 4PP
☎ (020) 8870 1717
🖷 (020) 8870 1818
🖰 www.createfood.co.uk
🖃 info@createfood.co.uk

"For the past 16 years our philosophy has always been to create events that exceed clients expectations" – that's the aim of this company which combines flexibility, experience, and reliability with superior service and stylish and delicious food.

Devils on Horseback
Church Hill Barn, Nether Wallop, Stockbridge, Hants SO20 8EU
☎ (01264) 783585
🖰 www.devilsonhorseback.com
🖃 gn@devilsonhorseback.com

Riding to the rescue of those in need of canapés, across London and the South. To help your budgeting, prices are quoted on a 'service included basis'.

deWintons
Unit 4, Sleaford St, London SW8 5AB
☎ (020) 7627 5550
🖰 www.dewintons.co.uk
🖃 info@dewintons.co.uk

An inventive and vibrant young catering company with a passion for food, an eye for details and a sense of occasion. They cater for canapé parties, directors' lunches, private dinners, weddings and picnics. For your event, they will relish the challenge to come up with something new and exciting.

Dish
Unit F, 63 Alscot Rd, London SE1 3AW
☎ (020) 7231 8304
🖰 www.dishcatering.co.uk
🖃 parties@dishcatering.co.uk

Great food, slick service and an event to remember – whether it is a cocktail reception at Dali Universe (where they are preferred caterer) to dining with the stars at Madame Tussaud's, or an exclusive private party or wedding – that's the aim of this business now celebrating half a decade in business.

Eat to the Beat

Studio 4-5, Garnett Close,
Watford WD24 7GN
☎ (01923) 211702
🖷 (01923) 211704
🖑 www.eattothebeat.com
✉ catering@eattothebeat.com

*"The UK's premier crew and
production caterer to the exhibition,
corporate, music, film and television
industries." They offer trained chefs,
temporary kitchens and vast logistical
experience to their clients to create
memorable events, often working
closely with sister company Chevalier
Event Design to offer a full range of
services.*

ECLARE Cuisine

Unit 1, Heliport Industrial Estate,
Lombard Rd, London SW11 3SS
☎ (020) 7223 8383
🖷 (020) 7223 8424
🖑 www.eclare.com
✉ cuisine@eclare.com

*Eclare is an exciting, modern caterer
owned by chef Martin Clare, catering
for an exclusive mix of private and
corporate events. Inspired menus and
a truly personal service makes Eclare
a much sought after caterer for
weddings, cocktail receptions, lunches
and dinners of every size.*

Epicure

Trident Business Centre,
Bickersteth Rd, London
SW17 9SH
☎ (020) 8288 8882
🖑 www.epicure.uk.com
✉ catering@epicure.uk.com

*Experienced quality caterers
providing wonderful modern stylish
food for parties, weddings and
corporate events at competitive
prices. They work with several
venues, event organisers, party
planners and marquee companies, so
are happy to provide a full service
from any event from canapés to a
barbecue or a full dinner.*

Eton Well

Unit 10, Thames View, Station Rd,
Abingdon OX14 3UJ
☎ (01491) 614159
🖷 (01491) 614993
🖑 www.etonwell.com
✉ info@etonwell.com

*"Sooner or later you will have Eton
Well!" Based in Oxfordshire the
company provides a full range of
personal and corporate catering
services – canapés, spit roasts,
buffets, banquets, office openings –
in and around Oxford, London and
the M4/M40 corridors.*

Felicitous

19 Kensington Park Rd, London
W11 2EU
☎ (020) 7243 4050
🖷 (020) 7243 4052
🖑 www.felicitouscatering.co.uk
✉ info@felicitouscatering.co.uk

*A head chef who includes Le Caprice,
Pétrus and the Criterion on his CV
adds lustre to this creative and
bespoke catering company, which
aims to suit individual occasions and
budgets. It is based in a gourmet deli
in Notting Hill (voted one of Food
Illustrated's "10 Best Delis") which
also features daily "dishes to go".*

Fizz

The Foundry, 156 Blackfriars Road, London SE1 8EN
☎ 0800 389 5584
🖷 (0870) 443 5005
🖰 www.fizz.uk.com
📧 events@fizz.uk.com

Privately owned and managed, this is a company with an established reputation and is a recommended caterer at many of London's leading venues. The service extends from complete design to stunning catering. The website includes sample menus, as well as panoramic views of venues.

Hunt Kendall Catering

Ham Polo Club, Petersham Rd, Richmond, Surrey TW10 7AH
☎ (020) 8334 0001
🖰 www.hunt-kendall.com
📧 nick@hunt-kendall.com

Catering for discerning private and corporate clients across the UK from a unique venue – Ham Polo Club – set in a rural oasis close to the centre of Richmond. At home base, they have a colonial pavilion, vine clad verandahs, a private enclosed garden and almost unlimited specs for marquees and parking – see Venues.

Freshampers

34-36 Gertrude St, London SW10 0JG
☎ (020) 7376 3185
🖰 www.freshampers.com
📧 enquiries@freshampers.com

Freshampers offers a new concept in event catering – completely self-contained freshly prepared food and drink hampers. These are perfect for all parties and corporate events as there are no labour costs to incur – it is all disposable. This was County Life's favourite summer hamper of 2003.

Jackson Gilmour

Unit 12 The Tramsheds, Coomber Way, Croydon CR0 4TQ
☎ (020) 8665 1855
🖰 www.jacksongilmour.com
📧 info@jacksongilmour.com

JACKSON *Gilmour*
CULINARY ART

GW8 Catering

3 Abingdon Rd, London W8 6AH
☎ (020) 7376 2191
🖰 www.gw8.co.uk
📧 david@goolies-bar.com
See advertisement on page opposite.

"Take a young, dynamic team who produce fabulous food. Add imaginative event ideas, impeccable service and elegant design. Result: Jackson Gilmour!"

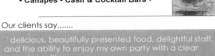

Lettice

18 Stannary Street, London
SE11 4AA
☎ 020 7820 1161
🖰 www.letticeparty.com
✉ info@letticeparty.com

Stephen Congdon recently relaunched his company under this new name. He is well known in corporate and private circles for his refreshing visual approach which is strongly influenced by modern design. The company creates beautiful and unusual effects with its own bespoke service equipment. A special team looks after weddings and private client business.

Mange on the Move

Unit 19, City North Trading Estate, Fonthill Rd, London N4 3HF
☎ (020) 7263 5000
🖨 (020) 7263 2233
🖰 www.mange.co.uk
✉ info@mange.co.uk

MANGE ON THE MOVE

For over 10 years, the company has provided stylish, robust food and imaginative event design. It is an approved supplier at several of London's top venues, and has a loyal corporate and private client-base. Other services offered by the Mange Group include 'drop-off' buffets, contemporary gift hampers and picnic boxes.

Lodge Catering

Unit 13, Mitre Bridge Industrial Estate, Mitre Way, London W10 6AU
☎ (020) 8960 5794
🖨 (020) 8964 8363
🖰 www.lodge-catering.co.uk
✉ lodge-catering@
lodge-catering.co.uk

LODGE
Catering

"The food was of an extremely high standard throughout the event, as was the service" – a customer comment on this wide-ranging service from a well-established firm, which brings a blend of innovative cuisine and personal service at some of London's top venues.

Mange Tout

38 Melgund Rd, London N5 1PT
☎ (020) 7609 0640
🖨 (020) 7503 5421
✉ audreyknight@
mangetout.demon.co.uk

Mange Tout caters for all occasions for numbers up to 350. The extensive choice of food includes vegetarian and ethnic menus and 'alternative' dishes, for customers to make up their own menus. Whatever the night, proprietor Audrey Knight will be happy to advise.

Mise-en-place
21 Battersea Rise, London SW11
1HG
☎ (020) 7228 4392
🖰 www.thefoodstore.co.uk
✉ simon@thefoodstore.co.uk
Small to medium-sized parties are the forte of this delicatessen-based caterer. They specialise in dinner parties, christenings, cocktail parties, picnics and "something special at the last minute".

Model Catering
697 Harrow Rd, London
NW10 5NY
☎ (020) 8964 1712
🖰 www.modelcatering.com
✉ info@modelcatering.com
Outside catering, party planning, fine dining and themed events of any size. Expertise in fashion shoots, film music, media, property launches, dinner parties and social functions. Clients include Ralph Lauren, Lord Lichfield, Mario Testino, Nike, Pathé, Columbia Tristar, 20th Century Fox, FHM, English Heritage, Barclays, Mercedes, Hamptons and Land Securities.

Mosimann's
4 William Blake Hse, Bridge Ln,
London SW11 3AD
☎ (020) 7326 8344
🖰 www.mosimann.com
✉ sales.enquiries
@mosimann.com

MOSIMANN'S
London

Anton Mosimann's inimitable and unique style is conveyed at events throughout the UK and overseas by this Royal Warrant-holding caterer, approved by many leading UK venues. The company can cater equally well for intimate private dinners, large cocktail parties or gala receptions, all tailored to personal preference and budgets.

The Moving Venue
Unit 10 Deptford Trading Estate,
Blackhorse Rd, London SE8 5HY
☎ (020) 8691 6661
🖰 www.movingvenue.com
✉ info@movingvenue.com
A well established corporate caterer which is on the 'approved' list of many of the top function venues. See advertisement on page 202.

Nicky Sherlock Catering
Hazeldene Manor, North Oakley,
Hampshire RG26 5TT
☎ 01256 780544
🖷 01256 782921
✉ nsccatering@btconnect.com
A well-established caterer and party planner, based in Hampshire but now covering London and the South. They offer modern menus in contemporary style, and believe thier team of chefs, co-ordinators and waiting staff maintain "an exceptional eye for detail".

The Original Chocolate Fountain
30 Belleville Road, London
SW11 6QT
☎ 020 7738 9191
🖷 020 7642 9122
🖰 www.the
originalchocolatefountain.com
✉ info@the
originalchocolatefountain.com
Heavenly and truly original! Delight your guests with a fountain of cascading glossy melted aromatic Belgian chocolate. Dip in strawberries, marshmallows or profiteroles and savour the moment! Complete the presentation with a special bespoke Perspex light box to create an eye-catching and unforgettable edible feature!

the

moving
venue

c a t e r e r s   l t d

Parsons Creative Food

107-108 Avro House, Havelock Terr, London SW8 4AS
☎ (020) 7720 3336,
Mobile 07885 248837
🖨 (020) 7720 8656
🖱 www.parsonscreativefood.co.uk
📧 katie@katie-parsons.ndo.co.uk
Since 1993 , the company has been arranging events, parties and weddings for up to 1000 guests. They enjoy developing a style to suit your event – contemporary or modern – and have an experienced team to attend to your requirements.

Pen

Unit 6, Ferrier Street, off Old York Road, London SW18 1SW
☎ (020) 8877 1977
🖱 www.pen-uk.com
📧 info@pen-uk.com
Innovative catering and detailed event management on every scale, now firmly established as "one of the most professional and creative event planners to be found".

The Pie Man Catering Company

Ventura House, 176-188 Acre Ln, London SW2 5UL
☎ (020) 7737 7799
🖱 www.the-pie-man.com
📧 sales@the-pie-man.com
A well established and versatile

caterer, with a shop in Chelsea, providing food for top-end parties both private and corporate. They offer a personal and friendly service for events of all sizes, whilst maintaining a flexible approach.

"rhubarb" Food Design

Unit 94, Battersea Business Centre, 103 Lavender Hl, London SW11 5QL
☎ (020) 7738 9272
🖱 www.rhubarb.net
📧 info@rhubarb.net
Established 7 years ago, "rhubarb" has grown into an extremely successful operation enjoying a reputation as "the frontrunner of London's catering scene". They concentrate on serving visually exciting food using only the finest quality seasonal produce, whether for an intimate gourmand dinner, a Moroccan buffet or a sit-down dinner for 1,000.

Richmond Caterers

17 Studley Grange Rd, London W7 2LU
☎ (020) 8567 9090
🖱 www.richmondcaterers.com
📧 info@richmondcaterers.com
Working at many of the top London venues, this is a firm constantly proving itself as one of the top party

caterers. With imagination and
experience they have built up a
strong following.

Scott Harris

The Arch, 324-325 Blucher Rd,
Camberwell, London SE5 0LH
☎ (020) 7701 2132
🖰 www.scottharris.co.uk
✉ scottharris@lineone.net

Scott Harris Ltd
Corporate & Private Caterers

*From business lunches for 6 guests to
cocktail parties for 600 – whatever
the event, the firm dedicates the*

same effort to ensuring perfect
events, ensuring the food tastes good,
is beautifully presented and served by
friendly staff.

Searcy's

124 Bolingbroke Grove, London
SW11 1DA
☎ (020) 7585 0505
🖰 www.searcys.co.uk
*A long-established firm, particularly
well known for having its own
premises at 30 Pavilion Rd SW1 (see
Venues), but which also undertakes
many outside catering assignments.
(They also run a number of
restaurants.)*

Table Talk

Friars Court, 17 Rushworth St,
London SE1 0RB
☎ (020) 7401 3200
🖳 (020) 7401 9500
🖰 www.tabletalk.co.uk
📧 info@tabletalk.co.uk
*Whether you are planning an
intimate celebration dinner or a
glamorous 1920's cocktail party, this
is a company which puts the finest
ingredients in the hands of the best
chefs to create a fabulous feast and
a memorable party .... Chic and
elegant or fun and funky, they will
look after your every need.*

Tamarind Outside Catering

Suite 18 MacMillan House,
96 Kensington High St,
London W8 4SG
☎ (020) 7082 0856
🖳 (020) 7082 0840
🖰 www.tamarindcatering.com
📧 sabrina@tamarindcatering.com

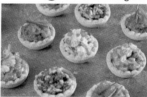

*Catering for private and corporate
events from 2-250 persons,
Tamarind offer superior quality
Indian food stemming from the
award-winning Tamarind Restaurant
in Mayfair. They can also provide
professional total event management,
arranging every aspect of your event,
from venue finding to the finishing
touches.*

Turtle Soup

No. 1 Lindsey St, Smithfield,
London EC1A 9HP
☎ 0870 780 6091
🖰 www.turtlesoup.biz
📧 helpme@turtlesoup.biz

*Progressive, dynamic and full of
sparkling-fresh new ideas, this is a
modern, vibrant catering company
which combines delicious food,
fabulous drinks, great service and
sensational venues to provide all the
very best ingredients for todays
events. For more information, visit the
funky website.*

urban kitchen

63-65 Goldney Rd,
London W9 2AR
☎ (020) 7286 1700
🖳 (020) 7286 1709
🖰 www.urban-kitchen.info
📧 kitchen@urban-
productions.co.uk
*Modern catering with generosity,
global style and a sassy crew of
energetic staff. Canapé receptions,
champagne parties, vodka hell-
raising and unforgettable dining are
all part of the mix that has attracted
a lot of big-name clients. Menu
suggestions includes organics, and
wild and fair trade menu options.*

Vama Direct

4 Chatfield Road, Battersea,
London SW11 3SE
☎ (020) 7801 1444
🖰 www.vama.co.uk
📧 ali@vama.co.uk
*Vama Direct where everything's
catered for... Vama's speciality is
themed Indian with an exotic touch,
a bespoke catering services that the
stars and celebrities use, offering
irreproachable levels of
professionalism and presentation.*

Melissa Webb

12 Southside , Stamford Brook,
London W6 0XY
☎ (020) 8741 7547,
Mobile 07966 440798
✉ mel@melissawebb.com
*A private company providing a
personalised service, and with an
array of clients who return again and
again for the glorious food, service
and style.*

Zafferano

Spaced Studios, 90 de Beauvoir
Rd, London N1 4EN
☎ (020) 7249 4455
🖰 www.zafferano.co.uk
✉ info@zafferano.co.uk
*Stylish caterer with a leaning towards
the simple, unfussy flavours of
modern Italian food, and with a
particular flair for canapés. From
hand picking the perfect waiters to
matching table linen with flowers,
they'll do it all, ensuring you complete
peace of mind. All that's left for you
to do is talk to your guests.*

2.2 CAKES

*The following firm is a specialist
which can take on almost any design.
Harrods and Selfridges also have
speciality cake departments, and a
number of the supermarket chains
(Waitrose and Safeway, for example)
have sample-books from which you
can order a surprisingly wide range of
special cakes.*

The Chelsea Cake Shop

66 Lower Sloane St, London SW1
8BP
☎ (020) 7730 6277
*Need a cake? Look no further! This
shop specialises in delicious,
handmade and individually crafted
cakes; fun and funky or classical and
traditional – in short a cake which
will make a real impact whatever the
occasion. Come in and discuss your
ideas, or choose from a large
collection of photographs. Open
Monday to Saturday.*

2.3 CATERING EQUIPMENT

*If you want to organise catering
yourself, but do not have enough
china, glasses or chairs, the following
companies will be able to help.
Practice differs from firm to firm as
regards charges for delivery, extra
charges for returning items dirty and
whether VAT is included in quoted
prices. As always, ensure that prices
you are comparing are quoted on a
similar basis.*

Speciality Linens

Unit 2, Albert Close Trading
Estate, Moss Ln, Whitefield,
Manchester M45 8EH
☎ (0161) 796 7111
🖷 (0161) 796 3337
🖰 www.specialitylinens.co.uk

Speciality Linens

*Specialists in fine and unusual table
cloths and chair covers. A bespoke
service is available, but apparently
many would-be bespoke customers
find that what they want is already
available from the extensive stock
range.*

Spikomat

Old Great North Road Industrial
Estate, Sutton-on-Trent, Newark,
Nottinghamshire NG23 6QS
☎ 01636 821123
🖰 www.skewers.co.uk
✉ sales@spikomat.co.uk
See advertisement on page 203.

Thorns Group

125 Brantwood Road, London
N17 0DX
☎ (020) 8801 4444
🖷 (020) 8801 4445
🖰 www.thorns.co.uk
✉ contact@thorns.co.uk
*With an unrivalled range of
banqueting chairs, tables, bar
furniture, dance floors, lounge suites,*

glassware and crockery plus extensive ranges of sophisticated sound and lighting equipment, Thorns can supply everything for the perfect party – no matter what the location or the theme.

2.4 STAFF

If you do not need caterers, but would like some staff to help out, the following will assist.

At Your Service
12 The Talina Centre, Bagleys Ln, London SW6 2BW
☎ (020) 7610 8610
🖑 www.ays.co.uk
📧 office@ays.co.uk
The largest event staffing and management company. They supply staff to many of the top caterers and party planners.

Gastronomique
Friars Court, 17 Rushworth St, London SE1 0RB
☎ (020) 7633 9363
🖨 (020) 7401 9500
📧 info@tabletalk.co.uk
"London's best kept entertaining secret", this company supplies permanent and temporary chefs and waiting staff for all types of private and corporate occasions – in London, across the UK and abroad. Whether it's for "home, work or play", they will seek out and supply the ideal person, however simple or extravagant the occasion.

SpokesModels
1 Elysium Gate, 126-128 New King's Rd, London SW6 4LZ
☎ (020) 7610 9966
🖨 (020) 7610 9234
🖑 www.spokesmodels.co.uk
📧 info@spokesmodels.co.uk

SPOKESMODELS

"An unrivalled calibre of event personnel" – gorgeous, intelligent and educated, confident communicators, quick thinkers and proactive team members – for your party, event,

show or campaign. In addition to their model looks, most of the staff also have a university education!

2.5 WINE

Almost all of the following will offer delivery (often free of charge), glass hire and sale-or-return (check the proportion you can send back). Many of them also supply ice. If you are buying drink in quantity you should certainly shop around – you may find that even the big chains will offer special terms for larger orders.

Berry Bros & Rudd
3 St James St, London SW1 1EG
☎ (020) 7396 9600
🖨 (020) 7396 9619
🖑 www.bbr.com
See advertisement on page 32.

Oddbins
31-33 Weir Road, Wimbledon SW19 8UG
☎ 0800 783 2834
🖑 www.oddbins.com

Eager to offer advice and help with party planning, this perennially popular chain of wine merchants has a host of stores across London, the rest of the UK and Ireland. They offer an eclectic and comprehensive range of alcohols, as well as extremely competitive discounts on champagnes, wines, spirits and beers.

Soho Wine Supply
18 Percy St, London W1T 1DX
☎ (020) 7636 8490
🖨 (020) 7636 8899
🖑 www.sohowine.co.uk
📧 info@sohowine.co.uk
A long-experienced merchant offering a carefully selected, competitively priced, range of Champagne, wine and spirits, whose stated aim is simply to offer value and quality at

every level. Helpful and knowledgeable staff are on hand to assist with any enquiries.

Virgin Wines
☎ 0870 164 9593
🖰 www.virginwines.com
See advertisement on page 208.

2.6 BARS

Bamboo
12 The Talina Centre, Bagleys Ln, London SW6 2BW
☎ (020) 7610 8606
🖰 www.ays.co.uk
🖂 bamboo@ays.co.uk
The inventors of event mixology, Bamboo's primary focus is on style, sophistication, service and the quality of ingredients. Bamboo supplies the party and events industry, with trained cocktail barmen with flair. Also drink consultancy and bespoke bar design and construction.

Bar Bazaar
C/O Helix 3D Ltd, 22 Sugar House Ln, London E15 2QS
☎ (07866) 589709
🖷 (0870) 758 6250
🖰 www.thebarbazaar.com
🖂 drink@thebarbazaar.com
See advertisement opposite title page.

3. THEMES & EQUIPMENT
3.1 Marquees
3.2 Florists
3.3 Equipment
3.4 Lighting
3.5 Lighting effects
3.6 Lasers
3.7 Fireworks
3.8 Themes & props
3.9 Furniture

3.1 MARQUEES

The most traditional type is the canvas tent supported by poles with external guy-ropes, but on constricted London sites, a clear-span (or frame) tent, which is free standing, will probably be more suitable. The structure is only the beginning and you should explore the types of linings available and the availability of furniture and, if appropriate, dance floors and heating. All but linings can, of course, be organised separately, but one-stop shopping will be much simpler.

London Garden Marquees
17 Ouseley Rd, London SW12 8ED
☎ (020) 8672 2580
A small hire company specialising in freestanding 4.5m x 3m marquees in yellow/navy stripe with red piping, (from £90). A quick and easy way of creating extra space in London, each one accommodates about 30 adults standing. Renowned for personalised service.

The London Marquee Company
5 Beechmore Rd, London SW11 4ET
☎ (020) 7610 1770
🖰 www.completeevents.co.uk
🖂 mhutchison@ completeevents.co.uk
Suppliers of luxurious marquees and temporary structures, for smart private or corporate events. They can also provide other related event services, including lighting, décor,

Harden's Party Guide for London, the leading resource for party planners at all levels, has teamed-up with Virgin, the largest independent online wine merchant in the world, to bring all our readers this great offer!

Introductory £20 voucher from Virgin Wines

You can use your voucher to mix yourself a case of 12 wines – if you don't like the wines, you don't pay!

To use your voucher, go to **www.virginwines.com/slurp**, click on 'claim a voucher' and enter the voucher code and password below. So make a note of the details now!

YOUR VOUCHER DETAILS

Voucher Code: VNTHAR
Password: champagne

You will need to use this voucher by 31/12/2004.

Virgin wines   HARDEN'S

theming, furniture, catering and entertainments. *(The London arm of Complete Events Marquee Solutions)*

3.2 FLORISTS

The following operators are specialists, often involved in lavish arrangements and theming. In some cases the firms are effectively designers of whole sets in which flowers may be the leading, but not the solo, performer – sharing the limelight with herbs, fruits, shells and other props.

Art of Flower

☎ (020) 7792 7982,
Mobile 07976 289969
🖐 www.artofflower.co.uk
📧 contact@artofflower.co.uk
A well reputed florist whose services range from large weddings at the top London venues to social functions of all sizes.

Detta Phillips

18 Redburn St, London SW3 4BX
☎ (020) 7498 2728
🖨 (020) 7498 8805
🖐 www.dettaphillips.com
📧 info@dettaphillips.com
A well reputed florist who takes on a diverse range of assignments, including launches, corporate events and weddings.

Pulbrook & Gould

Liscartan House, 127 Sloane St, London SW1X 9AS
☎ (020) 7730 0030
🖐 www.pulbrookandgould.com
Traditionally regarded as one of the very best of the big-name, shop-based florists – it was the training ground for many of the leading names who now have their own businesses. See advertisement on page 13.

RVH Floral Design

Unit 8, Tun Yard, Peardon St, London SW8 3HT
☎ (020) 7720 6774
🖐 www.rvhfloraldesign.com
📧 info@rvhfloraldesign.com

Over the past seventeen years, Rob Van Helden has established a reputation as one of London's top florists. By looking after his clients personally – consulting and nurturing them – he "adds extra value to his already priceless service".

Wild at Heart

Turquoise Island, 222 Westbourne Grove, London W11 2RJ
☎ (020) 7727 3095
🖐 www.wildatheart.com
📧 flowers@wildatheart.com
For all your traditional and contemporary floral requirements. Innovative and stylish flowers for offices, hotels, restaurants and the fashion industry, and fabulous flowers for weddings, parties and corporate events.

3.3 EQUIPMENT

Fisher Productions
118 Garratt Lane, London
SW18 4DJ
☎ (020) 8871 1978
🖷 (020) 8871 1988
🖰 www.fisherproductions.co.uk
🖂 dom@fisherproductions.co.uk
*Established in 1985 and widely
regarded as an industry leader, this
company supplies overall production
services, lighting design (both internal
and external), set design and
construction and equipment hire.*

Maiden Management
1 Elysium Gate,
126-128 New Kings Rd,
London SW6 4LZ
☎ (020) 7610 6234
🖷 (020) 7610 9234
🖰 www.maidenmanagement.com
🖂 info@maidenmanagement.com
*Established in 1997, an independent
event management company and
production house. Sound systems,
lighting and screens for hire – if
required, creative management too.*

Theme Traders
The Stadium, Oaklands Rd,
London NW2 6DL
☎ (020) 8452 8518
🖰 www.themetraders.com
🖂 projects@themetraders.com

theme **traders**™
+44 (0) 20 8452 8518

*Everything from popcorn warmers to
chill-out tables and cushions, this is a
company with a big name for its full
range of specialist event services
including prop hire, scenery, lighting,
costumes and greenery, as well as a
full party planning service. Visit the
website for more information.*

3.4 LIGHTING

Event Lighting & Design Company
B101 Tower Bridge Business
Complex, 100 Clements Rd,
London SE16 4DG
☎ (020) 7498 3385
🖷 (020) 7498 0006
🖰 www.eventlight.co.uk
🖂 barney@eventlight.co.uk

*One of London's leading suppliers of
beautiful lighting to the high-end
private and corporate party scene.
Their friendly and professional team
offers a complete design and
installation service (including
technical production).*

3.5 LIGHTING EFFECTS

Gekko Effects
103 Thomas More House,
Barbican, London EC2Y 8BU
☎ 07970 748626
🖰 www.gekkoeffects.com
🖂 info@gekkoeffects.com
*Whether for a Christmas Party,
Fashion Show or Wedding, flame-light
special effects and props will bring
your theme to life. Units come in all
sizes and colours, and specific décor
packages include Moroccan,
Halloween and Valentine's, but
custom-made effects can be supplied
to fit any theme.*

Starlight Design
12 Gateway Trading Est, Hythe Rd,
London NW10 6RJ
☎ (020) 8960 6078
🖰 www.starlightdesign.co.uk
🖂 info@starlightdesign.co.uk
*Creative experience blended with flair
together with practical technical
knowledge ensures delivery on all
aspects of event lighting. Decorative
interiors, sophisticated nite-club*

effects, dramatic floodlighting and all the cables and power you could ever need are available from one company, whose aim it is "to add creative illumination to every event".

3.6 LASERS

Laser Hire
☎ (0121) 236 2243,
Mobile 07836 526 834
🖰 www.laserhire.co.uk
✉ info@laserhire.co.uk
Adding extra excitement to any event for over 20 years. The firm can supply combined packages for shows and displays incorporating lasers, lighting effects, waterscreens, high-powered slide and video projection, fireworks and pyrotechnics. They have been supplying professional services for 20 years. Mention this guide, and they'll offer you an extra 5% discount.

3.7 FIREWORKS

The Firework Co.
Gunpowder Plot, Bridge St, Uffculme, Devon EX15 3AX
☎ (01884) 840504
🖰 www.thefirework.co.uk
✉ sales@thefirework.co.uk
Four thousand displays over 15 years provide party organisers with the comfort of a high level of experience from this firm, which emphasises the high levels of advice it offers, and the highest standards of safety .

Starlight Design
12 Gateway Trading Est, Hythe Rd, London NW10 6RJ
☎ (020) 8960 6078
🖰 www.starlightdesign.co.uk
✉ info@starlightdesign.co.uk
The company's own computerised firing system allows perfect synchronisation of fireworks with dramatic music, and has made them the principal supplier of display fireworks for the private market, and used by many event organisers. Their special skills are most apparent when

creating spectacular shows incorporating projections, fountains and lasers.

3.8 THEMES & PROPS

Amazing Parties
Unit 30, The Old Brickworks, Plumpton Green, nr Lewes, East Sussex BN7 3DF
☎ 0870 7591901
🖰 www.amazingpartythemes.com
✉ sales@
 amazingpartythemes.com
"Design, build and management, while you enjoy.", from a firm with over 7000 props and 1000 backdrops, and two decades of experience in creating memorable events around the globe. See the website for examples of past events, and inspiration for your own.

Helix 3D
22 Sugar House Ln, London E15 2QS
☎ 0870 758 6262
🖷 0870 758 6250
🖰 www.helix3d.co.uk
✉ info@helix3d.co.uk

Quality design and build solutions for the events industry. Using a combination of fresh young talent and the latest technology, they will take on any brief and have extensive industrial facilities and an experienced construction management team to turn concepts into reality, "on schedule and on budget".

Party Packages

62 Beechwood Road, South
Croydon, Surrey CR2 0AA
☎ (020) 8657 2813
🖱 www.partypackagesltd.co.uk
✉ info@partypackagesltd.co.uk
*With 30 different themes – including
Wild West, Hollywood, James Bond,
Arabian and Space – the company
has the props, backdrops, games,
bands, table decorations and so on to
offer you a complete package. Or if
you don't want to go for a 'package',
you can have a 'pick and mix' deal.*

Theme Traders

The Stadium, Oaklands Rd,
London NW2 6DL
☎ (020) 8452 8518
🖱 www.themetraders.com
✉ projects@themetraders.com
See advertisement below.

3.9 FURNITURE

Thorns Group

125 Brantwood Road, London
N17 0DX
☎ (020) 8801 4444
🖨 (020) 8801 4445
🖱 www.thorns.co.uk
✉ contact@thorns.co.uk
*Thorns is a single-source supplier for
all furniture and catering equipment
hire requirements. Their bespoke
service is supported by over a million
items of stock – including tables,
chairs, crockery, glassware and linen
– meaning they can supply
everything from a small private
celebration to a banquet for more
than 10,000 guests!*

4. ENTERTAINMENT

4.1 ENTERTAINMENT

If you have the budget, do consider whether a few hundred pounds spent on performers, perhaps some musicians, a magician or a caricaturist, might not help turn your party into a truly memorable event.

Music is, of course, the most common type of entertainment. The best way of finding the right musicians for your event is to go to an agency – they should be able to find not only a good band, but also one which is right for the party concerned.

Many of the agencies and consultancies below deal with entertainers of all types. Most of the general agencies can provide a disco and many of them can provide casinos and other themed events.

Barn Dance & Line Dance Agency

62 Beechwood Road, South Croydon, Surrey CR2 0AA
☎ (020) 8657 2813
🖥 www.barn-dance.co.uk
📧 info@barn-dance.co.uk
Try a barn dance, line dance, Ceilidh (Kaylee) or Hoedown for your next party – the only form of entertainment that actively encourages participation. Emphasis is on the fun side, and the company has access to over 900 bands and callers across the UK, and can always find something local to your event. Prices start at £175.

Carousel Entertainment & Event Mgt

18 Westbury Lodge Close, Pinner, Middlesex HA5 3FG
☎ (0870) 751 8688
🖨 0870 751 8668
🖥 www.carouselentertainments.co.uk
📧 info@carouselentertainments.co.uk
High-quality entertainment and event management for all corporate and private events. An enthusiastic team of consultants utilise their extensive experience and talent to offer a complete customised service to suit every brief and budget.

Carte Blanche

78 Cecil Rd, London SW19 1JP
☎ (020) 8543 8557
🖥 www.carteblancheinfo.com
📧 paul@carteblancheinfo.com
One of the UK's busiest party bands. Lineups of different sizes – 5-piece to 10-piece – are available. Also Tribute sets (eg 70s disco, Abba, Blues Brothers etc). Lookalike/soundalikes – Robbie Williams, Freddie Mercury, Tom Jones, Kylie, and so on – can sing with the band

THE CHOIR

4 Drake House, Dolphin Square, London SW1V 3NN
☎ (020) 7798 8579,
Mobile 07771 727586
📧 roebuckwebb@aol.com
Talented vocalists who perform accapella arrangements of rock, pop, jazz, blues, hymns and carols. Everyone is an experienced performer having toured with the likes of Pink Floyd, Eric Clapton, Tina Turner, Jools Holland and many more – terrific voices, unique vocal arrangements and passionate performances.

Function Junction

7 Market Square, Bicester, Oxon OX26 6AA
☎ 0800 034 3232
🖥 www.functionjunction.co.uk
📧 info@functionjunction.co.uk
Specialists in live music for parties, receptions and corporate events of all

kinds, capable of providing any sort of music for any sort of event – satisfied customers range from Joan Collins to the the John Lewis Partnership! The website allows you to hear clips of selected bands, or you can ring for sample CDs of appropriate entertainers.

Gekko Entertainments

103 Thomas More House, Barbican, London EC2Y 8BU
☎ 07816 921186
🖷 (020) 7053 2143
🖰 www.
   gekkoentertainments.com
🖃 info@
   gekkoentertainments.com
Finding the unusual and unique is this company's speciality - whether it is celebrity speakers, hosts for an awards ceremony, bands, comics, circus acts or musicians. If the act doesn't already exist, they will create a unique one-off performance for your evening, both in the UK and internationally.

Harp4u.co.uk

27 Donovan Avenue, Muswell Hill, London N10 2JU
☎ (020) 8365 2285
🖷 (020) 8883 8961
🖰 www.harp4u.co.uk
Sheila Watts plays popular music from shows and films, classical pieces and folk tunes as backdrop or solo spots. She wears long silk dresses to match your colour scheme, and inside her harp is a microphone which plugs into a sound system for large events!

Peter Johnson Entertainments

Hastings Rd, Hawkhurst, Kent TN18 4RT
☎ (01580) 754822
🖰 www.peterjohnson.co.uk
🖃 enquiries@peterjohnson.co.uk
Unusual party entertainment a speciality. Chocolate fountains, ice sculptures, ice rinks, indoor laser shooting, simulators (racing, skiiing, etc.) casino tables, giant scalextrics, rodeo bulls, dance bands, jazz bands, steel bands, string quartets, human statues, robots, caricaturists, close-up magicians, clowns, jugglers, stiltwalkers. If that's not enough, a 52-page brochure is available.

London Music Agency

16 Lancer Way, Billericay, Essex CM12 0XA
☎ (01277) 633030
🖰 www.londonmusicagency.co.uk
🖃 enquiries@
   londonmusicagency.co.uk
To complete your entertainments, anything musical from a cocktail pianist, harpist, jazz trio/quartet or string quartet to a superior discotheque or function band. Also, caricaturists and magicians plus many more unusual entertainments. Free brochure available.

Merlin Entertainments

29 Norwood Drive, North Harrow, Middx HA2 7PF
☎ (020) 8866 6327
🖃 merlin.wizard@btconnect.com
A supplier of all manner of children's and adult magicians everywhere for over 20 years, family-run by Magic Circle member Geoff Donald and son Clive, and numbering many local authorities and top companies among its customers. To conjure up a brochure, call (or email merlin.wizard@btconnect.com).

Partyjazz

26 Harold Rd, London E11 4QY
☎ (020) 8539 5229
🖷 (020) 8556 9545
🖰 www.partyjazz.co.uk
🖃 info@partyjazz.co.uk
A small music agency, able to provide bands of all sizes.

Sardi's Entertainment Consultants

6 Redbridge Ln East, Redbridge, Ilford IG4 5ES
☎ (020) 8551 6720/
(020) 8518 3925
🖰 www.sardisonline.com
🖃 mail@sardisonline.com
Together with Smarty Party Company, offers a complete party planning package. No job is too big

or too small – from dinner dances and cabaret nights to fun-days and children's parties. Entertainment includes bands, discos, clowns, caricaturists, silhouettists, magicians, casinos and much more. Also balloon decorations and bombonières.

spectacular voices. For an unforgettable performance of beautiful music "Three Tenors"-style, look no further than Scott, Jem and Stuart – what you see is what you get! See advertisement on page 216.

Sound Advice
30 Artesian Road, London
W2 5DD
☎ (020) 7229 2219
⌂ www.soundadvice.uk.com
✉ info@soundadvice.uk.com
"The leading provider of music at private and corporate events". Having just celebrated 21 years in business, and with gigs including Paul McCartney's wedding and HM The Queen's private Jubilee Party, and assignments with Rod Stewart, Bryan Ferry and Ronan Keating, under their belt, it would be difficult to argue!

Spotlight Entertainments
Chantersell, Nether Lane, Nutley, East Sussex TN22 3LA
☎ (01825) 713213
🖨 08701 229112
⌂ www. spotlightentertainments.com
✉ cs@spotlight-ents.com
Ten years' experience of supplying innovative entertainment, for everything from weddings and small private dinner parties to high-profile corporate functions. Party bands, steel bands, jazz, classical ensembles, strolling entertainers, cabaret acts, after dinner speakers, equipment hire. Many unusual ideas including stiltwalking insects, stunt artistes, Chinese acrobats and comedy pickpockets. Efficient and reliable service.

TENORS Un LIMITED
P.O. Box 35843, London E11 3WJ
☎ (020) 8534 6926
⌂ www.tenorsunlimited.com
✉ contact@tenorsunlimited.com

The best of popular opera, Neapolitan songs and crooner classics, with charm, wit and

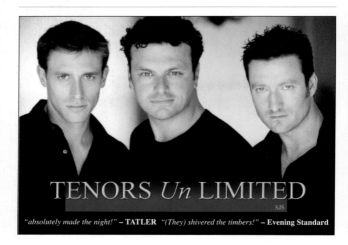

TENORS *Un* LIMITED

"absolutely made the night!" – **TATLER** *"(They) shivered the timbers!"* – **Evening Standard**

4.2 ENTERTAINMENT, MURDER MYSTERY

Accidental Productions
36 Barratt Av, London N22 7EZ
☎ (020) 8881 8000
🖰 www.accidental.co.uk
🖂 julie@accidental.co.uk
Accidental Productions offer Murder Mysteries, Themed Treasure Hunts, Gregarious Game Shows, Fantastic Film Days, Preposterous Pantomimes, Wacky Waiters, Still (but living) Statues and Raunchy Raids. Excellent entertainment for your next conference, staff party or client hospitality. Aside from the one-off events, they can create original road shows for product launches or customer awareness campaigns. 'Discreet, clever, funny, outrageous' (Publicity Matters) Make sure your next event is no accident!

Clive Panto Productions
Waters Edge, 1 Frogmill, Hurley, Berks SL6 5NL
☎ (01628) 826999
🖰 www.clivepanto.co.uk
🖂 murder@clivepanto.co.uk
See advertisement opposite.

4.3 DISCOS

William Bartholomew Party Organising
23 The Talina Centre, Bagleys Ln, London SW6 2BW
☎ (020) 7731 8328
🖶 (020) 7384 1807
🖰 www.wbpo.com
🖂 mail@wbpo.com

This is one of the top party planners – see their advertisement on the back flap – but they are also particularly well known for their discos.

Maiden Management
1 Elysium Gate, 126-128 New Kings Rd, London SW6 4LZ
☎ (020) 7610 6234
🖶 (020) 7610 9234
🖰 www.maidenmanagement.com
🖂 info@maidenmanagement.com
Established back in 1997, this is an independent event management

VISIT US AT: **www.hardens.com**

company and production house.
Fabulous disco systems and DJ's for
hire, to suit your event.

Mobile Music Company

18 Cosgrove Close, Winchmore
Hill, London N21 3BQ
☎ (020) 8882 6977
🖷 (020) 8882 2907
🖱 www.
  mobilemusiccompany.co.uk
📧 slewis@
  mobilemusiccompany.co.uk
See advertisement below.

Sounds Good to Me (Sound Division Group)

Montague House, 389 Liverpool
Road, Islington, London N1 1NP
☎ 020 7609 3999
🖱 www.sgtm.co.uk

*Suppliers of superior disco
entertainment for all manner of
functions for over 15 years.
Assignments range from private
engagements – including weddings,
birthdays, anniversaries etc. – to
large corporate black tie or themed*
*events. Highly experienced DJs and
the latest professional equipment
help create a thoroughly professional
performance, with crystal clear sound
reproduction and a vibrant, colourful
light show. See advertisement
opposite the title page (page 2).*

4.4 CORPORATE ENTERTAINMENT

West End Events

61-63 Great Queen St, London
WC2B 5DA
☎ (020) 7404 4232
🖱 www.westendevents.co.uk
📧 info@westendevents.co.uk
*Organising an office Christmas party?
Want to go on a Murder Mystery
Weekend? Just want to enjoy some
fun on an Abba theme night? Then
check out our website
www.westendevents.co.uk or call the
events team for that perfect night
out. From £49 per person.*

4.5 WINE TASTING

The Cellar Society
Unit 1, Bard Rd, London W10 6TP
☎ (020) 8960 2622
🖰 www.cellarsociety.com
✉ will@cellarsociety.com
"Wine tasting with a difference. The hottest thing in business entertainment. Exquisite food, fine and rare wines. The perfect corporate evenings, relaxation and informality… stylish, informative, fashionable and exciting." (The Times) Events include: The Grape Gameshow, Masterclass Gastronomica, Beer Hunter, Revolution!, Mercato, Wine Trader and Masterclass.

4.6 CASINOS & INDOOR AMUSEMENTS

1st call Viva Vegas
144a Old South Lambeth Rd, London SW8 1XX
☎ (020) 7820 0999
🖰 www.vivavegas.co.uk
✉ david@vivavegas.co.uk

The UK's no. 1 Casino and games company with over 50 full-size Casino tables, one-arm bandit slot machines, private party casino sets, corporate games (including 8 lane Scalextric tracks), shooting games, Giant Board games and the latest driving and amusement simulators.

4.7 MASSAGE & BEAUTY

Feet First
13 Raynham Rd, London W6 0HY
☎ 0870 2418243
🖨 0870 706 1785
🖰 www.feetfirst-therapies.co.uk
✉ feetfirst@pavilion.co.uk
Pamper your guests with all types of beauty treatments and complementary therapy treatments! The company uses only use natural products, and offers everything from pedicures and holistic facials to Indian head massage. Clients include JP Morgan, Citibank, Channel 5 and Soho House.

4.8 HOT TUBS

The London Hot Tub Company
320 Devonshire Road, Forest Hill, London SE23 3TH
☎ (020) 8699 8985
🖰 www. thelondonhottubcompany.com
✉ info@ thelondonhottubcompany.com

All your portable Hot Tub Rental needs! Whether it's a large event with tubs in different locations or a small private party. And their design team will help create a "themed immersive environment" to accompany the tubs themselves!

4.9 TOASTMASTERS

One of the most difficult events at larger parties is marshalling the guests so that they are in the right place at the right time. A toastmaster – apart from his traditional rôle of introducing speakers and so on – can be very useful as a 'sheepdog'.

Richard Birtchnell

6 Holbein Mews, Lower Sloane St, London SW1W 8NN
☎ (020) 7730 1074
🖨 (020) 7824 8169
🖱 www.londontoastmaster.com
📧 info@londontoastmaster.com

Richard Birtchnell has been producing and directing live events for over 30 years. So, when you book him, you get much more than a toastmaster – not only a master of ceremonies with a strong, clear voice and an eye for detail, but also an event expert and master of logistics!

John Hollingsworth

148 Park Crescent, Erith DA8 3DY
☎ (01322) 341465
🖱 www.johnhollingsworth.net
📧 john.hollingsworth1@ntlworld.com

A past President of the Society of London Toastmasers, and experienced in all types of functions, including banquets, weddings, conferences and exhibitions. Available worldwide. "Whenever you need a focal point for speeches or announcements, you will need the 'Man in the Red Coat'!"

4.10 CARICATURISTS

Photography is not the only way of capturing people – why not consider the services of an on-the-spot caricaturist? The following have a lot of experience in the business.

Steven Garner

9 Garden Farm, West Mersea, Essex CO5 8DU
☎ (01206) 383198
🖱 www.stevengarner.com
📧 stevengarner@caricaturist.freeserve.co.uk

Steve has over 20 years experience as a "live" caricaturist, entertaining at parties, exhibitions, dinners and balls. He has worked at most major hotels and venues, and his previous clients include Saatchi and Saatchi, Disney and KPMG. A quick caricature takes approximately four to five minutes.

Matthew Lawrence

☎ 07946 525501
🖱 www.mattart.co.uk
📧 matt@mattart.co.uk

Matt has been an established caricaturist on the party circuit for over 10 years. He is sure to charm and entertain your guests, and his drawings are guaranteed to help your guests take home fond memories of your event.

4.11 CHILDREN'S ENTERTAINMENT

There are many children's entertainers who help amuse the kids at parties – some of them are happy to take over the whole event. Local recommendations are probably the best way to find a clown or puppeteer to brighten up your child's party – an alternative is to approach

one of the general agencies listed under entertainments. The following are specialists in looking after kids.

Crafty Arty Parties

Buckland Newton, Dorchester, Dorset DT2 7RP
☎ (01300) 345397
🖨 (01300) 345554
🖰 www.craftyarty.co.uk

"Glittering events where kids make stuff", that's the theme of this kids' entertainments company recently featured in a national 5 page Harry Potter party shoot for Party Magazine. Other blue chip clients include Harrods, Cartoon Network, VW, Disney Paris and hopefully you! Small or large parties, UK or overseas.

Crechendo Events

1 Grange Mills, Weir Road, London SW12 0NE
☎ (020) 8772 8140
🖰 www.crechendo.com/events
✉ events@crechendo.com
Tailormade functions for children of all ages. Corporate events and weddings a speciality. The company offers complete Event Management from themed entertainment, venue search, catering and production.

5. INSURANCE

It's certainly worth talking to your broker, but surprisingly few people seem to be involved with event insurance. The following is one of the few specialists.

Event Insurance Services

Event House 20A, Headlands Business Park, Ringwood , Hampshire BH24 3PB
☎ 0800 515980
🖰 www.events-insurance.co.uk
✉ info@events-insurance.co.uk

(event insurance services

Shows, events, exhibitions and weddings – this is a firm which specialises in and can meet requirements of the entire event spectrum, protecting events with coverage for public liability, employer's liability and the property in which events are held, as well as cancellations.

6. INVITATIONS

Hand Scripted Productions

13 Calton Rd, New Barnet, Herts EN5 1BY
☎ (020) 8440 2582
🖨 (020) 8449 9266
✉ melsharpe1@aol.com
Invitations for all occasions, engraved or thermo printed
Matching response sets and thank you cards
Order of service, menus, seating plans and place cards
Calligraphy by hand or computer generated.
"23 years of unsurpassed service"
melsharpe1@aol.com

Historystore

29 Churton St, London SW1V 2LY
☎ (020) 7976 6040
🖰 www.historystore.ltd.uk
✉ claire@historystore.ltd.uk
Be different! Special stationery designed especially for you from the firm's unique archive – invitations, menus, name-place cards, with added calligraphy for that personal touch. Your wish is their command! You can visit either the gallery or the website for examples.

Alastair Lockhart

97 Walton St, London SW3 2HP
☎ (020) 7589 0000
✉ parties@alastairlockhart.com
Original invitations in all shapes and sizes for parties all over the world. Printed and engraved wedding invitations and social stationery are the speciality of this charming Chelsea shop.

Papyrus

48 Fulham Rd, London SW3 6HH
☎ (020) 7584 8022
🖰 www.papyrus.uk.com
✉ sales@papyrus.uk.com

PAPYRUS
PRINTERS & STATIONERS

From traditional copperplate to stylish contemporary invitations – through to completely outrageous! The company's award-winning design studio will start your party off on absolutely the right note, extending the same high level of service whether you are are in Britain or across the world. From its own print-works, the company also supplies its shops with exclusive 'ready to wear' invitations, placecards, menus, and so on.

The Wren Press

1 Chelsea Wharf, 15 Lots Rd, London SW10 0QJ
☎ (020) 7351 5887
🖨 (020) 7352 7063
🖰 www.wrenpress.com
✉ orders@wrenpress.com
Royal Warrant holders who specialise in creating and printing the finest stationery. The in-house designers and printers are able to produce an extensive and unique range of entertaining and social stationery of the highest quality. The selection includes personal and wedding stationery, corporate and private invitations, birth announcements and Christmas cards.

7. PHOTOGRAPHERS

BRD Associates
4 The Berries, Hawkinge, Kent
CT18 7PY
☎ (01303) 893341
🖰 www.brd.uk.com
🖃 brian@brd.uk.com

Experienced event, conference and party photographer used by many of London and the South East's premier venues and party organisers. Long experience of corporate, government, celebrity (and royally attended) events. No weddings.

Joshua Millais
1 Durham Terrace, London W2
5PB
☎ (020) 7792 3218,
Mobile 07932 152 794
🖰 www.joshuamillias.com
Fifteen years' experience, specialising in people, parties and portraits. (Also corporate, studio and interiors photography.)

8. TRANSPORT

8.1 Cars
8.2 Other vehicles

8.1 CARS

Eccentric, classic, impressive or merely practical …

Corporate Chauffeur
The Clockhouse, St Johns Lye, St Johns, Woking, Surrey GU21 7SE
☎ 01483 228028
🖰 www.ccc-chauffeur.co.uk
🖃 info@ccc-chauffeur.co.uk
Specialists in event transportation and corporate travel. Their range includes S class Mercedes, Range Rovers and MPV's.

A Vintage Occasion
45 Sugden Road,
London SW11 5EB
☎ (020) 7223 8635
🖰 www.avintageoccasion.com
🖃 info@avintageoccasion.com
Exotic chauffeur driven vehicles from a bygone age. Vintage, Classic and Modern saloons, limousines and convertibles for every special occasion. Period buses and modern luxury coaches of all sizes.

8.2 OTHER VEHICLES

Atlas Helicopters
Daedalus Airfield , Hangar 'H', Lee On Solent, Hants PO13 9NY
☎ 023 9255 6688
🖷 023 9255 6644
🖰 www.atlashelicopters.co.uk
🖃 atlas.helis@virgin.net
Add a different dimension to your event. Include a sightseeing tour, transport to a sporting event or even a helicopter dining trip. View your party or event venue from the air or partake in an Aerial Treasure Hunt. Helicopters are a versatile way of livening up you party, as well as an ideal promotional and marketing tool.

The Coach Connection

9 Oldfield Rd, Bath BA2 3ND
☎ (01225) 448184
🖳 (01225) 789833
🖱 www.coachconnection.co.uk
📧 info@coachconnection.co.uk

A company which can source a range of coaches and cars which can be sourced at competitive prices. The website shows the full scope of what's on offer.

9. ATTIRE

9.1 Costume hire
9.2 Evening dress hire

9.1 COSTUME HIRE

Theme Traders

The Stadium, Oaklands Rd,
London NW2 6DL
☎ (020) 8452 8518
🖱 www.themetraders.com
📧 projects@themetraders.com

theme **traders**™
+44 (0) 20 8452 8518

Every imaginable costume as well as large quantities of matching sets, promotional costumes and a mobile wardrobe service. Also vast stocks of props, scenery, furniture and lighting for parties and events as well as full party planning. Visit the website for more information.

9.2 EVENING DRESS HIRE

One Night Stand

8 Chelsea Manor Studios, Flood
St, London SW3 5SR
☎ (020) 7352 4848
🖱 www.onenightstand.co.uk
Evening dress hire for women, from an enormous choice, and catering for sizes 6 to18. Appointments are necessary.

VISIT US AT: www.hardens.com

INDEXES

VENUES BY TYPE

Halls

Central
Africa Centre (WC2)
Banqueting House (SW1)
Central Hall Westminster (SW1)
Conway Hall (WC1)
Gray's Inn (WC1)
Lincoln's Inn (WC1)
London Scottish (SW1)
The London Welsh Centre (WC1)
The Queen Elizabeth II Conference
  Centre (SW1)
Royal Green Jackets (W1)
Royal Horticultural Halls (SW1)
Staple Inn (WC1)
Westminster Cathedral Hall (SW1)

West
Amadeus Centre (W9)
Brompton Oratory – St Wilfrid's
  Hall (SW7)
Chelsea Old Town Hall (SW3)
Duke of York's HQ (SW3)
Ealing Town Hall (W5)
Fulham Town Hall (SW6)
Hammersmith Town Hall (W6)
Philbeach Hall (SW5)
Porchester Centre (W2)
St Peter's Hall (W11)

North
Alexandra Palace & Park (N22)
The Business Design Centre (N1)
Cecil Sharp House (NW1)

South
Academy of Live & Recorded
  Arts (SW18)
BAC (SW11)
Blackheath Concert Halls (SE3)
Chatham Hall (SW11)
Hop Exchange (SE1)
St Thomas' Hospital (SE1)
Wandsworth Civic Suite (SW18)

East
Barnard's Inn Hall (EC1)
Bishopsgate Institute (EC2)
Cabot Hall (E14)
Inner Temple Hall (EC4)
Middle Temple Hall (EC4)
St Bartholomew's Hospital (EC1)
St Botolph's Hall (EC2)
St Bride Foundation Institute (EC4)
St John's Gate (EC1)
Stoke Newington Town Hall (E8)

Outside London
Forty Hall (Middx)
Royal Holloway College (Surrey)
Windsor Guildhall (Berks)

Banqueting halls

Central
Café Royal (W1)
New Connaught Rms (WC2)
One Whitehall Place (SW1)
RICS (SW1)

West
Commonwealth Conference & Events
  Centre (W8)
Royal Hospital Chelsea (SW3)

North
Lord's (NW8)
Regency Banqueting Suite (N17)
Royal Majestic Suite (NW6)

South
Guy's Hospital (SE1)
The Oval (SE11)

East
The Brewery (EC1)
Gibson Hall (EC2)
Stratford Old Town Hall (E15)

Outside London
Addington Palace (Surrey)

Livery halls

South
Glaziers' Hall (SE1)

East
Apothecaries' Hall (EC4)
Armourers' & Braisers' Hall (EC2)
Bakers' Hall (EC3)
Barber-Surgeons' Hall (EC2)
Brewers' Hall (EC2)
Butchers' Hall (EC1)
Carpenters' Hall (EC2)
Chartered Accountants' Hall (EC2)
Clothworkers' Hall (EC3)
Coopers' Hall (EC2)
Drapers' Hall (EC2)
Dyers' Hall (EC4)
Farmers' & Fletchers' Hall (EC1)
Fishmongers' Hall (EC4)
The Founders' Hall (EC1)
Goldsmiths' Hall (EC2)
Grocers' Hall (EC2)
Guildhall (EC2)
Haberdashers' Hall (EC1)
Innholders' Hall (EC4)
The Insurance Hall (EC2)
Ironmongers' Hall (EC2)
Mercers' Hall (EC2)
Merchant Taylors' Hall (EC2)
Painters' Hall (EC4)
Pewterers' Hall (EC2)
Saddlers' Hall (EC2)
Salters' Hall (EC2)
Skinners' Hall (EC4)
Stationers' Hall (EC4)
Tallow Chandlers' Hall (EC4)
Watermen's Hall (EC3)
Wax Chandlers' Hall (EC2)

Houses

Central
The Artworkers Guild (WC1)
Arundel House (WC2)
BMA House (WC1)
Il Bottaccio (SW1)
Canning House (SW1)
Dartmouth House (W1)
Fitzroy Square (W1)
Home House (W1)

The House of St Barnabas-in-
  Soho *(W1)*
Lancaster House *(SW1)*
Motcomb's Townhouse *(SW1)*
Six Hamilton Place *(W1)*
Spencer House *(SW1)*
30 Pavilion Road *(SW1)*
32 Craven St *(WC2)*
28 Portland Place *(W1)*
Two Temple Place *(WC2)*

West
Chiswick House *(W4)*
Fulham House *(SW6)*
Fulham Palace *(SW6)*
Kensington Palace *(W8)*
Kent House *(SW7)*
Leighton House *(W14)*

North
Avenue House *(N3)*
Canonbury Academy *(N1)*
Kenwood House *(NW3)*
Kenwood House, Old Kitchen *(NW3)*
Lauderdale House *(N6)*

South
Devonport House *(SE10)*
Eltham Palace *(SE9)*
Queen's House *(SE10)*

East
Dr Johnsons' House *(EC4)*
Hamilton House *(EC4)*
Honourable Artillery Co *(EC1)*
The Newsroom *(EC1)*
One New Inn Square *(EC2)*
Sutton House *(E9)*

Outside London
Amberley Castle *(W Sussex)*
Blenheim Palace *(Oxon)*
Easthampstead Park Conference
  Centre *(Berks)*
Great Fosters *(Surrey)*
Ham House *(Surrey)*
Hampton Court Palace *(Surrey)*
Hever Castle *(Kent)*
Marble Hill House *(Surrey)*
The Old Palace *(Herts)*
Osterley Park & House *(Middx)*
Penshurst Place & Gardens *(Kent)*
Stonor *(Oxon)*
Syon Park (Conservatory) *(Middx)*
Syon Park (House) *(Middx)*
Wrotham Park *(Herts)*

Museums

Central
British Museum *(WC1)*
Cabinet War Rooms *(SW1)*
The Dickens' House Museum *(WC1)*
The Gilbert Collection *(WC2)*
Guards Museum *(SW1)*
London Transport Museum *(WC2)*
Sir John Soane's Museum *(WC2)*
Theatre Museum *(WC2)*

West
Hogarth's House *(W4)*
National Army Museum *(SW3)*
Natural History Museum *(SW7)*
Science Museum *(SW7)*
Victoria & Albert Museum *(SW7)*

North
Estorick Collection *(N1)*
Freud Museum *(NW3)*
The London Canal Museum *(N1)*
Royal Air Force Museum *(NW9)*

South
Bramah Tea & Coffee Museum *(SE1)*
Cutty Sark *(SE10)*
Design Museum *(SE1)*
Fan Museum *(SE10)*
Fashion & Textile Museum *(SE1)*
Firepower - The Royal Artillery
  Museum *(SE18)*
Horniman Museum *(SE23)*
Imperial War Museum *(SE1)*
Museum of Garden History *(SE1)*
National Maritime Museum *(SE10)*
The Old Operating Theatre, Museum
  & Herb Garret *(SE1)*
Royal Observatory *(SE10)*

East
Geffrye Museum *(E2)*
Museum of London *(EC2)*
Museum in Docklands *(E14)*

Outside London
Kew Bridge Steam Museum *(Middx)*
River & Rowing Museum *(Oxon)*
Whitewebbs Museum of
  Transport *(Middx)*

Galleries

Central
Courtauld Gallery *(WC2)*
Curwen Gallery *(W1)*
ICA *(SW1)*
The Imagination Gallery *(WC1)*
Mall Galleries *(SW1)*
The Music Room *(W1)*
National Portrait Gallery *(WC2)*
The October Gallery *(WC1)*
Photographers' Gallery *(WC2)*
Proud Galleries *(WC2)*
Royal Academy of Arts *(W1)*
Tate Britain *(SW1)*
Wallace Collection *(W1)*

West
Royal College of Art *(SW7)*
Serpentine Gallery *(W2)*
Will's Art Warehouse *(SW6)*

South
Bankside Gallery *(SE1)*
Dali Universe *(SE1)*
Delfina Galleries *(SE1)*
Dulwich Picture Gallery *(SE21)*
Hayward Gallery *(SE1)*
Jerwood Space *(SE1)*
The Pump House Gallery *(SW11)*
The Saatchi Gallery *(SE1)*
South London Gallery *(SE5)*
Tate Modern *(SE1)*

East
The AOP Gallery *(EC2)*
Barbican Art Gallery *(EC2)*
The Candid Arts Trust *(EC1)*
Prenelle Gallery *(E14)*
291 Gallery *(E2)*
Whitechapel Art Gallery *(E1)*

VISIT US AT: www.hardens.com

Tourist attractions

North
The London Planetarium (NW1)
London Zoo (NW1)
Madame Tussaud's (NW1)

South
The Clink (SE1)
London Aquarium (SE1)
The London Dungeon (SE1)
London Eye (SE1)
London Wetland Centre (SW13)
Shakespeare's UnderGlobe (SE1)
Winston Churchill's Britain at
   War (SE1)

East
Mudchute Park & Farm (E14)
HM Tower of London (EC3)

Outside London
Chessington World of
   Adventures (Surrey)
Kew (Royal Botanic) Gardens (Surrey)
Legoland Windsor (Berks)
Thorpe Park (Surrey)
West Wycombe Caves (Bucks)
Whipsnade Wild Animal Park (Beds)

Colleges & Universities

Central
Goodenough College (WC1)
King's College (WC2)
London School of Economics (WC2)
Royal College of Pathologists (SW1)
Royal College of Radiologists (W1)
University of London Union (WC1)
University of Westminster (NW1)

West
Imperial College (SW7)
Royal College of Music (SW7)

North
Highgate School (N6)
Regent's College (NW1)
Royal College of Physicians (NW1)

South
Dulwich College (SE21)
Froebel College (SW15)
Goldsmiths College (SE14)
King's College School (SW19)
King's College, King's Cuisine
   Restaurant (SE1)
Whitelands College (SW15)

East
Queen Mary College (E1)
Queen Mary Students' Union (E1)

Outside London
Eton College (Dorney Lake) (Berks)
Harrow School (Middx)
Spring Grove House (Middx)

Institutions

Central
BAFTA (W1)
Chartered Institute of Public Finance
   & Accountancy (WC2)

Church House (SW1)
The Geological Society of
   London (W1)
Institute of Directors (SW1)
Institute of Electrical Engineers (WC2)
The Law Society (WC2)
No 4 Hamilton Place (W1)
One Birdcage Walk (SW1)
One Great George Street (SW1)
Royal Academy of Engineering (SW1)
Royal Institute of British
   Architects (W1)
Royal Institution of Great
   Britain (W1)
Royal Society of Arts (WC2)
RUSI Building (SW1)
School of Pharmacy (WC1)

West
Le Bistrot de L'Institut Français (SW7)
Institut Français (SW7)
Royal Geographical Society (SW7)

East
Baltic Exchange (EC3)
College of Arms (EC4)
Lloyd's of London (EC3)
Scotch Malt Whisky Society (EC1)
Trinity House (EC3)

Moored boats

Central
RS Hispaniola (WC2)
TS Queen Mary (WC2)
HQS Wellington (WC2)

South
HMS Belfast (SE1)
The Golden Hinde (SE1)

East
Leven is Strijd (E14)
HMS President (EC4)
The Regalia (EC4)

Outside London
SS Great Britain (Bristol)

Theatres

Central
Adelphi Theatre (WC2)
Albery Theatre (WC2)
Aldwych Theatre (WC2)
Apollo Victoria Theatre (SW1)
Arts Theatre (WC2)
Bloomsbury Theatre (WC1)
Cochrane Theatre (WC1)
The Coliseum (WC2)
The Comedy Store (SW1)
Comedy Theatre (SW1)
Dominion Theatre (W1)
Duchess Theatre (WC2)
Fortune Theatre (WC2)
Haymarket Theatre (SW1)
London Palladium (W1)
Lyceum Theatre (WC2)
New Ambassadors Theatre (WC2)
Palace Theatre (W1)
Phoenix Artist Club (WC2)
Phoenix Theatre (WC2)
Queen's Theatre (WC2)
Royal Court Theatre (SW1)

Royal Opera House *(WC2)*
Shaftesbury Theatre *(WC2)*
Theatre Royal, Drury Lane *(WC2)*
The Villiers Theatre *(WC2)*
Wyndham's Theatre *(WC2)*

West
Canal Café Theatre *(W2)*
Hammersmith Apollo *(W6)*
Royal Albert Hall *(SW7)*
20th Century Theatre *(W11)*

North
Hoxton Hall *(N1)*
Jongleurs at Camden Lock *(NW1)*
King's Head Theatre *(N1)*
Little Angel Theatre *(N1)*
New End Theatre *(NW3)*
Tricycle Theatre *(NW6)*
UCS Theatre *(NW3)*
Union Chapel *(N1)*
Upstairs at the Gatehouse *(N6)*

South
BFI London IMAX Cinema *(SE1)*
Greenwich Playhouse *(SE10)*
Greenwich Theatre *(SE10)*
Jongleurs (Battersea) *(SW11)*
Latchmere Theatre *(SW11)*
Polka Theatre for Children *(SW19)*
Royal National Theatre *(SE1)*
Shakespeare's Globe *(SE1)*

East
Bridewell Theatre *(EC4)*
Jongleurs at Bow Wharf *(E3)*
Mermaid Theatre *(EC4)*
Sadler's Wells Theatre *(EC1)*

Miscellaneous

Central
Aldwych Station *(WC2)*
Audi Forum *(W1)*
Berry Bros & Rudd *(SW1)*
Christie's *(SW1)*
The Commonwealth Club *(WC2)*
Congress Centre *(WC1)*
Coram's Fields *(WC1)*
Covent Garden Market *(WC2)*
Fortnum & Mason *(W1)*
Funland *(W1)*
Hamleys Playground *(W1)*
Harrods *(SW1)*
Hellenic Centre *(W1)*
International Coffee
   Organisation *(W1)*
Kensington Place *(W8)*
London Astoria *(WC2)*
The Place *(WC1)*
Rex Cinema & Bar *(W1)*
Royal Astronomical Society *(W1)*
St Mary's Church *(W1)*
The Sanctuary *(WC2)*
Savile Club *(W1)*
Somerset House *(WC2)*
Sotheby's *(W1)*
St Martin In The Fields *(WC2)*
Thomas Goode *(W1)*
The Union Club *(W1)*
Waterstone's Piccadilly *(W1)*
Wellington Arch *(W1)*
Westminster Abbey Garden *(SW1)*
Westminster Boating Base *(SW1)*

West
Apartment 195 *(SW3)*
The Chelsea Gardener *(SW3)*
Chelsea Physic Garden *(SW3)*
Chelsea Village *(SW6)*
First Bowl Queensway *(W2)*
Gunnersbury Park *(W3)*
The Irish Centre *(W6)*
Orangery (Holland Park) *(W8)*
Orangery (Kensington Palace) *(W8)*
Riverside Studios *(W6)*
Royal Parks Agency *(W2)*
Trailfinders Sports Club *(W13)*
Westway Studios *(W11)*
The Worx *(SW6)*

North
Alexandra Palace Ice Rink *(N22)*
The British Library *(NW1)*
Burgh House *(NW3)*
The Decorium *(N22)*
Diorama *(NW1)*
Gainsborough Studios *(N1)*
Jackson's Lane Community
   Centre *(N6)*
The London Art House *(N1)*
The Magic Circle *(NW1)*
The Tram Studios *(NW1)*

South
Battersea Park *(SW11)*
The Bridge SE1 *(SE1)*
Bridges Wharf *(SW11)*
Brockwell Lido *(SE24)*
City Hall - London's Living
   Room *(SE1)*
The Conservatory *(SW11)*
The Coronet *(SE1)*
Cottons Atrium *(SE1)*
Crystal Palace Park *(SE20)*
Earlsfield Library *(SW18)*
Greenwich Yacht Club *(SE10)*
Kingswood House *(SE21)*
LABAN *(SE8)*
Mega Bowl *(SW2)*
Mosimann's Academy *(SW11)*
Namco *(SE1)*
Neal's Lodge *(SW18)*
The Old Royal Naval College *(SE10)*
Simon Drake's House of Magic *(SE17)*
Southwark Cathedral *(SE1)*
Streatham Ice Arena *(SW16)*
Surrey Docks Watersports
   Centre *(SE16)*
Tower Bridge *(SE1)*
Vinopolis – City of Wine *(SE1)*
Winchester House *(SW15)*

East
Barbican Centre *(EC2)*
Broadgate Estates *(EC2)*
The Chainstore *(E14)*
Circus Space *(N1)*
Docklands Sailing & Watersports
   Centre *(E14)*
East Wintergarden *(E14)*
The Energy Clinic *(E1)*
ExCel *(E16)*
Lee Valley Cycle Circuit *(E10)*
London Capital Club *(EC4)*
London Stock Exchange *(EC2)*
The London Underwriting
   Centre *(EC3)*
LSO St Luke's *(EC1)*

Newham City Farm (E16)
Old Billingsgate (EC3)
Old Spitalfields Market (E1)
St Andrew's Court House (EC4)
St Etheldreda's Crypt (EC1)
St Paul's Cathedral (EC4)

Outside London

Ascot Racecourse (Berks)
Big Brother House (Herts)
Brighton Royal Pavilion (E Sussex)
Denbies Wine Estate (Surrey)
Elstree Film Studio (Herts)
Epsom Downs (Surrey)
Ham Polo Club (Surrey)
The Hop Farm Country Park (Kent)
Painshill (Surrey)
Pinewood Studios (Bucks)
Queen's Eyot (Berks)
Raven's Ait Island (Surrey)
Temple Island (Oxon)
Twickenham Experience (Middx)

Clubs

Central

The Academy (WC1)
Adam Street (WC2)
The Agency (WC2)
Annabel's (W1)
Arts Club (W1)
The Caledonian Club (SW1)
Carlton Club (SW1)
Cavalry & Guards Club (W1)
East India Club (SW1)
The Fox Club (W1)
Groucho Club (W1)
Lansdowne Club (W1)
The Mayfair Club (W1)
Monte's (SW1)
Mosimann's Belfry (SW1)
National Liberal Club (SW1)
The New Cavendish Club (W1)
Oxford & Cambridge Club (SW1)
Poetry Society (WC2)
Ronnie Scotts (W1)
The Royal Air Force Club (W1)
Royal Over-Seas League (SW1)
Soho House (W1)
St Stephen's Club (SW1)
University Women's Club (W1)
The Wellington Club (SW1)

West

The Cobden Club (W10)
Hurlingham Club (SW6)
Polish Club (SW7)
Polish Social & Cultural
  Association (W6)
Raffles (SW3)
Victory Services Club (W2)

North

Red Rose Comedy Club (N7)

South

Bank of England Sports Club (SW15)
London Rowing Club (SW15)
Roehampton Club (SW15)

East

The Broadgate Club (EC2)
City Club (EC2)
Fifteen05 (EC4)

The Little Ship Club (EC4)
Lloyd's Club (EC3)

Nightclubs

Central

Browns Club (WC2)
Café de Paris (W1)
CC Club (W1)
China White (W1)
Denim (WC2)
Digress (W1)
Elysium (W1)
The End (WC1)
Equinox at the Empire (WC2)
5 Cavendish Square (W1)
The London Hippodrome (WC2)
The Mean Fiddler (WC2)
On Anon (W1)
Pacha (SW1)
Red Cube (WC2)
Rock Garden (WC2)
Sound (W1)
St Moritz (W1)
Sugar Reef (W1)
Sway (WC2)
Tantra (W1)
Tiger Tiger (SW1)

West

Crazy Larry's (SW10)
Embargo (SW10)
FireHouse (SW7)
Hammersmith Palais (W6)
The Roof Gardens (W8)
606 Club (SW10)

North

The Camden Palace (NW1)
The Cross (N1)
Egg (N7)
Electric Ballroom (NW1)
WKD (NW1)

South

The Fridge (SW2)
The Ministry of Sound (SE1)
Studio 33 (SE11)
Wessex House (SW11)

East

Aquarium (EC1)
Cargo (EC2)
Fabric (EC1)
Turnmills (EC1)

Wine bars

Central

Balls Brothers (SW1)
Bung Hole (WC1)
Shampers (W1)
Vats (WC1)

West

Gyngleboy (W2)
Hollands (W11)

South

Archduke Wine Bar (SE1)
Balls Brothers (SE1)
Boot & Flogger (SE1)
Hop Cellars (SE1)
The Mug House (SE1)

East
Gow's Restaurant (EC2)
Bleeding Heart (EC1)
Ochre (EC4)
Corney & Barrow (E14)
Bangers (EC2)
Leadenhall Wine Bar (EC3)
Jamies Pavilion (EC2)

Bars & Pubs

Central
Amber (W1)
The Antelope (SW1)
The Argyll Arms (W1)
Bar Red (W1)
Buzz Bar (WC2)
Calthorpe Arms (WC1)
Cittie of Yorke (WC1)
The Clachan (W1)
The Crown & Two Chairmen (W1)
The Dog & Duck (W1)
Duke of Albemarle (W1)
The Freemason's Arms (WC2)
Glassblower (W1)
The Glasshouse Stores (W1)
The Golden Lion (SW1)
The Player (W1)
The Plough (WC1)
Shelleys (W1)
Star Tavern (SW1)
The Sun (WC2)
The Tattershall Castle (SW1)
Two Chairmen (SW1)
Walkers of St James's (SW1)
Waxy O'Connors (W1)

West
Aragon House (SW6)
The Atlas (SW6)
Beach Blanket Babylon (W11)
Coopers Arms (SW3)
The Cross Keys (SW3)
Lonsdale (W11)
Phene Arms (SW3)
The Station (W10)
The White Horse (SW6)

North
Hoxton Square Bar & Kitchen (N1)
Prince of Wales (NW1)
Slug & Lettuce (N1)
The Wells (NW3)

South
Alma (SW18)
The Anchor (SE1)
Bar M (SW15)
Crown & Greyhound (SE21)
Doggetts Coat & Badge (SE1)
George Inn (SE1)
The Old Thameside Inn (SE1)
Putney Bridge (SW15)
Ship (SW18)
The Litten Tree (SW15)
Southwark Tavern (SE1)
The East Hill (SW18)
Trafalgar Tavern (SE10)

East
Bedroom Bar (EC2)
Captain Kidd (E1)
The Crown Tavern (EC1)
Dickens Inn (E1)

Home (EC2)
The Lamb Tavern (EC3)
Liquid Lab (EC1)
Loungelover (E1)
Ye Olde Cheshire Cheese (EC4)

Restaurants

Central
Atlantic Bar & Grill (W1)
Atrium (SW1)
The Avenue (SW1)
Bam-Bou (W1)
Bank Westminster (SW1)
Benares (W1)
Bentleys (W1)
Boisdale (SW1)
Boudin Blanc (W1)
Break For The Border (W1)
Browns (W1)
Café du Jardin (WC2)
Chez Gérard, Dover Street (W1)
Chez Gérard, Opera Terrace (WC2)
Chintamani (SW1)
Christopher's (WC2)
Chuen Cheng Ku (W1)
The Cinnamon Club (SW1)
The Circus (W1)
The Criterion (W1)
Deca (W1)
Detroit (WC2)
Dover Street Restaurant & Bar (W1)
Drones (SW1)
Eddalino (W1)
Elena's L'Etoile (W1)
L'Escargot (W1)
Footstool (SW1)
Le Gavroche (W1)
Gay Hussar (W1)
The Guinea Grill (W1)
Hakkasan (W1)
The Halkin (SW1)
Heights Bar & Restaurant (W1)
Ikkyu (W1)
Imperial China (WC2)
L'Incontro (SW1)
The Ivy (WC2)
Just St James (SW1)
Ken Lo's Memories of China (SW1)
Kettners (W1)
The Langley (WC2)
Levant (W1)
Lindsay House (W1)
The Little Square (W1)
Mela (WC2)
Mimmo d'Ischia (SW1)
Mint Leaf (SW1)
Mirabelle (W1)
Mitsukoshi (SW1)
Momo (W1)
Mon Plaisir (WC2)
Mr Kong (WC2)
New World (W1)
Noble Rot (W1)
115 at Hodgson's (WC2)
Opium (W1)
L'Oranger (SW1)
Paxton's Head (SW1)
Pattersons's (W1)
Pétrus (SW1)
Pizza On The Park (SW1)
PizzaExpress (W1)

Pomegranates *(SW1)*
La Porte des Indes *(W1)*
Quilon *(SW1)*
Quo Vadis *(W1)*
La Rascasse *(W1)*
Rocket *(W1)*
Rules *(WC2)*
Sartoria *(W1)*
Scotts *(W1)*
Shepherd's *(SW1)*
Shumi *(SW1)*
Simpsons-in-the-Strand *(WC2)*
Six-13 *(W1)*
Sketch *(W1)*
So.uk Soho *(W1)*
Souk *(WC2)*
Spaghetti House *(W1)*
The Square *(W1)*
Strictly Hush *(W1)*
Teca *(W1)*
Texas Embassy Cantina *(SW1)*
Tuttons *(WC2)*
Wiltons *(SW1)*
Yming *(W1)*
Zen Central *(W1)*

West

Babylon *(W8)*
Barbarella *(SW6)*
Belvedere *(W8)*
Bombay Brasserie *(SW7)*
Borscht & Tears *(SW3)*
Bonchurch Brasserie *(W10)*
Brasserie St Quentin *(SW3)*
Brinkley's *(SW10)*
Busabong Too *(SW10)*
Bush Bar & Grill *(W12)*
Cactus Blue *(SW3)*
Café Lazeez *(SW7)*
Cheyne Walk Brasserie *(SW3)*
Cibo *(W14)*
The Collection *(SW3)*
Le Colombier *(SW3)*
Costa's Grill *(W8)*
Da Mario *(SW7)*
Dan's *(SW3)*
E&O *(W11)*
Eight Over Eight *(SW3)*
Electric Brasserie (& Electric House Club) *(W11)*
Foxtrot Oscar *(SW3)*
Goolies *(W8)*
Henry J Beans *(SW3)*
Jason's *(W9)*
Julie's Restaurant & Wine Bar *(W11)*
Launceston Place *(W8)*
Mao Tai *(SW6)*
The Townhouse *(SW3)*
Notting Hill Brasserie *(W11)*
Patio *(W12)*
Pissarro's on the River *(W4)*
PizzaExpress *(W11)*
PJ's Bar & Grill *(SW3)*
Poissonnerie de l'Avenue *(SW3)*
Sugar Hut *(SW6)*
Le Suquet *(SW3)*
The Vale *(W9)*
The White House *(SW4)*
Wine Gallery *(SW10)*
Wódka *(W8)*
Woody's *(W9)*

North

The Almeida *(N1)*

Cuba Libre *(N1)*
Engineer *(NW1)*
Frederick's *(N1)*
Lemonia *(NW1)*
Le Mercury *(N1)*
Odette's *(NW1)*
Pasha *(N1)*
PizzaExpress *(N1)*
Queen Mary Garden *(NW1)*
Seashell *(NW1)*
Shillibeer's *(N7)*
William IV *(NW10)*
ZeNW3 *(NW3)*

South

Balham Bar & Kitchen *(SW12)*
Baltic *(SE1)*
Bankside Restaurant *(SE1)*
The Battersea Barge Bistro *(SW8)*
Belair House *(SE21)*
Bengal Clipper *(SE1)*
Bombay Bicycle Club *(SW12)*
Caper Green *(SE10)*
Chez Bruce *(SW17)*
Depot *(SW14)*
Le Gothique *(SW18)*
MVH *(SW13)*
Niksons *(SW11)*
The People's Palace *(SE1)*
PizzaExpress *(SW11)*
Polygon Bar & Grill *(SW4)*
Le Pont de la Tour *(SE1)*
RSJ *(SE1)*

East

Abbaye *(EC1)*
Aquarium *(E1)*
Bar Bourse *(EC4)*
Threadneedles *(EC2)*
Bow Wine Vaults *(EC4)*
Café du Marché *(EC1)*
Cicada *(EC1)*
City Miyama *(EC4)*
Coq d'Argent *(EC2)*
The Don *(EC4)*
Fox & Anchor *(EC1)*
Frocks *(E9)*
Great Eastern Dining Rooms *(EC2)*
Imperial City *(EC3)*
Just Gladwins *(EC3)*
Just The Bridge *(EC4)*
Lightship *(E1)*
The Medieval Banquet *(E1)*
Nylon *(EC2)*
1 Blossom Street *(E1)*
1 Lombard Street *(EC3)*
La Paquerette *(EC2)*
PizzaExpress *(E1)*
The Place Below *(EC2)*
Plateau *(E14)*
Prism *(EC3)*
Simpsons Tavern *(EC3)*
Singapura *(EC2)*
Smith's of Smithfield *(EC1)*
St John *(EC1)*
Sweetings *(EC4)*
Tatsuso *(EC2)*
Throgmorton's *(EC2)*
Les Trois Garçons *(EC2)*
Wapping Food *(E1)*
White's *(EC4)*

Outside London
Hampton Court Palace (The Tiltyard) (Surrey)

Hotels

Central
Athenaeum Hotel (W1)
The Berkeley (SW1)
The Berkshire (W1)
The Berners Hotel (W1)
The Bonnington in Bloomsbury (WC1)
Brown's Hotel (W1)
The Cadogan (SW1)
Carlton Tower (SW1)
Charlotte Street Hotel (W1)
The Chesterfield Mayfair (W1)
Churchill (W1)
City Inn Westminster (SW1)
Claridge's (W1)
The Connaught (W1)
Covent Garden Hotel (WC2)
Cumberland Hotel (W1)
The De Vere Cavendish St James's (SW1)
Dolphin Square Hotel (SW1)
The Dorchester (W1)
Dukes Hotel (SW1)
Durrants Hotel (W1)
Four Seasons Hotel (W1)
The Goring (SW1)
The Grafton (W1)
The Grosvenor House Hotel (W1)
Hampshire Hotel (WC2)
Hilton on Park Lane (W1)
Holiday Inn London Regent's Park (W1)
Holiday Inn – Mayair (W1)
InterContinental London (W1)
Jolly Hotel St Ermins (SW1)
The Kenilworth (WC1)
The Lanesborough (SW1)
Langham Hilton (W1)
London Marriott (W1)
London Marriott Hotel Park Lane (W1)
Mandarin Oriental Hyde Park (SW1)
The Mayfair Inter-Continental (W1)
Le Meridien (W1)
Le Meridien Russell Hotel (WC1)
The Metropolitan (W1)
Millennium London Mayfair (W1)
The Montcalm Hotel (W1)
The Mountbatten (WC2)
One Aldwych (WC2)
Park Lane Hotel (W1)
Portman Hotel (W1)
Renaissance London Chancery Court Hotel (WC1)
The Ritz (W1)
The Rubens (SW1)
The Savoy (WC2)
The Selfridge Hotel (W1)
Sheraton Belgravia (SW1)
Sheraton Park Tower (SW1)
St Martin's Lane Hotel (WC2)
The Stafford (SW1)
Strand Palace Hotel (WC2)
Swissôtel London the Howard (WC2)
Thistle Victoria Hotel (SW1)
The Trafalgar (SW1)
Waldorf Hotel (WC2)

The Washington (W1)
The Westbury (W1)

West
Basil Street Hotel (SW3)
The Capital (SW3)
Conrad Hotel (SW10)
Harrington Hall (SW7)
The Hempel (W2)
Hilton London Paddington (W2)
Kensington Rooms (SW7)
London Metropole (W2)
The Milestone Hotel & Apartments (W8)
Millennium Gloucester Hotel (SW7)
Number Sixteen (SW7)
The Ramada Jarvis London West (W5)
The Rembrandt Hotel (SW7)
Royal Garden Hotel (W8)
Royal Lancaster (W2)
Thistle Kensington Palace Hotel (W8)
Vanderbilt Hotel (SW7)

North
Hendon Hall Hotel (NW4)
The Landmark (NW1)
Marriott Maida Vale (NW6)
White House Hotel (NW1)

South
Cannizaro House (SW19)
Hilton London Docklands (SE16)
London Marriott County Hall Hotel (SE1)

East
Britannia International Hotel (E14)
Four Seasons Canary Wharf (E14)
Great Eastern Hotel (EC2)
Tower Thistle (E1)

Outside London
The Carlton Mitre Hotel (Surrey)
Cliveden (Berks)
The Grove (Herts)
Le Meridien Selsdon Park (Surrey)
Monkey Island Hotel (Berks)
Pennyhill Park Hotel (Surrey)
The Petersham (Surrey)

Conference centres

Central
Aeonian (WC1)
Bloomsbury Square Training Centre (WC1)
The CBI Conference Centre (WC1)
Kingsway Hall (WC2)
The Lincoln Centre (WC2)
The Mary Sumner House (SW1)
Park Crescent Conference Centre (W1)
Portland Place Conference Centre (W1)
Robert Wilson Black Centre (SW1)
76 Portland Place (W1)
St Paul's Church (W1)
United Grand Lodge of England (WC2)

West
Kensington Town Hall (W8)
Mayfair Conference Centre (W2)

VISIT US AT: www.hardens.com

North

White Hart Lane Conference
   Centre (N17)

East

City Conference Centre (EC2)
The City Presentation Centre (EC1)
City University (EC1)
The Hatton (EC1)
Inmarsat (EC1)
The Old Sessions House (EC1)
Royal Statistical Society (EC1)

Outside London

Warren House (Surrey)

VENUES LICENSED FOR WEDDINGS

Central

Arundel House (WC2)
Athenaeum Hotel (W1)
The Avenue (SW1)
The Berkeley (SW1)
The Berners Hotel (W1)
BMA House (WC1)
Brown's Hotel (W1)
The Cadogan (SW1)
Café de Paris (W1)
Café Royal (W1)
The Caledonian Club (SW1)
Canning House (SW1)
Carlton Club (SW1)
Carlton Tower (SW1)
The Chesterfield Mayfair (W1)
Church House (SW1)
Churchill (W1)
Claridge's (W1)
The Commonwealth Club (WC2)
Congress Centre (WC1)
Dartmouth House (W1)
Dolphin Square Hotel (SW1)
The Dorchester (W1)
Dukes Hotel (SW1)
Fortnum & Mason (W1)
Four Seasons Hotel (W1)
The Goring (SW1)
Gray's Inn (WC1)
The Grosvenor House Hotel (W1)
Groucho Club (W1)
Hilton on Park Lane (W1)
Home House (W1)
The House of St Barnabas-in-
   Soho (W1)
Institute of Directors (SW1)
Institute of Electrical Engineers (WC2)
InterContinental London (W1)
Jolly Hotel St Ermins (SW1)
Kingsway Hall (WC2)
The Lanesborough (SW1)
Langham Hilton (W1)
Lansdowne Club (W1)
The Law Society (WC2)
London Marriott (W1)
London Palladium (W1)
Mandarin Oriental Hyde Park (SW1)
The Mayfair Inter-Continental (W1)
Le Meridien (W1)
Millennium London Mayfair (W1)
Mosimann's Belfry (SW1)
National Liberal Club (SW1)
New Connaught Rms (WC2)
One Aldwych (WC2)
One Great George Street (SW1)
One Whitehall Place (SW1)
Park Lane Hotel (W1)
Portman Hotel (W1)
The Queen Elizabeth II Conference
   Centre (SW1)
TS Queen Mary (WC2)
Renaissance London Chancery Court
   Hotel (WC1)
The Ritz (W1)
Royal Opera House (WC2)
Royal Society of Arts (WC2)
St Mary's Church (W1)
The Savoy (WC2)
Soho House (W1)

Spencer House (SW1)
The Stafford (SW1)
Swissôtel London the Howard (WC2)
30 Pavilion Road (SW1)
28 Portland Place (W1)
Waldorf Hotel (WC2)

West

Belvedere (W8)
Chelsea Old Town Hall (SW3)
Chelsea Village (SW6)
Chiswick House (W4)
Conrad Hotel (SW10)
Ealing Town Hall (W5)
Fulham Palace (SW6)
Fulham Town Hall (SW6)
Hammersmith Town Hall (W6)
Harrington Hall (SW7)
The Hempel (W2)
Hilton London Paddington (W2)
Hurlingham Club (SW6)
Kensington Town Hall (W8)
The Milestone Hotel &
   Apartments (W8)
Millennium Gloucester Hotel (SW7)
Orangery (Holland Park) (W8)
Porchester Centre (W2)
The Ramada Jarvis London West (W5)
The Rembrandt Hotel (SW7)
The Roof Gardens (W8)
Royal Garden Hotel (W8)
Royal Geographical Society (SW7)
Vanderbilt Hotel (SW7)

North

Alexandra Palace & Park (N22)
Avenue House (N3)
Burgh House (NW3)
The Decorium (N22)
Frederick's (N1)
Gainsborough Studios (N1)
Hendon Hall Hotel (NW4)
Highgate School (N6)
Kenwood House, Old Kitchen (NW3)
The Landmark (NW1)
Lauderdale House (N6)
London Zoo (NW1)
Madame Tussaud's (NW1)
Queen Mary Garden (NW1)
Union Chapel (N1)
White Hart Lane Conference
   Centre (N17)
William IV (NW10)

South

Academy of Live & Recorded
   Arts (SW18)
Alma (SW18)
BAC (SW11)
Bank of England Sports Club (SW15)
Belair House (SE21)
HMS Belfast (SE1)
Blackheath Concert Halls (SE3)
Cannizaro House (SW19)
Crown & Greyhound (SE21)
Delfina Galleries (SE1)
Devonport House (SE10)
Dulwich College (SE21)
Eltham Palace (SE9)
Glaziers' Hall (SE1)
The Golden Hinde (SE1)
Le Gothique (SW18)
Guy's Hospital (SE1)
Hilton London Docklands (SE16)

Jerwood Space (SE1)
Kingswood House (SE21)
London Eye (SE1)
London Marriott County Hall
   Hotel (SE1)
The Ministry of Sound (SE1)
National Maritime Museum (SE10)
The Old Royal Naval College (SE10)
The Old Thameside Inn (SE1)
The Oval (SE11)
The Pump House Gallery (SW11)
Queen's House (SE10)
Tower Bridge (SE1)
Trafalgar Tavern (SE10)
Vinopolis – City of Wine (SE1)
Wandsworth Civic Suite (SW18)
Winchester House (SW15)

East

Aquarium (E1)
Barbican Art Gallery (EC2)
Barbican Centre (EC2)
The Brewery (EC1)
Britannia International Hotel (E14)
Cabot Hall (E14)
City Club (EC2)
Corney & Barrow (EC2)
Four Seasons Canary Wharf (E14)
Great Eastern Hotel (EC2)
Honourable Artillery Co (EC1)
Middle Temple Hall (EC4)
Sadler's Wells Theatre (EC1)
Stationers' Hall (EC4)
Sutton House (E9)
Tower Thistle (E1)
291 Gallery (E2)

Outside London

Addington Palace (Surrey)
Amberley Castle (W Sussex)
Ascot Racecourse (Berks)
Blenheim Palace (Oxon)
Brighton Royal Pavilion (E Sussex)
The Carlton Mitre Hotel (Surrey)
Cliveden (Berks)
Denbies Wine Estate (Surrey)
Easthampstead Park Conference
   Centre (Berks)
Epsom Downs (Surrey)
Great Fosters (Surrey)
The Grove (Herts)
Ham House (Surrey)
Harrow School (Middx)
Hever Castle (Kent)
The Hop Farm Country Park (Kent)
Kew (Royal Botanic) Gardens (Surrey)
Legoland Windsor (Berks)
Le Meridien Selsdon Park (Surrey)
Monkey Island Hotel (Berks)
The Old Palace (Herts)
Osterley Park & House (Middx)
Pennyhill Park Hotel (Surrey)
Penshurst Place & Gardens (Kent)
Pinewood Studios (Bucks)
Raven's Ait Island (Surrey)
Spring Grove House (Middx)
SS Great Britain (Bristol)
Stonor (Oxon)
Syon Park (Conservatory) (Middx)
Syon Park (House) (Middx)
Twickenham Experience (Middx)
Warren House (Surrey)
Whipsnade Wild Animal Park (Beds)

VISIT US AT: www.hardens.com

Windsor Guildhall *(Berks)*

VENUES WITH HIRER'S CHOICE OF CATERER

Central

Aldwych Station *(WC2)*
Aldwych Theatre *(WC2)*
Arts Club *(W1)*
The Artworkers Guild *(WC1)*
Il Bottaccio *(SW1)*
Browns Club *(WC2)*
Canning House *(SW1)*
Central Hall Westminster *(SW1)*
The Chesterfield Mayfair *(W1)*
Christie's *(SW1)*
Cochrane Theatre *(WC1)*
The Comedy Store *(SW1)*
Congress Centre *(WC1)*
Conway Hall *(WC1)*
Covent Garden Market *(WC2)*
Curwen Gallery *(W1)*
The Dickens' House Museum *(WC1)*
Elysium *(W1)*
Equinox at the Empire *(WC2)*
Fitzroy Square *(W1)*
Haymarket Theatre *(SW1)*
International Coffee
  Organisation *(W1)*
Lincoln's Inn *(WC1)*
London Astoria *(WC2)*
London Scottish *(SW1)*
Mall Galleries *(SW1)*
The Mary Sumner House *(SW1)*
The Mayfair Club *(W1)*
The Mean Fiddler *(WC2)*
The Music Room *(W1)*
New Connaught Rms *(WC2)*
The October Gallery *(WC1)*
One Whitehall Place *(SW1)*
Proud Galleries *(WC2)*
Ronnie Scotts *(W1)*
Royal Court Theatre *(SW1)*
Shaftesbury Theatre *(WC2)*
St Moritz *(W1)*
Staple Inn *(WC1)*
Theatre Museum *(WC2)*
Thomas Goode *(W1)*
United Grand Lodge of England *(WC2)*
Westminster Boating Base *(SW1)*
Westminster Cathedral Hall *(SW1)*

West

Apartment 195 *(SW3)*
Brompton Oratory – St Wilfrid's
  Hall *(SW7)*
Canal Café Theatre *(W2)*
Crazy Larry's *(SW10)*
Duke of York's HQ *(SW3)*
Ealing Town Hall *(W5)*
Embargo *(SW10)*
First Bowl Queensway *(W2)*
Fulham House *(SW6)*
Fulham Palace *(SW6)*
Fulham Town Hall *(SW6)*
Gunnersbury Park *(W3)*
Hammersmith Palais *(W6)*
Hammersmith Town Hall *(W6)*
Hilton London Paddington *(W2)*
Hogarth's House *(W4)*
Institut Français *(SW7)*
The Irish Centre *(W6)*
Philbeach Hall *(SW5)*
Porchester Centre *(W2)*
Royal College of Art *(SW7)*

St Peter's Hall *(W11)*
20th Century Theatre *(W11)*
Westway Studios *(W11)*
Will's Art Warehouse *(SW6)*
The Worx *(SW6)*

North

Alexandra Palace Ice Rink *(N22)*
Avenue House *(N3)*
The Camden Palace *(NW1)*
Canonbury Academy *(N1)*
The Cross *(N1)*
The Decorium *(N22)*
Diorama *(NW1)*
Electric Ballroom *(NW1)*
Estorick Collection *(N1)*
Freud Museum *(NW3)*
Gainsborough Studios *(N1)*
Hendon Hall Hotel *(NW4)*
Highgate School *(N6)*
Hoxton Hall *(N1)*
Jackson's Lane Community
    Centre *(N6)*
Jongleurs at Camden Lock *(NW1)*
Little Angel Theatre *(N1)*
The London Canal Museum *(N1)*
New End Theatre *(NW3)*
Red Rose Comedy Club *(N7)*
Regency Banqueting Suite *(N17)*
Tricycle Theatre *(NW6)*
Union Chapel *(N1)*
Upstairs at the Gatehouse *(N6)*
White House Hotel *(NW1)*

South

BAC *(SW11)*
Bankside Gallery *(SE1)*
Battersea Park *(SW11)*
Bramah Tea & Coffee Museum *(SE1)*
Chatham Hall *(SW11)*
The Conservatory *(SW11)*
Cottons Atrium *(SE1)*
Crystal Palace Park *(SE20)*
Dali Universe *(SE1)*
Dulwich College *(SE21)*
Earlsfield Library *(SW18)*
Firepower - The Royal Artillery
    Museum *(SE18)*
The Fridge *(SW2)*
The Golden Hinde *(SE1)*
Goldsmiths College *(SE14)*
Greenwich Yacht Club *(SE10)*
Hop Exchange *(SE1)*
Jongleurs (Battersea) *(SW11)*
King's College School *(SW19)*
Kingswood House *(SE21)*
London Rowing Club *(SW15)*
The Old Operating Theatre, Museum
    & Herb Garret *(SE1)*
Polka Theatre for Children *(SW19)*
The Pump House Gallery *(SW11)*
South London Gallery *(SE5)*
Streatham Ice Arena *(SW16)*
Studio 33 *(SE11)*
Surrey Docks Watersports
    Centre *(SE16)*
Wandsworth Civic Suite *(SW18)*
Winston Churchill's Britain at
    War *(SE1)*

East

The AOP Gallery *(EC2)*
Aquarium *(EC1)*
Barnard's Inn Hall *(EC1)*

Bridewell Theatre *(EC4)*
Broadgate Estates *(EC2)*
The Candid Arts Trust *(EC1)*
The Chainstore *(E14)*
Circus Space *(N1)*
Dr Johnsons' House *(EC4)*
The Energy Clinic *(E1)*
Fabric *(EC1)*
Gibson Hall *(EC2)*
Hamilton House *(EC4)*
Jongleurs at Bow Wharf *(E3)*
Lee Valley Cycle Circuit *(E10)*
Merchant Taylors' Hall *(EC2)*
Mermaid Theatre *(EC4)*
Middle Temple Hall *(EC4)*
Mudchute Park & Farm *(E14)*
Newham City Farm *(E16)*
The Newsroom *(EC1)*
Old Billingsgate *(EC3)*
Old Spitalfields Market *(E1)*
Prenelle Gallery *(E14)*
HMS President *(EC4)*
Queen Mary Students' Union *(E1)*
Royal Statistical Society *(EC1)*
Salters' Hall *(EC2)*
St Botolph's Hall *(EC2)*
St Bride Foundation Institute *(EC4)*
St John's Gate *(EC1)*
Stoke Newington Town Hall *(E8)*
Stratford Old Town Hall *(E15)*
Turnmills *(EC1)*
291 Gallery *(E2)*
Whitechapel Art Gallery *(E1)*

Outside London

Elstree Film Studio *(Herts)*
Eton College (Dorney Lake) *(Berks)*
Kew Bridge Steam Museum *(Middx)*
Marble Hill House *(Surrey)*
Painshill *(Surrey)*
Spring Grove House *(Middx)*
Whitewebbs Museum of
    Transport *(Middx)*

VENUES WITH OUTSIDE AREAS

Central

The Academy *(WC1)*
Arts Club *(W1)*
Arundel House *(WC2)*
BMA House *(WC1)*
Boisdale *(SW1)*
Café Royal *(W1)*
Canning House *(SW1)*
Chez Gérard, Dover Street *(W1)*
Chez Gérard, Opera Terrace *(WC2)*
The Circus *(W1)*
City Inn Westminster *(SW1)*
The Connaught *(W1)*
Coram's Fields *(WC1)*
Dartmouth House *(W1)*
Denim *(WC2)*
The Dickens' House Museum *(WC1)*
Dolphin Square Hotel *(SW1)*
The Dorchester *(W1)*
Four Seasons Hotel *(W1)*
Gray's Inn *(WC1)*
Guards Museum *(SW1)*
RS Hispaniola *(WC2)*
Home House *(W1)*
The House of St Barnabas-in-
   Soho *(W1)*
ICA *(SW1)*
The Imagination Gallery *(WC1)*
Institute of Electrical Engineers *(WC2)*
Jolly Hotel St Ermins *(SW1)*
Lancaster House *(SW1)*
Langham Hilton *(W1)*
Lansdowne Club *(W1)*
Lincoln's Inn *(WC1)*
Millennium London Mayfair *(W1)*
Mirabelle *(W1)*
Mosimann's Belfry *(SW1)*
National Liberal Club *(SW1)*
The New Cavendish Club *(W1)*
No 4 Hamilton Place *(W1)*
The October Gallery *(WC1)*
On Anon *(W1)*
Park Crescent Conference
   Centre *(W1)*
Portland Place Conference
   Centre *(W1)*
Proud Galleries *(WC2)*
TS Queen Mary *(WC2)*
The Ritz *(W1)*
Rock Garden *(WC2)*
Royal College of Pathologists *(SW1)*
Royal Institute of British
   Architects *(W1)*
Royal Opera House *(WC2)*
Savile Club *(W1)*
Sheraton Park Tower *(SW1)*
Soho House *(W1)*
Somerset House *(WC2)*
Sound *(W1)*
Spencer House *(SW1)*
St Martin's Lane Hotel *(WC2)*
St Stephen's Club *(SW1)*
The Stafford *(SW1)*
Staple Inn *(WC1)*
Swissôtel London the Howard *(WC2)*
Tate Britain *(SW1)*
Texas Embassy Cantina *(SW1)*
The Trafalgar *(SW1)*
28 Portland Place *(W1)*
University Women's Club *(W1)*
HQS Wellington *(WC2)*

Wellington Arch *(W1)*
Westminster Abbey Garden *(SW1)*
Westminster Boating Base *(SW1)*

West

Aragon House *(SW6)*
Belvedere *(W8)*
Brinkley's *(SW10)*
Café Lazeez *(SW7)*
The Chelsea Gardener *(SW3)*
Chelsea Physic Garden *(SW3)*
Chiswick House *(W4)*
Cibo *(W14)*
Commonwealth Conference & Events
   Centre *(W8)*
Conrad Hotel *(SW10)*
Dan's *(SW3)*
Duke of York's HQ *(SW3)*
Fulham Palace *(SW6)*
Gunnersbury Park *(W3)*
The Hempel *(W2)*
Henry J Beans *(SW3)*
Hogarth's House *(W4)*
Hollands *(W11)*
Hurlingham Club *(SW6)*
Imperial College *(SW7)*
Jason's *(W9)*
Kensington Palace *(W8)*
Kent House *(SW7)*
Leighton House *(W14)*
Number Sixteen *(SW7)*
Orangery (Holland Park) *(W8)*
Orangery (Kensington Palace) *(W8)*
Phene Arms *(SW3)*
Polish Club *(SW7)*
Riverside Studios *(W6)*
The Roof Gardens *(W8)*
Royal Geographical Society *(SW7)*
Royal Hospital Chelsea *(SW3)*
Royal Parks Agency *(W2)*
Serpentine Gallery *(W2)*
St Peter's Hall *(W11)*
The Station *(W10)*
Trailfinders Sports Club *(W13)*
Victoria & Albert Museum *(SW7)*
The White Horse *(SW6)*
The Worx *(SW6)*

North

Alexandra Palace & Park *(N22)*
Avenue House *(N3)*
The British Library *(NW1)*
Canonbury Academy *(N1)*
Cecil Sharp House *(NW1)*
The Cross *(N1)*
Egg *(N7)*
Engineer *(NW1)*
Estorick Collection *(N1)*
Frederick's *(N1)*
Freud Museum *(NW3)*
Gainsborough Studios *(N1)*
Hendon Hall Hotel *(NW4)*
Highgate School *(N6)*
Jackson's Lane Community
   Centre *(N6)*
Kenwood House *(NW3)*
King's Head Theatre *(N1)*
Lauderdale House *(N6)*
The London Canal Museum *(N1)*
London Zoo *(NW1)*
Lord's *(NW8)*
Marriott Maida Vale *(NW6)*
Prince of Wales *(NW1)*
Queen Mary Garden *(NW1)*

Regent's College (NW1)
Royal Air Force Museum (NW9)
Royal College of Physicians (NW1)
Royal Majestic Suite (NW6)
UCS Theatre (NW3)
White Hart Lane Conference
    Centre (N17)
William IV (NW10)
WKD (NW1)

South

Academy of Live & Recorded
    Arts (SW18)
The Anchor (SE1)
Archduke Wine Bar (SE1)
Bank of England Sports Club (SW15)
The Battersea Barge Bistro (SW8)
Battersea Park (SW11)
Belair House (SE21)
HMS Belfast (SE1)
Bridges Wharf (SW11)
Brockwell Lido (SE24)
Caper Green (SE10)
Cannizaro House (SW19)
Chatham Hall (SW11)
City Hall - London's Living
    Room (SE1)
The Conservatory (SW11)
Crown & Greyhound (SE21)
Crystal Palace Park (SE20)
Cutty Sark (SE10)
Design Museum (SE1)
Devonport House (SE10)
Doggetts Coat & Badge (SE1)
Dulwich College (SE21)
Dulwich Picture Gallery (SE21)
Eltham Palace (SE9)
Firepower - The Royal Artillery
    Museum (SE18)
Froebel College (SW15)
The Golden Hinde (SE1)
Le Gothique (SW18)
Greenwich Playhouse (SE10)
Greenwich Yacht Club (SE10)
Hayward Gallery (SE1)
Hilton London Docklands (SE16)
Horniman Museum (SE23)
Jerwood Space (SE1)
King's College School (SW19)
Kingswood House (SE21)
LABAN (SE8)
Latchmere Theatre (SW11)
London Aquarium (SE1)
London Rowing Club (SW15)
London Wetland Centre (SW13)
The Ministry of Sound (SE1)
Museum of Garden History (SE1)
National Maritime Museum (SE10)
Neal's Lodge (SW18)
The Old Royal Naval College (SE10)
The Old Thameside Inn (SE1)
Polka Theatre for Children (SW19)
The Pump House Gallery (SW11)
Queen's House (SE10)
Roehampton Club (SW15)
Royal National Theatre (SE1)
Royal Observatory (SE10)
The Saatchi Gallery (SE1)
Ship (SW18)
Simon Drake's House of Magic (SE17)
South London Gallery (SE5)
St Thomas' Hospital (SE1)
Studio 33 (SE11)

Tate Modern (SE1)
Whitelands College (SW15)
Winchester House (SW15)

East

Apothecaries' Hall (EC4)
Aquarium (E1)
Balls Brothers (EC3)
Barber-Surgeons' Hall (EC2)
Barbican Centre (EC2)
Barnard's Inn Hall (EC1)
Bleeding Heart (EC1)
The Brewery (EC1)
Broadgate Estates (EC2)
Cabot Hall (E14)
The Candid Arts Trust (EC1)
Captain Kidd (E1)
The Chainstore (E14)
Circus Space (N1)
City Club (EC2)
Coq d'Argent (EC2)
The Crown Tavern (EC1)
Docklands Sailing & Watersports
    Centre (E14)
Drapers' Hall (EC2)
Four Seasons Canary Wharf (E14)
Geffrye Museum (E2)
Gibson Hall (EC2)
Haberdashers' Hall (EC1)
Honourable Artillery Co (EC1)
Inner Temple Hall (EC4)
Ironmongers' Hall (EC2)
Jongleurs at Bow Wharf (E3)
Lee Valley Cycle Circuit (E10)
Leven is Strijd (E14)
Loungelover (E1)
LSO St Luke's (EC1)
Merchant Taylors' Hall (EC2)
Middle Temple Hall (EC4)
Mudchute Park & Farm (E14)
Museum of London (EC2)
Newham City Farm (E16)
Old Billingsgate (EC3)
Old Spitalfields Market (E1)
La Paquerette (EC2)
Prenelle Gallery (E14)
HMS President (EC4)
Queen Mary College (E1)
Salters' Hall (EC2)
Simpsons Tavern (EC3)
Singapura (EC4)
Skinners' Hall (EC4)
Smith's of Smithfield (EC1)
St Botolph's Hall (EC2)
St Bride Foundation Institute (EC4)
St Paul's Cathedral (EC4)
Stratford Old Town Hall (E15)
Tallow Chandlers' Hall (EC4)
291 Gallery (E2)

Outside London

Addington Palace (Surrey)
Amberley Castle (W Sussex)
Ascot Racecourse (Berks)
Big Brother House (Herts)
Blenheim Palace (Oxon)
Brighton Royal Pavilion (E Sussex)
The Carlton Mitre Hotel (Surrey)
Chessington World of
    Adventures (Surrey)
Cliveden (Berks)
Denbies Wine Estate (Surrey)
Easthampstead Park Conference
    Centre (Berks)

VISIT US AT: www.hardens.com

Epsom Downs *(Surrey)*
Eton College (Dorney Lake) *(Berks)*
Forty Hall *(Middx)*
Great Fosters *(Surrey)*
The Grove *(Herts)*
Ham House *(Surrey)*
Ham Polo Club *(Surrey)*
Hampton Court Palace *(Surrey)*
Hampton Court Palace (The
 Tiltyard) *(Surrey)*
Harrow School *(Middx)*
Hever Castle *(Kent)*
The Hop Farm Country Park *(Kent)*
Kew (Royal Botanic) Gardens *(Surrey)*
Kew Bridge Steam Museum *(Middx)*
Legoland Windsor *(Berks)*
Marble Hill House *(Surrey)*
Le Meridien Selsdon Park *(Surrey)*
Monkey Island Hotel *(Berks)*
The Old Palace *(Herts)*
Osterley Park & House *(Middx)*
Painshill *(Surrey)*
Pennyhill Park Hotel *(Surrey)*
Penshurst Place & Gardens *(Kent)*
Pinewood Studios *(Bucks)*
Queen's Eyot *(Berks)*
Raven's Ait Island *(Surrey)*
Royal Holloway College *(Surrey)*
Spring Grove House *(Middx)*
Stonor *(Oxon)*
Syon Park (Conservatory) *(Middx)*
Syon Park (House) *(Middx)*
Temple Island *(Oxon)*
Thorpe Park *(Surrey)*
Twickenham Experience *(Middx)*
West Wycombe Caves *(Bucks)*
Whipsnade Wild Animal Park *(Beds)*
Whitewebbs Museum of
 Transport *(Middx)*
Windsor Guildhall *(Berks)*
Wrotham Park *(Herts)*

VENUES WITH MARQUEE SITES

Central
The Academy *(WC1)*
Churchill *(W1)*
Coram's Fields *(WC1)*
Gray's Inn *(WC1)*
Guards Museum *(SW1)*
Home House *(W1)*
The House of St Barnabas-in-
 Soho *(W1)*
Lancaster House *(SW1)*
Lansdowne Club *(W1)*
No 4 Hamilton Place *(W1)*
Royal Institute of British
 Architects *(W1)*
Somerset House *(WC2)*
St Stephen's Club *(SW1)*
Staple Inn *(WC1)*
Westminster Abbey Garden *(SW1)*
Westminster Boating Base *(SW1)*

West
Aragon House *(SW6)*
Belvedere *(W8)*
Chelsea Physic Garden *(SW3)*
Chiswick House *(W4)*
Commonwealth Conference & Events
 Centre *(W8)*
Duke of York's HQ *(SW3)*
Fulham Palace *(SW6)*
Gunnersbury Park *(W3)*
The Hempel *(W2)*
Imperial College *(SW7)*
Kensington Palace *(W8)*
Orangery (Holland Park) *(W8)*
Orangery (Kensington Palace) *(W8)*
Polish Club *(SW7)*
Riverside Studios *(W6)*
The Roof Gardens *(W8)*
Royal Geographical Society *(SW7)*
Royal Hospital Chelsea *(SW3)*
Serpentine Gallery *(W2)*
The Station *(W10)*
Trailfinders Sports Club *(W13)*
The White Horse *(SW6)*

North
Alexandra Palace & Park *(N22)*
The British Library *(NW1)*
Cecil Sharp House *(NW1)*
The Decorium *(N22)*
Egg *(N7)*
Estorick Collection *(N1)*
Freud Museum *(NW3)*
Gainsborough Studios *(N1)*
Highgate School *(N6)*
London Zoo *(NW1)*
Queen Mary Garden *(NW1)*
Regent's College *(NW1)*
Royal Air Force Museum *(NW9)*

South
Academy of Live & Recorded
 Arts *(SW18)*
Bank of England Sports Club *(SW15)*
Battersea Park *(SW11)*
Belair House *(SE21)*
Bridges Wharf *(SW11)*
Brockwell Lido *(SE24)*
Caper Green *(SE10)*
Cannizaro House *(SW19)*
The Conservatory *(SW11)*
Crown & Greyhound *(SE21)*

Crystal Palace Park (SE20)
Devonport House (SE10)
Dulwich College (SE21)
Firepower - The Royal Artillery
    Museum (SE18)
The Golden Hinde (SE1)
Le Gothique (SW18)
Greenwich Yacht Club (SE10)
Horniman Museum (SE23)
Imperial War Museum (SE1)
King's College School (SW19)
Kingswood House (SE21)
London Aquarium (SE1)
London Wetland Centre (SW13)
The Ministry of Sound (SE1)
Museum of Garden History (SE1)
National Maritime Museum (SE10)
The Old Royal Naval College (SE10)
The Pump House Gallery (SW11)
Queen's House (SE10)
Roehampton Club (SW15)
The Saatchi Gallery (SE1)
Ship (SW18)
South London Gallery (SE5)
Southwark Cathedral (SE1)
St Thomas' Hospital (SE1)
Whitelands College (SW15)
Winchester House (SW15)

East
Apothecaries' Hall (EC4)
The Brewery (EC1)
The Candid Arts Trust (EC1)
The Chainstore (E14)
Circus Space (N1)
Docklands Sailing & Watersports
    Centre (E14)
ExCel (E16)
Gibson Hall (EC2)
Honourable Artillery Co (EC1)
Inner Temple Hall (EC4)
Jongleurs at Bow Wharf (E3)
Lee Valley Cycle Circuit (E10)
Leven is Strijd (E14)
Merchant Taylors' Hall (EC2)
Middle Temple Hall (EC4)
Mudchute Park & Farm (E14)
Newham City Farm (E16)
Old Billingsgate (EC3)
Old Spitalfields Market (E1)
The Regalia (EC4)
Stratford Old Town Hall (E15)
291 Gallery (E2)

Outside London
Addington Palace (Surrey)
Amberley Castle (W Sussex)
Ascot Racecourse (Berks)
Big Brother House (Herts)
Blenheim Palace (Oxon)
Chessington World of
    Adventures (Surrey)
Cliveden (Berks)
Denbies Wine Estate (Surrey)
Easthampstead Park Conference
    Centre (Berks)
Eton College (Dorney Lake) (Berks)
Forty Hall (Middx)
Great Fosters (Surrey)
The Grove (Herts)
Ham House (Surrey)
Ham Polo Club (Surrey)
Hampton Court Palace (Surrey)
Harrow School (Middx)

Hever Castle (Kent)
The Hop Farm Country Park (Kent)
Kew (Royal Botanic) Gardens (Surrey)
Legoland Windsor (Berks)
Marble Hill House (Surrey)
Monkey Island Hotel (Berks)
The Old Palace (Herts)
Osterley Park & House (Middx)
Painshill (Surrey)
Penshurst Place & Gardens (Kent)
Pinewood Studios (Bucks)
Queen's Eyot (Berks)
Royal Holloway College (Surrey)
Stonor (Oxon)
Syon Park (Conservatory) (Middx)
Syon Park (House) (Middx)
Temple Island (Oxon)
Thorpe Park (Surrey)
Twickenham Experience (Middx)
West Wycombe Caves (Bucks)
Whipsnade Wild Animal Park (Beds)
Whitewebbs Museum of
    Transport (Middx)
Wrotham Park (Herts)

ROOM CAPACITIES

CAPACITY LISTS

*Note: particularly with hotels, it may
be possible to divide rooms to provide
a smaller space.*

Function rooms listed by standing capacity

* largest entry for venue

£E

2000	British Museum *(Great Court*)*
1000	British Museum *(Hotung Gallery)*
	Home House *(Max*)*
800	Royal Academy of Arts *(Summer Exhibition*)*
750	Blenheim Palace *(State Rms*)*
700	Victoria & Albert Museum *(Dome*)*
600	Tate Britain *(Manton Entrance*)*
500	Hampton Court Palace *(Max*)*
450	Fishmongers' Hall *(Max*)*
	Spencer House *(Max*)*
400	Courtauld Gallery *(Max*)*
	Hampton Court Palace *(Great Hall)*
	Royal Academy of Arts *(Private Rms)*
	Tate Britain *(Rm 15 or Rm 9)*
	Two Temple Place *(Max*)*
	Victoria & Albert Museum *(Raphael Gallery)*
350	British Museum *(Egypt & Nereid Rms)*
	The Gilbert Collection *(Silver Gallery*)*
	Hampton Court Palace *(Cartoon Gallery)*
	Lancaster House *(Long Gallery*)*
	National Portrait Gallery *(Contemporary Galleries*)*
	Tate Britain *(Sackler Octagon)*
300	Blenheim Palace *(Orangery)*
	HM Tower of London *(New Armouries*)*
	Victoria & Albert Museum *(Gamble Rm or Silver Gallery)*
	Wallace Collection *(Main Galleries*)*
250	Annabel's *(Max*)*
	Cliveden *(Max*)*
	Courtauld Gallery *(Fine Rms or Great Rm)*
	Eltham Palace *(Great Hall*)*
	Kenwood House *(Orangery*)*
	HM Tower of London *(White Tower)*
	Wallace Collection *(Sculpture Garden)*
200	British Museum *(Restaurant)*
	Home House *(Asylum, Drawing Rm or Garden)*
	Lancaster House *(Grand Hall)*
	Tate Britain *(Clore Gallery Foyer)*
	Two Temple Place *(The Great Hall)*
185	Chiswick House *(Courtyard Marquee*)*
180	Blenheim Palace *(Marlborough)*
170	Cliveden *(Great Hall)*
160	Home House *(Front & Eating Room)*
150	Chiswick House *(First floor (6 Rms))*
	Hampton Court Palace *(Public Dining Rm)*
	Lancaster House *(Music Rm)*
	National Portrait Gallery *(Portrait Restaurant or Victorian Galleries)*
	Royal Observatory *(Max*)*
	HM Tower of London *(Medieval Palace)*
	Wrotham Park *(Drawing Rm*)*
120	Eltham Palace *(Drawing Rm)*
	Lancaster House *(State Dining Rm)*
	Syon Park (House) *(Long Gallery*)*
	Tate Britain *(Rex Whistler Restaurant)*
100	National Portrait Gallery *(Tudor Gallery)*
	HM Tower of London *(Royal Fusiliers Association Rm)*
	Wrotham Park *(Dining Rm)*
80	Chiswick House *(Domed Saloon)*
	Eltham Palace *(Dining Rm)*
	Hampton Court Palace *(Banqueting House)*
	Home House *(Eating Rm or Front Parlour)*

	Sir John Soane's Museum *(Max*)*
	HM Tower of London *(Jewel House)*
75	Cliveden *(French Dining Rm)*
60	Victoria & Albert Museum *(Morris Rm)*
50	Lancaster House *(Eagle Rm)*
	Wrotham Park *(Saloon)*
40	Lancaster House *(Gold Rm)*
25	Tate Britain *(Lodge)*

£M-E

10000	Royal Hospital Chelsea *(Grounds*)*
2800	Coram's Fields *(Max*)*
2500	Royal Lancaster *(Max*)*
2430	Old Billingsgate *(Grand Hall*)*
2000	Science Museum *(Making The World Modern* or Wellcome Wing)*
	Somerset House *(Courtyard*)*
1700	The Grosvenor House Hotel *(Great Rm*)*
1500	The Business Design Centre *(Main Hall*)*
	Chelsea Village *(Exhibition Space*)*
	Guildhall *(Max*)*
	London Aquarium *(Max*)*
	Royal Albert Hall *(Cabaret or Ball*)*
	Royal Lancaster *(Nine Kings Suite)*
	The Saatchi Gallery *(Max*)*
1400	Coram's Fields *(Split Facility)*
	InterContinental London *(Grand Ballroom*)*
	Royal Air Force Museum *(Max*)*
1300	Royal Lancaster *(Westbourne Suite)*
1250	Hilton on Park Lane *(Grand Ballroom*)*
1200	Addington Palace *(Max*)*
	Natural History Museum *(Central Hall*)*
	Park Lane Hotel *(Ballroom*)*
1000	Cumberland Hotel *(Production Box*)*
	Dali Universe *(Max*)*
	The Dorchester *(Ballroom*)*
	Harrods *(Food Halls or Georgian Restaurant*)*
	Hayward Gallery *(Max*)*
	Imperial War Museum *(Max*)*
	National Maritime Museum *(Neptune Court*)*
	Old Spitalfields Market *(With Marquee*)*
	Royal Air Force Museum *(Main Aircraft Hall)*
	The Saatchi Gallery *(Members Terrace)*
900	Guildhall *(Great Hall)*
	Smith's of Smithfield *(Max*)*
	Thorpe Park *(Dome*)*
800	Chelsea Village *(Galleria)*
	Fortnum & Mason *(Max*)*
	The Grosvenor House Hotel *(Ballroom)*
	InterContinental London *(Westminster)*
	Just St James *(Max*)*
	Kew (Royal Botanic) Gardens *(New Palace Marquee Site*)*
	Museum of London *(Max*)*
	The Queen Elizabeth II Conference Centre *(Benjamin Britten Lounge*)*
	The Savoy *(Lancaster Rm*)*
750	Inner Temple Hall *(Garden*)*
	InterContinental London *(Byron & Parks Suites)*
	Old Billingsgate *(Arches or Terrace)*
	The Saatchi Gallery *(Main Gallery)*
	Westway Studios *(Max*)*
725	Middle Temple Hall *(Max*)*
720	Elysium *(Max*)*
715	Café de Paris *(Max*)*
700	Christie's *(Max*)*
	East Wintergarden *(Max*)*
	Goldsmiths' Hall *(Max*)*
	Great Eastern Hotel *(Max*)*
	The Hempel *(Max*)*
	Hilton on Park Lane *(Wellington Ballroom)*
	Millennium London Mayfair *(Ballroom*)*
	Portman Hotel *(Ballroom*)*
	Sketch *(Max*)*
670	Carlton Tower *(Ballroom*)*
650	Chelsea Village *(Drakes Suite)*
	The Commonwealth Club *(Max*)*
	Four Seasons Hotel *(Ballroom*)*
	Royal Garden Hotel *(Max*)*
	Shakespeare's UnderGlobe *(Underglobe*)*

640	Millennium Gloucester Hotel *(Century Suite*)*
600	Carlton Club *(Max*)*
	Gibson Hall *(Hall*)*
	Guildhall *(Old Library)*
	Lincoln's Inn *(Great Hall*)*
	Madame Tussaud's *(World Stage*)*
	Merchant Taylors' Hall *(Max*)*
	The Old Royal Naval College *(Painted Hall*)*
	Penshurst Place & Gardens *(Max*)*
	Royal Opera House *(Vilar Floral Hall*)*
	Science Museum *(East Hall)*
590	Westway Studios *(Studio 2)*
550	Barbican Centre *(Max*)*
	Royal Garden Hotel *(Palace Suite)*
500	Atlantic Bar & Grill *(Max*)*
	Banqueting House *(Main Hall*)*
	Christie's *(Great Rm)*
	Circus Space *(Combustion Chamber*)*
	Cumberland Hotel *(Carlisle Suite)*
	Dulwich Picture Gallery *(Max*)*
	Fortnum & Mason *(Food Hall)*
	Goldsmiths' Hall *(Livery Hall)*
	Hurlingham Club *(Broom House Suite or Quadrangle Suite*)*
	Just St James *(Just St James)*
	The Landmark *(Ballroom*)*
	Legoland Windsor *(The Pavilions*)*
	The London Underwriting Centre *(Atrium*)*
	Merchant Taylors' Hall *(Great Hall)*
	Middle Temple Hall *(Hall)*
	Millennium Gloucester Hotel *(Cotswold Suite or Decade Suite)*
	Mint Leaf *(Max*)*
	Natural History Museum *(Earth Galleries)*
	Old Billingsgate *(Gallery or Mezzanine)*
	The Old Royal Naval College *(Queen Mary Ante Rm)*
	La Porte des Indes *(Max*)*
	La Rascasse *(Restaurant*)*
	The Roof Gardens *(Max*)*
	Royal Albert Hall *(The Gallery)*
	Royal College of Physicians *(Garden*)*
	Royal Hospital Chelsea *(Great Hall)*
	Royal Institute of British Architects *(Florence Hall*)*
	Science Museum *(Flight Gallery)*
	Stonor *(Front Lawn*)*
	Tate Modern *(Turbine Hall*)*
	Westminster Abbey Garden *(College Garden*)*
450	Gainsborough Studios *(Max*)*
	Hilton London Paddington *(Great Western Suite*)*
	Jerwood Space *(Max*)*
	LABAN *(Ampitheatre* or Concourse)*
	Renaissance London Chancery Court Hotel *(Ballroom*)*
	Threadneedles *(Max*)*
400	1 Lombard Street *(Max*)*
	The Avenue *(Max*)*
	Barbican Centre *(Garden Rm)*
	The Berkeley *(Ballroom*)*
	Il Bottaccio *(Gallery)*
	The Business Design Centre *(Gallery Hall)*
	China White *(Max*)*
	Claridge's *(Ballroom*)*
	Dover Street Restaurant & Bar *(Max*)*
	Drapers' Hall *(Livery Hall*)*
	Great Eastern Hotel *(Great Eastern)*
	Harrington Hall *(Harrington*)*
	The Hempel *(Garden Square)*
	Imperial War Museum *(Main Atrium)*
	Inner Temple Hall *(Hall)*
	Institute of Directors *(Nash*)*
	InterContinental London *(Piccadilly)*
	London Aquarium *(Terrace (with marquee))*
	The London Dungeon *(Max*)*
	Mandarin Oriental Hyde Park *(Ballroom*)*
	The Mayfair Inter-Continental *(Crystal Rm*)*
	Le Meridien *(Max*)*
	One Whitehall Place *(Gladstone Library*)*
	Penshurst Place & Gardens *(Baron's Hall)*
	The People's Palace *(Max*)*
	Raven's Ait Island *(Max*)*
	Royal Air Force Museum *(Battle of Britain Hall)*
	Royal College of Physicians *(Osler Rm)*
	Royal Opera House *(Terrace)*
	The Savoy *(Abraham Lincoln & Manhattan Rms)*
	Science Museum *(Challenge of Materials)*
	Sotheby's *(Max*)*
	Stationers' Hall *(Livery Hall*)*
	Tate Modern *(Level 3 Concourse)*
	Thorpe Park *(Lake Side Hospitality Area)*
380	London Zoo *(Aquarium or Prince Albert Suite*)*
375	Banqueting House *(Undercroft)*
350	BFI London IMAX Cinema *(Max*)*
	Chintamani *(Max*)*
	Circus Space *(Generating Chamber)*
	Clothworkers' Hall *(Livery Hall*)*
	The Collection *(Max*)*
	Dali Universe *(Dali A)*
	Dulwich Picture Gallery *(Soane Building)*
	The Energy Clinic *(Lobby*)*
	Haberdashers' Hall *(Courtyard Orangery*)*
	The Imagination Gallery *(Atrium and Restaurant*)*
	The Landmark *(Music Rm)*
	LSO St Luke's *(Jerwood Hall*)*
	Museum of London *(London Befort Gallery or World City Gallery)*
	The Savoy *(River Rm)*
	Serpentine Gallery *(Max*)*
	St Martin's Lane Hotel *(Restaurant*)*
320	Cabinet War Rooms *(Churchill Museum*)*
312	Royal Air Force Museum *(Cosford Rm)*
300	5 Cavendish Square *(Max*)*
	Benares *(Max*)*
	Chessington World of Adventures *(Glade or Hospitality Marquee*)*
	Coq d'Argent *(Outdoor Terraces*)*
	Firepower - The Royal Artillery Museum *(Gunnery Hall*)*
	Four Seasons Hotel *(Garden Rm)*
	Gibson Hall *(Garden)*
	Gray's Inn *(Hall*)*
	Guildhall *(Art Gallery)*
	Haberdashers' Hall *(Livery Hall)*
	Jerwood Space *(Gallery & Glasshouse)*
	Kensington Palace *(Orangery*)*
	Kent House *(The Sanctuary*)*
	Kew (Royal Botanic) Gardens *(Temperate House)*
	LABAN *(Bonnie Bird Theatre or Studio Theatre)*
	The Landmark *(Drawing Rm)*
	The Law Society *(Common Rm*)*
	London Aquarium *(Atlantic)*
	The London Art House *(Manor Garden Hall*)*
	The London Planetarium *(Max*)*
	London Zoo *(Bugs)*
	Millennium Gloucester Hotel *(Conservatory)*
	National Liberal Club *(Dining Rm or Smoking Rm*)*
	Noble Rot *(Max*)*
	The Old Palace *(Great Hall or The Old Riding School*)*
	One Whitehall Place *(Whitehall Suite)*
	Orangery (Kensington Palace) *(Max*)*
	Prism *(Max*)*
	Queen's House *(Max*)*
	River & Rowing Museum *(Max*)*
	Royal Air Force Museum *(Loching Rm or The Halton Gallery)*
	Royal College of Physicians *(Dorchester Library)*
	Sadler's Wells Theatre *(Mezzanine Area*)*
	Salters' Hall *(Max*)*
	Savile Club *(Members Dining Rm & Ballroom*)*
	Skinners' Hall *(Banquet Hall*)*
	Smith's of Smithfield *(Top Floor)*
	Stonor *(Croquet Lawn)*
	Tate Modern *(Cafe 7)*
	Theatre Museum *(Max*)*
	Westway Studios *(Studio 4)*
280	Aldwych Station *(Max*)*
	Just St James *(Just Oriental)*
250	Audi Forum *(Whole Space*)*
	The Berners Hotel *(Thomas Ashton Suite*)*
	Christopher's *(Max*)*
	City Hall - London's Living Room *(London's Living Rm*)*
	The Collection *(Mezzanine)*

PRIVATE VENUES | STANDING CAPACITY

The Commonwealth Club (Lower Ground Hall)
Coram's Fields (Party Chalet 2)
The Criterion (Max*)
Dali Universe (White Space)
The Dorchester (Orchid)
Elysium (Club Rm)
Funland (Max*)
Geffrye Museum (Museum Galleries*)
Grocers' Hall (Livery Hall*)
Guildhall (The Crypts)
Ham House (Orangery Garden (Marquee)*)
Hever Castle (Pavilion*)
The Imagination Gallery (Gallery)
Innholders' Hall (Max*)
The Landmark (Empire Rm or Gazebo (in the Atrium))
Lincoln's Inn (Old Hall)
London Stock Exchange (Top Floor*)
London Zoo (Lion Terrace or Reptile House)
Madame Tussaud's (Blush)
Mandarin Oriental Hyde Park (Carlyle Suite)
Marriott Maida Vale (Regent Suite*)
Mirabelle (Max*)
Museum of London (Lord Mayor's Gallery)
National Liberal Club (David Lloyd George or Terrace)
Natural History Museum (North Hall)
One Whitehall Place (Reading And Writing Rms)
Opium (Max*)
Park Lane Hotel (Tudor Rose Rm)
Raven's Ait Island (Britannia Suite)
Royal Hospital Chelsea (State Apartments)
Saddlers' Hall (Max*)
Science Museum (Space Gallery)
Sketch (Gallery)
Theatre Museum (Paintings Gallery)
Thorpe Park (Thorpe Belle)
Tower Bridge (Walkways*)
HQS Wellington (Quarterdeck*)

245 Le Meridien (Georgian)
240 30 Pavilion Road (Max*)
220 The Newsroom (Lecture Theatre*)
Scotts (Restaurant*)
215 Hakkasan (Max*)
200 Addington Palace (Great Hall)
Apothecaries' Hall (Hall*)
Arts Club (Dining Rm*)
Arundel House (Rm With A View*)
Barbican Centre (Conservatory)
BMA House (Members Dining Rm*)
Brighton Royal
     Pavilion (Banqueting Rm (and Great Kitchen)*)
Broadgate Estates (Arena*)
Cabinet War Rooms (Auditorium)
The Caledonian Club (Members Dining Rm*)
Carlton Club (Churchill Rm)
Christie's (Rm 1)
The Circus (Max*)
Claridge's (Drawing Rm, French Salon or Mirror Rm)
Clothworkers' Hall (Reception Room)
Cumberland Hotel (Gloucester)
Dali Universe (Modern Masters)
The Dorchester (The Terrace)
Estorick Collection (Max*)
FireHouse (Max*)
Fortnum & Mason (St James's Rm)
Four Seasons Canary Wharf (Ballroom*)
Gainsborough Studios (South Studio)
Gibson Hall (Garden Rm)
Goldsmiths' Hall (Drawing Rm & Exhbition Rm)
Great Fosters (Tithe Barn And Painted Hall*)
Hilton on Park Lane (Coronation Suite)
Inner Temple Hall (Parliament Chamber)
Just Gladwins (Max*)
Just St James (Just The Gallery)
Kensington Rooms (Rm 9*)
The Mayfair Inter-Continental (Danziger Suite)
Merchant Taylors' Hall (Cloisters, Drawing Rm or Parlour)
Le Meridien (Edwardian)
Le Meridien Selsdon Park (Terrace Suite*)
Millennium Gloucester Hotel (Ashburn Suite)
Momo (Max*)
Old Billingsgate (Well)

Pennyhill Park Hotel (Balmoral*)
Raffles (Max*)
River & Rowing Museum (Thames Rm)
Roehampton Club (Max*)
Royal Air Force Museum (Art Gallery)
Royal Lancaster (Gloucester Suite)
Sadler's Wells Theatre (Cable & Wireless Rm)
Salters' Hall (Mail Hall)
The Sanctuary (Max*)
Somerset House (Seamen's Waiting Hall)
Thomas Goode (Shop*)
United Grand Lodge of England (Vestibule*)
The Wellington Club (Max*)
180 5 Cavendish Square (Nightclub)
Cutty Sark (Lower Hold or Tween Decks*)
Haberdashers' Hall (Reception Gallery)
Harrington Hall (Turner & Constable)
The Lanesborough (Belgravia*)
Mosimann's Belfry (Coutts Rm*)
Swissôtel London the
     Howard (Fitzalan Suite*)
HQS Wellington (Court Rm)
175 Chelsea Village (Trophy Rm)
The Hempel (I-Thai Restaurant (and Shadow Bar))
170 Kensington Palace (Queens Gallery or State Apartments)
Lloyd's Club (Restaurant)
160 Café de Paris (Restaurant & Mezzanine)
Institute of Directors (Burton or Waterloo)
Royal Opera House (Crush Rm)
150 5 Cavendish Square (Ground Floor Bar or Restaurant)
Bam-Bou (Max*)
Belair House (Max*)
The Berkeley (Belgravia)
BMA House (Douglas Black)
Il Bottaccio (Club Gallery)
Cabinet War Rooms (Plant Rm)
Chessington World of Adventures (Keg)
Christie's (Rm 2)
Coram's Fields (Party Chalet)
Cumberland Hotel (Clarence)
Dali Universe (Dali B)
Dover Street Restaurant & Bar (Lower Bar)
Dulwich Picture Gallery (Linbury Rm)
Elysium (Restaurant & VIP Rm)
Firepower - The Royal Artillery
     Museum (History Gallery)
Four Seasons Hotel (Oak Rm)
Gray's Inn (Large Pension Rm)
Great Fosters (Orangery)
Grocers' Hall (Piper Rm)
The Grosvenor House Hotel (Albemarle)
The Halkin (Belgravia)
Harrington Hall (Reynolds & Landseer)
The Hempel (Room No 17)
Innholders' Hall (Hall)
Jerwood Space (Space 1 or Space 2)
Kensington Rooms (Media Rm)
Kew (Royal Botanic)
     Gardens (Gallery (entire ground floor))
Leighton House (Studio*)
London Aquarium (Shark Tank)
London Capital Club (Oriental Rm*)
London Zoo (Bear Mountain or Raffles Suite)
LSO St Luke's (Crypt Café)
Le Meridien Selsdon Park (Sir Edward Heath Rm)
The Metropolitan (Met Bar*)
Monkey Island Hotel (River Rm*)
Museum of London (Medieval Gallery)
National Maritime Museum (Orangery, Royal Observatory or Southern Parlors)
Natural History Museum (Darwin Centre)
The Old Royal Naval
     College (King William Restaurant)
Pasha (Max*)
Queen's House (Great Hall)
Quo Vadis (Warhol Rm*)
Raven's Ait Island (Thames Suite)
Royal College of Pathologists (Lecture Rm*)
Royal College of Physicians (Platt Rm)
Sartoria (Max*)
Savile Club (Members Dining Rm)

VISIT US AT: www.hardens.com

Sheraton Park Tower (Trianon Rm*)
Smith's of Smithfield (Cocktail Bar)
St Martin's Lane Hotel (Light Bar or The Studio)
Stationers' Hall (Court Rm)
Tate Modern (East Rm, Level 3 or Members Rm)
United Grand Lodge of England (Board Rm)
Westway Studios (Studio 3)
White's (Max*)
Windsor Guildhall (Guildhall Chamber*)

140   The Almeida (Max*)
The Carlton Mitre Hotel (Pavilion*)
Great Eastern Hotel (Bishopsgate)
Roehampton Club (Roehampton Rm)

130   Chelsea Village (Jimmys)
Drapers' Hall (Court Dining)
Motcomb's Townhouse (Max*)
Plateau (Max*)
Royal Garden Hotel (Kensington Suite)

125   Armourers' & Braisers' Hall (Livery Hall*)
The Grosvenor House Hotel (Stratton Suite)
Middle Temple Hall (Parliament Chamber)

120   28 Portland Place (Heggie Rm or Sainsbury's Rm*)
30 Pavilion Road (Ballroom or Stone Hall)
32 Craven St (Max*)
Barbican Centre (Conservatory Terrace)
The Berners Hotel (Fitzrovia Suite)
Big Brother House (Max*)
Café de Paris (Restaurant)
Cannizaro House (Viscount Melville Suite*)
Canonbury Academy (Long Gallery*)
Drapers' Hall (Court Rm)
Dukes Hotel (Marlborough Suite*)
Hampshire Hotel (Penthouse*)
Inner Temple Hall (Luncheon Rm)
The Law Society (Old Council Chamber)
Legoland Windsor (Creation Centre or JFK Drawing Rm)
The London Underwriting Centre (Hospitality Suite)
Le Meridien (Regency)
Millennium London Mayfair (Turner Fine Dining Rm)
Noble Rot (Member's Bar)
Park Lane Hotel (Oak Rm)
Pennyhill Park Hotel (Windsor & Eton)
Penshurst Place & Gardens (Sunderland Rm)
Queen's House (Undercroft)
The Savoy (Beaufort)
Sketch (Parlour)
Skinners' Hall (Old Court Rm, Outer Hall or Roof Garden)
Theatre Museum (Foyer)
Wax Chandlers' Hall (Hall*)
HQS Wellington (Model Rm)

100   28 Portland Place (Harben Rm)
Addington Palace (Winter Garden Suite)
Armourers' & Braisers' Hall (Drawing Rm)
Arts Club (Bar & Conservatory or Garden Rm)
Baltic Exchange (Dining Rm*)
Belair House (Restaurant)
Berry Bros & Rudd (Max*)
BMA House (Prince's Rm)
Brighton Royal Pavilion (Queen Adelaide Suite)
Broadgate Estates (Exchange Square)
Carlton Tower (Garden Rm)
The Commonwealth Club (Cinema Rm)
The Dorchester (Holford or Park Suite)
Elysium (Amber Bar)
Fitzroy Square (Max*)
Le Gavroche (Max*)
Hever Castle (Tudor Suite)
LABAN (Medium Studio)
The Lanesborough (Wellington Rm)
Lightship (Max*)
The London Art House (Baroque Hall, Rococo Rm or Tadema Terrace)
London Marriott County Hall Hotel (George V* or Library Lounge)
Mandarin Oriental Hyde Park (Roseberry Rms)
Le Meridien Selsdon Park (Surrey Rm)
Middle Temple Hall (Smoking Rm)
Millennium London Mayfair (Manhattan)
Monte's (Restaurant)

Museum of London (Eighteenth Century Gallery)
MVH (Max*)
The Old Royal Naval College (Admirals Residence)
One Aldwych (Rms 1 & 2*)
One New Inn Square (Max*)
Portman Hotel (Gloucester Suite)
Queen's House (SW Parlour)
Renaissance London Chancery Court Hotel (Lower Ground Floor Suite)
The Ritz (Garden or Marie Antoinette Suite*)
Royal Albert Hall (Victoria Rm)
Royal College of Pathologists (Council Rm)
Royal Institute of British Architects (Conference Rm)
Sadler's Wells Theatre (Rehearsal Studios)
Salters' Hall (Court Rm)
Savile Club (Ballroom)
Swissôtel London the Howard (Arundel Suite)
Tower Bridge (Engine Rms)
Westminster Abbey Garden (St Catherine's Chapel Garden)
Windsor Guildhall (Maidenhead Rm)

90   Brighton Royal Pavilion (Great Kitchen)
Café de Paris (VIP Rm)
London Marriott Hotel Park Lane (Oxford Suite (divisable by 3)*)
Le Meridien (Adam)
Le Meridien Selsdon Park (Kent Rm)
The Newsroom (Exhibition or Scott Rm)
Renaissance London Chancery Court Hotel (Ground Floor Suite)
Royal Academy of Engineering (Max*)

80   32 Craven St (Level 1)
Addington Palace (Lecture Rm)
Arts Club (Drawing Rm)
Barnard's Inn Hall (Max*)
Carlton Tower (Water Garden)
Christopher's (Bar or Private Dining Rm)
Claridge's (Kensington)
Fan Museum (Museum*)
Four Seasons Canary Wharf (River Rm)
The Grosvenor House Hotel (Spencer Rm)
Hilton on Park Lane (Serpentine Rm)
InterContinental London (Windsor Suite)
Kensington Palace (Victorian Garden Rooms)
Kent House (Marbled Foyer or Rutland Rm)
London Stock Exchange (Blue Rm)
The Metropolitan (Dining-Meeting Rm)
Millennium London Mayfair (Waterloo Rm)
Momo (Kemia Bar)
Mosimann's Academy (Thinking Rm*)
One Whitehall Place (Meston Suite or River Rm)
The Petersham (Meeting Rm*)
Prism (Cocktail Bar)
Queen's House (Orangery Suite)
Royal Academy of Engineering (Conference Rm or Dining Rm)
Royal Garden Hotel (Lancaster Suite)
The Savoy (Pinafore)
Stationers' Hall (Stock Rm)
Thorpe Park (Neptunes Chamber)
Wellington Arch (Max*)

75   Covent Garden Hotel (Meeting Rm 1*)
Fortnum & Mason (Burlington Rm)
Haberdashers' Hall (Court Rm)
London Aquarium (Rainforest)
Middle Temple Hall (Queen's Rm)
Sadler's Wells Theatre (Cahn Lecture Th)
The Stafford (The Cellar*)

70   28 Portland Place (Adam's Rm)
Atlantic Bar & Grill (Chez Cup or Dicks Bar)
Belair House (Bar)
Brighton Royal Pavilion (King William IV Rm or Large Adelaide)
Canonbury Academy (Denby Suite)
Carlton Club (Cabinet Rm)
The Commonwealth Club (Blue Rm)
Gainsborough Studios (North Studio)
Hakkasan (Lounge Bar)
Ham House (Orangery (Restaurant))
Harrington Hall (Stubbs)
Hever Castle (Inner Hall)

VISIT US AT: www.hardens.com

Imperial War Museum (Boardroom 1)	Royal Garden Hotel (Bertie's Bar)
The Landmark (Champagne Rm)	The Savoy (Gondoliers)
Leighton House (Arab Hall)	Skinners' Hall (Parlour)
Mandarin Oriental Hyde Park (Asquith Rm or Balfour Rm)	Smith's of Smithfield (Private Rm)
Mosimann's Belfry (Parmigiani Fleurier Rm)	The Stafford (Panel Rm & Sutherland Rm)
Penshurst Place & Gardens (Buttery)	Temple Island (Indoors*)
The Petersham (River Rm)	The Trafalgar (Strategy)
Prism (Mezzanine)	45 Covent Garden Hotel (Meeting Rm 2)
Royal Institute of British Architects (South Rm)	The Law Society (Fleet)
Sartoria (Private Rms (both))	Monkey Island Hall (Garden Rm)
St Martin's Lane Hotel (The Backroom)	40 The Academy (Garden*)

67 Charlotte Street Hotel (Rm 1*)
65 Café de Paris (Blue Bar)
The Caledonian Club (Stuart)
Dover Street Restaurant & Bar (Upper Bar)
The Fox Club (Max*)
London Capital Club (Boardroom)
The Trafalgar (Roof & Bar Garden*)
60 1 Lombard Street (Private Rm)
30 Pavilion Road (Library)
The Berners Hotel (Tyburn Rm)
The Business Design Centre (Executive Centre)
Cannizaro House (Queen Elizabeth Rm)
Canonbury Academy (Queen Elizabeth)
The Dorchester (Pavilion)
Fitzroy Square (1 Space)
Four Seasons Hotel (Pine Rm)
Institute of Directors (Trafalgar II/St James II)
Kensington Rooms (Studio Rm)
Kent House (Library)
Kew (Royal Botanic) Gardens (Cambridge Cottage Lounge)
The Landmark (Tower Suite)
The Lanesborough (Westminster Rm)
The Law Society (Chancery)
The Milestone Hotel & Apartments (Windsor Suite*)
National Liberal Club (Lady Violet)
Osterley Park & House (Brewhouse*)
Painshill (Visitor Building*)
Park Lane Hotel (Orchard Suite)
Pennyhill Park Hotel (Parkview)
Raven's Ait Island (Lambourne Rm)
Roehampton Club (Garden Rm)
Scotts (Cocktail Bar)
Sheraton Park Tower (Buckingham Rm)
Somerset House (Hermitage Rms)
The Trafalgar (Boardroom or Resolution)
United Grand Lodge of England (Drawing Rm)
Wax Chandlers' Hall (Courtroom)
55 Four Seasons Canary Wharf (City Rm)
The Halkin (Private Dining Rm)
Renaissance London Chancery Court Hotel (Staple Inn Rm & Gray's Inn Rm)
50 Addington Palace (Library, Music Rm or Wellington Rm)
Apothecaries' Hall (Court Rm or Parlour)
Arundel House (Conference Rm)
Bam-Bou (Black Lounge Bar)
Carlton Club (Disraeli Rm or Macmillan Rm)
Great Eastern Hotel (Chancery)
Harrington Hall (Sutherland)
Hilton London Paddington (Thunderbolt)
Institute of Directors (Trafalgar I)
The London Art House (Orangery)
London Marriott County Hall Hotel (Queen Mary)
The Mayfair Inter-Continental (Berkeley Suite)
Merchant Taylors' Hall (Kings Gallery or Library)
Le Meridien Selsdon Park (Solarium)
The Milestone Hotel & Apartments (Cheniston Restaurant)
Monte's (Nightclub)
Motcomb's Townhouse (Belgravia Rm)
One Aldwych (Rm 3)
One Whitehall Place (Cellar)
Park Lane Hotel (Mirror Rm)
The Petersham (Terrace Rm)
Portman Hotel (Berkeley Suite or Bryanston Suite)
Quo Vadis (Modigliani)
Royal College of Radiologists (Max*)

Addington Palace (Empire Rm)
Amberley Castle (Great Rm*)
Arundel House (4th Floor Conference Rm)
The Berkeley (Mulberry)
Brighton Royal Pavilion (Small Adelaide)
The Caledonian Club (Blue Rm)
Cannizaro House (Blue Rm)
Carlton Club (Lirary)
The Dorchester (Penthouse)
Fan Museum (Orangery)
Hampshire Hotel (Drawing Rm)
Hilton on Park Lane (Argyll Rm)
Institute of Directors (St James's II)
London Marriott Hotel Park Lane (Hyde Park Suite or Meeting Foyer)
Marble Hill House (Tetra Hall*)
Marriott Maida Vale (Carlton Suite)
Millennium London Mayfair (Grosvenor Suite)
Mosimann's Academy (Library)
Motcomb's Townhouse (Lounge or Mclue Suite)
Plateau (Private Rm)
Prism (Orangery)
Roehampton Club (Centenary Board Rm)
Royal College of Pathologists (Seminar Rm)
Sheraton Park Tower (Balmoral or Explorers)
The Stafford (Sutherland Rm)
36 Monkey Island Hotel (Spencer Rm)
35 Café de Paris (Red Bar)
Canonbury Academy (Wentworth)
Hilton London Paddington (McGyver)
Royal Albert Hall (Prince Of Wales)
Sartoria (Private Rm (x2))
The Savoy (Mikado)
30 5 Cavendish Square (Black Bar)
The Academy (Conservatory)
Arts Club (Board Rm)
Cannizaro House (Oak Rm)
The Capital (Eaton*)
The Carlton Mitre Hotel (Cardinal Wolsey)
Hampshire Hotel (Burley or Romsey)
Hilton London Paddington (Red Star)
Imperial War Museum (Boardroom 2)
Innholders' Hall (Court Rm)
LABAN (Meeting Rm)
The Lanesborough (Wilkins Rm)
London Capital Club (Gresham Rm)
Le Meridien (Chelsea or Mayfair)
MVH (Hell)
Number Sixteen (Conservatory*)
Park Lane Hotel (Drawing Rm)
Portman Hotel (Library)
Queen's House (Loggia)
Royal Albert Hall (Henry Cole Rm)
Royal College of Radiologists (Robens Rm)
Savile Club (Elgar Rm)
The Savoy (Patience)
The Stafford (Pink Rm & Argyll Rm)
Theatre Museum (Beard Rm)
Windsor Guildhall (Ascot Rm)
25 Charlotte Street Hotel (Rm 2)
Claridge's (St James's)
Dukes Hotel (Sheridan Rm)
Great Eastern Hotel (Broadgate or Moorgate)
The Hempel (Jade Rm)
Mosimann's Belfry (Veuve Cliquot Rm)
The Savoy (Iolanthe)
Threadneedles (Stirling or Capital)
20 32 Craven St (Level 2)
The Academy (Boardroom)
Covent Garden Hotel (Private)
The Energy Clinic (Smallest Area)

Hever Castle *(Music Rm)*
The Milestone Hotel & Apartments *(Safari Suite)*
The Stafford *(Argyll Rm)*
Tower Bridge *(Bridge Master's Dining Rm)*
18 Haberdashers' Hall *(Luncheon Rm)*
The Savoy *(Sorcerer)*
16 Monkey Island Hotel *(Boardroom)*
15 The Milestone Hotel & Apartments *(Conservatory)*
One Aldwych *(Suite 500)*
The Petersham *(Rose Rm)*
12 Amberley Castle *(King Charles Rm)*
10 The Academy *(Library)*
The Berkeley *(Knightsbridge)*
Charlotte Street Hotel *(Library)*
The Dorchester *(Library)*
London Capital Club *(Marco Polo or Wren)*
Monkey Island Hotel *(Wedgewood)*
6 Monkey Island Hotel *(Temple)*

£M

7250 Alexandra Palace & Park *(Max*)*
6500 Alexandra Palace & Park *(Great Hall)*
5000 Battersea Park *(British Genius Site*)*
3000 Café Royal *(Max*)*
2500 Alexandra Palace & Park *(West Hall)*
2100 The Coronet *(Max*)*
1900 London Metropole *(Monarch or King's Suite*)*
1770 Tiger Tiger *(Max*)*
1750 Alexandra Palace Ice Rink *(Max*)*
1500 Alexandra Palace & Park *(Palm Court)*
Ascot Racecourse *(Ascot Pavilion (subdivisible) *)*
The Camden Palace *(Max*)*
Commonwealth Conference & Events Centre *(Comm Galleries*)*
1200 Namco *(Max*)*
Royal National Theatre *(Max*)*
1100 London Metropole *(Palace Suite)*
1000 CC Club *(Max*)*
The Decorium *(Emperor Suite*)*
Horniman Museum *(Max*)*
London Marriott *(Westminster Ballroom*)*
Lord's *(Nursery Pavilion*)*
Sugar Reef *(Max*)*
850 The Brewery *(Porter Tun*)*
800 Cabot Hall *(Hall*)*
The Camden Palace *(Main Auditorium)*
Congress Centre *(Congress Hall*)*
Lloyd's of London *(Captain's Rm*)*
Museum in Docklands *(Max*)*
Pacha *(Max*)*
Topsail Charters *(Waverly (Static)*)*
The Tram Studios *(Studio 104*)*
750 291 Gallery *(Max*)*
720 Waxy O'Connors *(Max*)*
700 The Brewery *(King George III)*
Central Hall Westminster *(Lecture Hall* or Library)*
One Great George Street *(Max*)*
TS Queen Mary *(Max*)*
Twickenham Experience *(Norm Try Line*)*
Vinopolis – City of Wine *(Great Halls*)*
Waldorf Hotel *(Adelphi Suite & Palm Court*)*
670 Red Cube *(Max*)*
Sway *(Max*)*
650 Mega Bowl *(Max*)*
Le Meridien Russell Hotel *(Warncliffe Suite*)*
Sugar Reef *(Bar)*
625 Sound *(Club Sound*)*
600 Ascot Racecourse *(Royal Enclosure Suite)*
Battersea Park *(Boules Area)*
Britannia International Hotel *(Grand Suite*)*
Café Royal *(Dubarry & Dauphin)*
Epsom Downs *(Blue Riband Rm*)*
Kensington Town Hall *(Great Hall*)*
The Mayfair Club *(Max*)*
Sound *(Restaurant & Bar)*
St Mary's Church *(Max*)*
Whipsnade Wild Animal Park *(Max*)*

550 Bridges Wharf *(Max*)*
Goodenough College *(Max*)*
Shakespeare's Globe *(Max*)*
Tantra *(Max*)*
Tower Thistle *(Tower Suite*)*
The Washington *(Max*)*
540 Café Royal *(Empire Napoleon)*
500 291 Gallery *(Main Gallery)*
Aquarium *(Club*)*
Barbican Art Gallery *(Max*)*
City Club *(Max*)*
Covent Garden Market *(North Hall*)*
Delfina Galleries *(Max*)*
Ealing Town Hall *(Victoria Hall*)*
Glaziers' Hall *(Hall*)*
Groucho Club *(Max*)*
The Hop Farm Country Park *(Dray Museum*)*
London Eye *(Max*)*
Lord's *(Banqueting Suite)*
The Medieval Banquet *(Max*)*
Mega Bowl *(First floor)*
Museum in Docklands *(2nd Floor Galleries)*
Namco *(Substation (lower level))*
Pinewood Studios *(Max*)*
Regent's College *(Gardens*)*
Royal National Theatre *(Olivier Stalls Foyer)*
Simpsons-in-the-Strand *(Max*)*
Wapping Food *(Max*)*
475 Nylon *(Max*)*
450 Commonwealth Conference & Events Centre *(Exhibition Hall)*
Institute of Electrical Engineers *(Riverside Restaurant*)*
Jongleurs at Camden Lock *(Max*)*
Langham Hilton *(Ballroom*)*
Sugar Reef *(Restaurant)*
Twickenham Experience *(Rose Rm)*
Vinopolis – City of Wine *(Mezzanine)*
420 Red Cube *(Lounge Bar)*
400 Alexandra Palace & Park *(Palace Restaurant)*
Aquarium *(Max)*
Baltic *(Max*)*
HMS Belfast *(Max*)*
Chartered Accountants' Hall *(Great Hall*)*
Chelsea Physic Garden *(Max*)*
The Cinnamon Club *(Max*)*
The Comedy Store *(Max*)*
Elstree Film Studio *(Max*)*
Epsom Downs *(Derby Suite)*
Hilton London Docklands *(London*)*
Holiday Inn London Regent's Park *(Cambridge & Oxford Suites*)*
Hop Exchange *(Max*)*
Horniman Museum *(Exhibition Gallery)*
London Transport Museum *(Main Gallery*)*
The Mayfair Club *(Satellite Bar & Cabaret)*
Museum of Garden History *(Max*)*
One Great George Street *(Great Hall)*
Red Cube *(Dance Floor)*
The Regalia *(Max*)*
Regent's College *(Refectory)*
So.uk Soho *(Max*)*
South London Gallery *(Inside And Marquee*)*
Twickenham Experience *(Invincibles or Spirit Of Rugby)*
350 Adam Street *(Max*)*
Ascot Racecourse *(Paddock Balcony)*
HMS Belfast *(Quarter Deck (Summer Evenings))*
Café Royal *(Louis)*
Carpenters' Hall *(Livery Hall*)*
Cavalry & Guards Club *(Max*)*
Central Hall Westminster *(Westminster)*
The Cobden Club *(Max*)*
Conrad Hotel *(Drake Suite*)*
Dartmouth House *(Max*)*
Delfina Galleries *(Exhibition Gallery)*
Elstree Film Studio *(Restaurant)*
Goodenough College *(Great Hall)*
Groucho Club *(First Floor (entire))*
Hamleys Playground *(Max*)*
Hendon Hall Hotel *(Pembroke Suite*)*
ICA *(Theatre*)*
Jolly Hotel St Ermins *(Max*)*

VISIT US AT: www.hardens.com

PRIVATE VENUES | STANDING CAPACITY

The Oval (Banqueting Suite* or KBCC)
Royal College of Music (Concert Hall*)
Royal National Theatre (Lyttelton Exhibition Level)
St Paul's Cathedral (Crypt*)
Vinopolis – City of Wine (Wine Odyssey Rms)
330 Twickenham Experience (Members Lounge)
Woody's (Max*)
300 The AOP Gallery (Max*)
Apollo Victoria Theatre (Whole Theatre*)
Cavalry & Guards Club (Coffee Rm)
Chelsea Physic Garden (With Marquee (Sat in Jun-Sep only))
Churchill (Chartwell Suite*)
City Club (Main Dining Rm)
Covent Garden Market (Central Avenue)
The Decorium (Caesar Suite)
Denim (Max*)
Doggetts Coat & Badge (Wine Bar*)
Hammersmith Apollo (Max*)
Hampton Court Palace (The Tiltyard) (Max*)
RS Hispaniola (Main Deck*)
The Hop Farm Country Park (White Banqueting Suite)
Inmarsat (Max*)
The Insurance Hall (Great Hall*)
Jongleurs (Battersea) (Max*)
Jongleurs at Bow Wharf (Max*)
London Metropole (Windsor)
National Army Museum (Art Gallery*, Atrium or Modern Army Gallery)
No 4 Hamilton Place (Max*)
Royal Majestic Suite (Ground Floor*)
The Selfridge Hotel (Selfridge Suite*)
Shakespeare's Globe (Main Foyer)
Six-13 (Max*)
South London Gallery (Inside)
St Bartholomew's Hospital (Great Hall*)
St Stephen's Club (Max*)
St Thomas' Hospital (Shepherd Hall*)
Theatre Royal, Drury Lane (Grand Saloon & Rotunda*)
Whipsnade Wild Animal Park (Griffin Suite or Phoenix Suite)
280 Butchers' Hall (Max*)
260 Bank of England Sports Club (Max*)
St John's Gate (Max*)
250 Amadeus Centre (Upper Hall*)
Aquarium (Café Bar)
Bank of England Sports Club (Restaurant)
Bank Westminster (Max*)
Barber-Surgeons' Hall (Great Hall*)
Basil Street Hotel (Parrot Club*)
Belvedere (Max*)
The Bonnington in Bloomsbury (Derby Suite*)
The Brewery (Queen Charlotte)
Britannia International Hotel (Royal Lounge)
The British Library (Terrrace Restaurant*)
Butchers' Hall (Great Hall)
Café Royal (Dauphin)
CC Club (Bar M)
Chartered Accountants' Hall (Restaurant)
Church House (Harvey Goodwin Suite* or Hoare Memorial Hall)
Conrad Hotel (Henley Suite)
Cottons Atrium (Max*)
Design Museum (Entrance Hall*)
East India Club (Max*)
Fashion & Textile Museum (Max*)
Forty Hall (Banqueting Suite*)
Greenwich Yacht Club (Function Rms*)
Ham Polo Club (Club House*)
Hilton London Docklands (Thames Suite)
Holiday Inn London Regent's Park (Oxford)
The Hop Farm Country Park (Max)
Horniman Museum (Gallery Sq & Centenary Gallery)
ICA (Nash & Brandon Rms)
Ironmongers' Hall (Hall*)
Jongleurs at Bow Wharf (Bar Risa)
Jongleurs at Camden Lock (Jongleurs)
Kensington Town Hall (Small Hall)
Langham Hilton (Palm Court)
Lansdowne Club (Ballroom*)
The Mayfair Club (Living Rm Bar)

No 4 Hamilton Place (Lecture Theatre)
Painters' Hall (Livery Hall*)
Queen's Eyot (Marquee*)
The Royal Air Force Club (Ballroom*)
Royal College of Music (Britten Theatre)
Royal Society of Arts (Max*)
Royal Statistical Society (Lecture Theatre*)
The Rubens (Max*)
Singapura (Main Rm*)
So.uk Soho (Souk Restaurant)
St Thomas' Hospital (Governors' Hall)
Staple Inn (Hall*)
Thistle Kensington Palace Hotel (Duchess*)
240 HMS Belfast (Ship Co's Dining Hall)
230 Carpenters' Hall (Reception Rm)
Royal Court Theatre (Main Restaurant*)
220 Bar Bourse (Max*)
Ealing Town Hall (Princes Hall)
Farmers' & Fletchers' Hall (Max*)
Royal National Theatre (Terrace Café)
Six Hamilton Place (Red Rm*)
200 Aldwych Theatre (Bar*)
Alexandra Palace & Park (Loneborough Rm)
BAFTA (Club Bars, David Lean Rm* or Foyer Bar)
Brewers' Hall (Max*)
The Broadgate Club (Rest*)
Browns (Max*)
The Camden Palace (Balcony)
Central Hall Westminster (Assembly)
Cheyne Walk Brasserie (Max*)
Churchill (Chartwell I)
City Club (Upper Smoking Rms)
College of Arms (Max*)
Congress Centre (Council Chamber or Marble Hall)
Delfina Galleries (Café Gallery)
Denbies Wine Estate (Garden Atrium Conservatory*)
Easthampstead Park Conference Centre (Downshire*)
Elstree Film Studio (Oscars Bar)
Epsom Downs (Jockey Club Rm)
Eton College (Dorney Lake) (Main Rm*)
Farmers' & Fletchers' Hall (Livery Hall)
Frederick's (Max*)
Glaziers' Hall (River Rm)
Goodenough College (Common Rm)
The Grafton (Warren Suite*)
Great Eastern Dining Rooms (Below 54*)
Groucho Club (Soho Rm)
The Hatton (Restaurant*)
Hellenic Centre (Great Hall*)
Jolly Hotel St Ermins (Ballroom)
Jongleurs (Battersea) (Bar Risa)
Just The Bridge (Max*)
Kingsway Hall (Max*)
The London Canal Museum (1st Floor*)
Loungelover (Max*)
Museum in Docklands (Chris Ellmers Gallery)
No 4 Hamilton Place (Argyll Rm & Hawker Rm)
The Old Sessions House (Westminster*)
One Birdcage Walk (Marble Hall*)
Pattersons's (Max*)
Pinewood Studios (Ballroom)
The Ramada Jarvis London West (Ballroom*)
Red Rose Comedy Club (Max*)
Regent's College (Herringham Hall)
Royal Majestic Suite (First Floor)
The Rubens (Old Masters Restaurant)
RUSI Building (Lecture Theatre*)
Simpsons-in-the-Strand (Regency Rm)
SS Great Britain (Dining Saloon*)
St John's Gate (Chapter Hall)
St Stephen's Club (Dining Rm)
Syon Park (Conservatory) (Great Conservatory*)
Waterstone's Piccadilly (Red Rm or Simpson's Rm*)
West Wycombe Caves (Banqueting Hall*)
White House Hotel (Albany*)
190 Butchers' Hall (Court Suite)
Rex Cinema & Bar (Bar*)
180 1 Blossom Street (Max*)
The Cobden Club (The Grand Hall)

The Geological Society of London (Lower Library*)
Guards Museum (Royal Gallery*)
Kenwood House, Old Kitchen (Max*)
Kingsway Hall (Keats & Milton Rms)
Royal National Theatre (Mezzanine)
RUSI Building (Duke of Wellington Rm)
Simon Drake's House of Magic (Max*)
Winchester House (River Rm*)
175 Commonwealth Conference & Events Centre (JBR)
Drones (Max*)
Ealing Town Hall (Queens Hall)
170 76 Portland Place (Catering Suite*)
Lonsdale (Max*)
TS Queen Mary (Admirals Suite)
Watermen's Hall (Max*)
165 Butchers' Hall (Reception Rm)
160 Church House (Bishop Partridge Hall)
London Metropole (Park Suite)
150 115 at Hodgson's (Max*)
291 Gallery (South Wing)
Albery Theatre (Max*)
Aquarium (Bang Bar or Restaurant)
Bank of England Sports Club (Redgates Lodge)
Belvedere (Lower level)
Brewers' Hall (Livery Hall)
The Brewery (Sugar Rms)
Café Royal (Derby & Queensbury)
Chelsea Physic Garden (Reception Rm)
The Chesterfield Mayfair (Royal Suite*)
City Conference Centre (Ocean Suite*)
The Cobden Club (Restaurant)
Conrad Hotel (Henley I)
Dartmouth House (Courtyard or Long Drawing Rm)
Denim (Basement)
Doggetts Coat & Badge (Terrace Bar)
Greenwich Yacht Club (Club House)
RS Hispaniola (Top Deck)
Holiday Inn London Regent's Park (Cambridge)
The Insurance Hall (Oftler Suite)
Jamies Pavilion (Max*)
Jolly Hotel St Ermins (Balcony (With Balloom Only))
Jongleurs at Camden Lock (Riverside Bar)
The Kenilworth (Bloomsbury Suite*)
Kew Bridge Steam Museum (Max*)
Langham Hilton (Portland Suite)
The Lincoln Centre (Break-out Area*)
London Palladium (Variety Bar)
London Wetland Centre (Observatory*)
Lyceum Theatre (Function Rm*)
The Mayfair Club (VIP Rm)
Museum in Docklands (Thames Highway Gallery)
Namco (Private Party Area)
National Army Museum (Lecture Theatre)
No 4 Hamilton Place (Council Rm & Bar)
One Great George Street (Smeaton Rm)
Orangery (Holland Park) (Max*)
Phoenix Artist Club (Dining Rm*)
Pissarro's on the River (Max*)
The Place (Café or Founders Studio*)
Prenelle Gallery (Main Gallery* or Outter Deck)
RICS (Lecture Hall*)
Royal Society of Arts (Benjamin Franklin Rm)
Royal Statistical Society (Basement)
Shaftesbury Theatre (Bars*)
Simpsons-in-the-Strand (Bishops' Rm)
Singapura (Main Rm)
St John (Max*)
St Stephen's Club (Garden)
Thistle Victoria Hotel (Gallery Rm*)
Waxy O'Connors (Cottage Bar)
The Westbury (Mount Vernon Rm*)
White House Hotel (Chester)
140 291 Gallery (Bar)
Cavalry & Guards Club (Peninsula Rm)
Vanderbilt Hotel (Victoria & Albert Suite*)
130 Commonwealth Conference & Events Centre (Gillette)
Fulham Palace (Max*)
Heights Bar & Restaurant (Max*)

London Wetland Centre (Waters Edge)
The Magic Circle (Devant Rm*)
St Andrew's Court House (Court Rm*)
125 The Grafton (Grafton)
Mayfair Conference Centre (Conservatory*)
Pewterers' Hall (Court Rm or Livery Rm*)
Pinewood Studios (Green Rm)
Quilon (Max*)
Sound (Blue Rm or Sound Bar)
120 Amadeus Centre (Lower Hall)
HMS Belfast (Gun Rm)
The Bonnington in Bloomsbury (York Rm)
Browns (Courtroom I)
Café du Jardin (Downstairs*)
Café du Marché (Upstairs*)
Café Royal (Grill Rm)
Churchill (Library)
City Inn Westminster (Private Dining*)
Congress Centre (Invision Suite)
The De Vere Cavendish St James's (Meeting Rm I*)
Doggetts Coat & Badge (Doggetts Bar)
The Don (Max*)
Elstree Film Studio (Marquee)
Freud Museum (Max*)
Glaziers' Hall (Library & Court Rm)
The Golden Hinde (Max*)
Horniman Museum (African Worlds/Natural History)
The Insurance Hall (New Rm)
The Ivy (Private Rm*)
The Kenilworth (Kenilworth Suite*)
Kenwood House, Old Kitchen (Brew House)
Kingsway Hall (Restaurant)
Lloyd's of London (Old Library)
Lonsdale (Downstairs)
The Montcalm Hotel (Maquis De Montcalm*)
The Oval (Long Rm)
The Player (Max*)
The Royal Air Force Club (Running Horse/Millennium Suite)
The Selfridge Hotel (Cleaveland)
Shakespeare's Globe (Balcony Rm or Upper Foyer)
Soho House (Bar*)
Spring Grove House (Max*)
St Paul's Cathedral (Conference Rm)
Tallow Chandlers' Hall (Max*)
Teca (Max*)
Trinity House (Court Rm* or Library)
Twickenham Experience (England Rugby International's Club Rm)
The Washington (Richmond Suite)
The Westbury (Pine Rm)
White House Hotel (Osnaburgh)
Winston Churchill's Britain at War (Max*)
110 Watermen's Hall (Freemen's Rm)
100 115 at Hodgson's (Cellar Wine Bar)
Adam Street (Gallery)
The Agency (Max*)
Alexandra Palace & Park (Palm Court 5)
Aquarium (Waterside Terrace)
Athenaeum Hotel (Macallan*)
Barber-Surgeons' Hall (Reception Rm)
Belvedere (Top level)
Bleeding Heart (The Tavern*)
The Bonnington in Bloomsbury (Balmoral, Derby or Jubilee)
Britannia International Hotel (Buckingham)
Brown's Hotel (Clarendon* or Niagra & Roosevelt combined)
Butchers' Hall (Taurus Suite)
Cabot Hall (Sebastian Rm)
Café Lazeez (Max*)
Chartered Accountants' Hall (Main Reception Rm)
City Club (Garden Rm)
Commonwealth Conference & Events Centre (Bradley)
Covent Garden Market (East Terrace)
Cuba Libre (Max*)
Dartmouth House (Ballroom)
Devonport House (Nelson & Hamilton*)
Dominion Theatre (Smirnoff Bar*)
Elstree Film Studio (The White House)

The Founders' Hall (Livery Hall*)
Frederick's (Garden Rm (Main Restaurant))
Fulham Palace (Drawing Rm or Great Hall)
The Goring (Archive Rm*)
RS Hispaniola (Board Rm)
Horniman Museum (Music Gallery or Victoria Conservatory)
Institute of Electrical Engineers (Common Rm, Lancaster Rm or Maxwell Suite)
The Insurance Hall (Council Chamber)
Ironmongers' Hall (Drawing Rm)
Jamies Pavilion (Wine Bar)
Kenwood House, Old Kitchen (Old Kitchen)
London Palladium (Cinderella Bar)
Lord's (Media Centre)
Museum of Garden History (Garden)
National Army Museum (Council Chamber)
The New Cavendish Club (Jubilee Rm*)
The Old Sessions House (Judges or London Rm)
One Great George Street (Brunel Rm or Council Rm)
Painters' Hall (Court Rm)
Palace Theatre (Dress Circle Bar*)
Pinewood Studios (Great Gatsby Rm)
Regent's College (Tuke Common Rm)
RICS (Members Club Rm)
Royal Society of Arts (Vault 1)
RUSI Building (Library)
The Selfridge Hotel (Cheviot)
Spring Grove House (Winter Garden Rm)
St John (Bar)
Tallow Chandlers' Hall (Livery Hall)
Tantra (Red Rm)
Thistle Kensington Palace Hotel (Marchioness)
University Women's Club (Library*)
Vanderbilt Hotel (Cleo's)
Woody's (Individual Floors (x3))

95 Jason's (Max*)
90 Avenue House (Drawing Rm*)
Bloomsbury Square Training Centre (Cellars Restaurant*)
Holiday Inn – Mayfair (Stratton Suite*)
Kensington Place (Private Rm*)
One Birdcage Walk (Council)
TS Queen Mary (Captains Quarters)
The Rubens (Van Dyke)
St Stephen's Club (Garden Rm)
Sweetings (Max*)
Syon Park (Conservatory) (Public Rms)
80 Adam Street (Rehearsal Rm)
Bank of England Sports Club (Balcony Bar or Green Rm)
Bloomsbury Square Training Centre (Ascham Rm)
Brewers' Hall (Court Rm)
The Brewery (City Cellars)
Brown's Hotel (Roosevelt)
Browns (Courtroom 2)
Bush Bar & Grill (Private Dining Rm*)
The Cadogan (Max*)
Café du Marché (Rendezvous)
Churchill (Marlborough Suite)
The Cinnamon Club (Private Dining Rm)
The City Presentation Centre (Theatre*)
Curwen Gallery (Max*)
The De Vere Cavendish St James's (Meeting Rm 3)
Durrants Hotel (Edward VII Rm*)
Ealing Town Hall (Nelson Rm)
Fortune Theatre (Bar*)
Freud Museum (House)
Hilton London Docklands (Battersea)
Ironmongers' Hall (Court Rm or Luncheon Rm)
Lansdowne Club (Shelburne Rm)
Lloyd's of London (Conference Rm)
Le Meridien Russell Hotel (Bedford Suite)
The Mountbatten (Earl Suite*)
Neal's Lodge (Max*)
The Old Sessions House (Jailers Rm)
One Birdcage Walk (Hinton Rm)
Oxford & Cambridge Club (Marlborough*)
Queen's Eyot (Clubhouse)

Queen's Theatre (Stalls Bar*)
The Royal Air Force Club (Presidents Rm)
Royal Statistical Society (Council Chamber)
The Rubens (Rembrandt Rm)
RUSI Building (Reading Rm)
Singapura (Max)
Soho House (Roof Deck)
St Thomas' Hospital (Consultant's Dining Rm)
Staple Inn (Council Chamber)
Tantra (VIP Area)
Thistle Victoria Hotel (Bessborough Rm)
Twickenham Experience (Committee Rm)
The Union Club (Dining Rm*)
University Women's Club (Drawing Rm)
75 Cactus Blue (Blue Room*)
Conrad Hotel (Harbour)
Sheraton Belgravia (Study and Library*)
Waterstone's Piccadilly (Emberton Rm)
70 76 Portland Place (Franklin)
The Agency (Main Bar)
Bleeding Heart (Bistro (ground floor))
Cabot Hall (St Lawrence Rm)
Chartered Accountants' Hall (Members' Rm)
Cicada (Max*)
Lonsdale (Genevieve (upstairs))
National Army Museum (Templer Galleries)
PJ's Bar & Grill (Max*)
The Place (Theatre Bar)
Royal Court Theatre (Balcony Bar)
Royal Society of Arts (Gallery)
SS Great Britain (Hayward Saloon)
St Stephen's Club (Bar)
Watermen's Hall (Court Rm)
65 Hamilton House (Max*)
London Marriott (Hamilton Rm)
Polygon Bar & Grill (Max*)
60 Bleeding Heart (Private Rm)
Britannia International Hotel (Balmoral)
Brown's Hotel (Kipling)
Cavalry & Guards Club (Waterloo Rm)
The Chesterfield Mayfair (Conservatory)
Cheyne Walk Brasserie (Salon/lounge/bar)
City Conference Centre (Council Rm)
College of Arms (Earl Marshal's Court)
Coopers' Hall (Max*)
Delfina Galleries (Studio Gallery)
Denim (Mezz or VIP Rm)
Devonport House (Drake)
The Don (Bistro or Restaurant)
Epsom Downs (Coronation Cup)
Goolies (Max*)
The Grafton (Arlington Suite)
Groucho Club (Gennaro Rm)
Hendon Hall Hotel (Garrick)
Hogarth's House (Max*)
Holiday Inn London Regent's Park (Trinity Suite)
Jason's (Restaurant)
Jongleurs at Camden Lock (Roof Terrace)
The Magic Circle (Club Bar)
Le Meridien Russell Hotel (Library or Ormond Suite)
The New Cavendish Club (Ante Rm)
No 4 Hamilton Place (Sopwith Rm)
Pattersons's (Function Rm)
Spring Grove House (Banks Suite)
Tallow Chandlers' Hall (Parlour)
The Townhouse (First Floor*)
Vanderbilt Hotel (Edwardian)
Waldorf Hotel (Aldwych)
The Washington (Richmond 1 (Winchester))
The Westbury (Brighton Rm)
55 Hilton London Docklands (Westminster)
50 Ascot Racecourse (King Edward VII)
Basil Street Hotel (Basil Rm)
The Berkshire (Sonning Suite*)
The Bonnington in Bloomsbury (Jack Frame)
Britannia International Hotel (Blenheim or Queens)
Browns (Courtroom 3)
The Cadogan (Langtry Dining)
The Camden Palace (Royal Box)
The Cinnamon Club (Mezzanine)

VISIT US AT: www.hardens.com

City Club (Salisbury Rm)
Commonwealth Conference & Events
   Centre (Tweedsmuir)
Dartmouth House (Small Drawing Rm)
Dominion Theatre (Garland Suite)
Farmers' & Fletchers' Hall (Reception Rm)
The Founders' Hall (Parlour)
Groucho Club (New Rm)
The Guinea Grill (Boardroom*)
Hellenic Centre (Conference Rm)
Holiday Inn London Regent's
   Park (Somerville)
Jolly Hotel St Ermins (Cameo)
Langham Hilton (Ambassador Rm or
   Regent/Welbeck Rms)
Leven is Strijd (Max*)
Loungelover (Red Area)
Ronnie Scotts (Max*)
Royal National Theatre (Olivier Circle Foyer)
Royal Society of Arts (Folkestone Rm or
   Tavern Rm)
Scotch Malt Whisky Society (Members' Rm*)
Spring Grove House (Music Rm)
St Andrew's Court House (Archive Rm)
St Bartholomew's
   Hospital (Henry VIII Committee Rm)
St Thomas' Hospital (Grand Committee Rm)
Tower Thistle (Raleigh or Spencer)
Wapping Food (Private Rm)

45 Avenue House (Dining Rm or Salon)
    Waxy O'Connors (Mezzanine)
40 115 at Hodgson's (Mezzanine)
    Balham Bar & Kitchen (Playroom Bar*)
    Britannia International Hotel (Beaufort)
    Brown's Hotel (Niagara)
    Chartered Institute of Public Finance
      & Accountancy (Committee Rm 4* or
      Council Chamber)
    Churchill (Randolph)
    College of Arms (Waiting Rm)
    The De Vere Cavendish St
      James's (Meeting Rm 4 or Meeting Rm 5)
    Devonport House (Collingwood)
    Durrants Hotel (Oak Rm)
    Easthampstead Park Conference
      Centre (Tawney)
    Epsom Downs (Double Boxes)
    Eton College (Dorney Lake) (Clubroom)
    Hendon Hall Hotel (Sheridan)
    Holiday Inn — Mayair (Presidential Suite)
    Jamies Pavilion (Restaurant)
    Jolly Hotel St Ermins (York or Clarence)
    London Marriott (John Adams Suite)
    London Palladium (VIP Rm)
    The Mountbatten (Viceroy)
    The Old Sessions House (Justices or
      Recorder Rm)
    Queen's Theatre (Dress Circle Bar)
    The Ramada Jarvis London
      West (Park View Rm)
    RICS (Gloucester)
    The Royal Air Force Club (Drawing Rm or
      Mezzanine Suite)
    The Rubens (Rubens)
    Scotch Malt Whisky Society (Still Rm)
    The Selfridge Hotel (Chitten)
    St Bartholomew's Hospital (Peggy Turner Rm or
      Treasurer's Rm)
    St Paul's Cathedral (Beehive)
    Theatre Royal, Drury Lane (Boardroom)
    Tower Thistle (Mortimer Suite)
    Vanderbilt Hotel (Vanderbilt)
    Waldorf Hotel (Executive Boardroom)
    Warren House (Conference Rm 2*)
    The Washington (Richmond 2 (Fairfax))
    The Westbury (Regency Rm)
    Winchester House (Library)
38 Loungelover (Rustic Area)
    Thistle Kensington Palace Hotel (Countess)
35 HMS Belfast (Admiral's Quarters)
    The Broadgate Club (Private Dining)
    Chartered Accountants'
      Hall (Small Reception Rm)
    The Decorium (Ante Suite)

Electric Brasserie (& Electric House
   Club) (Playroom*)
Hendon Hall Hotel (Johnson)
Hilton London Docklands (Albert)
The Rubens (Library)
The Selfridge Hotel (Drawing Rm)
Thistle Victoria Hotel (Warwick Rm)
Tower Thistle (Beaufort)
30 The Berkshire (Sandhurst Suite)
    Cabot Hall (Cape Breton Rm)
    The Cadogan (Langtry Sitting)
    The Chesterfield Mayfair (Library)
    Church House (Westminster)
    City Conference Centre (Arctic or Indian)
    The Don (Private Rm)
    Farmers' & Fletchers' Hall (Court Rm)
    Fulham Palace (Ante Rm)
    The Hop Farm Country Park (Roundels)
    Horniman Museum (Performance Space)
    Kingsway Hall (Chaucer)
    Lansdowne Club (Findlay Rm)
    London Marriott (Grosvenor Suite)
    London Palladium (Argyll Suite)
    Mega Bowl (Balcony)
    New Ambassadors Theatre (Max*)
    One Great George
      Street (Stephenson Rm & President's Dining Rm)
    Prenelle Gallery (Library)
    Putney Bridge (Max*)
    Royal National Theatre (Ashcroft)
    Singapura (Large Mezzanine)
    Thistle Kensington Palace Hotel (Princess)
    Thistle Victoria Hotel (Belgrave)
    The Townhouse (Basement)
27 Scotch Malt Whisky Society (Tasting Rm)
25 Alexandra Palace & Park (Palm Court 1)
    The Chesterfield Mayfair (Stanhope Suite)
    Electric Brasserie (& Electric House
      Club) (Study)
    Elstree Film Studio (Board/Green Rm)
    The Goring (Drawing Rm)
    London Eye (Per Capsule)
    The Old Sessions House (Clerks)
    Oxford & Cambridge Club (Edward VII)
    Royal National Theatre (Richardson Rm)
    Royal Statistical Society (New Meeting Rm)
    The Selfridge Hotel (Conservatory)
    Thistle Kensington Palace Hotel (Baroness)
24 Rules (Green Rm*)
22 Lansdowne Club (Sun Rm)
20 Athenaeum Hotel (Ardmore or Richmond Suite)
    The Bonnington in
      Bloomsbury (Committee Rm)
    Brown's Hotel (Lord Byron)
    Cabot Hall (Newfoundland Rm)
    Cavalry & Guards Club (Double Bridle Rm)
    City Club (Masterman/Wellington Rms)
    City Conference Centre (Committee Rm)
    Dominion Theatre (Milburn Suite)
    Durrants Hotel (Armfield Rm)
    Epsom Downs (Single Boxes)
    The Geological Society of
      London (Council Rm)
    Holiday Inn — Mayair (Buckingham or Burlington)
    Loungelover (Baroque Rm)
    The New Cavendish Club (Library)
    St John's Gate (Prior's Dining Rm)
    Theatre Royal, Drury
      Lane (Royal Retiring Rm & Ante Rm)
    Thistle Victoria Hotel (Wilton Rm)
    Waldorf Hotel (Westminster)
15 Church House (Jubilee)
    Langham Hilton (Cumberland Rm)
14 Butchers' Hall (Commitee Rm)
    Tower Thistle (Lewin)
12 The Geological Society of
    London (Arthur Homes Rm)
    Singapura (Private Rm)
    Thistle Victoria Hotel (Hanover)
10 Brewers' Hall (Committee Rm)
    Chartered Institute of Public Finance
      & Accountancy (Committee Rm 5)

	The De Vere Cavendish St
	James's (Meeting Rm 2)
	Holiday Inn London Regent's Park (Churchill or Pembroke Suite)
8	Butchers' Hall (Library)
	Singapura (Small Mezzanine)
6	Butchers' Hall (George Adams)

£B-M

3000	Honourable Artillery Co (Marquee*)
2230	Hammersmith Palais (Max*)
2180	Equinox at the Empire (Max*)
2000	The Chainstore (Max*)
	Crystal Palace Park (Max*)
	London Astoria (Max*)
	Trailfinders Sports Club (Marquees*)
	The Worx (Max*)
1855	The London Hippodrome (Auditorium*)
1800	Fabric (Max*)
	Royal Horticultural Halls (Lawrence Hall*)
1500	The Bridge SE1 (Rm 1*)
	Streatham Ice Arena (Max*)
	Whitechapel Art Gallery (Max*)
1495	On Anon (Max*)
1200	Riverside Studios (Max*)
1064	ExCel (Platinum Suite*)
1000	Blackheath Concert Halls (Max*)
	Egg (Max*)
	Hammersmith Town Hall (Assembly Hall*)
	Harrow School (Shepherd Churchill Hall*)
	New Connaught Rms (Grand Hall & Balmoral*)
800	Buzz Bar (Max*)
	The Cross (Max*)
	The End (Max*)
	Studio 33 (Max*)
	Whitechapel Art Gallery (Lower Gallery)
700	Goldsmiths College (Stretch Bar*)
	Royal Horticultural Halls (Lindley Hall)
650	Whitechapel Art Gallery (Upper Gallery)
630	Porchester Centre (Ballroom*)
600	BAC (Grand Hall*)
	Blackheath Concert Halls (Great Hall)
	Regency Banqueting Suite (Max Banquet Rm*)
	Riverside Studios (Studios 1 & 2)
	Royal College of Art (Max*)
	White Hart Lane Conference Centre (Whites Suite*)
520	Thames Luxury Charters – moving venue (Dixie Queen*)
500	The Bridge SE1 (Rm 2)
	Cargo (Max*)
	Cecil Sharp House (Kennedy Hall*)
	Fulham Town Hall (Grand Hall*)
	Imperial College (Main Dining Hall*)
	The Langley (Max*)
	Mall Galleries (Main Gallery*)
	Queen Mary College (Max*)
	Royal College of Art (Henry Moore Gallery)
	Stoke Newington Town Hall (Assembly Rm*)
	Texas Embassy Cantina (Max*)
490	Stratford Old Town Hall (Main Hall*)
450	Balls Brothers (Max*)
	Break For The Border (Max*)
	Fifteen05 (Max*)
	London School of Economics (Max*)
	New Connaught Rms (Balmoral)
	Victory Services Club (Max*)
400	The Anchor (Terrace*)
	The Chelsea Gardener (Max*)
	Chelsea Old Town Hall (Main Hall*)
	Crazy Larry's (Max*)
	Dulwich College (Christison Hall and Upper Dining Rms*)
	Le Gothique (Max*)
	Highgate School (School Dining Hall*)
	Home (Max*)
	King's College, King's Cuisine Restaurant (Max*)
	Mermaid Theatre (Blackfriars Rm*)
	Royal Geographical Society (Max*)

	Shillibeer's (Max*)
	Southwark Cathedral (Courtyard*)
	The Station (Garden*)
	William IV (Max*)
350	Abbaye (Max*)
	Bishopsgate Institute (Max*)
	Conway Hall (Large Hall*)
	Duke of York's HQ (Max*)
	George Inn (Max*)
	Honourable Artillery Co (Albert Rm)
	King's College (Great Hall)
	The Music Room (Exhibition Hall*)
	New Connaught Rms (Edinburgh)
	Polish Club (Max*)
	HMS President (Ballroom*)
	Royal College of Art (Gulbenkian Upper Gallery)
	Royal Green Jackets (Hall*)
	St Martin In The Fields (Max*)
	Westminster Boating Base (Max*)
	The Worx (Studio 2)
340	Digress (Max*)
300	Academy of Live & Recorded Arts (Great Hall*)
	Archduke Wine Bar (Max*)
	Balls Brothers (Banqueting Suite)
	Beach Blanket Babylon (Max*)
	The Bridge SE1 (Rm 3)
	City University (Level Six Suite*)
	George Inn (Courtyard)
	Goldsmiths College (Bar Revolution)
	Hoxton Hall (Whole Ground Floor*)
	Hoxton Square Bar & Kitchen (Max*)
	The Irish Centre (Hall*)
	King's College School (Great Hall*)
	The London Hippodrome (Balcony – Restaurant)
	London Scottish (Hall*)
	School of Pharmacy (Refectory*)
	Trafalgar Tavern (Nelson Suite*)
	Victory Services Club (Carisbrooke Hall)
	White Hart Lane Conference Centre (Box Norm)
	Whitelands College (Ruskin Dining Hall*)
	The Worx (Studio 1)
278	Egg (Middle Floor)
250	Bankside Restaurant (Max*)
	Bar M (Bar M or River Rm*)
	Bar Red/5-6 Kingly St/W1 (Max*)
	Caper Green (including Garden*)
	Footstool (Max*)
	Fulham Town Hall (Concert Hall)
	Le Gothique (Patio)
	Home (Basement Bar)
	Honourable Artillery Co (Long Rm)
	Kingswood House (Golden Rm, Jacobean Rm*)
	New Connaught Rms (York)
	Riverside Studios (Studio 3)
	Rocket (Max*)
	Royal Holloway College (Founder's Dining Hall* or Picture Gallery)
	Texas Embassy Cantina (Upstairs)
	Trailfinders Sports Club (Pavilion Hall)
	University of Westminster (Max*)
	The Villiers Theatre (Max*)
	The White House (Max*)
	Will's Art Warehouse (Max*)
240	20th Century Theatre (Max*)
	Duke of York's HQ (London Irish Mess)
	Egg (Ground Floor)
235	Thames Luxury Charters – moving venue (Elizabethan)
228	ExCel (Waterfront Rms)
220	Fifteen05 (Great Hall)
	Union Chapel (Studio Theatre*)
208	Digress (Basement)
200	Abbaye (Basement Restaurant)
	BAC (Lower Hall)
	The Battersea Barge Bistro (Max*)
	Beach Blanket Babylon (Bar)
	Bridewell Theatre (Theatre*)
	The Bridge SE1 (Rm4)
	Browns Club (Ground Floor Bar & Dance Floor*)
	The Candid Arts Trust (Basement Gallery or Ground Floor Gallery*)

The Clink *(Max*)*
The Coliseum *(Dutch Bar or Terrace Bar*)*
The Cross *(Garden)*
Dickens Inn *(Nickleby Suite*)*
Docklands Sailing & Watersports
   Centre *(Function Room)*
Dolphin Square Hotel *(Restaurant*)*
Dulwich College *(Great Hall)*
Egg *(Loft Bar)*
Embargo *(Max*)*
Fulham House *(Main Hall*)*
Guy's Hospital *(Atrium*)*
Harrow School *(Shepherd Churchill Rm)*
Highgate School *(Big School)*
Home *(Ground Floor Restaurant)*
Levant *(Max*)*
The Little Ship Club *(Max*)*
London School of
   Economics *(Senior Dining Rm)*
PizzaExpress *(Max*)*
Polish Club *(Ballroom or Restaurant)*
Polka Theatre for Children *(Foyer or
   Studio Theatre*)*
Regency Banqueting Suite *(Amber Rm)*
Riverside Studios *(Café-Bar)*
Royal Over-Seas
   League *(Hall of India & Pakistan*)*
Strand Palace Hotel *(Exeter Suite*)*
Throgmorton's *(Oak Rm*)*
University of Westminster *(Deep End)*
The Villiers Theatre *(Lower Supper Rm/Bar)*
186 Studio 33 *(Purple Rm)*
180 Aragon House *(Max*)*
     Guy's Hospital *(Robens Suite)*
     Lauderdale House *(Max*)*
     Proud Galleries *(Max*)*
175 Detroit *(Max*)*
165 606 Club *(Max*)*
160 Froebel College *(Portrait Rm*)*
150 Abbaye *(Wine Bar)*
     Academy of Live & Recorded
       Arts *(Le Gothique)*
     Arts Theatre *(Bar or Restaurant*)*
     Bakers' Hall *(Max*)*
     Bankside Gallery *(Max*)*
     Blackheath Concert Halls *(Recital Rm)*
     Buzz Bar *(Bourbon Street)*
     Canning House *(Drawing Rm*)*
     Caper Green *(inside only)*
     Chelsea Old Town Hall *(Small Hall)*
     Chez Gérard, Opera Terrace *(Max*)*
     Dulwich College *(Lower Hall)*
     Equinox at the Empire *(Empire Lounge)*
     Greenwich Playhouse *(Bar*)*
     Hammersmith Town Hall *(Small Hall)*
     Liquid Lab *(Max*)*
     The Mary Sumner House *(Conference Hall*)*
     Photographers' Gallery *(Max*)*
     Porchester Centre *(Baths)*
     HMS President *(Quarter Deck)*
     Riverside Studios *(Terrace)*
     Royal College of Art *(Entrance Gallery,
       Gulbenkian Lower Gallery or
       Senior Common Rm Dining Rm)*
     Royal Geographical Society *(Main Hall or
       New Map Rm)*
     Royal Institution of Great
       Britain *(Long Library & Red Corridor*)*
     Royal Over-Seas League *(St Andrew's Hall)*
     St Botolph's Hall *(Upper Hall*)*
     St Martin In The Fields *(Gallery)*
     Thames Luxury Charters – moving
       venue *(Golden Salamander)*
     University of Westminster *(Fyvie Hall)*
     White Hart Lane Conference
       Centre *(Oak Rm)*
     William IV *(Bar 1)*
140 Brompton Oratory – St Wilfrid's
     Hall *(St Wilfrid's Hall and Billiards Rm)*)*
     Cecil Sharp House *(Trefusis Hall)*
     Egg *(Courtyard)*
     Hoxton Hall *(Theatre)*
     Maidenhead Steam Navigation – moving
       venue *(Georgian*)*

Studio 33 *(Cristal Rm or Lounge Bar)*
135 Amber *(Max*)*
130 Da Mario *(Max*)*
120 The Artworkers Guild *(Max*)*
     Bakers' Hall *(Livery Hall)*
     Browns Club *(Brown's Studio)*
     Chelsea Old Town Hall *(Cadogan Suite)*
     The Cross Keys *(First Floor Gallery*)*
     Dulwich College *(Pavilion Salle)*
     Froebel College *(Terrace Rm)*
     Gunnersbury Park *(Orangery*)*
     The House of St Barnabas-in-Soho *(Max*)*
     Latchmere Theatre *(Max*)*
     The Little Ship Club *(Dining Rm)*
     Mela *(Ground Floor*)*
     Mermaid Theatre *(River Rm)*
     PizzaExpress *(Private Rm or Section)*
     HMS President *(Wardroom)*
     Royal Institution of Great
       Britain *(Main Library)*
     Southwark Cathedral *(Library or Restaurant)*
     The Station *(Conservatory)*
     Surrey Docks Watersports
       Centre *(Quay Rm/Quay Lounge*)*
     William IV *(Function Rm)*
110 Maidenhead Steam Navigation – moving
     venue *(Southern Comfort)*
100 20th Century Theatre *(Reception Rm)*
     Apartment 195 *(Lounge*)*
     Bar Red/5-6 Kingly St/W1 *(Downstairs)*
     Bedroom Bar *(Max*)*
     Le Bistrot de L'Institut Français *(Max*)*
     Bloomsbury Theatre *(Foyer*)*
     Bramah Tea & Coffee Museum *(Max*)*
     Bridewell Theatre *(Bar)*
     Browns Club *(VIP Rm I)*
     The Conservatory *(Max*)*
     Conway Hall *(Small Hall)*
     Docklands Sailing & Watersports
       Centre *(Bar)*
     Dolphin Square Hotel *(Chichester)*
     Dr Johnsons' House *(Max*)*
     Greenwich Theatre *(Bar*)*
     Gunnersbury Park *(Terrace Rm)*
     Hammersmith Town Hall *(Marble Gallery)*
     Institut Français *(Library*)*
     King's College School *(Boathouse or Dalziel Rm)*
     Kingswood House *(Charles Suite)*
     The Little Ship Club *(Club Rm Bar)*
     The London Hippodrome *(Private Function Rm)*
     Mall Galleries *(East Gallery)*
     PizzaExpress *(Section)*
     Royal Green Jackets *(Club Bar)*
     St Peter's Hall *(Café or Upper Hall*)*
     Thames Luxury Charters – moving
       venue *(Edwardian)*
     Trafalgar Tavern *(Trafalgar Club)*
     Victory Services Club *(El Alamein Rm)*
     The Villiers Theatre *(Mezzanine Supper Rm)*
     Whitelands College *(Boardroom)*
     Whitewebbs Museum of Transport *(Max*)*
     William IV *(Garden)*
     The Worx *(Studio 4)*
90 Burgh House *(Music Rm*)*
    The Sun *(Max*)*
85 PizzaExpress *(Upstairs)*
80 Aragon House *(Function Rm)*
    Bow Wine Vaults *(Max*)*
    Dulwich College *(Old Library)*
    Floating Boater – moving
     venue *(Prince Regent*)*
    Fulham House *(Dining Rm)*
    The House of St Barnabas-in-
     Soho *(Council Rm)*
    Hoxton Square Bar & Kitchen *(Private Room)*
    Institut Français *(Salon de Réception)*
    Maidenhead Steam Navigation – moving
     venue *(Belle)*
    Mall Galleries *(North Gallery)*
    Paxton's Head *(Basement Bar*)*
    PizzaExpress *(Upstairs)*
    Polish Club *(Terrace)*

VISIT US AT: www.hardens.com

	HMS President (Embankment Bar)
	Royal Institution of Great
	Britain (Conversation Rm)
	The Station (Private Rm)
	Stratford Old Town
	Hall (Council Chamber)
	Streatham Ice Arena (Function Rm)
	Trafalgar Tavern (Hawke & Howe Bar)
	Victory Services Club (Trafalgar Rm)
	Whitechapel Art Gallery (Café)
77	Studio 33 (Upper Lounge)
75	Blackheath Concert Halls (Café Bar)
	King's College (Council Rm)
	The Lady Daphne – moving
	venue (Stationary*)
	Queen Mary Garden (Prince Regent Rm)
	Shillibeer's (Private Rm)
	Tuttons (Larger Vault*)
70	Bakers' Hall (Ante Rm)
	Bar M (The Cellar Bar)
	Browns Club (VIP Rm II)
	Canning House (Library)
	Fifteen05 (Gallery of City Bar)
	The Little Ship Club (Library)
	Mela (Private Rm (downstairs))
	Poetry Society (Restaurant & Basement*)
	Royal Institution of Great
	Britain (Ante Rm)
	Strand Palace Hotel (Essex Suite or Grenville Suite)
	Stratford Old Town
	Hall (Conference Rm)
	Studio 33 (Champagne Bar)
65	Cecil Sharp House (Bar)
60	The Antelope (Max*)
	Bakers' Hall (Court Rm)
	Beach Blanket Babylon (Bar Area)
	Bonchurch Brasserie (Private Rm*)
	Bow Wine Vaults (Bistrot)
	Gunnersbury Park (Temple)
	Highgate School (Undercroft)
	Honourable Artillery Co (Queen's Rm)
	London School of
	Economics (Senior Common Rm)
	London Scottish (Officers' Mess or Queen Elizabeth Rm)
	The Music Room (Gallery)
	New Connaught Rms (Durham)
	The Old Operating Theatre,
	Museum & Herb Garret (Max*)
	PizzaExpress (Bar, Private Rm, Section or Section)
	Royal Geographical
	Society (Council Rm or Tea Rm)
	Ship (Garden*)
	St Peter's Hall (North Hall)
	The Vale (Bar*)
54	The Lady Daphne – moving
	venue (Afloat)
50	The Anchor (Mrs Thrale's Rm)
	Archduke Wine Bar (Bridge Rm)
	The Battersea Barge
	Bistro (Upper Deck)
	The Candid Arts Trust (Banquet Rm)
	Cecil Sharp House (Storrow Hall)
	Crazy Larry's (Vip Rm)
	The Dickens' House Museum (Max*)
	Digress (Lounge)
	Dolphin Square Hotel (Anson)
	George Inn (Old Bar)
	Guy's Hospital (Court Rm)
	Henry J Beans (Max*)
	Jason's Trip – moving
	venue (Lady Rose*)
	Kingswood House (Vestey)
	The Langley (The Vault)
	Liquid Lab (Mezzanine or Basement)
	Maidenhead Steam Navigation
	– moving venue (Pink Champagne)
	New Connaught Rms (Penthouse)
	PizzaExpress (Downstairs or Section)
	Southwark Cathedral (Seminar Rm)
	Strand Palace Hotel (Drake Suite)

	Victory Services Club (Allenby Rm)
48	Jason's Trip – moving venue (Holland)
45	The Coliseum (Chairman's)
	PizzaExpress (Section)
	Royal Over-Seas
	League (Mountbatten Rutland or Wrench)
	St Botolph's Hall (Lower Hall)
40	Docklands Sailing & Watersports
	Centre (Teaching Rm)
	The House of St Barnabas-in-Soho
	(Withdrawing Rm)
	Imperial College (Solar)
	The Mary Sumner
	House (Mary Sumner Rm)
	PizzaExpress (Private Rm)
36	Jason's Trip – moving
	venue (Lace Plate)
35	Chez Gérard, Dover Street (Max*)
	Jason's Trip – moving venue (Jason)
	Royal Institution of Great
	Britain (Council Rm)
30	Archduke Wine Bar (Conservatory)
	Chez Gérard, Dover
	Street (Private Rm)
	The Coliseum (Stall Rm)
	Floating Boater – moving
	venue (Lapwing)
	King's College (Committee Rm)
	PizzaExpress (Private Rm)
	Royal Over-Seas League (Bennet-Clark)
	Ship (Max)
	The Worx (Studio 3)
25	Apartment 195 (Cellar)
	PizzaExpress (Upstairs)
	Victory Services Club (Chetwode Rm)
20	Digress (Booths x 5)
	The House of St Barnabas-in-
	Soho (Records Rm)
	Kingswood House (Hannen Rm)
	Stratford Old Town
	Hall (Mayors Parlour)
15	Dolphin Square Hotel (Blake)
	Royal Over-Seas League (Park)
14	The Mary Sumner
	House (Syndicate Rm)
12	The Coliseum (Arlen Rm)
	Maidenhead Steam Navigation
	– moving venue (Fringilla)
10	Apartment 195 (TV Rm)

£B

1500	The Ministry of Sound (Max*)
	Turnmills (Max*)
1200	Electric Ballroom (Max*)
1100	The Fridge (Max*)
1000	The Mean Fiddler (Max*)
800	Queen Mary College (Max*)
	Wandsworth Civic Suite (Civic Suite*)
750	Polish Social & Cultural
	Association (Max*)
	Queen Mary Students'
	Union (e1 Nightclub*)
700	The Ministry of Sound (Box)
600	Park Crescent Conference
	Centre (Theatre*)
	University of London
	Union (Rm 101*)
500	First Bowl Queensway (Sega World*)
	The Ministry of Sound (Main Bar)
	Queen Mary
	College (Charterhouse Square)
400	Corney & Barrow (Max*)
	First Bowl Queensway (Ice Rink)
350	Balls Brothers (Max)
	Brockwell Lido (Marquee Site*)
330	Hop Cellars (Max*)
300	Cittie of Yorke (Main Bar*)
	City Pipe (see Davy's) (Max*)
	Corney & Barrow (Max)
	Crown & Greyhound (Garden*)

The Old Thameside Inn *(Ground Floor*)*
Philbeach Hall *(Max*)*
Queen Mary College *(The Octagon)*
Rock Garden *(Gardening Club Nightclub*)*
Turnmills *(Juno Lucina)*
Westminster Cathedral Hall *(Max*)*
275 Queen Mary Students' Union *(Drapers Arms)*
255 WKD *(Max*)*
250 Balls Brothers *(Max or Max)*
Bangers (see Davy's) *(Max*)*
Bung Hole (see Davy's) *(Max*)*
Chiv (see Davy's) *(Max*)*
City Flogger (see Davy's) *(Max*)*
Colonel Jaspers (see Davy's) *(Max*)*
Crown Passage Vaults (see Davy's) *(Max*)*
Kettners *(Max*)*
London Rowing Club *(Max*)*
The London Welsh Centre *(Main Hall*)*
Park Crescent Conference
Centre *(Portland Rm)*
Rock Garden *(Rock Garden)*
Skinkers (see Davy's) *(Max*)*
The Tattershall Castle *(Max*)*
Vineyard (see Davy's) *(Max*)*
200 Balls Brothers *(Max, Max, Max or Max)*
Bishop of Norwich (see Davy's) *(Max*)*
Champagne Charlies (see Davy's) *(Max*)*
Chopper Lump (see Davy's) *(Max*)*
City Boot (see Davy's) *(Max*)*
Colonel Jaspers (see Davy's) *(Max)*
Corney & Barrow *(Max)*
Davy's of Creed Lane (see Davy's) *(Max*)*
Diorama *(Max*)*
Habit (see Davy's) *(Max*)*
Heeltap & Bumper (see Davy's) *(Max*)*
Lees Bag (see Davy's) *(Max*)*
The Ministry of Sound *(Balcony Max)*
Mudchute Park & Farm *(Max*)*
Ochre *(Max*)*
Polish Social & Cultural
Association *(Lowiczanka Restaurant or
Malinova Rm)*
Queen Mary College *(Bar Med or The Old Library)*
St Bride Foundation Institute *(Bridewell Hall*)*
Tappit-Hen (see Davy's) *(Max*)*
Truckles Of Pied Bull Yard (see
Davy's) *(Max*)*
University of London Union *(Gallery Bar)*
Wessex House *(Max*)*
170 The Ministry of Sound *(VIP Bar)*
St Etheldreda's Crypt *(Max*)*
150 Balls Brothers *(Max)*
Brockwell Lido *(Café-restaurant)*
City FOB (see Davy's) *(Max*)*
Cooperage (see Davy's) *(Max*)*
Corney & Barrow *(Max or Max)*
Crown & Greyhound *(Max)*
The Crown Tavern *(Max*)*
Glassblower *(Max*)*
The Glasshouse Stores *(Max*)*
Hop Cellars *(Bar or Porter Rm)*
Jackson's Lane Community Centre *(Max*)*
Leadenhall Wine Bar *(Max*)*
The Mug House (see Davy's) *(Max*)*
The October Gallery *(Main Gallery*)*
The Old Thameside Inn *(Cellar Bar)*
Park Crescent Conference Centre *(Bistro or
Gulbenkian)*
Phene Arms *(Garden*)*
Polish Social & Cultural
Association *(Club Disco)*
Pulpit (see Davy's) *(Max*)*
Tapster (see Davy's) *(Max*)*
University of London Union *(Bar 101)*
Walkers of St James's *(Max*)*
Ye Olde Cheshire Cheese *(Cellar Bar*)*
144 First Bowl
Queensway *(10 Pin Bowling (per game))*
130 Balls Brothers *(Weekday function)*
Slug & Lettuce *(Max*)*
Vats *(Max*)*
120 The Atlas *(Max*)*
Balls Brothers *(Max)*

Borscht & Tears *(Max*)*
Cittie of Yorke *(Cellar Bar)*
Corney & Barrow *(Max or Max)*
Crown & Greyhound *(Private Rm (large))*
The Crown & Two Chairmen *(Upstairs Bar*)*
Dock Blida (see Davy's) *(Max*)*
Earlsfield Library *(Max*)*
The Golden Lion *(Max*)*
Gow's Restaurant *(Max*)*
Jackson's Lane Community
Centre *(Dance Studio)*
The Litten Tree *(Function Rm 1*)*
St Moritz *(Max*)*
Tappit-Hen (see Davy's) *(Wine Rms)*
University of London Union *(Palms Rm)*
WKD *(Mezzanine)*
100 Balls Brothers *(Weekday function)*
Boot & Flogger (see Davy's) *(Max*)*
Chatham Hall *(Max*)*
Corney & Barrow *(Max)*
The Crown Tavern *(Outside)*
The Freemason's Arms *(Max*)*
Glassblower *(Top Bar)*
Kettners *(Edward Rm)*
The Lamb Tavern *(Dining Rm* or The Dive)*
Leadenhall Wine Bar *(Main Rm)*
The London Welsh Centre *(Bar)*
The Mug House (see Davy's) *(Bar)*
La Paquerette *(Terrace*)*
Prince of Wales *(Max*)*
Shampers *(Max*)*
80 Alma *(Max*)*
Balls Brothers *(Weekday function)*
Chiv (see Davy's) *(Dining Rm)*
Cittie of Yorke *(Front Bar)*
The Glasshouse Stores *(Large Side)*
Jackson's Lane Community Centre *(Multi-
purpose Rm)*
The Litten Tree *(Basement Bar)*
The Ministry of Sound *(Baby Box)*
The October Gallery *(Top Floor Theatre)*
St Bride Foundation Institute *(Blackfriars Rm or
Farringdon Rm)*
Vats *(Restaurant)*
The White Horse *(Private Rm*)*
75 Bangers Too (see Davy's) *(Max*)*
Hollands *(Conservatory*)*
Hop Cellars *(Malt Rm)*
70 The Argyll Arms *(Max*)*
Bung Hole (see Davy's) *(Private Rm)*
The Clachan *(Highland Bar*)*
Corney & Barrow *(Max)*
The Pump House Gallery *(Max*)*
Shelleys *(Max*)*
Southwark Tavern *(Cellar Bar*)*
Ye Olde Cheshire Cheese *(Johnson's Bar)*
60 Balls Brothers *(Weekday function)*
Calthorpe Arms *(Private Rm*)*
Captain Kidd *(The Observation Deck*)*
Corney & Barrow *(Max)*
Mudchute Park & Farm *(Café)*
Ochre *(Function Rm)*
Shampers *(Restaurant)*
Simpsons Tavern *(Courtyard*)*
50 The Crown Tavern *(Function Rm)*
The Glasshouse Stores *(Small Side)*
Leadenhall Wine Bar *(Top Floor)*
Newham City Farm *(Rm*)*
Simpsons Tavern *(Max)*
Star Tavern *(Bar*)*
Two Chairmen *(Max*)*
45 The Golden Lion *(Theatre Rm)*
The Plough *(Max*)*
40 Duke of Albemarle *(Max*)*
Grapeshots (see Davy's) *(Max*)*
The October Gallery *(Club)*
Simpsons Tavern *(Amy's Bar or Wine Bar)*
St Bride Foundation Institute *(Salisbury Rm)*
30 The Dog & Duck *(Max*)*
Wandsworth Civic Suite *(Reception Rm)*
25 The East Hill *(Max*)*

Jackson's Lane Community
Centre *(Youth Space)*
Ye Olde Cheshire Cheese *(Director's Rm)*
20 Phene Arms *(Bistro or Upstairs Terrace)*
15 St Bride Foundation Institute *(Caxton)*
10 Balls Brothers *(Private Rm)*

Function rooms listed by seated capacity

* largest entry for venue

£E

750	Hampton Court Palace *(Max*)*
450	British Museum *(Max*)*
400	Victoria & Albert Museum *(Raphael Gallery*)*
320	Blenheim Palace *(State Rms*)*
300	British Museum *(Great Court)*
280	Hampton Court Palace *(Great Hall)*
250	Royal Academy of Arts *(Summer Exhibition*)*
	Victoria & Albert Museum *(Dome)*
240	HM Tower of London *(New Armouries*)*
230	Blenheim Palace *(Orangery)*
220	Hampton Court Palace *(Cartoon Gallery)*
200	Eltham Palace *(Great Hall*)*
	Tate Britain *(Rm 15 or Rm 9*)*
180	Fishmongers' Hall *(Max*)*
	The Gilbert Collection *(Silver Gallery*)*
170	British Museum *(Egypt & Nereid Rms)*
	Cliveden *(Max*)*
150	British Museum *(Restaurant)*
	Chiswick House *(Courtyard Marquee*)*
	Home House *(Garden*)*
	Lancaster House *(Long Gallery*)*
	Spencer House *(Max*)*
	Victoria & Albert Museum *(Gamble Rm)*
125	Annabel's *(Max*)*
120	Home House *(Front & Eating Room)*
	Syon Park (House) *(Great Hall*)*
	Wallace Collection *(Great Gallery or Main Galleries*)*
	Wrotham Park *(Drawing Rm*)*
110	Cliveden *(Terraced Dining Rm)*
100	The Gilbert Collection *(Max)*
	National Portrait Gallery *(Portrait Restaurant or Victorian Galleries*)*
	Royal Academy of Arts *(Private Rms)*
	Two Temple Place *(The Great Hall*)*
	Wallace Collection *(Sculpture Garden)*
90	Blenheim Palace *(Marlborough)*
	Spencer House *(Great Rm)*
80	British Museum *(Hotung Gallery)*
	Chiswick House *(First floor (6 Rms))*
	Courtauld Gallery *(Fine Rms*)*
	Kenwood House *(Orangery*)*
	National Portrait Gallery *(Contemporary Galleries)*
	Syon Park (House) *(State Dining Rm)*
	Tate Britain *(Rex Whistler Restaurant)*
78	Lancaster House *(Music Rm)*
72	Home House *(Eating Rm)*
70	HM Tower of London *(Royal Fusiliers Association Rm)*
	Wrotham Park *(Dining Rm)*
67	Lancaster House *(State Dining Rm)*
60	Cliveden *(French Dining Rm)*
	Eltham Palace *(Drawing Rm)*
	Royal Observatory *(Max*)*
50	Eltham Palace *(Dining Rm)*
	Hampton Court Palace *(Banqueting House or Public Dining Rm)*
48	Chiswick House *(Domed Saloon)*
40	Home House *(Front Parlour)*
	Royal Academy of Arts *(General Assembly Rm)*
	Victoria & Albert Museum *(Morris Rm)*
	Wallace Collection *(Dining Rm or State Rm)*
36	Spencer House *(Lady Spencer's Rm)*
32	Blenheim Palace *(Audenarde Rm, Malplaquet or Ramillies)*
30	Sir John Soane's Museum *(Max*)*
24	Lancaster House *(Eagle Rm)*
	Spencer House *(Dining Rm or Music Rm)*
20	Cliveden *(Macmillan Boardroom)*
16	Lancaster House *(Gold Rm)*
15	The Gilbert Collection *(Russian Gate Rm)*
10	Tate Britain *(Lodge)*

£M-E

1700	The Grosvenor House Hotel (Great Rm*)
1600	Royal Albert Hall (Cabaret or Ball*)
1500	The Business Design Centre (Main Hall*)
1400	Coram's Fields (Max*)
	Old Billingsgate (Grand Hall*)
1250	Hilton on Park Lane (Grand Ballroom*)
1050	Royal Lancaster (Max*)
1000	Addington Palace (Max*)
	Old Spitalfields Market (With Marquee*)
	Royal Lancaster (Westbourne Suite)
880	The Queen Elizabeth II Conference Centre (Fleming & Whittle Rms*)
850	Somerset House (Courtyard)
780	Royal Lancaster (Nine Kings Suite)
750	Cumberland Hotel (Production Box*)
	InterContinental London (Grand Ballroom*)
704	Guildhall (Great Hall*)
700	Coram's Fields (Split Facility)
650	Park Lane Hotel (Ballroom*)
	Thorpe Park (Dome*)
600	Kew (Royal Botanic) Gardens (New Palace Marquee Site*)
	Natural History Museum (Central Hall*)
550	Portman Hotel (Ballroom*)
510	The Dorchester (Ballroom*)
500	Chelsea Village (Exhibition Space*)
	East Wintergarden (Max*)
	The Grosvenor House Hotel (Ballroom)
	The Grove (Amber*)
	Harrods (Georgian Restaurant*)
	National Maritime Museum (Neptune Court*)
	Old Billingsgate (Terrace)
	The Old Royal Naval College (Painted Hall*)
	The Queen Elizabeth II Conference Centre (Benjamin Britten Lounge or Fleming Rm)
	The Savoy (Lancaster Rm*)
	Science Museum (Making The World Modern* or Wellcome Wing)
	Westway Studios (Max*)
470	Just St James (Max*)
460	Millennium London Mayfair (Ballroom*)
450	Chelsea Village (Galleria)
432	Millennium Gloucester Hotel (Century Suite*)
430	InterContinental London (Westminster)
426	Royal Garden Hotel (Palace Suite*)
408	The Landmark (Ballroom*)
400	Banqueting House (Main Hall*)
	The Business Design Centre (Gallery Hall)
	Carlton Tower (Ballroom*)
	Cumberland Hotel (Carlisle Suite)
	Four Seasons Hotel (Max*)
	Imperial War Museum (Max*)
	Madame Tussaud's (World Stage*)
	Royal Air Force Museum (Main Aircraft Hall*)
	Tate Modern (Turbine Hall*)
392	Middle Temple Hall (Max*)
380	Guildhall (Old Library)
	Hurlingham Club (Quadrangle Suite*)
360	Hurlingham Club (Broom House Suite)
	The Landmark (Max)
	Royal Albert Hall (Arena)
350	Royal Opera House (Vilar Floral Hall*)
	Science Museum (Flight Gallery)
	Stonor (Front Lawn*)
340	Dover Street Restaurant & Bar (Max*)
	The Landmark (Music Rm)
330	Renaissance London Chancery Court Hotel (Ballroom*)
320	Cabinet War Rooms (Churchill Museum*)
	Circus Space (Combustion Chamber*)
	Lincoln's Inn (Great Hall*)
	The Mayfair Inter-Continental (Crystal Rm*)
310	Millennium Gloucester Hotel (Cotswold Suite)
300	Atlantic Bar & Grill (Max*)
	Chelsea Village (Drakes Suite)
	Chessington World of Adventures (Glade or Hospitality Marquee*)
	Dali Universe (Max*)
	Gibson Hall (Hall*)
	The Hempel (Garden Square*)

	Hilton on Park Lane (Wellington Ballroom)
	Imperial War Museum (Main Atrium)
	Legoland Windsor (The Pavilions*)
	Middle Temple Hall (Hall)
	Millennium Gloucester Hotel (Decade Suite)
	Old Billingsgate (Gallery or Mezzanine)
	La Porte des Indes (Max*)
	Raven's Ait Island (Max*)
	Royal Hospital Chelsea (Great Hall*)
	Thorpe Park (Lake Side Hospitality Area)
	Westway Studios (Studio 2)
292	The Mayfair Inter-Continental (Mayfair Theatre)
290	Merchant Taylors' Hall (Great Hall*)
288	Barbican Centre (Garden Rm*)
284	Royal Institute of British Architects (Jarvis Hall*)
280	Merchant Taylors' Hall (Max)
	Royal Air Force Museum (Battle of Britain Hall)
270	Shakespeare's UnderGlobe (Underglobe*)
250	China White (Max*)
	Drapers' Hall (Max*)
	Gainsborough Studios (Max*)
	Ham House (Orangery Garden (Marquee)*)
	Inner Temple Hall (Hall*)
	Institute of Directors (Nash*)
	London Aquarium (Atlantic*)
	Le Meridien (Max*)
	Royal Institute of British Architects (Florence Hall*)
	The Saatchi Gallery (Main Gallery*)
	Science Museum (Challenge of Materials)
	Sotheby's (Max*)
240	Café de Paris (Restaurant & Mezzanine*)
	Claridge's (Ballroom*)
	Harrington Hall (Harrington*)
	LABAN (Ampitheatre, Bonnie Bird Theatre* or Studio Theatre)
	London Zoo (Prince Albert Suite*)
	Le Meridien (Georgian)
	The People's Palace (Max*)
	Royal College of Physicians (Osler Rm*)
230	Great Eastern Hotel (Great Eastern*)
	Mandarin Oriental Hyde Park (Ballroom*)
	Westminster Abbey Garden (College Garden*)
228	One Whitehall Place (Gladstone Library*)
224	Clothworkers' Hall (Livery Hall*)
	The Commonwealth Club (Max*)
	Drapers' Hall (Livery Hall)
220	Goldsmiths' Hall (Livery Hall*)
	InterContinental London (Piccadilly)
	The Law Society (Max*)
	The London Underwriting Centre (Atrium*)
	The Old Palace (Great Hall or The Old Riding School*)
	One Whitehall Place (Whitehall Suite)
	Raven's Ait Island (Britannia Suite)
	The Roof Gardens (Max*)
	Stonor (Croqret Lawn)
210	Haberdashers' Hall (Livery Hall*)
205	Stationers' Hall (Livery Hall*)
200	The Berkeley (Ballroom*)
	Il Bottaccio (Gallery*)
	Christie's (Great Rm*)
	The Collection (Mezzanine*)
	Dali Universe (Dali A)
	The Energy Clinic (Max*)
	Four Seasons Canary Wharf (Ballroom*)
	Hakkasan (Max*)
	Hilton London Paddington (Great Western Suite*)
	InterContinental London (Byron & Parks Suites)
	Just St James (Just St James)
	Kent House (The Sanctuary*)
	Kew (Royal Botanic) Gardens (Temperate House)
	London Aquarium (Terrace (with marquee))
	The London Art House (Manor Garden Hall*)
	Millennium Gloucester Hotel (Conservatory)
	Mint Leaf (Max*)
	Park Lane Hotel (Tudor Rose Rm)
	Royal Opera House (Clore Studio)
	Sadler's Wells Theatre (Max*)
	The Savoy (Abraham Lincoln & Manhattan Rms)

PRIVATE VENUES | SEATED CAPACITY

	Science Museum (East Hall)		The Mayfair Inter-Continental (Danziger Suite)
	St Martin's Lane Hotel (Restaurant*)		Monkey Island Hotel (River Rm*)
	Tate Modern (Cafe 7)		National Liberal Club (Dining Rm)
	Thorpe Park (Thorpe Belle)		Natural History Museum (Spencer Gallery)
	Westway Studios (Studio 4)		The Old Royal Naval
180	The Avenue (Max*)		College (King William Restaurant)
	Carlton Club (Max*)		Prism (Max*)
	Great Fosters (Tithe Barn And Painted Hall*)		Queen's House (Great Hall*)
	The Landmark (Drawing Rm or Empire Rm)		Roehampton Club (Roehampton Rm)
	Marriott Maida Vale (Regent Suite*)		Royal Opera House (Crush Rm)
	Le Meridien (Edwardian)		Salters' Hall (Mail Hall*)
	Le Meridien Selsdon Park (Terrace Suite*)		The Savoy (River Rm)
	Natural History Museum (Earth Galleries or		Sheraton Park Tower (Trianon Rm*)
	North Hall)		Swissôtel London the
	Roehampton Club (Max*)		Howard (Fitzalan Suite*)
	HQS Wellington (Max*)		Tower Bridge (Walkways*)
170	1 Lombard Street (Max*)		Windsor Guildhall (Guildhall Chamber*)
	Gray's Inn (Hall*)	115	Mosimann's Belfry (Dining Rm*)
	Pennyhill Park Hotel (Balmoral*)		Noble Rot (Max*)
	La Rascasse (Restaurant*)	110	Circus Space (Generating Chamber)
	Royal Air Force Museum (Cosford Rm or		Elysium (Restaurant & VIP Rm*)
	The Halton Gallery)		Harrington Hall (Reynolds & Landseer)
	Skinners' Hall (Banquet Hall*)		Royal Garden Hotel (The Tenth' Restaurant)
160	Arts Club (Max*)	108	Royal Garden Hotel (Kensington Suite)
	The Berners Hotel (Thomas Ashton Suite*)	100	BMA House (Members Dining Rm*)
	The Criterion (Max*)		Cannizaro House (Max*)
	Grocers' Hall (Livery Hall*)		Christopher's (Max*)
	Guildhall (The Crypts)		City Hall - London's Living
	The Law Society (Common Rm)		Room (London's Living Rm*)
	Savile Club (Members Dining Rm & Ballroom*)		Cumberland Hotel (Gloucester)
150	Arts Club (Dining Rm)		Dali Universe (Dali B, Modern Masters or White Space)
	Banqueting House (Undercroft)		The Dorchester (The Terrace)
	Barbican Centre (Conservatory)		Firepower - The Royal Artillery
	Benares (Restaurant*)		Museum (Gunnery Hall* or Theatre)
	Coq d'Argent (Outdoor Terraces*)		Gibson Hall (Garden Rm)
	The Dorchester (Orchid)		Grocers' Hall (Piper Rm)
	Dulwich Picture Gallery (Soane Building*)		Hampshire Hotel (Penthouse*)
	Four Seasons Hotel (Garden Rm)		Harrington Hall (Turner & Constable)
	Gainsborough Studios (South Studio)		The Imagination Gallery (Atrium and Restaurant
	Hever Castle (Pavilion*)		or Gallery)
	Jerwood Space (Max*)		Jerwood Space (Gallery & Glasshouse)
	Just St James (Just Oriental)		Kensington Rooms (Rm 9*)
	Kensington Palace (Orangery*)		Kent House (Max)
	Mandarin Oriental Hyde Park (Carlyle Suite)		The Lanesborough (Belgravia*)
	National Liberal Club (Max*)		Lightship (Max*)
	One Whitehall Place (Reading And Writing Rms)		London Zoo (Raffles Suite)
	Orangery (Kensington Palace) (Max*)		Madame Tussaud's (Blush)
	Penshurst Place & Gardens (Baron's Hall*)		Le Meridien (Regency)
	Royal Opera		Millennium Gloucester Hotel (Ashburn Suite)
	House (Royal Opera House Café & Restaurant)		Momo (Max*)
	Sartoria (Max*)		Museum of London (Max*)
	Serpentine Gallery (Max*)		Natural History Museum (Darwin Centre)
	Sketch (Gallery*)		Pennyhill Park Hotel (Windsor & Eton)
	HQS Wellington (Court Rm)		Raven's Ait Island (Thames Suite)
140	Arundel House (Rm With A View*)		River & Rowing Museum (Thames Rm*)
	Cabinet War Rooms (Auditorium)		Royal Air Force Museum (Art Gallery)
	The Circus (Max*)		Royal College of Physicians (Platt Rm)
	Hilton on Park Lane (Coronation Suite)		Royal Hospital Chelsea (State Apartments)
	The Imagination Gallery (Max*)		The Sanctuary (Max*)
	Just St James (Just The Gallery)		Somerset House (Seamen's Waiting Hall)
	Scotts (Restaurant*)		Tate Modern (East Rm or Level 3)
139	Saddlers' Hall (Max*)		Theatre Museum (Paintings Gallery*)
130	Apothecaries' Hall (Hall*)		Westway Studios (Studio 3)
	Chintamani (Max*)	98	The Almeida (Max*)
	Lincoln's Inn (Old Hall)	96	Cannizaro House (Viscount Melville Suite)
	The London Planetarium (Max*)		Claridge's (Drawing Rm, French Salon or Mirror Rm)
	Mirabelle (Max*)		Cumberland Hotel (Clarence)
	National Liberal Club (David Lloyd George)		Drapers' Hall (Court Dining)
	Royal Air Force Museum (Loching Rm)	95	Four Seasons Hotel (Oak Rm)
	Smith's of Smithfield (Max*)	92	Carlton Club (Churchill Rm)
125	Coram's Fields (Party Chalet 2)	90	30 Pavilion Road (Stone Hall)
120	30 Pavilion Road (Great Hall)		Brighton Royal
	Addington Palace (Great Hall)		Pavilion (Banqueting Rm (and Great Kitchen)*)
	Babylon (Max*)		The Carlton Mitre Hotel (Pavilion*)
	The Caledonian Club (Members Dining Rm*)		Gray's Inn (Large Pension Rm)
	Chessington World of Adventures (Keg)		Inner Temple Hall (Parliament Chamber)
	The Commonwealth Club (Lower Ground Hall)		Kent House (Rutland Rm)
	Dover Street Restaurant & Bar (Lower Bar)		LABAN (Medium Studio)
	Fortnum & Mason (St James's Rm*)		The Landmark (Gazebo (in the Atrium))
	The Grosvenor House Hotel (Albemarle)		London Stock Exchange (Top Floor*)
	The Grove (Ivory)		Plateau (Max*)
	Just Gladwins (Max*)		Quo Vadis (Warhol Rm*)
	The London Dungeon (Max*)		Sadler's Wells Theatre (Cable & Wireless Rm)

Science Museum (Directors Suite or Space Gallery)
St Martin's Lane Hotel (The Studio)
Swissôtel London the Howard (Arundel Suite)
88 Great Eastern Hotel (Bishopsgate)
87 Innholders' Hall (Hall*)
85 Belair House (Restaurant*)
84 28 Portland Place (Heggie Rm or Sainsbury's Rm*)
Kensington Rooms (Media Rm)
Penshurst Place & Gardens (Sunderland Rm)
80 5 Cavendish Square (Restaurant*)
Armourers' & Braisers' Hall (Livery Hall*)
Audi Forum (Whole Space*)
Bam-Bou (Max*)
The Berners Hotel (Fitzrovia Suite)
Big Brother House (Max*)
Brighton Royal Pavilion (Queen Adelaide Suite)
Cabinet War Rooms (Plant Rm)
Chelsea Village (Trophy Rm)
Cutty Sark (Tween Decks*)
The Energy Clinic (Lobby)
Estorick Collection (Max*)
Great Fosters (Orangery)
The Halkin (Max*)
The Hempel (I-Thai Restaurant (and Shadow Bar))
Institute of Directors (Burton)
Jerwood Space (Space 1 or Space 2)
Kew (Royal Botanic)
    Gardens (Gallery (entire ground floor))
Leighton House (Studio*)
Merchant Taylors' Hall (Drawing Rm or Parlour)
Le Meridien Selsdon Park (Sir Edward Heath Rm)
Millennium London
    Mayfair (Turner Fine Dining Rm)
Monte's (Restaurant*)
Park Lane Hotel (Oak Rm)
Portman Hotel (Gloucester Suite)
Royal Academy of
    Engineering (Conference Rm*)
Royal College of Pathologists (Lecture Rm*)
The Savoy (Beaufort)
Smith's of Smithfield (Top Floor)
Stationers' Hall (Court Rm)
Strictly Hush (Zanzibar*)
Theatre Museum (Foyer)
Thomas Goode (Shop*)
White's (Max*)
76 Threadneedles (Max*)
75 Coram's Fields (Party Chalet)
74 Haberdashers' Hall (Court Rm)
72 28 Portland Place (Harben Rm)
Drapers' Hall (Court Rm)
One Whitehall Place (Meston Suite)
Royal Garden Hotel (Lancaster Suite)
70 Addington Palace (Winter Garden)
Atlantic Bar & Grill (Chez Cup)
Christie's (Rm 1 or Rm 2)
Le Gavroche (Max*)
Geffrye Museum (Museum Galleries*)
Goldsmiths' Hall (Drawing Rm & Exhibition Rm)
The Grosvenor House Hotel (Stratton Suite)
Lightship (Lower Deck)
Le Meridien (Adam)
Middle Temple Hall (Parliament Chamber)
The Newsroom (Lecture Theatre*)
Raffles (Max*)
Renaissance London Chancery Court
    Hotel (Lower Ground Floor Suite)
Royal Albert Hall (Victoria Rm)
Royal Institute of British
    Architects (Conference Rm)
Royal Lancaster (Gloucester Suite)
68 One Whitehall Place (River Rm)
66 Barbican Centre (Conservatory Terrace)
64 The Commonwealth Club (Cinema Rm)
Dukes Hotel (Marlborough Suite*)
Hever Castle (Tudor Suite)
LSO St Luke's (Crypt Café*)
Renaissance London Chancery Court
    Hotel (Ground Floor Suite)
60 28 Portland Place (Adam's Rm)
Addington Palace (Lecture Rm)
Arts Club (Garden Rm)

Berry Bros & Rudd (Max*)
Il Bottaccio (Club Gallery)
Brighton Royal Pavilion (King William IV Rm)
Carlton Tower (Garden Rm)
Chelsea Village (Jimmys)
The Commonwealth Club (Blue Rm)
The Dorchester (Park Suite)
Dukes Hotel (Max)
Dulwich Picture Gallery (Linbury Rm)
Fitzroy Square (2nd Space*)
Four Seasons Canary Wharf (River Rm)
Ham House (Orangery (Restaurant))
Institute of Directors (Waterloo)
The Lanesborough (Wellington Rm)
Legoland Windsor (JFK Drawing Rm)
London Aquarium (Shark Tank)
The London Art House (Baroque Hall or
    Rococo Rm)
London Capital Club (Oriental Rm*)
London Marriott County Hall
    Hotel (George V*)
The London Underwriting
    Centre (Hospitality Suite)
Le Meridien Selsdon Park (Surrey Rm)
Millennium London Mayfair (Manhattan or
    Waterloo Rm)
Mint Leaf (Private Rm)
Museum of London (Eighteenth Century Gallery)
National Maritime Museum (Royal Observatory)
Opium (Max*)
Osterley Park & House (Brewhouse*)
Pasha (Max*)
Savile Club (Ballroom or Members Dining Rm)
Tower Bridge (Engine Rms)
Wax Chandlers' Hall (Hall*)
57 Dyers' Hall (Max*)
56 Fortnum & Mason (Burlington Rm)
55 Amberley Castle (Queens Rm*)
Canonbury Academy (Long Gallery*)
FireHouse (Max*)
The Law Society (Old Council Chamber)
Notting Hill Brasserie (Main Restaurant*)
L'Oranger (Max*)
54 The Berkeley (Belgravia)
52 The Caledonian Club (Stuart)
50 32 Craven St (Level 1*)
Addington Palace (Wellington Rm)
Atlantic Bar & Grill (Dicks Bar)
Baltic Exchange (Dining Rm*)
Barnard's Inn Hall (Max*)
Brighton Royal Pavilion (Large Adelaide)
Claridge's (Kensington)
The Dorchester (Holford)
Dover Street Restaurant & Bar (Upper Bar)
The Energy Clinic (Largest Area)
Inner Temple Hall (Luncheon Rm)
Institute of Directors (Trafalgar II/St James II)
Kew (Royal Botanic)
    Gardens (Cambridge Cottage Lounge)
The Law Society (Chancery)
Le Meridien Selsdon Park (Kent Rm)
Mosimann's Belfry (Coutts Rm)
National Maritime Museum (Orangery or
    Southern Parlors)
Noble Rot (Member's Bar)
The Old Royal Naval
    College (Admirals Residence)
Park Lane Hotel (Mirror Rm or Orchard Suite)
Portman Hotel (Berkeley Suite or Bryanston Suite)
Queen's House (SW Parlour)
Raven's Ait Island (Lambourne Rm)
The Ritz (Marie Antoinette Suite*)
Roehampton Club (Garden Rm)
Royal College of Pathologists (Council Rm)
The Savoy (Pinafore)
Skinners' Hall (Old Court Rm)
Thorpe Park (Neptunes Chamber)
HQS Wellington (Quarterdeck)
48 32 Craven St (Max)
Four Seasons Hotel (Pine Rm)
Hilton London Paddington (McGyver or
    Thunderbolt)
Mirabelle (Chinese)
One Aldwych (Rms 1 & 2*)

PRIVATE VENUES | SEATED CAPACITY

46 Pennyhill Park Hotel (Parkview)
St Martin's Lane Hotel (The Backroom)
Stationers' Hall (Stock Rm)

45 Harrington Hall (Stubbs or Sutherland)
Hilton on Park Lane (Serpentine Rm)
The Metropolitan (Max*)
La Rascasse (Semi-private Area)
Sketch (Lecture Rm)

44 The Stafford (The Cellar*)

42 The Hempel (Room No 17)

40 1 Lombard Street (Private Rm)
Addington Palace (Library or Music Rm)
Amberley Castle (Great Rm)
Arundel House (4th Floor Conference Rm or Conference Rm)
Belair House (Bar)
The Berners Hotel (Tyburn Rm)
Brighton Royal Pavilion (Great Kitchen)
Canonbury Academy (Denby Suite)
Christopher's (Private Dining Rm)
The Dorchester (Pavilion)
Gainsborough Studios (North Studio)
Great Eastern Hotel (Chancery)
The Grosvenor House Hotel (Spencer Rm)
The Grove (Silk)
Hever Castle (Castle Dining Rm)
Hilton London Paddington (Red Star)
Imperial War Museum (Boardroom 1)
Institute of Directors (Trafalgar I)
InterContinental London (Windsor Suite)
Kent House (Library)
The Lanesborough (Westminster Rm)
Legoland Windsor (Creation Centre)
Lloyd's Club (Restaurant*)
The London Art House (Orangery)
London Marriott County Hall Hotel (Library Lounge)
London Marriott Hotel Park Lane (Oxford Suite (divisable by 3)*)
Mandarin Oriental Hyde Park (Roseberry Rms)
The Metropolitan (Dining-Meeting Rm)
Mosimann's Academy (Thinking Rm*)
Museum of London (Medieval Gallery)
MVH (Max*)
The Petersham (River Rm* or Terrace Rm)
Portland Place Conference Centre (Max*)
Prism (Mezzanine)
Queen's House (Orangery Suite)
La Rascasse (Private Rm)
Renaissance London Chancery Court Hotel (Staple Inn Rm & Gray's Inn Rm)
Royal Academy of Engineering (Dining Rm)
Sartoria (Private Rms (both))
The Stafford (Panel Rm & Sutherland Rm)
Temple Island (Indoors*)
The Trafalgar (Resolution*)
Windsor Guildhall (Maidenhead Rm)

38 The Wellington Club (Max*)

37 Sketch (Parlour)

36 BMA House (Prince's Rm)
Cannizaro House (Queen Elizabeth Rm)
Carlton Club (Cabinet Rm)
The Halkin (Private Dining Rm)
The Landmark (Champagne Rm or Tower Suite)
Sheraton Park Tower (Buckingham Rm)
Thomas Goode (Chairman's Rm)
Wellington Club (Max*)

35 One New Inn Square (Max*)

34 London Marriott Hotel Park Lane (Hyde Park Suite)
The Milestone Hotel & Apartments (Max*)

33 Mirabelle (Pine Rm)

32 L'Incontro (Private Rm*)
Notting Hill Brasserie (Semi-Private Areas By Bar)

30 Addington Palace (Empire Rm)
Brighton Royal Pavilion (Small Adelaide)
Cannizaro House (Blue Rm)
Canonbury Academy (Queen Elizabeth)
Carlton Tower (Water Garden)
Claridge's (Amarillis)
Covent Garden Hotel (Meeting Rm 1*)
Fan Museum (Orangery*)
Four Seasons Canary Wharf (City Rm)

Great Eastern Hotel (Moorgate)
Institute of Directors (St James's II)
The Law Society (Fleet)
Leighton House (Dining Rm)
Lightship (Main Deck)
London Aquarium (Rainforest)
Mandarin Oriental Hyde Park (Asquith Rm or Balfour Rm)
The Mayfair Inter-Continental (Berkeley Suite)
Merchant Taylors' Hall (Kings Gallery or Library)
Mimmo d'Ischia (Private Rm*)
Monkey Island Hotel (Garden Rm)
Mosimann's Belfry (Parmigiani Fleurier Rm)
Motcomb's Townhouse (Belgravia Rm*)
National Liberal Club (Lady Violet)
One Aldwych (Rm 3)
Penshurst Place & Gardens (Buttery)
Quo Vadis (Modigliani)
Royal Academy of Engineering (Council Chamber)
Royal Institute of British Architects (South Rm)
Sadler's Wells Theatre (Fonteyn Rm)
Salters' Hall (Court Rm)
The Savoy (Gondoliers)
The Trafalgar (Boardroom)
HQS Wellington (Model Rm)

28 30 Pavilion Road (Library)
London Stock Exchange (Blue Rm)
The Milestone Hotel & Apartments (Cheniston Restaurant)

26 Arts Club (Drawing Rm)
Christopher's (Small Dining Rm)
Marriott Maida Vale (Carlton Suite)
Smith's of Smithfield (Private Rm)
Windsor Guildhall (Ascot Rm)

25 Innholders' Hall (Court Rm)
Kensington Rooms (Studio Rm)
Marble Hill House (Tetra Hall*)
Le Meridien (Chelsea)
Royal Albert Hall (Prince Of Wales)

24 5 Cavendish Square (Private Dining Rm)
Baltic Exchange (Boardroom)
Canonbury Academy (Wentworth)
Carlton Club (Disraeli Rm or Macmillan Rm)
Dover Street Restaurant & Bar (Alcove)
The Milestone Hotel & Apartments (Windsor Suite)
Plateau (Private Rm)
Portman Hotel (Library)
Royal College of Radiologists (Council Chamber*)
The Savoy (Patience)
Sketch (Lecture Rm (Library))
The Stafford (Sutherland Rm)

22 Apothecaries' Hall (Court Rm)
The Caledonian Club (Selkirk)
The Capital (Cadogan*)
The Circus (Private Dinin Rm)
The Connaught (Regency Carlos Suite*)
Middle Temple Hall (Queen's Rm)
Notting Hill Brasserie (Large Private Rm)
Park Lane Mews (Smart Rms)
Royal Institute of British Architects (Aston)
Scotts (Club Rm)
Somerset House (Hermitage Rms)

20 Armourers' & Braisers' Hall (Court Rm)
Baltic Exchange (Chairman's Rm)
Bam-Bou (Black Lounge Bar)
Benares (Private Rm)
The Berkeley (Mulberry)
Charlotte Street Hotel (Rm I*)
The Fox Club (Max*)
The Grove (Garden Rm)
LABAN (Meeting Rm)
The Lanesborough (Wilkins Rm)
Legoland Windsor (Boardroom)
London Capital Club (Boardroom)
London Marriott County Hall Hotel (Queen Mary)
Le Meridien (Mayfair)
Millennium London Mayfair (Grosvenor Suite)
Mitsukoshi (Western Rm*)

VISIT US AT: www.hardens.com

Mosimann's Academy *(Library)*
Motcomb's Townhouse *(Mclue Suite)*
One Whitehall Place *(Thames Suite)*
L'Oranger *(Private Rm)*
Park Lane Hotel *(Drawing Rm)*
Le Pont de la Tour *(Private Rm*)*
Prism *(Library)*
The Ritz *(Trafalgar Suite)*
Royal Albert Hall *(Henry Cole Rm)*
Royal College of Pathologists *(Seminar Rm)*
Royal Institute of British Architects *(Canal Chamber or Committe Rm)*
Sartoria *(Private Rm (x2))*
Stationers' Hall *(Ante Rm)*
Strictly Hush *(Kenya)*
The Trafalgar *(Strategy)*
Wax Chandlers' Hall *(Courtroom)*
Zen Central *(Private Rm*)*

18 The Academy *(Boardroom*)*
Cannizaro House *(Oak Rm)*
Carlton Club *(Lirary)*
Claridge's *(St James's)*
Deca *(Private Rm*)*
The Dorchester *(Penthouse)*
Haberdashers' Hall *(Luncheon Rm)*
Marriott Maida Vale *(Hamilton Suite)*
Monkey Island Hotel *(Spencer Rm)*
The Savoy *(Mikado)*
The Square *(Private Rm*)*
Wiltons *(Private Rm*)*

16 The Almeida *(Private Rm)*
Carlton Tower *(Boardroom)*
The Commonwealth Club *(Glass Dining Rm)*
Hampshire Hotel *(Burley or Romsey)*
The Hempel *(Jade Rm)*
Hilton on Park Lane *(Argyll Rm)*
Monkey Island Hotel *(Boardroom)*
Monte's *(Private Dining Rm)*
The Petersham *(Cellars)*
Sheraton Park Tower *(Explorers)*
Threadneedles *(Stirling or Capital)*

15 MVH *(Hell)*
Quo Vadis *(Giacommeti)*
Royal Institute of British Architects *(Professional Gallery)*
Sadler's Wells Theatre *(Cripplegate Rm or Sackler Rm)*
Strictly Hush *(Tangiers)*

14 28 Portland Place *(Founder's Rm)*
Bam-Bou *(Private Rms (2))*
Belair House *(Conservatory)*
Covent Garden Hotel *(Meeting Rm 2)*
Great Eastern Hotel *(Broadgate)*
The Grove *(Zebrano)*
Imperial War Museum *(Boardroom 2)*
The London Art House *(Redon Rm)*
London Capital Club *(Gresham Rm)*
Mosimann's Belfry *(Gucci Rm)*
Pétrus *(Max*)*
La Porte des Indes *(Private Rm 1)*
Roehampton Club *(Centenary Board Rm)*
Royal College of Radiologists *(Robens Rm)*
The Stafford *(Argyll Rm or Pink Rm & Argyll Rm)*

12 32 Craven St *(Level 2)*
Amberley Castle *(King Charles Rm)*
Arts Club *(Board Rm)*
Babylon *(Private Rm)*
Baltic Exchange *(Churchill)*
Benares *(Private Rm)*
The Caledonian Club *(Oval)*
Charlotte Street Hotel *(Private Dining Rm or Rm 2)*
Claridge's *(Davies)*
The Connaught *(Georgian Rm)*
Cutty Sark *(Master's Saloon)*
Dukes Hotel *(Sheridan Rm)*
The Lanesborough *(Wine Cellar)*
London Marriott County Hall Hotel *(Boardroom)*
The Milestone Hotel & Apartments *(Safari Suite)*
Millennium Gloucester Hotel *(Boardroom)*
Mimmo d'Ischia *(Private Rm)*

Mitsukoshi *(Tatami Rm)*
One Whitehall Place *(Cellar)*
Quo Vadis *(Rossini Rm)*
Savile Club *(Elgar Rm)*
The Savoy *(Iolanthe)*
Sheraton Park Tower *(Balmoral)*
Skinners' Hall *(Parlour)*
Tower Bridge *(Bridge Master's Dining Rm)*

10 32 Craven St *(Level 3)*
The Berkeley *(Knightsbridge)*
Cannizaro House *(Boardroom)*
The Capital *(Eaton)*
City Miyama *(Private Rm*)*
Claridge's *(Salon)*
Covent Garden Hotel *(Private)*
Great Eastern Hotel *(Monument)*
Hampshire Hotel *(Drawing Rm)*
The London Art House *(Albert Moore Lounge)*
London Capital Club *(Marco Polo)*
London Stock Exchange *(Syndicate Rm)*
The Milestone Hotel & Apartments *(Conservatory)*
Monkey Island Hotel *(Wedgewood)*
Mosimann's Belfry *(Veuve Cliquot Rm)*
Number Sixteen *(Conservatory*)*
One Aldwych *(Dome Suite)*
The Petersham *(Rose Rm)*
La Porte des Indes *(Private Rm 2)*
River & Rowing Museum *(Henley Rm)*
Royal Academy of Engineering *(Meeting Rm 1 or Meeting rm 2)*
Royal Institute of British Architects *(Student Gallery)*
Royal Opera House *(Trust Dining Rms (x8, of which 4 interlink))*

8 Benares *(Private Rm)*
Hampshire Hotel *(Milton)*
London Capital Club *(Wren)*
The Milestone Hotel & Apartments *(Map Rm or Oratory)*
Monkey Island Hotel *(Temple)*
Notting Hill Brasserie *(Small Private Rm)*
Shumi *(Max*)*
The Stafford *(Panel Rm or Pink Rm)*
Threadneedles *(Traders)*

6 City Miyama *(Private Rm x2))*
Claridge's *(Chef's Table)*
The Savoy *(Sorcerer)*

5 The Academy *(Library)*
4 City Miyama *(Private Rm (x2))*
Mosimann's Belfry *(Davidoff Rm)*
2 Mosimann's Belfry *(Mont Blanc Rm)*

£M

5500	Alexandra Palace & Park *(Great Hall*)*
2500	Café Royal *(Max*)*
2350	Central Hall Westminster *(Max*)*
2200	Alexandra Palace & Park *(West Hall)*
2000	Battersea Park *(British Genius Site*)*
1500	Commonwealth Conference & Events Centre *(Comm Galleries*)*
1200	Ascot Racecourse *(Ascot Pavilion (subdivisible)*)*
	Ham Polo Club *(Marquee*)*
1100	London Metropole *(Monarch or King's Suite*)*
1046	Phoenix Theatre *(Max*)*
700	Lord's *(Nursery Pavilion*)*
660	The Brewery *(Porter Tun*)*
600	London Marriott *(Westminster Ballroom*)*
	London Metropole *(Palace Suite)*
550	Central Hall Westminster *(Great Hall)*
	Vinopolis – City of Wine *(Great Halls*)*
540	Café Royal *(Empire Napoleon)*
	The Decorium *(Max*)*
520	The Decorium *(Emperor Suite)*
500	Ascot Racecourse *(Royal Enclosure Suite)*
	Battersea Park *(Boules Area)*
	Britannia International Hotel *(Grand Suite*)*
	Central Hall Westminster *(Lecture Hall or Library)*
	Kensington Town Hall *(Great Hall*)*
	The Medieval Banquet *(Max*)*

PRIVATE VENUES | SEATED CAPACITY

	Pinewood Studios *(Max*)*
	Tower Thistle *(Tower Suite*)*
420	Waldorf Hotel *(Adelphi Suite & Palm Court*)*
400	The Brewery *(King George III)*
	Cabot Hall *(Hall*)*
	Café Royal *(Dubarry & Dauphin)*
	The Comedy Store *(Max*)*
	Epsom Downs *(Blue Riband Rm*)*
	Lord's *(Banqueting Suite)*
	Regent's College *(Gardens*)*
	Topsail Charters *(Waverly (Static)*)*
	The Tram Studios *(Studio 104*)*
	Twickenham Experience *(Invincibles or Rose Rm*)*
	Whipsnade Wild Animal Park *(Max*)*
375	Ealing Town Hall *(Victoria Hall*)*
350	The Coronet *(Max*)*
	Le Meridien Russell Hotel *(Warncliffe Suite*)*
	The Oval *(KBCC*)*
	Twickenham Experience *(Norm Try Line)*
	Vinopolis – City of Wine *(Mezzanine)*
330	Lloyd's of London *(Captain's Rm*)*
320	Twickenham Experience *(Spirit Of Rugby)*
300	Goodenough College *(Max*)*
	Hilton London Docklands *(London*)*
	The Hop Farm Country Park *(Dray Museum*)*
	Horniman Museum *(Exhibition Gallery*)*
	Langham Hilton *(Ballroom*)*
	Royal College of Music *(Concert Hall*)*
	Sound *(Restaurant & Bar*)*
	St Mary's Church *(Max*)*
	Sugar Reef *(Restaurant*)*
280	No 4 Hamilton Place *(Max*)*
270	Elstree Film Studio *(Restaurant*)*
	Holiday Inn London Regent's Park *(Max*)*
	Shakespeare's Globe *(Max*)*
	Simpsons-in-the-Strand *(Max*)*
260	Delfina Galleries *(Max*)*
	Ham Polo Club *(Club House)*
	Institute of Electrical Engineers *(Max*)*
	One Great George Street *(Great Hall*)*
255	The British Library *(Auditorium & Foyer*)*
250	291 Gallery *(Main Gallery*)*
	Alexandra Palace & Park *(Palace Restaurant)*
	Ascot Racecourse *(Paddock Balcony)*
	Bombay Brasserie *(Max*)*
	Bridges Wharf *(Max*)*
	The Camden Palace *(Main Auditorium*)*
	Central Hall Westminster *(Westminster)*
	Chartered Accountants' Hall *(Great Hall*)*
	Chelsea Physic Garden *(With Marquee (Sat in Jun-Sep only)*)*
	Delfina Galleries *(Exhibition Gallery)*
	Glaziers' Hall *(Hall*)*
	Hop Exchange *(Max*)*
	The Hop Farm Country Park *(Max)*
	London Metropole *(Windsor)*
	The Mayfair Club *(Satellite Bar & Cabaret*)*
	Museum of Garden History *(Max*)*
	No 4 Hamilton Place *(Lecture Theatre)*
	The Regalia *(Max*)*
	Ronnie Scotts *(Max*)*
	South London Gallery *(Inside And Marquee*)*
240	Café Royal *(Louis)*
	Churchill *(Chartwell Suite*)*
	Commonwealth Conference & Events Centre *(Exhibition Hall)*
	Hendon Hall Hotel *(Pembroke Suite*)*
	The Oval *(Banqueting Suite)*
	Royal National Theatre *(Lyttelton Exhibition Level*)*
220	Carpenters' Hall *(Livery Hall*)*
	Congress Centre *(Congress Hall*)*
	Ealing Town Hall *(Princes Hall)*
	RS Hispaniola *(Main Deck*)*
	The Hop Farm Country Park *(White Banqueting Suite)*
	Institute of Electrical Engineers *(Riverside Restaurant)*
	Royal Majestic Suite *(Ground Floor*)*
216	The Selfridge Hotel *(Selfridge Suite*)*
200	Adam Street *(Max*)*
	BAFTA *(David Lean Rm*)*
	Church House *(Max*)*

	Conrad Hotel *(Drake Suite* or Henley Suite)*
	Cottons Atrium *(Max*)*
	Denbies Wine Estate *(Garden Atrium Conservatory*)*
	Design Museum *(Collection Gallery*)*
	Epsom Downs *(Derby Suite)*
	Goodenough College *(Great Hall)*
	Hampton Court Palace (The Tiltyard*)*
	Hellenic Centre *(Great Hall*)*
	Hilton London Docklands *(Thames Suite)*
	Jolly Hotel St Ermins *(Max*)*
	Jongleurs at Camden Lock *(Jongleurs*)*
	Lord's *(Long Rm)*
	Nylon *(Max*)*
	Red Cube *(Max*)*
	Regent's College *(Refectory)*
	Sound *(Club Sound)*
	South London Gallery *(Inside)*
	St Paul's Cathedral *(Crypt*)*
	St Thomas' Hospital *(Shepherd Hall*)*
	Whipsnade Wild Animal Park *(Griffin Suite or Phoenix Suite)*
190	St Bartholomew's Hospital *(Great Hall*)*
186	The Decorium *(Caesar Suite)*
180	Bank of England Sports Club *(Restaurant*)*
	The Brewery *(Queen Charlotte)*
	Easthampstead Park Conference Centre *(Max*)*
	The Insurance Hall *(Max*)*
	Jolly Hotel St Ermins *(Ballroom)*
	Pacha *(Max*)*
	Painters' Hall *(Livery Hall*)*
	The Ramada Jarvis London West *(Ballroom*)*
	The Rembrandt Hotel *(Max*)*
	Winchester House *(River Lawn*)*
175	Wapping Food *(Max*)*
170	Bengal Clipper *(Max*)*
	Britannia International Hotel *(Royal Lounge)*
	Butchers' Hall *(Max*)*
168	Ironmongers' Hall *(Hall*)*
165	Butchers' Hall *(Great Hall)*
160	Amadeus Centre *(Upper Hall*)*
	Forty Hall *(Banqueting Suite)*
	The Insurance Hall *(Great Hall)*
	Museum in Docklands *(Chris Ellmers Gallery*)*
	Royal National Theatre *(Olivier Stalls Foyer)*
	The Rubens *(Old Masters Restaurant*)*
	Thistle Kensington Palace Hotel *(Duchess*)*
	White House Hotel *(Albany*)*
150	Belvedere *(Max*)*
	Bombay Brasserie *(Conservatory)*
	The Bonnington in Bloomsbury *(Derby Suite*)*
	The British Library *(Terrace Restaurant)*
	Browns *(Max*)*
	CC Club *(Max*)*
	Central Hall Westminster *(Assembly)*
	Church House *(Harvey Goodwin Suite)*
	The Cinnamon Club *(Max*)*
	Delfina Galleries *(Café Gallery)*
	East India Club *(Max*)*
	Fashion & Textile Museum *(Max*)*
	The Hatton *(Restaurant*)*
	Holiday Inn London Regent's Park *(Oxford)*
	Kingsway Hall *(Max*)*
	Lansdowne Club *(Ballroom*)*
	One Birdcage Walk *(Marble Hall*)*
	Pinewood Studios *(Ballroom)*
	TS Queen Mary *(Admirals Suite*)*
	Queen's Eyot *(Marquee*)*
	Red Cube *(Lounge Bar)*
	RUSI Building *(Lecture Theatre*)*
	Simpsons-in-the-Strand *(Regency Rm)*
	Singapura *(Main Rm*)*
	SS Great Britain *(Dining Saloon*)*
	Syon Park (Conservatory) *(Great Conservatory*)*
	Waterstone's Piccadilly *(Simpson's Rm*)*
	ZeNW3 *(Max*)*
147	Red Cube *(Restaurant)*
144	HMS Belfast *(Ship Co's Dining Hall*)*
	Churchill *(Chartwell I)*
	London Metropole *(Park Suite)*
140	76 Portland Place *(Catering Suite*)*

VISIT US AT: www.hardens.com

Bank Westminster (Max*)
Basil Street Hotel (Parrot Club*)
Bleeding Heart (Max*)
Dartmouth House (Max*)
Epsom Downs (Jockey Club Rm)
Frederick's (Max*)
The Grafton (Warren Suite*)
Greenwich Yacht Club (Function Rms*)
National Army Museum (Art Gallery* or Atrium)
The Royal Air Force Club (Ballroom*)
132 Ealing Town Hall (Queens Hall)
130 76 Portland Place (Max)
Aeonian (Dining Rm*)
Alexandra Palace & Park (Loneborough Rm)
Barber-Surgeons' Hall (Great Hall*)
Cavalry & Guards Club (Coffee Rm*)
Church House (Hoare Memorial Hall)
Mao Tai (Max*)
Royal Court Theatre (Main Restaurant*)
The Washington (Restaurant (Madisons)*)
Winchester House (Front Lawn)
125 City Conference Centre (Ocean Suite*)
Farmers' & Fletchers' Hall (Livery Hall*)
St Thomas' Hospital (Governors' Hall)
120 Café Royal (Dauphin)
The Chesterfield Mayfair (Royal Suite*)
The Cobden Club (Restaurant*)
Commonwealth Conference & Events
Centre (Gillette)
Eton College (Dorney Lake) (Main Rm*)
Glaziers' Hall (River Rm)
Greenwich Yacht Club (Club House)
Groucho Club (First Floor (entire)*)
ICA (Nash & Brandon Rms*)
Just The Bridge (Max*)
The Kenilworth (Bloomsbury Suite*)
Kew Bridge Steam Museum (Max*)
London Transport Museum (Lecture Theatre or Main Gallery*)
No 4 Hamilton Place (Argyll Rm & Hawker Rm)
The Old Sessions House (Westminster*)
Pissarro's on the River (Max*)
Royal National Theatre (Terrace Café)
Royal Society of Arts (Max*)
Singapura (Main Rm)
Six Hamilton Place (Red Rm*)
St Stephen's Club (Dining Rm*)
Staple Inn (Hall*)
Sway (Max*)
Tantra (Max*)
Theatre Royal, Drury Lane (Grand Saloon & Rotunda*)
Trinity House (Library*)
Winchester House (River Rm)
115 City Club (Main Dining Rm*)
110 The Cobden Club (Max)
Easthampstead Park Conference Centre (Downshire)
Royal National Theatre (Mezzanine)
100 1 Blossom Street (Max*)
The AOP Gallery (Max*)
Aquarium (Restaurant*)
Baltic (Max*)
Bar Bourse (Max*)
Bombay Brasserie (Main)
The Brewery (Sugar Rms)
The Broadgate Club (Rest*)
Browns (Courtroom 1)
Café Lazeez (Max*)
Café Royal (Derby & Queensbury)
The Cobden Club (The Grand Hall)
Commonwealth Conference & Events Centre (JBR)
Dartmouth House (Long Drawing Rm)
The Don (Max*)
Elstree Film Studio (Oscars Bar)
Glaziers' Hall (Library & Court Rm)
Goodenough College (Common Rm)
The Goring (Max*)
Jolly Hotel St Ermins (Balcony (With Balloon Only))
Ken Lo's Memories of China (Max*)
Kensington Town Hall (Small Hall)
Kingsway Hall (Keats & Milton Rms)

Langham Hilton (Portland Suite)
The London Canal Museum (1st Floor*)
London Wetland Centre (Waters Edge*)
The Mayfair Club (Living Rm Bar)
One Great George Street (Smeaton Rm)
Pinewood Studios (Green Rm)
Quilon (Max*)
Regent's College (Herringham Hall)
RICS (Lecture Hall*)
Royal Society of Arts (Benjamin Franklin Rm)
Royal Statistical Society (Lecture Theatre*)
Shaftesbury Theatre (Bars*)
Shakespeare's Globe (Café)
St John (Max*)
St John's Gate (Chapter Hall*)
Tallow Chandlers' Hall (Livery Hall*)
Thistle Victoria Hotel (Gallery Rm*)
Vanderbilt Hotel (Victoria & Albert Suite*)
Waterstone's Piccadilly (Red Rm)
97 Tallow Chandlers' Hall (Max)
96 The Selfridge Hotel (Cleaveland)
95 Simon Drake's House of Magic (Max*)
90 Devonport House (Nelson & Hamilton*)
Groucho Club (Soho Rm)
RS Hispaniola (Top Deck)
The Insurance Hall (Oftler Suite)
Pattersons's (Max*)
Syon Park (Conservatory) (Public Rms)
Vanderbilt Hotel (Cleo's)
Waxy O'Connors (Cottage Bar*)
White House Hotel (Chester)
85 291 Gallery (South Wing)
84 Cavalry & Guards Club (Peninsula Rm)
80 Bank of England Sports Club (Redgates Lodge)
Belvedere (Top level)
Boisdale (Max*)
The Bonnington in Bloomsbury (Jubilee)
Brasserie St Quentin (Max*)
Brewers' Hall (Livery Hall*)
Café Royal (Grill Rm)
Chartered Accountants' Hall (Restaurant)
Chelsea Physic Garden (Max)
Cheyne Walk Brasserie (Max*)
Church House (Bishop Partridge Hall)
Congress Centre (Council Chamber)
Dartmouth House (Ballroom)
The De Vere Cavendish St James's (Meeting Rm 1*)
Drones (Max*)
Elstree Film Studio (Marquee)
The Founders' Hall (Livery Hall*)
Fulham Palace (Drawing Rm or Great Hall*)
The Grafton (Grafton)
Guards Museum (Royal Gallery*)
Holiday Inn London Regent's Park (Cambridge)
Horniman Museum (Gallery Sq & Centenary Gallery or Victoria Conservatory)
The Kenilworth (Kenilworth Suite)
Kenwood House, Old Kitchen (Brew House* or Old Kitchen)
Launceston Place (Max*)
The Magic Circle (Devant Rm*)
The Mountbatten (Max*)
The New Cavendish Club (Jubilee Rm*)
One Great George Street (Brunel Rm or Council Rm)
Orangery (Holland Park) (Max*)
The Oval (Long Rm)
The Place (Café*)
TS Queen Mary (Captains Quarters)
The Rubens (Van Dyke)
RUSI Building (Duke of Wellington Rm)
Sound (Blue Rm)
Spring Grove House (Winter Garden Rm*)
St Andrew's Court House (Court Rm*)
Sugar Hut (Max*)
Twickenham Experience (England Rugby International's Club Rm)
Vinopolis – City of Wine (Wine Odyssey Rms)
The Westbury (Mount Vernon Rm*)
75 Ealing Town Hall (Nelson Rm)
Mayfair Conference Centre (Conservatory*)

Teca *(Max*)*
72 Brown's Hotel *(Clarendon*)*
The Selfridge Hotel *(Cheviot)*
Watermen's Hall *(Freemen's Rm*)*
70 115 at Hodgson's *(Max*)*
Avenue House *(Drawing Rm*)*
Bleeding Heart *(The Tavern)*
Bombay Bicycle Club *(Max*)*
The Bonnington in Bloomsbury *(York Rm)*
Britannia International Hotel *(Buckingham)*
Brown's Hotel *(Niagra & Roosevelt combined)*
Butchers' Hall *(Taurus Suite)*
Café du Jardin *(Downstairs*)*
Commonwealth Conference & Events
    Centre *(Bradley)*
Conrad Hotel *(Henley I)*
Dan's *(Max*)*
Doggetts Coat & Badge *(Wine Bar*)*
Epsom Downs *(Boardroom)*
Frederick's *(Garden Rm (Main Restaurant))*
Heights Bar & Restaurant *(Max*)*
Julie's Restaurant & Wine Bar *(Max*)*
The Old Sessions House *(Judges)*
One Birdcage Walk *(Courses Rm or
    Lower Dining Rm)*
Oxford & Cambridge Club *(Marlborough*)*
Pewterers' Hall *(Court Rm or Livery Rm*)*
Pinewood Studios *(Great Gatsby Rm)*
Royal Majestic Suite *(First Floor)*
Shakespeare's Globe *(Balcony Rm)*
Six-13 *(Max*)*
St Paul's Cathedral *(Conference Rm)*
Thistle Kensington Palace
    Hotel *(Marchioness)*
The Washington *(Richmond Suite)*
White House Hotel *(Osnaburgh)*
Wódka *(Max*)*
69 Avenue House *(Stephens Rm)*
65 Polygon Bar & Grill *(Max*)*
64 City Inn Westminster *(Private Dining*)*
60 Amadeus Centre *(Lower Hall)*
Athenaeum Hotel *(Macallan*)*
HMS Belfast *(Gun Rm)*
Belvedere *(Lower level)*
Browns *(Courtroom 2)*
Butchers' Hall *(Court Suite)*
Cabot Hall *(Sebastian Rm)*
Cactus Blue *(Mezzanine*)*
Café du Marché *(Upstairs*)*
Café Lazeez *(Downstairs)*
Chelsea Physic Garden *(Reception Rm)*
Cibo *(Max*)*
Conrad Hotel *(Aquasia)*
Cuba Libre *(Max*)*
Dartmouth House *(Restaurant)*
Doggetts Coat & Badge *(Doggetts Bar)*
Durrants Hotel *(Max*)*
Eddalino *(Max*)*
L'Escargot *(Barrel Vault Rm*)*
The Golden Hinde *(Max*)*
Horniman Museum *(Music Gallery)*
Institute of Electrical
    Engineers *(Maxwell Suite)*
The Insurance Hall *(New Rm)*
Ironmongers' Hall *(Drawing Rm)*
The Ivy *(Private Rm*)*
Jason's *(Max*)*
Jongleurs at Camden Lock *(Roof Terrace)*
Loungelover *(Max*)*
The Montcalm Hotel *(Maquis De Montcalm*)*
The Mountbatten *(Earl Suite)*
No 4 Hamilton Place *(Council Rm & Bar)*
The Old Sessions House *(Jailers Rm)*
One Birdcage Walk *(Council or Hinton Rm)*
Prenelle Gallery *(Main Gallery* or Outter Deck)*
Queen's Eyot *(Clubhouse)*
The Rembrandt
    Hotel *(Elizabeth & Victoria (Queen Suite))*
The Royal Air Force Club *(Presidents Rm)*
Royal Society of Arts *(Vault I)*
The Rubens *(Rembrandt Rm)*
RUSI Building *(Library)*
Six-13 *(Lower Ground Floor)*

Sound *(Sound Bar)*
Spring Grove House *(Banks Suite)*
Thistle Victoria Hotel *(Bessborough Rm)*
Trinity House *(Court Rm)*
The Union Club *(Dining Rm*)*
The Westbury *(Pine Rm)*
55 Adam Street *(Gallery)*
50 291 Gallery *(Restaurant)*
Alexandra Palace & Park *(Palm Court 5)*
Aquarium *(Bang Bar)*
Bank of England Sports Club *(Green Rm)*
Bentleys *(Max*)*
Bleeding Heart *(Private Rm)*
The Bonnington in Bloomsbury *(Derby)*
Bush Bar & Grill *(Private Dining Rm*)*
The Cadogan *(Max*)*
Café Lazeez *(Upstairs)*
CC Club *(Bar M)*
Chartered Accountants'
    Hall *(Main Reception Rm)*
Churchill *(Library or Marlborough Suite)*
The Cinnamon Club *(Private Dining Rm)*
City Club *(Garden Rm)*
Conrad Hotel *(Harbour)*
Dartmouth House *(Small Drawing Rm)*
The De Vere Cavendish St
    James's *(Meeting Rm 3)*
Denim *(Basement*)*
Devonport House *(Drake)*
The Don *(Restaurant)*
Durrants Hotel *(Edward VII Rm)*
Goolies *(Max*)*
The Goring *(Archive Rm)*
Groucho Club *(Gennaro Rm)*
Hellenic Centre *(Conference Rm)*
Holiday Inn London Regent's
    Park *(Trinity Suite)*
Holiday Inn – Mayfair *(Stratton Suite*)*
Ironmongers' Hall *(Court Rm or Luncheon Rm)*
The Lincoln Centre *(Break-out Area*)*
Lloyd's of London *(Conference Rm)*
London Palladium *(Cinderella Bar or Variety Bar*)*
Lonsdale *(Max*)*
Lord's *(Media Centre)*
The Magic Circle *(Club Rm)*
The Medieval Banquet *(Alcove)*
Le Meridien Russell Hotel *(Library)*
Museum in Docklands *(Thames Highway Gallery)*
National Army Museum *(Lecture Theatre)*
Neal's Lodge *(Max*)*
Phoenix Artist Club *(Dining Rm*)*
Regent's College *(Tuke Common Rm)*
The Rembrandt Hotel *(Elizabeth)*
Royal Statistical Society *(Basement)*
Simpsons-in-the-Strand *(Bishops' Rm)*
Singapura *(Max*)*
Spring Grove House *(Music Rm)*
SS Great Britain *(Hayward Saloon)*
Les Trois Garçons *(Max*)*
University Women's Club *(Drawing Rm or
    Library*)*
Vanderbilt Hotel *(Edwardian)*
Waterstone's Piccadilly *(Emberton Rm)*
Waxy O'Connors *(Restaurant)*
West Wycombe Caves *(Banqueting Hall*)*
48 Epsom Downs *(Coronation Cup)*
Kensington Place *(Private Rm*)*
Le Meridien Russell Hotel *(Ormond Suite)*
46 Dan's *(Restaurant)*
45 The Brewery *(City Cellars)*
Brinkley's *(Private Rm I*)*
Elstree Film Studio *(The White House)*
Julie's Restaurant & Wine Bar *(Gothic Rm)*
RSJ *(Private Rm (Basement)*)*
40 The Agency *(Main Bar*)*
Ascot Racecourse *(King Edward VII)*
Bank of England Sports Club *(Balcony Rm)*
Bank Westminster *(Private Rms (combined))*
Bleeding Heart *(Bistro (ground floor))*
The Bonnington in Bloomsbury *(Balmoral)*
Brown's Hotel *(Kipling, Niagara or Roosevelt)*
Browns *(Courtroom 3)*
Cabot Hall *(St Lawrence Rm)*

Cactus Blue *(Blue Room)*
Café du Marché *(Rendezvous)*
Chartered Institute of Public Finance
   & Accountancy *(Max*)*
City Club *(Salisbury Rm)*
Dan's *(Garden)*
Delfina Galleries *(Studio Gallery)*
Doggetts Coat & Badge *(Terrace Bar)*
The Don *(Bistro)*
Drones *(Private Rm)*
The Grafton *(Arlington Suite)*
Hendon Hall Hotel *(Garrick)*
Holiday Inn London Regent's
   Park *(Somerville)*
Jason's *(Restaurant)*
Jolly Hotel St Ermins *(Cameo)*
Langham Hilton *(Ambassador Rm or
   Regent/Welbeck Rms)*
Lansdowne Club *(Shelburne Rm)*
London Marriott *(Hamilton Rm)*
National Army Museum *(Templer Galleries)*
The New Cavendish Club *(Ante Rm)*
No 4 Hamilton Place *(Sopwith Rm)*
The Old Sessions House *(London Rm)*
PJ's Bar & Grill *(Max*)*
The Ramada Jarvis London
   West *(Park View Rm)*
Royal Statistical Society *(Council Chamber)*
RUSI Building *(Reading Rm)*
Staple Inn *(Council Chamber)*
Tower Thistle *(Raleigh or Spencer)*
Yming *(Max*)*

38 Loungelover *(Rustic Area)*
    National Army Museum *(Council Chamber)*
37 Lindsay House *(Max*)*
    Watermen's Hall *(Court Rm)*
36 The Cadogan *(Langtry Dining)*
    Easthampstead Park Conference
       Centre *(Harwich)*
    Epsom Downs *(Double Boxes)*
    Le Meridien Russell Hotel *(Bedford Suite)*
    The Selfridge Hotel *(Cotswold)*
35 Groucho Club *(New Rm)*
    Jamies Pavilion *(Wine Bar*)*
    The Mayfair Club *(VIP Rm)*
    Painters' Hall *(Court Rm)*
    Scotch Malt Whisky Society *(Members' Rm*)*
34 Chartered Institute of Public Finance
       & Accountancy *(Council Chamber)*
    Julie's Restaurant & Wine Bar *(Garden Rm)*
32 Carpenters' Hall *(Luncheon Rm)*
    City Conference Centre *(Council Rm)*
    Coopers' Hall *(Max*)*
    Frederick's *(Clarence Rm)*
    Niksons *(Max*)*
    Shepherd's *(Private Rm*)*
    St Stephen's Club *(Garden Rm)*
    Wódka *(Private Rm)*
30 115 at Hodgson's *(Mezzanine)*
    76 Portland Place *(Herschel)*
    Avenue House *(Dining Rm or Salon)*
    Baltic *(Private Dining Rm)*
    Basil Street Hotel *(Basil Rm)*
    Bloomsbury Square Training
       Centre *(Cellars Restaurant*)*
    The Bonnington in Bloomsbury *(Jack Frame)*
    The Chesterfield Mayfair *(Conservatory)*
    Churchill *(Randolph)*
    The Cinnamon Club *(Mezzanine)*
    Le Colombier *(Private Rm*)*
    Commonwealth Conference & Events
       Centre *(Tweedsmuir)*
    Curwen Gallery *(Max*)*
    Dan's *(Conservatory)*
    Denim *(Mezz)*
    Easthampstead Park Conference
       Centre *(Windsor)*
    L'Escargot *(Private Rm)*
    Freud Museum *(House*)*
    The Guinea Grill *(Boardroom*)*
    Hendon Hall Hotel *(Johnson or Sheridan)*
    Institute of Electrical Engineers *(Common Rm)*
    Jolly Hotel St Ermins *(York or Clarence)*

Launceston Place *(Private Area)*
London Palladium *(VIP Rm)*
London Wetland Centre *(Bird Hide or
   Observatory)*
Odette's *(Conservatory*)*
The Old Sessions House *(Justices or
   Recorder Rm)*
One Great George
   Street *(Stephenson Rm & President's Dining Rm)*
Pattersons's *(Function Rm)*
The Place *(Founders Studio)*
The Rembrandt Hotel *(Princes)*
Royal National Theatre *(Ashcroft)*
Royal Society of Arts *(Folkestone Rm or
   Tavern Rm)*
The Rubens *(Rubens)*
Sheraton Belgravia *(Restaurant*)*
Singapura *(Large Mezzanine)*
Soho House *(Dining Rm*)*
Le Suquet *(Private Rm 1*)*
Sweetings *(Max*)*
Tallow Chandlers' Hall *(Parlour)*
Theatre Royal, Drury Lane *(Boardroom)*
Tower Thistle *(Mortimer Suite)*
Waldorf Hotel *(Executive Boardroom)*
The Washington *(Richmond 1 (Winchester))*
Waxy O'Connors *(Mezzanine)*
The Westbury *(Brighton Rm)*
Whipsnade Wild Animal Park *(Unicorn)*

28 Boisdale *(Back Bar)*
    Chartered Accountants' Hall *(Members' Rm)*
    Mao Tai *(Private Rm)*
    Mon Plaisir *(Private Rm*)*
26 1 Blossom Street *(Grand Salon)*
    The Berkshire *(Sonning Suite*)*
    St Thomas' Hospital *(Consultant's Dining Rm)*
25 Busabong Too *(Mezzanine*)*
    Easthampstead Park Conference
       Centre *(Tawney or Wylie)*
    Elstree Film Studio *(Board/Green Rm)*
    Eton College (Dorney Lake) *(Clubroom)*
    The Founders' Hall *(Parlour)*
    The Hop Farm Country Park *(Roundels)*
    Jamies Pavilion *(Restaurant)*
    Ken Lo's Memories of
       China *(Private Rms (combined))*
    London Marriott *(John Adams Suite)*
    The Selfridge Hotel *(Chitten)*
    Wapping Food *(Private Rm)*
    The Washington *(Richmond 2 (Fairfax))*
    ZeNW3 *(Private Rm)*
24 Atrium *(Private Rm*)*
    Belvedere *(Mezzanine)*
    Chartered Institute of Public Finance
       & Accountancy *(Committee Rm 4)*
    Doggetts Coat & Badge *(Boardroom)*
    The Don *(Private Rm)*
    Durrants Hotel *(Oak Rm)*
    Elena's L'Etoile *(Private Rm*)*
    Gay Hussar *(First Floor*)*
    Hilton London Docklands *(Copenhagen)*
    Julie's Restaurant & Wine Bar *(Banqueting Rm)*
    RICS *(Gloucester)*
    RSJ *(Private Rm (Ground Floor))*
    Rules *(Green Rm*)*
    Scotch Malt Whisky Society *(Still Rm)*
    St Thomas' Hospital *(Grand Committee Rm)*
23 The Insurance Hall *(Council Chamber)*
22 Boisdale *(Jacobite Rm)*
    Bombay Bicycle Club *(Private Rm)*
    Britannia International Hotel *(Balmoral,
       Blenheim or Queens)*
    Sheraton Belgravia *(Max)*
    Syon Park (Conservatory) *(Priate Dining Rm)*
    Warren House *(Meeting Rm 3*)*
20 115 at Hodgson's *(CWB Private Rm)*
    Bank Westminster *(Private Rms (x2))*
    HMS Belfast *(Admiral's Quarters)*
    Brewers' Hall *(Court Rm)*
    Brinkley's *(Private Rm 2 or Private Rm 3)*
    Britannia International Hotel *(Beaufort)*
    The Broadgate Club *(Private Dining)*
    Brown's Hotel *(Lord Byron)*
    Church House *(Westminster)*

VISIT US AT: www.hardens.com

City Conference Centre (Arctic or Indian)
The De Vere Cavendish St
  James's (Meeting Rm 4 or Meeting Rm 5)
The Decorium (Ante Suite)
Devonport House (Collingwood)
The Geological Society of
  London (Council Rm*)
Holiday Inn – Mayair (Presidential Suite)
Horniman Museum (Performance Space)
Lansdowne Club (Findlay Rm)
Leven is Strijd (Max*)
Lindsay House (Private Rm)
Lonsdale (Genevieve (upstairs))
Loungelover (Red Area)
The Mountbatten (Viceroy)
Poissonnerie de l'Avenue (Bar or Private Rm*)
The Royal Air Force Club (Drawing Rm or
  Mezzanine Suite)
The Selfridge Hotel (Drawing Rm)
Six-13 (Private Rm)
Spring Grove House (Board Rm)
St Andrew's Court House (Archive Rm)
Sugar Reef (Private Dining Rm)
Tantra (Private Dining Rm)
Thistle Kensington Palace Hotel (Countess or
  Princess)
Thistle Victoria Hotel (Warwick Rm)
Tower Thistle (Beaufort)
Trinity House (Luncheon Rm)
The Westbury (Regency Rm)

18 Brasserie St Quentin (Private Rm)
The Cadogan (Langtry Sitting)
Cavalry & Guards Club (Waterloo Rm)
Chartered Accountants'
  Hall (Small Reception Rm)
The Cobden Club (Private Rm)
E&O (Max*)
Farmers' & Fletchers' Hall (Court Rm)
Frederick's (Sussex Rm)
Groucho Club (Mackintosh)
Hamilton House (Max*)
Oxford & Cambridge Club (Edward VII)
Rules (King Edward VII Rm)
Sheraton Belgravia (Study and Library)
St Bartholomew's
  Hospital (Henry VIII Committee Rm or Treasurer's Rm)
St John (Private Rm)

17 The Rubens (Library)

16 The Agency (Conference Rm)
Balham Bar & Kitchen (Max*)
The Chesterfield Mayfair (Library)
Chez Bruce (Private Rm*)
Cibo (Private Rm)
Elena's L'Etoile (Private Rm (x2))
Imperial City (Private Vault*)
Julie's Restaurant & Wine Bar (Conservatory)
The Montcalm Hotel (Montagu Suite or
  Portman Suite)
Royal Statistical Society (New Meeting Rm)
Rules (Charles Dickens Rm)
Scotch Malt Whisky Society (Tasting Rm)
Le Suquet (Private Rm 2)
Thistle Victoria Hotel (Belgrave)
Waterstone's Piccadilly (Boardroom)
Winchester House (Turner Rm)

15 The London Canal Museum (Private Rm)
London Marriott (Grosvenor Suite)
Spring Grove House (Captain Cook's Rm)
St John's Gate (Council Chamber)
St Paul's Cathedral (Beehive)
Thistle Kensington Palace Hotel (Baroness)

14 Bentleys (Private Rm)
Browns (Private Rm)
Butchers' Hall (Committee Rm)
City Club (Masterman/Wellington Rms)
Eight Over Eight (Max*)
Electric Brasserie (& Electric House
  Club) (Playroom*)
The Founders' Hall (Masters & Clerks)
Launceston Place (Private Rm)
Lindsay House (Private Rm)
Painters' Hall (Painted Chamber)

The Ramada Jarvis London
  West (Park Mews)
Royal National Theatre (Richardson Rm)
Royal Statistical Society (Old Meeting Rm)
St Bartholomew's Hospital (Peggy Turner Rm)
Warren House (Meeting Rm 2)

12 1 Blossom Street (Garden Salon)
76 Portland Place (Faraday Rm)
Athenaeum Hotel (Ardmore or Bowmore)
Atrium (Private Rm)
Barber-Surgeons' Hall (Court Rm)
The Berkshire (Sandhurst Suite)
Cabot Hall (Cape Breton Rm or Newfoundland Rm)
Chartered Institute of Public Finance
  & Accountancy (Committee Rm 5)
Cibo (Private Rm)
City Inn Westminster (Sky Lounge)
Dan's (Private Rm)
Devonport House (Churchill)
Durrants Hotel (Armfield Rm)
Gay Hussar (Second Floor)
The Geological Society of
  London (Arthur Homes Rm)
The Goring (Drawing Rm)
The Grafton (Torrington)
Holiday Inn – Mayair (Buckingham or Burlington)
Julie's Restaurant & Wine Bar (Moroccan Rm)
Ken Lo's Memories of China (Private Rm (x2))
Kingsway Hall (Chaucer)
Lansdowne Club (Sun Rm)
The New Cavendish Club (Library)
Pomegranates (Private Rm*)
Singapura (Private Rm)
Spring Grove House (Directors Rm)
St John's Gate (Prior's Dining Rm)
Thistle Victoria Hotel (Wilton Rm)
Vanderbilt Hotel (Vanderbilt)

11 The New Cavendish Club (Boardroom)

10 Adam Street (Private Rm)
Alexandra Palace & Park (Palm Court 1)
Browns (Courtroom 4 or Private Rm)
Church House (Jubilee)
City Club (Hardwick Rm)
City Conference Centre (Committee Rm)
The De Vere Cavendish St
  James's (Meeting Rm 2)
Electric Brasserie (& Electric House
  Club) (Study)
Epsom Downs (Single Boxes)
Holiday Inn London Regent's Park (Churchill
  or Pembroke Suite)
Julie's Restaurant & Wine Bar (The Gallery)
Odette's (Private Rm)
The Rembrandt Hotel (Victoria)
The Selfridge Hotel (Conservatory)
Trinity House (Reading Rm)
Les Trois Garçons (Private Rm)
The Wells (Max*)
Whipsnade Wild Animal Park (Pegasus)

8 Athenaeum Hotel (Richmond Suite)
Browns (Private Rm)
Butchers' Hall (Library)
Cavalry & Guards Club (Double Bridle Rm)
The Chesterfield Mayfair (Stanhope Suite)
The Goring (Breakfast Rm)
The Insurance Hall (President's Rm)
The Royal Air Force Club (Boardroom)
Sheraton Belgravia (Meeting Rm or Study)
Singapura (Small Mezzanine)
Tatsuso (Western*)
Thistle Victoria Hotel (Hanover)
Warren House (Meeting Rm 4)

6 1 Blossom Street (Red Rm (no smoking))
Athenaeum Hotel (Apartments)
Brewers' Hall (Committee Rm)
Butchers' Hall (George Adams)
Tatsuso (Tatami Rm)
Tower Thistle (Lewin)
Warren House (Library)

4 Browns (Private Rm)

£B-M

2500 Honourable Artillery Co *(Marquee*)*
1500 Crystal Palace Park *(Max*)*
1000 The Chainstore *(Max*)*
850 Harrow School *(Shepherd Churchill Hall*)*
800 Equinox at the Empire *(Max*)*
      Royal Horticultural Halls *(Lawrence Hall*)*
700 New World *(Max*)*
600 Blackheath Concert Halls *(Great Hall*)*
530 New Connaught Rms *(Grand Hall & Balmoral*)*
500 Imperial China *(Max*)*
450 The London Hippodrome *(Auditorium*)*
      Porchester Centre *(Ballroom*)*
      Royal College of Art *(Max*)*
      Royal Horticultural Halls *(Lindley Hall)*
420 Imperial College *(Main Dining Hall*)*
400 BAC *(Grand Hall*)*
      Hammersmith Town Hall *(Assembly Hall*)*
      Regency Banqueting Suite *(Main Banquet Rm*)*
      Riverside Studios *(Studios 1 & 2*)*
      Royal College of Art *(Henry Moore Gallery)*
      Stoke Newington Town Hall *(Assembly Rm*)*
      Thames Luxury Charters – moving
        venue *(Dixie Queen*)*
      White Hart Lane Conference
        Centre *(Whites Suite*)*
      Whitechapel Art Gallery *(Lower Gallery*)*
350 The Bridge SE1 *(Rm 1*)*
      Dulwich
        College *(Christison Hall and Upper Dining Rms*)*
320 Shillibeer's *(Max*)*
300 Break For The Border *(Max*)*
      Cecil Sharp House *(Kennedy Hall*)*
      Duke of York's HQ *(Max*)*
      Egg *(Max*)*
      Highgate School *(School Dining Hall*)*
270 Honourable Artillery Co *(Albert Rm)*
250 Academy of Live & Recorded
        Arts *(Great Hall*)*
      City University *(Max*)*
      Fulham Town Hall *(Grand Hall*)*
      Le Gothique *(Max*)*
      King's College, King's Cuisine
        Restaurant *(Max*)*
      Mall Galleries *(Main Gallery*)*
      New Connaught Rms *(Edinburgh)*
      Stratford Old Town Hall *(Main Hall*)*
      Victory Services Club *(Max*)*
240 Texas Embassy Cantina *(Max*)*
230 New Connaught Rms *(Balmoral)*
      Royal Geographical Society *(Max*)*
220 Fifteen05 *(Max*)*
      Union Chapel *(Studio Theatre*)*
      Victory Services Club *(Carisbrooke Hall)*
200 Archduke Wine Bar *(Max*)*
      The Bridge SE1 *(Rm 2)*
      Caper Green *(including Garden*)*
      Dulwich College *(Great Hall)*
      Fabric *(Max*)*
      New World *(Private Rm)*
      PizzaExpress *(Max*)*
      HMS President *(Ballroom*)*
      Royal College of Art *(Gulbenkian Upper Gallery)*
      Royal Green Jackets *(Hall*)*
      Royal Holloway College *(Founder's Dining Hall*)*
      Royal Over-Seas
        League *(Hall of India & Pakistan*)*
      Trafalgar Tavern *(Nelson Suite*)*
      Whitechapel Art Gallery *(Upper Gallery)*
      Whitelands College *(Ruskin Dining Hall*)*
      The Worx *(Max*)*
192 Conway Hall *(Large Hall*)*
184 City University *(Level Six Suite)*
180 Chelsea Old Town Hall *(Main Hall*)*
      King's College School *(Great Hall*)*
      Kingswood House *(Golden Rm, Jacobean Rm*)*
      London Scottish *(Hall*)*
      Thames Luxury Charters – moving
        venue *(Elizabethan)*
175 The London Hippodrome *(Balcony – Restaurant)*
172 Honourable Artillery Co *(Long Rm)*

160 Abbaye *(Max*)*
      The Clink *(Max*)*
      Dickens Inn *(Nickleby Suite*)*
      Highgate School *(Big School)*
      The Irish Centre *(Hall*)*
      The Music Room *(Exhibition Hall*)*
      Trailfinders Sports Club *(Pavilion Hall*)*
      Westminster Boating Base *(Max*)*
      White Hart Lane Conference
        Centre *(Box Norm)*
150 The Anchor *(Max*)*
      The Artworkers Guild *(Max*)*
      Bankside Restaurant *(Max*)*
      The Chelsea Gardener *(Max*)*
      Docklands Sailing & Watersports
        Centre *(Function Rm*)*
      Fifteen05 *(Great Hall)*
      Fulham House *(Concert Hall)*
      George Inn *(Max*)*
      Le Gothique *(Patio)*
      Mermaid Theatre *(Blackfriars Rm*)*
      New Connaught Rms *(York)*
      Queen Mary Garden *(Rose Garden Restaurant*)*
      Riverside Studios *(Studio 3)*
      School of Pharmacy *(Refectory*)*
      St Martin In The Fields *(Max*)*
      The Villiers Theatre *(Max*)*
      Will's Art Warehouse *(Max*)*
      William IV *(Max*)*
      The Worx *(Studio 2)*
140 Balls Brothers *(Banqueting Suite*)*
      Egg *(Courtyard)*
      Fulham House *(Main Hall*)*
      King's College *(Great Hall*)*
      Strand Palace Hotel *(Exeter Suite*)*
135 606 Club *(Max*)*
      Depot *(Max*)*
130 Bar M *(River Rm*)*
      Da Mario *(Max*)*
      Polish Club *(Ballroom*)*
      Royal Geographical Society *(Education Centre)*
      St Paul's Church *(Church Rm*)*
125 Abbaye *(Basement Restaurant)*
120 20th Century Theatre *(Max*)*
      BAC *(Lower Hall)*
      Bishopsgate Institute *(Max*)*
      Footstool *(Max*)*
      Guy's Hospital *(Robens Suite*)*
      Levant *(Max*)*
      PizzaExpress *(Max)*
      Polish Club *(Restaurant)*
      Regency Banqueting Suite *(Amber Rm)*
      Riverside Studios *(Café-Bar)*
      Royal Holloway College *(Picture Gallery)*
      Texas Embassy Cantina *(Upstairs)*
      University of Westminster *(Deep End*)*
110 Home *(Ground Floor Restaurant*)*
      Souk *(Max*)*
105 Dolphin Square Hotel *(Restaurant*)*
104 The Villiers Theatre *(Lower Supper Rm/Bar)*
100 Bar M *(Bar M)*
      The Battersea Barge Bistro *(Max*)*
      Beach Blanket Babylon *(Max*)*
      Blackheath Concert Halls *(Recital Rm)*
      Brompton Oratory – St Wilfrid's
        Hall *(St Wilfrid's Hall and Billiards Rm*)*
      The Candid Arts Trust *(Basement Gallery or
        Ground Floor Gallery*)*
      Caper Green *(inside only)*
      Cecil Sharp House *(Trefusis Hall)*
      Chelsea Old Town Hall *(Small Hall)*
      Crazy Larry's *(Max*)*
      Egg *(Ground Floor or Middle Floor)*
      Froebel College *(Portrait Rm*)*
      The Langley *(Max*)*
      Lauderdale House *(Max*)*
      The Little Ship Club *(Dining Rm*)*
      London School of Economics *(Max*)*
      The Mary Sumner House *(Conference Hall*)*
      Pizza On The Park *(Max*)*
      Riverside Studios *(Terrace)*
      Royal Geographical Society *(Main Hall)*
      Throgmorton's *(Oak Rm*)*

White Hart Lane Conference
    Centre *(Oak Rm)*
William IV *(Garden)*
The Worx *(Studio 1)*
90 Academy of Live & Recorded
    Arts *(Le Gothique)*
The Coliseum *(Dutch Bar*)*
Dulwich College *(Lower Hall)*
Royal Institution of Great
    Britain *(Main Library*)*
Victory Services Club *(El Alamein Rm)*
86 Harrow School *(Shepherd Churchill Rm)*
80 The Bridge SE1 *(Rm 3)*
Canning House *(Drawing Rm*)*
The Coliseum *(Terrace Bar)*
Greenwich Playhouse *(Bar*)*
Gunnersbury Park *(Orangery*)*
Hammersmith Town Hall *(Small Hall)*
Hoxton Hall *(Theatre* or Whole Ground Floor)*
Kingswood House *(Charles Suite)*
Maidenhead Steam Navigation – moving
    venue *(Georgian*)*
Photographers' Gallery *(Max*)*
The Place Below *(Max*)*
Royal College of Art *(Gulbenkian Lower Gallery or*
    Senior Common Rm Dining Rm)
Royal Over-Seas League *(St Andrew's Hall)*
Southwark Cathedral *(Restaurant*)*
St Botolph's Hall *(Upper Hall*)*
St Peter's Hall *(Upper Hall*)*
The Station *(Private Rm*)*
Stratford Old Town Hall *(Council Chamber)*
Surrey Docks Watersports
    Centre *(Quay Rm/Quay Lounge*)*
University of Westminster *(Fyvie Hall)*
Whitewebbs Museum of Transport *(Max*)*
77 Bakers' Hall *(Livery Hall*)*
76 PizzaExpress *(Section)*
75 Bakers' Hall *(Max)*
Dulwich College *(Pavilion Salle)*
Mall Galleries *(East Gallery)*
74 Mela *(Ground Floor*)*
72 Duke of York's HQ *(London Irish Mess)*
70 Bankside Gallery *(Max*)*
The Cross Keys *(Conservatory*)*
Docklands Sailing & Watersports
    Centre *(Bar)*
Dolphin Square Hotel *(Chichester)*
Embargo *(Max*)*
London School of
    Economics *(Senior Dining Rm)*
PizzaExpress *(Upstairs)*
HMS President *(Wardroom)*
St Martin In The Fields *(Gallery)*
The Station *(Conservatory)*
Thames Luxury Charters – moving
    venue *(Golden Salamander)*
Victory Services Club *(Trafalgar Rm)*
William IV *(Restaurant)*
66 Imperial College *(Council Rm)*
60 Abbaye *(Wine Bar)*
Apartment 195 *(Lounge*)*
Arts Theatre *(Restaurant*)*
Froebel College *(Terrace Rm)*
Gunnersbury Park *(Terrace Rm)*
The House of St Barnabas-in-
    Soho *(Council Rm*)*
Latchmere Theatre *(Max*)*
Maidenhead Steam Navigation – moving
    venue *(Southern Comfort)*
Mermaid Theatre *(River Rm)*
PizzaExpress *(Private Rm)*
Royal Geographical Society *(New Map Rm)*
Southwark Cathedral *(Library)*
St Paul's Church *(Blue Lounge)*
Thames Luxury Charters – moving
    venue *(Edwardian)*
Whitechapel Art Gallery *(Café)*
56 Strand Palace Hotel *(Essex Suite or Grenville Suite)*
55 Aragon House *(Max*)*
George Inn *(George)*
PizzaExpress *(Section or Upstairs)*
Shillibeer's *(Private Rm)*

50 20th Century Theatre *(Reception Rm)*
The Anchor *(Upper Chart Rm)*
Blackheath Concert Halls *(Café Bar)*
Bow Wine Vaults *(Restaurant*)*
The Bridge SE1 *(Rm4)*
Burgh House *(Music Rm*)*
The Conservatory *(Max*)*
Equinox at the Empire *(Empire Lounge)*
Imperial China *(Private Rm)*
Institut Français *(Library*)*
The London Hippodrome *(Private Function Rm)*
Mall Galleries *(North Gallery)*
The Music Room *(Gallery)*
New Connaught Rms *(Durham)*
PizzaExpress *(Section)*
Queen Mary Garden *(Prince Regent Rm)*
St Peter's Hall *(Café)*
Streatham Ice Arena *(Function Rm*)*
Tuttons *(Max*)*
The White House *(Max*)*
48 Strand Palace Hotel *(Drake Suite)*
The Villiers Theatre *(Mezzanine Supper Rm)*
46 Honourable Artillery Co *(Queen's Rm)*
45 Beach Blanket Babylon *(Restaurant)*
Floating Boater – moving
    venue *(Prince Regent*)*
Greenwich Theatre *(Bar*)*
PizzaExpress *(Upstairs)*
Wine Gallery *(Private Rm*)*
40 Le Bistrot de L'Institut Français *(Max*)*
Bonchurch Brasserie *(Private Rm*)*
Conway Hall *(Small Hall)*
The Cross Keys *(First Floor Gallery)*
Fifteen05 *(Gallery of City Bar)*
Guy's Hospital *(Court Rm)*
Highgate School *(Undercroft)*
Hoxton Square Bar & Kitchen *(Private Room*)*
Imperial College *(Dining Rm (170 Queensgate))*
King's College School *(Boathouse or Dalziel Rm)*
Lemonia *(Private Rm*)*
The Little Ship Club *(Library)*
The Mary Sumner House *(Max)*
Mr Kong *(Private Basement*)*
New Connaught Rms *(Penthouse)*
Paxton's Head *(Pan-Asian Canteen*)*
PizzaExpress *(Private Rm or Private Rm)*
Poetry Society *(Restaurant & Basement*)*
HMS President *(Embankment Bar)*
Royal Geographical Society *(Tea Rm)*
Royal Over-Seas League *(Wrench)*
Stratford Old Town Hall *(Conference Rm)*
The Sun *(Max*)*
Trafalgar Tavern *(Trafalgar Club)*
William IV *(Function Rm)*
36 Jason's Trip – moving venue *(Lady Rose*)*
35 Beach Blanket Babylon *(Chapel)*
Gunnersbury Park *(Temple)*
The Lady Daphne – moving venue *(Afloat or*
    Stationary*)
PizzaExpress *(Downstairs or Section)*
Royal Institution of Great
    Britain *(Conversation Rm)*
34 Foxtrot Oscar *(Max*)*
George Inn *(Talbot)*
Mela *(Private Rm (downstairs))*
The Vale *(Private Rm*)*
32 Royal Over-Seas League *(Mountbatten Rutland)*
30 The Anchor *(Lower Chart Rm)*
Archduke Wine Bar *(Bridge Rm)*
Bow Wine Vaults *(Bistrot)*
Chez Gérard, Dover Street *(Mezzanine*)*
Engineer *(Large Rm*)*
Frocks *(Basement*)*
Fulham House *(Dining Rm)*
Institut Français *(Salon de Réception)*
London Scottish *(Queen Elizabeth Rm)*
PizzaExpress *(Private Rm, Private Rm or Section)*
Polish Club *(Terrace)*
Rocket *(Private Rm*)*
St Peter's Hall *(North Hall)*
Tuttons *(Larger Room)*
The Worx *(Studio 4)*
29 The Candid Arts Trust *(Banquet Rm)*

28 Jason's Trip – moving venue (Lace Plate)
Maidenhead Steam Navigation – moving
venue (Belle or Pink Champagne)
The White House (Private Rm)
25 The Antelope (Max*)
Cecil Sharp House (Storrow Hall)
Chez Gérard, Dover Street (Max)
Coopers Arms (Private Rm*)
Dr Johnsons' House (Max*)
Fox & Anchor (Private Rm*)
The Mary Sumner House (Mary Sumner Rm)
PizzaExpress (Section)
24 Docklands Sailing & Watersports
Centre (Teaching Rm)
Dolphin Square Hotel (Anson)
Royal Geographical Society (Council Rm)
22 The Anchor (Shakespeare Rm)
Bakers' Hall (Court Rm)
City University (Tait Meeting Rms)
Floating Boater – moving venue (Lapwing)
20 Archduke Wine Bar (Conservatory)
Boudin Blanc (Private Rm*)
Burgh House (Library)
The Coliseum (Chairman's)
The House of St Barnabas-in-
Soho (Withdrawing Rm)
Imperial China (Private Rms (x2))
London School of
Economics (Senior Common Rm)
London Scottish (Officers' Mess)
Royal Institution of Great
Britain (Council Rm)
Ship (Max*)
Southwark Cathedral (Seminar Rm)
St Paul's Church (Portman Rm)
Tuttons (Smaller Vault)
Wine Gallery (Private Rm (x2))
18 Engineer (Mirror Rm)
16 Ikkyu (Tatami Rm*)
PizzaExpress (Upstairs)
Royal Over-Seas League (Bennet-Clark)
15 Apartment 195 (Cellar)
Chez Gérard, Dover Street (Private Rm)
The Dickens' House Museum (Max*)
14 Bakers' Hall (Ante Rm)
Boudin Blanc (Private Rm)
The Coliseum (Stoll Rm)
The Little Ship Club (Claude Worth Rm)
The Little Square (Max*)
The Vale (Private Rm)
12 Guy's Hospital (Emily MacManus Hse or Lounge)
Maidenhead Steam Navigation – moving
venue (Fringilla)
The Mary Sumner House (Syndicate Rm)
11 Royal Over-Seas League (Park)
10 The House of St Barnabas-in-
Soho (Records Rm)
Rocket (Private Rm)
The Worx (Studio 3)
8 The Coliseum (Arlen Rm)
The Little Ship Club (Chart Rm)
The White House (Private Rm)

£B

900 The Ministry of Sound (Max*)
520 Wandsworth Civic Suite (Civic Suite*)
400 Chuen Cheng Ku (Max*)
300 Brockwell Lido (Marquee Site*)
280 Wandsworth Civic Suite (Civic Hall)
240 Wandsworth Civic Suite (Banqueting Hall)
220 Park Crescent Conference
Centre (Theatre*)
Philbeach Hall (Max*)
200 Bangers (see Davy's) (Max*)
The Ministry of Sound (Box)
Polish Social & Cultural
Association (Malinova Rm)
Queen Mary College (The Octagon* or
The Old Library)
Turnmills (Juno Lucina*)

Westminster Cathedral Hall (Max*)
180 Chuen Cheng Ku (Rm 1)
Queen Mary Students' Union (Drapers Arms*)
160 The Ministry of Sound (Main Bar)
150 City Pipe (see Davy's) (Max*)
The London Welsh Centre (Main Hall*)
The Ministry of Sound (Balcony Bar)
Polish Social & Cultural
Association (Lowiczanka Restaurant)
Queen Mary College (The Gallery)
Spaghetti House (Max*)
Wessex House (Max*)
140 Queen Mary College (Bar Med)
120 Africa Centre (Main Hall*)
City Flogger (see Davy's) (Max*)
Colonel Jaspers (see Davy's) (Max*)
Crown Passage Vaults (see Davy's) (Max*)
Ochre (Max*)
St Etheldreda's Crypt (Max*)
100 Balls Brothers (Max)
Borscht & Tears (Max*)
Brockwell Lido (Café-restaurant)
Chopper Lump (see Davy's) (Max*)
Chuen Cheng Ku (Rm 2)
Cittie of Yorke (Main Bar*)
Colonel Jaspers (see Davy's) (Max)
Corney & Barrow (Max*)
Davy's of Creed Lane (see Davy's) (Max*)
Habit (see Davy's) (Max*)
Hop Cellars (Max*)
Leadenhall Wine Bar (Max*)
Lees Bag (see Davy's) (Max*)
London Rowing Club (Max*)
Pulpit (see Davy's) (Max*)
Skinkers (see Davy's) (Max*)
St Bride Foundation Institute (Bridewell Hall*)
University of London Union (Rm 101*)
Vineyard (see Davy's) (Max*)
Walkers of St James's (Max*)
90 Balls Brothers (Max)
Corney & Barrow (Max, Max or Max)
Gow's Restaurant (Max*)
Hop Cellars (Porter Rm)
Kettners (Max*)
85 City Boot (see Davy's) (Max*)
80 Bishop of Norwich (see Davy's) (Max*)
Chatham Hall (Max*)
Chiv (see Davy's) (Max*)
Corney & Barrow (Max or Max)
Crown & Greyhound (Private Rm (large)*)
Earlsfield Library (Max*)
The October Gallery (Main Gallery*)
Park Crescent Conference
Centre (Portland Rm)
Patio (Max*)
Rock Garden (Piazza Seating Restaurant*)
Truckles Of Pied Bull Yard (see
Davy's) (Max*)
Turnmills (Café Gaudi or Las Brassas)
75 Jackson's Lane Community
Centre (Dance Studio*)
Tapster (see Davy's) (Max*)
Vats (Max*)
74 Simpsons Tavern (Restaurant*)
70 Corney & Barrow (Max)
Heeltap & Bumper (see Davy's) (Max*)
The Lamb Tavern (Dining Rm*)
Park Crescent Conference Centre (Bistro)
The Pump House Gallery (Max*)
65 Cittie of Yorke (Cellar Bar)
Dock Blida (see Davy's) (Max*)
The Mug House (see Davy's) (Max*)
The White Horse (Winter Marquee*)
60 Alma (Max*)
Balls Brothers (Weekday function or
Weekday function)
Bangers Too (see Davy's) (Max*)
Chuen Cheng Ku (Rm 3)
Corney & Barrow (Max)
Davy's at Canary Wharf (see
Davy's) (Private Rm*)
Hollands (Max*)
Leadenhall Wine Bar (Main Rm)

VISIT US AT: www.hardens.com

La Paquerette *(Max*)*
WKD *(Mezzanine*)*
Ye Olde Cheshire Cheese *(Cellar Bar* or Williams Rm)*
55 Borscht & Tears *(Restaurant)*
Hop Cellars *(Restaurant)*
50 Balls Brothers *(Max)*
Captain Kidd *(The Observation Deck*)*
Cooperage (see Davy's) *(Max*)*
Corney & Barrow *(Max)*
Diorama *(Max*)*
The Freemason's Arms *(Max*)*
Glassblower *(Top Bar*)*
Hop Cellars *(Malt Rm)*
Kettners *(Edward Rm)*
Le Mercury *(Private Rm*)*
The Mug House (see Davy's) *(Bar)*
Newham City Farm *(Rm*)*
The October Gallery *(Top Floor Theatre)*
La Paquerette *(Terrace)*
Slug & Lettuce *(Max*)*
St Bride Foundation Institute *(Blackfriars Rm or Farringdon Rm)*
Vats *(Restaurant)*
The White Horse *(Private Rm)*
48 Simpsons Tavern *(Grill)*
45 The Mug House (see Davy's) *(Restaurant)*
Shampers *(Restaurant*)*
44 Corney & Barrow *(Max)*
40 The Atlas *(Max*)*
Balls Brothers *(Max)*
Chiv (see Davy's) *(Dining Rm)*
Chuen Cheng Ku *(Rm 4)*
Cittie of Yorke *(Front Bar)*
The Clachan *(Highland Bar*)*
The Crown & Two Chairmen *(Upstairs Bar*)*
The Golden Lion *(Max*)*
Hollands *(Conservatory)*
Jackson's Lane Community Centre *(Multi-purpose Rm)*
Leadenhall Wine Bar *(Top Floor)*
Mudchute Park & Farm *(Max*)*
Ochre *(Function Rm)*
Patio *(Basement)*
Rock Garden *(Ground Floor Restaurant)*
Shelleys *(Max*)*
Spaghetti House *(Private Floor (x 2))*
37 Star Tavern *(Bar*)*
36 Calthorpe Arms *(Private Rm*)*
Rock Garden *(1st Floor Restaurant)*
35 Phene Arms *(Max*)*
The White Horse *(Restaurant)*
30 The Argyll Arms *(Max*)*
Bishops Parlour (see Davy's) *(Max*)*
Borscht & Tears *(Downstairs)*
Davy's at Canary Wharf (see Davy's) *(Private Rm)*
Duke of Albemarle *(Max*)*
Gyngleboy (see Davy's) *(Max*)*
Kettners *(Blue Rm)*
The Ministry of Sound *(Baby Box)*
Mudchute Park & Farm *(Café)*
Phene Arms *(Upstairs Rm)*
The Plough *(Max*)*
Seashell *(Downstairs Rm*)*
Southwark Tavern *(Cellar Bar*)*
25 Costa's Grill *(Private Rm*)*
The East Hill *(Max*)*
The Golden Lion *(Theatre Bar)*
23 Crusting Pipe (see Davy's) *(Private Rm*)*
20 Hollands *(Balcony Bar)*
16 Balls Brothers *(2 Private Rms)*
Phene Arms *(Upstairs Terrace)*
14 St Bride Foundation Institute *(Salisbury Rm)*
12 Balls Brothers *(Private Rm, Private Rm or Private Rm 2)*
Bottlescrue (see Davy's) *(Private Rm*)*
Kettners *(Soho Rm)*
10 Balls Brothers *(Private Rm)*
Boot & Flogger (see Davy's) *(Private Rm*)*
Crusting Pipe (see Davy's) *(Private Rm)*
The October Gallery *(Club)*
Ye Olde Cheshire Cheese *(Director's Rm)*
8 Balls Brothers *(Private Rm 2)*
Davy's Wine Vaults (see Davy's) *(Private Rm*)*
7 Balls Brothers *(Private Rm 2)*
6 The Mug House (see Davy's) *(Private Rm)*
St Bride Foundation Institute *(Caxton)*

Function rooms listed by capacity for dinner dances

* largest entry for venue

£E

320	Blenheim Palace (State Rms*)
250	Victoria & Albert Museum (Dome*)
200	National Portrait Gallery (Contemporary Galleries*)
150	Eltham Palace (Great Hall*)
132	Spencer House (Max*)
130	Chiswick House (Courtyard Marquee*)
125	Annabel's (Max*)
120	Home House (Front & Eating Room*)
100	Two Temple Place (The Great Hall*)
80	Chiswick House (Max)
	Syon Park (House) (Great Hall*)

£M-E

1700	The Grosvenor House Hotel (Great Rm*)
1200	Coram's Fields (Max*)
1000	Hilton on Park Lane (Grand Ballroom*)
	Old Billingsgate (Grand Hall*)
	Old Spitalfields Market (With Marquee*)
	Royal Albert Hall (Cabaret or Ball*)
	Royal Lancaster (Max*)
800	Addington Palace (Max*)
704	Guildhall (Great Hall*)
700	Coram's Fields (Split Facility)
650	InterContinental London (Grand Ballroom*)
	Royal Lancaster (Nine Kings Suite)
600	Cumberland Hotel (Production Box*)
	Kew (Royal Botanic) Gardens (New Palace Marquee Site*)
	Natural History Museum (Central Hall*)
	The Queen Elizabeth II Conference Centre (Fleming Rm*)
	Thorpe Park (Dome*)
520	Royal Lancaster (Westbourne Suite)
500	The Grosvenor House Hotel (Ballroom)
	National Maritime Museum (Max*)
	The Old Royal Naval College (Max*)
	Park Lane Hotel (Ballroom*)
	Portman Hotel (Ballroom*)
	Westway Studios (Max*)
450	The Dorchester (Ballroom*)
	East Wintergarden (Max*)
	The Grove (Amber*)
	Science Museum (Wellcome Wing*)
400	Chelsea Village (Exhibition Space* or Galleria)
	Royal Air Force Museum (Max*)
380	Banqueting House (Main Hall*)
	Hurlingham Club (Quadrangle Suite*)
375	The Savoy (Lancaster Rm*)
360	Carlton Tower (Ballroom*)
	Cumberland Hotel (Carlisle Suite)
	Millennium London Mayfair (Ballroom*)
	Royal Garden Hotel (Palace Suite*)
350	Imperial War Museum (Max*)
	Madame Tussaud's (World Stage*)
	Science Museum (Making The World Modern)
348	The Landmark (Ballroom*)
	Millennium Gloucester Hotel (Century Suite*)
320	Cabinet War Rooms (Churchill Museum*)
	Circus Space (Combustion Chamber*)
310	The Landmark (Max)
300	Dali Universe (Max*)
	Four Seasons Hotel (Ballroom*)
	InterContinental London (Westminster)
	Merchant Taylors' Hall (Max*)
	Raven's Ait Island (Max*)
	Science Museum (Flight Gallery)
	Stonor (Front Lawn*)
280	Hurlingham Club (Broom House Suite)
	Legoland Windsor (The Pavilions*)
	Lincoln's Inn (Great Hall*)

	Royal Air Force Museum (Battle of Britain Hall)
	Thorpe Park (Lake Side Hospitality Area)
270	Renaissance London Chancery Court Hotel (Ballroom*)
	Shakespeare's UnderGlobe (Underglobe*)
260	Barbican Centre (Garden Rm*)
	Gibson Hall (Hall*)
250	Chessington World of Adventures (Glade or Hospitality Marquee*)
	Gainsborough Studios (Max*)
	Ham House (Max*)
	Imperial War Museum (Main Atrium)
	London Aquarium (Atlantic*)
	The Mayfair Inter-Continental (Crystal Rm*)
	Merchant Taylors' Hall (Great Hall)
	Millennium Gloucester Hotel (Cotswold Suite or Decade Suite)
240	London Zoo (Prince Albert Suite*)
228	One Whitehall Place (Gladstone Library*)
225	Guildhall (Old Library)
	Middle Temple Hall (Hall*)
220	Chelsea Village (Drakes Suite)
	Raven's Ait Island (Britannia Suite)
210	Le Meridien (Georgian*)
200	Dali Universe (Dali A)
	Harrington Hall (Harrington*)
	Hilton London Paddington (Great Western Suite*)
	Hilton on Park Lane (Wellington Ballroom)
	Kew (Royal Botanic) Gardens (Temperate House)
	LABAN (Ampitheatre, Bonnie Bird Theatre* or Studio Theatre)
	London Aquarium (Terrace (with marquee))
	The London Art House (Manor Garden Hall*)
	Mandarin Oriental Hyde Park (Ballroom*)
	La Porte des Indes (Max*)
	Science Museum (East Hall)
	Stonor (Croqret Lawn)
192	Claridge's (Ballroom*)
180	Carlton Club (Max*)
	Institute of Directors (Nash*)
	The Landmark (Music Rm)
	Natural History Museum (Earth Galleries)
	The Old Palace (Great Hall*)
	Roehampton Club (Max*)
	The Roof Gardens (Max*)
	Thorpe Park (Thorpe Belle)
176	Great Eastern Hotel (Great Eastern*)
175	Stationers' Hall (Livery Hall*)
170	The Commonwealth Club (Max*)
	Gray's Inn (Hall*)
	Pennyhill Park Hotel (Balmoral*)
	Royal Air Force Museum (Cosford Rm or The Halton Gallery)
	Skinners' Hall (Max*)
160	The Berkeley (Ballroom*)
	The Criterion (Max*)
	Four Seasons Canary Wharf (Ballroom*)
	Great Fosters (Tithe Barn And Painted Hall*)
	Guildhall (The Crypts)
	The Old Palace (The Old Riding School)
	One Whitehall Place (Whitehall Suite)
	Savile Club (Members Dining Rm & Ballroom*)
150	Il Bottaccio (Gallery*)
	Gainsborough Studios (South Studio)
	The Law Society (Common Rm*)
	Le Meridien (Edwardian)
	Le Meridien Selsdon Park (Terrace Suite*)
	Millennium Gloucester Hotel (Conservatory)
	Natural History Museum (North Hall)
	Park Lane Hotel (Tudor Rose Rm)
	Penshurst Place & Gardens (Max*)
	Queen's House (Max*)
	The Savoy (Abraham Lincoln & Manhattan Rms)
	Sketch (Gallery*)
	HQS Wellington (Court Rm*)
140	The Imagination Gallery (Max*)
	National Liberal Club (Max*)
130	Hever Castle (Pavilion*)
	The London Planetarium (Max*)
	Royal Air Force Museum (Loching Rm)
	Smith's of Smithfield (Max*)
125	Coram's Fields (Party Chalet 2)

PRIVATE VENUES | DINNER-DANCE CAPACITY

120	30 Pavilion Road (Max*)
	Arts Club (Dining Rm*)
	The Berners Hotel (Thomas Ashton Suite*)
	Cabinet War Rooms (Auditorium)
	The Caledonian Club (Max*)
	The Dorchester (Orchid)
	Fortnum & Mason (St James's Rm*)
	Four Seasons Hotel (Garden Rm)
	Kew (Royal Botanic)
	Gardens (Gallery (entire ground floor))
	The Landmark (Drawing Rm or Empire Rm)
	Monkey Island Hotel (River Rm*)
	Prism (Max*)
	Roehampton Club (Roehampton Rm)
	Sartoria (Max*)
	The Savoy (River Rm)
	Skinners' Hall (Banquet Hall)
	Temple Island (Outdoors (with marquee)*)
	Tower Bridge (Walkways*)
	Windsor Guildhall (Guildhall Chamber*)
110	Circus Space (Generating Chamber)
	Elysium (Max*)
	The Grove (Ivory)
	Marriott Maida Vale (Regent Suite*)
	Royal Garden Hotel ('The Tenth' Restaurant)
105	Mosimann's Belfry (Max*)
100	Arundel House (Rm With A View*)
	BMA House (Members Dining Rm*)
	Chessington World of Adventures (Keg)
	Chintamani (Max*)
	The Commonwealth Club (Lower Ground Hall)
	Cutty Sark (Lower Hold*)
	Dali Universe (White Space)
	Goldsmiths' Hall (Livery Hall*)
	The Grosvenor House Hotel (Albemarle)
	Hilton on Park Lane (Coronation Suite)
	The London Dungeon (Max*)
	Momo (Max*)
	Museum of London (Lord Mayor's Gallery*)
	The Old Royal Naval
	College (King William Restaurant)
	Raven's Ait Island (Thames Suite)
	River & Rowing Museum (Thames Rm*)
	Theatre Museum (Paintings Gallery*)
92	Carlton Club (Churchill Rm)
90	The Carlton Mitre Hotel (Max*)
	Lincoln's Inn (Old Hall)
	London Stock Exchange (Top Floor*)
	National Liberal Club (David Lloyd George)
85	Belair House (Restaurant*)
	Harrington Hall (Turner & Constable)
	Mosimann's Belfry (Dining Rm)
84	28 Portland Place (Heggie Rm or Sainsbury's Rm*)
80	Addington Palace (Great Hall)
	The Dorchester (The Terrace)
	Great Eastern Hotel (Bishopsgate)
	The Hempel (Max*)
	The Mayfair Inter-Continental (Danziger Suite)
	Le Meridien Selsdon Park (Sir Edward Heath Rm)
	Monte's (Max*)
	Pennyhill Park Hotel (Windsor & Eton)
	Royal Garden Hotel (Kensington Suite)
	Sheraton Park Tower (Trianon Rm*)
	Smith's of Smithfield (Top Floor)
	Swissôtel London the
	Howard (Fitzalan Suite*)
75	Coram's Fields (Party Chalet)
70	The Carlton Mitre Hotel (Pavilion)
	Chelsea Village (Trophy Rm)
	Great Fosters (Orangery)
	Harrington Hall (Reynolds & Landseer)
	Mandarin Oriental Hyde Park (Carlyle Suite)
	Le Meridien (Regency)
	Millennium Gloucester Hotel (Ashburn Suite)
	One Whitehall Place (Reading And Writing Rms)
	Raffles (Max*)
	Royal Lancaster (Gloucester Suite)
	Tower Bridge (Engine Rms)
65	Noble Rot (Max*)
60	Arts Club (Garden Rm)
	Baltic Exchange (Dining Rm*)
	Il Bottaccio (Club Gallery)

	Cabinet War Rooms (Plant Rm)
	The Caledonian Club (Members Dining Rm)
	Cannizaro House (Viscount Melville Suite*)
	Four Seasons Hotel (Oak Rm)
	Hampshire Hotel (Penthouse*)
	The Hempel (I-Thai Restaurant (and Shadow Bar))
	Institute of Directors (Burton)
	LABAN (Medium Studio)
	The Lanesborough (Belgravia*)
	Legoland Windsor (JFK Drawing Rm)
	Savile Club (Ballroom or Members Dining Rm)
	St Martin's Lane Hotel (The Studio*)
50	Addington Palace (Winter Garden)
	The Dorchester (Park Suite)
	Millennium London
	Mayfair (Turner Fine Dining Rm)
	The Newsroom (Lecture Theatre*)
	Park Lane Hotel (Oak Rm)
	Raven's Ait Island (Lambourne Rm)
	Renaissance London Chancery Court
	Hotel (Lower Ground Floor)
	Roehampton Club (Garden Rm)
	Swissôtel London the Howard (Arundel Suite)
48	32 Craven St (Max*)
45	Dukes Hotel (Marlborough Suite*)
40	Gainsborough Studios (North Studio)
	The Grosvenor House Hotel (Stratton Suite)
	Institute of Directors (Waterloo)
	The Lanesborough (Wellington Rm)
	Millennium London Mayfair (Manhattan or
	Waterloo Rm)
	MVH (Max*)
	The Old Royal Naval
	College (Admirals Residence)
	Renaissance London Chancery Court
	Hotel (Ground Floor Suite)
	Royal Garden Hotel (Lancaster Suite)
36	Wellington Arch (Max*)
35	One New Inn Square (Max*)
32	Hilton London Paddington (Thunderbolt)
30	London Marriott Hotel Park
	Lane (Oxford Suite (divisable by 3)*)
	National Liberal Club (Lady Violet)
28	Hilton London Paddington (McGyver)
24	Hilton London Paddington (Red Star)

£M

5000	Alexandra Palace & Park (Great Hall*)
2000	Alexandra Palace & Park (West Hall)
	Battersea Park (British Genius Site*)
1500	Commonwealth Conference & Events
	Centre (Comm Galleries*)
1000	Ascot Racecourse (Ascot Pavilion (subdivisible)*)
900	London Metropole (Monarch or King's Suite*)
600	London Metropole (Palace Suite)
570	London Marriott (Westminster Ballroom*)
550	The Brewery (Porter Tun*)
500	The Decorium (Max*)
	The Medieval Banquet (Max*)
	Pinewood Studios (Max*)
466	The Decorium (Emperor Suite)
450	Ascot Racecourse (Royal Enclosure Suite)
	Britannia International Hotel (Grand Suite*)
	Café Royal (Dubarry & Dauphin or Empire Napoleon*)
	Tower Thistle (Tower Suite*)
	Vinopolis – City of Wine (Great Halls*)
420	Waldorf Hotel (Adelphi Suite & Palm Court*)
400	Kensington Town Hall (Great Hall*)
	Regent's College (Gardens*)
	The Tram Studios (Studio 104*)
	Whipsnade Wild Animal Park (Max*)
375	Ealing Town Hall (Victoria Hall*)
360	Epsom Downs (Blue Riband Rm*)
350	Cabot Hall (Hall*)
	Lord's (Banqueting Suite*)
320	Twickenham Experience (Invincibles*)
300	The Brewery (King George III)
	Central Hall Westminster (Lecture Hall* or
	Library)
	The Coronet (Max*)
	Horniman Museum (Exhibition Gallery*)

Lloyd's of London *(Captain's Rm*)*
Le Meridien Russell Hotel *(Warncliffe Suite*)*
The Oval *(KBCC*)*
Sound *(Restaurant & Bar*)*
St Mary's Church *(Max*)*
Twickenham Experience *(Norm Try Line or Rose Rm)*
280 Twickenham Experience *(Spirit Of Rugby)*
270 Elstree Film Studio *(Max*)*
Shakespeare's Globe *(Max*)*
Vinopolis – City of Wine *(Mezzanine)*
250 Bridges Wharf *(Max*)*
The Camden Palace *(Main Auditorium*)*
Commonwealth Conference & Events Centre *(Exhibition Hall)*
Delfina Galleries *(Max*)*
Hilton London Docklands *(London*)*
Holiday Inn London Regent's Park *(Cambridge & Oxford Suites*)*
The Hop Farm Country Park *(Dray Museum*)*
The Mayfair Club *(Max*)*
The Regalia *(Max*)*
220 Ealing Town Hall *(Princes Hall)*
Langham Hilton *(Ballroom*)*
One Great George Street *(Great Hall*)*
200 291 Gallery *(Main Gallery*)*
Alexandra Palace & Park *(Palace Restaurant)*
Ascot Racecourse *(Paddock Balcony)*
BAFTA *(Max*)*
Chartered Accountants' Hall *(Great Hall*)*
Congress Centre *(Congress Hall*)*
Cottons Atrium *(Max*)*
Delfina Galleries *(Exhibition Gallery)*
Denbies Wine Estate *(Garden Atrium Conservatory*)*
Design Museum *(Max*)*
Glaziers' Hall *(Hall*)*
Hendon Hall Hotel *(Pembroke Suite*)*
Hop Exchange *(Max*)*
The Hop Farm Country Park *(Max)*
Institute of Electrical Engineers *(Riverside Restaurant*)*
Red Cube *(Max*)*
Regent's College *(Refectory)*
The Selfridge Hotel *(Selfridge Suite*)*
Simpsons-in-the-Strand *(Max*)*
Whipsnade Wild Animal Park *(Griffin Suite or Phoenix Suite)*
180 Bank of England Sports Club *(Restaurant*)*
Café Royal *(Louis)*
Central Hall Westminster *(Westminster)*
Churchill *(Chartwell Suite*)*
Conrad Hotel *(Drake Suite*)*
Epsom Downs *(Derby Suite)*
Hellenic Centre *(Great Hall*)*
Hilton London Docklands *(Thames Suite)*
The Oval *(Banqueting Suite)*
Painters' Hall *(Max*)*
The Ramada Jarvis London West *(Ballroom*)*
The Rembrandt Hotel *(Max*)*
Royal Majestic Suite *(Ground Floor*)*
Winchester House *(River Lawn*)*
160 Conrad Hotel *(Henley Suite)*
Hampton Court Palace (The Tiltyard) *(Max*)*
Museum in Docklands *(Chris Ellmers Gallery*)*
Pacha *(Max*)*
The Rubens *(Old Masters Restaurant*)*
150 Barbarella *(Max*)*
The Bonnington in Bloomsbury *(Derby Suite*)*
The Decorium *(Caesar Suite)*
RS Hispaniola *(Max*)*
The Hop Farm Country Park *(White Banqueting Suite)*
Jolly Hotel St Ermins *(Ballroom*)*
Museum of Garden History *(Max*)*
No 4 Hamilton Place *(Lecture Theatre*)*
Pinewood Studios *(Ballroom)*
Queen's Eyot *(Marquee*)*
South London Gallery *(Inside*)*
SS Great Britain *(Dining Saloon*)*
St Thomas' Hospital *(Shepherd Hall*)*
Syon Park (Conservatory) *(Great Conservatory*)*
White House Hotel *(Albany*)*
140 Bank Westminster *(Max*)*
Bleeding Heart *(Max*)*
Dartmouth House *(Max*)*
London Metropole *(Windsor)*
130 Holiday Inn London Regent's Park *(Oxford)*
Royal Court Theatre *(Main Restaurant*)*
Tantra *(Max*)*
125 Goodenough College *(Great Hall*)*
120 Basil Street Hotel *(Parrot Club*)*
The Brewery *(Queen Charlotte)*
Britannia International Hotel *(Royal Lounge)*
The British Library *(Terrrace Restaurant*)*
Church House *(Harvey Goodwin Suite*)*
Epsom Downs *(Jockey Club Rm)*
Farmers' & Fletchers' Hall *(Livery Hall*)*
Forty Hall *(Banqueting Suite*)*
Frederick's *(Max*)*
The Grafton *(Warren Suite*)*
The Insurance Hall *(Great Hall*)*
Just The Bridge *(Max*)*
Kingsway Hall *(Restaurant*)*
Lansdowne Club *(Max*)*
TS Queen Mary *(Admirals Suite*)*
The Royal Air Force Club *(Running Horse/Millennium Suite*)*
Six Hamilton Place *(Max*)*
St Stephen's Club *(Dining Rm*)*
Thistle Kensington Palace Hotel *(Duchess*)*
Trinity House *(Max*)*
The Washington *(Restaurant (Madisons)*)*
110 Butchers' Hall *(Great Hall*)*
Easthampstead Park Conference Centre *(Max*)*
Greenwich Yacht Club *(Function Rms*)*
100 76 Portland Place *(Catering Suite*)*
Alexandra Palace & Park *(Loneborough Rm)*
Amadeus Centre *(Upper Hall*)*
The Brewery *(Sugar Rms)*
CC Club *(Max*)*
Commonwealth Conference & Events Centre *(Gillette)*
Delfina Galleries *(Café Gallery)*
Ealing Town Hall *(Queens Hall)*
Fashion & Textile Museum *(Max*)*
The Kenilworth *(Bloomsbury Suite*)*
Kew Bridge Steam Museum *(Max*)*
London Transport Museum *(Lecture Theatre or Main Gallery*)*
London Wetland Centre *(Waters Edge*)*
The Mayfair Club *(Living Rm Bar)*
Regent's College *(Herringham Hall)*
Royal Society of Arts *(Max*)*
96 HMS Belfast *(Ship Co's Dining Hall*)*
90 Adam Street *(Max*)*
The Chesterfield Mayfair *(Royal Suite*)*
City Club *(Main Dining Rm*)*
The Cobden Club *(Max*)*
Pattersons's *(Max*)*
St Thomas' Hospital *(Governors' Hall)*
Syon Park (Conservatory) *(Public Rms)*
80 Brewers' Hall *(Livery Hall*)*
Café Royal *(Derby & Queensbury)*
Central Hall Westminster *(Assembly)*
Chartered Accountants' Hall *(Restaurant)*
Churchill *(Chartwell I)*
Commonwealth Conference & Events Centre *(JBR)*
Fulham Palace *(Great Hall*)*
Glaziers' Hall *(Library & Court Rm)*
The Grafton *(Grafton)*
Holiday Inn London Regent's Park *(Cambridge)*
Horniman Museum *(Gallery Sq & Centenary Gallery or Victoria Conservatory)*
ICA *(Nash & Brandon Rms*)*
The Kenilworth *(Kenilworth Suite)*
No 4 Hamilton Place *(Argyll Rm & Hawker Rm)*
Simpsons-in-the-Strand *(Regency Rm)*
Singapura *(Main Rm*)*
Staple Inn *(Max*)*
Thistle Victoria Hotel *(Gallery Rm*)*
Vanderbilt Hotel *(Victoria & Albert Suite*)*

	Warren House *(Max*)*
	White House Hotel *(Chester)*
72	Britannia International Hotel *(Buckingham)*
70	115 at Hodgson's *(Max*)*
	Avenue House *(Drawing Rm*)*
	The Bonnington in Bloomsbury *(York Rm)*
	Devonport House *(Nelson & Hamilton*)*
	Epsom Downs *(Boardroom)*
	RS Hispaniola *(Top Deck)*
	Kensington Town Hall *(Small Hall)*
	Kingsway Hall *(Keats & Milton Rms)*
	The Old Sessions House *(Judges*)*
	TS Queen Mary *(Captains Quarters)*
	Royal Majestic Suite *(First Floor)*
64	City Inn Westminster *(Private Dining*)*
62	The Washington *(Richmond Suite)*
60	Amadeus Centre *(Lower Hall)*
	HMS Belfast *(Gun Rm)*
	Bloomsbury Square Training Centre *(Cellars Restaurant*)*
	Café Royal *(Grill Rm)*
	Cuba Libre *(Max*)*
	The De Vere Cavendish St James's *(Meeting Rm 1*)*
	Durrants Hotel *(Max*)*
	Loungelover *(Max*)*
	The Montcalm Hotel *(Maquis De Montcalm*)*
	One Great George Street *(Smeaton Rm)*
	Oxford & Cambridge Club *(Max*)*
	Prenelle Gallery *(Main Gallery*)*
	Royal Society of Arts *(Benjamin Franklin Rm)*
	The Selfridge Hotel *(Cleaveland)*
	Twickenham Experience *(England Rugby International's Club Rm)*
	The Westbury *(Mount Vernon Rm*)*
50	Denim *(Basement*)*
	The Mountbatten *(Earl Suite*)*
	Regent's College *(Tuke Common Rm)*
	RUSI Building *(Duke of Wellington Rm*)*
	Singapura *(Max)*
	Thistle Kensington Palace Hotel *(Marchioness)*
	Vanderbilt Hotel *(Cleo's)*
	Warren House *(Conference Rm 1)*
	West Wycombe Caves *(Banqueting Hall*)*
	White House Hotel *(Osnaburgh)*
45	Avenue House *(Salon)*
40	Athenaeum Hotel *(Macallan*)*
	The Brewery *(City Cellars)*
	Devonport House *(Drake)*
	Goolies *(Max*)*
	The Insurance Hall *(New Rm)*
	The Old Sessions House *(London Rm)*
	The Rembrandt Hotel *(Elizabeth & Victoria (Queen Suite))*
	The Westbury *(Pine Rm)*
36	Britannia International Hotel *(Blenheim)*
30	CC Club *(Bar M)*
	Denim *(Mezz)*
	Hendon Hall Hotel *(Garrick)*
	Pattersons's *(Function Rm)*
	Vanderbilt Hotel *(Edwardian)*
24	Britannia International Hotel *(Queens)*
20	Loungelover *(Red Area)*
10	Whipsnade Wild Animal Park *(Unicorn)*
	Whipsnade Wild Animal Park *(Pegasus)*

£B-M

2500	Honourable Artillery Co *(Marquee*)*
1000	The Chainstore *(Max*)*
	Crystal Palace Park *(Max*)*
750	Royal Horticultural Halls *(Lawrence Hall*)*
600	Equinox at the Empire *(Max*)*
520	Thames Luxury Charters – moving venue *(Dixie Queen*)*
500	Harrow School *(Shepherd Churchill Hall*)*
450	The London Hippodrome *(Auditorium*)*
	Porchester Centre *(Ballroom*)*
400	BAC *(Grand Hall*)*
	Stoke Newington Town Hall *(Assembly Rm*)*

380	New Connaught Rms *(Grand Hall & Balmoral*)*
350	Hammersmith Town Hall *(Assembly Hall*)*
	Royal College of Art *(Henry Moore Gallery*)*
	Royal Horticultural Halls *(Lindley Hall)*
300	Blackheath Concert Halls *(Great Hall*)*
	Cecil Sharp House *(Kennedy Hall*)*
	Dulwich College *(Christison Hall and Upper Dining Rms*)*
	Highgate School *(School Dining Hall*)*
	Honourable Artillery Co *(Albert Rm)*
	Regency Banqueting Suite *(Max*)*
	White Hart Lane Conference Centre *(Whites Suite*)*
275	Conway Hall *(Large Hall*)*
250	Break For The Border *(Max*)*
	Duke of York's HQ *(Max*)*
	Riverside Studios *(Studios 1 & 2*)*
230	Fulham Town Hall *(Grand Hall*)*
	Thames Luxury Charters – moving venue *(Elizabethan)*
220	Union Chapel *(Studio Theatre*)*
	Victory Services Club *(Carisbrooke Hall*)*
200	Academy of Live & Recorded Arts *(Great Hall*)*
	Dulwich College *(Great Hall)*
	Egg *(Max*)*
	Fabric *(Max*)*
	Fifteen05 *(Max*)*
	Le Gothique *(Max*)*
	Highgate School *(Big School)*
	Stratford Old Town Hall *(Main Hall*)*
	The Worx *(Max*)*
180	King's College School *(Great Hall*)*
	Trafalgar Tavern *(Nelson Suite*)*
175	The London Hippodrome *(Balcony – Restaurant)*
170	New Connaught Rms *(Edinburgh)*
	Royal Holloway College *(Founder's Dining Hall*)*
160	Abbaye *(Max*)*
	The Clink *(Max*)*
	Dickens Inn *(Nickleby Suite*)*
	New Connaught Rms *(Balmoral)*
	HMS President *(Ballroom*)*
	Trailfinders Sports Club *(Pavilion Hall*)*
	Westminster Boating Base *(Max*)*
150	Academy of Live & Recorded Arts *(Le Gothique)*
	The Anchor *(Max*)*
	King's College, King's Cuisine Restaurant *(Max*)*
	London Scottish *(Hall*)*
	Mermaid Theatre *(Blackfriars Rm* or Studio)*
	Royal Green Jackets *(Max*)*
	Thames Luxury Charters – moving venue *(Golden Salamander)*
	Whitelands College *(Ruskin Dining Hall*)*
140	Chelsea Old Town Hall *(Main Hall*)*
	Egg *(Courtyard)*
	King's College *(Great Hall*)*
	Strand Palace Hotel *(Exeter Suite*)*
130	Da Mario *(Max*)*
	Royal Geographical Society *(Max*)*
120	BAC *(Lower Hall)*
	Balls Brothers *(Banqueting Suite*)*
	Fifteen05 *(Great Hall)*
	Honourable Artillery Co *(Long Rm)*
	Levant *(Max*)*
	White Hart Lane Conference Centre *(Box Norm)*
	Will's Art Warehouse *(Max*)*
110	Fulham House *(Main Hall*)*
	The Irish Centre *(Hall*)*
	Maidenhead Steam Navigation – moving venue *(Max*)*
	St Martin In The Fields *(Max*)*
100	The Battersea Barge Bistro *(Max*)*
	Bishopsgate Institute *(Max*)*
	Blackheath Concert Halls *(Recital Rm)*
	Cecil Sharp House *(Trefusis Hall)*
	Egg *(Ground Floor or Middle Floor)*
	Fulham Town Hall *(Concert Hall)*
	Lauderdale House *(Max*)*
	The Little Ship Club *(Max*)*

New Connaught Rms *(York)*
Royal College of Art *(Gulbenkian Upper Gallery)*
Royal Over-Seas
   League *(Hall of India & Pakistan*)*
School of Pharmacy *(Refectory*)*
Thames Luxury Charters – moving
   venue *(Edwardian)*
Throgmorton's *(Oak Rm*)*
The Worx *(Studio 1)*

95 The Coliseum *(Dutch Bar*)*
90 White Hart Lane Conference
   Centre *(Oak Rm)*
80 Chelsea Old Town Hall *(Small Hall)*
   The Coliseum *(Terrace Bar)*
   Greenwich Playhouse *(Bar*)*
   Guy's Hospital *(Robens Suite*)*
   Hoxton Hall *(Whole Ground Floor*)*
   Maidenhead Steam Navigation – moving
      venue *(Georgian)*
   Royal Over-Seas League *(St Andrew's Hall)*
   Whitewebbs Museum of Transport *(Max*)*
70 Royal College of Art *(Gulbenkian Lower Gallery)*
60 Apartment 195 *(Lounge*)*
   Dulwich College *(Lower Hall or Pavilion Salle)*
   Equinox at the Empire *(Empire Lounge)*
   Latchmere Theatre *(Max*)*
   Maidenhead Steam Navigation – moving
      venue *(Southern Comfort)*
   Stratford Old Town Hall *(Council Chamber)*
56 Strand Palace Hotel *(Essex Suite & Grenville Suite)*
53 Aragon House *(Max*)*
50 Dolphin Square Hotel *(Restaurant*)*
   Maidenhead Steam Navigation – moving
      venue *(Pink Champagne)*
   St Botolph's Hall *(Upper Hall*)*
   St Martin In The Fields *(Gallery)*
   Thames Luxury Charters – moving
      venue *(Max)*
48 Strand Palace Hotel *(Drake Suite)*
40 Conway Hall *(Small Hall)*
   Kingswood House *(Charles Suite*)*
36 Jason's Trip – moving venue *(Lady Rose*)*
24 Jason's Trip – moving venue *(Lace Plate)*

£B

460 Wandsworth Civic Suite *(Civic Suite*)*
240 Wandsworth Civic Suite *(Banqueting Hall)*
220 Wandsworth Civic Suite *(Civic Hall)*
200 Polish Social & Cultural
   Association *(Malinova Rm*)*
160 The Ministry of Sound *(Main Bar*)*
   Polish Social & Cultural
   Association *(Ball Rm)*
150 City Pipe (see Davy's) *(Max*)*
   Corney & Barrow *(Max*)*
   The London Welsh Centre *(Main Hall*)*
110 Polish Social & Cultural
   Association *(Lowiczanka Restaurant*)*
100 Balls Brothers *(Max)*
   Cittie of Yorke *(Main Bar*)*
   Hop Cellars *(Max*)*
   London Rowing Club *(Max*)*
   Skinkers (see Davy's) *(Max*)*
   St Bride Foundation Institute *(Bridewell Hall*)*
   St Etheldreda's Crypt *(Max*)*
90 Gow's Restaurant *(Max*)*
80 Crown & Greyhound *(Private Rm (large)*)*
   Walkers of St James's *(Max*)*
75 Jackson's Lane Community
   Centre *(Dance Studio*)*
70 Heeltap & Bumper (see Davy's) *(Max*)*
65 The Mug House (see Davy's) *(Max*)*
60 Balls Brothers *(Weekday function or
      Weekday function)*
   The October Gallery *(Main Gallery*)*
   WKD *(Mezzanine*)*
50 Balls Brothers *(Max)*
   Captain Kidd *(Max*)*
   Cooperage (see Davy's) *(Max*)*
   St Bride Foundation Institute *(Blackfriars Rm or
      Farringdon Rm)*

Function rooms listed by capacity for theatre style

* largest entry for venue

40 The Atlas *(Max*)*
   Cittie of Yorke *(Cellar Bar)*
   Jackson's Lane Community Centre *(Multi-
      purpose Rm)*
14 St Bride Foundation Institute *(Salisbury Rm)*

£E

320 British Museum *(Max*)*
300 Eltham Palace *(Great Hall*)*
200 Lancaster House *(Long Gallery*)*
   National Portrait Gallery *(Max*)*
190 Tate Britain *(Auditorium*)*
150 Two Temple Place *(Long Gallery* or The Great Hall)*
   Wrotham Park *(Drawing Rm*)*
120 Blenheim Palace *(Marlborough*)*
100 Wrotham Park *(Dining Rm)*
80 Eltham Palace *(Drawing Rm)*
70 Blenheim Palace *(Spencer Churchill)*
   Home House *(Eating Rm*)*
30 Blenheim Palace *(Audenarde Rm, Malplaquet or
      Ramillies)*
20 Cliveden *(Macmillan Boardroom*)*

£M-E

5200 Royal Albert Hall *(Cabaret or Ball*)*
1400 Coram's Fields *(Max*)*
1000 Addington Palace *(Max*)*
750 Royal Albert Hall *(Arena)*
725 The Saatchi Gallery *(Council Chamber*)*
700 Coram's Fields *(Split Facility)*
600 Thorpe Park *(Dome*)*
550 Royal Garden Hotel *(Palace Suite*)*
500 The Business Design Centre *(Auditorium or
      Gallery Hall*)*
450 BFI London IMAX Cinema *(Max*)*
   Millennium London Mayfair *(Ballroom*)*
430 Science Museum *(Imax Cinema*)*
400 Hurlingham Club *(Broom House Suite or
      Quadrangle Suite*)*
   Legoland Windsor *(The Pavilions*)*
   Merchant Taylors' Hall *(Great Hall*)*
   Middle Temple Hall *(Hall*)*
   Royal Hospital Chelsea *(Chapel*)*
   Royal Opera House *(Linbury Studio Theatre*)*
   The Saatchi Gallery *(Main Gallery)*
380 Hilton London
   Paddington *(Great Western Suite*)*
375 Drapers' Hall *(Livery Hall*)*
360 LSO St Luke's *(Jerwood Hall*)*
350 Royal Opera House *(Vilar Floral Hall)*
340 Kensington Palace *(State Apartments*)*
320 Royal College of Physicians *(Osler Rm*)*
310 Circus Space *(Combustion Chamber*)*
300 Chelsea Village *(Galleria*)*
   Gainsborough Studios *(Max*)*
   The Grove *(Amber*)*
   Institute of Directors *(Nash*)*
   The Old Palace *(Great Hall or The Old Riding School*)*
   Thorpe Park *(Lake Side Hospitality Area)*
294 LABAN *(Bonnie Bird Theatre*)*
270 Museum of London *(Lecture Theatre*)*
   Shakespeare's UnderGlobe *(Underglobe*)*
250 Il Bottaccio *(Gallery*)*
   Chessington World of Adventures *(Glade*)*
   Inner Temple Hall *(Hall*)*
   London Aquarium *(Atlantic*)*
   The London Art House *(Manor Garden Hall*)*
240 Haberdashers' Hall *(Livery Hall*)*
220 Kew (Royal Botanic)
   Gardens *(Lecture Theatre*)*
   One Whitehall Place *(Gladstone Library*)*
200 Addington Palace *(Great Hall)*

Arundel House (Rm With A View*)	Arts Club (Garden Rm *)
Chessington World of Adventures (Hospitality Marquee)	Arundel House (Conference Rm)
Circus Space (Generating Chamber)	The Commonwealth Club (Cinema Rm)
Four Seasons Canary Wharf (Ballroom*)	Great Eastern Hotel (Bishopsgate)
Great Eastern Hotel (Great Eastern*)	Kew (Royal Botanic) Gardens (Cambridge Cottage Lounge)
LABAN (Ampitheatre)	LABAN (Medium Studio)
London Aquarium (Terrace (with marquee))	The Lanesborough (Wellington Rm)
Marriott Maida Vale (Regent Suite*)	Legoland Windsor (JFK Drawing Rm)
One Whitehall Place (Whitehall Suite*)	The London Art House (Baroque Hall)
Penshurst Place & Gardens (Baron's Hall*)	London Stock Exchange (Theatre*)
Raven's Ait Island (Britannia Suite*)	Osterley Park & House (Hall)
Sketch (Gallery*)	Portman Hotel (Gloucester Suite*)

196 Stationers' Hall (Livery Hall*)

180 Brighton Royal Pavilion (Music Rm*)
Kent House (The Sanctuary*)
Sadler's Wells Theatre (Lillian Bayliss Theatre*)
HQS Wellington (Court Rm*)

170 Gainsborough Studios (South Studio)
Royal Opera House (Clore Studio)

150 Carlton Club (Churchill Rm*)
The Commonwealth Club (Max*)
Dali Universe (White Space*)
Hever Castle (Pavilion*)
Kensington Palace (Victorian Garden Rooms*)
Monkey Island Hotel (River Rm*)
Swissôtel London the Howard (Fitzalan Suite*)

140 Cabinet War Rooms (Auditorium*)
The Energy Clinic (Largest Area*)
The Grove (Ivory)
Roehampton Club (Roehampton Rm*)

125 Coram's Fields (Party Chalet 2)

120 The Carlton Mitre Hotel (Pavilion*)
City Hall - London's Living Room (London's Living Rm*)
The Commonwealth Club (Thorne Rm)
Dulwich Picture Gallery (Linbury Rm*)
Inner Temple Hall (Parliament Chamber)
Innholders' Hall (Hall*)
Institute of Directors (Burton)
Merchant Taylors' Hall (Parlour)
National Maritime Museum (Lecture Theatre*)
Natural History Museum (Darwin Centre or Spencer Gallery*)
One Whitehall Place (Reading And Writing Rms)
Penshurst Place & Gardens (Sunderland Rm)
Royal Garden Hotel (Kensington Suite)
Salters' Hall (Mail Hall*)
Stationers' Hall (Court Rm)
Swissôtel London the Howard (Arundel Suite)

110 Savile Club (Ballroom, Members Dining Rm or Members Dining Rm & Ballroom*)

100 BMA House (Douglas Black or Members Dining Rm*)
Drapers' Hall (Court Dining or Court Rm)
Firepower - The Royal Artillery Museum (Theatre*)
The Hempel (I-Thai Restaurant (and Shadow Bar)*)
Institute of Directors (Waterloo)
Kent House (Max)
LABAN (Studio Theatre)
The Lanesborough (Belgravia*)
Merchant Taylors' Hall (Drawing Rm)
Osterley Park & House (Brewhouse*)
Raven's Ait Island (Thames Suite)
Royal College of Pathologists (Lecture Rm*)
Royal Institute of British Architects (Conference Rm*)
Sadler's Wells Theatre (Cable & Wireless Rm)
Science Museum (Directors Suite)
Tate Modern (East Rm*)

90 28 Portland Place (Heggie Rm or Sainsbury's Rm*)
Addington Palace (Winter Garden)
Canonbury Academy (Long Gallery*)
The Grove (Silk)
Haberdashers' Hall (Court Rm)
Kensington Rooms (Rm 9*)
Millennium London Mayfair (Turner Fine Dining Rm)
The Newsroom (Lecture Theatre* or Scott Rm)
St Martin's Lane Hotel (The Studio*)

80 28 Portland Place (Harben Rm)
Addington Palace (Library)

Sheraton Park Tower (Trianon Rm*)
Theatre Museum (Studio Theatre*)
United Grand Lodge of England (Board Rm or Vestibule*)
Wax Chandlers' Hall (Hall*)

75 Coram's Fields (Party Chalet)
Four Seasons Canary Wharf (River Rm)
London Stock Exchange (Top Floor)
Millennium London Mayfair (Manhattan)

72 Hilton London Paddington (Thunderbolt)
London Marriott Hotel Park Lane (Oxford Suite (divisable by 3)*)
Millennium London Mayfair (Waterloo Rm)

70 28 Portland Place (Adam's Rm)
32 Craven St (Level 1*)
Addington Palace (Lecture Rm)
Baltic Exchange (Dining Rm*)
BMA House (Prince's Rm)
Dali Universe (Modern Masters)
Estorick Collection (Max*)
Inner Temple Hall (Luncheon Rm)
Kensington Rooms (Media Rm)
Kent House (Rutland Rm)
The London Art House (Rococo Rm)
Middle Temple Hall (Parliament Chamber)
Royal Institute of British Architects (South Rm)

67 Charlotte Street Hotel (Private Screening Rm*)

65 One Whitehall Place (Meston Suite or River Rm*)

64 Hever Castle (Tudor Suite)

60 Addington Palace (Wellington Rm)
Chelsea Village (Trophy Rm*)
The Commonwealth Club (Blue Rm)
Dukes Hotel (Marlborough Suite*)
Hilton London Paddington (McGyver)
London Aquarium (Shark Tank)
The Old Royal Naval College (Admirals Residence*)
One Aldwych (Rms 1 & 2*)
Roehampton Club (Garden Rm)
Royal Garden Hotel (Lancaster Suite)
Royal Institute of British Architects (Council Chamber)
Salters' Hall (Court Rm)
St Martin's Lane Hotel (The Backroom)
Stationers' Hall (Stock Rm)
Thorpe Park (Neptunes Chamber or Thorpe Belle)
United Grand Lodge of England (Drawing Rm)

55 The Lanesborough (Westminster Rm)

53 Covent Garden Hotel (Screening Rm*)

50 Addington Palace (Empire Rm)
Il Bottaccio (Club Gallery)
Cabinet War Rooms (Plant Rm)
Canonbury Academy (Denby Suite)
Gainsborough Studios (North Studio)
Great Eastern Hotel (Chancery)
The Hempel (Room No 17)
Imperial War Museum (Boardroom 1*)
Institute of Directors (Trafalgar II/St James II)
Merchant Taylors' Hall (Kings Gallery)
Middle Temple Hall (Queen's Rm)
Mosimann's Academy (Demonstration Kitchen*)
Royal College of Pathologists (Council Rm)

48 Hilton London Paddington (Red Star)
The London Art House (Orangery)

45 Arundel House (4th Floor Conference Rm)

44 Monkey Island Hotel (Garden Rm)

40 Addington Palace (Music Rm)
Amberley Castle (Great Rm*)
Audi Forum (Meeting Rm*)

	Great Eastern Hotel (Moorgate)	1402	Shaftesbury Theatre (Max*)
	Great Fosters (Conference Centre*)	1396	Palace Theatre (Auditorium*)
	Institute of Directors (Trafalgar I)	1200	Aldwych Theatre (Auditorium*)
	Kent House (Library)	1150	Royal National Theatre (Max*)
	The London Art House (Art Studio)	1100	London Metropole (Palace Suite)
	London Stock Exchange (Blue Rm)	990	Queen's Theatre (Auditorium*)
	Marriott Maida Vale (Carlton Suite)	895	Haymarket Theatre (Max*)
	Monkey Island Hotel (Spencer Rm)	860	Kensington Town Hall (Great Hall*)
	One New Inn Square (Max*)	826	The Decorium (Emperor Suite*)
	Portland Place Conference	800	Albery Theatre (Max*)
	Centre (Grosvenor or Tavistock*)	790	Comedy Theatre (Max*)
	Roehampton Club (Centenary Board Rm)	782	Wyndham's Theatre (Max*)
	Royal Institute of British	600	St Mary's Church (Max*)
	Architects (Aston or Committe Rm)		Whipsnade Wild Animal Park (Max*)
	Sheraton Park Tower (Buckingham Rm)	570	The Coronet (Max*)
	HQS Wellington (Model Rm)	550	Britannia International Hotel (Grand Suite*)
36	Carlton Club (Cabinet Rm)		Tower Thistle (Tower Suite*)
35	Carlton Club (Disraeli Rm or Macmillan Rm)	540	Café Royal (Empire Napoleon*)
	The Lanesborough (Wilkins Rm)	500	Central Hall Westminster (Lecture Hall or
	Portland Place Conference		Library)
	Centre (Cavendish)		Congress Centre (Congress Hall*)
	Queen's House (SW Parlour*)		Lord's (Nursery Pavilion*)
32	Canonbury Academy (Queen Elizabeth)	470	Duchess Theatre (Max*)
30	Arts Club (Board Rm)	468	Royal College of Music (Concert Hall*)
	Carlton Club (Lirary)	460	Commonwealth Conference & Events
	The Carlton Mitre Hotel (Cardinal Wolsey)		Centre (Main Auditorium*)
	Four Seasons Canary Wharf (City Rm)		Institute of Electrical
	Institute of Directors (St James's II)		Engineers (Lecture Theatre*)
	LABAN (Meeting Rm)	450	Goodenough College (Max*)
	One Aldwych (Screening Rm)	432	Fortune Theatre (Auditorium*)
	Royal College of Pathologists (Seminar Rm)	403	New Ambassadors Theatre (Max*)
	Sadler's Wells Theatre (Fonteyn Rm)	400	291 Gallery (Main Gallery*)
	Wax Chandlers' Hall (Courtroom)		Cabot Hall (Hall*)
25	Charlotte Street Hotel (Rm I)		The Comedy Store (Max*)
	Imperial War Museum (Boardroom 2)		Horniman Museum (Exhibition Gallery*)
	One Aldwych (Rm 3)		One Great George Street (Great Hall*)
	Royal Institute of British		Royal College of Music (Britten Theatre)
	Architects (Professional Gallery)		The Tram Studios (Studio 104*)
	Savile Club (Elgar Rm)		Twickenham Experience (Rose Rm*)
	Sheraton Park Tower (Explorers)		Vinopolis – City of Wine (Mezzanine*)
24	London Marriott Hotel Park	360	Café Royal (Dubarry & Dauphin)
	Lane (Hyde Park Suite)	350	Hendon Hall Hotel (Pembrake Suite*)
	Portland Place Conference	325	Chartered Accountants' Hall (Great Hall*)
	Centre (Chiswick)	300	Glaziers' Hall (Hall*)
22	Park Lane Hotel (Smart Rms*)		Goodenough College (Great Hall)
	The Trafalgar (Resolution*)		Inmarsat (Max*)
20	BMA House (Alexander Fleming or Edward Jenner)		Jongleurs at Camden Lock (Max*)
	The Hempel (Jade Rm)		Lord's (Banqueting Suite)
	Kensington Rooms (Studio Rm)		Royal National Theatre (Lyttelton Exhibition Level)
	The London Art House (Albert Moore Lounge)		Whipsnade Wild Animal Park (Griffin Suite or
	LSO St Luke's (Clore Rms)		Phoenix Rm*)
	Merchant Taylors' Hall (Library)	284	International Coffee
	Sheraton Park Tower (Balmoral)		Organisation (Council Chamber*)
18	Haberdashers' Hall (Luncheon Rm)	270	Jongleurs at Bow Wharf (Max*)
	St Martin's Lane Hotel (Front Rm)		Shakespeare's Globe (Max*)
	The Trafalgar (Boardroom or Strategy)		Waldorf Hotel (Adelphi Suite & Palm Court*)
16	BMA House (James Young Simpson)	255	The British Library (Auditorium & Foyer*)
	St Martin's Lane Hotel (Board Rm)	250	The Bonnington in Bloomsbury (Derby Suite*)
15	32 Craven St (Level 2)		Central Hall Westminster (Westminster)
	Dukes Hotel (Sheridan Rm)		London Metropole (Windsor)
	Royal Astronomical Society (Meeting Rm*)		National Army Museum (Art Gallery*)
14	28 Portland Place (Founder's Rm)		Twickenham Experience (Spirit Of Rugby)
	The Academy (Boardroom*)		Vinopolis – City of Wine (Great Halls)
	BMA House (Joseph Lister)	241	One Great George Street (Telford Theatre)
12	Amberley Castle (King Charles Rm)	230	The Decorium (Caesar Suite)
	Charlotte Street Hotel (Rm 2)		UCS Theatre (Theatre*)
	London Stock Exchange (Video Conference Rm)	220	Café Royal (Louis)
10	Hampshire Hotel (Drawing Rm*)		Carpenters' Hall (Livery Hall*)
	London Stock Exchange (Syndicate Rm)	214	One Birdcage Walk (Lecture Theatre*)
	Royal Institute of British	213	BAFTA (Princess Anne Theatre*)
	Architects (Student Gallery)	200	BAFTA (David Lean Rm)
			Britannia International Hotel (Royal Lounge)
			The CBI Conference Centre (Methven*)
£M			CC Club (Max*)
			Church House (Harvey Goodwin Suite*)
			Design Museum (Collection Gallery*)
3719	Hammersmith Apollo (Max*)		Painters' Hall (Livery Hall*)
2572	Apollo Victoria Theatre (Whole Theatre*)		The Rembrandt Hotel (Max*)
2350	Central Hall Westminster (Great Hall*)		Royal Society of Arts (Great Rm*)
2190	Dominion Theatre (Auditorium*)		Royal Statistical Society (Lecture Theatre*)
2100	Lyceum Theatre (Theatre*)		The Selfridge Hotel (Max*)
1700	London Metropole (Monarch or King's Suite*)		Sound (Restaurant & Bar*)
1500	Adelphi Theatre (Max*)		St Thomas' Hospital (Governors' Hall*)

45 ICA *(Cinema 2)*
42 The Selfridge Hotel *(Chitten)*
40 76 Portland Place *(Herschel)*
 The Bonnington in Bloomsbury *(Jack Frame)*
 Britannia International Hotel *(Blenheim or Queens)*
 Chartered Accountants' Hall *(Members' Rm)*
 Chartered Institute of Public Finance & Accountancy *(Committee Rm 4*)*
 Denbies Wine Estate *(Lecture Rm)*
 Easthampstead Park Conference Centre *(Tawney)*
 The Lincoln Centre *(Presentation 2)*
 The New Cavendish Club *(Ante Rm)*
 The Old Sessions House *(Justices or Recorder Rm)*
 One Birdcage Walk *(Courses Rm)*
 Royal Society of Arts *(Tavern Rm)*
 Thistle Victoria Hotel *(Warwick Rm)*
 Warren House *(Conference Rm 2)*
 Whipsnade Wild Animal Park *(Unicorn)*
35 The Decorium *(Ante Suite)*
 Hendon Hall Hotel *(Johnson or Sheridan)*
 Royal National Theatre *(Ashcroft)*
 Scotch Malt Whisky Society *(Still Rm*)*
 Tower Thistle *(Mortimer Suite)*
32 City Conference Centre *(Council Rm)*
30 Aeonian *(Rm 3)*
 Avenue House *(Dining Rm or Salon)*
 Britannia International Hotel *(Balmoral or Beaufort)*
 Brown's Hotel *(Roosevelt)*
 Coopers' Hall *(Max*)*
 Easthampstead Park Conference Centre *(Windsor or Wylie)*
 Farmers' & Fletchers' Hall *(Court Rm)*
 Hamilton House *(Max*)*
 Horniman Museum *(Performance Space)*
 Ironmongers' Hall *(Luncheon Rm)*
 Lansdowne Club *(Findlay Rm)*
 The Montcalm Hotel *(Montagu Suite or Portman Suite)*
 One Great George Street *(Stephenson Rm & President's Dining Rm)*
 The Place *(Theatre Bar)*
 The Royal Air Force Club *(Drawing Rm or Mezzanine Suite)*
 Singapura *(Large Mezzanine)*
 Thistle Victoria Hotel *(Belgrave)*
 Waldorf Hotel *(Aldwych)*
 Whipsnade Wild Animal Park *(Pegasus)*
26 International Coffee Organisation *(Committee Rm)*
 Kingsway Hall *(Chaucer)*
25 Barber-Surgeons' Hall *(Court Rm)*
 Cabot Hall *(Cape Breton Rm)*
 The CBI Conference Centre *(Rm 1 or Rm 2)*
 City Conference Centre *(Arctic or Indian)*
 The De Vere Cavendish St James's *(Meeting Rm 4 or Meeting Rm 5)*
 The Founders' Hall *(Parlour)*
 International Coffee Organisation *(Meeting Rms)*
 The Old Sessions House *(Clerks)*
 Thistle Victoria Hotel *(Wilton Rm)*
 Tower Thistle *(Beaufort)*
24 Devonport House *(Collingwood)*
 Doggetts Coat & Badge *(Boardroom*)*
 Scotch Malt Whisky Society *(Tasting Rm)*
22 London Wetland Centre *(Meeting Rm)*
20 The Bonnington in Bloomsbury *(Committee Rm)*
 Denim *(Mezz)*
 The Geological Society of London *(Council Rm)*
 The New Cavendish Club *(Library)*
 Royal National Theatre *(Richardson Rm)*
 Royal Statistical Society *(New Meeting Rm)*
 Thistle Victoria Hotel *(Hanover)*
18 Sutton House *(Linenfold Rm)*
16 The Agency *(Conference Rm*)*
 Waterstone's Piccadilly *(Emberton Rm)*
15 Brown's Hotel *(Kipling)*
 Cabot Hall *(Newfoundland Rm)*

 St Andrew's Court House *(Archive Rm)*
14 Butchers' Hall *(Commitee Rm)*
 Waterstone's Piccadilly *(Boardroom)*
12 The Lincoln Centre *(Central Boardroom)*
 Singapura *(Private Rm)*
 Warren House *(Meeting Rm 1)*
10 The Agency *(Board Rm)*
 The Ramada Jarvis London West *(Boardroom*)*
8 Butchers' Hall *(Library)*
6 The Agency *(Library)*
 Butchers' Hall *(George Adams)*

£B-M

2000 Honourable Artillery Co *(Marquee*)*
 London Astoria *(Max*)*
1000 Union Chapel *(Auditorium*)*
950 Hammersmith Town Hall *(Assembly Hall*)*
750 Harrow School *(Speech Rm*)*
 Royal Geographical Society *(Theatre*)*
700 New Connaught Rms *(Grand Hall & Balmoral*)*
650 BAC *(Grand Hall*)*
600 Union Chapel *(Auditorim (downstairs))*
550 Bloomsbury Theatre *(Venue*)*
500 Conway Hall *(Large Hall*)*
 White Hart Lane Conference Centre *(Whites Suite*)*
486 Dulwich College *(Great Hall*)*
450 Dulwich College *(Christison Hall and Upper Dining Rms)*
430 Royal Institution of Great Britain *(Faraday Lecture Theatre*)*
420 Greenwich Theatre *(Max*)*
400 Chelsea Old Town Hall *(Main Hall*)*
 Dulwich College *(Max)*
360 Arts Theatre *(Auditorium*)*
 City University *(Oliver Thompson Lecture Theatre*)*
350 The Bridge SE1 *(Rm 1*)*
 University of Westminster *(Old Cinema*)*
314 Cochrane Theatre *(Auditorium*)*
300 Fulham Town Hall *(Grand Hall*)*
 Honourable Artillery Co *(Albert Rm)*
 New Connaught Rms *(Balmoral or Edinburgh)*
 Polka Theatre for Children *(Main Theatre*)*
 Tricycle Theatre *(Cinema*)*
278 Egg *(Middle Floor*)*
270 St Paul's Church *(Church Rm*)*
250 Academy of Live & Recorded Arts *(Great Hall*)*
 King's College *(Great Hall*)*
 The Villiers Theatre *(Max*)*
 White Hart Lane Conference Centre *(Box Norm)*
 The Worx *(Max*)*
240 Egg *(Ground Floor)*
 Tricycle Theatre *(Theatre)*
224 London Scottish *(Max*)*
220 Union Chapel *(Studio Theatre)*
210 New Connaught Rms *(York)*
200 The Bridge SE1 *(Rm 2)*
 Duke of York's HQ *(London Irish Hall*)*
 Fabric *(Max*)*
 Fulham Town Hall *(Concert Hall)*
 Royal Horticultural Halls *(Lecture Theatre*)*
 Whitelands College *(Ruskin Dining Hall*)*
 The Worx *(Studio 1 or Studio 2)*
190 University of Westminster *(Portland Hall AD)*
184 City University *(Level Six Suite)*
180 BAC *(Lower Hall)*
 The Music Room *(Max*)*
 Strand Palace Hotel *(Exeter Suite*)*
160 Highgate School *(Big School*)*
 The Mary Sumner House *(Conference Hall*)*
 The Music Room *(Exhibition Hall)*
154 Whitelands College *(Lecture Theatre)*
150 Chelsea Old Town Hall *(Small Hall)*
140 Egg *(Courtyard)*
 Hoxton Hall *(Theatre* or Whole Ground Floor)*
 The Irish Centre *(Hall*)*
130 Honourable Artillery Co *(Long Rm)*

	Upstairs at the Gatehouse (Max*)
125	University of Westminster (Fyvie Hall)
120	Canning House (Drawing Rm*)
	Dulwich College (Lower Hall)
110	Dulwich College (Old Library)
104	Whitechapel Art Gallery (Lecture Theatre*)
100	Bakers' Hall (Livery Hall*)
	The Bridge SE1 (Rm 3)
	The Coliseum (Terrace Bar*)
	Conway Hall (Small Hall)
	Fulham House (Main Hall*)
	Little Angel Theatre (Auditorium)
	Royal Institution of Great Britain (Bernard Sunley Theatre)
	St Botolph's Hall (Upper Hall*)
90	St Paul's Church (Blue Lounge)
85	Dolphin Square Hotel (Chichester*)
84	Greenwich Playhouse (Theatre*)
80	Dolphin Square Hotel (Restaurant)
	Dulwich College (Pavilion Salle)
	Latchmere Theatre (Max*)
	Polka Theatre for Children (Studio Theatre)
	Southwark Cathedral (Library*)
	Victory Services Club (Trafalgar Rm*)
	White Hart Lane Conference Centre (Oak Rm)
77	New End Theatre (Max*)
70	Canning House (Library)
	Stratford Old Town Hall (Conference Rm*)
67	Imperial College (Council Rm*)
60	Bakers' Hall (Court Rm)
	Burgh House (Music Rm*)
	Canal Café Theatre (Theatre*)
	Strand Palace Hotel (Essex Suite or Grenville Suite)
55	New Connaught Rms (Durham)
50	The Bridge SE1 (Rm4)
	Fulham House (Dining Rm)
	Honourable Artillery Co (Queen's Rm)
	King's College (Council Rm)
	Royal Institution of Great Britain (Main Library)
	Whitewebbs Museum of Transport (Max*)
	The Worx (Studio 4)
44	London Scottish (Queen Elizabeth Rm)
43	Dolphin Square Hotel (Anson)
40	London Scottish (Officers' Mess)
	The Mary Sumner House (Mary Sumner Rm)
	New Connaught Rms (Penthouse)
	Southwark Cathedral (Seminar Rm)
	Strand Palace Hotel (Drake Suite)
30	Docklands Sailing & Watersports Centre (Teaching Rm*)
	King's College (Committee Rm)
	St Paul's Church (Portman Rm)
	Victory Services Club (Allenby Rm)
25	Victory Services Club (Chetwode Rm)
22	City University (Tait Meeting Rms)
20	The Coliseum (Chairman's)
	Dolphin Square Hotel (Blake)
	The Music Room (Gallery)
	Stratford Old Town Hall (Mayors Parlour)
	The Worx (Studio 3)
15	Apartment 195 (Cellar*)
14	The Coliseum (Stoll Rm)
10	Apartment 195 (TV Rm)

110	Park Crescent Conference Centre (Portland Rm)
60	The Ministry of Sound (VIP Bar)
	St Bride Foundation Institute (Blackfriars Rm or Farringdon Rm)
50	Diorama (Max*)
	The White Horse (Private Rm*)
30	Wandsworth Civic Suite (Reception Rm)
25	St Bride Foundation Institute (Salisbury Rm)
12	St Bride Foundation Institute (Caxton)
10	Balls Brothers (Private Rm*)

£B

748	Wandsworth Civic Suite (Civic Suite*)
428	Wandsworth Civic Suite (Civic Hall)
350	Wandsworth Civic Suite (Banqueting Hall)
320	Park Crescent Conference Centre (Theatre*)
220	The Ministry of Sound (Box*)
	University of London Union (Rm 101*)
200	The London Welsh Centre (Main Hall*)
167	Jackson's Lane Community Centre (Theatre*)
150	St Bride Foundation Institute (Bridewell Hall*)
130	University of London Union (Palms Rm)
120	King's Head Theatre (Max*)

ALPHABETICAL INDEX
OF SERVICES

ALPHABETICAL INDEX

VISIT US AT: www.hardens.com